INTRODUCTION TO PERSONALITY

Sixth Edition

INTRODUCTION TO PERSONALITY

Sixth Edition

Walter Mischel

Columbia University

with contributions by

Robert Plomin
Institute of Psychiatry
London

Harcourt Brace College Publishers

Fort Worth   Philadelphia   San Diego   New York   Orlando   Austin   San Antonio
Toronto   Montreal   London   Sydney   Tokyo

Publisher	Earl McPeek
Executive Editor	Carol Wada
Market Strategist	Kathleen Sharp
Developmental Editor	steve Norder
Project Editor	Michele Tomiak
Art Director	David Day
Production Manager	Andrea A. Johnson

Cover: MATISSE, Henri
The Swimmer in the Aquarium {La nageuse dans l'auqarium}
Plate XII from *Jazz,* by Henri Matisse. Paris, E. Tériade, 1947.
Pochoir, printed in color, each double page: 16 5/8 × 25 5/8" (42.2 × 65.1cm).
The Museum of Modern Art, New York. The Louis E. Stern Collection.
Photograph ©1999 The Museum of Modern Art, New York

ISBN: 0-15-505169-5
Library of Congress Catalog Card Number: 98-87604

Address for Orders
Harcourt Brace College Publishers, 6277 Sea Harbor Drive, Orlando, FL 32887-6777
1-800-782-4479

Address for Editorial Correspondence
Harcourt Brace College Publishers, 301 Commerce Street, Suite 3700, Fort Worth, TX 76102

Web Site Address
http://www.hbcollege.com

Harcourt Brace College Publishers will provide complimentary supplements or supplement packages to those adopters qualified under our adoption policy. Please contact your sales representative to learn how you qualify. If as an adopter or potential user you receive supplements you do not need, please return them to your sales representative or send them to: Attn: Returns Department, Troy Warehouse, 465 South Lincoln Drive, Troy, MO 63379.

Printed in the United States of America

8 9 0 1 2 3 4 5 6 7   039   9 8 7 6 5 4 3 2 1

Harcourt Brace College Publishers

Historically, the field of personality as presented in textbooks could be seen as an accumulating collection of alternative points of view and strategies, often in conflict with one another. That can be discouraging to students who seek a coherent perspective, and it can be dismaying to researchers and teachers who would like to help build and teach a cumulative science rather just another viewpoint or mini-theory.

That is why it seems particularly exciting to this author that the field now may be evolving into what promises to become a genuinely cumulative and coherent science of personality. In such a field, seemingly discrepant positions and findings on both personality dispositions and personality mechanisms and dynamics can be understood and reconciled within a coherent unifying broader framework. While the full form and reality of that potential evolution remains to be seen, its outline at least seems to be becoming visible. This edition of **Introduction to Personality** is devoted to trying to advance this broader perspective and unifying theoretical framework, in which some of the best aspects of diverse perspectives can be reconciled, and to convey this coherent view of personality to the student.

Specifically, there are major changes in the content and organization of this sixth edition of the text, and they are more extensive than those made in any of the earlier editions. These changes reflect the remarkably exciting and prolific developments that have occurred in the past decade in personality psychology and related areas. Many of these advances in the field impact directly our understanding of the nature of personality. They include discoveries coming from diverse sources: behavior genetics, social evolutionary theory, trait theory and the Big Five, social cognitive theory, cognitive neuroscience, and findings at the interface of personality and social psychology.

To take account of these developments appropriately, the sixth edition includes approximately one third new material. It is a revision that is intended not only to make this text timely and up to date for the moment but also to capture the promising new directions into which the field seems to be moving at the turn into the next century. It also tries to offer the student a perspective through which to see and make sense of the essentials of what is known about personality. And it attempts to do so without excessive length, in fact, with only 18 rather than 19 chapters, by pruning material that is no longer central. It does so, for example, by eliminating whole chapters previously devoted to such topics as aggression, while integrating the essential findings and concepts wherever they fit best.

The most notable substantive change comes from the collaboration with Professor **Robert Plomin** of the Institute of Psychiatry in London, a world leader in the field of behavior genetics, in the revision of *Part III, Trait and Biological Approaches*. This section of the text has been extensively revised and now also includes an additional chapter that is needed, given how much has been learned in recent years in this area. Professor Plomin contributed materials and drafts particularly for Chapters 8 and 9, which provide a state-of-the-art perspective on the role of genetics in human personality. The resulting chapters contain the essentials of the latest scientific developments, in a style and at a level accessible to the undergraduate with virtually no background in science. In the same spirit, Part III now also includes the exciting current developments in the evolutionary perspective to personality.

Advances in recent years also have revitalized some basic concepts from the classic *psychodynamic approaches* and *phenomenological approaches*. Many topics central to these approaches are again of major interest but now are studied with better, more rigorous methods. Examples include the unconscious, mental and emotional processing at multiple levels of awareness, defenses, the therapeutic value of self-disclosure and support, and the role of the self and of self-discrepancies.

Part VI, Social Cognitive-Affective Approaches, also has undergone major revision to take account of the theoretical and empirical advances in that extremely active area of the field. Notable changes here include great attention to the role of affect, emotion, goals and motivation, and new findings on the nature of personality coherence and its behavioral expressions. The development of the Cognitive Affective Personality System (CAPS) model also provides a fresh route for understanding personality dynamics and dispositions within this framework. The approach is illustrated with both clinical and research examples that are particularly meaningful to undergraduates.

This revision gives these diverse developments the attention they merit and shows the links between current findings and concepts and their classic antecedents. My overarching goal is to indicate some routes toward a unifying cumulative approach to personality, and I hope this text provides a step in that direction.

The Instructors Manual/Test Bank, prepared by Sheri R. Levy of Columbia University, has been updated to coincide with the new edition. The manual contains an extended case study that helps students to utilize and apply what is learned in the text and lectures. Students can be invited to view the case from the various perspectives—and to identify the common themes that emerge. The Test Bank portion of the manual consists of virtually all new questions to reflect the changes made to the textbook. Questions for each chapter are divided by type to include 50 multiple-choice (except for Chapter 1), 25 true/false, 5 discussion, and 5 written response. The items are designed to assess student knowledge of the theoretical concepts, important empirical findings, history of the field of personality, and mechanisms or processes that underlie personality.

Thanks are due to many people for help with manuscript development and preparation. I am particularly grateful to Dr. Sheri Levy for preparation of the Instructor's Manual and Test Bank. I also thank her as well as Dr. Anita Sethi, Lisa Schwartz, and Sandra Testa for thoughtful and informative drafts summarizing selected research topics and invaluable assistance with diverse other chores and challenges essential in the preparation of this edition. Helpful early comments concerning the fifth edition and direction for the sixth edition were provided by Edward E. Abramson (California State University, Chico), Nancy Dixon (Tennessee Technological University), and Stanley Woll (California State University, Fullerton). At Harcourt Brace, the staff—most notably Carol Wada, steve Norder, Michele Tomiak, David Day, and Andrea Johnson—proved to be exceptionally helpful and constructive in the transformation of the manuscript into this textbook.

Walter Mischel
Columbia University
July 1998

BRIEF CONTENTS

CONTENTS

INTRODUCTION TO PERSONALITY

Sixth Edition

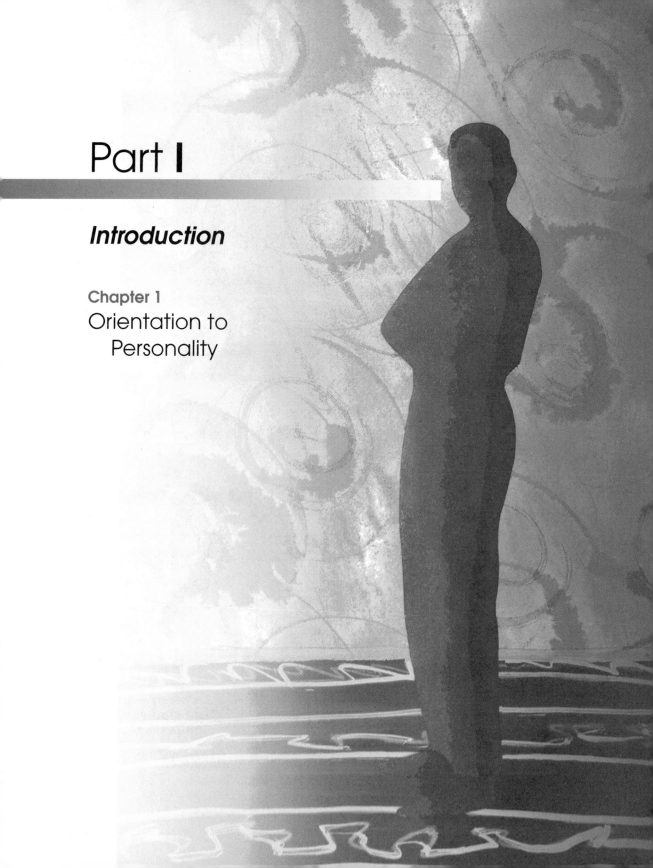

Part I

Introduction

Chapter 1
Orientation to Personality

Orientation to Personality

WHAT IS PERSONALITY?

Individual Differences.   Charles and Jane both are college freshmen taking an introductory course in economics. Their instructor returns the midterm examination in class, and both receive a D grade. Right after class, Charles goes up to the instructor and seems distressed and upset: He sweats as he talks, his hands tremble slightly, he speaks slowly and softly, almost whispering. His face is flushed, and he appears to be on the edge of tears. He apologizes for his "poor performance," accusing himself bitterly: "I really have no good excuse—it was so stupid of me—I just don't know how I could have done such a sloppy job." He spends most of the rest of the day alone in his dormitory, cuts his classes, and writes a long entry in his diary.

Jane, on the other hand, rushes out of the lecture room at the end of class and quickly starts to joke loudly with her friend about the economics course. She makes fun of the course, comments acidly about the instructor's lecture, and seems to pay little attention to her grade as she strides briskly to her next class. In that class (English composition), Jane participates more actively than usual and, surprising her teacher, makes a few excellent comments. This example illustrates a well-known fact: Different people respond differently to similar events. One goal of personality psychology is to find and describe those *individual differences* among people that are psychologically meaningful and stable.

Describing and Predicting.   Both students received a D, yet each reacted differently to the experience. How consistent are these differences? Would Charles and Jane show similar differences in their responses to a D in physical education? Would each respond similarly if they were fired from their part-time jobs? Would Charles also be apologetic and self-effacing if he received a personal rebuff from a close friend? Will Jane treat a poor grade the same way when she is a senior?

What do the observed differences in the reactions of the two students to their grade suggest about their other characteristics? That is, on the basis of what we know about them already, can we predict accurately other differences between them? For example, how do they also differ in their academic goals and in their past achievements and failures? Do they generally show different degrees of anxiety about tests?

Underlying Processes: What Causes the Differences? Explaining and Understanding.   In addition to mapping out the differences among people in terms of their characteristic ways of behaving—that is, thinking, feeling, and acting—personality

3

psychologists try to understand the psychological structures and the mechanisms or processes that underlie these differences. They ask: Why did Jane and Charles react so differently to the same event? What within each person leads to his or her distinctive ways of behaving? How are these distinctive patterns maintained, and how might they be changed? What must we know about the mind and personality of each person to under-stand—and perhaps sometimes even predict—what he or she will think and feel and do under particular conditions? Personality psychologists ask questions of this sort as they pursue the goal of trying to explain and understand the observed psychological differ-ences among people.

Alternative Meanings of "Personality".

But what *is* personality? Many people have asked that question, but few agree on an answer. The term *personality* has many definitions, but no single meaning is accepted universally.

In popular usage, personality is often equated with social skill and effectiveness. In this usage, personality is the ability to elicit positive reactions from other people in one's typical dealings with them. For example, we may speak of someone as having "a lot of personality" or a "popular personality," and advertisements for glamour courses promise to give those who enroll "more personality."

Less superficially, personality may be taken to be an individual's most striking or dominant characteristic. In this sense a person may be said to have a "shy personality" or a "neurotic personality," meaning that his or her dominant attribute appears to be shyness or neurosis.

More formal definitions of personality by psychologists also have shown little agreement. Influential personality theorists tell us that personality is:

> . . . the dynamic organization within the individual of those psychophysical systems that determine his characteristic behavior and thought (Allport, 1961, p. 28
> . . . a person's unique pattern of traits (Guilford, 1959, p. 5).
> . . . the most adequate conceptualization of a person's behavior in all its detai (McClelland, 1951, p. 69).

As these examples imply, in the past there may have been as many different mean-ings of the term *personality* as there are theorists who have tried to define it. Neverthe-less, a common theme runs throughout most definitions of personality: "Personality" usually refers to the distinctive patterns (including thoughts as well as "affects," that is, feelings and emotions and actions) that characterize each individual enduringly. Dif-ferent theorists use the concepts and language of their theories to carve their preferred formulations of personality. These different views of personality will become increas-ingly clear throughout this book as we examine the concepts and findings of personal-ity psychologists.

Toward a Unifying Definition of Personality.

In spite of the differences that continue to exist among alternative approaches to personality, as the science matures there is a growing consensus about the findings and concepts that have stood the test of time and the discoveries that seem most solid. Consequently, the field may be at a point where both a unifying conception of personality and, more modestly, at least a broadly acceptable definition are becoming possible. A good candidate for such a definition was offered by Pervin (1996, p. 414):

> Personality is the complex organization of cognitions, affects, and behaviors that gives direction and pattern (coherence) to the person's life. Like the body, personality consists of both structures and processes and reflects both nature (genes) and nurture (experience). In addition, personality includes the effects of the past, including memories of the past, as well as constructions of the present and future.

THE FIELD OF PERSONALITY PSYCHOLOGY

Within the discipline of psychology, personality is a field of study rather than a particular aspect of the individual. Although there are many different approaches to personality, there is general agreement about what the study of personality must include. Traditionally, "Personality is that branch of psychology which is concerned with providing a systematic account of the ways in which individuals differ from one another" (Wiggins, 1979, p. 395). The traditional focus is on individual differences in basic tendencies, qualities, or dispositions.

Individual Differences and Underlying Processes

Individual differences are always a core part of the definition of this field, but they are not necessarily the whole of it. Thus ". . . the term 'personality psychology' does not need to be limited to the study of differences between individuals in their consistent attributes. . . . Personality psychology must also . . . study how people's [thoughts and actions] . . . interact with—and shape reciprocally—the conditions of their lives" (Mischel, 1980, p. 17).

This expanded view recognizes that human tendencies are a crucial part of personality. But it also asserts the need to study the basic processes of adaptation through which people interact with the conditions of their lives in their unique patterns of coping with and transforming their psychological environment. This view of personality focuses not only on *personal tendencies* but also on *psychological processes* (such as learning, motivation, and thinking) that interact with *biological-genetic processes* to influence the individual's distinctive patterns of adaptation throughout the life span.

No other area of psychology covers as much territory as the field of personality does; personality study overlaps extensively with neighboring areas. The field of personality is at the crossroads of most areas of psychology; it is the meeting point among the study of human development and change, of abnormality and deviance, of competence and fulfillment, of emotions and thought, of learning, of social relations, and even of the biological foundations that underlie human qualities. The breadth of the field is not surprising because for many psychologists the object of personality study has been nothing less than the total person. Given such an ambitious goal, the student cannot expect to find simple definitions of personality.

Although the boundaries between personality psychology and other parts of psychology are fuzzy, personality theories do tend to share certain distinctive goals;

namely, they generally try to "integrate many aspects of human behavior into a single theoretical framework. Not satisfied with an inventory of psychological facts, personality theorists derive and explain these facts from a central theme" (Bavelas, 1978, p. 1).

Themes in Personality Theory

What should that central theme be? What should a good theory of personality contain and exclude? How should such a theory be built? How can one best analyze and study human behavior? The answers to all these questions are controversial. In dealing with them, different theorists throughout this book will compete for your attention, interest, and even loyalty.

Personality theorists not only tend to cover large areas and seek broad integrations, they also tend to deal with questions of central personal, philosophical, and practical importance. It is personality theorists who typically have grappled with such questions as: What are the basic causes underlying everyday interpersonal behavior? What are the roots of and best treatments for psychological disorders? What is "healthy," adaptive, creative personal functioning, and how can it be facilitated? What are the most fundamental, universal, enduring psychological qualities of human nature? How do they arise, change, or maintain themselves throughout the life cycle? Given the scope and personal implications of these questions, it is no wonder that personality theories (and theorists!) tend to provoke intense controversies. Sometimes the arguments are so heated that it becomes difficult to examine the questions objectively and to move beyond debate to research. Yet it is only through research that the psychological study of personality can build a view of the individual and of types of persons based on science rather than on speculation.

A History of Diverse Approaches to Personality

Historically, most psychologists in the field of personality share certain basic interests but also tend to favor and adapt one or more of a number of fundamentally different approaches, in part because they focus on different questions. To illustrate, let us briefly consider a concrete case: that of Jane, the college student we already met.

Jane's test scores indicate that she is very bright, and yet she is having serious difficulties in college. She suffers severe anxiety about examinations and is plagued by an enduring tendency to be overweight. In spite of her chubbiness, there is wide agreement that she is a very attractive person. Her boyfriend describes her as a "knockout"; her roommate says she is a very genuine person whose "inside is as beautiful as her outside." Jane's parents and sister see her as intelligent, sincere, and artistic. Her father thinks she may be experiencing an identity crisis but says, "She'll come through with flying colors." Jane says, "I remember being pretty lonely [as a very young child]. I started turning into myself in seventh grade and often hated what I saw . . . what really excited me was painting and music." In college, she says, "I still don't have a major—I don't even have a meaning. I'm still searching. . . ."

Table 1.1
Some Basic and Enduring Questions in Personality Psychology

1. What is given to the human being by inheritance (nature); what is acquired through experience with the environment (nurture)? How do nature and nurture—genes and socialization—interact in the course of development?

2. What are the best units for conceptualizing and studying people? Examples of the possible units include situations, physical responses, thoughts or cognitions, needs, conflicts, emotional states, inferred motives, and dispositions.

3. How stable and enduring are particular psychological qualities? How easily can they be changed? By what means? For what ends should such change be attempted?

4. Does what we do and think and feel characteristically depend mostly on the individual or on the situation? How do the two interact? How can one best understand and study the important social interactions between person and environment?

5. What basic, general principles emerge from the study of personality? How do these principles inform us about the causes of the person's behavior and the ways to understand, to modify, and/or to predict what individuals will be like and what they will really do in different situations?

6. What are the basic psychological processes through which individuals construct, interpret, and understand their social-personal world and come to deal with it in stable cognitive, emotional, and behavior patterns that characterize them stably?

Faced with a case such as Jane's, most psychologists try to understand and explain the basic causes of her behavior, including her thoughts and feelings. Many also would want to predict her future behavior as accurately and as fully as possible. With Jane, and everyone in general, they are interested in questions such as those listed in Table 1.1. Applying the issue of nature versus nurture to Jane, for example, raises some important questions. To what extent has inheritance produced her current problems and qualities, including her personal characteristics, her tendencies to be anxious, artistic, and overweight? If genes do play a significant role in determining such qualities, to what degree can Jane still change her own characteristics and behavior? What methods would be best to achieve this change? What role can she herself have as an active agent making such change? Most students of personality want to explain the causes of behavior, but they differ in the types of causes they emphasize, in the methods they use, and in the kinds of behavior on which they focus.

Personality Theories: Alternative Approaches

Some personality psychologists are most concerned with theory and generate ideas about the causes and nature of personality. Each theorist conceptualizes personality somewhat differently. Obviously, Sigmund Freud's view of personality, which emphasized unconscious motives, is very different from the formulations of early behaviorists, who stressed learned habits. Indeed, the concepts employed by such widely differing theories may have almost nothing in common.

Some personality psychologists believe that human behaviors have their roots in unconscious motives from one's distant past. Others focus on the individual's present relationships and current experiences. Although some theorists search for signs of character traits that are not directly observable, others attend to the person's overt actions—the things the individual does—and seek to sample them as directly and precisely as possible.

A few of the many theoretical alternatives for conceptualizing the same behavior are shown in Figure 1.1. The same behavior—Jane's becoming tense in response to an exam scheduled for tomorrow—is open to diverse interpretations about the reasons underlying her upset. Is Jane's reaction a sign of her more generalized fearfulness? Is it a symptom of an underlying problem provoked or symbolized in some complex way by the exam? Is it part of a learned pattern of exam fears and poor habits for studying? Is it related to more basic conflicts and insecurities about herself?

Conceptualizations about the meaning of behavior are more than idle games; they guide the ways we think about ourselves and the solutions we seek in efforts to better our lives. For example, if Jane's tension reflects unconscious conflicts and fears, it might help her to get better insights into her own motives. In contrast, if Jane's behavior reflects poor study skills, it might be better for her to learn ways of reducing exam-related tensions (for example, by learning to relax) while also mastering more effective ways of studying.

Students are easily puzzled by a field in which different theorists may fail to agree even about the meaning of the same behavior. It may help, however, to recognize that lack of agreement in this instance merely means that the same events can be construed in many different ways. The events are tangible and real enough: Nature goes on "minding its own business"; the events of life keep on happening no matter how

Figure 1.1
Examples of Alternative Conceptualizations about the Mechanisms (Reasons) Underlying the Same Behavior

Situation	Conceptions about possible underlying mechanisms	Response
Jane is at her desk preparing for an exam tomorrow.	Jane is a generally fearful person with diffuse anxieties. Jane really fears "success" and unconsciously wants to fail. Jane has learned to fear exams and has poor study habits. Jane's upset reflects her identity crisis about herself as a person.	Jane becomes increasingly tense and cannot study effectively.

people understand them. People behave and act continuously, but the meaning of those actions and the reasons for them may be conceptualized from many vantage points and for many purposes by different theorists.

From Grand Theories to General Approaches to Personality

In the first half of this century, grand theories of personality were developed by innovators such as Sigmund Freud who proposed distinctive conceptions of the nature of personality, typically based on their own personal and clinical experience. Early personality theorists, like Freud, usually worked as therapists treating psychologically disturbed and distressed individuals and used their cases as the basis for generalizing broadly to the nature of personality as they construed it.

In the second half of this century, personality psychology grew into a substantial field within the larger discipline of psychology. Researchers working with both normal and disturbed populations developed and applied increasingly sophisticated scientific methods to address many central issues in personality psychology. Increasingly it became possible to examine important questions about personality with research evidence.

In spite of the growth of personality psychology as a field of scientific research, most theories of personality do not lend themselves to precise scientific testing that allows them to be either supported or disconfirmed clearly on the basis of empirical studies (Meehl, 1990, 1995). There are many reasons for this, ranging from the difficulty of specifying the theoretical premises in testable terms to various types of experimental and statistical limitations in conducting and evaluating the test results. Because it is difficult to firmly reject or support a given theory on the basis of empirical studies, theories often function more like general guidelines or orientations for studying personality and interpreting the results from a particular perspective or framework. This, however, does not diminish their importance and their implications for those who care about personality.

While theories may not lend themselves to clear support or disconfirmation, they provide an orientation and perspective that stimulate different types of research within the field and different types of real-life applications of everyday potential significance. Most notably, they lead to different forms of therapy or intervention designed to modify or enhance personality constructively — with major differences among approaches in what is considered "constructive." They also lead to different approaches to assessing personality and to thinking about persons, including oneself, and thus matter a great deal to the image one develops of personality and individuality itself.

Toward a Coherent Perspective

To the beginning student, the fact that there are different approaches to personality may seem bewildering. When entering a new field one may simply want to get "The Truth" without the complexities of considering different viewpoints. A little reflection, however, leads one to a basic conclusion: The individual is influenced by many determinants, and human behavior reflects the continuous interaction of many forces both in the person and in the environment or situation (Mischel & Shoda, 1998).

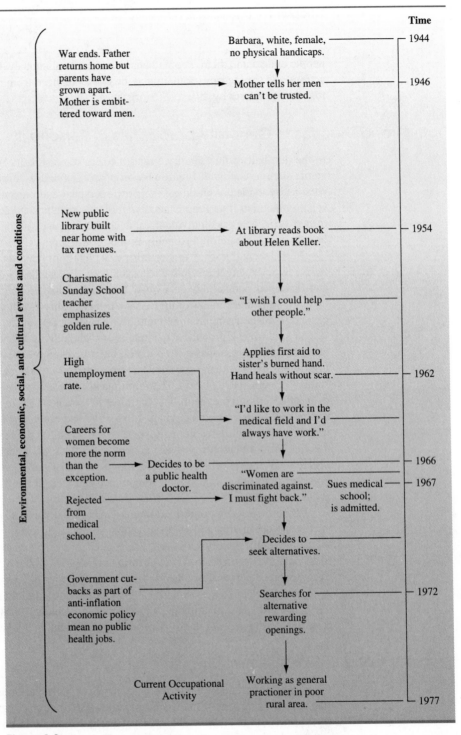

Figure 1.2

Many Factors, Both in Barbara and in Her Environment, Interacted and Combined to Influence Her Progress toward Her Present Occupation

SOURCE: Adapted from Krumboltz, J. D., Mitchell, A. M., & Jones, G. B. (1976). A social learning theory of career selection. *The Counseling Psychologist, 6,* 71-81.

Consider, for example, how a person chooses a career. The many influences on such a choice might include inherited and acquired abilities and skills, interests, and a wide range of specific experiences and circumstances. We can see this in the case of Barbara, a person whose decision to become a general practitioner of medicine in a poor rural area was affected by many factors throughout her life, as Figure 1.2 illustrates. If human behavior is determined by so many forces—both in the person and in the environment—it follows that a focus on any one of them is likely to have limited value.

Often our understanding improves when information from many perspectives and sources is taken into account. With Jane's anxiety about examinations, for example, it is informative to focus on her immediate fears and the conditions that currently evoke them. But it also may be worthwhile to examine the history of those fears, relating them to other aspects of her changing life. To use a historical focus, however, does not make it pointless to study the biological mechanisms involved in Jane's anxiety or to investigate the role of heredity in her tendency to be fearful or to study how she thinks and processes information when she is emotionally upset.

Alternative approaches, then, can complement one another constructively, increasing our total understanding and knowledge of individual cases and of personality as a whole. At times, to be sure, they can also produce critical findings that contradict each other and generate real conflicts. But those are some of the most exciting moments in science and often set the stage for dramatic progress.

OVERVIEW OF THIS BOOK: FIVE APPROACHES TO PERSONALITY

Personality psychology is rich in ideas, theories, and findings that advance and refine the understanding of human beings. In this book you will learn some of the major theoretical approaches to personality. We will survey some of the main concepts developed to describe and understand the important psychological differences among people, and we will consider the concepts and findings that are central to diverse views of human nature. The range of these concepts is great, with much research relevant to each. To capture the essentials, this text is organized into the five major approaches to personality that emerged from a century of work in psychology as a science and profession. Each part presents the main concepts, methods, and findings associated with that approach, and each focuses attention on distinctive aspects of personality. In combination, the five approaches provide an overview of the many complex and diverse aspects of human personality. Let us briefly preview each.

Psychodynamic Approaches: Uncovering Underlying Motives

The psychodynamic orientation focuses on psychological processes of personality interpreted as a largely unconscious struggle within the mind. It conceptualizes unconscious internal forces, or **psychodynamics,** within the personality that clash and conflict and reach compromises in a delicate balance; the individual's distinctive problems and behaviors, often in the form of symptoms, emerge from the underlying conflicts and the unconscious attempts to resolve them. For example, the compulsion to wash one's hands many times even when they are clean may reflect deep hidden wishes and conflicts beyond the victim's own awareness and understanding. Likewise, victims of traumatic experiences, such as sexual abuse in early childhood, may be tormented by fragmented memories and anxieties that return in nightmares and symptoms. The challenge is to unravel the meaning of the observed and often seemingly bizarre behaviors in order to help the victims achieve greater awareness and understanding of them and become able to cope with them rationally.

Although psychodynamic approaches have importantly influenced clinical psychology and psychotherapy for many years, some of their main ideas have suffered from being cast in a form that made them difficult to test scientifically. Consequently, the approach became separated from many of the mainstream developments in personality psychology. In recent years, however, there has been a renewal of interest in ideas about the unconscious and complex mental representations, motivations, and emotional reactions, stimulated by the development of increasingly sophisticated models of the mind in cognitive psychology. These developments make it possible to revisit and reconceptualize some of the contributions and insights of psychodynamic approaches, allowing them to be incorporated into current personality theory.

Trait and Biological Approaches: Dispositions, Genes, Biochemistry, and Evolution

People readily characterize one another in terms of personality traits: friendly, assertive, submissive, conscientious, and so on. Enduring personal qualities are the essence of trait concepts, and it is assumed that people are consistent and stable with regard to at least some important traits. A major goal is to discover the set of traits that apply to most people and on which they are relatively consistent. Psychologists in these approaches believe that they are well on their way to identifying the most important traits of personality. They compare individuals with regard to these traits in terms of the degree to which each trait characterizes him or her.

In addition to identifying and describing important individual differences, researchers within this approach explore their biological-genetic bases. They study the role of heredity in personality, for example, by comparing the degree of trait similarity found in identical twins who were raised apart versus in those who were raised together within the same home. Research increasingly points to the important role of genes in personality, providing much encouragement for this approach and calling attention to the complex interplay between genetic influences and environmental-situational influences. Likewise, there are exciting prospects about biochemical methods for influencing personality, with potential therapeutic applications for people suffering from severe psychological problems.

Still another route for connecting personality to its biological roots comes from the evolutionary theory. This theory—so basic for all science—is providing fresh insights as it is applied to understanding why particular personality characteristics and individual differences developed. It also addresses how traits and behavioral dispositions are expressed in relation to the problems posed by the environment and to such evolutionary challenges as finding and retaining a mate, reproducing, and surviving.

Phenomenological Approaches: The Self and the Internal View

Phenomenological approaches in part arose as a humanistically oriented protest against earlier views of personality. These approaches insist that people are not merely passively molded by internal and external forces that shape what they become. Instead, phenomenologists focus on the individual's perceptions and interpretations of the meaning of events and on each individual's own subjective experiences and feelings as he or she encounters those events. Honest self-awareness of what one is experiencing and self-acceptance of genuine feelings, in this view, are key ingredients of personal growth and fulfillment. People are capable of knowing themselves, of being their own best experts, and self-knowledge and self-acceptance become the route to realizing one's human potential fully.

In its contemporary form, this approach (particularly popular in the 1960s) has achieved a new life and vitality. One of its favorite concepts, the self, has become a major focus of research and has a central role in most accounts of personality. Its influence is seen in thinking on topics that range from self-esteem, self-control, and emotional self-regulation to interpersonal relations and the impact of culture and other people on self-concepts.

Behavioral Approaches: Experimental Analysis of Behavior

Early behavioral approaches provided the sharpest conflicts with the phenomenological approach and further stimulated its development. Traditionally, behavioral approaches to personality emphasized that all that we can ever observe directly about people is their behavior, that is, what they say and do, including their physiological responses. Even the most interesting inferences about motives, traits, or internal experiences rest upon observations of what the person says and does under various circumstances: We have no way of knowing what goes on inside other persons except by observing carefully what they say and do.

Behavioral approaches focus on an important behavior relevant to concepts about personality and then analyze the situations or conditions that seem to control that behavior, using experiments to test the effects. They have been especially useful for understanding the conditions through which behaviors relevant to personality are learned and can be modified. The results have been applied to help

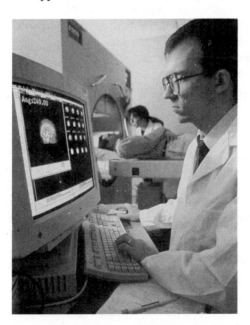

Advances in brain imaging offer a new way to study mental activity.

people overcome a variety of serious personal difficulties, ranging from common but debilitating fears, to weight problems, to learning deficits and handicaps, to increasing personal assertiveness.

In their original forms, these approaches drew mostly on classic types of learning such as conditioning. In a completely new direction, behavioral approaches are seen now in the rapid developments in cognitive neuroscience, the study of mental processes and the brain structures and functions that underlie them. For example, advances in brain imaging make it possible to see the areas of the brain that become activated during different mental activities, such as when thinking about emotion-arousing events. These new methods make it possible to analyze mental functions previously considered too mysterious for behavioral study with the objective methods of science.

Recent versions of the behavioral approach also have expanded so that they now deal more with social and interpersonal behaviors and problems using cognitive and social concepts and methods that go beyond the earlier conceptions of learning theories. In their present forms, these approaches remain relevant by supplementing their original methods with more contemporary developments originally designed to overcome their limitations, particularly as developed by the cognitive social approaches described next.

Cognitive Social Approaches: The Mind in Social Interaction

In the past 30 years the approaches called "cognitive social" (or "social cognitive") have emerged. As the name suggests, the focus here is on the social and cognitive aspects of personality, and much has been borrowed from and built upon findings from other areas of psychology. This reaching out to adjacent areas, including social, cognitive, and developmental psychology, has been intentional, part of an effort to construct a comprehensive account of personality processes based on the strongest foundations available. Thus although these approaches have generated novel concepts, methods, and much research, they are rooted in elements from each of the earlier approaches and try to integrate them into a coherent view of personality.

Rather than reflecting the exclusive views of any single theorist, these approaches emerged from the work of many theorists who shared common themes and goals. These diverse researchers and theorists were unified, however, in a focus on the individual's ways of thinking and processing information (*cognitive processes*) as determinants of his or her distinctive and meaningful patterns of experience and social behavior. Most recently, efforts have been made to go beyond the social and cognitive aspect of personality and to incorporate feelings, affects, and emotions within the same framework.

Toward an Integration: Emergence of a Cumulative Comprehensive Approach?

Each of the above approaches allows a view of particular aspects of personality and focuses on those features, studying them in depth but often neglecting or underestimating the other aspects. In recent years, however, personality psychologists seem to be crossing more freely over what used to be rigid boundaries dividing the major theoretical approaches. As one reviewer of ongoing work within diverse research orientations put it:

> Their research programs frequently inform one another. The complementary findings are beginning to portray a coherent (albeit incomplete) picture of personality structure and functioning. Personality psychologists have found common ground (Cervone, 1991, p. 371).

A more comprehensive view of the person seems to be emerging that seeks to incorporate many of the insights and findings from each of the diverse approaches within one unifying broader framework (e.g., Cervone, 1991; Mischel & Shoda, 1998). If this trend continues, it promises to be an exciting moment for the field. It suggests that personality psychology is becoming a science in which knowledge and insights are cumulative, allowing each generation of researchers to revise earlier conclusions, often radically, but nevertheless to build progressively on one another's foundations. If so, major contributions provided by each of the approaches to personality will ultimately become more integrated, retaining those elements that stand the test of time and research as the science matures.

In the same vein, there also are indications that boundaries are being crossed productively between personality psychology and related fields, both at more molar, social-cultural levels of analysis (e.g., Nisbett, 1997) and at more molecular levels, particularly in cognitive neuroscience and in behavioral genetics (Plomin, DeFries, McClearn, & Rutter, 1997; Rothbart, Derryberry, & Posner, 1994; Rothbart, Posner, & Gerardi, 1997). It has long been the hope of personality psychology that it could some day provide an integrated view of the person that at least begins to capture the complexity and depth of its subject matter: Optimists in the field are beginning to think that day might not be too far off. The last sections of this text, drawing on findings and concepts from all of the approaches discussed in earlier pages, present recent efforts in this direction.

STUDYING PERSONALITY

To convert personality theories from speculations about people into ideas that can be studied scientifically, we must be able to put them into *testable* terms. It is basic to science that any conceptualization must be potentially testable. This is what makes science different from the simple assertion of opinions. Perhaps the most distinctive feature of modern personality psychology has been its concern with studying ideas about people by actually putting those ideas to the test.

Testing the Limits of Approaches

When theorists develop their ideas, they often try to extend them as far as possible to probe their relevance for diverse areas of life. Such a stretching of concepts can be extremely fruitful for builders of theories because it helps them to generalize and to see how widely their ideas apply. Thus the theorist may try to make his or her ideas about the "unconscious" or the "self" or "early experience" serve to explain many different human phenomena. One or two favorite concepts may be used to deal with everything from love to hate, from birth trauma to fears about death, from deep disturbance to great achievement. While such an extension of ideas may be of use to the theorist, the student should ask, "Does it fit? How does the theorist know? What would we have to do to discover whether he or she is right or wrong? What are the consequences of thinking about it that way?" Likewise, efforts to measure and analyze personality supply information not only about the people who are measured but also about the meaning of the ideas and methods used in the measurement process. What we learn about 10 children from their answers to an intelligence test, for example, tells us something about the test and the concept of "intelligence" as well as something about the children.

Such an analytical, skeptical attitude is the heart of the scientific approach. It is a necessary attitude if we want to go beyond learning what different theorists say about human nature and personality to testing their ideas so that we can discriminate among those that have no substance and those that are worthy of further study. To test theoretical ideas to find the ones worth retaining, it is necessary to turn from theories to methods, applications, and findings. Therefore, for each theoretical approach we will consider those methods of personality study associated with that conception. We will describe the main methods of assessing persons favored by each approach and examine their relevance for understanding individuals. We also will consider some of the main research findings stimulated by each approach.

Practical (Therapeutic) Applications

Personality theories are often *applied* to help improve the psychological qualities of our lives. Even people whose problems are not severe enough to seek help from professionals still search for ways to live their lives more fully and satisfyingly. But what constitutes a fuller, more satisfying life? Given the diversity and complexity of human strengths and problems, it seems evident that simple notions of psychological adequacy in terms of "good adjustment" or "sound personality" are naïve. More adequate definitions of "adaptation" and "abnormality," of "mental health" and "deviance," hinge on the personality theory that is used as a guide. The theoretical conceptions discussed provide distinctive notions about the nature of psychological adequacy and deviance. Each also dictates the strategies chosen to try to change troublesome behaviors and to encourage better alternatives.

Many personality psychologists are concerned about practical questions. They tend to concentrate on searching for useful techniques to deal with the implications of personality for human problems, such as depression, anxiety, and poor health, and to foster more advantageous patterns of coping and growth. In addition to having enormous practical and social importance, attempts to understand and change behaviors provide one of the sharpest testing grounds for ideas about personality. These efforts include different forms of psychotherapy, drugs and physical treatments, various special learning programs, and changes in the psychological environment to permit people to develop to their full potential. Research on these topics informs us about the usefulness and implications of different ideas about personality change. The concepts, methods, and findings relevant to personality change and growth will be discussed at many points as they apply to each of the major approaches.

Resistance to a Science of Personality

Efforts to study personality scientifically face many problems. On the one hand, it seems fascinating to try to gain insight into the causes of one's own behavior and the roots of one's own personality. But at the same time we may resist actually achieving such an understanding and seeing ourselves objectively. Many scholars feel that it does violence to a person's complexity and "humanness" to study and "objectify" him or her in the framework of science. Instead, they suggest that perhaps the most perceptive and provoking studies of personality are found in great literary creations, such as the characters of a great novel.

People do not perceive themselves entirely objectively. Thus although it may be fashionable to say in public that human behavior, like that of other organisms, is "lawfully determined," privately the laws of nature may seem to be operating on everyone except oneself. Subjectively, while other people's behavior may be seen as controlled by "variables" or "conditions," one's own important thoughts, feelings, dreams, and actions may seem to defy such control and to resist scientific analysis.

Even within the field of personality psychology, there is some resistance to "objectifying" personality. For every personality psychologist who believes that people must be studied under carefully controlled experimental conditions, there is another who believes that individuals can be understood only by investigating them under "naturalistic," lifelike conditions. As one sensitive student of people noted, lives are "too human for science, too beautiful for numbers, too sad for diagnosis, and too immortal for bound journals" (Vaillant, 1977, p. 11).

Some personality psychologists commit themselves to quantitative, statistical techniques for gathering information from large groups. Others rely on intuition and subjective judgments based on lengthy personal experience with a few people. Some urge us to concentrate on "peak experiences"—moments of personal, spiritual, or religious climax and fulfillment. Others prefer to study simpler behaviors under conditions that permit a clearer analysis of causation. For example, they prefer to study the responses of a young child to specific instructions under the closely controlled conditions of a testing room at school. Different experts favor different techniques of investigation, but all of them generally share a conviction that ultimately theoretical ideas about personality and human behavior must be tested and applied.

Sources of Information about the Person

Psychologists guided by different approaches obtain information about people from many sources and through a number of strategies. Just as alternative approaches can and do complement one another, so do the different methods employed in personality psychology provide useful information for answering different questions. One of the most frequently used sources of information for the personality psychologist (sometimes called the **personologist**) is the **test.** A test is any standardized measure of behavior, including school achievement tests, mental ability tests, and measures of personal qualities, such as anxiety or friendliness. Table 1.2 shows an example of a test question used to measure self-reported anxiety. Some tests are *questionnaires* or *ratings* that may be answered directly

Table 1.2

Typical Test Item from a Questionnaire Used to Measure Self-Reported Anxiety

Situation 1 of the S-R Inventory of General Trait Anxiousness
"You Are in Situations Where You Are Being Evaluated by Other People"

(We are primarily interested in your reactions *in general* to those situations where you are being evaluated by other people. This includes situations at work, in sports, in social situations, etc.)

Mark one of the five alternative degrees of reaction or attitude for each of the following 9 items.

	Very much ←→ Not at all				
Seek experiences like this	1	2	3	4	5
Perspire	1	2	3	4	5
Have an "uneasy feeling"	1	2	3	4	5
Look forward to these situations	1	2	3	4	5
Get fluttering feeling in stomach	1	2	3	4	5
Feel tense	1	2	3	4	5
Enjoy these situations	1	2	3	4	5
Heart beats faster	1	2	3	4	5
Feel anxious	1	2	3	4	5

SOURCE: Adapted from Endler, N. S., Edwards, J. M. & Vitelli, R. (1989). *Endler multidimensional anxiety scales: Manual.* Los Angeles, CA. Western Psychological Services.

by the subject or by others who have observed the subject. Other tests involve *performance measures* (such as tests of arithmetic ability or spatial skills).

Another valuable source of information is the **interview**—a verbal exchange between the subject and the examiner. Some interviews are tightly structured and formal: The examiner follows a fixed, prescribed format. For example, in research to survey people's sexual activities, the interviewer might follow a standard series of questions, starting with questions about the subject's earliest experiences and going on to inquiries about current practices. Table 1.3 shows some typical questions from such an interview.

Table 1.3

Typical History-Taking Questions from a Survey of Sexual Activities and Attitudes

In adolescence, to which parent did you feel closest? Why?

In your school years, did you have special friends? Mostly boys? Mostly girls? Were your schools coeducational?

When did you first find out how babies are conceived and "where they come from"? How did you learn this? How did you react?

When did you start to date? Did you date in groups or on single dates?

NOTE: These questions are similar to those used in Masters, W. H., & Johnson, V. (1970). *Human sexual inadequacy.* Boston: Little, Brown.

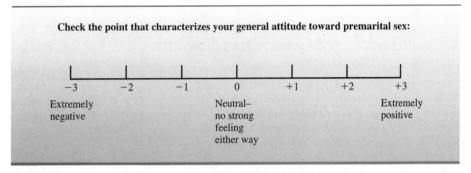

Figure 1.3
Any Attribute That Can Be Assigned Two or More Values Is Called a "Variable."
Here Is an Example of Attitude toward Premarital Sex Treated as a Seven-Point
Variable

Responses to paper-and-pencil tests and to interviews are widely used sources of information but are by no means the only ones. Valuable information also comes from *nonverbal responses,* such as changes in facial expression. Psychologists also study performance in special situations in which they can systematically observe selected behaviors. For example, they might investigate the frequency and intensity with which subjects engage in physical aggression, as when children are given a chance to attack a large inflated doll or adults have an opportunity to punish another person. Similarly, they might study responses to a solicitor who asks for charitable donations or reactions to someone who needs help and appears to be in distress. **Physiological measures,** such as heart rate, types of brain waves, amount of sweating, and degree of sexual arousal, can also provide valuable information. For an ingenious combination of methods used to study the ways in which obese and non-obese people differ, see *In Focus 1.1.*

The data that psychologists who study personality collect, regardless of their source, are conceptualized as **variables.** A variable is an attribute, quality, or characteristic that can be given two or more values. For example, a psychological variable might be an attitude toward premarital sex treated in terms of two values—positive or negative. Of course, the same variable could also be categorized into finer units such as seven points on a single scale in which 0 is neutral, +3 is extremely positive, and −3 is extremely negative (Figure 1.3).

Correlation: What Goes with What?

One way to study personality is to try to find relations among variables. Often, two or more variables seem to be associated—seem to "go together"—in such a way that when we know something about one variable, we can usually make a good guess about the other variables. For example, people who are taller generally tend to weigh more; when we know how tall someone is, we can roughly predict the person's weight. This "going together," this "co-relationship" or joint relationship between variables, is what

IN FOCUS 1.1 | *Individual Differences in Emotionality: Obese versus Normals*

There are great individual differences in the intensity of emotional responses made to any situation. The sight of blood may cause one person to faint while another remains calm. The importance of individual differences in emotionality has been illustrated by studies that compare the reactions of obese people with those of normal-weight people (Schachter & Rodin, 1974). Obese and normal-weight male college students listened to one of two kinds of tape-recorded material: neutral or emotionally disturbing. The emotionally neutral tapes invited the listener to think about rain or about seashells. The emotionally disturbing tapes detailed horrible images of the bombing of Hiroshima (for example, the skin of the victims coming off) or the listener's death as a result of leukemia (such as the incapacitating weakness and the terrible pain). Immediately after listening to the tape, the participants were asked the following five questions designed to measure emotionality:

1. Are you experiencing any palpitations?
2. Do you think your breathing rate is faster than usual?
3. Are you feeling generally upset?
4. Are you experiencing any anxiety?
5. Do you feel emotionally aroused?

Subjects responded to each of these questions by marking a scale numbered from 0 to 100, with 0 meaning "not at all" and 100 meaning "extremely."

Comparisons show that the obese individuals were more disturbed by the emotional tapes than were the normal-weight ones (see Figure 1.4). Note, however, that in their responses to neutral tapes, the obese were *less* emotional than the normals. In another study, when threatened with painful shock, obese individuals described themselves as more nervous than did normals (Schachter, Goldman, & Gordon, 1968). Although the

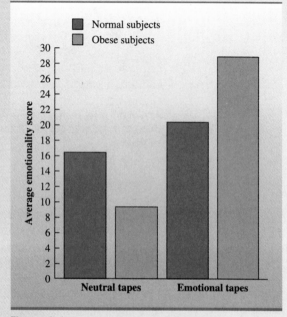

Figure 1.4
Emotional Responses of Normal and Obese People After Listening to Neutral and Emotional Tapes

SOURCE: Adapted from by Schachter S., and Rodin, J. (1974), *Obese humans and rats.* Potomac, MD: Erlbaum.

differences in emotionality between obese and normals in both these studies were too large to be due to chance, there were great differences among the individuals in each group. Emotionality depends on many variables both in the person and in the situation, and body weight is only one relatively small influence.

psychologists mean by the term **correlation.** Correlations are discovered by searching for answers to specific questions such as: Do attitudes toward premarital sex relate to subsequent marital adjustment? Is depression related to age? Do college grades relate to income in later life? A correlational study seeks not only to answer such questions with "yes" or "no," but also to provide a quantitative estimate of the degree of relatedness.

Correlations are called *positive* when a high magnitude of one variable is associated with a high magnitude of the other variable. For example, there is a positive correlation between the number of years of schooling a person has had and that person's ultimate socioeconomic level: the more schooling, the higher the person's socioeconomic level, and vice versa. A negative correlation, on the other hand, occurs when a high magnitude of one variable tends to be associated with a relatively low magnitude of the other variable. For example, there is a negative correlation between a person's intelligence and how satisfied he or she will be in doing a dull job.

The degree of relationship or correlation may be expressed quantitatively by a number called a **correlation coefficient,** symbolized by the letter r. Theoretically, a correlation coefficient can go from no correlation whatsoever, expressed as 0, to a perfect positive correlation ($+1$) or a perfect negative correlation (-1). In fact, correlations that are even close to perfect are very rare in psychology, showing that although many psychological variables are, indeed, associated with one another, the association usually is not very strong. Correlations of about .30 to .50, either positive or negative, are fairly common in psychology. Such correlations may allow predictions that significantly exceed chance guesses, but they are still far from perfect. Statistical computations are used to evaluate the strength, or "statistical significance," of particular correlation coefficients and to determine how far a given association exceeds that which would be expected by chance.

Correlations are useful, but they do not indicate cause and effect. Suppose a positive correlation were found between the income level of parents and the IQ level of their children. You could not conclude from this that income causes intelligence; the correlation would only alert you to the many things that might make the two tend to occur together. For example, the correlation might partly reflect the enriched environment or special privileges that more affluent parents could provide. Correlations can, however, be used to make predictions. For instance, one study used correlational methods to try to predict which students would be among the 500 who drop out of American medical schools each year (Gough & Hall, 1975). Among the best predictors were poor scores on a quantitative ability test and poor premedical grades.

Interpreting Correlations

Correlations, whether positive or negative, are almost never perfect. How can the less-than-perfect correlation, the one that falls somewhere between 0 and $+1.00$, be interpreted? The first thing to keep in mind is that a correlation is not a perfect percentage. A correlation of .50, for example, between shyness and femininity, does not mean that 50% of the variation of scores on the shyness measure (that is, in the differences among persons on the measure) is accounted for, or explained, by the relation with scores of the femininity measure. Nor is a correlation of .50 twice as strong as a correlation of .25.

Correlations tend to seem more powerful than they actually are. Unless a correlation is practically 1.00, many individuals who score relatively high on one variable will score relatively low on the other, making individual predictions difficult, inaccurate, or even impossible. The correlations typically found in psychological research tend to be moderate in strength, and therefore predictions of scores on one variable from the score on the other variable are moderately accurate.

Technically, one can estimate the percentage of the variance that the two distributions of scores have in common by squaring the correlation coefficient and multiplying by 100. For example, if the correlation is .50, then $.50^2 \times 100 = 25\%$. A correlation of .50 between "shyness" and "femininity," for example, means that 25% of the variation in shyness scores is accounted for by the femininity scores and the reverse. If the correlation between the two scores had been .25, then only about 6% of the variance would have been accounted for: 94% of the variance (of the individual differences in scores) would remain unexplained. A correlation of .25 is thus only one-fourth as strong as a correlation of .50.

Experimentation: Trying to Control the Phenomenon

To study cause-and-effect relations systematically, many psychologists favor the **experiment**—the basic method of science. An experiment is an attempt to manipulate or alter one variable of interest so that its impact can be determined. To do that, one tries to control all other conditions so that their influences can be discounted; then the effects of the variable of interest can be measured. The main limitation of the experiment in psychology is that to achieve good control over extraneous conditions the experimenter may have to set up situations that are so artificial and simplified that they have no resemblance to real life. The challenge of good experimentation in psychology is to achieve a reasonable degree of control without distorting the phenomenon one wants to study. Because the ethics of good research further limit the phenomena one can or should experiment upon, there are serious constraints on the types of experiments possible. Nevertheless, as will be seen throughout the text, personality researchers have managed to do many useful and relevant experiments.

The **independent variable** is the stimulus or condition that the experimenter systematically manipulates or varies in order to study its effects. It is called the independent variable because it does not depend on the subject's behavior; its presence or absence, increase or decrease, occur regardless of what the subject does. For example, to study altruism, one might expose subjects to a confederate who solicits contributions for a charity. The confederate might dress well and present a high-status appearance when soliciting half of the subjects and dress in a sloppy, low-status fashion with the other half. This variable—the solicitor's appearance—would be independent of the subject's behavior; it would be determined solely by the experimenter to see how it influences the subject's behavior.

The **dependent variable** is the aspect of a subject's behavior that is observed after the experimenter has manipulated the independent variable. It is a measure of the subject's response to the independent variable. In the altruism example it might be the amount of money that subjects promise to give the solicitor.

For many purposes **control groups** are essential in experimentation. Control groups are like the **experimental group** except for one crucial difference: They get no independent variable manipulation or treatment. They therefore provide comparisons for evaluating the effects of the experimental treatments that are given to the experimental groups. In the study of academic attitudes and course performance (see *In Focus 1.2*), for example, the inclusion of control groups made it possible to show that the measured improvement in grades and attitudes was not just due to taking tests, involvement in a prediction study, or the passage of time.

Experimenters want to select groups of subjects who are comparable or matched in all respects, such as sex, age, intelligence, and general background so that these factors can be ruled out as the causes of any differences found in the dependent variable. All subjects receive the same treatment with the crucial exception of the one factor that the investigator varies. Because it is usually difficult or impossible to match subjects who are assigned to different conditions, assignments may be made by **randomization,** that is, on a purely chance basis, as by flipping a coin or picking names out of a hat. The psychologist recognizes that there will be great individual differences among the subjects in any one group but assumes that by using many subjects and as-

IN FOCUS 1.2   *An Illustrative Experiment: Improving Course Performance*

To illustrate some of the basic features of a psychological experiment, let us consider a classic study by Meichenbaum and Smart (1971). They investigated the academic performance and attitudes of first-year engineering students who were working at an academic level so low that it endangered their continuation in school. The researchers tested the hypothesis that these students could be helped to do better if they increased their expectations for academic success. For this experiment the investigators randomly assigned the students to serve as subjects in one of three groups after the end of the first semester.

The subjects in one group received the experimental treatment designed to increase their expectancies. They were informed by the counseling service that tests they had taken earlier showed they were "late bloomers" whose mental abilities would soon reach a fuller development. They were also told that their test results predicted a high likelihood of academic success for them by the end of their first year. In the second group subjects were told that their test results permitted no definite predictions for either better or worse performance. This

group was called the "no-prediction control" group. The third group was called the "assessment control" group; its members had taken the same tests but were not given any expectation manipulation or prediction. The two control groups served as comparisons to see whether the experimental treatment would produce more improvement than that which might result from the students' just knowing that they were participating in a special prediction study or even from merely taking the tests.

Grades and measures of attitudes toward the school courses were obtained at the end of the year for all subjects. The results showed that in two out of four courses the students who had been told to expect success improved their grades more than did those in the two control groups. On the attitude measures, the students who expected to succeed also reported greater interest in their course work and more confidence about school work compared with both control groups. The study thus gave good evidence that by increasing their expectancy for academic success, borderline students could be helped both to do better academic work and to feel more positive about it.

signing them to the groups at random, these differences will average out. For example, although there may be great differences in intelligence among the subjects who participate in a study, if they are all assigned to groups randomly, the number of bright and dull ones in each should be approximately equal so that the average level of intelligence for all groups will be similar and thus matched. In the study of course performance (*In Focus 1.2*) the assignment of subjects to groups in a strictly random fashion ruled out the possibility that the three groups differed in some way beyond the treatments they were given.

Often a special control is required in psychological studies. Suppose, for example, an investigator wanted to test a drug intended to reduce anxiety. She would find some anxious subjects, administer specific dosages of the drug in the form of pills, and then test for reduced anxiety levels on such measures as self-reported tension or ability to cope with stress. But the subjects' improvement on these measures might reflect little more than their hopes and expectations that the drug would help them. Therefore, it is important to have at the same time another group, this one consisting of subjects who take an inactive substance, called a **placebo,** instead of the active drug. In the **single-blind method** the subjects do not know whether they are receiving the active treatment or some control treatment such as a sugar pill that looks like the real drug but is inert (inactive).

Of course, experimenters, just like subjects, may also be biased by their own hopes and expectations. For example, the researcher who wants to prove the value of a new drug for reducing anxiety might be fooled into seeing improvement where there is none. To avoid this type of error, the experimenter must not know which subjects receive the real treatment and which ones serve as placebo controls. She might employ an independent third party to keep track of which subjects receive which treatment. The method of keeping the experimenter as well as the subject ignorant of the group to which each subject is assigned is called the **double-blind method.**

To assess the effect of an experimental treatment, the researcher compares the results obtained with the experimental group (the one that actually received the treatment) with the results obtained from the control group. Suppose there is a difference, and the average score in the experimental group is, say, five points higher than the average score in the control group. What may one conclude? Very little, unless one can be sure that this difference is greater than the difference that would be expected just on the basis of chance. For example, if you correctly predicted how a tossed coin would land a few times, you could still not conclude that you had a special ability to predict heads or tails unless you could demonstrate your skill at a level that was clearly greater than chance. It is the same in experimentation: The differences found between experimental groups and controls must be shown to exceed chance. Statistics are used to calculate quantitative estimates of the degree to which a given finding or difference reflects more than a chance effect—in short, the degree to which it is *statistically significant.* Even if a finding is beyond chance, however, the psychologist needs to evaluate its strength or power. For example, given that a particular treatment decreases fear more than no treatment at all, how powerful is it? Statistical analyses can help evaluate the impact of particular experimental variables and judge their relative strength as well as their occurrence at a level significantly beyond chance. Some of the main terms used in psychological research are summarized in Table 1.4.

Table 1.4
The Language of Personality Research

Term	Definition
Variable	Any attribute or quality that can be given two or more values, such as degree of friendliness.
Correlation	The degree of relationship or association between two or more variables. For example, the degree to which people who are friendly in one situation are likely to be friendly in another situation.
Independent variable	The event, condition, or treatment that is systematically varied by the experimenter.
Dependent variable	A measure of the response to the independent variable.
Control (control group)	The condition against which the effects of the experimental treatment are compared. For example, the control subjects might receive an inert substance while those in the experimental group get a drug.
Randomization	The distribution of subjects into different groups (experimental or control) on a purely chance or random basis.
Single-blind technique	A method in which subjects are not informed of the group or treatment into which they have been placed. This is done so that subjects in different groups will have comparable expectations about the study.
Double-blind technique	In this method neither the subjects nor the experimenters know the group or treatment to which subjects are assigned. For example, neither the subjects nor the experimenters know who received the real drug or the inert substance until all the data have been collected and recorded.
Statistical significance	An effect, relationship, or difference that significantly exceeds that which might be expected by chance (as shown by a statistical test).

Differences between Groups: But Are They "Significant"?

In sum, psychologists must routinely decide whether a difference found between two or more groups is "significant" or whether it is merely the result of chance. The two groups being compared may be preselected to differ in some characteristic, like sex, birth order, or socioeconomic class; or individuals may be assigned at random to groups that receive different instructions, drugs, experiences of success or failure, or other treatment. The performances of these groups on some criterion (measure or standard) are then compared. If descriptive statistics suggest that there are differences, inferential statistics are used to help determine the degree to which the results reflect more than chance, or random, differences.

If first-born children in a sample of families score higher on IQ tests than later-born children, can we conclude that first-born children are brighter than later-born children? Or suppose that children instructed to "think happy" while waiting for a reward are able to wait longer than those in groups instructed to "think sad" or given no instructions at all. Is the difference in waiting times between the two groups greater than might be expected by chance?

Statistical tests of significance help to answer such questions; they indicate how trustworthy the differences between groups are. If, for example, the average delay times for groups of children given different instructions on what to think about during the interval are large enough, it is reasonable to assume that they are probably not the result of chance inclusion in one group of more children who would delay regardless of their instructions. Statistical tests of significance tell us how large the differences must be before we can conclude that they have not occurred by chance. To answer such questions, statistics are used to test the significance of an observed difference between the means of two groups. Whether or not the difference is significant—that is,

Concealed video cameras and one-way mirrors allow unobtrusive observation by researchers who remain unseen by participants.

beyond chance—depends not only upon the size of this mean difference but also upon the variation (variability) in the scores being compared.

For example, a sample of girls may be more "dependent" (in mean scores) than boys on a measure of "help seeking." But, if the variability *within* each sex is very high (and some boys are much more dependent than some girls), the difference in means may not be significant. On the other hand, even if the mean difference between the sexes is small, it still may be highly significant if the variability within each group is very small.

Statistics are used to estimate the probability that the obtained difference between the means of the groups is due to chance. The resulting probability is expressed as a p value; it indicates the number of times that the obtained effect or difference might be expected by chance. For example, a p of .05 indicates that the result would be expected by chance 5 times in 100 (or 1 chance in 20). It is conventionally agreed by researchers that a p smaller than .05 ($p < .05$) will be considered statistically significant, while a p larger than .05 ($p > .05$) is not going to be considered a reliable, beyond-chance finding. Obviously, the smaller the p value, the greater the confidence that an effect is really significant. A p of .001, for example, indicates that the result would be expected by chance only once in 1,000 times, while a p of .10 means that there is only 1 chance in 10 that the effect is merely accidental.

Naturalistic Observation: Moving out of the Lab

Often experimentation is not possible or not desirable. Just as astronomers cannot manipulate the actions of heavenly bodies, psychologists often cannot—or should not—manipulate certain aspects of human behavior. For example, one could not or would not create home environments in which children become delinquent or marital conflicts are provoked. Although such phenomena cannot be manipulated as independent variables, often they can be observed closely and systematically. Ethical considerations often prevent psychologists from trying to create powerful, lifelike experimental treatments in the laboratories (see Consent Form, Figure 1.5).

Even when some variables can be manipulated, the investigator often prefers to observe behavior as it naturally occurs, without any scientific interference. Some of the most informative work using this method, called *naturalistic observation,* comes from students of animal behavior, who unobtrusively observe the moment-by-moment lives of such animals as chimpanzees in their natural environment. Such methods have been adapted to study families interacting in their own homes (Patterson, 1990). In a somewhat similar fashion, but usually on a smaller scale, unseen observers may study children from behind a one-way mirror in such settings as a playroom or a preschool class (Mischel, Shoda, & Rodriguez, 1989). Of course, observation is a commonplace method in everyday life; through observation we form impressions and learn about events and people. The distinguishing feature of observation as a scientific tool is that it is conducted as precisely, objectively, and systematically as possible.

Part I • Introduction

CONSENT FORM

FOR PARTICIPATION IN AN EXPERIMENT IN _____
PSYCHOLOGY IN THE LABORATORY OF _____

1. In this experiment, you will be asked to
2. The benefit we hope to achieve from this work
3. The risks involved (if any)

CONSENT AGREEMENT

I have read the above statement and am consenting to participate in the experiment of my own volition. I understand that I am free to discontinue my participation at any time without suffering disadvantage. I understand that if I am dissatisfied with any aspect of this program at any time, I may report grievances anonymously to _____

Signed: _____
Date: _____

Figure 1.5
A Typical Consent Form for Participation in a Psychological Study. Ethical Standards Require That Participation in Research Come Only After Volunteers Understand the Task and Freely Consent

Sampling Daily Life Experiences

In recent years, many personality researchers have moved outside the lab to study people's daily experiences by obtaining their self-reported reactions to daily experiences that cannot be observed directly (Tennen, Suls, & Affleck, 1991). A good example is found in studies that ask for reports of positive and negative mood experienced in daily life (Diener, Smith, & Fujita, 1995). Studies like these use various types of self-

Table 1.5
Illustrative Methods for Sampling Daily Life Experiences

Method	Examples	Source
Preprogrammed time samples	Digital watch alarm signals time for subjects to record their tasks, behavior, and perceptions at the moment	Cantor, Norem, Langston, Zirkel, Fleeson, & Cook-Flannagan, 1991
Systematic diaries	Self-reports of reactions to daily stressors (e.g., overload at work, family demands, arguments)	Bolger & Schilling, 1991
Sampling emotions, symptoms, and other internal states	Self-ratings of emotional states (e.g., pessimistic–optimistic, full–hungry); occurrence and duration of symptoms (e.g., backache, headache); reported personal strivings and well-being	Larsen & Kasimatis, 1991; Emmons, 1991; Diener et al., 1995; David et al., 1997

recording and self-reports by subjects to sample daily events and emotional reactions to them as they occur in everyday life (see Table 1.5). For example, they use daily mood measures on which subjects indicate the degree to which they experienced various emotions (such as enjoyment/fun, pleased; depressed/blue) in each reporting period (Larsen & Kasimatis, 1991). Such reports can be linked to other aspects of

IN FOCUS 1.3 *Locating the Case of Gary in the Text for Each Approach*

Because material on Gary occurs wherever it is relevant to a particular approach, it appears in many places within the text. To help the reader find Gary W. within the context of each approach, the location of case materials and interpretations for him throughout the book is summarized in this *In Focus*. Students with an interest in the individual personality and in clinical psychology may wish to consult this material to view it as a whole in order to gain perspective on all the approaches to the same person. Such an overview of the differences among approaches in studying the same individual will be most meaningful after completing a reading of the text.

The chapters indicated contain case material and interpretations about the same case, Gary W., who will be assessed and conceptualized with the methods and concepts distinctive to each major approach to personality.

Approach	Location
Psychodynamic	Chapter 4
Trait-Biological	Chapter 7
Phenomenological	Chapter 11
Behavioral	Chapter 13
Social Cognitive	Chapter 18

Case Studies: Gary W., the Text's Case

Finally, in *case studies* the focus is on one individual assessed intensively. A variety of data sources may be used to study the person. For example, interviews, questionnaires, tests, observations, and diaries may be included. The study may deal with just one aspect of a person's life (reactions to divorce, for example) or may try to provide broad coverage of long periods or even an entire life.

In this text you will learn about the case method through an actual case, "Gary W." Gary's personality and the information made available about him is based on his clinical files but was modified sufficiently in order to protect confidentiality. The case will be used to provide concrete examples of how clinical psychologists, working within each of the major theoretical approaches presented in the text, conceptualize the same individual in their own terms, drawing on their own preferred methods. Therefore, the text presents not only information obtained directly from Gary but also a conceptualization of his personality written by psychologists from each perspective, using the methods and concepts they prefer. The placement of these case materials and interpretations in the text is shown in *In Focus 1.3*.

Methods like those described in this section are essential for the scientific study of persons, but they are merely the tools in the service of ideas. Throughout this text these ideas will be presented, followed by the methods used to explore their implications and the findings they yielded.

experience, such as minor illnesses and psychological well-being (e.g., Emmons, 1991). Likewise, daily reports of everyday reactions to various stressors and hassles, such as interpersonal conflicts at home, can be related to other measures of personality (Bolger & Schilling, 1991; David, Green, Martin, & Suls, 1997). Experience samples also are used to study reactions to common life problems such as adjusting to college life in terms of such personal tasks as getting good grades and making friends (e.g., Cantor et al., 1991).

SUMMARY

1. To psychologists, personality is a field of study rather than a particular aspect of people. Personality psychology is a field of great breadth. It overlaps with the neighboring areas of human development, creativity and abnormality, emotions, cognition, learning, and social relations. This book is an introduction to

the field of personality. It surveys personality theories and their applications, as well as personal adaptation and basic coping processes.

2. Traditionally, much attention has been devoted to theories about human nature. Personality theories differ in their degree of emphasis on the past and the present, the conscious and the unconscious, the directly observable and the relatively unobservable. The essence of a scientific approach to personality is to test various ideas, to evaluate the evidence supporting them, and to seek better ones. It is this potential testability of personality theory that differentiates a science of personality from the simple assertion of opinions or beliefs.

3. Complex human behavior has many determinants. It is the result of the interaction among various qualities in the person and the situation, often over long periods of time. Information about various types of determinants from many alternative perspectives helps to improve our total understanding. Sometimes, however, different approaches to personality come into conflict, and it is from such conflict that progress in science is often stimulated.

4. Specific personality theories have stimulated more general approaches to personality that can be grouped into five major categories. This text is organized into parts that present, in sequence, these five approaches: psychodynamic, trait and biological, phenomenological, behavioral, and cognitive social. Each approach provides basic concepts as well as strategies for seeking information about people and for changing maladaptive behavior in constructive ways. The successes achieved by these applications and the research they generated reflect the value (and limitations) of the personality concepts that guide them. Contemporary personality research investigates psychological differences among individuals and the processes that underlie them.

5. Different approaches favor different methods; each has distinct uses for getting particular types of information. Paper-and-pencil tests, interviews, performance in special situations, and physiological measures and other nonverbal responses are all among the sources of information used. Regardless of its source, any information may be treated as a variable, which is defined as a characteristic or quality that can be given two or more noticeably different values, such as high and low.

6. Individual differences were illustrated in a study of how obese versus normal-weight individuals react emotionally to the same situation. The obese individuals reported more emotionality than normal subjects when listening to emotionally disturbing material but less when listening to neutral material.

7. A correlation is an expression of the relationship between two variables (for example, the association between people's height and their weight). When the correlation is zero, there is no relationship between the two variables. In a positive correlation, the variables are related in such a way that a high value for one is associated with a high value for the other. In a negative correlation, a high value for one variable is associated with a low value for the other.

8. Statistical techniques are needed to evaluate whether or not the relationship between two or more variables is statistically significant—that is, greater than would be expected by chance. If two variables are significantly related, then a prediction may be made about one on the basis of knowledge of the other. Correlations, however, cannot provide an answer to the question of cause and effect. Two variables may be associated even though neither one causes the other.

9. In the experiment, the basic method of science, the researcher systematically manipulates one treatment or variable while holding all other conditions constant. The group that receives the treatment or is exposed to this one variable is called the "experimental group" (treatment group). A "control group" does not receive the treatment so that it can serve as a comparison. The assignment of subjects to experimental or control groups is usually done at random to avoid bias (any difference between groups in any respect other than the experimental variable).

10. An independent variable is the variable or treatment that is administered systematically by the experimenter, independently of the subject's behavior. The dependent variable is the subject's response to the independent variable. A placebo is an inert substance that may be given to control group subjects in an experiment testing the efficacy of a drug. In the single-blind method, subjects do not know whether they are in the control or experimental group. In the double-blind method, neither the experimenter nor the subjects know who is in the treatment or control groups.

11. In recent years many personality researchers have moved outside the lab and devised measures to study experiences and behaviors as they unfold. These methods include daily diary records and self-reports of emotional reactions, symptoms, and other behavior as they occur. Case studies provide another useful tool for studying persons in depth. The case study of Gary W. will be used to illustrate the five major approaches throughout the text. Each approach provides different types of information about Gary, and each views him in terms of its own conception of personality and has its favorite methods.

Part II

Psychodynamic Approaches

Psychodynamic Theories: Freud's Conceptions

It is a mistake to think that Freud's ideas about sexuality in the young child or the existence of deep unconscious wishes about a parent are especially difficult for the modern person to accept. Far more unacceptable today is his idea that we human beings really can neither know ourselves nor one another: We are trapped in our solitary systems of fantasy, full of misperceptions and self-deceptions, driven by early blueprints that prevent us from seeing clearly. Most tragic in this vision is that while much in life and in our own desires urges us to connect to others, the psychoanalyst is convinced that we really cannot (Malcom, 1982, p. 6). This disturbing conclusion had its beginnings not in a philosopher's speculations, but in Sigmund Freud's experiences as a Viennese physician a century ago.

Curiously, Freud started his career in medicine with research on cocaine. In 1884 the properties of this new drug intrigued him, partly because it helped him to get some relief from his own episodes of depression. When he became aware of cocaine's dangers, he soon gave it up, both for personal use and as a research problem. Studying for six months with the neurologist Jean Charcot in Paris in 1885, he became interested in the use of hypnosis to help patients deal with various nonorganic symptoms of "nervous disorders," particularly "hysteria."

Freud's own pioneering breakthroughs began from his clinical observations of patients he was seeing in his private practice when he returned to Vienna. Imagine scenes like this one in his consulting room on a pleasant residential street in the Vienna of 1905. Sigmund Freud is presented with a young girl who feels compelled to rinse out her washbasin over and over, dozens of times after each time she washes herself. She cannot stop, even though the basin is obviously clean. Her habit becomes so intense and upsetting that her whole life revolves around it. Why? Another woman appears to be physically well upon examination, yet she is able to sit in only one chair, clings to it for hours, and leaves it only with the greatest of difficulty. Why? A young boy becomes terrified of horses, although he himself was never hurt by one. Why? Still another patient appears to be blind, although tests of her vision show that her eyes and visual system are undamaged. Again, why? It was puzzles like these that intrigued the young genius—the Viennese physician Sigmund Freud (1856–1939)—who invented psychoanalysis, reshaped the field of psychology, and influenced many later developments in all the social sciences and in Western concepts of human nature.

**Sigmund Freud
(1856–1939)**

From these puzzles Freud created a theory and a treatment method that changed our view of personality, health, and the mind itself. Working as a physician treating disturbed people in Vienna at the turn of the century, he formulated a theory that upset many cherished assumptions about human nature and startled the neo-Victorian world. Before Freud, people's behavior was believed to be under their conscious and rational control. Freud turned that conception upside down. Rather than seeing consciousness as the core of the mind, Freud compared personality with an iceberg: Only the tip shows itself overtly; the rest lies below. Rather than viewing the person as a supremely rational being, he saw people as driven by impulses and striving to satisfy deep and lasting sexual and aggressive urgings. Rather than relying on people's reports about themselves as accurate self-representation, he interpreted what they said and did as highly indirect, disguised, symbolic representations of unconscious underlying forces.

In the course of more than 40 years of active writing and clinical research, Freud developed a theory of personality, a method of treatment for personality disturbances, and a wealth of clinical observations based on his therapeutic experiences as well as on his analyses of himself. Freud based both his theory and his psychoanalytic treatment on his extensive clinical observation of disturbed persons. He first noted certain **sensory anesthesias,** which are losses of sensory ability, as in blindness, deafness, or loss of feeling in a body part. He also found patients with motor paralyses that seemed to have no neurological origin. He proposed that these symptoms expressed a way of defending against unacceptable unconscious wishes. For example, a soldier who cannot admit his fear of facing battle develops a motor paralysis without a neurological basis. Or a young bride, unable to admit her hostility to her husband, becomes confined to her chair, although she shows no physical disease. All these examples illustrate **hysteria.** The fundamental feature of hysteria, according to Freud, is the presence of massive repression and the development of a symptom pattern that indirectly or symbolically expresses the repressed needs and wishes. On the basis of careful clinical observations, Freud gradually developed his theory of personality, continuously changing his ideas in the light of his growing clinical experiences and insights.

BASIC ASSUMPTIONS: UNCONSCIOUS MENTAL DETERMINISM

Two key assumptions underlie much of Freud's conception:

First, his unique innovation was to propose that behavior is never accidental: It is *psychologically determined.* Freud's work with mental patients convinced him that their bizarre behavior was meaningful and determined by underlying mental continuities that persist in the personality.

Second, these continuities in personality function outside the zone of the person's complete consciousness. They are *unconscious causes* that determine actions, but without the actor's full awareness.

The Unconscious

Freud the scientist was driven to try to explain the irrational behavior he witnessed in his patients. They seemed compelled to do things that they could not explain or sometimes even remember. Most puzzling, he could not attribute their symptoms to organic causes such as brain injuries or physical diseases: Physically they were intact. They were consciously trying to stop their symptoms, desperate to relieve them, but they simply could not control them. Freud's insight was to propose that some unconscious "counterwill" or irrational force was behind the symptom psychologically: The battles between the conscious will and the unconscious counterwill became the war of mental life in his theory.

Around the year 1900, Freud first divided mental processes into three types that vary in the degree to which they are available to awareness: conscious, preconscious, and unconscious (Freud, 1905). We are instantly aware of our conscious thoughts. The immediately available level of consciousness refers to what is in one's attention at a given moment. The many events that we can bring into attention more or less easily, from the background music on the radio to memories of things experienced years ago, are **preconscious.** Thus even though we are not aware of preconscious thoughts at a given moment, we can bring them into awareness voluntarily and fairly easily. In contrast, outside this range of the potentially available lies the **unconscious.** This third zone is not responsive to our deliberate efforts at recall, and it is the layer that was Freud's core concern. Because their content is threatening, unconscious mental activities are kept unconscious by a mechanism of repression that works actively to keep them away from our awareness, so that we simply are unable to raise them into consciousness.

The Roads to the Unconscious

Freud was eager to find methods for his work that would make his ideas more than abstract claims or beliefs. It was through these methods that his conception achieved its richness and ultimately made its enormous impact. If the unconscious mind was so important for understanding psychological causes, then the challenge was how to get to it.

Dreams.   Freud probed the unconscious most deeply through his explorations of dreams. He saw his 1899 book, *The Interpretation of Dreams,* like the adventures of a Columbus of the mind, a voyage into the darkest regions. The dream, Freud proposed, was the dreamer's unconscious effort to fulfill a wish that could not be expressed more directly. The analyst's task was to discover the hidden secrets underneath the surface content of the dream. To uncover those buried meanings, the analyst must overcome the dreamer's own resistance to facing himself or herself honestly, no matter how frightening or ugly the discoveries might prove to be.

In his voyage into the unconscious, Freud proceeded by scrutinizing his own dreams to try to face the motivations deep within his own personality. Unflattering self-revelation often resulted. In one dream, for example, Freud is troubled by fears about plagiarizing and dreams about himself being treated as a thief stealing overcoats in lecture halls (Roazen, 1974, p. 99). Through such self-analysis, Freud constructed his theory of the unconscious and the devious self-deceptions with which people try to disguise their own wishes from themselves.

In *The Interpretation of Dreams,* Freud elaborately built the case that in the dream we can find the hidden fulfillment of a desire that the person is trying to avoid experiencing consciously. Interestingly, this insight into the wish-fulfilling nature of dreams also led to the view that dreams, rather than disturbing sleep, actually function as the "guardians" of sleep. More than 50 years later, experiments discovered that in fact people need their dreams and become deeply troubled if their sleep is deprived of the phases in which dreaming naturally occurs (Roazen, 1974).

Neurotic Symptoms.   From his pioneering theory of dreams, Freud moved on to analyze the meaning of neurotic symptoms. He argued that, like dreams, these other expressions of the unconscious also reflected a mix of unacceptable wishes (sexual and aggressive impulses) compromised by the inhibiting forces of the mental censors blocking their direct expression. By allowing the unconscious wishes to become conscious, Freud believed that their indirect expression as symptoms could be reduced. His ideas about treatment followed from this insight.

The main sources of anxiety for Freud were the person's own unconscious sexual desires and aggressive impulses. He saw both sexual and aggressive urgings as basic human impulses or instincts, part of our heritage. He believed that sexuality does not begin with puberty but is visible early in childhood. It shows itself also in the young girl's affection for her father and the boy's infantile desires for his mother. Emotional attitudes, moreover, arise in these early relations, as expressed in the **Oedipus complex,** symbolized in the father–son conflicts of ancient Greek myths.

In the face of the objections and prudishness of the Victorian Age, he insisted that the route to self-acceptance was the honest recognition of one's instinctual sexuality and aggressiveness: Avoiding self-deception was the key. Making the unconscious impulses conscious was the road to health. The symptoms, Freud believed, were simply the indirect and sometimes symbolic expression of the unacceptable impulses that the person was unable to face consciously.

Free Association.   Much of Freud's thinking was built on the analysis of dreams, but that was not the only method he favored. Another road to the unconscious, sometimes called the "royal road," became the therapeutic method of **free association.** In this method the patient, reclining on a couch, is encouraged to simply say anything and everything that comes to mind, no matter what it is or how irrational it might seem, without censoring it.

By allowing unconscious material to be expressed freely, the patient, assisted by the analyst in the close relationship or "transference" they build, begins to let the unconscious become conscious. Although "resistance" to this process occurs often, it is gradually "worked through" until the unacceptable wishes can be faced. Then the patient is freed from having to manifest them indirectly through such symptoms as hysterical paralysis or other neurotic expressions.

PSYCHIC STRUCTURE: ANATOMY OF THE MIND

To understand how we deal with unconscious wishes, Freud (1933) also developed an "anatomy" of the mind, which occupied him in the early part of the 1920s. This led to the structural view of personality consisting of three "institutions" or "agencies" of the mental personality: the id, ego, and superego. These institutions are formed in the course of early experience, with the superego, the last one in the sequence, crystallized some time after the sixth year, approximately.

These three agencies are closely linked to the three layers of consciousness. The id is in the unconscious layer, characterized by mental processes outside one's awareness, the ego is predominantly conscious, and the superego includes a mix of conscious and unconscious processes. Although the three parts interact intimately, each has its own characteristics, which are summarized in Table 2.1 and discussed next.

Table 2.1
The Freudian Conception of Mental Structure

Structure	Consciousness	Contents and Function
Id	Unconscious	Basic impulses (sex and aggression); seeks immediate gratification regardless of consequences; impervious to reason and logic; immediate, irrational, impulsive
Ego	Predominantly conscious	Executive mediating between id impulses and superego inhibitions; tests reality; seeks safety and survival; rational, logical, taking account of space and time
Superego	Both conscious and unconscious	Ideals and morals; strives for perfection; incorporated (internalized) from parents; observes, dictates, criticizes, and prohibits; imposes limitations on satisfactions; becomes the conscience of the individual

The Id: At the Core

The **id** is the mental agency that contains everything inherited, especially the instincts. It is the basis of personality, the energy source for the whole system, and the foundation from which the ego and superego later develop. The id, according to Freud, is the innermost core of personality, and it is closely linked to biological processes.

The id's instincts have their source biologically within the excitation states of the body. They act like drives, pressing for discharge (release). They are motivated, in the sense that their *aim* is to seek reduction, that is, to lower the state of excitation. Usually drive reduction requires an external *object* in the outside world, including, of course, people—primarily the mother for most infants. Instinctual drives are biological and inborn, but the objects involved in attempts to reduce the drives depend on the individual's particular early experiences.

The Pleasure Principle.   Increases in energy from internal or external stimulation produce tension and discomfort that the id cannot tolerate. The id seeks immediate tension reduction, regardless of the consequences. This tendency toward immediate tension reduction is called the **pleasure principle.** The id obeys it, seeking immediate satisfaction of instinctual wishes and impulses, regardless of reason or logic or consequences.

Sexual and Aggressive Instincts.   Freud (1940) believed the impulses of the id to be chiefly *sexual* and *aggressive instincts.* He classified these impulses or instincts into the categories of *life,* or sexual instincts, and *death,* or aggressive instincts. The psychological representations of these instincts are wishes, and they often are irrational and unconscious.

Primary Process Thinking.   To discharge tension, the id forms an internal image or hallucination of the desired object. The hungry infant, for example, may conjure up an internal representation of the mother's breast. The resulting image is considered a wish fulfillment, similar to the attempted wish fulfillment that Freud believed characterized normal dreams and the hallucinations of psychotics. **Primary process thinking** was Freud's term for such direct, reality-ignoring attempts to satisfy needs irrationally. Because mental images by themselves cannot reduce tension, the ego develops.

The Ego: Tester of Reality

The **ego** is a direct outgrowth of the id. Freud described its origin this way:

> Under the influence of the real external world around us, one portion of the id has undergone a special development. From what was originally a cortical layer, equipped with the organs for receiving stimuli and with arrangements for acting as a protective shield against stimuli, a special organization has arisen which henceforward acts as an intermediary between the id and the external world. To this region of our mind we have given the name of *ego* (Freud, 1933, p. 2).

The ego is in direct contact with the external world. It is governed by considerations of safety, and its task is preservation of the organism. The ego wages its battle for survival against both the external world and the internal instinctual demands of the id. In this task it has to continuously differentiate between the mental representations of wish-fulfilling images and the actual outer world of reality. In its search for food or sexual release, for example, it must find the appropriate tension-reducing objects in the environment so that tension reduction can actually occur. That is, it must go from image to object and get satisfaction for id impulses while simultaneously preserving itself.

The Reality Principle.   The ego's function is governed by the **reality principle,** which requires it to test reality and to delay discharge of tension until the appropriate object and environmental conditions are found. The ego operates by means of a "secondary process" that involves realistic, logical thinking and planning through the use of the higher or cognitive mental processes. That is, while the id seeks immediate tension reduction by such primary process means as wish-fulfilling imagery and direct gratification of sexual and aggressive impulses, the ego, like an executive, mediates between the id and the world, testing reality and making decisions about various courses of available action. For example, it delays impulses for immediate sexual gratification until the environmental conditions are appropriate.

Freud believed the ego was the only hope for the world, the part of the mind that would allow humans to emerge from the irrationality and primitivism of being driven wildly by their biological impulses. The ego was the way toward a life of reason: "Where id was," Freud wrote, "there shall ego be," and psychoanalysis was the road for that transformation from the person's domination by impulsivity to rationality and insightfulness.

The Superego: High Court in Pursuit of Perfection

Freud's third mental structure was the superego. He wrote:

> The long period of childhood, during which the growing human being lives in dependence on his parents, leaves behind it as a precipitate the formation in his ego of a special agency in which this parental influence is prolonged. It has received the name of *superego.* In so far as this superego is differentiated from the ego or is opposed to it, it constitutes a third power which the ego must take into account (Freud, 1933, p. 2).

Thus the **superego** is the agency that internalizes the influence of the parents. It represents the morals and standards of society that have become part of the internal world of the individual in the course of the development of personality. The superego is the conscience, the judge of right and wrong, of good and bad, in accord with the internalized standards of the parents and thus, indirectly, of society. It represents the ideal. Whereas the id seeks pleasure and the ego tests reality, the superego seeks perfection. The superego, for Freud, involved the internalization of parental control in the form of self-control. For example, the individual with a well-developed superego resists "bad" or "evil" temptations, such as stealing when hungry or killing when angry, even when there are no external constraints (in the form of police or other people) to stop him.

The superego develops around age five out of the human infant's long period of helplessness and extreme dependency on caregivers. The young child desperately fears the possible loss of this early love; the threat of parents withdrawing protection and gratification is terrifying. At first this fear is rooted in the objective anxiety of losing love and satisfaction due to the child's own actions (being "bad"). In time, an active *identification* occurs as the child incorporates the parental images and commands into itself psychologically. As the parental wishes become incorporated, through this process the conscience becomes an internal voice rather than an external control.

Once fully developed, the superego can become a compelling and even irrational force of its own, just as demanding as the id. Examples of this force are seen in severe depressions characterized by extreme self-hatred and self-destructiveness. The tyranny of the superego is thus added to the demandingness of the id. It is the burden of the ego to continuously try to compromise among these competing forces while testing the waters of "reality."

CONFLICT AND ANXIETY

Conflict

According to Freud (1915), the three parts of the psychic structure—id, ego, and superego—are always in dynamic conflict. The term *dynamics* refers to this continuous interaction and clash between id impulses seeking release and inhibitions or restraining forces against them—an interplay between driving forces and forces that inhibit them. These forces and counterforces propel personality.

The id's drive for immediate satisfaction of impulses reflects human nature: People are motivated to avoid pain and achieve immediate tension reduction. This drive for immediate satisfaction of instinctual demands leads to a clash between the individual and the environment. Conflict develops to the degree that the environment and its representatives in the form of other persons, notably the parents in childhood, and later the superego, punish or block immediate impulse expression.

Persons in time come to incorporate into their superegos the values by which they are raised, largely by internalizing parental characteristics and morals. In Freud's view, perpetual warfare and conflict exist between humans and environment. Insofar as societal values become **internalized** as part of the person, this warfare is waged internally among the id, ego, and superego, and it produces anxiety.

Three Types of Anxiety

Freud (1933) distinguished three kinds of anxiety. In **neurotic anxiety** the person fears that his instincts will get out of control and cause him to behave in ways that will be punished. In **moral anxiety** the person feels conscience-stricken or guilty about unacceptable things that she feels she has done or even contemplates. Both neurotic and moral anxiety are derivatives of reality anxiety, the fear of real dangers in the external world.

The sequence of events in reality anxiety is simple: A danger exists in the external world, the person perceives it, and this perception evokes anxiety. This sequence may be summarized as:

external danger → perception of danger → reality anxiety

Because anxiety is painful (tension producing), we try to reduce it as quickly as possible. Usually we try to cope with anxiety by anticipating and fighting dangers by realistic means: locking doors to keep out intruders, getting physical checkups to guard our health, cleansing wounds to prevent infection, seeking shelter against the elements. When realistic methods fail (or cannot be found), unrealistic **defense mechanisms** may be tried unconsciously. Defenses are used especially in the internal struggle, where the individual tries to cope with his or her own unacceptable wishes. These defenses serve as disguises through which people hide their motives and conflicts from themselves as well as from others.

BASIC DEFENSE MECHANISMS

Most Freudian analysts now see the defense mechanisms as the core of psychodynamics. These are the processes through which the ego does much of its peace-keeping work. They are the mechanisms through which the ego tries to subordinate the impulses, test reality, and accommodate the demands of the superego in the lifelong internal war within the psyche.

Making distinctions among Freud's three types of anxiety requires complex judgments.

Psychodynamic theorists emphasize that when a threat becomes especially serious, it may lead to intense inhibitions. In the psychodynamic view, such defensive inhibition is desperate and primitive. It is a massive, generalized, inhibitory reaction rather than a specific response to the particular danger. This **denial** defense occurs when the person can neither escape nor attack the threat. If the panic is sufficient, the only possible alternative may be to deny it. Outright denial may be possible for the young child, who is not yet upset by violating the demands of reality testing. When the child becomes too mature to deny objective facts in the interests of defense, denial becomes a less plausible alternative and repression may occur.

Repression

In psychodynamic theory **repression** usually refers to a particular type of denial: ". . . the forgetting, or ejection from consciousness, of memories of threat, and especially the ejection from awareness of impulses in oneself that might have objectionable consequences" (White, 1964, p. 214).

Repression was one of the initial concepts in Freud's theory and became one of its cornerstones. Freud (1920) believed that the mechanisms of denial and repression were the most fundamental or primitive defenses and played a part in other defenses. Indeed, he thought that other defenses started with a massive inhibition of an impulse, which was followed by various elaborations (see Table 2.2).

Freud based his ideas concerning repression and defense on his clinical observations of hysterical women at the turn of this century. Recall that he noted that some of these patients seemed to develop physical symptoms that did not make sense neurologically. For example, in an hysterical difficulty called "glove anesthesia," the patient showed an inability to feel in the hands—a symptom that is impossible neurologically. In their 1895 studies of hysteria, Freud and his associate Breuer hypnotized some of the patients and found, to their great surprise, that when the origins and meanings of hysterical symptoms were talked about under hypnosis, the symptoms tended to disappear. This finding proved beyond any doubt that the symptoms were not caused by organic damage or physical defects.

Partly to understand hysteria, Freud developed his theory of unconscious conflict and defense. In his view, such symptoms as hysterical blindness and hysterical anesthesias reflected defensive attempts to avoid painful thoughts and feelings by diversionary preoccupation with apparently physical symptoms. Freud thought that the key

Table 2.2

Definitions and Examples of Some Defense Mechanisms

Mechanism	Definition	Example
Repression	Massive inhibition of a threatening impulse or event by rendering it unconscious (beyond awareness)	Guilt-producing sexual wishes are "forgotten"
Projection	Unacceptable aspects of oneself are attributed to someone else	Projecting one's own unacceptable sexual impulses by attributing them to one's boss
Reaction formation	Anxiety-producing impulse is replaced by its opposite in consciousness	Unacceptable feelings of hate are converted into "love"
Rationalization	Making something more acceptable by attributing it to more acceptable causes	Blaming an aggressive act on "being overworked" rather than on feeling angry
Sublimation	Expression of a socially unacceptable impulse in socially acceptable ways	Becoming a soldier to hurt others; becoming a plumber to indulge in anal desires

mechanism in this blocking was *unconsciously motivated repression.* Through repression the basic impulses that are unacceptable to the person are rendered unconscious and thereby less frightening. Because such diversionary measures are inherently ineffective ways of dealing with anxiety-provoking impulses, these impulses persist. The impulses continue to press for release in disguised and distorted forms that are called "symptoms."

Although Freud was concerned with extreme examples of this mechanism, repression also can be seen in many mild forms, as in the following example. Jim, a 13-year-old, has a girlfriend with whom he has had a few happy "dates," but she fails to show up on the movie line after having promised to be there. Jim convinces himself that he feels no anger, is not annoyed, and just "doesn't care." Yet he explodes later at dinner with his family and gets into a squabble with his little sister. If Jim privately knows he is just trying to cover his irritation and upset, then repression is not a relevant explanation for what he is doing. On the other hand, if his anger is evident to those who know him well but truly hidden from his own awareness, then repression may be at work as a defense. This hypothesis is strengthened if Jim also shows resistance to efforts by his mother to suggest, for example, that he may be upset by the broken date. In genuine repression if you push the person to face the underlying feelings that are being avoided unconsciously, it may only increase the defensive attempts to reject the interpretation and avoid the emotion. That tends to make the defense more elaborate and even irrational. In this type of example, when the person is no longer a young child and the threat is relatively mild, repression is unlikely to be very deep. The depth and desperation of the defense tend to be greater, however, in infancy or early childhood or when the threats are profoundly frightening and the organism is highly vulnerable.

Projection

In **projection,** the person's own unacceptable impulses are inhibited and the source of the anxiety is attributed to another person. For example, one's own angry feelings are attributed to one's innocent friend. Or a man who is attracted to his brother's wife sincerely believes she is trying to seduce him at a family gathering. Projection presumably gives relief because it reduces anxiety.

Reaction Formation

Replacement in consciousness of an anxiety-producing impulse by its opposite is another defense termed **reaction formation.** For example, people frightened by their own sexual impulses may become actively involved in a "ban the filth" vigilante group. They use their energy to vigorously censor books and movies they consider obscene. Through projection and reaction formation, the id impulses are expressed, but in a disguise that makes them acceptable to the ego.

A mother who was herself a leading psychoanalyst describes reaction formation as a mechanism shown by her own children in their early development (Monro, 1955). As a psychoanalyst, she was especially sensitive to the possible problems faced in the anal stage and the impulses activated then. She therefore allowed her children considerable freedom to express their infantile anal interests with few inhibitions. After experiencing that early phase of freedom, however, the children seemed to undergo an opposite pattern spontaneously. Now they began to exhibit overcleanliness to the point of finickiness, wanting everything to be "super clean," orderly, and neat. They found dishwater disgusting, for example, and insisted on refilling the sink with clean water repeatedly in spite of an extreme water shortage in the county. Likewise, they refused to clean up the puppy's "mistakes," and, as their insightful mother put it, "The reaction of finicking disgust, very genuinely experienced, was clearly related to the positive pleasures recently renounced. Housekeeping became much smoother as reaction formation involving an extreme if somewhat spotty orderliness also gave way to advancing maturity" (Monro, 1955, p. 252).

Rationalization

Another defense mechanism is the **rationalization** of feelings by making self-deceiving excuses. Thus, a man who has unconscious, deeply hostile impulses toward his wife might invent elaborate excuses that serve to disrupt and even destroy their relationship without ever admitting his true feelings. For example, he might invoke explanations such as "pressures at the office," "a hectic schedule," or "worrying about inflation and politics" as reasons for staying away from home. In doing so, he experiences little guilt over (and might even feel justified in) ignoring, avoiding, and frustrating his wife.

Sublimation

Sublimation, according to Freud, is an ego defense that is particularly significant in the development of culture. It consists of a displacement or redirection of impulses from an object (or target) that is sexual to one that is social in character. Suppose, for example, that masturbation becomes too threatening to the young child. He or she may sublimate (or transform) these impulses into a socially acceptable form, such as horseback riding and other athletics.

PSYCHODYNAMICS OF DEFENSE AND NEUROSIS

Psychodynamics

Psychodynamics are the processes through which personality works. They concern three continuous tasks of the ego: (1) the control of unacceptable impulses from the id; (2) the avoidance of pain produced by internal conflict in the efforts to control and master those unacceptable impulses; and (3) the attainment of a harmonious integration among the diverse components of personality in conflict. Much of Freud's own energy was directed at understanding how the instinctual components of the personality system work as the id impulses seek satisfaction. The essence of Freudian personality dynamics is the transformation of motives: The basic impulses persist and press for discharge, but the objects at which they are directed and the manner in which they are expressed are transformed (1917). Freud thought that these transformations involved a finite amount of energy that was contained in the person.

Libido.   This energy (called **libido**) is "cathected" (attached or fixed) on aspects of the internal and external environment. The energy available to the organism may be

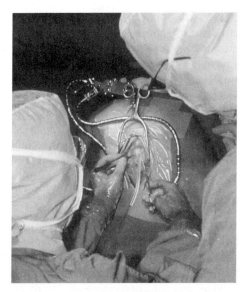

The concept of sublimation suggests that sexual and aggressive impulses may be redirected from their original objects and displaced to socially acceptable activities and careers.

continuously transformed, fixed onto different "objects" (note that "objects" was a term that for Freud included people and not just inanimate things). However, the total amount of energy is conserved and stable. Freud's energy system thus was consistent with the hydraulic models of 19th-century physics.

Equilibrium. The id was seen as a kind of dynamo, and the total mind (or psyche) was viewed as a closed system motivated to maintain equilibrium: Any forces that were built up required discharge. The discharge could be indirect. Instinctual impulses could be *displaced* from one object to another, for instance, from one's parents to other authority figures or more remotely, from the genitals, for example, to phallic symbols.

Transformation of Motives. Some of these transformations or displacements are shown in Figure 2.1. For

Figure 2.1
The Psychodynamic Transformation of Motives: Examples of Displacement in the Form of Sublimation

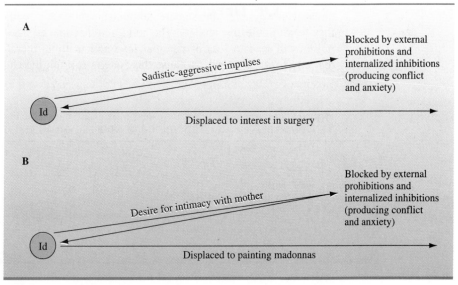

example, if sadistic aggressive impulses are too threatening to self-acceptance, they might be transformed into a more socially sanctioned form, such as an interest in surgery. Likewise, sexual wishes toward the mother might be displaced into a career of painting madonnas, as some Freudians think happened among certain Renaissance painters. Freud (1909) himself suggested such dynamics in the case of Leonardo da Vinci.

In sum, psychodynamics involve a continuous conflict between id impulses seeking discharge and defenses designed to transform these wishes into an acceptable form for the person. In the course of these transformations, energy is exchanged and directed toward different objects, mediated by the mechanisms of defense.

When Defenses Fail: Neurotic Anxiety and Conflict

Sometimes the defenses that disguise basic motives may become inadequate and the person becomes disturbed. But even under the usual circumstances of everyday life the defenses are occasionally penetrated and the person betrays himself (Freud, 1901). Such betrayals of underlying motives are seen when defenses are relaxed, as in dream life during sleep or in jokes and slips of the tongue. The defense process involves distortion and displacement; private meanings develop as objects and events become symbols representing things quite different from themselves. It is believed that these meanings are partially revealed by behavioral "signs" or symptoms that may symbolize disguised wishes and unconscious conflicts. For example, phobias such as the fear of snakes may reflect basic sexual conflicts; in this case, the feared snake has symbolic meaning.

Development of Neurotic Anxiety.   It is now possible to consider the Freudian conception of how neurotic anxiety may develop. The sequence here (depicted in Figure 2.2) begins with the child's aggressive or sexual impulses that seek direct release. These efforts at discharge may be strongly punished and blocked by dangers or threats (for example, intense parental punishment such as withdrawal of love). Hence, they lead to objective anxiety. The child may become especially afraid that these impulses will lead to loss of parental love and in time, therefore, may come to fear his or her own impulses. Because this state is painful, the child tries to repress these

Figure 2.2
Sequence in Freudian Conception of Neurotic Anxiety

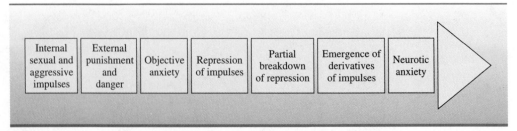

impulses. If the ego is weak, the repression is only partly successful and the instinctual impulses persist. Unless expressed in some acceptable form, these impulses become increasingly "pent up," gradually building up to the point where they become hard to repress. Consequently, there may be a partial breakdown of repression, and some of the impulses may break through, producing some neurotic anxiety. Anxiety, in this view, functions as a danger signal, a warning to the individual that repressed impulses are starting to break through the defenses. Rather than emerging directly, however, the unacceptable impulses express themselves indirectly in disguised and symbolic ways.

The Meaning of Neurotic Acts. Freud felt that the symbolic meaning of behavior was clearest in neurotic acts. He cited the case of a girl who compulsively rinsed out her washbasin many times after washing. Freud thought that the significance of this ceremonial act was expressed in the proverb, "Don't throw away dirty water until you have clean." He interpreted the girl's action as a warning to her sister, to whom she was very close, "not to separate from her unsatisfactory husband until she had established a relationship with a better man" (Freud, 1959, vol. 2, p. 28).

Another patient was able to sit only in a particular chair and could leave it only with much difficulty. In Freud's analysis of her problem, the chair symbolized the husband to whom she remained faithful. Freud saw the symbolic meaning of her compulsion in her sentence, "It is so hard to part from anything (chair or husband) in which one has once settled oneself" (Freud, 1959, vol. 2, p. 29). Thus the important object of conflict—the husband—was transformed into a trivial one—the chair. Freud cited these and many similar cases as evidence for the view that neurotic behaviors express unconscious motives and ideas symbolically. The clinician's task, then, is to decipher the unconscious meaning of the patient's behavior and to discover the conflicts and dynamics that might underlie seemingly irrational behavior patterns (see Table 2.3).

Table 2.3
Possible Meanings of Some Behavioral Signs According to Freudian Theory

Behavioral Sign	Possible Underlying Meaning
Fear of snakes	Sexual conflicts concerning genitals
Compulsive cleanliness	Reaction against anal impulses
Obsessive thought: "My mother is drowning."	Imperfectly repressed hostility toward mother
Paranoid jealousy	Homosexual wishes
Preoccupation with money	Problems around toilet training
Crusading against obscenity	Reaction formation against own unacceptable wishes

Traumatic Seeds: Origins of Neuroses

In Freud's view, serious problems, such as the neuroses, and the roots of the symptoms that characterize them begin in early childhood:

> . . . It seems that neuroses are acquired only in early childhood (up to the age of six), even though their symptoms may not make their appearance till much later. The childhood neurosis may become manifest for a short time or may even be overlooked. In every case the later neurotic illness links up with the prelude in childhood.
>
> . . . The neuroses are, as we know, disorders of the ego; and it is not to be wondered at if the ego, so long as it is feeble, immature and incapable of resistance, fails to deal with tasks which it could cope with later on with the utmost ease. In these circumstances instinctual demands from within, no less than excitations from the external world, operate as 'traumas,' particularly if they are met halfway by certain innate dispositions (Freud, 1933, pp. 41–42).

As these quotations indicate, neuroses were seen as the products of early childhood traumas plus innate dispositions. But even the behavior of less disturbed persons was believed to reflect expressions of underlying unconscious motives and conflicts. These manifestations could be seen in the "psychopathology of everyday life"—the occurrence of meaningful but common unconscious expressions, as discussed next.

The Psychopathology of Everyday Life: "Mistakes" That Betray

Some of Freud's most fascinating—and controversial—ideas involved the elaboration of possible hidden meanings that might underlie such common occurrences as slips of the tongue, errors in writing, jokes, and dreams. In Freud's (1901, 1920)

Table 2.4
Examples of Behaviors Motivated by Unconscious Wishes

Behavior	Unconscious Wish	Transformation Involved
Slip of tongue: "May I 'insort' (instead of 'escort') you?"	To insult	Condensation (insult + escort = "insort")
Slip of tongue: "Gentlemen, I declare a quorum present and herewith declare the session *closed*."	To close the meeting	Association of opposites (open = closed)
Dream of disappointment in quality of theater tickets, as result of having gotten them too soon	I married too soon; I could have gotten a better spouse by waiting.	Symbolism (getting tickets too soon = marrying too soon)
Dream of breaking an arm	Desire to break marriage vows	Conversion into visual imagery (breaking vows = breaking an arm)

SOURCE: Freud, S. (1920). *A general introduction to psychoanalysis.* New York: Boni and Liveright.

Table 2.5
Some Freudian Dream Symbols and Their Meanings

Dream Symbol	Meaning
King, queen	Parents
Little animals, vermin	Siblings
Travel, journey	Dying
Clothes, uniforms	Nakedness
Flying	Sexual intercourse
Extraction of teeth	Castration

SOURCE: Freud, S. (1920). *A general introduction to psychoanalysis.* New York: Boni and Liveright.

view, "mistakes" may be unconsciously motivated by impulses that the individual is afraid to express directly or openly. To show that mistakes may really be motivated by underlying wishes, Freud pointed out many instances in which even the attempt to "correct" the error appears to betray a hidden, unacceptable meaning. In one case, for example, an official introduced a general as "this battle-scared veteran" and tried to "correct" his mistake by saying "bottle-scarred veteran." Other examples are summarized in Table 2.4. Some common Freudian dream symbols are shown in Table 2.5.

Motivational Determinism: Unconscious Causes

By now it should be clear that Freudian psychoanalytic theory offers the view that behavior is motivationally determined. The causal chain can be complex and indirect.

Events in one area of the personality exert their effects on another, but every behavior, no matter how trivial, has its ultimate motivational cause. Suppose, for example, a man fights with his wife about money, is personally fussy about his appearance, and becomes very upset when he loses his umbrella. These seemingly different bits of behavior might actually be motivated by a common cause. Much of psychoanalytic assessment and therapy is a search for such underlying causes. A psychodynamic explanation of behavior consists of finding the motives that produced it. The focus is not on behavior, but on the motivations that it serves and reflects.

Freudians tend to believe in **motivational determinism:** All behavior, even the seemingly most absurd or trivial (like losing an umbrella), is motivated and significant. They may view any behavior as a sign of basic, largely unconscious forces. This means that your most important motives are primarily unconscious. You may be victimized by these hidden motives and perceive them only through the distortions of defensive maneuvers used in ways only dimly known to you. The basic psychodynamics arise early in life during the stages of psychosexual development, and they shape your future and how you will deal with the world.

PSYCHOSEXUAL STAGES AND PERSONALITY DEVELOPMENT

Freud believed that every person normally progresses through five **psychosexual stages.** During the first five years of life, pleasure is successively focused on three zones of the body as the oral, anal, and phallic stages unfold. Then comes a quiet latency period of about five or six years. Finally, if progress through each stage has been successful, the person reaches the mature or genital stage after puberty. But special problems at any stage may retard or arrest (fixate) development and leave enduring marks on the person's character throughout life.

The Oral Stage

The **oral stage** occurs during the first year of life, when body pleasure is focused on the mouth and on the satisfactions of sucking, eating, and biting in the course of feeding (but see *In Focus 2.1*). The dependent, helpless person is said to be fixated at this stage, when the infant is totally dependent upon others for satisfaction of his or her needs.

According to Freud, the oral stage is divided into two periods: (1) sucking and (2) biting and chewing. Later character traits develop from these earliest modes of oral pleasure. More specifically, oral incorporation (as in sucking and taking in milk in the first oral period) becomes the prototype of such pleasures as those gained from the acquisition of knowledge or possessions. In his view, the gullible person (who is "easily taken in") is fixated at the oral, incorporative level of personality. The sarcastic, bitingly argumentative person is fixated at the second oral period—the sadistic level associated with biting and chewing.

The Anal Stage

In the second year of life, the **anal stage** is marked by a shift in body pleasure to the anus and by a concern with the retention and expulsion of feces. According to Freud, during toilet training the child has his first experience with imposed control: The manner in which toilet training is handled may influence later personal qualities and conflicts. For example, extremely harsh, repressive training might produce a person characterized by obstinacy, stinginess, and a preoccupation with orderliness and cleanliness.

The Phallic Stage

The **phallic stage** is the period in which the child observes the difference between male and female and experiences what Freud called the Oedipus complex. This occurs at about age five. Freud thought that both boys and girls love their mother as the satisfier of their basic needs and resent their father as a rival for their mother's affections.

In addition, the boy fears castration by the father as punishment for desiring his mother sexually. This **castration anxiety** is so terrifying that it results in the

IN FOCUS 2.1   *How Oral Is the Infant?*

Although the feeding situation is a critical phase of early development, it is only one part of the total relationship between the growing organism and the world. Thus the baby is more than an "oral" creature. Babies respond to stimulation of the mouth, lips, and tongue, but in addition, they see, hear, and feel, obtaining stimulation visually, aurally, and from being handled.

Convinced that in spite of an abundance of theories, personality psychology has much too little real data, Professor Burton L. White of Harvard University began by carefully observing infants as they lay in their cribs. (The subjects were physically normal infants in an orphanage.) He and his colleagues recorded the quantity and quality of visual-motor activity to study the babies' attention. On the basis of these observations, they plotted the development of the infants' tendency to explore the visual surroundings, as depicted in Figure 2.3. The findings surprised the investigators:

One important revelation for me which resulted from these weekly observations was that, contrary to my academically bred expectations, infants weren't really very oral during the first months of life. In fact, between two and six months, a far more appropriate description would be that they are visual-prehensory creatures. We observed subject after subject spend dozens of hours watching first his fists, then his fingers, and then the interactions between hands and fingers. Thumb-sucking and mouthing were rarely observed except for brief periods when the infant was either noticeably upset or unusually hungry (White, 1967, p. 207).

These observations point up how much more we need to know about the details of the infant's activities before we can reach conclusions about what events characterize early development. It may be, as this investigator's comments imply, that the "oral" infant will turn out to be much more attentive and active and less oral and passive than was believed in early formulations. Indeed, close observation of young children suggests a dramatic increase in the infant's competence by the second or third month. More wakefulness and alertness, greater receptivity to stimulation, more directed attention, and less fussing begin to characterize the baby (Sroufe, 1977). Stimulation becomes less unsettling and may be sought out actively as the baby becomes more and more attentive, even to its own movements.

Figure 2.3
The Development of the Tendency to Explore the Surround

SOURCE: Adapted from White, B. L., & Held, R. (1966). Plasticity of sensorimotor development in the human infant. In J. F. Rosenblith & W. Allinsmith (Eds.), *The Causes of Behavior II*, pp. 60–70. Boston: Allyn and Bacon.

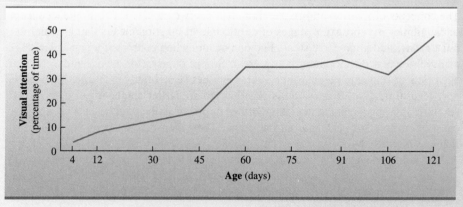

repression of the boy's sexual desire for his mother and hostility toward his father. To reduce the anxiety of possible castration by the father, the boy tries to become like him or to identify with him, gradually internalizing the father's standards and values as his own.

Identification with the father in turn helps the boy gain some indirect (vicarious) satisfaction of his sexual impulses toward his mother. In this last phase of the Oedipus complex of the male, the superego reaches its final development as the internalized standards of parents and society: The opposition to incest and aggression becomes part of his own value system.

In the female, **penis envy,** resulting from the discovery that she lacks the male organ, is the impetus to exchange her original love object—the mother—for a new object—the father. Unlike the boy's Oedipus complex, which is repressed through fear, the girl—having nothing to lose—persists in her sexual desire for her father. This desire does, naturally, undergo some modification because of realistic barriers.

The Latency Period

After the phallic stage, a **latency period** develops. Now there is less overt concern with sexuality; the child represses his or her memories of infantile sexuality and forbidden sexual activity by making them unconscious.

The Genital Stage

The genital stage is the final, mature stage of psychosexual development. Now the person is capable of genuine love for other people and can achieve adult sexual satisfactions. No longer characterized by the selfishness (narcissism) and mixed, conflicting feelings that marked the earlier stages, he or she can relate to others in a mature, heterosexual fashion. But before he or she reaches the **genital stage,** excessive stress or overindulgence may cause the person to become fixated at earlier levels of psychosexual development.

Fixation and Regression

The concepts of **fixation** and **regression** are closely connected with Freud's conceptualization of psychosexual stages of development. Fixation means that a sexual impulse is arrested at an early stage. Fixation occurs when conflict at a particular stage of psychosexual development is too great. Severe deprivation or overindulgence at a particular stage or inconsistent alterations between indulgence and deprivation may lead to fixation. Regression is reversion to an earlier stage. When individuals' resolutions of problems at any stage of development is inadequate, later stress may cause them to regress to that earlier stage. They then display behavior typical of that less mature period.

In sum, personality is intimately related to the individual's mode of coping with problems at each stage of psychosexual development. The result is reflected in the nature of character formation, symptoms, and relations with other people.

Freud's Theory of Identification

Parts of Freud's theory of psychosexual stages have been modified and even rejected in recent years. Some of his closely related concepts regarding identification, however, have continued to be influential.

Early personality development occurs in the setting of the family. In that context you saw that Freud strongly emphasized the child's attachment to the mother and the rivalry between son and father for her attentions. This triangle of relations, called the Oedipal situation, is the basis for identification with the standards of the parent. This identification process Freud attributed to two mechanisms that operate during psychosexual development.

Anaclitic identification is based on the intense dependency of a child on his mother, beginning early in the course of the infant's development. Because of the helplessness of the infant, his dependency upon his caretaker is profound. Identification for girls is based mainly on this early love or dependency relation with the mother. In anaclitic identification the child must first have developed a dependent love relationship with her caretaker (usually the mother). Later, when the mother begins to withdraw some of her nurturant attention, the child tries to recapture her by imitating and reproducing her in actions and fantasy.

For boys, dependency or "anaclitic" identification with the mother is followed later by *identification with the aggressor.* The "aggressor" is the father during the Oedipal phase of development. Identification with the aggressor is motivated by fear of harm and castration by the punitive father in retribution for the son's fantasies and his sexual wishes toward the mother. Freud described the situation vividly:

> . . . When a boy (from the age of two or three) has entered the phallic phase of his libidinal [sexual] development, is feeling pleasurable sensations in his sexual organ and has learnt to procure these at will by manual stimulation, he becomes his mother's lover. He wishes to possess her physically in such ways as he has divined from his observations and intuitions about sexual life, and he tries to seduce her by showing her the male organ which he is proud to own. In a word, his early awakened masculinity seeks to take his father's place with her; his father has hitherto in any case been an envied model to the boy, owing to the physical strength he perceives in him and the authority with which he finds him clothed. His father now becomes a rival who stands in his way and whom he would like to get rid of (Freud, 1933, p. 46).

The hostile feelings that the boy experiences in the Oedipal situation create great anxiety in him; he desires the mother but fears castration from the father. To defend against the anxiety, he resolves the Oedipal conflict, repressing his aggressive wishes against his father and trying to become more like him. It is as though the boy believes that if he *"is"* the father he cannot be hurt by him. Identification with the aggressor requires that the boy have a strong (but ambivalent) relation with the father. In this relationship, love for the father is mixed with hostility because the father possesses the mother and interferes with the son's urges. Freud thought that through identification with the aggressor, boys develop a stricter superego.

IMPACT OF FREUD'S THEORIES

Freud's Image of the Person

It is not simple—and is probably impossible—to capture the essence of Freud's conceptions. Freud built a dramatic image of what a person might be, inventing a sweeping and novel theoretical system. Freud saw the person as struggling with himself and the world, blocked by anxieties, conflicted, and plagued by his own unacceptable wishes and unconscious secrets. This picture has captivated the imagination of many laymen as well as clinicians. Consequently, it has had an enormous impact on philosophical as well as psychological conceptions of human nature. In Freud's view, humans are not the unemotional, rational beings that Victorian society thought they were. Instead, people are torn by unconscious conflicts and wishes that push them in seemingly puzzling ways.

Freud's emphasis on unconscious impulses as the most basic determinants of behavior is seen in an analogy in which the relation of the id and the ego is likened to that between a horse and its rider:

> . . . The horse provides the locomotive energy, and the rider has the prerogative of determining the goal and of guiding the movements of his powerful mount towards it. But all too often in the relations between the ego and the id we find a picture of the less ideal situation in which the rider is obliged to guide his horse in the direction in which it itself wants to go (Freud, 1933, p. 108).

Thus in Freud's psychology the id is stubborn and strong and often the ego cannot really control it effectively.

Freud believed that the environment is less important than inborn instincts in the dynamics of personality. He thought that external stimuli make fewer demands and, in any event, can always be avoided. In contrast, one's own impulses and needs cannot be escaped. Consequently, he made instinctual impulses the core of personality. Psychodynamic theories also have shaped ideas about adaptation, deviance, and personality change. And they have done this more than any other psychological approach.

Freud's View of the Healthy Personality

For Freud, a healthy personality showed itself in the ability to love and work and required a harmony among id, ego, and superego. Referring to the goal of psychotherapy, Freud wrote, "Where id was, there shall ego be." He meant that for the healthy personality, rational choice and control replace irrational, impulse-driven compulsion. A healthy personality also required mature (genital) psychosexual development. In the healthy person, for Freud, genital sexuality replaces earlier forms of psychosexuality. That is, the healthy individual is one who achieves psychosexual maturity, having progressed through the psychosexual stages of development.

From the psychodynamic perspective, adequate adaptation requires insight into one's unconscious motives. Persons who can cope adequately are the ones who can face their impulses and conflicts without having to resort to massive unconscious defenses that sap psychic energy in the service of distorting either wishes or reality itself. Symptoms represent the return of unsuccessfully repressed materials, reemerging to torture the person in disguised forms; breakdowns represent the inadequacy of defenses to deal with unconscious conflicts. If the ego fails to achieve sufficient strength to cope with the demands of external reality and the internal pressures of id and superego as they wage their warfare, the person becomes ill.

In Freud's words (1940, pp. 62–63):

> . . . The ego has been weakened by the internal conflict; we must come to its aid. The position is like a civil war which can only be decided by the help of an ally from without. The analytical physician and the weakened ego of the patient, basing themselves upon the real external world, are to combine against the enemies, the instinctual demands of the id, and the moral demands of the superego. We form a pact with each other. The patient's sick ego promises us the most candor, promises, that is, to put at our disposal all of the material which his self-perception provides; we, on the other hand, assure him of the strictest discretion and put at his service our experience in interpreting material that has been influenced by the unconscious. Our knowledge shall compensate for his ignorance and shall give his ego once more mastery over the lost provinces of his mental life. This pact constitutes the analytic situation.

Behaviors as Symptoms

The Freudian approach views an individual's problematic behavior as symptomatic (rather than of main interest in its own right). It searches for the possible causes of these symptoms by making inferences about the underlying personality dynamics. For example, an individual who has a bad stutter might be viewed as repressing hostility, one with asthma as suffering from dependency conflicts, and one with snake fears as victimized by unconscious sexual problems. This focus on the meaning of behavior as a symptom (sign) guides the psychodynamic strategy for understanding both normal and abnormal behavior. Thus the psychodynamically oriented clinician seeks to infer unconscious conflicts, defense structure, problems in psychosexual development, and the symbolic meaning and functions of behavior.

Many features of the traditional psychodynamic approach to adaptation and deviance are illustrated in the Freudian conceptualization of Gary (pp. 90–92). The report refers to Gary's fear of injury, his anxiety in social situations and fear of public speaking, and his problems in forming close relations. Rather than conceptualizing these behaviors as problems in their own right, they are viewed as signs (symptoms) that reflect (often very indirectly) such hypothetical, inferred problems as his "castration anxiety," "need for control," "unresolved Oedipal themes," "brittle defenses," and "basic insecurity."

PSYCHOANALYTIC TREATMENT

The psychodynamic approach to treatment has had an enormous influence on American psychiatry and clinical psychology. Its major version is **psychoanalysis** or psychoanalytic therapy, a form of psychotherapy originally developed by Freud and practiced by psychoanalysts.

Traditionally, in psychoanalysis several weekly meetings, each about an hour long, are held between the therapist and client (or "patient"), often for a period of many years. The treatment is based on the premise that neurotic conflict and anxiety are the result of repressed (unconscious) impulses. The aim is to remove the repression and resolve the conflict by helping patients achieve insight into their unconscious impulses.

Free Association and Dream Interpretation

To uncover unconscious material (or lift the repression) the techniques of **free association** and **dream interpretation** are used in traditional psychoanalysis. As was noted before, in free association the patient, usually reclining on a couch, is instructed to report whatever comes to mind without screening or censoring his or her thoughts in any way. Here is a fragment of free association from a psychotherapy session as an example: "I wonder how my mother is getting along. You know how she and I don't get along. Once when I was about twelve she and I were having an argument—I can't remember what it was about—argument 1001. Anyway, the phone rang and one of her darling friends offered her two tickets to the matinee performance of a ballet that day. What a day. She refused them to punish me. For a change! I don't think I even saw a ballet until I was grown up and married. Joe took me. I still get sad when I think about it. I could cry. All blue. It reminds me of all the times when I felt. . . ."

Any difficulties or blocks in free association are considered as important as the material that is easily produced. These difficulties are interpreted as **resistances,** caused by unconscious defenses blocking access to material central to the patient's problems, and the person is encouraged to continue with the free association.

According to psychoanalytic theory, the ego's defense mechanisms are relaxed during sleep, making dreams an avenue to express repressed material. But the defenses still operate to distort the content of dreams, so interpretation is necessary to unravel their meaning. In treatment, the interpretation of blocks in association and of dreams is done carefully so that the patient continues to relax the defenses. When the patient's resistances to facing unconscious conflicts and true motives are fully overcome, the therapeutic goal of making the unconscious conscious is gradually realized.

The Transference Relationship and Working Through

The therapist in psychoanalysis is supposed to create an atmosphere of safety by remaining accepting and noncritical. Therapists deliberately reveal little about themselves and remain shadowy figures who often sit behind the patient and outside his view in order to facilitate a **transference** relationship. Transference is said to occur when the patient responds to the therapist as if he or she were the patient's father, mother, or some other important childhood figure. Feelings and problems initially experienced in childhood relations with these figures are transferred to the relationship with the therapist. Transference is regarded as inevitable and essential by most psychoanalysts. In the transference, the therapist demonstrates to patients the childhood origins of their conflicts and helps them to work through and face these problems. Here in the words of a distinguished psychoanalyst (Colby, 1951) is an example of how the transference is used and interpreted (p. 113):

The manner in which a patient acts and feels about his therapist is a bonanza of psychological information. In subtracting the inappropriate from appropriate responses the therapist has a first-hand, immediately observable illustration of the patient's psychodynamics in an interpersonal relationship. . . .

A woman from an old Southern family broke away in late adolescence from family ties and values. She became a nomadic Bohemian vigorously opposed to all authority. She expressed her feelings by zealous work in Anarchist societies and other radical movements. In therapy she often told of fearlessly challenging policemen and openly sneering at successful businessmen.

Yet her behavior toward the therapist was in marked contrast to this. She was very respectful, nonaggressive and acquiescent—all attitudes she faintly remembers having as a child toward her parents until adolescence. The therapist's concept was that the patient unconsciously saw him as a feared and loved parent who must not be antagonized. She really feared authority as a source of punishment.

The insight to be achieved by the patient in psychoanalysis is not a detached, rational, intellectual understanding. People must work through their problems in the transference relationship. **Working through** involves repeated reexamination of basic problems in different contexts until one learns to handle them more appropriately and understands their emotional roots.

A Century After Freud: Trauma and Dissociation Revisited

Freud's theory of the origin of neurosis emphasized the importance of childhood traumas—intense emotional experiences that the person cannot deal with and that "exert a disintegrating effect on the mind" (Spiegel, Koopman, & Classen, 1994, p. 11). Freud held that traumatic experiences can induce not only severe anxiety but also dissociative states of the sort he reported in his clinical observations of hysterical patients who, you will recall, developed physical symptoms (like "glove anesthesia") that made no sense neurologically.

Although these ideas continue to be controversial, they also have stimulated extensive contemporary research on reactions to acute stress, called **traumatic experiences.** These are experiences that abruptly and severely disrupt the person's normal daily routine, suddenly threatening him or her with physical injury or death, as happens under war conditions, in earthquakes, or to victims of violent crimes. In contemporary research it has been possible to document and study these experiences systematically. The results of these new studies in part support many of Freud's insights and in part serve to modify and improve the treatment procedures to help the victims deal with their traumas more effectively (e.g., Metcalfe & Jacobs, 1998; Roth & Newman, 1990; Spiegel & Cardena, 1990, 1991).

In the contemporary view, consistent with Freud, when traumas profoundly endanger the victim's core beliefs about himself and the world, dissociative reactions may occur to keep the threat outside full awareness, split off from the rest of one's experience. Consequently, treatment is aimed at helping the person to integrate the experience and to manage the painful emotions. Freud originally emphasized simply helping the person to re-experience and repeat the event and its emotions in the transference relationship and to express or release them in the "working through" process.

Traumatic experiences may be induced by such extreme events as wars that shatter normal life routines.

Current approaches take another step. Called **cognitive restructuring,** the focus is on reinterpreting the meaning of the event in a way that allows the person to deal with it. It involves helping the person to give up the sense of control over the event that often creates inappropriate guilt:

> A rape victim will apply hindsight and berate herself for having left the car to go to the store, as though she could have known that the attack would happen. A soldier who survived a rocket attack may feel he traded his safety for that of a comrade who died. . . . Therapy is aimed at helping the victim acknowledge and bear the emotional distress which comes with traumatic memories, grieving the loss of control which occurred at the time and thereby admitting the uncomfortable sense of helplessness (Spiegel et al., 1994, p. 18).

In short, in contemporary applications of Freud's ideas about traumas and disassociation, the focus is on helping the person to acknowledge the trauma itself; to bear and reinterpret the memories of the traumatic events; and to cast them into a more meaningful perspective with less self-blame. In these efforts, hypnosis, which Freud originally explored deeply but then abandoned as a technique, is often used, and support is given and encouraged, for example, by strengthening interpersonal relationships. These treatment features are characteristic of the "ego psychology" which grew out of, and builds upon, Freud's work, discussed in the next chapter.

This chapter has merely sketched the outline of Freud's conceptions. The applications of these ideas for the assessment and treatment of persons probably have been greater than those of any other psychological theory. Consequently, an adequate view of the implications of Freud's psychodynamic theory and of its current status cannot be achieved until these applications are examined in the following chapters.

SUMMARY

1. The most influential psychodynamic theory has been that of Sigmund Freud. Freud's theory and method of treating personality disturbances were based on extensive clinical observations of neurotic persons and on self-analysis. These led him to the unconscious as a key component of personality and to dreams as a window into the unconscious wishes of the dreamer.

2. In Freud's view, the id, ego, and superego form the structure of the personality. The id is the primary, instinctual core. It obeys the "pleasure principle," seeking immediate gratification of impulses. The ego mediates between the instinctual demands of the id and the outer world of reality. Its energy is derived from the id, and it operates by means of "secondary processes": logical thinking and rational planning. The ego tests reality, localizing the appropriate objects for gratification in the environment so that tension reduction can occur. The superego represents the internalized moral standards of the society, achieved through the internalization of parental control and characteristics in the course of socialization.

3. Personality dynamics involve a perpetual conflict between the id, ego, and superego. This conflict is accompanied by continuous transformations of the finite amount of energy or libido contained in the person. The basic conflict is between the person's instinctual impulses and learned inhibitions

and anxieties regarding their expression. The major determinants of behavior are unconscious and irrational: Individuals are driven by persistent, illogical demands from within.

4. The desire for immediate gratification of sexual and aggressive instincts puts the person in conflict with the environment. The conflict becomes internal when the person has incorporated the prohibitions of the culture.

5. This struggle between impulse and inhibition produces anxiety. Defenses may be used by the ego when it is unable to handle anxiety effectively. Transformed by these defenses, the person's unacceptable impulses and unconscious motives express themselves indirectly or symbolically in disguised forms.

6. Freud's theory of personality development includes a series of psychosexual stages: oral, anal, phallic, and genital, so named for the erogenous zone which characterizes each. Later personality traits develop according to the individual's experience at each of these stages of maturation.

7. Anaclitic identification and identification with the aggressor are two Freudian identification mechanisms. The first is based on the intense dependency of a child on the mother; the second, on identification with castration by his father as punishment for his incestuous desires for his mother.

8. According to Freud, the psychic battle rages continuously from birth as people struggle with unacceptable wishes, internalized standards, and unconscious conflicts. Healthy individuals, however, achieve a kind of truce within themselves by substituting rational choice for id impulse. This requires both insight into one's own unconscious motives and arrival at the final stage of psychosexual development. The result is an adult who is able to love and to work.

9. The goal of psychoanalysis (or psychoanalytic therapy) is to make the unconscious conscious. The principal techniques used are free association and dream interpretation, both of which help uncover unconscious material when defense mechanisms are relaxed. This process requires several years and a strong transference relationship between the patient and the psychoanalyst. Psychoanalysts seek to uncover unconscious conflicts and to examine them so they can be worked through and resolved. When these conflicts are reduced, anxiety is relieved.

Ego Psychology and Object Relations

"Psychoanalysis was a well-guarded fortress, and most psychologists had little interest in scaling its walls . . . [in contrast] today . . . 'pluralism' characterizes contemporary psychoanalysis" (Westen, 1990, p. 21).

The boundaries of the psychodynamic approach have become increasingly elastic, as many in this tradition have become interested in new ideas about personality that go well beyond Freud's original contributions. This chapter presents some of the main ideas of theorists who retained much of Freud's psychodynamic orientation but transformed its focus and shape in crucial ways. These "neo-Freudians" or post-Freudians represent a wide range of innovations. They began with Freud's own followers at the start of the 20th century and moved on to some radical departures from his ideas by leaders in current psychodynamic psychology (Westen, 1998).

COMMON THEMES: TOWARD EGO PSYCHOLOGY AND THE SELF

Although each neo-Freudian writer has made a distinctive contribution, certain common themes emerge, especially in recent years. These themes suggest a gradual shift in focus, summarized in Table 3.1. Less attention is paid to Freud's ideas about the basic sexual and aggressive instincts of the id, and the id itself is given a less dominant role. This shift is accompanied by an expansion of the concept and functions of ego and "self," to the point where the newer theoretical trends have been named **ego psychology** and its practitioners are called ego psychologists.

Ego psychologists now pay more attention to the ego and its defense maneuvers and less attention to the role of underlying id impulses as determinants of most human behavior. They recognize that the ego has crucial conflict-free functions. These ego functions are relatively independent of underlying unconscious motivations. They are directly in the service of the coping process and to some degree free of the intrapsychic drama produced by the instincts as they seek expression. Conflict-free ego functions are seen in the normal operation of much of our everyday perception, memory, language, and thought.

With this growth of the role of ego, the person is viewed as a more competent, potentially creative problem solver, engaged in much more than the management of instincts that press for discharge. The neo-Freudians, as Table 3.1 suggests, also saw human development as a more continuous process that extends throughout the life span.

Table 3.1
Post-Freudian Developments: Some Characteristics of the Neo-Freudians

Less Attention To	More Attention To
Id and instincts	Ego and self
Purely intrapsychic causes and conflicts	Social, interpersonal causes; relationship issues
Earliest childhood	Later developments throughout the life span; adult functioning
Psychosexual stages	Social forces and positive strivings; the role of the culture and society

More than the product of early psychosexual experiences, personality began to be viewed as a lifelong development, rooted in social and interpersonal relations and in the context of culture and society. Much human striving began to be seen as motivated by social and personal goals as well as by the satisfaction of primitive instincts. (See *In Focus 3.1* for one example.)

You have seen that for Freud, the id and the instincts were the dominant aspects of the total personality. The ego was subservient to the id's instinctual wishes, even in healthy personalities. More recent theorists in the psychoanalytic tradition have put more emphasis on social variables shaping personality and less on the role of instincts. These neo-Freudian ego psychologists assert a "conflict-free sphere" of the ego (Hartmann, Kris, & Loewenstein, 1947; Rapaport, 1951). In their view, the ego has its own sources of energy and follows a course of development independent of the id and the instincts. That is, some portion of ego functioning is not determined by the attempt to avoid conflict between the id and the demands of society: It deals, instead, with the ego's reality-oriented tasks (Kihlstrom, 1987, 1990).

Let us now consider some of the major relevant theorists to illustrate the range and nature of their ideas about personality, starting with the highly controversial Carl Jung.

Carl Jung

Born in 1875, Carl Jung was brought up in Basel, Switzerland, the son of a pastor in the Swiss Reformed Church. Upon earning his medical degree from the University of Basel, he began his career in psychology at the Psychiatric Institute in Zurich. Jung began as an admirer and associate of Freud but later became a dissenter and developed his own theory of psychoanalysis and his own method of psychotherapy. His approach became known as **analytical psychology.** Although it retains Freud's unconscious processes, it claims a **collective unconscious** — an inherited foundation of personality. The contents of the collective unconscious are **archetypes** or "primordial images." Unlike the personal unconscious, whose contents were once conscious but have been forgotten or repressed, the contents of the collective unconscious have never been in consciousness. Therefore, the contents of the collective unconscious are not individually acquired; they are due to heredity. Examples of archetypes include God, the Young

Motives Outside the Id: Competence Motivation—and Beyond

At the same time that the neo-Freudian analysts were expanding the conception of ego functions, psychologists also were beginning to call attention to the importance of human needs and motives beyond the Freudian id impulses of sex and aggression. Most relevant for ego psychologists are such so-called higher-order motives as curiosity, the need for stimulation, and the desire for play and adventure. All these may be seen as parts of a more basic motive: the desire for competence (White, 1959). Everyday activities such as a child's exploring, playing, talking, and even crawling and walking, according to Robert White, reflect the desire for mastery and effective functioning; they are satisfying for their own sake (intrinsically) and create in the person a feeling of efficacy. White argues the point in these words:

> If in our thinking about motives we do not include this overall tendency toward active dealing, we draw the picture of a creature that is helpless in the grip of its fears, drives, and passions; too helpless perhaps even to survive, certainly too helpless to have been the creator of civilization. It is in connection with strivings to attain competence that the activity inherent in living organisms is given its clearest representation—the power of initiative and exertion that we experience as

a sense of being an agent in the living of our lives. This experience may be called a *feeling of efficacy* (White, 1972, p. 209).

In sum, **competence motivation** is a desire for mastery of a task for its own sake and may apply to such diverse tasks as running, piano playing, juggling, chess, or the mastery of a new surgical procedure. According to White, the desire for mastery arises independently of other biological drives (such as hunger and sex) and is not derived from them. Moreover, people engage in activities that satisfy competence needs for the sake of the activity, not for the sake of any external reward such as the praise, attention, or money to which it may lead. The concept of competence motivation is valuable in emphasizing the enormous range of creative activities that humans pursue and appear to enjoy in their own right. It is, however, only one of many newer directions explored by psychodynamic theorists in their focus on the functions of the ego. These include higher-order nonphysiological motives and needs—such as achievement, intimacy, and power—and diverse life goals and projects that range from going to college to building a career and a family (Emmons, 1997).

Potent Hero, the Wise Old Man, the Earth Mother, the Fairy Godmother, and the Hostile Brethren. They occur in myths, art, and dreams of all mankind.

In Jung's view, the psyche included not only a conscious side but also a covert or **shadow aspect** that is unconscious. Personal growth involves an unfolding of this shadow and its gradual integration with the rest of the personality into a meaningful, coherent life pattern. The unconscious of every female includes a masculine, assertive element (the **animus**). The unconscious of every male includes a feminine, passive element (the **anima**). To be constructively masculine or feminine, individuals of each sex must recognize and integrate these opposite sex elements within themselves (see Table 3.2).

Jung described four basic ways of experiencing (contacting) the world: *sensing, intuition, feeling,* and *thinking,* summarized in Table 3.3. According to Jung, people differ consistently in the degree to which they emphasize each way of experiencing. One person, for example, might typically prefer intuitive leaps with little abstract

Table 3.2
Examples of Jungian Concepts

The Collective Unconscious: Found in everyone and said to contain inherited memories and ancestral behavior patterns

Archetypes: Basic elements or primordial images forming the collective unconscious, manifested in dreams and myths (for example, Earth Mother, the Wise Old Man)

The Animus: The masculine, assertive element in the unconscious of every woman

The Anima: The feminine, passive element in the unconscious of every man

The Mandala: Usually a circular shape, symbolizing the self, and often divided into four parts

thought. Another might know the world mostly through his or her senses with little use of either intuition or reason. In addition, Jung suggested **extraversion-introversion** (discussed further in Chapter 6). Like the four ways of experiencing, these two attitudes of extraversion-introversion are divided: One is dominant in the conscious life while the other influences the unconscious side of the personality.

Jung broadened the concept of psychic energy. He did not exclude the sexual instinct of Freudian theory but thought it was only one among many instincts. Jung placed great emphasis on the goal-directed nature of personality and believed that human behavior cannot be explained entirely by past history. For Jung, the meaning of behavior became fully intelligible only in terms of its end products or final effects; we need to understand humans not only in terms of their past but also in the light of their purposes and goal strivings.

Jung, like Freud, emphasized symbolic meanings. He believed, for example, that "abnormal behaviors" are expressions of the unconscious mind. Some examples of these expressions are shown in Table 3.4, and they reveal clear overlap with Freud's thinking. Also like Freud, Jung thought that abnormal behaviors were merely one way in which the contents of the unconscious may reveal themselves. More often, he felt, they are expressed in dreams.

Table 3.3
Jung's Four Ways of Experiencing the World

Ways of Experiencing	Characteristics
Sensing	Knowing through sensory systems
Intuition	Quick guessing about what underlies sensory inputs
Feeling	Focus on the emotional aspects of experience—its beauty or ugliness, pleasantness or unpleasantness
Thinking	Abstract thought, reasoning

**Carl Gustav Jung
(1875–1961)**

Jung went beyond Freud, however, in his increasing fascination with dreams as unconscious expressions of great interest in their own right. (He believed that this contrasts with their use merely as starting points for saying whatever comes to mind, that is, "free associations," discussed in Chapter 4.) As Jung put it: ". . . I came increasingly to disagree with free association as Freud first employed it; I wanted to keep as close as possible to the dream itself, and to exclude all the irrelevant ideas and associations that it might evoke" (Jung, 1964, p. 28).

In the same direction, Jung became intrigued by the unconscious for its own sake. He viewed the unconscious not just as the source of instincts. For him it was a vital, rich part of everyone's life, more significant than the conscious world, full of symbols communicated through dreams. The focus of Jungian psychology became the study of people's relations to their unconscious. Jung's method taught individuals to become more receptive to their own dreams and to let their unconscious serve as a guide for how to live.

Jung's conception of personality is complex, more a set of fascinating observations than a coherent theory. His observations often dwelled on the multiple, contradictory forces in life: "I see in all that happens the play of opposites" (1963, p. 235). Yet he also was one of the first to conceptualize a *self* that actively strives for oneness and unity. He believed that to achieve unity and wholeness, the individual must become increasingly aware of the wisdom available in his or her personal and collective unconscious and must learn to live in harmony with it. Jung saw the self (the striving for wholeness) as an archetype that is expressed in many ways. The expressions of the

Table 3.4
Examples of Unconscious Symbolic Meanings Believed to Underlie Abnormal Behavior ("Symptoms") According to Jung

Behavior	Underlying Meaning
Asthma attack	"She can't breathe the atmosphere at home"
Vomiting	"He can't digest—(some unpleasant fact)"
Spasm and inability to swallow	"He can't swallow it"
Leg paralysis	"She can't go on any longer"

SOURCE: Jung, C. G. (1964). *Man and his symbols.* Garden City, NY: Doubleday.

Figure 3.1
A Mandala

striving for wholeness include the **mandala** (a magic circle archetype shown in Figure 3.1) and various religious and transcendental experiences. He devoted much of his life to the study of these expressions in preindustrial societies, alchemy, mythology, dreams, and symbols. His ideas continue to fascinate many psychologists and are being applied to topics that range from "feminist consciousness" (Lyons, 1997) to the role of the spiritual in healing (Molina, 1996). However, his ideas remain difficult to study with the methods most psychologists favor.

Alfred Adler

Like Freud, Alfred Adler also was born in Austria, 14 years after Freud—in 1870. He earned his degree as a doctor of medicine in 1895. After a brief period as an ophthalmologist, he practiced psychiatry, joining Freud's Vienna circle of associates at the turn of the century. A highly independent, even rebellious person, Adler broke from Freud after 10 years and began his own psychoanalytic movement, ultimately as a founder of the Society for Individual Psychology.

Adler's contributions have suffered an ironic fate. Much of what he said has become so widely accepted and seems so plausible that it has been incorporated into the everyday ideas and terms, the ordinary wisdom that we intuitively have about psychology. Some of these concepts are so common as to risk becoming clichés. Nevertheless, while the popularity of Adler's ideas makes them less distinctive, they remain important even in contemporary thinking about personality.

It is often said that every personality theory captures best the personality of the theorist who created it. Adler's own childhood was marked by chronic illness and hostile relations with his five siblings. Interestingly, both these themes—physical weakness, or "organ inferiority," and **sibling rivalry**—became central concepts in his theory. Adler's theory begins with a recognition of the infant's profound *helplessness,* a state that makes him or her especially vulnerable to any biological *organ inferiority* or weakness. This biological vulnerability becomes the root for a psychological state that endures in the person and that has central importance in Adler's theory: *feelings of inferiority.*

It is the struggle to overcome these inferiority feelings that provides the underlying motivation for lifelong compensatory strivings. Throughout the life course, the person tries to make up for the perceived deficit by reaching for superiority, by striving for perfection. The particular attitude the person adopts toward the inevitable state of inferiority, rather than the deficit itself, was most important for Adler; given a courageous attitude, a perceived deficit can become a positive asset. We all know dramatic examples of personal victories in overcoming biological deficits. Demosthenes was the ancient Greek who achieved fame as a great orator, overcoming a childhood stutter, and more than one great athlete reached the Olympics after long efforts to compensate for early concerns with physical weakness or illness. If the person fails to develop effective compensations, the risk is that he or she will suffer from an **inferiority complex.**

Adler's *compensatory motivation* contrasts sharply with the id impulses, sexual and aggressive in nature, featured as the driving forces in Freud's theory. It is a much more social psychological view of motivation. It is rooted in a biological deficit but goes much beyond that origin. Adler also showed this more social orientation in other parts of his theory in which he is alert to cultural influences and social, interpersonal situations. He saw the rivalry among siblings within the family as an important part of development. Thus he viewed the family as the context for significant relationships and conflicts beyond those captured in the Oedipal triangle of mother-father-child that was central for Freud. Indeed, Adler's ideas were notable as a major break from concern with inborn impulses and hereditary causes to focus on the environmental forces and the social world as determinants of personality development. The specific ways in which the person tries to strive for his or her goals in the striving for superiority show a basic unity. This *unity of function* develops as a distinctive *style of life;* it originates in infancy and is characterized in the organism's functioning consistently. Although the individual functions with consistency, the pattern that makes up the style of life can be modified. This happens when the person changes the goals toward which the whole pattern of striving is directed.

The striving for perfection plays a great role for Adler, but it is matched by his concern for the individual's *social feeling* or *social interest,* qualities vital for the healthy, well-functioning personality. This focus on the positive, adaptive aspects of personality development is also seen in two other Adlerian concepts: *courage* and *common sense.* Taken together, social feeling, courage, and common sense constitute the set of characteristics that mark well-functioning, healthy persons.

In Adler's view of compensatory motivation, the striving to excel may be a way of overcoming early feelings of inferiority.

Such persons cope with the realities of life, including their inevitable helplessness and inferiority, with confidence and constructive strivings, without excessive fear but also without unrealistic fantasies. In contrast, the unhealthy personality abandons appropriate effort and avoids facing realistic difficulties by a retreat into increasingly grandiose fantasies. These fantasies are defensive in the sense that they widen the gap to reality and provide an unrealistic avoidance of failure.

The positive qualities of social feeling, courage, and common sense are natural states: Every person is capable of having them spontaneously unless they are blocked or frustrated badly in the course of development. For example, the excessively *pampered child* may develop a style of life characterized by extreme demandingness, while the severely *rejected child* may live life in a world seen as dangerous and hostile.

To help overcome this type of damage, the therapist in the Adlerian approach provides the encouragement and sympathetic understanding that allows the patient to face life more realistically and effectively. In this supportive atmosphere, the patient can abandon "mistaken" strivings for fantastic superiority and stop the retreat from reality to begin to face life with common sense, courage, and social feeling.

Erich Fromm

Erich Fromm (1941, 1947) helped to expand Freudian concepts to the individual as a member of society. Freud saw personality development as a reaction to satisfactions

**Erich Fromm
(1900–1980)**

and frustrations of physiological drives. In contrast, for Fromm people are primarily social beings to be understood in terms of their relations to others. According to Fromm, individual psychology is fundamentally social psychology. People have psychological qualities, such as tendencies to grow, develop, and realize potentialities, that result in a desire for freedom and a striving for justice and truth. Thus human nature has a force of its own that influences social processes.

Fromm's explanation of character traits illustrates the difference between Freud's biological orientation and Fromm's social orientation. Fromm criticized Freud's idea that fixation at certain pleasure-giving stages is the cause of later character traits. According to Fromm, character traits develop from experiences with others. Psychosexual problems and attitudes are rooted in the whole of the character structure. They are expressions in the language of the body of an attitude toward the world that is socially conditioned. According to Freud, culture is the result of societal suppressions of instinctual drives. Fromm also believed that culture is molded by the structure and substance of a given society but does not focus on suppression of drives as the point of origin. For Fromm, the dominant character traits of the people in a society become forces shaping the social process and the culture itself.

Another major point of departure from Freud is Fromm's belief that ideals like truth, justice, and freedom can be genuine strivings and not simply rationalizations of biological motives. Freud's psychology is a psychology of instinctual drives that defines pleasure in terms of tension reduction. Fromm's psychology tries to make a place for positive attributes, such as tenderness and the human ability to love, and implies that these human needs have a force of their own. He believes that character is not the result of passive adaptation to social conditions. It is a dynamic adaptation on the basis of elements that either are biologically inherent in human nature or have become inherent as the result of historic evolution.

Erik Erikson

The psychoanalyst Erik Erikson (1963) has proposed stages of development that call attention to problems of social adaptation (Table 3.5). As children grow up, they face a wider range of human relationships. The solution of the specific problems at each of eight **psychosocial stages** (rather than psychosexual stages) determines how adequate they will become as adults. Erikson's focus on psychosocial development reflects the

Table 3.5
Erikson's Stages of Psychosocial Development

Stage and Age	Psychosocial Crisis	Optimal Outcome
I. Oral-sensory (first year of life)	Trust vs. mistrust	Basic trust and optimism
II. Muscular-anal (second year)	Autonomy vs. shame, doubt	Sense of control over oneself and the environment
III. Locomotor-genital (third through fifth year)	Initiative vs. guilt	Goal-directedness and purpose
IV. Latency (sixth year to start of puberty)	Industry vs. inferiority	Competence
V. Puberty and adolescence	Identity vs. role confusion	Reintegration of past with present and future goals, fidelity
VI. Early adulthood	Intimacy vs. isolation	Commitment, sharing, closeness, and love
VII. Young and middle adulthood	Generativity vs. self-absorption	Production and concern with the world and future generations
VIII. Mature adulthood	Integrity vs. despair	Perspective, satisfaction with one's past life, wisdom

SOURCE: Adapted from Erikson, E. (1963). *Childhood and society.* New York: Norton.

growing neo-Freudian emphasis on broad social and cultural forces rather than instinctual drives alone.

At each stage of development, Erikson hypothesizes a psychosocial "crisis." This crisis arises from the person's efforts to solve the problems at that stage. For example, in the first stage of life (the "oral-sensory" stage of the first year) the crisis involves "trust versus mistrust." Erikson hypothesizes that at this stage the child's relation to its mother forms basic attitudes about "getting" and "giving." If the crisis is properly resolved, the experiences at this stage lay the foundation for later trust, drive, and hope.

Erikson's stages extend beyond infancy to include crises of adolescence and adulthood. He sees development as a process that extends throughout life, rather than being entirely determined in the early years. In this developmental process, "ego identity" is central:

> The integration . . . of ego identity is . . . more than the sum of the childhood identifications. It is the accrued experience of the ego's ability to integrate all identifications with the vicissitudes of the libido, with the aptitudes developed out of endowment, and with the opportunities offered in social roles (Erikson, 1963, p. 261).

The underlying assumptions of his view of development are:

> (1) that the human personality in principle develops according to steps predetermined in the growing person's readiness to be driven toward, to be aware of, and to interact with, a widening social radius; and (2) that society, in principle, tends to be so constituted as to

**Erik H. Erikson
(1902-1994)**

meet and invite this succession of potentialities for interaction and attempts to safeguard and to encourage the proper rate and the proper sequence of their enfolding (Erikson, 1963, p. 270).

Erikson's ideas have become popular in many parts of our culture. His thoughts concerning the "identity crises" of adolescence, for example, are discussed widely. Indeed the phrase **identity crisis** has become a part of everyday speech. Both provocative and literate, Erikson's ideas have influenced concepts of human nature and the general intellectual culture. Erikson believes that all young people must generate for themselves some "central perspective and direction" that gives them a meaningful sense of unity and purpose. This perspective integrates the remnants of their childhood with the expectations and hopes of adulthood (Erikson, 1968). This sense of identity involves a synthesis of how individuals have come to see themselves and their awareness of what the important other people in their lives expect them to be.

THE RELATIONAL SELF: OBJECT RELATIONS THEORY

In the past two decades, psychodynamic theory and practice have undergone particularly important transformations. While many psychologists remain within an essentially psychoanalytic framework, many have moved far beyond Freud and his immediate followers. These innovators are changing how they think about personality, the roots of mental health, and ways to help troubled people.

The basic orientation of this relational approach has emerged clearly in an integrative review of this movement (Cashdan, 1988; Greenberg & Mitchell, 1983). There have been different variations in this shift. Leaders include such psychoanalysts as Melanie Klein (one of the earliest innovators) in England and, more recently, Otto Kernberg (1976, 1984) and Heinz Kohut (1971, 1977) in the United States. In this section we will emphasize the common themes of change that seem to be emerging in this movement.

The approach is called **object relations theory** and therapy (Cashdan, 1988), and the first point to note is that the "objects" in the language of this theory are simply other human beings. The term *objects* is a leftover from classic psychoanalysis, and *significant others* essentially could substitute for it. The important shift from classic

The developing self is defined from the start in relational, interpersonal terms in Kohut's theory.

psychoanalysis to object relations theory is that while the former focused on the instinctual drives, the latter focuses on the relationships to significant other people (i.e., object relations).

The most important object for the developing child generally and unsurprisingly is the mother. It is in the context of the young child's relationship with the mother that the **relational self** begins to originate and emerge. Note that the self is defined from the start in relational or interpersonal terms. That redefinition also fits the relational view of the self in current research on how people cognitively (mentally) process information about themselves (e.g., Andersen, 1997), as discussed in Part VI. (See *In Focus 3.2.*)

"Good-Bad Splitting"

Within psychodynamic theory, one of the first to address the mother-child relationship in great depth was Melanie Klein, a British psychoanalyst who was Freud's contemporary. A theme that still persists from Klein's work is her clinical observation that the young child tends to divide the world into good and bad. Klein saw the core conflict throughout life as a struggle between positive feelings of love and negative feelings of hate. Her insight that in this conflict people tend to "split" the world into benevolent and malevolent components has been integrated into much current relational theorizing about personality structure and development.

IN FOCUS 3.2   *A Cognitive Reconceptualization of the Relational Self and Transference*

In recent years, concepts like the relational self and transference have been reconceptualized in light of current theory and findings on how memory works.

The Relational Self

According to researchers who study the self from this modern memory theory framework, self-knowledge includes all the thoughts (cognitions) and feelings (affects) that develop about oneself. It consists of information that is stored and organized in memory as a cognitive-affective (mental and emotional) representation. This knowledge representation is closely connected in the memory system to knowledge representations about the significant other people in one's life (e.g., Andersen, Reznik, & Chen, 1997; Linville & Carlston, 1994), making these two types of information directly associated. Consequently, when the representation of a particular significant other is activated (e.g., you interact with or think about your mother), aspects of your own self-representation also become activated mentally. These close connections in memory make the self intrinsically *relational* and interpersonal: In a sense, the significant others to whom one is close become part of one's personal identity. Thus the self-definition and sense of self evolves from and is linked to the important relationships in one's life.

As the self develops in relation to a particular significant other person, expectations also develop about the most likely interactions that will occur with him or her. Consequently, the relational self comes to include knowledge of interpersonal scripts about the expected pattern of self-other interaction, based on those earlier experiences. For example, an adolescent may come to expect that interactions with her mother on certain topics are likely to play out along predictable lines (e.g., more hassles, more guilt, more avoidance). These scripts

become reactivated in future interactions with the significant other or with other people who remind you of that person (Andersen et al., 1997).

Transference

The notion of the *relational self*, conceptualized in terms of memory representations that connect self-knowledge with representations of significant others, also has revived interest in the psychodynamic concept of transference, now recast in social-cognitive terms. In that view, when one develops relationships with new people, *transference* readily occurs. That happens to the degree that representations of significant others in memory are activated by the newly encountered person. Feeling attracted to—or repelled by—the newly encountered person and easily making all sorts of inferences about his or her qualities (that may or may not turn out to be accurate) can be understood in terms of the particular significant other representation that is being triggered by and applied to the new person (Andersen et al., 1997; Andersen & Chen, 1998). If the psychiatrist's manner reminds the patient of her father, the cognitive-affective representation of the father and of the patient's self in relation to him also may become easily activated and brought to mind.

Note that this view of transference is compatible with Freud's (1912/1958) claim that the individual's mental representations of significant others, most notably the parents in early childhood, profoundly influence relationships to new people (including the psychoanalyst in the treatment process). It is different, however, because it views how this process happens in terms of social-cognitive information processing rather than as a reflection of the psychosexual drives and conflicts favored in psychodynamic theory (as discussed in Part VI).

Klein spoke of a nourishing "good breast" and an empty "bad breast" in the child's conflict-ridden representation of the mother. This notion has remained in a variety of contemporary psychodynamic ideas about "good" and "bad" self-representations, internal representations of the self and of other people. It is part of the belief that from infancy on there is a tendency to somehow "split" or partition experiences in good-bad, gratifying-frustrating terms (Cashdan, 1988), fragmenting rather than integrating them into a coherent whole. When these splits are severe, therapy seeks to help the person integrate them.

Internalizing Maternal Interactions: Early Representations

Building on this idea, one of the most influential object relations theorists, Otto Kernberg (1984), sees the mother-child relationship as giving rise to and characterized by **"bipolar representations."** Each of these bipolar representations is made up of the child's image of itself, its image of the significant other person (the mother), and the feelings activated when the interaction occurs. If the child experiences deprivation during the interaction, it will emotionally color that bipolar representation negatively. If satisfaction is experienced in the interaction, a positive bipolar representation will result. The bipolar representations are internalized or, in Kernberg's biological metaphor, "metabolized" as a result of the experienced interactions. These internalizations produce different types of unique consequences within the child at different points in development. The bipolar representations that accumulate in this fashion become the basic internalized units of mental structures. They serve as lenses or templates through which the developing person views the emerging self in relation to others (Cashdan, 1988). Subsequent relationships, in turn, are seen and experienced through the templates provided by these earlier internalized representations.

Like Freud, object relations theorists focus on the importance of the early years. Unlike Freud's emphasis on how the instinctual drives are expressed and managed in the first few years, however, these theorists stress the type of caretaking relationship that develops with the early caretaker, usually the mother. This early relationship becomes the basic framework for the perception and experience of later relationships. The details of this developmental process have received increasing research attention by child psychologists. They are researching the quality and varieties of early attachment relations between mother and child (Ainsworth et al., 1978; Sroufe & Fleeson, 1986) and tracing their consequences in the course of development (see *In Focus 3.3*).

The Development of Self

Briefly, development is seen as a process in which the newborn begins in a world that is experienced as "split" into "good" (gratifications) and "bad" (tensions) feelings. In this early world, "objects" (other people, including the mother) are not yet differentiated. Emotional splitting of experiences and objects in good-bad, positive-negative terms continues throughout later life.

The most important object, the mother, soon begins to be represented by the young child internally as an image. With cognitive development and the growth of language skills, the child can start to internalize not only a maternal image but also maternal conversation in the form of an inner dialogue. Some of these early conversations are audible. You know this if you have ever heard the conversations youngsters sometimes have

IN FOCUS 3.3　*Attachment Theory: The Roots of Object Relations*

The Attachment Relationship

A half-century ago, John Bowlby, a British psychiatrist, was seeing a three-year-old in analysis. He was being supervised by the psychoanalyst Melanie Klein, who refused to allow him to meet with the child's mother. Bowlby was frustrated by this experience because, in contrast to his supervisors, he believed that parents' behavior had an important role in the development of children's personality. He felt that psychoanalysts focused too much on children's fantasy lives at the expense of attention to what was happening in their real lives (Ainsworth & Bowlby, 1991). Concurrently, he had become interested in the work of animal researchers who found that the young of various species could become attached to something separate from that which fed them and would seek proximity to that figure in times of distress. This work suggested to Bowlby that attachment was a separate, independent goal from feeding and that it was important for psychological and physical well-being. Building on and synthesizing these ideas, he developed his now-famous attachment theory (Holmes, 1993). This theory is consistent with object relations theory in giving center stage to the relationship between the young child and the primary caregiver (Bowlby, 1982). For Bowlby, however, the psychological characteristics of the "object" (the primary caregiver, usually the mother) were crucial, and he emphasized the experienced relationship between the child and the mother.

Internal Working Models

Based on experiences in this relationship, the child develops **internal working models.** These are mental representations of others, of the self, or of relationships which guide subsequent experience and behavior. Children who have had positive, gratifiying experiences with significant others in their environment will develop internal working models of others as responsive and giving and of themselves as competent and worthy of affection; those who have had painful or unsatisfying experiences develop internal models that reflect those troubled relationships.

The Strange Situation

Inspired by Bowlby, Mary Ainsworth developed the *Strange Situation* to examine patterns of infant-parent attachment in everyday situations among 8½- to 12-month-olds (e.g., Stayton & Ainsworth, 1973; Ainsworth, Blehar, Waters, & Wall, 1978). Ainsworth chose to conduct her study in a "strange" setting, that is, one unfamiliar to the baby, because she found that most American children were accustomed to the frequent comings and goings of their mothers throughout the day. Placed in an unfamiliar setting, however, and confronted with stress, young children were expected to exhibit more clearly their characteristic attachment behaviors.

with themselves as they praise or scold their own performance, saying "good boy" or "no, no" aloud to themselves. This internal dialogue is especially evident during toilet training and other early exercises in the development of self-regulation.

In time, the internalizations of maternal images and conversations become the foundations of the developing "self." You can see this development, for example, in the increasing use of "I" in the child's speech. The child's utterance changes from "Jane wants ice cream" to the personal pronoun in which "I" want it, "I" eat it, "I" am bad.

In this conception, emotional splitting continues as an aspect of the developing self: "Just as early splitting of the mother creates a split in the maternal presence, so the split in the inner maternal presence creates a split in the self. Early splits give birth

The Strange Situation assesses individual differences in the baby's quality of attachment relations. The child is introduced to a novel playroom environment with the mother and a stranger and is exposed to different levels of availability of the mother, from present and involved with the child, to present and mildly preoccupied, to absent. The child is separated from the mother twice during the Strange Situation; once left with the stranger and once left alone.

Types of Attachment

Three main patterns of behavior were identified in this situation. Babies who avoided the mother throughout the paradigm as well as on reunion were considered insecure-avoidant, or *A* babies. Those who were able to greet the mother positively upon reunion and then return to play, and who attended to the mother and desired interaction with her throughout the procedure, were termed securely-attached, or *B* babies. Infants whose reunion behavior seemed to be a combination of contact-seeking and anger, and who were difficult to comfort upon reunion, were classified as the *C* or insecure-resistant (or insecure-ambivalent) babies. These children displayed interaction-resistant behavior, but, once contact was attained, they showed contact-maintaining behaviors.

Data from home visits conducted before the Strange Situation revealed that the different types of babies experienced different patterns of maternal responsiveness. For example, mothers of infants rated as securely attached responded most quickly and consistently to their babies'

crying. Mothers of resistant babies were inconsistent in their responsiveness, while the responsiveness of mothers of avoidant children varied with the context: They were unresponsive to bids for contact and comfort and controlling and intrusive in reponse to their children's attempts at independent play.

Long-Term Consequences

Research over the ensuing years has provided more data on these classifications. For example, children rated secure are more likely to remain confident and flexibly organized when faced with an insurmountable task as preschoolers (Arend, Gove, & Sroufe, 1979) and can suggest strategies for coping with the absence of a parent as 6-year-olds (Main, Kaplan, & Cassidy, 1985). Additionally, five-year-olds with a history of a secure relationship with the mother are less likely to exhibit negative interactions with a peer (Youngblade & Belsky, 1992). Many other links have been found and they seem to extend into adulthood. Studies of adult attachment suggest that individuals may carry specific attachment styles with them in relationships throughout life (e.g., Fraley & Shaver, 1997; Kobak & Sceery, 1988). For example, college students rated secure (by interview measures) were rated by their friends as more warm and nurturant (Bartholomew & Horowitz, 1991). Ultimately, these styles are thought to influence the way one parents one's own children (Main & Goldwyn, 1984).

to later splits" (Cashdan, 1988, p. 48). In time, individuals come to view themselves as "good" or "bad" depending on their earlier good-bad emotional experiences of splitting. The sense of self-esteem—or its lack—that ultimately emerges characterizes how persons feel about themselves. It is both the consequence of the earlier experiences and the determinant of much of what is experienced later in the course of life.

As the splitting process continues, a variety of identity splits occur. They yield such important categories as one's sexual identity, career identity, identity as a parent, and so on. Each is colored emotionally in good-bad terms. The emotional splitting represented by the enduring concern with goodness-badness never ends. When it is maladaptively tilted toward a badness imbalance, it continues to corrode the person's relationships. The therapeutic process, in turn, is viewed as the method for undoing the imbalance, recognizing and overcoming inner conflicts, and developing a more integrated and positive image of the self.

HEINZ KOHUT'S THEORY OF OBJECT RELATIONS AND THE SELF

> . . . man can no more survive psychologically in a psychological milieu that does not respond empathically to him, than he can survive physically in an atmosphere that contains no oxygen (Kohut, 1977, p. 85).

The object relations theorists share several themes, as the previous section showed. One leader in this movement, Heinz Kohut, is selected in this section for further attention because his work is seen as especially influential for changing views of the healthy and the disturbed personality. Kohut, a psychiatrist who received his medical training at the University of Vienna, went on to psychoanalytic training and teaching in Chicago, where he gained recognition as a theorist and clinician in the 1970s.

In Kohut's view, profound changes in the family and culture throughout the century have occurred: Psychoanalysis and psychodynamic theory must be responsive to them. An important change, he believes, is that Freud's patients typically came from a Western civilization in which life was concentrated in the home and family unit. Families tended to expose their children to "emotional overcloseness" (Kohut, 1977, p. 269), and these intense emotional relations in turn often produced neurotic problems involving internal conflicts such as in the Oedipus complex. The developing child was likely to be trapped in too much intimacy, too much stimulation, too much intrusiveness.

In contrast, children now are more likely to see parents at most in leisure hours and to develop much less clear role definitions and models: "The environment which used to be experienced as threateningly close, is now experienced more and more as threateningly distant . . ." (Kohut, 1977, p. 271). While personal problems used to arise from being too stimulated emotionally by parents, even erotically as in Freud's case of "Little Hans" (Freud, 1963), now youngsters tend to be *under*stimulated and may search for erotic sensations and other strong experiences to fill the emotional emptiness of their lives and to try to escape loneliness and depression.

Kohut's thinking has led the way for a new psychoanalytic interest in the self and for the treatment of problems such as disorders of the self. Rather than being driven by unconscious conflicts and impulses, Kohut sees patients today as often deprived of **"empathic mirroring"** and ideal "objects" or tar-

**Heinz Kohut
(1913–1981)**

gets for suitable identification. Because their parents were walled off from them emotionally or too involved with their own narcissistic needs, they did not provide the necessary models for healthy development of the self and for the formation of meaningful, responsive relationships in adulthood.

People fear the destruction of the self when they don't feel the empathic human responses from the important others ("self objects") in their lives. Kohut compares this state to being deprived of "psychological oxygen." The availability of empathic reactions from self objects is as vital to the survival of the self as the presence of oxygen is to the survival of the body:

> What leads to the human self's destruction is its exposure to the coldness, the indifference of the nonhuman, the nonempathical responding world (Kohut, 1984, p. 18).

What is feared most is not so much physical death, but a world in which our humanness would end forever (Kohut, 1980, 1984). In the same vein, Kohut does not see Freud's castration anxiety as the ultimate human anxiety: ". . . the little boy's manifest horror at the sight of the female genitals is not the deepest layer of this experience . . . behind it and covered by it lies a deeper and even more dreadful experience—the experience of the faceless mother, that is, the mother whose face does not light up at the sight of her child" (Kohut, 1984, p. 21).

The "disintegration anxiety" from a nonempathic, nonhuman environment, taken to the extreme, is seen in the inorganic, stainless steel and plastic heart experienced so terrifyingly in a dream reported by one of Kohut's patients (Kohut, 1984, p. 19). In his "stainless steel world" dream, Mr. U was in an ice tunnel with walls from which large glistening strands of ice went down to the ground and up to the ceiling. It was like an enormous model of the human heart, large enough to be walked around in (like one in a museum the patient knew well). Walking within this icy heart, Mr. U felt the anxiety of an oncoming but unnamed danger to which he was exposed, all alone, except for a shadowy figure to whom he appealed but who was unresponsive. In a flash, he was pulled through a crack in the wall into a cityscape that was blindingly bright—a landscape that was utterly unreal, with busy but completely unapproachable people all around: a "stainless steel world" in the patient's own words, in a science fiction scene with no escape, no communication, trapped forever, unreachable in a world of cold-heartedness.

Reinterpretation of the Oedipal Period

Kohut's theory also leads to a reinterpretation of such Freudian constructs as the "Oedipal period." In his view, during this period the girl fears confrontation from a father who is nonempathic and sexually seductive instead of affectionate and accepting. In the same period she fears a mother who is competitive and hostile rather than reflecting that she is proud of the child and pleased by her.

In parallel fashion, during the same period the boy fears confrontation from a mother who is nonempathic and sexually seductive rather than affectionate and accepting of him. He also fears confrontation from a father who is competitive and hostile with him rather than pleased and proud.

Table 3.6
Kohut's Characteristics of the Self

Defective Self	Healthy Personality
Fragmented experience of love (sexual fantasies)	Feels glow of healthy pleasure in appropriate sexual functioning
Fragmented assertiveness (hostile fantasies)	Able to be self-confidently assertive in pursuit of goals

Kohut's Healthy Self

In Kohut's theory, if parents fail to respond empathically and healthily to their child in this phase of development, it sets up a defect in the self. As a result, the child develops a tendency to experience sexual fantasies and the fragments of love rather than love. Likewise, the child with a defective self also tends to experience hostile fantasies and only the fragments of assertiveness rather than appropriate assertiveness. The individual's typical internal reaction to these experiences becomes great anxiety. These characteristics of the defective self contrast with those of a healthy, normal personality, which, instead of anxiety and fragmented experiences, feels the glow of appropriate sexual functioning and assertiveness, as summarized in Table 3.6.

APPROACHES TO RELATIONAL THERAPY

The new focus on the relational nature of personality has stimulated many alternative approaches to psychotherapy that go far beyond Freud's original ideas. For example, it has led therapists to conduct couples' group therapy from an object-relations standpoint (Feld, 1997). Two developments, both relational in theory but very different in practice, are seen in Kohut's own approach and, in contrast, in "family therapies," also considered here.

The Road to Cure: Relational Therapy and Restoration of the Self

It follows from this conception that the goal of the analytic therapy process becomes the restoration of the self. Led by theorists like Kohut, **relational therapy** (our abbreviation for "object relations therapy") has emerged as a coherent approach to conceptualizing personality problems and treating them therapeutically. It is a psychodynamic approach in the sense that its roots are in earlier psychoanalytic theories. Like them, its focus is on the individual's often unconscious, long-standing conflicts and defenses. It is distinctive, however, in three ways. It sees the history of these problems in early relationships, especially with the mother. It sees their expression in current relationships. Finally, it conceptualizes their treatment as a process that emphasizes the relationship within the therapeutic experience.

In this approach, the therapeutic process requires formation of an empathic relationship with the analyst. The therapist actively and empathically "engages" the patient to build a close therapeutic relationship. Interpretation and confrontation of basic relational problems occur in this supportive context. Note that this focus on the carefully nurtured empathic relationship contrasts with the "blank screen" image of the traditional Freudian analyst. Unlike the Freudian patient who free associates while reclining on a couch, with the therapist sitting behind the patient, in relational therapy, the two face each other and interact actively, the therapist providing empathic support as well as gradual confrontation.

Kohut's therapy is considered relational in the sense just described, but it is still limited to the therapist-client interaction without directly involving the relationships currently within the family. The latter requires going beyond the two-person psychodynamic situation itself, as seen dramatically in such developments as family therapy, discussed next.

Treating Interactions and Relationships: Family Therapy

Family therapy is a promising approach to treatment, based in part on modern psychodynamic theory of the sort developed by the neo-Freudians. In family therapy, the problem is seen as residing in the family's system of interactions rather than within the child. The goal of therapy is a transformation in the family system—allowing family members to relate to one another in more adaptive ways (Minuchin, Lee, & Simon, 1996). This family therapy approach is illustrated nicely in efforts to treat **anorexia nervosa,** the psychophysiological problem of self-starvation (Minuchin, Roseman, & Baker, 1978). For example, the therapist may challenge the family's notion that the

For Kohut, the modern child's life is characterized not by too much parenting and intimacy but by loneliness.

daughter is sick and the parents are helpless. The problem is recast for them as one in which both parents and daughter are involved in a fight for control. This reorientation mobilizes the parents to treat their daughter as a rebellious adolescent, not as an invalid. Specific therapeutic strategies are directed toward challenging maladaptive family characteristics. For example, all family members are encouraged to speak for themselves or not to speak if they so choose. The protectiveness valued by the family may be redefined to include the protection of each member's individuality. Overprotection may be challenged directly by pointing out, for instance, that the child can take her coat off herself or even by explicitly stating that excessive protection robs the individual of her right to try and fail, learning how to cope in the process. The tendency of the family to avoid conflict may be challenged by insisting that two family members who disagree discuss their disagreement without the possibility of intervention by other family members to diffuse the conflict. The therapist's role is to maintain or even increase the conflict and to prevent intrusion or escape. Thus, instead of simply treating the individual as having a problem, the entire family is seen as in need of learning new and healthier ways of relating to one another—an approach far different from the original strategies Freud favored (Minuchin & Nichols, 1994). The focus has shifted from individual psychodynamics to the dynamics of the family as a social system.

Relational Problems Expressed in Pathology: The Case of Anorexia

To illustrate the types of problems that relational therapists treat and how they conceptualize them, let us consider the following case illustration of the disorder called anorexia nervosa. In this now relatively common problem, often found in American adolescent girls, persons may starve themselves virtually to death even in the midst of plenty and with no initial physical illness responsible for the starvation.

> Debby M. was 14 years old when she decided she wanted to be a fashion model and went on a diet. Gradually, she eliminated more and more foods until, one year later, she ate only cottage cheese, carrots, diet soda, and water. Her weight dropped from 115 to 81 pounds and her menstrual periods stopped. During this time Debby became excessively active physically. She would wake up at around 5 a.m. and jog two to three miles before getting ready for school, jogging another two to three miles in the afternoon when she returned home. Weekends were spent at the community swimming pool or practicing alone on the tennis court. She had always been a good student and continued to get excellent grades (often studying past midnight), but she withdrew from school activities and spent little or no time with friends. Her parents describe her as a good girl: they are proud of her grades and cannot explain why she will not eat. On her pediatrician's recommendation, Debby has been hospitalized. After careful physical examination, no organic cause has been found for her refusal to eat. Debby is diagnosed as having anorexia nervosa (Minuchin, Roseman, & Baker, 1978).

As Debby's case illustrates, anorexia nervosa occurs most often in middle-class females and usually begins during adolescence. Symptoms include a loss of over 25% of total body weight, cessation of menstruation, excessive activity, below normal body temperature, denial of hunger, fear of gaining weight, and a distorted body image. From 10 to 15% of these cases die of self-inflicted starvation.

A group of psychologists working with people who have this disorder report similarities in the way the families of these patients function (Minuchin, Roseman, & Baker, 1978). There are some distinctive family characteristics which appear to encourage and maintain anorexia nervosa. For example, the family members are overinvolved (enmeshed) with one another. Changes within one member or between two members affect other members too much. In addition, the relationships between parents and children, brothers and sisters, and husband and wife become so intertwined that they may become ineffective and inappropriate. The enmeshed family's excessive togetherness and sharing intrude on individual autonomy, and family members have poorly differentiated perceptions of one another and often of themselves. The family's overprotectiveness retards the child's development of autonomy and competence. In turn, the "sick" child may use her symptoms to control and manipulate the family. While normal families are able to disagree, these families are characteristically unable to confront their differences to the extent of negotiating a resolution. They avoid conflict, deny the existence of problems, or diffuse the disagreements that do occur, including the battles over the child's refusal to eat sometimes to the point of death.

SUMMARY

1. In general, the psychoanalytic followers of Freud have de-emphasized the role of instincts and psychosexual stages. They have concerned themselves more with the social milieu and the ego. Their conception of human nature has been less deterministic, less drive oriented, and more humanistic.

2. One especially striking departure from Freud is the psychology of Jung. Jung emphasized the unconscious and its symbolic and mystical expressions. He focused on dreams and on human beings' need to achieve unity through greater awareness of their collective and personal unconscious.

3. Freud saw sex and aggression as the basic human motives. Beginning with the neo-Freudians and continuing to the present, psychologists have expanded the list of human wishes by adding many higher-order motives. These motives, such as competence, are purely psychological and have no specific physiological bases. A good example of a higher-order motive is competence motivation, which is the desire for mastery of a task for its own sake.

4. Freud's theory has many implications for our view of the human being. The impact and value of this theory cannot be judged fully until we examine its applications.

5. Adler's theories provide another significant departure from Freud. Based on his own personal experience, Adler saw individuals as struggling from birth to overcome profound feelings of helplessness and inferiority and striving for perfection. This compensatory motivation, and not id impulses, guides behavior and fuels psychological development. According to Adler, people are social beings who are influenced more by cultural influences and personal relations than by sexual and aggressive instincts.

6. Fromm likewise saw people primarily as social beings who can be understood best in relation to others. People are not simply victims of biological urges. Instead, Fromm invests them with the ability to grow, to develop, to reach potentialities. Culture does not exist to stifle instinctual drives; instead, it is a product of the people in the society.

7. Erikson revises and broadens Freud's ideas about developmental stages. Erikson views social adaptation, not unconscious sexual urges, as the key force underlying development that takes place over

an entire lifetime. Most critical during this development is the evolution of "ego identity," which involves the incorporation of past experiences and future hopes, and which directs people through life.

8. Object relations theories are one of the most important recent developments in psychoanalytic theory. Prominent object relations theorists, primarily Kernberg and Kohut, emphasize the mental representation of the self and other persons. These mental representations develop in the early relationship with the primary caregiver. They are characterized by emotional splits into good and bad components or "bipolar representations." According to Kohut, troubled people have experienced a lack of "empathic mirroring": Psychotherapy in this framework tries to provide such empathic care, to enhance damaged self-esteem, and to help the person find suitable objects for identification.

9. Although many traditional approaches to personality change still emphasize insight and awareness of unconscious motives and feelings, more current approaches focus on the relational aspects of people. Relational therapy, as practiced by the object relations theorists, and family therapy, which concentrates on more current life problems and relationships, are two primary examples.

10. Current research on memory information about one's self supports the view of the self in relational interpersonal terms: What we know about ourselves is often contextualized in our relations with significant others.

Psychodynamic Personality Assessment

This chapter considers some of the major contributions of the psychodynamic approach to the assessment of persons. In it you will find examples of how psychologists in this orientation have approached personality assessment and the study of lives and tried to understand individuals seeking psychological help.

As the previous two chapters described, Freud's original theories have been modified and even transformed in many different directions over the years both by disciples and by revisionists. It therefore is not surprising to also find many variations in how psychodynamic ideas are applied to assess and understand people. This chapter begins by illustrating some of the earlier applications of the approach for the assessment of individuals and then considers some of the more recent developments.

The ideas and methods presented in this chapter are already a firm part of the field's historical past. They also remain important influences on much contemporary thought about personality, with only minor modification. For many other psychologists today, however, psychodynamic contributions provide foundations for quite new directions and substantial change, as you will see in later chapters.

GLOBAL PSYCHODYNAMIC ORIENTATION

Freudian psychology was especially exciting because it promised a way to understand and to treat each complex individual with the depth that he or she deserves. The preceding two chapters gave you a sense of some of the main concepts that underlie the psychodynamic approach to personality. Guided by these concepts, one tries to help the person to reveal unconscious motives, conflicts, and other dynamics. In this approach, the objective is to uncover disguises and defenses, to read the symbolic meanings of behaviors, and to find the unconscious motives that underlie action. In this way the clinician tries to find the distinctive qualities that characterize the individual.

The Core Beneath the Mask

Psychodynamic theorists recognized that a person's overt actions across seemingly similar situations often seem inconsistent. They felt, however, that these inconsistencies in behavior were merely superficial because beneath them were underlying motives that actually drove the person consistently over the years. The basic motives persist across diverse settings, but their overt expressions are disguised. Therefore, the task is to find the person's fundamental motives and dynamics under the defensive distortions of the overt behavior. The challenge is to discover the basic core hidden behind the mask, to find the truth beneath the surface. But how?

Minimizing the Situation: In Search of Underlying Dynamics

Psychodynamically oriented psychologists hoped that dynamic patterns would, under ambiguous conditions, penetrate the person's defenses and reveal themselves. Therefore techniques were developed in which cues in the situation are kept vague and unclear. These beliefs about the importance of stimulus ambiguity guide assessment. If you experience such an assessment, you will not be asked detailed and structured questions. Instead, psychodynamic inquiries tend to be open-ended probes that leave your task unclear so that underlying motives and dynamics can emerge.

Such assessment tries to reconstruct the person's history. These historical reconstructions deal with the ways in which the person handled sexual and aggressive impulses during childhood at each psychosexual stage. Clues are also sought about traumatic experiences, defenses, and basic character traits.

The Case of Gary W.

Approaches to personality become most meaningful when applied to an actual person. In this text, each of the major approaches will be applied to the same individual. Gary W. is not an unusual person, except in the sense that everyone is unique. He is presented here as a case example of an essentially normal human being whose characteristics and history are neither dramatically bizarre nor especially exciting. Often case histories serve to illustrate rare and even esoteric qualities—the strange sex criminal, the twisted neurotic, the split personality. Our purpose in considering Gary, however, is not to display odd bits of abnormality, not to shock and titillate, but rather to make concrete the methods and ideas created to deal with personality. So that our concepts and techniques do not become too abstract, we must apply them to daily life and examine their relevance—and occasionally their irrelevance—for understanding the particular individual (and not just people in general). For this reason we have selected Gary as an ordinary person, one among hundreds of millions. Still, like all individuals, he is unique enough to surprise us occasionally, complex enough to defy pat explanations, troubled enough to encounter problems, and human enough to be confused about himself, at least some of the time, and even more often to confuse those who try to understand him.

As we proceed, you will get new information regarding Gary W. so that the contributions of different personality perspectives and data can be appreciated more fully. In later chapters Gary's case will be interpreted according to the different approaches available for studying personality. (As an exercise, you may find it interesting to apply each approach to yourself by writing down how you see yourself from that perspective.) Our first information about Gary will be limited to a few background facts that introduce him, provided when he was first seen by a psychologist.

Gary W. was born in Boston 25 years ago. He comes from an old New England family of moderate means. His father is a businessman; his mother described herself as a homemaker. Both parents are alive and are currently divorcing. Gary has an older and now married brother who is a successful physician.

After attending a private boarding school as an adolescent, Gary went to Hilson College. His record was good but not outstanding. On tests of intellectual ability, Gary's scores indicated he was of superior intelligence. After graduating he worked at various jobs for three years, part of that time abroad. He then returned to seek a master's degree in business. Currently he is in graduate school and still unmarried.

We have already noted that psychodynamic assessors often begin by trying to reconstruct the person's history. How did Gary handle sexual and aggressive impulses during childhood? What were his struggles at each psychosexual stage? What are his defenses and basic character traits? The following excerpts are taken from a psychodynamic report about Gary W., based on interviews and test situations that will be discussed later in this chapter, interpreted from a Freudian view.

Gary W.: The Psychodynamic View—Freudian Interpretation

Oedipal themes abound in the case of Gary W., although he has grown a long way toward resolving them. W. emotionally describes his feeling that his father was his "severest critic" and that he is his mother's favorite. He says that he no longer sees adults as all-knowing, and he refers to his father as mellowed and "out of it." He reports warmth and affection for his mother, although these feelings are mixed.

In his own sibling relationships, Gary seems to have displaced much of his rivalry with his father onto his older brother. W. describes great outbursts of anger vented on Charles with obvious intent to injure. He compares Charles with their father and says that the two are alike in many respects. He is on better terms with Charles since the latter was in a car crash in which he was hurt. (This in some respects parallels his present hostile condescension, rather than competitive hostility, toward the father who has proved himself a failure in business.)

A recent revival of the Oedipal situation occurred when Gary's girlfriend left him for his roommate. She may well have symbolized his mother to him more than is usual: She is older, was married before, and has a child from the previous marriage. After he had confessed his love to her, she told him that she had been seeing his roommate. W. felt humiliated and "wounded in my vanity," because these events went on "behind my back." His feelings are reminiscent of the chagrin felt by the little boy when he realizes his father's role vis-à-vis his mother. W. attempted to resolve his anger by recognizing that he was not in a position financially to marry her, whereas his roommate was. His apparent satisfaction that his roommate after all has not married her, and that they may have broken up, also is consistent with the conceptualization that this relationship was filled with Oedipal themes.

The incomplete resolution of the Oedipal conflict is further evident in W.'s fear of injury and physical illness, in the depression that has followed a motorcycle accident (castration anxiety)—and in the distinction he makes between girlfriends ("good girls") and sex objects ("fast girls"). Incomplete identification with his father, whether a cause or a result of this unresolved situation, is apparent. His search for a strong male figure is evident in his reactions to the headmaster and teacher at boarding school, described respectively as "a very definite, determined sort of person" and "not the sort of man you could push around." He is quite openly disparaging of his father, albeit on intellectual grounds. (This tends to be W.'s typical style.)

According to Gary, his mother sees sex as something bad and nasty. This report, as well as his suggestion that his mother has undermined his father's masculinity, may represent wishes that his mother may not be responsive to his father. He himself may regard sexuality ambivalently—his sexual experiences seem to involve much parental rebellion, and he keeps his sex objects separate from his affections. When he speaks about sex, he talks crudely of "making it."

Gary's anxiety in social situations in general, and his fear of public speaking in particular, are further indices of his basic insecurity and his brittle defenses. He is concerned that he will be found lacking. The underlying castration anxiety is expressed symbolically in his comment that when he stands up to speak in public, he is afraid "the audience is ready to chop my head off," and when there is a possibility of debate, that he will be "caught with my pants down."

Gary shows some concern about homosexuality. He mentions it spontaneously when talking about friendship, and his descriptions of living in close proximity with other males include tension, friction, and annoyance. This anxiety is illustrated in his uncomfortable relationship to his current roommate. His first two responses to cards on the Rorschach are also interesting in this connection. Laughter accompanies the statement that two figures are "grinding their bottoms." The perception of animals rather than human figures further serves as a defense to reduce his anxiety. Paranoid tendencies appear in both the fantasy and interview material (for example, seeing "eyes" on the Rorschach) and suggest some projection of the homosexual conflict.

The battle being waged between impulses, reality, and conscience are evidenced by Gary's concern with control and his obsessive-compulsive traits. W. makes a tenuous distinction between passion and reason, rejecting the former and clinging to the latter. He extends this distinction to interpersonal relations, drawing a line between "companionship" and "love." He reports an inability to empathize and form good object-relations. An example of repression of affect is W.'s difficulty in expressing anger. In this area, as in others, he tends to intellectualize as a way to systematize and control anxiety. His problems in expressing anger may also be reflected in his speech difficulties and in his verbal blocks, especially in public and social situations.

Instinctual elements arise to disturb the tenuous control gained by secondary processes. He complains that he sometimes gets drunk when he should be accomplishing things. He says he admires people with enough self-discipline not to drink, smoke, and sleep late. He speaks of trying to force himself not to do the things that he knows are bad for him and that interfere with his long-range objectives.

The need to control is also apparent in his performance and behavior on many of the psychological tests, where his approach is analytic rather than imaginative and his expressive movements are tight and controlled. (His attention to detail and his constant intellectualization of real feeling on the Rorschach, his hobby of insect study, and his admission that often "trivialities" bother him for a long time add up to a picture of restriction and repression in the service of anxiety reduction.) There is an anal retentive aspect of this need to control, which comes out rather clearly in his interaction with the assessor when he says testily, "Didn't you show that to me already—are you trying to squeeze more out of me?" A further compulsive trait is W.'s frequent counting and the way he rigidly breaks his ability self-ratings down into component parts and strives to ensure complete accuracy and coverage of whatever he is discussing about himself.

The need for control may circle back to castration anxiety. The two themes come together in W.'s fear of physical injury and in his fear of losing his brain capacity. The culmination of these two fears occurred when W.'s motorcycle failed him, and he is still preoccupied with this incident. He relates these fears more directly to the Oedipal conflict when, in the phrase association test, he links anger at his brother with fear of losing his mind.

Note that the focus in this report is on hypothesized underlying dynamics. It is implicitly assumed that sexual and aggressive motives and unconscious conflicts widely affect many behaviors. Statements about behavior tend to be relatively global and undifferentiated. The emphasis is on unacceptable impulses and defenses for coping with the anxiety they arouse. There is also an attempt to link current sexual and aggressive problems to relations with the parents and to Oedipal problems in early childhood.

This report provides a way of seeing meaning and unity throughout Gary's diverse behaviors. For example, his relations with his brother and with women became part of his larger efforts to cope with Oedipal problems. Indeed, a main attraction of psychodynamic theory is that it offers a systematic, unified view of the individual. It views him as an integrated, dynamic creature: When his underlying core personality is revealed, his seemingly diverse, discrepant behaviors become meaningful, and all fit into the total whole. It becomes easy to see why such an elegant conceptual system is attractive. But the key question for scientifically oriented students is: Do psychodynamic reports of the kind made about Gary provide accurate and useful insights?

Relying on the Clinician

Psychodynamic interpretations depend more on intuitions than on tests. The rules for relating behavioral signs to unconscious meanings are not spelled out and require clinicians to form their own judgments based on clinical experience and the "feel" of the case. The merit of such assessments depends on two things. First, it depends on the evidence supporting the techniques upon which the psychologist relies. Second, it depends on the value of clinical judgment itself. Because psychodynamic theories rest on the belief that the core of personality is revealed by highly indirect behavioral signs, evidence for the value of these indirect signs of personality is most important. We next review some of the main clinical methods that have been studied in the search for valuable signs of personality. Probably the most important of these methods are the projective techniques.

Dreams and Free Association

Free association and the analysis of dreams are the methods of personality study that come most directly from Freud's work. Both methods are used in the context of the patient-therapist meetings during psychoanalysis.

In free association, you are instructed to give your thoughts complete freedom and to report daydreams, feelings, and images, no matter how incoherent, illogical, or meaningless they might seem. This technique may be employed either with a little prompting or by offering brief phrases ("my mother . . ."; "I often . . .") as a stimulus to encourage associations (see *In Focus 4.1*).

Freud believed that dreams were similar to the patient's free associations. He thought the dream was an expression of the most primitive workings of the mind. Dreams were interpreted as fulfilling a wish or discharging tension by inducing an image of the desired goal. Freud felt that through the interpretation of dreams, he was penetrating into the unconscious.

PROJECTIVE METHODS AND INTERVIEWS

Free association and dream analysis, while remaining the basic tools of orthodox psychoanalytic therapy, have had only indirect impacts for the personality assessments

IN FOCUS 4.1   *Encouraging Free Association*

The following passages illustrate some typical instructions and responses in the process of encouraging free association during psychoanalytic interviews. The patient complains that she does not have any thoughts at the moment.

THERAPIST: It may seem that way to you at first, but there are always some thoughts there. Just as your heart is always beating, there's always some thought or other going through your mind.

PATIENT: Your mentioning the word "heart" reminds me that the doctor told my mother the other day she had a weak heart.

In a later interview the same woman became silent again and could not continue.

THERAPIST: Just say what comes to you.

PATIENT: Oh, odds and ends that aren't very important.

THERAPIST: Say them anyway.

PATIENT: I don't see how they could have much bearing. I was wondering what sort of books those are over there. But that hasn't anything to do with what I'm here for.

THERAPIST: One never can tell, and actually you're in no position to judge what has bearing and what hasn't. Let me decide that. You just report what comes into your mind regardless of whether you think it's important or not (Colby, 1951, p. 153).

---

conducted by most psychologists. These techniques have been used for research purposes (Antrobus, 1991; Klinger, 1977; Singer & Bonanno, 1990) and as parts of larger projects for the intensive assessment of individuals. They have not, however, been widely adopted in personality study. They are considered too time consuming and are believed to require extensive contact with the subject to establish a comfortable atmosphere before they can be used profitably. Most personality psychologists currently believe it is uneconomical to devote much time to gathering dream data and free-association material. While intrigued by these methods, many personality psychologists have been influenced more by projective tests.

Characteristics of Projective Techniques

The main characteristic of **projective methods** is the way in which the testing situation is usually structured so that the task is *ambiguous*. Typically, there are also attempts to *disguise the purpose* of the test (Bell, 1948; Exner, 1993), and the person is given *freedom to respond* in any way that he or she likes.

In projective testing, assessors present you with ambiguous stimuli and ask ambiguous questions. For example, they ask, "What might this be?" "What could this remind you of?" [while showing an inkblot] or say, "Create the most imaginative story that you can [showing a picture], including what the people are thinking and feeling, what led up to this situation, and how it all comes out." Or they read words and ask you to "say the first thing that comes to mind."

The same stimulus materials with different instructions could be used nonprojectively by asking you to trace the blots, count the pictures, or spell the words in the association list. Similarly, almost any test item can be used projectively with appropriate instructions. Some stimuli, of course, lend themselves more readily than others to projective use, primarily because they more easily evoke a wide range of responses. Therefore, fairly vague stimuli such as inkblots, unclear pictures, barely audible sounds, clay, plastic materials, and paint have been favorites. Some differences between projective techniques and more objective, structured performance tests (such as tests of achievement and ability) are shown in Figure 4.1.

Projective techniques have been favored by psychoanalytically oriented assessors because they assumed that the "unconscious inner life" is at least partially revealed in responses to the projective test situation. The assumptions underlying projective tests reflect the influences of psychoanalytic theory: the emphasis on the unconsciously motivated nature of behavior, the importance of unconscious material, and the conception that the person has a central, enduring "core" or basic personality organization. This core personality is reflected more or less pervasively in the person's behavior, according to psychodynamic theory. And this core is most readily revealed through free responses in an ambiguous, nonthreatening situation of the kind created by projective tests (MacFarlane & Tuddenham, 1951).

Figure 4.1
Some Differences between an Objective Performance Test and a Projective Test
In objective performance tests, the person must choose between definite right or wrong answers. In projective tests, the stimulus and instructions are ambiguous, and the person has greater freedom to respond in accord with his or her interpretation of the stimulus.

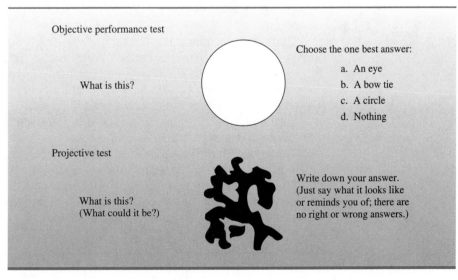

Traditionally, projective techniques are presented with special efforts to disguise their purposes. This practice reflects the belief that projective data reveal unacceptable unconscious aspects of the person. Presumably the person has erected defensive maneuvers that prevent the expression of these impulses unless the defenses are relaxed. But although the general characteristics and purposes of projective tests are widely agreed upon, there is much uncertainty about the actual nature of the "projection" that occurs in response to these tests.

Probably the two most influential and popular projective techniques have been the Rorschach and the Thematic Apperception Test (TAT). A 1995 survey with replies from over 400 clinical psychologists across a variety of settings indicated that the Rorschach and TAT still remain among the most commonly used personality assessment procedures in everyday clinical practice (Watkins, Campbell, Nieberding, & Hallmark, 1995).

The Rorschach

Developed by the psychiatrist Hermann Rorschach in 1921, the **Rorschach test** consists of a series of inkblots on 10 separate cards (Figure 4.2). Some of the blots are black and white, and some colored. The person is instructed to look at the inkblots one at a time and to say everything that the inkblot could resemble or look like. The examiner then generally conducts an inquiry into the details of the person's interpretation of each blot.

Gary's Reactions to Two of the Rorschach Inkblot Cards

RESPONSE: This looks like two dogs, head-to-foot (laughs), licking each other.
That's about it, that's all.

INQUIRY ANSWERS (TO THE QUESTION "WHAT ABOUT THE INKBLOT MADE YOU THINK OF TWO DOGS?"): They're sort of fuzzy . . . kinda shapeless. It was the dark skin and the furry effect that made me think of it.

RESPONSE: Didn't we have this one already?
This could be an ogre laughing—his head thrown back and he's laughing, his eyes and mouth wide open.
These over here look like insects, tsetse flies in fact, with tiny, tiny legs, and small, delicate and rather beautiful wings.
That's it, that's enough.

INQUIRY ANSWERS: It's the shagginess and the hugeness, the massiveness of the shape. The wings over here, head here.

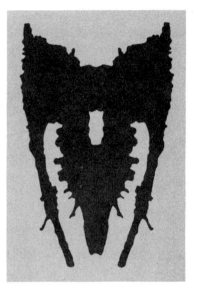

Figure 4.2
Inkblot Similar to Those in the Rorschach Test

Responses may be scored for location (the place on the card that the response refers to) and such determinants as the physical aspects of the blot (such as shape, color, shading, or an expression of movement) that suggested the response (Exner, 1993). The originality of the responses, the content, and other characteristics also may be scored and compared with those of other people of similar age. The interpreter may try to relate these scores to aspects of personality, such as creative capacity, contact with reality, and anxiety.

The Thematic Apperception Test (TAT)

The **Thematic Apperception Test** or **TAT** was developed by Morgan and Murray in the Harvard Psychological Clinic research program during the 1930s, and it is still popular in clinical work. The test consists of a series of pictures and one blank card (see Figure 4.3). The cards are presented one at a time.

Figure 4.3
Picture Similar to Those in the TAT

If you take this test, you will be told that it is a story-telling test and that you are to make up a story for each picture: "Tell what has led up to the event shown in the picture, describe what is happening at the moment, what the characters are feeling and thinking, and then give the outcome." You are encouraged to give free reign to your imagination and to say whatever comes to mind. Typically, the length of time before the subject begins telling the story and the total time for each story are recorded.

As the name of the test suggests, it is expected that people will interpret an ambiguous stimulus according to their individual readiness to perceive in a certain way ("apperception"). Furthermore, the themes that recur in these imaginative productions are thought to reflect the person's underlying conflicts and problems. Special scoring keys have been designed for use with the TAT (Bellack & Abrams, 1997; McClelland et al., 1953; Mussen & Naylor, 1954). Usually the stories are not scored formally, however, and instead are used "clinically," the clinician interpreting the themes intuitively in accord with his or her personality theory (Rossini & Moretti, 1997).

Two of Gary's Stories from the TAT

Card depicting two men: Two men have gone on a hunting trip. It is dawn now and the younger one is still sound asleep. The older one is watching over him. Thinking how much he reminds him of when he was young and could sleep no matter what. Also, seeing the boy sleeping there makes him long for the son he never had. He's raising his hand about to stroke him on the forehead. I think he'll be too embarrassed to go ahead with it. He'll start a fire and put on some coffee and wait for the younger man to wake up.

Card depicting young man and older woman: This depicts a mother-son relationship. The mother is a strong, stalwart person. Her son is hesitating at the doorway. He wants to ask her advice about something but isn't sure whether it's the right thing to do. Maybe he should make up his own mind. I think he'll just come in and have a chat with her. He won't ask her advice but will work things out for himself. Maybe it's a career choice, a girlfriend. I don't know what, but whatever it is, he'll decide himself. He'll make his own plans, figure out what the consequences will be, and work it out from there.

The Interview

The oldest method for studying personality is the interview, and it remains the most favored for psychodynamic research and assessment (Watkins et al., 1995). Its usefulness as an assessment tool depends on many considerations, including how the interview is guided and structured and how the interviewee's responses are recorded, coded, and interpreted. Each of these steps requires attention to the same issues that apply to other methods that rely on the clinician's judgment, as was just discussed for projective techniques.

Psychodynamically oriented interviewers tend to structure their sessions like projective methods so that the interviewee has considerable freedom to respond and go in any direction. Questions usually are open-ended (such as "Tell me about yourself"), and the goals or purpose are left ambiguous. Probes, when they occur, are aimed at underlying motives (for example, "I wonder *why* you felt that. . . ."). Most of the talking is done by the interviewee.

In recent years, unobtrusive video and sound recording has made the interview a method that is more open to manageable scoring, coding, and data analysis. These procedures often can be made even more flexible by computerized programs. The interview, therefore, is being used with renewed interest in efforts to systematically improve psychodynamic assessment (Horowitz et al., 1989; Perry & Cooper, 1989), as discussed later in this chapter.

MURRAY AND THE HARVARD PERSONOLOGISTS: PIONEERS OF ASSESSMENT

The psychodynamic approach stimulated many innovations in personality assessment. One of the most extensive and imaginative efforts unfolded under the leadership of Henry A. Murray, Robert W. White, and their many colleagues at the Harvard Psychological Clinic in the 1940s and 1950s. This group, which became known as the **Harvard personologists,** provided a rare model for the intensive psychodynamic study of individual lives and devoted itself to the portrayal of persons in depth. The Harvard personologists were influenced strongly by Freud. They also were influenced by "biosocial" organismic views that emphasized the wholeness, integration, and adaptiveness of personality. They synthesized these influences into a distinct assessment style that became widely respected by other psychologists.

Studying Lives in Depth

The Harvard group focused on intensive studies of small samples of subjects. In one project (Murray et al., 1938), researchers studied Harvard college undergraduates over a period of many years and gathered data on their personality development and maturation at many points in their lives. The techniques included administering projective and other tests of many kinds at many different times. They also gathered extensive

Table 4.1
Examples of Topics Included in the Study of Lives by the Harvard Personologists

Personal history (early development, school and college, major experiences)

Family relations and childhood memories (including school relations, reactions to authority)

Sexual development (earliest recollections, first experiences, masturbation)

Present dilemmas (discussion of current problems)

Abilities and interests (physical, mechanical, social, economic, erotic)

Aesthetic preferences (judgments, attitudes, tastes regarding art)

Level of aspiration (goal setting, reactions to success and failure)

Ethical standards (cheating to succeed, resistance to temptation)

Imaginal productivity (reactions to inkblots)

Musical reveries (report of images evoked by phonograph music)

Dramatic productions (constructing a dramatic scene with toys)

SOURCE: Based on Murray, H. A., Barrett, W. G., & Homburger, E. (1938). *Explorations in personality.* New York: Oxford University Press.

biographical data on each person, obtaining their autobiographical sketches, observing their behavior directly, and conducting elaborate interviews with them. These methods probed ingeniously and thoroughly into many topics and most facets of their lives (see Table 4.1). The results often provided rich narratives of life histories, as in Robert White's *Lives in Progress* (1952), which traced several lives over many years.

Assessment Strategy: Diagnostic Council

The assessors in the Harvard clinical studies were experienced psychologists who interpreted their data clinically. Usually a group of several assessors studied each subject. To share their insights they pooled their overall impressions at a staff conference or "diagnostic council." These councils became a model for clinical practice. In them a case conference was conducted in detail and in depth about each individual. On the basis of the council's discussions, inferences were generated about each subject's personality. They inferred basic needs, motives, conflicts, and dynamics; attitudes and values; main character strengths and liabilities. Each piece of information served as a sign of the individual's personality and was interpreted by the council of assessors.

Selecting U.S. Spies: The OSS Assessment Project

This clinical strategy is illustrated in one of the important applied projects of the personologists—their effort to select officers for the supersensitive Office of Strategic Services (OSS) during World War II. OSS officers in World War II had to perform critical and difficult secret intelligence assignments, often behind enemy lines and under great stress. The personologists obviously could not devote the same lengthy time to studying OSS candidates that they had given to Harvard undergraduates in the relaxed prewar days in Cambridge. Nevertheless, they attempted to use the same general strategy of global clinical assessment. For this purpose, teams of assessors studied small groups of OSS candidates intensively, usually for a few days or a weekend, in special secret retreats or "stations" located in various parts of the country. Many different measures were obtained on each candidate.

One of the most interesting innovations was the situational test. In this procedure, participants were required to perform stressful, lifelike tasks under extremely difficult conditions. For example, "The Bridge" task required building a wooden bridge under simulated dangerous field conditions and under high stress and anxiety. But such situational tests were not used to obtain a sample of the participant's bridge-building skills. Instead, the clinicians made deep inferences, based on the behavior observed during the task, about each individual's underlying personality. It was these inferences of unobserved attributes or dispositions, rather than the behavior actually observed in the sampled situation, that entered into the assessment report and became the bases for clinical predictions. In this fashion, behavior samples and situational tests were transformed into inferences about underlying dispositions.

To illustrate, in the *Assessment of Men* by the OSS staff (1948), the bridge-building situation was used to answer questions like these (p. 326):

> Who took the lead in finally crossing the chasm? And why did he do it? Was it to show his superiority? Why did each of the others fall back from the trip? Did they fear failure?

It is obvious that the chief value of this situation was to raise questions about personality dynamics that required an explanation on the basis of the personality trends already explored. If these could not supply a reasonable explanation, then new information had to be sought, new deductions made.

In the situational test, just as on the projective test, behavior was interpreted as a clue revealing personality. Although behavior was sampled and observed, the observations served mainly as signs from which the researchers inferred the motives that prompted the behaviors.

From Situational Tests to Psychodynamic Inferences

In the global clinical assessment strategy, the assessors form their impressions of the person on the basis of many data sources: performance on various projective and objective tests, the autobiography and total personal history, and reactions to thorough interviews. Several assessors study the same person and each generates his or her own clinical impressions. Later, at a conference, the assessors discuss and share their interpretations and pool their judgments. Gradually they synthesize their impressions and achieve consensus, jointly arriving at a conceptualization of each subject's overall personality structure and dynamics (like the psychodynamic conceptualization of Gary given earlier in this chapter). To predict the person's behavior in a new situation (for example, under attack behind enemy lines), they try to infer, from the personality they have hypothesized, how such an individual would probably react to the stresses of that situation. This global assessment model is schematized in Figure 4.4. It depicts the

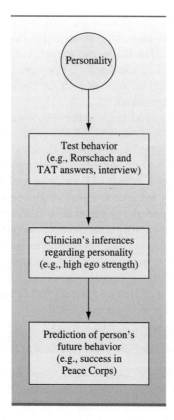

Figure 4.4
Global Psychodynamic Assessment   The clinician infers the subject's personality from his test behavior and predicts his future behavior by judging how a person with that personality would probably react to specific future situations.

strategy of using test behavior to generate inferences about the underlying personality. The prediction of future behavior is based on judgments of how a person with that particular personality would probably act. The test behavior itself is used as a sign of the underlying personality.

Uncovering New Motives: The Multiple Determinants of Personality

The Harvard personologists also developed the TAT and used it as a method not only for clinical assessment, but also for research into a variety of motives. Perhaps most important for the advancement of psychodynamic theory, Henry Murray called attention to the finding that sex and aggression were by no means the only basic motives revealed by the study of fantasies in depth. His influential investigation, "Explorations in Personality" (1938), suggested that a comprehensive assessment of personality required taking account of the following points:

1. A multiplicity of human needs and motives is revealed by in-depth studies of lives. Although sex and aggression have retained an important place among the human motivations recognized by Freud's successors, additional motives and wishes may be hypothesized.

2. These additional motives are called **higher-order motives** because unlike such basic biological needs as hunger and thirst, they do not involve specific physiological changes (such as increased salivation or stomach contraction). Instead, they are seen as psychological desires (wishes) for particular goals or outcomes that have value for the individual. Many theorists have hypothesized a variety of higher-order motives, such as the organism's needs for competence (White, 1959), for achievement, and for stimulation. Table 4.2 shows examples of needs inferred by Henry Murray and associates (1938) in their classical listing. Many of these motives have been investigated in detail (e.g., Emmons, 1997; Koestner & McClelland, 1990); see, for example, *In Focus 4.2*.

3. Situational pressures (called "environmental presses" by Murray) exert important effects on personality that interact with the individual's needs in complex ways.

4. A broad strategy of assessment that uses many judges and multiple methods greatly enriches insights into the complexity of lives. It also reveals that many determinants influence personality development.

The Harvard model for studying personality stimulated many research programs that helped clarify and specify the types of nonbiological higher needs that Murray's group had identified. One good example was the motivation for competence—the need to be effective in its own right—described first by Robert White (discussed in Chapter 3), which plays a major role in current motivational theory (Dweck, 1990). Other examples of specific human needs studied include the *need for affiliation* (McAdams & Constantion, 1983), the *need for control* (Glass, 1977), and the need to endow experience with meaning, called *need for cognition* (Cacioppo & Petty, 1982), and diverse other goals, motives, and personal projects that drive people and motivate behavior (e.g., Emmons, 1997).

Table 4.2
Some Nonphysiological Human Needs Hypothesized by Henry Murray

Abasement (to comply and accept punishment	Humiliation avoidance
Achievement (to strive and reach goals quickly and well)	Nurturance (to aid or protect the helpless)
	Order (to achieve order and cleanliness)
Affiliation (to form friendships)	Play (to relax)
Aggression (to hurt another)	Rejection (to reject disliked others)
Autonomy (to strive for independence)	Seclusion (to be distant from others)
Counteraction (to overcome defeat)	Sentience (to obtain sensual gratification)
Defendance (to defend and justify oneself)	Sex (to form an erotic relationship)
Deference (to serve gladly)	Succorance (to ask for nourishment, love, aid)
Dominance (to control or influence others)	Superiority (to overcome obstacles)
Exhibition (to excite, shock, self-dramatize)	Understanding (to question and think)
Harm avoidance (to avoid pain and injury)	

SOURCE: Based on Murray, H. A., Barrett, W. G., & Homburger, E. (1938). *Explorations in personality.* New York: Oxford University Press.

Research Application of the TAT: Assessing the Need for Achievement

David C. McClelland and his colleagues (1953) investigated fantasies from stories told on the TAT. The motive of greatest interest to them was the need to achieve (**n Ach**), defined as competition with a standard of excellence.

They studied this need extensively by scoring achievement imagery in stories to TAT cards (see Figure 4.5). If, for example, the person creates stories in which the hero is studying hard for a profession and strives to improve himself, to compete against standards of excellence, and to advance far in his career, the story gets high n Ach scores. This technique has become an important way of measuring the motive to achieve. It is not employed widely with individuals in clinical assessment, but it has been used often in research (Atkinson, 1958) and yielded a rich network of meaningful relationships.

Projective themes and fantasies are interesting in their own right, but their relations to other behaviors tend to be complex and indirect. Thoughts and fantasies as measured through projective and story-telling techniques, such as the TAT, usually relate only modestly with measures of relevant overt behavior. For example, achievement concerns measured from TAT stories in which the character strives hard to achieve and compete against high standards of excellence predict, but only in limited ways, such other measures of achievement as grades or vocational achievements (McClelland, 1966; Skolnick, 1966). About 25% of the predicted relationships were supported, and many interesting associations have been found between achievement themes on the TAT and other measures, sometimes over long periods of time, although usually the findings are not strong. Such results are valuable for research and are of value in the study of group differences and broad trends. McClelland (1961), for example, has found intriguing relations between TAT achievement themes and many economic and social measures of achievement orientation in different cultures. His work suggests that careful measures of motives allow some impressive predictions of achievement performance and other important social behaviors (McClelland, 1985).

Applied to the individual case, however, we cannot assume that fantasy themes revealed on projective tests

are reflected directly in the person's nontest behavior. Gary might show relatively little achievement striving on the stories he tells to the TAT; nevertheless, he might feel driven to achieve outstandingly in financial and business activities. Moreover, his achievement orientation in business might not be generalized to other areas. For example, he might show much less concern with achievement in intellectual pursuits and social relations.

Figure 4.5
A TAT Card Developed by David C. McClelland for Measuring the "Need to Achieve"

ASSESSING PSYCHODYNAMIC ASSESSMENT

The explorations of the Harvard personologists made it plain that research was needed to demonstrate the usefulness of clinical "judges." Do they actually agree in their independent interpretations of the underlying meaning of the behaviors they observe? How useful and accurate are their interpretations? These questions are especially important for psychodynamic assessment because they rely so heavily on interpretation.

Many different methods have been employed to study psychodynamic assessment (Mischel, 1968; Peterson, 1968; Rorer, 1990). Many psychologists insist that such assessments require individualized judgments of the meaning of the person's total personality configuration. This kind of assessment involves intuitive judgments about the underlying meaning of behavior patterns and their relations. Such global assessment requires experienced clinicians guided by theory as well as by intuition and draws on many data sources rather than on just one or two tests.

Assessing Projective Methods

In one direction, a great deal of research investigated the usefulness of the favored psychodynamic assessment method: the projective tests. For many years the field was full of workers eagerly trying to invent projective devices. This search for stimulus materials that would elicit rich data about personality resulted in a flood of techniques (Exner, 1993; Wiggins, 1973; Zubin, Eron, & Schumer, 1965).

While it has been relatively simple to invent projective devices, it has been extremely difficult to establish what they measure. The initial aim and hope was to create a "situationless" situation in which only the core or central aspects of personality would emerge (Frank, 1939). The data elicited by these techniques, however, instead of providing a royal road to the unconscious, seem to include a mixture of verbal responses, momentary states, bits of autobiography, and so on. Projective response, like most other behavior, is "subject to conscious control and distortion" and therefore does not necessarily provide a reflection of personality (Holmes, 1974, p. 328, 1992).

Just what is projected in response to the stimuli employed by projective devices is unclear (Murstein, 1963; Zubin, Eron, & Schumer, 1965). What the person's answers mean is open to diverse clinical interpretations and depends heavily on the theoretical preferences and subjective judgments of the interpreter.

Interjudge Reliability. Both scores and interpretations based on projective techniques usually depend extensively on the clinician's judgments about the meaning of the responses as signs of underlying traits in the subject. *Interjudge agreement,* called **interjudge reliability,** must be demonstrated whenever there are subjective judgments, as with projective data. Such reliability decreases to the extent that highly subjective interpretations are required by the judge. That is, reliability is likely to be low when judgments depend upon the intuitions of the interpreter. For example, "old man strangling boy on couch" in a TAT story might be categorized as reflecting underlying "psychopathic trends," "defense against repressed homosexuality," or "hostile acting-out," depending on the interpreter's subjective judgments. Such interpretation may be influenced by projection on the part of the interpreter.

Manuals with explicit instructions for scoring help to increase agreement among judges. Agreement is also better when judges are trained with examples and sample scoring decisions so that they can learn to make similar judgments.

Accuracy and Usefulness.

Generally, predictions based on personality inferences from projective data tend to be less accurate than those more easily available from cheaper and simpler data such as self-reports and background information from the person (Mischel, 1968; Peterson, 1968; Wiggins, 1973). Some researchers, while recognizing the practical limitations of projective testing, continue to be fascinated by the projective situation as a method for studying personality. They see such tests as the Rorschach as providing a kind of perceptual test or an interview setting. In these situations they seek to study persons clinically or to conduct research on the mechanisms of projection (Zubin, Eron, & Schumer, 1965). It is not clear just how most psychologists now use projective tests, but their popularity in everyday clinical practice remained strong when last surveyed (Wade & Baker, 1977). Unfortunately, this popularity is not well supported by research findings within a psychodynamic framework. As a comprehensive review of 50 years of work concluded in 1990: ". . . the huge literature on the psychodynamic interpretation of these instruments has shown their utility to be negative" (Rorer, 1990, p. 698).

Finally, regardless of the research results, many psychologists still use and rely on techniques like the Rorschach and the TAT, often employing them more like an interview than a standardized test. They point out that these devices simply provide a set of ambiguous stimuli to which the person reacts; clinicians then build their assessments in part on their interpretations of the dynamic meanings revealed by the test behavior.

There also has been some renewed research interest in projective methods, particularly in the Rorschach. Some of its advocates have discussed the processes that characterize the experience of people who take the Rorschach test. For example, Exner (1989) considered in great detail the cognitive processes employed by the typical subject interpreting an inkblot. The same psychologist also has developed a comprehensive system for scoring and interpreting test responses (Exner, 1986, 1993). For example, a pattern in which the respondent sees more shading in the blot than movement and has a high proportion of "morbid" perceptions (e.g., dead animals) is considered, in combination with other items, to be an indication of depression. Such interpretations have come under attack, however, for often being inaccurate (Carlson, Kula, & St. Laurent, 1997).

There also continue to be many more general problems, such as inconsistent agreement among coders on the scores that respondents should receive (Viglione, 1997; Wood, Nezworski, & Stejskal, 1996). Proponents of the Rorschach argue that no score can be interpreted in isolation and acknowledge that the Rorschach is best used in combination with other measures (Exner, 1996). In short, while often interesting and suggestive, most of the research on the Rorschach and other projective techniques is still not convincingly and consistently supported by statistical evidence. The results are enough to retain and encourage its devoted followers, but not to persuade its critics (Rorer, 1990).

Combining Clinical Judges and Tests

In clinical practice, many psychologists tend to rely on a fairly standard battery of personality tests and techniques for the assessment of most problems. Perhaps, to obtain good results, the clinician has to draw on all these diagnostic aids. This set of procedures usually includes the Rorschach inkblots and often also the TAT and a standard personality questionnaire (the MMPI, discussed in Chapter 7). Many clinicians also ask the client to complete a series of unfinished sentences, to draw some pictures, and to participate in a short interview. Responses to all these tests then are interpreted clinically. Researchers have tried to analyze the relative contributions of the different parts of the total procedure as it is used in the clinic.

Kostlan (1954), for example, studied which of the most common data sources and data combinations allow the clinician to make the best personality inferences. He selected four popular sources of clinical information: the social case history, the MMPI, the Rorschach, and an incomplete sentence test (on which the person must finish such sentence stems as "I feel . . ."). Twenty experienced clinical psychologists were the judges, and each was assigned data for five outpatients at a psychiatric clinic. The study found that the minimal identifying facts on the fact sheet (age, marital status, etc.) provided inferences that were not surpassed in accuracy by judgments based on any other data source or combination unless the clinician also had the social case history. Thus only inferences from data that included the social history were more accurate than those from the identifying data alone.

Golden (1964) studied the gains when experienced clinicians combine the Rorschach, TAT, and MMPI tests as opposed to using them singly. He found that the accuracy of clinical inferences did not increase as a function of the number of tests used, nor were there any differences among tests or pairs of tests. In another study, none of the tests improved predictions available from biographical data alone, and student nurses predicted as well as clinicians (Soskin, 1959).

How well do experienced clinicians reach agreement with one another in the inferences that they derive from standard data sources? A classic study of clinical judgments examined the inferences made by expert clinicians from each of five sources (Little & Schneidman, 1959). The sources included the Rorschach, the TAT, a standard personality questionnaire, and case histories. Agreement among judges about personality dynamics was only slight. On the whole, the investigators found their results "distressing" (p. 26). No matter how fascinating inferences about personality dynamics may seem intuitively, they cannot be useful when expert judges cannot agree about them. Results like these have been the rule rather than the exception (Goldberg & Werts, 1966; Mischel, 1968; Peterson, 1968; Rorer, 1990).

Alternative Psychodynamic Interpretations of Gary W.

One concrete implication of these results is that the psychodynamic meaning of the same information may be interpreted quite differently depending on the specific theory and biases of the particular psychologist. This is especially likely when broad inferences are made about a person's deep, unobservable psychodynamics. For example, if a disciple of Alfred Adler assesses Gary W., he may find evidence for an inferiority complex and sibling rivalry from the same observations that lead a Freudian to infer castration anxiety and an Oedipal complex. Likewise, in the same set of responses, Kohut's student may see Gary's fragmented self and his cry for empathic mirroring of his feelings.

Many psychologists now view such pluralism of alternative views as a welcome development. It encourages the frank recognition that the same "facts" about a person are indeed open to multiple interpretations from different perspectives. Each view may contribute a somewhat different vision of the individual from a different angle, and no one view is necessarily exclusively correct or absolute. Accepting this kind of pluralism, personality psychologists seek to be more open-minded, flexible, and eclectic in their approach, rejecting interpretations that insist on any single perspective to the exclusion of plausible alternatives.

The Complexity of Personality Judgments

In spite of many negative research findings on judgmental accuracy, many clinicians have faith in their judgments about psychodynamics. Is confidence about inferences related to their accuracy? Oskamp (1965) found that judges became more confident of their judgments as they received more information about a case. However, although self-confidence increased with information, accuracy did not. Moreover, clinicians may confidently agree with one another about the meaning of cues, even when the cues are not accurate indicators (Chapman & Chapman, 1969; Mirels, 1976).

In a well-designed study, psychodynamic formulations of the same cases were generated by two different teams of clinicians (DeWitt, Kaltreider, Weiss, & Horowitz, 1983). A third group of clinicians then tried to match the corresponding formulations from the two teams for each of the cases. The results again were disappointing. A clinician who studied the psychodynamic formulation of a given case by one team could not recognize that case from the psychodynamic formulation of the same case developed by the other team of clinicians. In other words, it was not possible to match accurately the psychodynamic formulations of the same case generated by the different clinicians.

CHALLENGES AND NEW DIRECTIONS

As you saw in the previous section, the results of psychodynamic assessment have been disappointing and, therefore, have challenged some of the main assumptions of the approach. They have also led to a number of interesting developments and promising new directions.

Studying the Judgment Process

The recognition that clinical judgments may be fallible and open to alternative interpretations has encouraged studies of the clinical judgment process itself. Researchers began to examine how people infer and judge personality (Gollwitzer & Moskowitz, 1997; Weiner, 1990) and the processes through which people form impressions of one another and of themselves (Anderson, 1965, 1974; Nisbett & Ross, 1980; Ross & Nisbett, 1991). These investigations reveal some of the complexities of the information processing that underlie social judgments in general and clinical inferences in particular.

In one interesting direction, Kahneman and Tversky (1973, 1984) have identified a number of rules or heuristics that guide—and sometimes may misguide—intuitive predictions, not just in professional clinicians, but in all of us. One rule, called the **availability heuristic,** refers to the relative availability, salience, or accessibility of events in the judge's mind. This heuristic leads us to think that the greater the availability of an event cognitively (mentally), the more likely it will occur in reality: The more easily we think of something, the more frequent we believe it to be. As a result, people who major in music may overestimate the number of music majors; New Yorkers may believe that almost everyone comes from New York; and those who think and talk a lot about mental illness may tend to overestimate the frequency of its occurrence in the population. A number of other judgment mechanisms have been identified by Tversky (1977) and by Nisbett and Ross (1980; Ross & Nisbett, 1991) that make it easier to understand how clinicians may feel very confident even when they are objectively quite inaccurate.

But many psychologists continue to blame the shortcomings of the particular clinicians, judges, or research. They do not believe the findings necessarily undermine the general psychodynamic approach (Erdelyi & Goldberg, 1979; Silverman, 1976; Westen, 1990). Consequently, most clinical psychologists (Watkins et al., 1995) still employ methods like the Rorschach and the TAT, rely on their intuitions, and continue to apply psychodynamic concepts to the analysis of individuals, hoping that better research in the future will provide better justification (Watkins et al., 1995).

Agreement for Less Inferential Judgments

In spite of such results undermining psychodynamic interpretations, careful research has shown that personality judgments can be linked clearly and significantly to such independent information as the person's own self-reports (Funder, 1987; Funder & Colvin, 1997; Jackson, Chan, & Stricker, 1979). These relations usually are found when the judges make simple ratings about the degree to which the person has particular personality traits (such as friendliness or aggressiveness, Chapter 6). While these findings provide little support for highly indirect global inferences about the individual's underlying psychodynamics (Mischel, 1968; Peterson, 1968; Rorer, 1990), they do show that judges can agree about what people are like. Agreement tends to be good as long as the judgments are descriptive (for example, "is conscientious") and do not require complex, indirect inferences about underlying motives or causes (see *In Focus 4.3*).

Consensual Thought Units in Psychodynamic Case Formulations

In recent years, psychologists in the psychodynamic orientation also have developed new ways to improve and demonstrate the usefulness of judgments relevant to clinical

IN FOCUS 4.3   *The Hazards of Interpretation: The Case of Dora Revisited*

Progress in science often is described as consisting of a series of breakthrough successes in a steady stream. In reality, many failures and mistakes tend to unevenly pave the way for the next success. Freud's famous case of Dora illustrates a failure in early psychoanalysis, but one from which much was learned for future progress.

Dora (really Ida Braun) was an 18-year-old suffering from signs of "hysteria," including an inexplicable cough, when Freud treated her in Vienna in the fall of 1900. In what became one of Freud's most notable failures, she terminated treatment after 11 weeks. Hanna S. Decker, a historian, shed new light on this case in 1990 in a book that places the case in its personal and historical context. In this reexamination of Dora's life, we see not only Dora, but turn-of-the-century women in Viennese society in their status as social inferiors. They were expected to conform rigidly to Victorian norms, and their lives were shaped largely by the men to whom they were related, not by their own qualities. In this historical context, Decker interprets the symptoms of hysteria as one of the few ways that women could express their pent-up anger and resentment at their victimization by both family and society.

Dora's mother was obsessive about cleanliness and order in the home and provided a cold, remote model. Although Dora originally was deeply devoted to her father, she became resentful as he became involved with a neighbor's wife, Mrs. K. Dora's life reached a crisis at age 15 when she reported to her parents that Mrs. K's husband was making sexual advances to her. Mr. K attributed these accusations to Dora's erotic fantasies. She became even more desperate when, to her amazement, her own father accepted this explanation. Now she felt that her father was "giving her" to Mr. K in return for allowing his affair with Mrs. K to continue.

Freud tried to deal with this case in 1900, when he had little therapeutic experience and had not yet grasped the complexity of the relationship between patient and therapist. He thus may have inadvertently added to Dora's despair by interpreting her feelings as reflecting unconscious attraction to Mr. K. This interpretation was one that Dora was quite unprepared to accept and "resisted" by fleeing from further therapy with Freud.

Decker's revisit to *Freud, Dora and Vienna, 1900* helps point out the hazards and complexities of psychoanalytic interpretation. It calls attention to a danger that many analysts themselves recognize increasingly. One cannot safely assume that a patient's resistance to an interpretation reflects only his or her unwillingness to accept unconscious impulses and conflicts. Psychoanalytic interpretations are by no means immune to the biases of the historical moment and even to the emotions and motivations of the analyst. Therefore, it is essential for the analyst to try to take those pressures and limitations into account seriously (Decker, 1990) by being alert to personal and cultural biases.

---

concerns. For example, it is easier to achieve consensus among clinicians if more specific and concrete descriptors are used as units in the case formulation. With this goal, specific *thought units* were coded from psychodynamic case formulations (Horowitz et al., 1989). Clinical judges watched videotaped interviews conducted by clinicians working with patients in brief psychodynamic therapy sessions. The judges viewing the tapes were encouraged to consider a number of topics in their own dynamic formulations. They were instructed to focus only on the most essential information, limiting their reports to one page after watching the tapes. They then discussed the case with one another for 30 minutes (somewhat like the Harvard personologists) and, if they wished, could rewrite their formulations.

The researchers identified the basic thought units that were mentioned often in these formulations and on which there was greatest agreement among the judges. An example of such a thought unit is "she wishes to accommodate others," based on such observations as her own self-description. These "consensual thought units" then were integrated into a composite case formulation. Such formulations describe the patient's treatment motivation (for example, to avoid divorce), the main difficulties experienced, self-perceptions, family background, and the like.

The formulations developed in this step-by-step, specific fashion made it possible to achieve a reasonable degree of agreement among judges. They also provided encouraging steps for achieving some accuracy in making specific predictions, such as the types of problems likely to be most distressing for a particular patient. The formulations, for example, allowed other raters to significantly predict some of the interpersonal problems that would be discussed later in treatment. Studies like this begin to show that agreement may be achieved in psychodynamic formulations if the clinicians are careful to use only specific descriptors on which there is good consensus. Consensus tends to be greatest when the units describe observed behavior, including what the patient says, while avoiding speculations about its possible underlying meaning.

SUMMARY

1. Psychodynamically oriented psychologists attempt to study personality in depth and try to eliminate situational interferences. They hope to bypass defenses and reach basic dynamics and motives. Guided by psychoanalytic theory, the traditional focus has been on reconstructions of early history, particularly the early handling of sexual and aggressive impulses. Inferences are made regarding personality in global, dynamic terms.

2. In the psychodynamic approach, the Rorschach and the TAT (Thematic Apperception Test) are projective tests that have been especially popular. The Rorschach consists of a series of complex inkblots. The subject says what the inkblots resemble or look like to him or her. The TAT consists of a series of ambiguous pictures for which subjects are asked to make up a story.

3. The main characteristics of projective techniques are that they are presented as ambiguous tasks for the subject; the purpose of the test is disguised, and the person is free to respond as he or she wishes. Clinicians then may interpret the meaning of the answers in accord with their theories and intuitions,

trying to infer the person's psychodynamics and personality from his or her responses. The most favored method of assessment, however, probably remains the interview, which psychodynamically oriented clinicians usually structure like a projective method, giving patients as much freedom as possible to express themselves.

4. The clinician is a central instrument in psychodynamic assessment. Harvard personologists have provided a model for the intensive clinical study of individuals. Trained assessors collected diverse data on each subject and, in council, made inferences about the individual's personality dynamics.

5. The study of achievement motives as expressed through TAT stories has been carefully developed. Research on the need for achievement as expressed in TAT themes has yielded an extensive network of correlations.

6. Several procedures have been devised to help interpret projective test responses. It is especially important to demonstrate interscorer consistency—the degree to which different judges arrive at the same

interpretive statements from the same test data. Manuals with clear instructions and practice training help increase agreement among judges.

7. Surprisingly but consistently, studies on the effect of clinical training do not show a clear advantage for trained judges in making global judgments. Research also indicates that the information from various clinical tests does not enable the experienced clinician to make more accurate predictions than he or she could have made from biographical data. Experienced judges may not agree with one another in their inferences about personality dynamics even when they are using the same test data from the same individual.

8. In an effort to achieve better consensus among clinicians, *thought units* were devised to define certain common feelings, such as "she wishes to accommodate others." Together with a patient's treatment motivation and circumstances, these thought units can help make a case formulation more systematic for research.

Psychodynamic Processes

ANXIETY AND UNCONSCIOUS DEFENSES
The Concept of Unconscious Repression
Repression versus Suppression
Studying Repression
Perceptual Defense
The Long History of Perceptual Defense
Limitations of Early Laboratory Studies

THE COGNITIVE UNCONSCIOUS
Early Experimental Evidence
The Risk of Excessive Skepticism: The Value of Self-Disclosure
Cognition without Awareness: Reformulating the Unconscious

IN FOCUS **5.1**

The Repressed Memory Debate
Selectivity in Attention
Processing Outside Awareness
Automaticity in Responding

A Kinder, Gentler Unconscious
Discrimination without Awareness?
Do We Know What We Think?
"Mommy and I Are One"
Optimistic Prospects for the Future of the Unconscious

PATTERNS OF DEFENSE: INDIVIDUAL DIFFERENCES IN COGNITIVE AVOIDANCE
Repression-Sensitization
Selective Attention
Blunting versus Monitoring Styles

IN FOCUS **5.2**

Matching the Medical Information to the Patient's Style
The Role of Control: When Don't You Want to Know?
Vigilance versus Avoidance as Learned Defenses

SUMMARY

In this chapter, we will focus on research relevant to the psychodynamic view of how people deal with anxiety and their unconscious modes of psychological defenses. We also will consider research on the approach pioneered by Freud and his followers. This research tells an important story for personality psychology because it has led to conclusions different from original hypotheses, and all of it has stimulated and challenged later developments throughout the field. Many of those ideas continue to influence how both professional psychologists and laypersons think about the nature of personality and the complexities of the mind, and therefore they deserve close attention.

ANXIETY AND UNCONSCIOUS DEFENSES

The psychodynamic view originally saw **anxiety** as the emotional reaction to the breakthrough into consciousness of unacceptable impulses. In more recent years, other theorists and neo-analysts within this framework have liberalized the definition. For example, in one version, the definition was recast into terms that treat it more as a learned fear that can become attached to many signals and events (Dollard & Miller, 1950).

Although different individuals experience anxiety in different ways, the following three elements often are found (Maher, 1966):

1. A conscious feeling of fear and danger without the ability to identify immediate objective threats that could account for these feelings.
2. A pattern of physiological arousal and bodily distress that may include miscellaneous physical changes and complaints (Cacioppo, Berntson, & Criter, 1997). Common examples include *cardiovascular* symptoms (heart palpitations, faintness, increased blood pressure, pulse changes); *respiratory* complaints (breathlessness, feeling of suffocation); and *gastrointestinal* symptoms (diarrhea, nausea, vomiting). If the anxiety persists, the prolonged physical reactions to it may have chronic effects on each of these bodily systems. In addition, the person's agitation may be reflected in sleeplessness, frequent urination, perspiration, muscular tensions, fatigue, and other signs of upset and distress (Chapita & Barlow, 1998).

3. A disruption or disorganization of effective problem solving and cognitive (mental) control, including difficulty in thinking clearly and coping effectively with environmental demands.

An outstanding characteristic of human beings, emphasized in psychodynamic theories, is that they can create great anxiety in themselves even when they are not in any immediate external danger. A man may be seated comfortably in his favorite chair, adequately fed and luxuriously sheltered, seemingly safe from outside threats, and yet torture himself with anxiety-provoking memories of old events, with terrifying thoughts, or with expectations of imagined dangers in years to come. He also can eliminate such internally cued anxiety within his own mind without altering his external environment, simply by avoiding or changing his painful thoughts or memories.

Does such avoidance of anxiety also occur unconsciously, outside the range of one's awareness? A core assumption of the psychodynamic view is that the answer to the question is clearly affirmative. After years of research, however, that answer still remains controversial.

Defense mechanisms are attempts to cope mentally (cognitively) with internal anxiety-arousing cues. Usually it has also been assumed, in line with Freudian theory, that these efforts are at least partly unconscious—that is, they occur without the person's awareness. Because this assumption is so basic, research in the psychodynamic approach has tried to clarify this process. Especially important have been studies of unconscious processes and mechanisms of defense, which are a focus of this chapter. Repression has received the greatest attention as an unconscious defense mechanism probably because of its theoretical importance in Freudian psychology. Because most theoretical issues and research studies have focused on repression rather than dealing with many defenses superficially, we will concentrate on this important one.

The Concept of Unconscious Repression

Most people sometimes feel that they actively try to avoid painful memories and ideas and struggle to "put out of mind" thoughts that are aversive to them. Common examples are trying not to think about a forthcoming surgical operation and trying to turn attention away from the unknown results of an important test. Psychologists often call such efforts to avoid painful thoughts "cognitive avoidance."

The existence of cognitive avoidance is widely recognized; few psychologists doubt that thoughts may be inhibited. However, the mechanisms underlying cognitive avoidance have been controversial. The basic controversy is whether or not cognitive avoidance includes an unconscious defense mechanism of "repression" that forces unacceptable material into an unconscious region without the person's awareness.

Repression versus Suppression

The psychoanalytic concept of repression as a defense mechanism is closely linked to the Freudian idea of an unconscious mind. The unconscious mind was seen by early Freudians as a supersensitive entity whose perceptual alertness and memory bank surpassed the same properties of the conscious mind (Blum, 1955). A chief function of the unconscious mind was to screen and monitor memories and the inputs to the senses. This screening served to inhibit the breakthrough of anxiety-arousing stimuli from the unconscious mind to the conscious or from the outside world to consciousness. Just as the conscious mind was believed capable of deliberately (consciously) inhibiting events by **suppression,** so the unconscious was considered capable of inhibition or cognitive avoidance at the unconscious level by repression.

Suppression occurs when one voluntarily and consciously withholds a response or turns attention away from it deliberately. Unconscious repression, in contrast, may function as an automatic guardian against anxiety, a safety mechanism that prevents threatening material from entering consciousness. Psychoanalysts have offered clinical evidence for the existence of repression in the form of cases in which slips of the tongue (**parapraxes**), jokes, dreams, or free associations seemed to momentarily bypass the defenses and betray the person, revealing a brief glimpse of repressed unconscious impulses.

Studying Repression

Repression has remained a cornerstone for most psychoanalysts (Erdelyi, 1985; Grunbaum, 1984), and it has been the subject of a great deal of research for many years. The early efforts to assess whether or not particular findings demonstrated the truth of Freud's concepts created more controversy than clarity. In more recent years it has been recognized that well-designed experiments on the topic of cognitive avoidance can provide useful information about cognitive processes and personality regardless of their direct relevance to the Freudian theory of repression (Kihlstrom, 1990; Westen, 1990, 1998).

Early experimental research on repression studied the differential recall of pleasant and unpleasant experiences (Jersild, 1931; Meltzer, 1930). These investigators seemed to assume that repression showed itself in a tendency to selectively forget negative or unpleasant experiences rather than positive ones. It was soon pointed out, however, that the Freudian theory of repression does not imply that experiences associated with unpleasant affective tone are repressed (Rosenzweig & Mason, 1934; Sears, 1936). Freudian repression, instead, was believed to depend on the presence of an "ego threat" (for example, a basic threat to self-esteem) and not on mere unpleasantness.

Later it also was recognized that to study repression adequately one should be able to demonstrate that when the cause of the repression (the ego threat) is removed, the repressed material is restored to consciousness (Zeller, 1950). This assumption was consistent with the psychoanalytic belief that when the cause of a repression is discovered by insight in psychotherapy, the repressed material rapidly emerges into the patient's consciousness. In other words, if the threat is eliminated, it becomes safe for the repressed material to return to awareness. Reports by psychoanalysts often have cited cases in which a sudden insight supposedly lifted a long-standing amnesia (memory loss).

Most experiments to show repression effects have been inconclusive. For example, when college students were threatened by taking a test described as measuring their unacceptable unconscious sexual conflicts, they tended to recall anxiety-arousing words less well. When the threat was removed (by revealing that the test was really not an index for such conflicts), recall improved (D'Zurilla, 1965). Does this mean that repression occurred? After much debate, it has become clear that the answer is "not necessarily"; other interpretations are at least equally plausible.

For example, reduced recall for threat-provoking information may simply reflect that the person is upset. Therefore, other thoughts, produced by the anxiety as the person worries, may interfere with recall. If the recall improves later when the threat is removed, it may only mean that the competing, anxious thoughts now no longer interfere with recall. It does not necessarily mean either that unconscious repression occurred or that awareness returned when the threat was removed (Holmes & Schallow, 1969; Tudor & Holmes, 1973).

Perceptual Defense

If unconscious repression is a mechanism that keeps painful material out of consciousness, one might also expect it to screen and block threatening perceptual inputs to the eyes and ears. Indeed, clinical reports from psychoanalysts suggest that in some cases of hysteria, massive repression may prevent the individual from perceiving (consciously registering) threatening stimuli such as sexual scenes or symbols.

One very severe instance of this would be hysterical blindness. In these cases, the individual seems to lose his or her vision although no physical damage to the eyes or to the perceptual system can be detected. Case reports have suggested that such psychological failures to see might be linked to traumatic sexual experiences with resulting repression of stimuli that might unleash anxiety. Although clinical case reports often provide suggestive evidence, they are never conclusive. To go beyond clinical impressions, researchers have tried to study possible anxiety-reducing distortions in perception experimentally. Because it was obviously both unfeasible and unethical to induce sexual traumas in human subjects, considerable ingenuity was needed to find even a rough experimental analog for perceptual defense.

The Long History of Perceptual Defense

In the 1940s and 1950s, a general research strategy was devised to explore perceptual defenses, guided by the then-prevalent faith in projective devices as methods for revealing conflict. Specifically, it was believed that persons who did not give sexual or aggressive responses to ambiguous stimuli must be defending against this type of ideation, especially if the same stimuli generally elicited many such responses from most normal people. Consequently, if a person failed to identify potentially threatening inputs to the senses, such as anxiety-arousing sexual words or threatening scenes, one inferred perceptual inhibition or defense.

To study this process, researchers presented threatening perceptual stimuli in decreasing degrees of ambiguity. They began at a point at which subjects could tell what the words were and could reasonably interpret them in many ways to a point of definiteness that permitted only one clearly correct interpretation. A helpful device for this purpose was the **tachistoscope,** a machine through which potentially threatening words (for example, "penis," "whore") and neutral words (for example, "house," "flowers") could be flashed at varying speeds. These stimulus words were presented on a screen very rapidly at first and then gradually exposed for increasingly long durations. The length of time required before each subject correctly recognized the stimulus served as the "defensiveness" score; the longer the time required to recognize threatening stimuli, the greater the subject's defensive avoidance tendencies were assumed to be.

In one classic study, college students viewed words presented tachistoscopically so rapidly that they could not perceive them consciously. The words were either emotional or neutral in meaning (McGinnies, 1949). Each student was asked what word had been seen after each exposure. If the answer was wrong, the same word was presented again at a slightly longer exposure time, and the subject again tried to recognize it. It was predicted that such taboo words as "penis" or "raped" would be anxiety-laden and therefore more readily inhibited than neutral words such as "apple." The results confirmed this prediction, showing greater perceptual defense (longer recognition times) for taboo words than for neutral words.

But these results also can be interpreted quite differently. As was noted long ago (Howes & Solomon, 1951), the perceptual situation places the subject in an embarrassing predicament. In the typical procedure, an undergraduate was brought to the laboratory by a professor or an assistant and then exposed to brief and unclear stimulus presentations by the tachistoscope. The task is essentially a guessing game in which the subject tries to discern the correct word from fleeting fragments. On the first trial of a word, for example, something like an "r" and "p" may be seen, and the subject may guess "rope." On the next trial, the subject may think, "Good grief, that looked something like 'rape'!" But rather than make this guess to a professor or an assistant in the academic atmosphere of a scientific laboratory, the subject may deliberately suppress the response. Instead of saying "rape," "rope" is offered again, and the taboo word is withheld until the subject is absolutely sure that this perception is correct.

In sum, a major problem in interpreting results from such studies is that it is extremely difficult to know whether subjects are slower to report some stimuli because they are unconsciously screening them from awareness. Even without such an unconscious mechanism, they may be inhibited about reporting such stimuli until they are absolutely sure, just to avoid embarrassment.

Limitations of Early Laboratory Studies

Understandably discouraged by the early experiments on unconscious processes, psychoanalytically oriented critics have been quite skeptical of the relevance of many of these studies for their theory (Erdelyi, 1993; Erdelyi & Goldberg, 1979). They argue that it is confusing and misleading to study single processes (such as repression) in isolation, outside the context of the person's total psychic functioning. Such critics believe that these experimental studies are at best suggestive but clinically irrelevant. They doubt that long-term psychodynamic processes can be studied under the artificial conditions of the typical laboratory experiment.

It is certainly true that the findings are limited by the artificiality of the measures typically used in such research. It is also risky to generalize from college sophomores in a laboratory to clinical populations and clinical problems. The mild anxiety induced by experimental threats to college students may have little relevance for understanding the traumas experienced by the young child trying to cope with Oedipal fantasies or the severely disturbed patient in the clinic.

Most experiments on repression provide only a remote analog of the motivational aspects of clinical repression in Freud's theory (Madison, 1960). Repression (or more broadly speaking, any defense) involves motives that were associated with traumatic childhood experiences for a particular individual. Thus many psychoanalytically oriented critics believe that evidence obtained from controlled experimental research conducted outside the clinical setting (such as the studies reviewed in the preceding sections) is largely irrelevant (Erdelyi, 1993). On the other hand, as we have seen (Chapter 4), the clinician's judgments and intuitive procedures for inferring unconscious dynamics, for example from projective tests, also have serious limitations (Rorer, 1990).

THE COGNITIVE UNCONSCIOUS

There have been many studies of unconscious repression and unconscious perception, but the conclusions that may be drawn from them have long remained controversial. Some clear themes, however, have emerged.

Early Experimental Evidence

Experiments to demonstrate repression and unconscious perception have been difficult to conduct and more difficult to interpret (Erdelyi, 1985; D'Zurilla, 1965). Most of the early studies yielded unclear and discouraging results. After more than 25 years of experiments, for example, one influential review of experimental research on repression led the reviewer to conclude that "there is no evidence to support the predictions generated by the theory of repression" (Holmes, 1974, p. 651). Two decades later, another review led him to the same conclusion (Holmes, 1992). But it is just as easy to conclude that all these studies were flawed.

The two main ways of looking at the research results are well summarized by Erdelyi (1985, pp. 104–105):

One may begin to understand why experimental psychology, in contrast to dynamic clinical psychology, has taken such a different stance on phenomena such as repression. Experimental psychology, in the service of simplification and control, has studied manifest events, specific memory episodes, or percepts (as in perceptual defense). It is not typical, however, for a normal college subject to resort in the laboratory to such drastic defenses as to block out a clear memory episode or perceptual experience. Consequently, experimental psychology has had great difficulty in demonstrating repression in the laboratory and has understandably taken a skeptical attitude towards this phenomenon. Clinicians, on the other hand, deal continually with latent (hidden) contents, and in this realm the selective blocking or distortion of information through context manipulation is utterly common-place. The clinician shakes his head in disbelief at the experimental psychologist, whose paltry methodology cannot even demonstrate a phenomenon as obvious and ubiquitous as repression. The experimentalist similarly shakes his head at the credulity of the psychodynamic clinician, who embraces notions unproven in the laboratory and which, moreover, rest on the presumed existence of unconscious, indeed, physically non-existent, latent contents.

In sum, most clinicians remain convinced that evidence for the unconscious is almost everywhere; in contrast, many experimental researchers have trouble finding it anywhere (see *In Focus 5.1*).

The Risk of Excessive Skepticism: The Value of Self-Disclosure

The debate about repressed memory (discussed in *In Focus 5.1*) raises important questions but also risks creating excessive skepticism, leading people to doubt all reports about repressed memories that become accessible. The danger is that by making the topic so controversial, many victims of abuse and trauma in childhood and later life may be ignored or undermined in their efforts to find and express the truth. Relevant here is the recent discovery that when people have had traumatic experiences it can greatly help them to discuss those memories candidly, rather than try to hide or suppress them. The process of talking or writing about these traumatic experiences not only helps one feel better by 'getting it off your chest,' as folk wisdom has long suggested, but also can profoundly improve one's health. For example, by simply writing about their traumatic experiences during a period of four days, essentially healthy college students improved their health following the study, with fewer visits to the health center and improved blood pressure and immune system functioning (Pennebaker, 1993; Pennebaker, Kiecolt-Glaser, & Glaser, 1988).

A dramatic illustration of the value of sharing traumatic experiences comes from work with patients suffering from advanced breast cancer that had already spread (Spiegel, Kraemer, Bloom, & Gottheil, 1989). The patients were divided into two conditions and both conditions, of course, received the usual medical care for cancer. In addition, however, people in the intervention received weekly supportive group therapy for a period of one year, sharing their experiences with others openly. The patients who had this experience survived almost twice as long (37 months) as those who did not. It would therefore be unfortunate if trauma victims failed to avail themselves of opportunities to appropriately air rather than conceal their experience.

Cognition without Awareness: Reformulating the Unconscious

Modern approaches to how people think and deal mentally with information, called *cognition,* allow a fresh view of the unconscious. Repression and perceptual defense are beginning to be seen as instances of the selectivity that occurs throughout cognition. Repression and perceptual defense can be studied more fruitfully when they are placed in this larger context of selective information processing (Bargh, 1997; Broadbent, 1977; Erdelyi, 1985; Kihlstrom, 1990).

IN FOCUS 5.1   *The Repressed Memory Debate*

Based on the Freudian premise that the human mind purposefully but unconsciously hides frightening or potentially damaging memories, repression is seen by many clinicians and reseachers as a major root of psychological dysfunction. But skeptics see it more as a fiction created by a biased theoretical perspective through which therapists may unwittingly damage their patients and their families (Loftus, 1993, 1994; Ofshe & Watters, 1993). While repressed memory continues to remain a controversial academic topic in psychology, it now also has become the center of a public debate that spread into the media.

Return of the Repressed

The public debate began in recent years when many people claimed that they had been the victims of childhood abuse of which they had been unaware until their repressed memories for the traumatic event were recovered, usually in the course of psychotherapy. The question raised then was: Are these recovered memories accurate or might they be false?

Although reported recovered memories of abuse have often produced great personal pain and been the bases for lawsuits and punishment of the alleged abusers, as the defense lawyers are quick to point out, the existence of repression itself remains controversial, as discussed in the text. On the one hand, a review of over 60 years of research led Holmes (1992) to still conclude that ". . . at the present time there is no controlled laboratory evidence supporting the concept of repression" (p. 95). Likewise, in a study of children (ages 5 to 10) who witnessed the murder of one of their parents, Malmquist (1986) reported that none of the children seemed to repress the memory: Instead they frequently focused on it.

Nevertheless, as also noted in the text, most sophisticated and highly experienced clinical practitioners still remain convinced that case studies compellingly document the existence of repression (Erdelyi, 1993). Supporting that view, some researchers make the case that memories for traumatic events from the early years of life, even after they have been forgotten, may reappear in adulthood under conditions of high stress (Jacobs & Nadel, 1985; Schooler, 1994, 1997; Schooler, Bendiksen, & Ambadar, 1997).

Did It Really Happen?

But even assuming that a defensive mechanism of repression occurs and in some cases is activated as a way of coping with such traumatic events as sexual abuse, there is a major problem in determining accurately whether a particular memory for a traumatic event is accurate or instead invented or grossly distorted. Modern memory research makes it clear that memories are not stored like videotapes on a shelf and later replayed. Rather, they are reconstructions of the past, and they are subject to being influenced by suggestions and cues from the outside world and the inside of one's mind, including one's own fantasies and speculations (e.g. Loftus, 1993, 1994; Ofshe, 1992). In short, memories can be created in people by suggestion and self-suggestion or by telling them that something occurred, often in ways that can even give the person confidence that they are based on reality (Loftus, 1993).

The Power of Suggestion

One worry is that false memories can be unwittingly strengthened by therapists, particularly if they believe, as Freud did, that problems tend to stem from the abuse that the patient suffered as a child. Guided by that belief, some therapists may too easily encourage their patients to explore their subconscious, searching for repressed memories that may not exist. In this search they may do what is sometimes called "memory work," using hypnosis, suggestive questioning, guided visualization, and dream interpretation (Loftus, 1994). Such exploration risks coming up with memories of traumas that are more invented than discovered. In that case, instead of helping victims to reclaim lost pieces of their lives, therapists may hurt innocent people and create rather than reduce distress.

Selectivity in Attention.   Selectivity and bias occur throughout mental functioning. It is found in our choice of the things to which we attend and the manner in which we organize, rehearse, and recall the flood of information that enters the sense receptors and the response that we ultimately generate (Erdelyi, 1974; Mischel, Ebbesen, & Zeiss, 1976). The study of information processing has shown, for example, that the individual's mood state may lead to the recall of more mood-congruent materials (Bower, 1981; Forgas, 1992; Isen et al., 1978). People who feel sad, for instance, are more likely to recall more negative material than do those in a happy mood. Current experiences and emotional states also may "prime" or activate other aspects of memory, triggering related concepts and feelings from earlier experiences (Higgins, 1990, 1997).

Processing Outside Awareness.   Modern theories of cognition and research on how people process information (Anderson, 1983) have made it clear that "it is not necessary for an object to be fully represented in consciousness before information about it can influence other units" (Kihlstrom, 1990, p. 448); not all aspects of the cognitive system are accessible to the person's awareness (Bornstein, Leone, & Galley, 1987).

Particularly, "procedural knowledge" (knowledge about how skills are enacted, e.g., how one manages to parallel park the car) may be largely outside one's awareness. Such unconscious procedural knowledge is *automatic,* in contrast to mental activity that is controlled, intentional, and effortful. Examples are the many routines that take place without actively engaging attention, whenever we do complex mental tasks in which a number of different cognitive activities "run off" at the same time, that is, automatically, independent of our intention and explicit self-instructions (Kahneman & Triesman, 1984).

Automaticity in Responding.   Even our social behavior, as well as our emotional responding, often is so overlearned that we react more or less automatically (Bargh, 1997), mindlessly ignoring relevant information in repeatedly encountered interpersonal situations to which we apply familiar scripts (Langer, 1978). Perhaps the most convincing body of evidence for the importance of the unconscious, broadly defined, comes from research showing that much (and perhaps most) of what we perceive, think, believe, feel, and do is automatic and done without conscious control or intention (Bargh, 1997). While it has long been evident that all sorts of activities, from driving to spelling and reading, may be enacted in ways that run off automatically, it has been surprising to find in recent years that the judgments, understandings, and reactions we have to ourselves and to other people also tend to be immediate and automatic.

For example, just seeing a few physical features may be enough to trigger automatic stereotypic reactions to members of social groups in the power minority — such as racial minorities, women, and the elderly (Bargh, 1997). Our automatic reactions go beyond stereotypes and may include patterns of action and feeling, as well as goals and intentions, that are pulled by trigger stimuli in the environment. Once set in motion, they may operate autonomously without requiring any conscious guidance or intentional control.

A Kinder, Gentler Unconscious

Thus on the one hand, current work on cognition has shed new light on the nature of the psychological unconscious, the aspects of mental life that unfold without our awareness, attention, intention, and effort; in that sense, much of what goes on in one's mind is not in the thinker's control and is outside consciousness (Westen, 1991). On the other hand, these discoveries do

> . . . not thereby support the essential propositions of psychoanalytic theory research on subliminal perception, motivated forgetting, and the like [and] offer little support for the Freudian conception of mental life . . . for example, that unconscious contents are sexual and aggressive in nature, and that unconscious processes are primitive and irrational (Kihlstrom, 1990, p. 447).

As Kihlstrom also notes, the view of nonconscious mental life in modern cognitive psychology gives it a significant role but yields a quite different image that is kinder, "gentler, and more rational—than the seething unconscious of Freud" (1990, p. 460).

Discrimination without Awareness?

Can people learn without awareness or consciousness? It would certainly be impressive evidence for the unconscious if important learning were shown to occur in people without their awareness. In a classic paper that is as relevant now as when it was written, Eriksen (1960) undertook an extensive survey and analysis of research on human learning without awareness. The results led him to conclude that learning at levels not available to conscious awareness (equated with verbal report) has not been shown adequately. Although some simple responses may be learned without awareness, in most forms of human learning and thought, awareness seems to play a major role (Dulany, 1962; Spielberger & DeNike, 1966).

Eriksen (1966) was one of the first to suggest that unpleasant or painful material may initially be consciously suppressed (rather than unconsciously repressed). Then after sufficient rehearsal, response suppression becomes automatic. It is also possible that even without a deliberate suppression mechanism, painful thoughts and memories are less likely to be evoked and covertly rehearsed because they are more aversive. Two decades later, some reviewers of the more recent evidence still agreed (Bandura, 1986).

The foregoing does not imply that people are aware of everything they do. During new learning, we usually feel aware and even "self-conscious," but once a behavior is mastered and overlearned, it often seems to flow smoothly and automatically without any subjective awareness whatsoever. We usually stay safely clear of hot stoves, cross busy streets only when the traffic lights are appropriate, and drive our cars for miles without self-conscious awareness of every step and discrimination made along the route. For example, learning to park a car may at first require great awareness and self-conscious attention to subtle positional cues. Many trials later, one is likely to be unaware of the procedure (unless startled by a sudden bump). And it is certainly true that without being aware of it, we very commonly bring our past knowledge to bear on how we act in the world. Consider, for example, how "automatically" we know what to expect and do in familiar situations, like birthday parties or restaurants (Schank & Abelson, 1977). Likewise, all sorts of stereotypes, emotions, and reaction patterns may come to be triggered automatically and almost acquire a life of their own, as Bargh (1997) has shown. But that does not mean that we are necessarily unaware of what we think and feel or incapable of accessing our thought processes when the right questions are asked (Bandura, 1986; Ericsson & Simon, 1980).

Do We Know What We Think?

There also have been experiments suggesting that people may make systematic errors without awareness (Dixon, 1981; Lewicki, 1986) and engage in "self-deception." In addition, they may respond to stimuli at a physiological level (through changes in the electrical activity in their skin) even when they seem unaware at the verbal level (Gur & Sackeim, 1979).

In a related direction, Nisbett and Wilson (1977) have argued that people often are not able to access their own cognitive processes and misidentify the causes of their own behavior. In one experiment, for instance, people were asked to evaluate articles of clothing. The results revealed that the clothing article in the right-hand position was evaluated more favorably. But when asked whether position had any effect on their choice, people vehemently and consistently denied it. We also may develop more positive feelings toward objects that were previously encountered without consciously knowing that the object is familiar to us. That is, simple exposure to the objects led to enhanced feelings for them, even when there was no recognition that the objects had been seen before (Wilson, 1979). Thus research from a number of directions suggests that sometimes we seem to have little insight into our own thought processes and are not fully aware of them (Kihlstrom, 1990; Lewicki, 1986; Westen, 1990).

On the other hand, careful reviews evaluating the evidence for people's inability to access how they think continue to be critical (Bandura, 1986). Bandura argues that the evidence that people cannot consciously know their own thinking processes actually reflects inadequate methods for probing their awareness (Ericsson & Simon, 1980). Thus the problem may not be that people are unaware of the steps that lead to what they think; researchers just may be continuously asking them the wrong questions, driven by their own hypotheses rather than by the subject's thought processes.

In sum, the existence and importance of nonconscious mental activity has been claimed in many studies of how people process information (Erdelyi, 1985, 1993; Kihlstrom, 1987, 1990; Nisbett & Wilson, 1977). Some of these studies suggest that we have limited access to our own thought processes. Some conclude that we can execute complex mental processes without awareness (Westen, 1990) and that the knowledge we acquire without awareness can further influence what we perceive, feel, and do (Bornstein et al., 1987; Lewicki, 1986). These studies, however, are still open to serious criticism (Bandura, 1986).

Notice also that most of these studies have been done with emotionally neutral information and therefore speak at most to a nonconscious level of mental activities quite different from Freud's psychodynamic unconscious. There is some compelling evidence, however, that emotional stimuli may be subject to unconscious processing.

Unpleasant words, for example, are less easily perceived than pleasant ones, even in carefully controlled experiments (Broadbent, 1977; Westen, 1985). Likewise, physiological measures of brain activity suggest that patients may respond distinctively to words that are relevant to their complaints, even when they are flashed too rapidly to be recognized by them consciously (Shevrin & Dickman, 1980). Most interesting, but also extremely controversial, are a few studies that do suggest deeply motivated unconscious effects (Horowitz & Stinson, 1995; Morokoff, 1985; Silverman & Weinberger, 1985), as illustrated next.

"Mommy and I Are One"

According to Silverman and Weinberger (1985), exposure to certain stimuli below the person's consciousness can encourage infantlike fantasies that may be therapeutic. Specifically, the authors proposed that the phrase "Mommy and I are one," when presented just below the level of awareness (**subliminally**) by rapid exposures (with a tachistoscope), should produce a feeling of oneness, like a young child feels with its mother. They hypothesized that subconscious activation of the fantasy would serve to reduce anxiety and be reflected in better functioning. In their research, for example, groups of schizophrenic men were exposed to either the phrase "Mommy and I are one" or to a control phrase, such as "People are walking." The phrases were flashed too quickly to be perceived consciously. Some groups of schizophrenic men who were exposed to the "Mommy" phrase showed reduced symptoms, supporting the researchers' hypothesis.

In a similar direction, a study with college women also demonstrated benign effects in response to the same messages presented at a level the researchers believed was below the students' conscious awareness. Students who were exposed to the "Mommy" stimulus, compared with the control group, were reported to lessen their defensiveness and anxiety, reflected in greater ability to reveal their feelings in a counseling session (Linehan & O'Toole, 1982). Likewise, students in another academic setting showed a significant improvement in math grades after they experienced the "Mommy and I are one" stimulation (Ariam & Siller, 1982). Taken collectively, these results are exciting for psychodynamic theory, although much further research will be needed before confident final conclusions are reached. The results from these studies remain controversial and have proved extremely difficult to reproduce by other investigators (Balay & Shevrin, 1988). The researchers emphasize, nevertheless, that they may have substantial implications for teaching, counseling, and psychotherapy if they are supported in future research.

Optimistic Prospects for the Future of the Unconscious

In conclusion, what can be said about the role of the unconscious in modern personality psychology? This question was addressed in a special series of articles in which research experts in the area reviewed what is known about the nature of the unconscious (e.g., Bruner, 1992; Erdelyi, 1992; Greenwald, 1992). Although there was no consistent agreement about how to characterize unconscious processes in terms of their precise role and significance, there was ". . . absolute agreement that exciting times, both in research and theory, are ahead for the unconscious" (Loftus & Klinger, 1992, p. 764). This optimism seems justified because methods and concepts in the research on this topic are starting to reach a level of sophistication that is appropriate for the complexity of the phenomena being studied (e.g., Lewicki, Hill, & Czyzewska, 1992). There is also growing attention to how such factors as the person's goals, emotional states, and needs influence memory (e.g., Higgins & Sorrentino, 1990; Kunda, 1990; Metcalfe & Jacobs, 1998; Singer & Salovey, 1993).

PATTERNS OF DEFENSE: INDIVIDUAL DIFFERENCES IN COGNITIVE AVOIDANCE

Cognitive avoidance of anxiety-provoking information is not only a basic process; it also is a dimension of personality on which people differ substantially and interestingly. Some people react to stimuli that arouse anxiety by avoiding them cognitively, but other people do not. For many years, individual differences in "defensive" patterns have been found (Bruner & Postman, 1947; Lazarus, 1976; Miller, 1987; Paulhus, Fridhandler, & Hayes, 1997).

Repression-Sensitization

The dimension on which these differences seemed to fall was a continuum of behaviors ranging from avoiding the anxiety-arousing stimuli to approaching them more readily and being extravigilant or supersensitized to them. The former end of the continuum included behaviors similar to the defensive mechanisms that psychoanalysts called denial and repression; the latter pattern — vigilance or sensitization to anxiety-provoking cues — seemed more like obsessive worrying. This dimension now has become known as the **repression-sensitization** continuum. Repression-sensitization became the focus of much research both as a dynamic process and as a personality dimension on which individuals might show consistent patterns.

In general, individuals show some consistency in their cognitive avoidance of anxiety-provoking cues such as threatening words (Eriksen, 1952; Eriksen & Kuethe, 1956). Consistency evidence usually has been strongest when extreme groups are preselected. In one study, reaction time and other measures of avoidance were obtained in the auditory recognition of poorly audible sentences that had sexual and aggressive content. People who were slow to recognize such sentences also tended to avoid sexual and aggressive materials in a sentence completion test (Lazarus, Eriksen, & Fonda, 1951). People who more readily recalled stimuli associated with a painful shock also tended to recall their failures; those who forgot one were more likely to forget the other (Lazarus & Longo, 1953). A tendency for some consistency in cognitive avoidance may exist at least when extremely high and low groups are selected (Eriksen,

1966). Correlations between cognitive avoidance on experimental tasks and various other measures of repression-sensitization also imply some consistency in these patterns (Byrne, 1964; McFarland & Buehler, 1997; Mischel, Ebbesen, & Zeiss, 1973, 1976), as discussed next.

Selective Attention

Individual differences in repression-sensitization have often been measured on a self-report questionnaire (Byrne, 1964). On this scale, people who describe themselves as having few problems or difficulties and who do not report themselves as highly sensitive to everyday stress and anxieties score high in repression, whereas those with an opposite pattern are called sensitizers.

Individual differences on this scale can predict selective attention to important personal information about the self. In one study, college students were exposed to personal information about themselves supposedly based on their own performance on personality tests they had taken earlier (Mischel, Ebbesen, & Zeiss, 1973). The results were made available to students in individual sessions in which each was left alone to look at descriptions of his or her personal liabilities (in one computer file) and personal assets (in another file). For example, the personality assets included such feedback as, "Affiliative, capable of cooperating and reciprocating deeply in relations with others. . . ." In contrast, the personality liabilities information included such descriptions as, "Nonperseverative, procrastination, and distractibility . . . resultant failures lead to greater and greater apathy. . . ." (Actually, all students received the same feedback, but in the debriefing session in which they were told the truth, it became clear that they had been convinced that the test results really described them; in fact, they believed the information had captured much about their personalities.)

The question was: Would repressors and sensitizers (as measured on the self-report questionnaire) exhibit different attentional patterns for the positive, self-enhancing information versus the negative, threatening information about themselves? There were clear differences.

These results are summarized in Figure 5.1. Sensitizers attended more to their liabilities and spent little time on their assets; in sharp contrast, repressors attended as much to their assets as to their liabilities. Later research suggests that repressors may be people who are especially sensitive to criticism and threat and use their defense to protect themselves against this vulnerability (Baumeister & Cairns, 1992).

When exposed equally to positive and negative information about themselves, repressors and sensitizers do not differ in their recall of the two types of information (Mischel, Ebbesen, & Zeiss, 1976). In general the repressors seemed to simply avoid attending to negative or threatening information and focused instead on their positive qualities as much as on their negative ones. Sensitizers manifested the opposite pattern, attending habitually more to their negative qualities and to potentially threatening information, spending little time on their personal strengths.

In sum, the repressors and the sensitizers differed in how they dealt with positive and negative ego-relevant information. But these differences seem linked to their

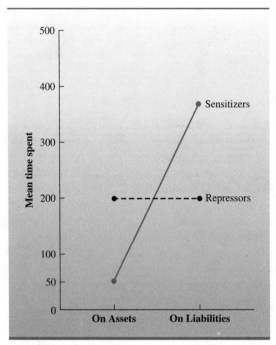

Figure 5.1
Attention Deployment by Sensitizers and Repressors Mean amount of time (in seconds) spent on assets and liabilities by sensitizers and by repressors.

SOURCE: Based on data in the control condition from Mischel, W., Ebbesen, E. B., & Zeiss, A. R. (1973). Selective attention to the self: Situational and dispositional determinants. *Journal of Personality and Social Psychology, 27,* 129–142.

attentional strategies, not to unconscious distortions in their memory: Both groups are able to recall threatening information about themselves with equal accuracy if they are made to attend equally to that information. Normally, however, the sensitizers tended to focus on negative self-relevant information, whereas the repressors tended to avoid it and preferred to think about happier things. When the situation prevents repressors from simply ignoring the threat they do begin to attend to it and worry anxiously about it (Baumeister & Cairns, 1992).

The two groups also differed in their self-descriptions: While repressors described themselves in positive, socially desirable terms, representing themselves consistently in a more favorable light, sensitizers painted a much more critical and negative self-portrait (Alicke, 1985; Joy, 1963). Most interesting, however, is that it is the repressor, not the sensitizer, who better fits the picture of the optimistic personality with a good mental and physical health prognosis: It is the sensitizers who may be more at risk. This is a surprising relationship from the perspective of psychodynamic theory, which has long assumed that accurate self-awareness and being in touch with one's personal limitations, anxieties, and flaws (i.e., sensitization) were important ingredients of the healthy personality. In contrast, repression and cognitive avoidance of negative information and threat were the hallmark of the brittle, vulnerable personality. It is, of course, likely that the massive emotional repression to which Freudians refer is quite different from the self-enhancing positive bias that seems to characterize repressors as identified on this scale. Likewise, the growth of self-awareness and accessibility of personal anxieties to which psychodynamic theory refers may also be different from "sensitization" measures on this scale. But as the next section also suggests (Miller, 1987), and as a great deal of work reported in later chapters shows (Seligman, 1990; Taylor & Brown, 1988; see Chapter 15), under many circumstances an attitude of emotional blunting that deliberately avoids threatening information may be highly adaptive, a symptom of mental health rather than of a fragile personality in need of insight.

Blunting versus Monitoring Styles

In a related direction, it has been shown that people differ considerably in their disposition to distract themselves or to monitor for (be alert to) danger signals (Miller, 1996). One promising scale tries to identify information-avoiders and information-seekers as two distinct coping styles. The **Miller Behavioral Style Scale (MBSS)** consists of four hypothetical stress-evoking scenes of an uncontrollable nature (Miller, 1981, 1987; Miller & Mangan, 1983). On this measure, people are asked to vividly imagine scenes like "You are afraid of the dentist and have to get some dental work done"; or "You are being held hostage by a group of armed terrorists in a public building"; or "You are on an airplane, 30 minutes from your destination, when the plane unexpectedly goes into a deep dive and then suddenly levels off. After a short time, the pilot announces that nothing is wrong, although the rest of the ride may be rough. You, however, are not convinced that all is well."

Each scene is followed by statements that represent ways of coping with the situation, either by **monitoring** or by **blunting.** Half of the statements accompanying each scene are of a monitoring variety. For example, in the hostage situation: "If there was a radio present, I would stay near it and listen to the bulletins about what the police were doing"; or, in the airplane situation: "I would listen carefully to the engines for unusual noises and would watch the crew to see if their behavior was out of the ordinary." The other half of the statements are of the blunting type. For example, in the dental situation: "I would do mental puzzles in my head"; or, in the airplane situation: "I would watch the end of the movie, even if I had seen it before." The subject simply marks all the statements following each scene that might apply to him.

Some people cope with unpleasant events by mentally "blunting" (distracting themselves).

IN FOCUS 5.2   *Matching the Medical Information to the Patient's Style*

Miller and Mangan (1983) gave the MBSS to gynecologic patients about to undergo colposcopy, a diagnostic procedure to check for the presence of abnormal (cancerous) cells in the uterus. Based on scale scores, patients were first divided into monitors or blunters. Half the women in each group were then given extensive information about the forthcoming procedure, and half were given (the usual) minimal information. Psychophysiological reactions (like heart rate), subjective reports, and observer ratings of arousal and discomfort were taken before, during, and after the procedures. The results revealed, again as expected, that monitors showed more arousal overall than blunters (for example, see Figure 5.2 for the physician's rating of patients' tension during the exam).

Most interesting, physiological arousal was reduced when the level of preparatory information was consistent with the patients' coping style. That is, physiological arousal was reduced for blunters who received minimal information and for monitors who received extensive information. The total results clearly show strong individual differences in informational preferences during the coping process when people are faced with threats. Most important, they showed that when monitors are told more and blunters are told less about an impending stress, each type is likely to cope with it best: Matching the information to the style can reduce the stress experienced and enhance resources.

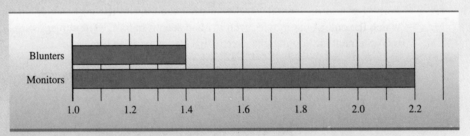

Figure 5.2
Doctor's Report—Tension During Exam

SOURCE: Miller, S. M., & Mangan, C. E. (1983). Cognition and psychopathology. In K. Dobson & P. C. Kendall (Eds.), *Cognition, stress, and health.* New York: Academic Press.

College students were threatened with a low probability shock and allowed to choose whether they wanted to monitor for information or distract themselves with music (Miller, 1981). As expected, the amount of time spent on information rather than on music was predicted reasonably well by an individual's MBSS score. In particular, the more blunting items endorsed on the scale, the less time the person spent listening to the information and the more to the music. Thus individuals differ in the extent to which they choose to monitor or distract themselves when faced with aversive events; and these differences in coping style were related to their questionnaire scores. These individual differences can have important implications, as seen in *In Focus 5.2.*

The Role of Control: When Don't You Want to Know?

Whether you react to potentially painful stimuli by trying to avoid them cognitively or by becoming vigilantly alert and monitoring them may depend in part on what you can do to control the threat. Consider first the situation in which a person receives aversive stimulation but cannot control its occurrence. That is, the individual can do nothing to change the objective circumstances to render the aversive or negative stimuli less painful through his or her own problem-solving actions. Examples of this frustrating dilemma would include most experimentally induced stress experiments in which the researcher administers painful but unavoidable electric shocks to the subject, confronts him with embarrassing words or pictures, provides him with insoluble problems, or deprives him of food for long periods of time.

Under all these conditions, the aversive stimulation is essentially inescapable (unless the subject terminates the situation altogether by abandoning the experiment). If the subject can have no control over the painful stimuli by means of his own instrumental actions such as problem solving, it may be most adaptive for him to avoid them cognitively and thus not think about them or attend to them. On the other hand, if escape from the noxious or distressing stimulation is possible and depends on the person's ability to find a solution (cognitively or physically), then monitoring vigilance or sensitization to the anxiety-arousing cues would be adaptive and often even essential for survival.

The foregoing speculations have received some experimental support. Reece (1954) tested people's recognition thresholds for various nonsense syllables in the first phase of his experiment. Thereafter, they underwent a training period during which some of the syllables were paired with electric shock. In the final phase of the study, the participants' recognition thresholds after training were assessed again. Post-training recognition thresholds for the syllables were longer if during training the syllable-shock combinations were inescapable (i.e., participants could do nothing to prevent them). In contrast, if they could escape shock during training by verbalizing the syllable as soon as it was presented, then the syllables were later recognized as rapidly as in a control group that received no shock. Similar evidence comes from a study by Rosen (1954), who controlled for the effect of the electric shock itself.

Thus, whether or not persons react to negative stimuli by avoiding them "defensively" in their cognitions and perceptions may depend on whether or not they believe that they can somehow cope with them by problem solving and action. If adaptive action seems impossible, cognitive suppressive attempts may be more likely. But if the painful cues can be controlled by the person's actions, then greater attention and vigilance to them may occur. This point is illustrated in a blunting-monitoring study that gave people a choice between stress-relevant information or distraction (Miller, 1979). The information was a warning signal for when an electric shock would come; the distraction was listening to music. Half the participants were led to believe the shock was potentially avoidable; the rest believed it was unavoidable. As Table 5.1 shows, when participants believed avoidance was possible, they preferred information; when they thought it was unavoidable, they preferred distraction. Other research has documented the many circumstances under which coping with problems is improved by the

Table 5.1
Number of Subjects Who Seek Information (Warning Signal) or Distraction
(Listen to Music) When Avoidance Is or Is Not Possible

	Information-Seeking	Distraction-Seeking
Avoidance possible	24	10
Avoidance not possible	11	23

SOURCE: Based on Miller, S. M. (1979). Coping with impending stress: Physiological and cognitive correlates of choice. *Psychopathology, 16,* 572–581.

selective avoidance of threatening information (Janis, 1971; Lazarus, 1976, 1990; Lazarus & Folkman, 1984).

Vigilance versus Avoidance as Learned Defenses

The previous section suggested that whether a person becomes cognitively vigilant or avoidant to anxiety-arousing cues may depend on whether or not he believes he can control the onset of danger. This conclusion refers to the person's subjective state, his personal beliefs about his ability to cope with threat through his own action. The subjective feeling that one can control the occurrence of dangerous outcomes is not achieved arbitrarily — it reflects, instead, the person's previous experiences and current condition. Depending on the exact learning history and the structure of the particular situation, he might react to anxiety cues either with vigilance or with avoidance.

Some of the conditions under which perceptual defense and perceptual vigilance may be learned have been carefully investigated. Covert responses such as thoughts and associations may be modified by punishment in the same fashion as overt responses (Eriksen & Kuethe, 1956). If a thought or association elicited by a stimulus is punished, then it tends to be inhibited and a new association becomes more likely. The recall or retrieval of memories may be hampered when the person expects punishment for recalling the material (Weiner, 1968). According to learning theory, if behaviors such as sexual and aggressive responses have been punished, they are more likely to become inhibited and to be replaced by other responses that, on the basis of prior learning, are less likely to produce painful consequences (Bandura, 1986).

In sum, the phenomena of cognitive avoidance may become less mysterious when they are seen as learned functional responses. Such learning involves suppression of thoughts, images, percepts, associations, or other cognitive events that have been punished. In turn, competing, unpunished responses will become more likely.

SUMMARY

1. The experience of anxiety often includes an unaccounted-for sense of fear, physiological arousal, and a disruption of mental processes. Conscious and unconscious defense mechanisms may be used to cope with anxiety-producing stimuli. In Freudian theory, repression has long been considered the most central unconscious mental defense against anxiety.

2. People can cognitively avoid internal anxiety-generating cues such as threatening thoughts. While the phenomenon of cognitive avoidance is widely recognized, a controversial issue is whether or not it involves a mechanism of unconscious repression.

3. The Freudian concept of defensive mechanisms refers to attempts to cope cognitively with internal anxiety-arousing cues without awareness—that is, unconsciously. According to this theory, repressed impulses are not eliminated but are only camouflaged; hence, they ultimately may return in disguised and distorted forms, such as "slips" of the tongue or symptoms.

4. The concept of repression has been the subject of extensive research for many years. Although studies have been interpreted as supporting the concept of repression, alternative interpretations usually are possible. For example, poorer learning under conditions of emotional upset and response interference due to stress may provide simpler explanations of the result.

5. Psychodynamic theory suggests that "perceptual defenses" produce anxiety-reducing distortions and avoidance in perception. Some researchers reasoned that if certain stimuli generally elicited many sexual or aggressive responses, then the *failure* to give such responses meant that the person must be inhibiting or defending against this type of ideation. Often a tachistoscope was used to present stimuli briefly, and the length of time required to recognize threatening stimuli (such as taboo words) was the measure of defensive avoidance. Methodological problems left the conclusions uncertain. For example, it is difficult to distinguish between the person's *report* and *perception*. The participants in a perceptual recognition situation may see the taboo stimulus but may deliberately suppress a response because of embarrassment about saying or admitting it. Conclusions from other experiments on unconscious defense have been limited by many similar methodological dilemmas.

6. Evidence from controlled experimental research on unconscious processes is often negative. Many psychoanalytically oriented critics, however, maintain that most of it is irrelevant, because of the artificiality of the measures usually employed and the hazards of generalizing from laboratory subjects to clinical populations and problems. Alternatively, the clinician's judgments and the intuitive procedures used for inferring the phenomena of unconscious dynamics have been questioned most seriously.

7. Currently, repression and perceptual defense are seen in terms of the selectivity involved in how information is processed. Mood has been shown to selectively influence the recall of emotionally relevant information without awareness by the subject. Some studies also suggest that people may not always be conscious of their thought processes and the reasons for their behavior. The structure of these studies, however, may have biased responses, and the person's awareness may not have been tested adequately. Some evidence does suggest that emotional stimuli may be subject to unconscious or automatic mental processing, and a few studies have reported deeply motivated unconscious effects of subliminally presented stimuli, but they remain extremely controversial.

8. A classic effort to assess the role of the unconscious has investigated learning to see if it can occur without awareness or consciousness. In general, while some simple conditioned responses may be learned without awareness, awareness usually plays a major role in most forms of human learning. Yet, although most learning may require awareness, once behavior is mastered, it often seems to proceed without subjective awareness.

9. Individuals' behaviors in reaction to stress tend either toward avoidance and minimization of the anxiety-producing stimulus (repression) or toward a hyper-sensitization or vigilance to it. Individual differences on such a dimension, called repression-sensitization, are manifested in how people attend to positive and negative information about the self, sensitizers tending to attend more to the negative and less to the positive. The two types do not differ, however, in their recall for such information.

Repressors attend more to positive feedback, see themselves favorably, and, interestingly, are usually the more mentally and physically healthy; whereas sensitizers tend to be preoccupied with negative feedback and are often self-critical. Similar patterns of individual differences are also found when comparing people in their tendency toward blunting (self-distraction) and toward monitoring (increased alertness) in a stressful situation. These differences in patterns of information-seeking when coping with stress may have significant implications for health.

10. Whether one reacts to a painful stimulus by trying cognitively to avoid it or by becoming vigilantly alert to it may depend partly upon what one can do to control the threat. If adaptive action seems impossible, cognitive suppression may be more likely. If, however, the potentially painful events can be controlled by the person's actions, then greater attention and vigilance to them may be found. Experimental research has explored the mechanisms through which perceptual defense and vigilance can be learned.

Summary Evaluation

Psychodynamic Approaches

This section summarizes the most basic contributions and limitations of psychodynamic approaches and reviews their mean features, which were presented throughout Part Two. As a review exercise and learning experience, try to add any other strengths or weaknesses you see. Illustrate each of the suggested contributions or limitations with examples or reasons. At the conclusion of the presentation of each major theoretical approach in this book, there is a similar summary evaluation for which you may want to conduct a similar exercise.

OVERVIEW

Some of the essentials of psychodynamic approaches are summarized in the Summary Overview table. The table reminds you that unconscious motives and psychodynamics within persons are viewed as the basic causes of their behavior, including their feelings, conflicts, and problems. Clinicians who have been trained within this perspective try to infer and interpret these causes from their overt "symptomlike" expressions in the individual's behaviors. These behaviors are diverse and include dreams, free associations, and responses to unstructured situations such as projective stimuli (for example, the Rorschach inkblots), which are especially favored sources of information within this perspective.

The responses from the person serve as indirect signs whose meaning and significance the clinician interprets. The role of the situation is deliberately minimized, guided by the belief that the more ambiguous the situation, the more likely it is that the individual's basic, underlying psychodynamics will be projected in how he or she interprets it and reacts.

The focus of research, like the focus of personality assessment and of psychotherapy within this perspective, is on the person's unconscious psychodynamics and defenses. Those defenses disguise the underlying motives and conflicts that must be revealed and confronted in order for the individual to function well. Personality change requires insight into the disguised (unacceptable to the person) unconscious motives and dynamics that underlie the behavioral symptoms, so that they can be made conscious, accepted, and managed more rationally. When that occurs, the symptoms

135

Summary Overview of Psychodynamic Approaches

Basic units:	Inferred motives and psychodynamics
Causes of behavior:	Underlying stable motives and their unconscious transformations and conflicts
Behavioral manifestations of personality:	Symptoms and irrational patterns of behavior (including dreams, "mistakes," and fantasies)
Favored data:	Interpretations by expert judges (clinicians)
Observed responses used as:	Indirect signs
Research focus:	Personality dynamics and psychopathology; unconscious processes; defense mechanisms; the fragmented self
Approach to personality change:	By insight into motives and conflicts underlying behavior
Role of situation:	Deliberately minimized or ambiguous

should diminish. In more recent work, however, increasing attention is being given to such concepts as the self, self-perception, and interpersonal relationship problems with significant others.

CONTRIBUTIONS AND LIMITATIONS

The Summary Evaluation table indicates some of the main contributions and limitations of this perspective. The impact of Freud's theory on society and on philosophy, as well as on the social sciences, is almost universally hailed as profound; its significance is frequently compared with that of Darwin's. Freud's monumental contributions have been widely acknowledged. He opened the topic of childhood sexuality, revolutionized conceptions of the human psyche, provided strikingly powerful metaphors for the mind and human condition, and pioneered 20th-century psychiatry with his approach to the treatment of psychological problems. The evidence relevant to Freud's

Summary Evaluation of Psychodynamic Approaches

Contributions	Limitations
Stimulating, broad (comprehensive), systematic theory; revolutionary reconceptualization of human psyche and human condition	Concepts difficult to test scientifically
Extensive intellectual influence, including in other disciplines (for example, history, literature); major impact on research; pioneered studies of unconscious processes and conflicts	Limited research support: a. for key concepts (e.g., repression, Oedipal complex b. for key methods (e.g., clinical inference by clinical experts, projective methods)
Profound influence on clinical practice, especially treatment; pioneered 20th-century psychiatry	Efficacy of therapy remains in dispute

theory as a scientific psychological system, however, has been questioned persistently (Grunbaum, 1984).

Although Freud attempted to create a general psychology, his main work was with conflict-ridden persons caught up in personal crises. Freud observed these tortured individuals under extremely artificial conditions: lying on a couch during the psychotherapy hour in an environment deliberately made as nonsocial as possible. This drastically restricted observational base helped to foster a theory that originally was almost entirely a theory of anxiety and internal conflict. It paid little attention to the social environment and to the interpersonal context of behavior. We have already seen that many of Freud's own followers attempted to modify that initial emphasis and to devise a more ego-oriented and social approach. That trend is continuing.

This newer "ego psychology" is characterized by a greater focus on development beyond early childhood to include the entire life span. It attends more to the role of interpersonal relations and society and to the nature and functions of the concepts of ego and "self" rather than to the id and its impulses. Freud's ideas thus have been going through a considerable continuing revolution that goes beyond his own writings to the extensions introduced by his many followers over the years.

The objects relations theories of analysts such as Kohut and Kernberg are especially important innovations that seem to be changing psychodynamic theories substantially. They emphasize the "self" (rather than the instincts and the unconscious defenses against their expression) and thus have some similarity to the self theories discussed in later parts of this text.

One of the main criticisms of Freud's theory is that it is hard to test. Unfortunately this criticism also applies (although to a lesser degree) to most of the later psychodynamic thinkers. That is true in part because psychodynamic constructs tend to have both the richness and the ambiguity of metaphors; while they may seem compelling intuitively, they are hard to quantify. Rooted in clinical experience and clinical language, the terms often are loose and metaphoric and convey different meanings in different contexts. The theory also requires the user to have available a clinical background with much experience and training as the framework and language on which the constructs draw.

Critics of these theories ask: Just what observations are required to conclude, for example, that an individual is fixated at the anal stage? Under what conditions may we conclude that he or she is not fixated at that stage? How can the extent or amount of fixation be assessed? Likewise, is the college student who commits himself to fight the "establishment" really "intellectualizing" his emotional conflicts with "authority figures" like his father and his "Oedipal problems," or is he truly motivated to undo political evils? What would he have to do to show that he is motivated by his professed idealism rather than by unconscious conflicts?

Often the answers to questions like these depend on the clinical judgments of trained experts. It therefore becomes essential to study how closely experts (who have the necessary training and experience to use the constructs meaningfully) really do agree with one another and how well they can support their opinions with evidence. These results generally have been disappointing in the opinion of the critics of this approach (e.g., Bandura, 1969, 1986; Grunbaum, 1984).

The harshest critics view Freud's theory as providing little more than labels. Such labels (for example, the "death wish") cannot be tested by any method. Bluntly, some of these concepts do not offer the possibility of ever being disconfirmed by research. One danger here is that people may believe that these labels are useful when, instead, they merely lead to sweeping generalities.

In spite of these problems, many attempts have been made to clarify Freudian constructs. Especially vigorous efforts have been made to deal with defense mechanisms and conflict, and to submit them to experimental study (e.g., Blum, 1953; Erdelyi, 1985; Holmes, 1974; Sears, 1943, 1944; Silverman, 1976; Westen, 1990, 1991). You already saw some of the research that psychoanalytic ideas have influenced, and you will see many more examples throughout the text.

Particularly exciting in recent years is the renewed interest in psychodynamic concepts such as the unconscious in light of new discoveries about mental processes (e.g., attention, thinking, and memory) emerging from the study of cognitive psychology. There are many interesting parallels, and people certainly are not aware of all the things that happen in their minds. Modern cognitive psychology has understandably stimulated a sympathetic reexamination of the nature of unconscious processes (e.g., Kihlstrom, 1990).

There is evidence that unconscious processes and events influence us massively. For example, individuals with amnesia continue to be affected by previous experiences although they cannot remember them (Kihlstrom, Barnhardt, & Tataryn, 1992). All sorts of information that influences how different individuals encode (interpret) and evaluate their social environments is acquired unconsciously (e.g., Lewicki, Hill, & Czyzewska, 1992). And the claim that most of what we feel and believe and do may be elicited or triggered automatically without consciousness is now accepted as a fact. Its significance, however, continues to be debated (Loftus & Klinger, 1992), and firm conclusions cannot be reached until further research explores more directly the relevance of nonconscious information processing for Freud's concepts about the unconscious mind (e.g., Erdelyi, 1992).

Although the research over the years in the psychodynamic framework has not yet found compelling experimental support for many of the original Freudian concepts, almost always it has led to useful insights. It often has proved psychodynamic ideas to be partly right as well as partly wrong: The challenge remains to identify the parts of this provocative theory that are valid and to separate clinical wisdom from the many assumptions that are not justified.

New Directions and Challenges

Psychodynamic approaches face a number of challenges and opportunities. If they respond "defensively," they will miss a rare chance to review themselves in ways that could allow psychodynamic contributions to be incorporated into personality psychology. To face these challenges constructively requires attention to the following:

1. Reformulating psychodynamic ideas about the unconscious in light of new findings on the nature of mental processes (cognition) from the psychological study of selective attention, perception, memory, thinking, and stress.

2. Revision of the psychodynamic theory of early personality development requires taking greater account of findings on the cognitive-perceptual competencies (and constraints) of the newborn.

3. The theory of psychosexual development also needs to further consider results from the studies of early attachment relationships with caretakers (e.g., Ainsworth, Blehar, Waters, & Wall, 1978; Sroufe & Fleeson, 1986) as well as from contemporary anthropology (e.g., Shweder & Sullivan, 1990).

4. Finally, this perspective would benefit from considering new information about the genetics of personality (discussed in Part Three) and from other areas of personality and social psychology that have been changing conceptions of the nature of personality, as discussed throughout the remainder of the text.

In conclusion, psychodynamic approaches offer important insights that are mixed together with unsubstantiated assumptions. The task is to separate the valid contributions from the lingering dogmas. Many psychologists within this approach have remained too isolated from relevant advances in other areas of personality psychology. They now need to revise psychodynamic theories to take into account these developments in ways that integrate their work with the larger field of personality psychology. Fortunately, this seems to be happening (Westen, 1998).

Part III

Trait and Biological Approaches

Trait Theories: Conceptions

"My father is a really great guy. He's absolutely dependable; I can always count on him."

"Nancy's very quiet and withdrawn. She never says hello to anybody. She's very unsure of herself."

"I've always wanted to succeed. Winning is everything. If you're not a winner, you're nobody."

Descriptions like those above are the stuff of trait psychology. We see trait psychology in everyday life whenever people describe and group the differences among themselves into slots or categories. We all tend to classify one another readily on many dimensions: Sex, race, religion, occupation, friendliness, and competitiveness are a few examples. Good-bad, strong-weak, friend-enemy, winner-loser—the ways of sorting and classifying human qualities seem virtually infinite.

A concern with classifying and naming things is also characteristic of most sciences in their early efforts to find order. Consider, for example, the classification system of biology, in which all life is sorted into genera and species. This effort to categorize also occurs in psychology, where, as the oldest and most enduring approach to individuality, it is known as the **trait approach.** Psychologists working from this perspective seek to label, measure, and classify people with the trait terms of everyday language (for example, friendly, aggressive, honest) in order to describe and compare their psychological attributes (John, 1990).

TYPES AND TRAITS

Traditionally, the essence of the trait approach has been the assumption that behavior is primarily determined by stable generalized **traits**—basic qualities of the person that express themselves in many contexts. Guided by this assumption, many investigators have searched vigorously for these traits. Perhaps the chief goal of trait psychology has been to find the person's position on one or more trait dimensions (for example, intelligence, introversion, anxiety) by comparing the individual with others under similar uniform conditions. Guided by the belief that positions on these dimensions tend to be stable across situations and over time, the focus in the study of individuality becomes the search to identify the person's basic traits.

Types: Sheldon and Jung

Some categorizations sort individuals into discrete categories or *types* (Eysenck, 1991; Matthews, 1984). In the ancient theory of temperaments, for example, the Greek physician Hippocrates assigned persons to one of four types of temperament: *choleric* (irritable), *melancholic* (depressed), *sanguine* (optimistic), and *phlegmatic* (calm, listless). In accord with the biology of his time (about 400 B.C.), Hippocrates attributed each temperament to a predominance of one of the bodily humors: yellow bile, black bile, blood, and phlegm. A choleric temperament was caused by an excess of yellow bile; a depressive temperament reflected the predominance of black bile; the sanguine person had too much blood; and phlegmatic people suffered from an excess of phlegm.

Other typologies have searched for constitutional types, seeking associations between physique and indices of temperament. Such groupings in terms of body build have considerable popular appeal, as seen in the prevalence of stereotypes linking the body to the psyche: Fat people are "jolly" and "lazy," thin people are "morose" and "sensitive," and so on.

Formal classifications of the possible links between personality and body type were developed by the German psychiatrist Kretschmer and more recently by an American physician, William H. Sheldon. Sheldon's classification has received the most attention. In 1942 he suggested three dimensions of physique and their corresponding temperaments. These are summarized in Figure 6.1.

As Figure 6.1 suggests, the endomorph is obese, the mesomorph has an athletic build, and the ectomorph is tall, thin, and stoop-shouldered. Rather than dividing peo-

Connections between body build and personality are often assumed. But are they valid?

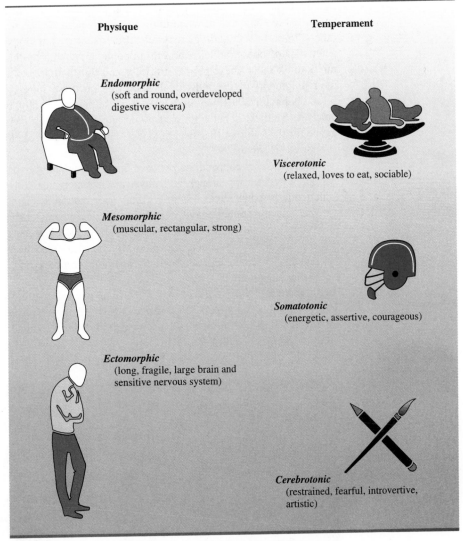

Physique

Endomorphic
(soft and round, overdeveloped digestive viscera)

Mesomorphic
(muscular, rectangular, strong)

Ectomorphic
(long, fragile, large brain and sensitive nervous system)

Temperament

Viscerotonic
(relaxed, loves to eat, sociable)

Somatotonic
(energetic, assertive, courageous)

Cerebrotonic
(restrained, fearful, introvertive, artistic)

Figure 6.1
Sheldon's Physique Dimensions and Their Associated Temperaments

ple into three distinct types, Sheldon considered every individual's status on each dimension. He developed a seven-point rating system for measuring body types. For example, a 7-3-1 would be high on endomorphy, moderate on mesomorphy, and low on ectomorphy, presumably with corresponding levels of the associated temperaments. Sheldon's typology thus was quite sophisticated, especially by comparison with earlier attempts.

Sheldon's ideas about the association between body build and temperament are supported to some extent when untrained people rate the personality characteristics of others. In part these findings may reflect the fact that stereotyped ideas about the characteristics of obese, athletic, and thin people are shared by the raters. For example, if raters think most obese people are jolly and thin people are sensitive, they may base their judgments of the individuals they rate on these stereotypes rather than on observed behavior. Thus they may rate an obese person as jolly, no matter how he or she behaves. Studies of behavior that avoid such stereotypes generally provide less evidence for the value of this system (Tyler, 1956) and leave Sheldon's theory largely unsupported (Herman, 1992).

Nevertheless, connections between body types and personality may be quite important. Physical appearance and physical characteristics certainly affect the ways in which others perceive us, what we can and cannot do, and, ultimately, even what we feel and experience about ourselves. Physical characteristics like strength, height, and muscularity affect the situations we select, the work and avocations we pursue, and the interests and values that we develop. But the relations between physique and particular personality characteristics tend to be more complex and indirect than the early typologies suggested.

One of the most famous typologies was devised by the Swiss psychiatrist Carl Jung. He grouped all people into **introverts** or **extraverts.** According to this typology, introverts withdraw into themselves, especially when encountering stressful emotional conflict, prefer to be alone, tend to avoid others, and are shy. Extraverts, in contrast, re-

Jung described the introvert as consistently shy and withdrawn.

act to stress by trying to lose themselves among people and social activity. They are drawn to occupations that allow them to deal directly with many people, such as sales, and are apt to be conventional, sociable, and outgoing.

The very simplicity that makes such typologies appealing also reduces their value. Such characteristics as blood or sex may be typed, but because each person's behaviors and psychological qualities are complex and variable, it is difficult to assign an individual to a single slot. Nevertheless, interesting and important typologies continue to be explored (see *In Focus 6.1*) and will be discussed later.

IN FOCUS 6.1 *Type A: A Typology That Predicts Coronary Disease*

In spite of recent significant declines in deaths due to coronary disease in American men, coronary disease remains the major cause of death in the United States. Many of the men killed by coronary disease are only 35 to 50 years old.

Psychologists and physicians have looked at the psychological variables that place individuals at higher risk of coronary heart disease. A coronary-prone behavior pattern was identified (Friedman & Roseman, 1974; Glass, 1977) and designated as *Type A*. This behavior pattern is characterized by:

1. Competitive Achievement Striving: Type A's are likely to be involved in multiple activities, to have numerous community and social commitments, and to participate in competitive athletics. In laboratory studies they are persistent and behave as though they believe that with sufficient effort they can overcome a variety of obstacles or frustrations.
2. Exaggerated Sense of Time Urgency: Type A's show great impatience and irritation at delay (for example, in a traffic jam, in a waiting line).
3. Aggressiveness and Hostility: Type A's may not be generally more aggressive than other people, but they become more aggressive under circumstances that threaten their sense of task mastery, for example, when under criticism or high time pressure.

Individuals who manifest these behaviors to a great degree are called Type A's; those who show the opposite patterns of relaxation, serenity, and lack of time urgency are designated as Type B. The two types differ in many ways, including in their family environments (Woodall & Matthews, 1989).

A number of studies have suggested that Type A people may have at least twice the likelihood of coronary heart disease as Type B people. They also smoke more and have higher levels of cholesterol in their blood. Type A people also tend to describe themselves as more impulsive, self-confident, and higher in achievement and aggression. Both Type A men and women fail to report physical symptoms and fatigue (Carver et al., 1976; Weidner & Matthews, 1978). This tendency to ignore symptoms may result in a Type A individual failing to rest or to seek medical care in the early phases of heart disease and may be one reason why these people push themselves into greater risk of premature coronary death. Identifying individuals at high risk for heart disease and teaching them to pay more attention to physical symptoms may be an important part of programs aimed at reducing the toll of heart disease.

There may be a less strong relationship between the total pattern of Type A behavior and coronary disease than was suggested initially, especially among high-risk subjects (Matthews, 1984). Rather than looking at the relationship between the Type A pattern as a whole and coronary disease, it may be more useful to isolate such specific components of the pattern as anger and hostility. These components were found to be related to coronary disease even in the more recent studies (Miller et al., 1996). In sum, it now seems that specific behaviors, rather than the more global typology, are linked to a higher risk of coronary disease.

Individual Differences on Dimensions

While typologies assume discontinuous categories (like male or female), traits are continuous dimensions like "friendliness" (see Figure 6.2). On such dimensions, differences among individuals may be arranged quantitatively in terms of the degree of the quality the person has (like degrees of "conscientiousness"). Psychological measurements usually suggest a continuous dimension of individual differences in the degree of the measured quality: Most people show intermediate amounts, and only a few are at each extreme, as Figure 6.2 shows. For example, on Jung's introversion-extraversion typology, individuals differ in the extent to which they show either quality but usually do not belong totally to one category or the other. It is therefore better to think of a psychological continuum of individual differences for most qualities.

Many psychologists who use a trait approach investigate such personality dimensions as aggressiveness, dependency, and the striving to achieve high standards of excellence. An example of such a dimension is "repression-sensitization," as was discussed in Chapter 5. Great differences have been found among people in the degree to which they show such dispositions.

The trait approach begins with the commonsense observation that individuals often differ greatly and consistently in their responses to the same psychological situation or stimulus. That is, when different people are confronted with the same event—the same social encounter, the same test question, the same frightening experience—each individual tends to react in a somewhat different way. The basic idea that no two people react identically to the same stimulus is shown schematically in Figure 6.3. Moreover, in

Figure 6.2
Examples of Discontinuous Categories (Types) and Continuous Dimensions (Traits)

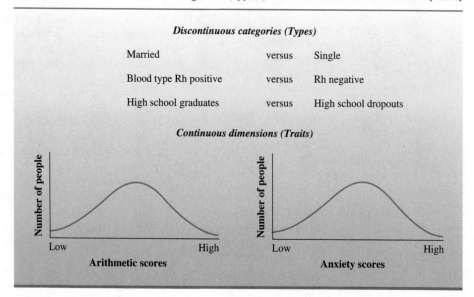

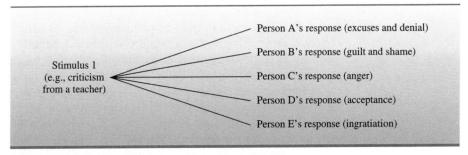

Figure 6.3
Individual Differences in Response to the Same Stimulus   The trait approach
emphasizes consistent differences among people in their response to the same
stimulus.

everyday life most of us are impressed with the distinctive *consistency* of one individual's responses over a wide variety of stimulus situations: We expect an "aggressive"
person to differ consistently from others in his or her responses to many stimuli. In its
simplest meaning, the term *trait* refers to consistent differences between the behavior
or characteristics of two or more people. Thus, "a trait is any distinguishable, relatively
enduring way in which one individual varies from another" (Guilford, 1959, p. 6).

In addition to using trait labels to describe individual differences, some theorists
also invoke the trait as an explanation: In their view the trait is the property within the
person that accounts for his or her unique but relatively stable reactions to stimuli.
Thus, the trait becomes a construct to explain behavior—a hypothesized reason for
enduring individual differences. Before examining formal trait theories, however, we
should consider how traits are used informally by people in daily life. Indeed, we are
all trait theorists in the sense that we generate ideas about our own dispositions and the
characteristics of other people.

Trait Attributions

When people describe one another in daily life, they spontaneously use trait terms. We
all characterize one another (and ourselves) with such terms as *aggressive, dependent,
fearful, introverted, anxious, submissive*—the list is almost endless. We see a person
behaving in a particular way—for example, sitting at a desk for an hour yawning—
and we attribute a trait—"unmotivated" or "lazy" or "bored" or "dull."

These simple trait attributions are often adequate to explain events for many
everyday purposes in commonsense psychology (Heider, 1958; Kelley, 1973; Ross &
Nisbett, 1991). In these commonsense explanations, traits are invoked not just as descriptions of what people do but also as the causes of their behavior. Thus, in everyday
practice, traits may be used first simply as adjectives describing behavior ("He behaves
in a lazy way"), but the description is soon generalized from the behavior to the person

("He *is* lazy") and then abstracted to "He has a lazy disposition" or "He is unmotivated." These descriptions pose no problems as long as their basis is recalled—he is construed as behaving in a lazy way and no more. A hazard in trait attribution is that we easily forget that nothing is explained if the state *we* have attributed to the person from his behavior ("He has a trait of laziness") is now invoked as the *cause* of the behavior from which it was inferred. We then quickly emerge with the tautology, "He behaves in a lazy way because he has a lazy disposition" or because he is "unmotivated."

The trait approach to formal personality study begins with the commonsense conviction that personality can be described with trait terms. But it extends and refines those descriptions by arriving at them quantitatively and systematically. Efforts to explain individual differences by formal trait theories face some of the same problems that arise when traits are offered as causes by the layman. However, numerous safeguards have been developed to try to control some of these difficulties (see Chapter 7).

Gordon Allport

One of the most outstanding trait psychologists was Gordon Allport, whose conceptions of traits have had an important influence for more than 30 years. In Allport's theory, traits have a very real existence: They are the ultimate realities of psychological organization. Allport favored a biophysical conception that

does not hold that every trait-name necessarily implies a trait; but rather that behind all confusion of terms, behind the disagreement of judges, and apart from errors and failures

of empirical observation, there are none the less *bona fide* mental structures in each personality that account for the consistency of its behavior (1937, p. 289).

According to Allport, traits are determining tendencies or predispositions to respond. These dispositions serve to integrate what would otherwise be dissimilar stimuli and responses. In other words, a trait is

a generalized and focalized neuropsychic system (peculiar to the individual) with the capacity to render many stimuli functionally equivalent, and to initiate and guide consistent (equivalent) forms of adaptive and expressive behavior (1937, p. 295).

Allport implied that traits are not linked to a small number of specific stimuli or responses but are relatively general and enduring: By uniting re-

Gordon Allport (1897–1967)

Stimuli		Responses
1. Meeting a stranger		1. outgoing, pleasant
2. Working with peers	Trait: friendliness	2. helpful, encouraging
3. Visiting family		3. warm, interested
4. Dating a girlfriend		4. attentive, thoughtful

Figure 6.4
An Example of a Trait as the Unifier of Stimuli and Responses

sponses to numerous stimuli, they produce fairly broad consistencies in behavior, as schematized in Figure 6.4.

Allport was convinced that some people have dispositions that influence most aspects of their behavior. He called these highly generalized dispositions **cardinal traits.** For example, if a person's whole life seems to be organized around goal achievement and the attainment of excellence, then achievement might be his or her cardinal trait. Less pervasive but still quite generalized dispositions are **central traits,** and Allport thought that many people are broadly influenced by central traits. Finally, more specific, narrow traits are called **secondary dispositions** or "attitudes."

Allport believed that one's pattern of dispositions or "personality structure" determines one's behavior. This emphasis on structure rather than environment or stimulus conditions is seen in his colorful phrase, "The same fire that melts the butter hardens the egg" (1937, p. 102). Allport was a pioneering spokesman for the importance of individual differences: No two people are completely alike, and, hence, no two people respond identically to the same event. Each person's behavior is determined by a particular trait structure.

According to Allport, traits never occur in any two people in exactly the same way: They operate in *unique* ways in each person. This conviction was consistent with his emphasis on the individuality and uniqueness of each personality. To the extent that any trait is unique within a person rather than common among many people, it cannot be studied by making comparisons among people. Consequently, Allport urged the thorough study of individuals through intensive and long-term case studies. He also believed, however, that because of shared experiences and common cultural influences, most persons tend to develop some *roughly* common kinds of traits: They can be compared on these common dispositions.

Many of Allport's theories were most relevant to the in-depth study of lives and experience rather than to the quantitative study of groups. He contributed to trait theory, but he was critical of many of the statistical methods and quantitative research strategies favored by other **trait theorists.** Nevertheless, his influence has been most important for the study of common "global" traits, for which he is still considered a model (Funder, 1991).

R. B. Cattell

Raymond B. Cattell (1950, 1965) is another important trait theorist. For Cattell, the trait is also the basic unit of study; it is a "mental structure," inferred from behavior, and a fundamental construct that accounts for behavioral regularity or consistency. Like Allport, Cattell distinguished between **common traits,** which are possessed by all people, and **unique traits,** which occur only in a particular person and cannot be found in another in exactly the same form.

Cattell also distinguished **surface traits** from **source traits** (see Table 6.1 for selected examples). Surface traits are clusters of overt or manifest trait elements (responses) that seem to go together. Source traits are the underlying variables that are the causal entities determining the surface manifestations. In research, trait elements (in the form of test responses or scores) are analyzed statistically until collections of elements that correlate positively in all possible combinations are discovered. This procedure, according to Cattell, yields surface traits.

For Cattell source traits can be found only by means of the mathematical technique of factor analysis (discussed further in Chapter 7). Using this technique, the investigator tries to estimate the factors or dimensions that appear to underlie surface variations in behavior. According to Cattell, the basic aim in research and assessment should be identification of source traits. In this view, these traits are divided between those that reflect environmental conditions (**environmental-mold traits**) and those that reflect constitutional factors (**constitutional traits**). Moreover, source traits may be either *general* (those affecting behavior in many different situations) or *specific*. Specific source traits are particularized sources of personality reaction that operate in one situation only, and Cattell pays little attention to them.

Cattell uses three kinds of data to discover general source traits: *life records,* in which everyday behavior situations are observed and rated; *self-ratings;* and *objective tests,* in which the person is observed in situations that are specifically designed to elicit responses from which behavior in other situations can be predicted. The data from all three sources are subjected to factor analysis. In his own work, Cattell shows a preference for factor analysis of life-record data based on many behavior ratings for large samples of persons. Some 14 or 15 source traits have been reported from such investigations, but only six have been found repeatedly (Vernon, 1964).

Raymond B. Cattell

Table 6.1
Surface Traits and Source Traits Studied by Cattell

Examples of surface traits (Cattell, 1950)	Integrity, altruism—dishonesty, undependability Disciplined thoughtfulness—foolishness Thrift, tidiness, obstinacy—lability, curiosity, intuition
Examples of source traits (Cattell, 1965)	Ego strength—emotionality and neuroticism Dominance—submissiveness

NOTE: These are selected and abbreviated examples from much longer lists.

In Cattell's system, traits may also be grouped into classes on the basis of how they are expressed. Those that are relevant to the individual's being "set into action" with respect to some goal are called **dynamic traits.** Those concerned with effectiveness in gaining the goal are **ability traits.** Traits concerned with energy or emotional reactivity are named **temperament traits.** Cattell has speculated extensively about the relationships among various traits and the development of personality (1965).

H. J. Eysenck

Hans J. Eysenck

The extensive research of the English psychologist Hans Eysenck has complemented the work of the American trait theorists in many important ways. Eysenck (1961, 1991) has extended the search for personality dimensions to the area of abnormal behavior, studying such traits as neuroticism. He also has investigated **introversion-extraversion** as a dimensional trait (although Carl Jung originally proposed "introvert" and "extravert" as personality *types*). Eysenck and his associates have pursued an elaborate and sophisticated statistical methodology in their search for personality dimensions. In addition to providing a set of descriptive dimensions, Eysenck and his colleagues have studied the associations between people's status on these dimensions and their scores on a variety of other personality and intellectual measures.

Eysenck emphasized that his dimension of introversion-extraversion is based entirely on research and "must stand and fall by empirical confirmation" (Eysenck & Rachman, 1965, p. 19). In his words:

The typical extravert is sociable, likes parties, has many friends, needs to have people to talk to, and does not like reading or studying by himself. He craves excitement, takes chances, often sticks his neck out, acts on the spur of the moment, and is generally an impulsive individual. He is fond of practical jokes, always has a ready answer, and generally likes change; he is carefree, easygoing, optimistic, and "likes to laugh and be merry." He prefers to keep moving and doing things, tends to be aggressive and loses his temper quickly; altogether his feelings are not kept under tight control, and he is not always a reliable person.

The typical introvert is a quiet, retiring sort of person, introspective, fond of books rather than people; he is reserved and distant except to intimate friends. He tends to plan ahead, "looks before he leaps," and mistrusts the impulse of the moment. He does not like excitement, takes matters of everyday life with proper seriousness, and likes a well-ordered mode of life. He keeps his feelings under close control, seldom behaves in an aggressive manner, and does not lose his temper easily. He is reliable, somewhat pessimistic and places great value on ethical standards.

Eysenck and his colleagues recognized that these descriptions may sound almost like caricatures because they portray "perfect" extraverts and introverts while in fact most people are mixtures who fall in the middle rather than at the extremes of the dimensions (see Figure 6.5). As Figure 6.5 shows, Eysenck suggested that the second

Figure 6.5
Dimensions of Personality   The inner ring shows the "four temperaments" of Hippocrates; the outer ring shows the results of modern factor analytic studies of the intercorrelations among traits by Eysenck and others (Eysenck & Rachman, 1965).

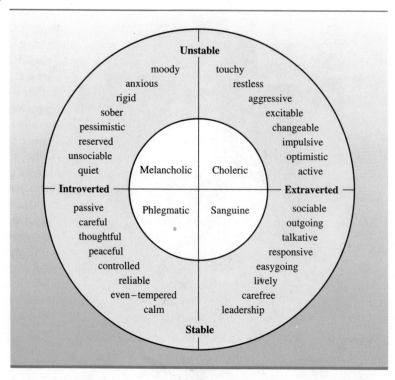

Table 6.2
Sexual Activities Reported by Introverted (I) and Extraverted (E) Students[a]

Activity	Males		Females	
	I	E	I	E
Masturbation at present	86	72	47	39
Petting:				
at 17	16	40	15	24
at 19	3	56	30	47
at present	57	78	62	76
Coitus (intercourse):				
at 17	5	21	4	8
at 19	15	45	12	29
at present	47	77	42	71
Median frequency of coitus per month (sexually active students only)	3.0	5.5	3.1	7.5
Coitus partners in the past 12 months (unmarried students only)				
one	75	46	72	60
two or three	18	30	25	23
four or more	7	25	4	17

[a]The numbers are the frequencies of endorsements by each group.

SOURCE: Based on data from Giese, H. & Schmidt, S. (1968). *Studenten sexualitat.* Hamburg: Rowohlt; cited in Eysenck, H. J. (1973). Personality and the law of effect. In D. E. Berlyne and K. B. Madsen (Eds.), *Pleasure, reward, preference.* New York: Academic Press.

major dimension of personality is **emotional stability** or **neuroticism.** This dimension describes at one end people who tend to be moody, touchy, anxious, restless, and so on. At the other extreme are people who are characterized by such terms as stable, calm, carefree, even-tempered, and reliable. As Eysenck stressed, the ultimate value of these dimensions will depend on the research support they receive.

To clarify the meaning of both dimensions, Eysenck and his associates have studied the relations between people's status on them and their scores on many other measures. An example of the results found is summarized in Table 6.2, which shows self-reported differences in the sexual activities of extraverts and introverts (reported in Eysenck, 1973). As expected, the extraverts generally reported earlier, more frequent, and more varied sexual experiences. While the groups differed on the average, there was still considerable overlap, making it difficult to predict any particular individual's behavior from his introversion-extraversion score alone. But the results of many studies of this type provide an increasingly comprehensive picture of Eysenck's dimensions. In addition, Eysenck's ideas are notable in stimulating a search for the biological foundations of dispositions (see *In Focus 6.2*).

COMMON FEATURES OF TRAIT THEORIES

Now consider the principal common characteristics of trait approaches.

In Search of the Biological Bases of Extraversion-Introversion

Hans Eysenck has led the way in trying to connect psychological dispositions to their biological foundations, focusing on the characteristics of extraverts versus introverts. According to Eysenck's theory (Eysenck, 1990; Eysenck & Eysenck, 1985, 1995), extraverts differ from introverts because of differences in their level of physiological arousal, specifically within the ascending reticular ascending system (ARAS). This system controls the level of stimulation that is transmitted to the central nervous system (CNS). In Eysenck's theory, introverts need only small amounts of stimulation to overstimulate their CNS, which then leads them to become withdrawn in their behavior. In extraverts, in contrast, the ARAS is not easily stimulated, which leads them to seek activities that will increase the level of stimulation, for example, by socializing more actively and seeking activies—such as parties—more than introverts.

Eysenck and colleagues tested this theory by conducting studies, which measured, for example, brain wave activity and cardiovascular activity. To illustrate, it was found that introverts show greater changes in their brain wave activity in response to low frequency tones, indicating their lower threshold for stimulation to the CNS, as the theory predicted (Stelmack & Achorn-Michaud, 1985). Although Eysenck's model of the biological mechanisms involved has been criticized for being too simplistic, his work is notable in trying to link personality to its biological foundations and it has received some support in later versions.

In related theorizing, for example, chemical injections and lesions observed in certain areas of the brain were used to pinpoint two neurological systems that seem to be involved in the differences between extraverts and introverts (Gray, 1991). These are the behavioral inhibition system (BIS), which according to these researchers is the more influential system in introverts, and the behavioral activation system (BAS), which is believed to be the more active system in extraverts (Gray, 1991). The theory suggests, for example, that because BAS is the more active system in extraverts they tend to focus on rewards and seek situations in which they could find them. This is in contrast to the more passive, avoidant behavior of introverts who are, in the theory, physiologically sensitized to punishment (e.g., Bartussek, Diedrich, Naumann, & Collet, 1993).

Generality and Stability of Traits

Trait theorists often disagree about the specific content and structure of the basic traits needed to describe personality, but their general conceptions have much similarity and they remain popular (Funder, 1991). They all use the trait to account for consistencies in an individual's behavior and to explain why persons respond differently to the same stimulus. Most view traits as dispositions that determine such behaviors. Each differentiates between relatively superficial traits (e.g., Cattell's surface traits) and more basic, underlying traits (e.g., Cattell's source traits). Each recognizes that traits vary in breadth or generality. Allport puts the strongest emphasis on the relative generality of common traits across many situations. Each theorist also admits trait fluctuations, or changes in a person's position with respect to a disposition. At the same time, each is committed to a search for relatively broad, stable traits.

Search for Basic Traits

Guided by the assumption that stable dispositions exist, trait psychologists try to identify the individual's position on one or more dimensions (such as neuroticism, extraversion). They do this by comparing people tested under standardized conditions. They believe that positions on these dimensions are relatively stable across testing situations and over long time periods. Their main emphasis in the study of personality is the development of instruments that can accurately tap the person's underlying traits. Less attention has been paid to the effects of environmental conditions on traits and behavior.

Inferring Traits from Behavioral Signs

In the search for dispositions one always *infers* traits from behavior—for example, from what people say about themselves on a questionnaire. The person's responses or behaviors are taken as *indicators* of underlying traits. The trait approach to personality is a "sign" approach in the sense that there is no interest in the test behavior itself. That is, test responses are of value not in their own right but only as *signs* of the traits that underlie them; test behavior is always used as a sign of nontest behavior (Loevinger, 1957). The trait psychologist is not interested in answers on an inventory or computerized score sheet for their own sake, but only in a subject's responses to a test as cues or signs of dispositions. It is therefore essential to demonstrate the relation between test behaviors and the traits they supposedly represent. We will consider efforts of this sort later (Chapter 7).

Quantification

A main feature of the trait approach has been its methodology. This methodology is "psychometric" in the sense that it attempts to measure individual differences and to quantify them. Psychometricians study persons and groups on trait dimensions by comparing their scores on tests. To do this, they sample many people, compare large groups under uniform testing conditions, and devise statistical techniques to infer basic traits (Chapters 7 and 8). Their methods over the years have become increasingly sophisticated and effective for meeting a wide range of measurement goals (e.g., Jackson & Paunonen, 1980; John, 1990).

TAXONOMY OF HUMAN ATTRIBUTES

A widely shared goal is to find a universal taxonomy or classification system for sorting the vast array of human attributes into a relatively small set of fundamental dimensions or categories on which most individual differences can be described. From this perspective, researchers attempt to identify "the most important individual differences in mankind" (Goldberg, 1973, p. 1). They assume that the most significant individual differences—those that are most important in daily human relationships—enter into the natural language of the culture as single-word trait terms. Using a variety of methods (discussed in Chapters 7 and 8) they try to identify basic trait terms in the language and to categorize them into comprehensive groupings. This classification task is an enormous one, given that thousands of trait terms (over 18,000 in one count) are found in English. The researchers hope that an extensive, well-organized vocabulary for describing human attributes in trait terms will lead to better theories of personality and better methods of personality assessment.

Psycholexical Approach

This research strategy is called the **psycholexical approach** and its basic data are the words in the natural language used to describe human qualities. In these studies, many people are asked to rate how well each of many trait terms describes or fits a particular person they know well. In some studies, this is a peer; in some studies, subjects rate how well the words describe them. In each study, the results are then analyzed to see which sets of trait terms tend to cluster or "go together" when individuals are described. Using statistical procedures called factor analysis (see Chapter 7), the researchers try to specify a small number of factors or dimensions that seem to capture the common element among adjectives that are closely associated.

This approach is illustrated in a comprehensive taxonomy of the domain of "interpersonal behavior" (Wiggins, 1979, 1980) that yielded the dimensions shown in Figure 6.6. Note that each dimension is bipolar, that is, has two opposite ends or poles. The

Figure 6.6
Wiggins' (1980) Taxonomy of the Interpersonal Domain

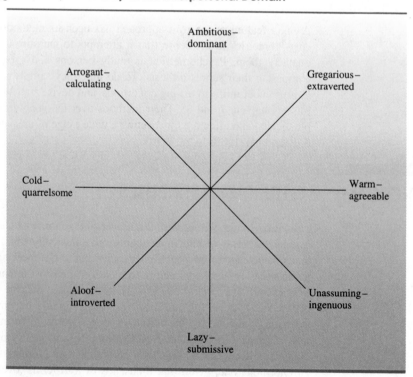

dimensions are structured in a circular pattern like a pie. Each pole is made up of a set of adjectives so that *Ambitious (Dominant),* for example, is defined with such terms as "persevering," "persistent," "industrious." The opposite pole, *Lazy (Submissive),* includes such terms as "unproductive," "unthorough," "unindustrious." Wiggins reports that these eight dimensions fit well the results of earlier descriptions of the interpersonal domain (Leary, 1957). They seem to be reasonably robust and useful when different samples of people are rated on them and continue to be revised and refined (Wiggins, Phillips, & Trapnell, 1989).

The "Big Five" Trait Dimensions

For many years in the long search for a "universal taxonomy" of traits, researchers disagreed actively as to which personality dimensions they should use to describe personality. Some proposed as many as 16; others, as few as two or three (Vernon, 1964).

More recently, however, consensus has grown among many researchers to focus on five dimensions of personality (Goldberg, 1991; John, 1990; McCrae & Costa, 1985, 1987) that emerge from ratings using English-language trait adjectives. These dimensions are neuroticism (for example, worrying and insecurity); extraversion (positive emotionality); openness to new experience; agreeableness; and conscientiousness, and they are shown in Table 6.3. They closely resemble similar dimensions initially proposed by

Robert R. McCrae

Paul T. Costa Jr.

Table 6.3
"Big Five" Trait Dimensions and Their Components

Trait Dimension (Factor)	Adjective Items[a]
I. Neuroticism (negative emotions, e.g., anxiety, depression)	Calm–worrying Unemotional–emotional Secure–insecure Not envious–jealous
II. Extraversion (positive emotionality)	Quiet–talkative Aloof–friendly Inhibited–spontaneous Timid–bold
III. Openness to experience (versus closed-minded)	Conventional–original Unadventurous–daring Conforming–independent Unartistic–artistic
IV. Agreeableness (versus antagonism)	Irritable–good natured Uncooperative–helpful Suspicious–trusting Critical–lenient
V. Conscientiousness (versus undirectedness)	Careless–careful Helpless–self-reliant Lax–scrupulous Ignorant–knowledgeable

[a]Illustrative adjectives describing the two ends of the scales that comprise the dimension

SOURCE: Adapted from McCrae, R. R., & Costa, P.T., Jr. (1987). Validation of the five-factor model of personality across instruments and observers. *Journal of Personality and Social Psychology, 52,* 81–90. Essentially similar results were found in John, O. P. (1990). The big-five factor taxonomy: Dimensions of personality in the natural language and questionnaires. In L. A. Pervin (Ed.), *Handbook of personality: Theory and research* (pp. 66–100). New York: Guilford Press; and in Normak, W. T. (1963). Toward an adequate taxonomy of personality attributes: Replicated factor structure in peer nomination personality ratings. *Journal of Abnormal and Social Psychology, 66,* 574–583.

Norman (1963) and found repeatedly in research. Each dimension includes a collection of bipolar rating scales, such as "calm–worrying" and "timid–bold," that refer to types of feelings or behaviors. For each dimension, Table 6.3 gives examples of the adjectives describing the two ends of some of the rating scales used.

To illustrate, in one study 187 college students rated how well each of 1,710 trait terms described him or her (Goldberg, 1991). Statistical analysis showed that these terms clustered into five major factors or dimensions much like those found by McCrae and Costa (1987) (Table 6.3). Thus, when people are described with trait terms, such as those shown in the table, a reliable clustering occurs consisting of five large descriptive categories. Now often called the **Big Five Structure,** these five factors seem to characterize major dimensions of personality in natural English-language words. Both personality trait questionnaires and personality ratings using these types of trait terms provide descriptions of persons that seem to fit these dimensions reasonably (Costa & McCrae, 1992; Costa, McCrae, & Dye, 1991).

FINDING MEANINGFUL PATTERNS OF INDIVIDUAL DIFFERENCES

Many researchers in the trait tradition also examine the relationships between an individual's position on personality dimensions and his or her behavior in other situations (Hogan, Johnson, & Briggs, 1997). For example, a group of school children may be tested for their intellectual abilities and also given questionnaires concerning beliefs and attitudes. In addition, they may be asked to rate themselves on a set of characteristics, and they may be rated by their teachers and their peers. The results are examined statistically to discover the associations (correlations) among all of the obtained measures. When very many associations emerge from this procedure, it often helps to simplify them by means of further statistical techniques. The findings of trait research help to illuminate what kinds of behaviors are most likely to occur together. The results help us to answer questions like these: Do aggressive children become aggressive adults? Are adolescent boys who are aggressive at home likely to be aggressive at school?

Prototypes: "Typical" People

Psychologists concerned with the classification of human attributes have also begun to identify how we judge the **prototypicality** or "typicality" of different members of a category, whether it is a trait category, such as one of the Big Five, or an everyday, "natural" category, such as the category "birds." To demonstrate the idea of typicality to yourself, think of the most typical, representative, or "birdlike" bird. You probably will think of a bird that is something like a robin or sparrow—not a chicken or an ostrich. The point is simply that some members of a category (in this case, birds) are better or more typical examples of a category: Some reds are "redder" than others, some chairs are more chairlike than others. This point has been elegantly documented for everyday categories of natural objects like furniture (Rosch et al., 1976). Thus, natural categories may be organized around *prototypical* examples (the best examples of the concept), with less prototypical or less good members forming a continuum away from the central one (Rosch, 1975; Tversky, 1977).

The important point here is that trait categories, like other categories, often are not well-defined, distinct, nonoverlapping categories in which each member of a category has all its defining features. (While many birds sing, not all do, and some nonbirds surely do.) Well-defined, nonoverlapping categories are built into artificial, logical systems, but they are rare in the real world. If we turn from the abstract world of logic and formal, artificial systems to common, everyday categories—to furniture, birds, and clothing—the categories become "fuzzy." As the philosopher Wittgenstein (1953) first pointed out, the members of common, everyday categories do not all share all of a set of single, essential features critical for category membership. If you closely examine a set of natural objects all labeled by one general term (like "birds") you will not find a single set of features that all members of the category share: Rather, a *pattern* of overlapping similarities—a *family resemblance* structure—seems to emerge.

"Typicality" and "family resemblance" and "fuzziness" also may characterize everyday judgments about categories of people (Cantor & Mischel, 1979; Cantor,

Mischel, & Schwartz, 1982; Chaplin, John, & Goldberg, 1988; John, 1990). When making these judgments while forming our everyday impressions of people, we seem able to agree about who is a more or less typical or even "ideal" kind of personality, just as we agree that a robin is a more birdlike bird than a chicken. For instance, such qualities as "sociable" and "outgoing" are the characteristics of a "typical extravert."

The study of prototypicality rules and family resemblance principles in judgments of people helps in understanding how consistency and coherence are perceived in spite of variations in behavior (Mischel, 1984). To illustrate, someone who really knows Rembrandt's work, who has seen dozens of his paintings, can easily identify whether a previously unseen painting is a real Rembrandt, an imitation, or a fake. The art expert seems able to extract a central distinctive gist from a wide range of variations. The same processes that permit such judgments must underlie how we identify personality coherence in the face of behavioral variability and agree that someone is or is not a "real" introvert, or an anxious neurotic, or a sincere, friendly person. One attractive feature of this prototypicality approach to traits is that it seems highly compatible with attempts to quantify interpersonal behavior into dimensions (John, Hampson, & Goldberg, 1991).

Act Trends: Traits as Summaries

Not all theorists view traits as causes. Buss and Craik (1983) moved away from the traditional trait view of dispositions as underlying internal causes (or explanations) of cross-situational consistencies in behavior. Instead, they see dispositions like the Big Five as summary statements of "act trends," not explanations. In this view, dispositions are natural categories made up of various acts. The acts within a category differ in the degree to which they are prototypical or ideal members. Perhaps most importantly, this view of dispositions emphasizes that dispositions do not provide explanations of behavior; instead, they are summary statements of behavioral trends that must themselves be explained (Buss & Craik, 1983; Pervin, 1994).

This revised view of dispositions reflects attempts to take account of the explanatory limitations of classical global trait theories like Allport's (1937), which have been widely criticized for several decades (Mischel, 1968; Ross & Nisbett, 1991; Pervin, 1994). It is a revision, however, that is by no means completely shared: Some voices still call for a return to the earlier approach to traits as global entities that provide adequate explanations (Funder, 1991).

Traits versus States

It is one thing to be irascible, quite another thing to be angry, just as an *anxious temper* is different from *feeling anxiety*. Not all men who are sometimes anxious are of an anxious temperament, nor are those who have an anxious temperament always feeling anxious. In the same way there is a difference between intoxication and habitual drunkenness . . .

Cicero (45 B.C.)

This ancient wisdom (quoted in Chaplin, John, & Goldberg, 1988) is used by modern trait theorists to illustrate a distinction that is often made, both intuitively and by trait psychologists, between *traits* and *states* (Chaplin, John, & Goldberg, 1988;

Eysenck, 1983). Both traits and states are terms that refer to the perceived attributes of people. Both refer to categories that have fuzzy boundaries, and both are based on prototypes or ideal exemplars (e.g., Cantor & Mischel, 1979). The difference between them is that prototypic traits are seen as enduring, stable qualities of the person over long time periods and as internally caused. In contrast, prototypic states refer to qualities that are only brief in duration and attributable to external causes, such as the momentary situation (Chaplin, John, & Goldberg, 1988). Examples of terms that people tend to classify as traits are gentle, domineering, and timid, while terms like infatuated, uninterested, and displeased tend to be seen as states.

Interaction of Traits and Situations

In recent years, it has been increasingly recognized that a comprehensive approach to the study of traits must deal seriously with how the qualities of the person and the situation influence each other—that is, their "interaction" (Higgins, 1990; Magnusson, 1990; Mischel & Shoda, 1995). The behavioral expressions of a person's traits depend on his or her psychological situation at the moment. For example, rather than exhibit aggression widely, an individual may be highly aggressive but only under some set of relatively narrow circumstances, such as when psychological demands are very high (Shoda, Mischel, & Wright, 1993; Wright & Mischel, 1987). Moreover, this aggressiveness may be expressed in some ways (such as verbally) but not in others (for example, physically). The implications of these specific interactions for contemporary personality theory will become evident when we consider the topic of interaction in later chapters.

SUMMARY

1. Since earliest times, people have labeled and classified one another according to their psychological characteristics. Typologies classify people into discrete categories. Among others, Hippocrates, Sheldon, and Jung have proposed typologies of personality, but the very simplicity that makes these typologies appealing also limits their value. An individual personality cannot be fitted neatly into one category or another.

2. Traits are continuous dimensions on which individual differences may be arranged quantitatively in accord with the amount of an attribute that the individual has.

3. In everyday life, people habitually use trait terms. They employ these terms not just to describe what people do but also to explain their behavior. We have not really explained anything, however, if after attributing a trait to a person on the basis of behavior, we later invoke that trait as the cause of the very behavior from which we inferred it.

4. Trait theorists conceptualize traits as underlying properties, qualities, or processes that exist in persons. Traits also are constructs to account for observed behavioral consistencies within persons and for the enduring and stable behavioral differences among them in their responses to similar stimuli (situations).

5. For Allport, traits are the ultimate realities of psychological organization. They are the mental structures that account for consistency in behavior. In his view, traits are predispositions to respond, and they serve to integrate what would otherwise be dissimilar stimuli and responses. Traits are relatively general and enduring, although they may range in generality from highly generalized cardinal traits through central to secondary traits or more specific "attitudes." An individual's "personality structure" is his or her pattern of dispositions or traits. Allport emphasized this structure, rather than the environment or stimulus conditions, in his analysis of human behavior. He stressed individual differences and the uniqueness of each person. Although he recognized some roughly common traits on which individuals can be compared, he urged the intensive study of the individual. He disapproved of many of the statistical methods and quantitative research strategies favored by other trait theorists.

6. Cattell distinguished between surface traits and source traits. Surface traits are identified by statistical correlations; source traits, by factor analysis. Through factor analysis Cattell tried to estimate the basic dimensions or factors underlying surface variations in behavior. Extensions of trait theory have been provided by Eysenck, who emphasizes the dimensions of introversion-extraversion and emotional stability (neuroticism).

7. In spite of their many differences, most trait theorists share the following theoretical assumptions and strategies:

   a. Traits are assumed to be general underlying dispositions that account for consistencies in behavior.

   b. Some traits are considered to be relatively superficial and specific; others that are more basic and widely generalized are assumed to produce consistencies across many situations.

   c. The predominant objective is the identification of underlying broad dispositions. Emphasis is on the measurement of an individual's position on one or more dimensions by means of objective instruments or tests administered under standard conditions.

   d. People's tested or sampled behaviors (including what they say about themselves) are viewed as signs of their underlying traits.

   e. To search for basic traits, a psychometric strategy is used that samples and compares large groups of subjects quantitatively under uniform conditions.

8. Researchers have long sought a universal taxonomy for classifying human attributes. In the psycholexical approach, people are asked to rate common trait words for how well they apply to various individuals, and the results are analyzed to identify basic dimensions of personality. The Big Five Structure emerged from these studies. It identifies five dimensions of personality: neuroticism, extraversion, openness to new experience, agreeableness, and conscientiousness. Each of these five broad dimensions (or factors) includes a number of specific personality characteristics represented as adjectives on a bipolar scale (for example, quiet–talkative, suspicious–trusting). Many trait researchers now agree that these five factors capture essential personality differences among individuals when they are described in terms of English trait adjectives.

9. In another approach to traits, the focus is on finding typical (prototypical or best) examples of particular categories about people. One tries to identify the pattern of overlapping similarities, "the family resemblance," shared by typical members of the category. For example, a typical extravert is sociable and outgoing. In this view, traits may be seen as summaries of behavior or "act trends," not as explanations of behavior. There is also increasing recognition that the qualities of the person interact with those of the situation(s) in which he or she functions.

Measuring Individual Differences

In this chapter you will learn how trait perspectives are applied to measure important individual differences. We begin by looking at the history of the trait approach to measurement. Later you will see some of the main methods that have grown from these theoretical roots. Most important, the trait approach has contributed basic concepts and measures to assess how individuals differ and to test hypotheses about their personalities. It permits a quantitative, orderly study of individual differences in an area that before had defied measurement.

Late in the 19th century, psychologists who pioneered the trait approach recognized the hazards of basing impressions of people on informal, subjective judgments about them. To avoid those dangers, they tried to go beyond casual impressions and to create more formal tests. Tests, they hoped, would measure important individual differences objectively and accurately. For these trait theorists any attempt to study personality without tests would be as naïve as a biological science without microscopes. Since the end of the 19th century there have been continuous efforts to study personality traits quantitatively by means of tests. This movement, often called the **psychometric trait approach,** has been one of the main forces in the study of personality; its roots extend far into the past and its implications for an understanding of personality are profound. It has yielded results that remain both important and controversial (Pervin, 1994; Rorer, 1990).

MEASURING INTELLIGENCE

Psychometric testing started in the psychological laboratories during the last decades of the 19th century. Sir Francis Galton was administering tests in his London laboratory as early as 1882 in an effort to establish an inventory of human abilities. He included measures of sensory acuity, reaction time, and strength of movement. His aim was to measure the resemblance between large numbers of related and unrelated persons to explore the role of inheritance. Galton also devised a questionnaire that was an important forerunner of those developed in later years.

James McKeen Cattell was an American psychologist who had a major role in the development of psychological testing. In 1890 Cattell suggested a standard series of tests for the study of mental processes. These tests were typical of the kind appearing at that time. They included measures of strength of grip, rate of arm movement, amount of pressure needed to produce pain on the forehead, reaction time for sound, and speed of color naming.

Tests of reading, judgment, and memory were also being used with some schoolchildren toward the end of the 19th century. A first attempt to evaluate test scores systematically is found in a study by T. L. Bolton that appeared in 1892. Bolton analyzed data from about 1,500 schoolchildren, comparing their memory spans with their teachers' estimates of their "intellectual acuteness." He found little correspondence. A 1901 monograph likewise reported disappointing results: The relationships found between Cattell's various tests at Columbia College and students' academic standing were negligible (Wissler, 1901).

The simple, specific sensorimotor measures popular in the laboratories at the end of the 19th century were important forerunners of later tests. But the tests favored during this period were laboratory-bound techniques for comparing individual differences on single measures rather than on organized scales. It was the development of intelligence testing in the early 20th century that made "psychometrics" a special and prominent field in its own right (Watson, 1959).

Intelligence Testing

Intelligence testing evolved in response to practical demands, mostly the need to separate the "uneducable" or severely retarded children into special schools that could give a simplified curriculum. In the 1890s, Alfred Binet, a Frenchman and a physician by training, began to try to measure intelligence. He wanted to discover how "bright" and

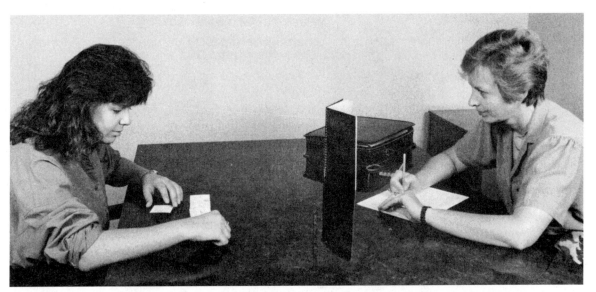

Intelligence testing may be useful for some purposes and populations, such as the prediction of grades earned in school, but also may have surprisingly limited value for many other goals.

"dull" children differ and started without any clear ideas about the nature of their difference. Binet and his associates believed that available tests lacked measures of complex processes and overemphasized sensory tasks. They hoped that individual differences in ability would be seen better in more complex tasks. Accordingly, they proposed a series of tests including measures of aesthetic appreciation, attention, comprehension, imagination, memory, mental imagery, moral feelings, muscular force, force of will, motor ability, suggestibility, and visual discrimination.

Ultimately, Binet's scales successfully differentiated children with respect to scholastic standing. The Binet scales were enthusiastically received because they seemed to fill the urgent need for a practical way to study mental processes. The test supplied a single overall score that offered a general and simple summary of mental status. It permitted ready comparisons among individuals in terms of their level of mental development. The Binet scales were revised and extended several times, most notably by Lewis M. Terman of Stanford University in 1916. Terman's revision pro-

Table 7.1
Sample Items Similar to Those on Tests Like the Stanford-Binet

Subtest	Sample Task
Absurdities	Identify what is wrong with a particular picture (e.g., a picture of a woman putting a telephone in the oven, a picture of a girl writing with a banana)
Analogies	Complete sentences that contain comparisons and contrasts (e.g., "A sock is to a foot as a glove is to a _____"; "A rooster is a male; a chicken is a _____")
Comprehension	Explain reasons behind social conventions (e.g., "Why do people brush their teeth?")
Digit reversal	Listen to five numbers read aloud and then recite them in reverse order
Memory	Repeat a sentence after hearing it read aloud Repeat a series of digits after hearing it read aloud Look at a series of pictures and then identify them from among others in the same order in which they were seen
Number series	Look at a series of numbers and complete the next three numbers in the series (e.g., 3, 6, 9 . . .)
Quantitative	Match, count, add, or order using blocks (e.g., take eight blocks out of a large pile of blocks; subtract three from eight using the blocks to illustrate computation)
Similarities	Listen to three words read aloud and tell how the first two words are alike but different from the third (e.g., table, chair, shirt)
Vocabulary	Define a word after hearing it read aloud (e.g., apple, believe, embarrassment, freedom)

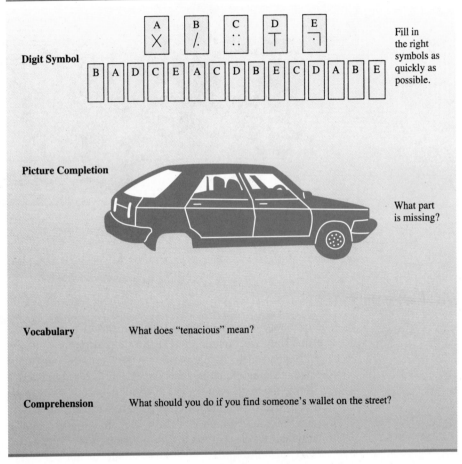

Figure 7.1
Items Similar to Those on Standard Intelligence Tests (Such as the Wechsler Intelligence Scale)

duced the now classic Stanford-Binet, which became a popular standard for all later work on mental ability testing (see Table 7.1).

Most of the developments in mental and personality testing have been influenced more or less directly by Binet's original work. Following his pioneering lead, an extremely influential series of intelligence scales that are still very popular was developed by David Wechsler. These scales assess the individual's standing in relation to many other people of the same age and have considerable practical value. The person's general **intelligence quotient** or **IQ** score summarizes the "full-scale" or total test achievement. The person's standing on the main subcomponents of the test also is computed. Items similar to those found on such IQ scales are presented in Figure 7.1.

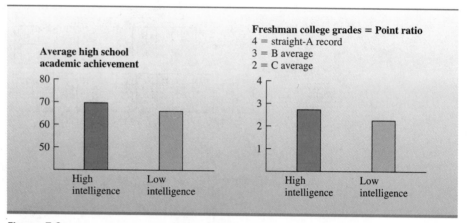

Figure 7.2
Academic Achievement in High School and in College for Groups of High and Low Intelligence

SOURCE: Wallach, M. A., & Wing, C. W., Jr. (1969). *The talented student.* New York: Holt.

What Is Intelligence?

The question remains: What is intelligence? At first, some testers tried to avoid this question simply by defining intelligence circularly as "whatever intelligence tests measure." Beyond such circular reasoning there is considerable disagreement about the nature and meaning of intelligence (e.g., Ceci, 1996; Sternberg, 1998).

Some theorists have argued that intelligence is a single *generalized mental ability* (called *g*) that is important for success in many mental tasks; others propose that it is made up of a large number of distinct, more *specific mental abilities* that are specific to particular tasks or problems. In a compromise, Thurstone (1938) suggested seven *primary mental abilities,* including verbal, memory, reasoning, and spatial abilities. Thurstone thought of them as distinct basic abilities that combine to determine performance on groups of complex tasks. In another direction, an extremely elaborate theory has been developed that suggests as many as 120 subcategories of intelligence (Guilford, 1967). The 120 subcategories represent elements of knowledge, skill for operating on these elements, and knowledge of the products (outcomes) of operations. Theorizing and research on the skills involved in intelligence continue actively (Baltes & Baltes, 1990; Cantor & Kihlstrom, 1987; Cantor, 1990; Sternberg, 1982, 1984, 1998).

At a simple, practical level, intelligence tests often predict later classroom achievements with reasonable accuracy (Ames & Walker, 1964). The practical value of intelligence tests for predictions and decisions beyond the classroom has often been assumed but with little proof (Cronbach, 1970). Consequently, one may legitimately criticize basing important nonschool decisions on such tests and seek better alternatives (e.g., Sternberg, 1989).

One large, classic study investigated the meaning of intelligence test scores from the verbal and mathematical portions of the **Scholastic Aptitude Test (SAT)** that most high school students take routinely (Wallach & Wing, 1969). As expected, they found the usual connection between high intelligence and superior academic performance in the classroom (see Figure 7.2).

The same researchers also examined the relations between intelligence and talented accomplishments outside the classroom in such areas as leadership, writing, science, and art. They found consistently that intelligence was unrelated to all measures of nonacademic accomplishment. In contrast, significant relations were found between nonclassroom achievements and simple measures of cognitive productivity or effort. (The productivity tests required subjects to generate ideas, for example, by naming as many uses as possible for everyday objects such as a chair, or by generating as many interpretations as possible of a series of abstract visual designs.) The authors concluded that the prediction of talent requires that we go beyond intelligence and include such considerations as the student's "cognitive vitality" or energy as one important ingredient of success beyond the classroom. A strongly motivated person, for example, might actually achieve more than a person whose test scores are 10 points higher but who is poorly motivated. Character sketches of two students, both with average intelligence but one with extremely high cognitive productivity and the other scoring low in this trait, are given in Table 7.2.

Table 7.2
Character Sketches of Students Differing in "Creativity" (Ideational Productivity) but Similar in Intelligence

John Ideational Productivity: Very High Intelligence: Average	Bob Ideational Productivity: Very Low Intelligence: Average
Involved in leadership roles in student government and other student organizations. Committed to activism and working with people.	Disappointed by high degree of liberalism on campus.
Political science major who gets good grades but is dispassionate toward the academic life. Feels an urgent need to "do something," to be effective in the practical world rather than extending his education past college.	Studies hard and although he occasionally questions his own diligence and wonders whether he would study so hard if not for his need to get good grades, he would not want any changes that would affect the prestige of his degree.
Wants to help teach others to find meaningful lives in society. "There are still people needed to teach values."	Desire for good grades is based on approval from family and others and on his career plans: getting into a good business school and then entering one of the many fields for which such preparation would qualify him.
Feels somewhat unsure about the future.	

SOURCE: Wallach, M. A., & Wing, C. W. (1969). *The talented student.* New York: Holt.

Other studies support the results of Wallach and Wing (1969) in showing that measures of academic ability may fail to predict real-life achievements outside the classroom to a surprising degree (Cantor & Kihlstrom, 1987; Gough, Hall, & Harris, 1963; Holland & Richards, 1965). Thus academic and nonacademic, artistic, scientific, and social achievements tend to be more independent than is often thought. An outstanding success in one field may be a painful failure in other endeavors, and school success may not generalize to success in life.

On the other hand, people who fail to complete schooling are less likely to succeed in the future; dropping out of high school is one of the best predictors of adjustment and occupational problems (Robbins, 1972). Poor classroom work or inadequate schooling are good ways to lock the door to many opportunities such as admission to professional and graduate schools and to the careers that they permit. Although children's scores on intelligence tests do not allow confident "long-term predictions for individual normal children," on the whole (for large groups), they do relate significantly to the ultimate level of education and occupation likely to be attained (McCall, 1977, p. 482).

Social and Practical Intelligence

In current work, the concept of intelligence is being refined and extended. The intelligence concept is being stretched to cover a wide range of different mental skills and different types of **domain specific knowledge and expertise** (Cantor, 1990; Cantor & Kihlstrom, 1987; Sternberg & Detterman, 1986). Important aspects of real-life competencies that are required for everyday effective coping, sometimes called **practical intelligence** or **social intelligence,** are receiving greater research attention. This new work calls attention to the sorts of everyday knowledge and social and cognitive skills that can be important for such life problems as figuring out how to be a good law student at Michigan, or an effective sales executive in a retail chain, or a more planful and organized person in everyday self-management. These new approaches to intelligence seek to identify key ingredients of real-life intelligence (Sternberg & Kolligian, 1990). They focus on three components of knowledge and understanding (Cantor & Kihlstrom, 1987).

Expertise.   The expertise component refers to the concepts and procedural rules needed to solve problems and to plan behavior. It consists of the type of knowledge and procedures that individuals need in order to be able to anticipate new situations and prepare for dealing with them.

Context.   A focus on context in intelligence requires a detailed analysis of the particular life contexts and tasks to which people direct their intelligence and effort. The types of contexts that will be relevant depend on the specific culture and persons studied. This focus, sometimes called "contextualism," makes it clear that a fair test of intelligence requires sampling the life tasks on which the individual's intelligence is customarily practiced. Thus, whether one is testing a person from another culture (e.g.,

The pragmatic aspects of intelligence refer to the diverse problem-solving strategies people use for meeting practical, real-life needs and goals.

newly arrived Vietnamese refugees in Los Angeles) or individuals from another subculture within the larger culture (e.g., young children versus middle-aged adults in middle-class urban America), appropriate contexts need to be selected.

Pragmatics (Practical Problem Solving for Multiple Goals).

"Intelligence is purposive. It is directed toward goals. . . ." (Sternberg, 1984, p. 272). **Pragmatics** refer to the practical aspects of intelligence through which people devise compromises for pursuing their goals realistically and flexibly. Because we all have many goals and only limited mental energies and capacities, our goals inevitably impose constraints and require that we divide our time and resources. Pragmatic solutions are ways of moving toward goals with methods that "suffice" but are necessarily imperfect. The focus on pragmatics shared by these new approaches to intelligence puts problem solving at the core of the intelligence construct itself (Cantor & Kihlstrom, 1987). It requires taking careful account of the person's changing life contexts, multiple goals, and particular culture. It suggests that intelligence is not "what intelligence tests measure," as has often been said about traditional IQ tests, but rather the mental (cognitive) strategies and skills and the knowledge, rules, and expertise people need to deal with life tasks in their real-world contexts.

Emotional Intelligence (EQ)

One example of the cognitive competencies relevant for daily experience is seen in the ability to purposefully delay immediate gratification in order to obtain a preferred but delayed outcome. This ability has been measured in preschool in what has become widely known as the "marshmallow test," described in a best-selling book about "emotional intelligence" by Daniel Goleman:

> Just imagine you're four years old and someone makes the following proposal: If you'll wait until after he runs an errand, you can have two marshmallows for a treat. If you can't wait until then, you can have only one—but you can have it right now. It is a challenge sure to try the soul of any four-year-old, a microcosm of the eternal battle between impulse and restraint, id and ego, desire and self-control, gratification and delay (Goleman, 1995, pp. 80–81).

IN FOCUS 7.1   *What EQ Is Not*

At the same time that the concept of intelligence and IQ became the target of increasing criticism, a related concept called Emotional Intelligence (EQ) has become popularly embraced. It was featured on a 1995 *Time* magazine cover that asked "What's your emotional intelligence (EQ)?" (but never said how you could find out) and served as the title of a worldwide best seller that promoted EQ over IQ (Goleman, 1995). The term itself, first introduced by Salovey and Mayer (1990), refers to a concept that has many meanings, diverse definitions, and no single measure to assess it. As Salovey (1997, APS) lamented, after all the popularizing, emotional intelligence is in danger of becoming a confused and ultimately lost idea. As he notes, it is sometimes equated with optimism, sometimes with persistence and zeal, sometimes even with having a 'good character' or being a dependable, nice person, and often with delay of gratification. And surely it is not equivalent to any of those. For example, the research on the measurement of delay of gratification in preschool and its links to later positive developmental outcomes cited in the text became abbreviated in the media as the "marshmallow test" and treated as if delaying on that measure in preschool was "the" route to guarantee success in later life. But while simplistic definitions like these do risk making the concept meaningless (and have parents eager to learn what they can do to make their preschoolers wait longer

for the marshmallows!), it would be a pity to lose it altogether.

There are many valuable ingredients in the EQ construct, most notably the recognition that social-emotional problem solving and competence are key aspects of adequate functioning. Although that may involve intelligence as traditionally defined, it goes beyond IQ to self-regulatory strategies and diverse social-emotional coping skills needed to effectively pursue long-term life goals in the face of adversity and frustration. It calls attention to the fact that in the course of development, in order to cope adequately, people need to be able to deal with emotional and motivational conflicts and challenges, not just with cognitive problem solving of the sort emphasized in schoolwork.

Like all complex psychological ideas, the concept of social-emotional intelligence cannot be defined by any single measure. Rather, it takes its meaning from the network of construct validation research that measures it, tests it, and progressively clarifies it by specifying just what it does and does not predict. And while at present it may be easier to say what EQ is not than to assess just what it is, it seems important to pursue this construct further to identify its ingredients more precisely. It is hoped this will be a step toward an enriched view of human ability broadly conceived to include the strategies that enable social-emotional-cognitive adaptation.

In fact, it has been found that the number of seconds a child waits in certain situations of this type in preschool may significantly predict such long-term academic outcomes as SAT scores as well as various social and cognitive competencies in early adulthood (Mischel, Shoda, & Rodriguez, 1989; Shoda, Mischel, & Peake, 1990). These results were statistically significant, surprisingly strong, and theoretically important, but they still do not allow confident predictions about individuals (see *In Focus 7.1*).

Intelligence, Family, and the SAT

The Scholastic Aptitude Test (SAT), a measure of verbal and quantitative skills, is given routinely to high school seniors and is used by colleges in their admissions decisions. The average score of high school seniors in 1962 was 490, but it has declined steadily, falling to about 450 by 1975. What accounts for the decline? Speculations about the possible reasons include an erosion of interest in basic language skills and the negative effects of television, but there is no hard evidence to support either of these interpretations. A fascinating alternative has been developed (Zajonc, Markus, & Markus, 1979; Zajonc, 1986).

Robert Zajonc speculated that the intellectual growth of each child depends on the total intellectual environment of the whole family. In turn, the total intellectual environment of the family may be defined as the average of the intellectual level of all its members (including the newborn). Note that intellectual level here does not mean IQ but refers instead to the absolute level of mental growth, or to the "mental age," of the members. Suppose, for example, that the intellectual level of a newborn first child in a family is 0 and the level of each parent has reached its maximum of 30 units. In that case, the child's intellectual environment will have an average value of 20. We arrive at that figure by simply adding the child's level (0) to that of each parent (30 + 30) and dividing by the total number in the family to obtain the average level, $(0 + 30 + 30) \div 3 = 20$.

Now consider what happens if a second child is born when the first child has reached a level of, let us say, 4 units. The intellectual environment entered by the second born will be:

$$\frac{0 + 4 + 30 + 30}{4} = 16$$

Suppose a third child is born when the first one has reached a level of 7 units and the second child is at a level of 3 units. The family's intellectual environment becomes a mere 14:

$$\frac{0 + 7 + 3 + 30 + 30}{5} = 14$$

The crucial point made by these examples is that each additional child depreciates the family's intellectual environment. It follows that intelligence declines with family size so that a family with fewer children is more likely to have brighter ones. Likewise, intelligence would decline with birth order, children who arrive later becoming less bright. Of greatest importance is the spacing between children. The shorter the spacing between siblings, the lower the intellectual environment will be that each addition to the family enters. A number of interesting predictions are made by the model, and they have received some promising support.

For example, the model predicts that twins should score lower on intelligence tests than nontwins because twins have the shortest possible gap in age of any siblings. Even if twins are the firstborn in the family used in our example, their intellectual environment at birth is only 15:

$$\frac{0 + 0 + 30 + 30}{4} = 15$$

Recall that in the same family, the intellectual environment of a firstborn child if he did not have a twin would be:

$$\frac{0 + 30 + 30}{3} = 20$$

No matter how young the firstborn nontwin would be at the birth of the second child, the intellectual level of his environment still would be greater than the environment of 15 into which the twins would be born.

In fact, twins do score consistently and significantly lower than singly born children on tests of intelligence such as the National Merit Scholarship Qualification Test (Breland, 1974). Moreover, twins whose co-twins were stillborn or died within the first four weeks score nearly as high on intelligence tests as singly born children (Record, McKeown, & Edwards, 1970). Might these effects be due to physiological differences that favor the surviving twin? That explanation seems unlikely because the birth weights (and general health) of twin pairs in which one twin dies early are lower than in pairs where both survive. Hence, differences in the intellectual environments of the children seem to be a more reasonable explanation of the total findings.

The drop in SAT scores since 1962 noted at the start of this section can be understood as reflecting the decline in the proportion of firstborns taking the test. As the number of firstborns decreased, so did the average SAT score. But now a new trend is beginning to appear. Families have been getting smaller and the proportion of firstborns is climbing. Zajonc predicted that these trends should be reflected in higher SAT scores beginning in the mid-1980s.

Zajonc's predictions made in 1976 seem to be receiving further support: The 1980s saw a rise in SAT scores, just as the theory prophesized. The continued decline in family size next led Zajonc to predict in 1986 that SAT scores should rise further until the end of the century and then level off and begin to decline (Zajonc, 1986). This prediction seems to be supported by the results so far (Zajonc & Mullally, 1997). Of course, changes in family size are only one of the many causes that may underlie these shifting test score patterns, but the fact that this theory leads to clear predictions that have received encouraging support so far will make it interesting to see how they fare in the future.

THE NATURE OF TRAIT TESTS

The traditional psychometric approach to the study of personality relies on tests to tap personality traits. These traits or dispositions are assumed to be quantifiable and scalable. As J. P. Guilford, a leading spokesman for the psychometric trait position, said:

> By [scalability] we mean that a trait is a certain quality or attribute, and different individuals have different degrees of it. . . . If individuals differ in a trait by having higher or

lower degrees of it, we can represent the trait by means of a single straight line. . . . Individual trait positions may be represented by points on the line (Guilford, 1959, pp. 64–65).

Personality Measurement: Early Roots

Early questionnaires to measure individual differences in personality arose in the wake of the successful measurement of intelligence and flourished especially during the 1920s and 1930s. Interest in self-description or self-report as a method of personality assessment was stimulated by an inventory devised during World War I (Watson, 1959). This was Woodworth's *Personal Data Sheet,* later known as the *Psychoneurotic Inventory.* It was aimed at detecting soldiers who would be likely to break down under wartime stress. Because it was impractical to give individual psychiatric interviews to recruits, Woodworth listed the kinds of symptoms psychiatrists would probably ask about in interviews. He then condensed them into a paper-and-pencil questionnaire of more than 100 items. Examples are: "Do you wet your bed at night?" and "Do you daydream frequently?" The respondent must answer "yes" or "no" to each question. Soldiers who gave many affirmative responses were followed up with individual interviews. This method was valuable as a simplified and economic alternative to interviewing all subjects individually. Often questionnaires are still employed as substitutes for interviews (Hogan, Johnson, & Briggs, 1997).

The Woodworth questionnaire was not used widely, but it was a forerunner of the many other self-report devices that flourished in the next two decades. These self-reports compared people usually with respect to a single summary score. This total score served as an index of their "overall level of adjustment," just as single scores or mental quotients were developed to describe the level of "general intelligence." In addition to efforts to assess adjustment, attempts to measure individuals on various personality dimensions soon became extremely popular.

Scoring: Allowing Comparisons

Traits like aggressiveness or introversion, or submissiveness or masculinity, for example, may be thought of as like physical dimensions. It is assumed that individuals differ from one another more or less enduringly in the degree (or amount) to which they possess each of these attributes. It is also assumed that at least some traits are *common* in the population. Measurement usually proceeds with respect to one trait at a time. On the basis of test results, each individual is assigned a point position on a single trait scale. It is generally assumed that most traits are scalable in some way and can be described quantitatively.

Given these assumptions, the challenge is to find the appropriate measure for important personality traits (Guilford, 1959). To illustrate, Figure 7.3 depicts a hypothetical profile of test scores on eight trait scales for one person. The profile suggests that this person's scores were highest on the "submissiveness" test, lowest on the "aggressiveness" test, and intermediate on the other measures.

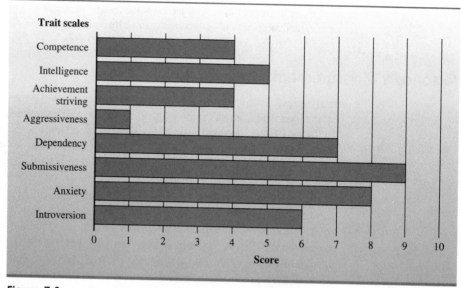

Figure 7.3
One Person's Hypothetical Test Profile on Eight Trait Scales

But what do these scores mean? Just how high or low is this person on each of these attributes? The scores have little meaning unless they can be compared with norms or with the scores of other people who took the same tests. Trait psychologists compare the scores of different people on one measure at a time, as Figure 7.4 illustrates. The figure shows a hypothetical distribution of scores for 230 people on a dependency scale.

Figure 7.4
Number of People at Each Score Level on a Dependency Test

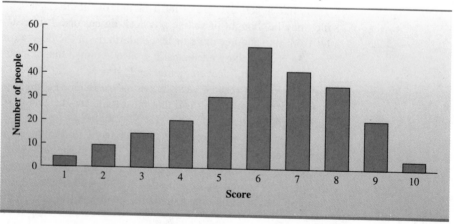

This person's dependency score was 7 (as shown in Figure 7.3). A comparison of this dependency score with the data in Figure 7.4 suggests that this score was the same as that of 40 of the 230 tested people. Only 60 people scored higher, and 130 scored lower than he did.

The meaning of these comparisons depends, of course, on many considerations, such as the appropriateness of the comparison sample. For example, how many of the 230 people were much older or younger than this individual? How many came from utterly different backgrounds or were of the opposite sex? Most important, the meaning of the scores depends on the nature and quality of the test.

Self-Reports and Ratings

Data about persons can be obtained from three sources: People may report or rate (judge) aspects of themselves; other people may judge the person; or performance may be elicited and observed directly.

Figure 7.5
Examples of Different Types of Structured Test Items

I have many fears.

Yes No Unsure (Circle your answer.)

Most police officers are really friendly.

−3 −2 −1 0 1 2 3

Strongly disagree … Strongly agree

(Circle the number that indicates your degree of agreement or disagreement.)

Falling in love can be more trouble than it's worth.

Never Rarely Sometimes Often Always

(Check the point that best fits your feeling.)

My anger at people usually is:

Very low Below average About average Above average Very high

(Check the point that best describes you.)

I suffer from many aches and pains.

1 2 3 4 5 6 7

Lowest … Highest

(Check the degree to which this statement is true for you.)

Psychometric inferences about traits usually have been based on self-reports. The term *self-report* refers to any statements people make about themselves; "structured" self-reports are statements in the form of restricted reactions to items. On structured self-report tests, respondents must react to sets of questions or items with one of a limited number of prescribed choices (e.g., "yes," "no," "strongly agree," "frequently," "don't know"). Examples are shown in Figure 7.5. These items contrast with open-ended or unstructured tests (like the projective devices in Chapter 4), on which subjects may supply their own reactions freely. The distinction between "structured" and "unstructured" or "open-ended" tests is a matter of degree only. The extent to which a test is structured depends on the items and the instructions to the subjects: Less structured techniques allow greater variation in response.

Many formats have been devised for trait ratings (see Figure 7.5). On some scales, for example, participants may be told that "7" indicates that the item is completely applicable to themselves and "1" indicates complete nonapplicability, and that they should check the point on the continuum that describes their own reactions. Scales like this ask people to express the extent of their agreement or disagreement with the particular item or to rate themselves with respect to the particular descriptions supplied. They may also be asked to judge the attributes of other people they know, for example, their peers at work or in school, on bipolar scales of adjectives like those used in the trait approach to personality dimensions (e.g., John, 1990; McCrae & Costa, 1987), as discussed in Chapter 6, and as the examples in Figure 7.6 illustrate. On each of many scales like this one, people rate themselves or their peers.

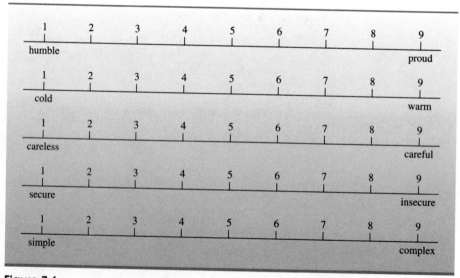

Figure 7.6

Examples of Adjective Scales Rate yourself for the degree to which these terms describe you. (Check the point that describes you best on each scale.)

SOURCE: Adapted as illustrations, selected from 40 adjective items used by McCrae and Costa (1985, 1987) to identify personality dimensions from ratings and questionnaires.

Objectivity: Are the Procedures Standardized?

Objectivity in the study of personality is the condition that exists when every observer (or "judge") who sees a particular sample of behavior (for example, a test answer sheet) draws the same conclusions from it. Objectivity depends on the entire testing procedure. That includes the interaction between the examiner and subject, the instructions and test items, the available response choices, and the scoring and interpretation procedures. Anything that enhances the uniformity of the testing conditions to which different subjects are exposed increases the objectivity of a test. Objectivity is also furthered by standardized (uniform) test materials, instructions, answer sheets, and scoring procedures. Effective standardization requires uniformity in other conditions that could affect test performance. Depending on what is being measured, these conditions may include the time of administration, the physical conditions under which measurement occurs, the sex of the examiner, and so on. The psychometrician thus attempts to make the stimulus material as uniform as possible by giving everyone the same standardized test and directions.

A lack of objectivity increases the risk of bias. It certainly would be unfair to test some people with a "friendly" examiner in a comfortable, relaxed setting but others with a "cold" examiner in a noisy, crowded room. Likewise, objectivity is reduced and fair comparisons among people are prevented if the test questions are changed on different occasions or scored differently depending on the prejudices of the tester or other momentary whims.

No matter how careful the attempt to maintain objectivity may be, it is beset with problems. In practice it has become increasingly evident that scores on any personality trait test are affected by all sorts of variables that are irrelevant to the trait the test is trying to measure. For example, even such gross examiner and participant characteristics as sex, as well as such subtler attributes as friendliness, may affect scores (Masling, 1960; Mischel, 1968). Other irrelevant characteristics of the respondent, such as his or her manner, may significantly affect the examiner's evaluation of the test results. There are many possible sources for bias. More attractive or appealing persons, for example, may be scored more liberally, even when scoring is relatively objective and standardized, as it is on intelligence tests (Masling, 1959).

In spite of some early hopes to the contrary, no psychological test provides anything remotely like a mental X-ray. A test merely yields a sample of behavior under particular conditions. The observed behavior is always elicited in a context— in a psychological situation. No matter how carefully standardized, the test is never able to eliminate or "control out" all determinants other than the trait of interest. The consistency and meaning of what is being sampled, therefore, must be demonstrated and cannot be assumed no matter how uniform the conditions may be for all people who take the test.

Correlations: What Relates to What?

The specific techniques for assessing the consistency and meaning of test behavior are considered in later chapters. At this point, just note that most applications of trait psychology involve a search for *correlations* among tests (Chapter 1). Such correlations simply examine the degree of association (relation) between the scores achieved by a group of individuals on one set of measures with their scores on another set. For example, do people who score high on Test 1 also tend to score high on Test 2, and do those who score low on Test 1 also score low on Test 2? To the degree that the relative position of individuals remains consistent across the measures, high correlations are obtained; conversely, when relative positions change easily, correlations decrease, indicating that responses to the two tests are not as closely related. When correlations between tests are high, responses on one test can be used to predict responses on the other; for example, if you succeed on 1 you are likely to succeed on 2. When correlations are low, one cannot predict performance (relative position) on one test from knowing scores on the other test.

Moderator Variables

The relations between any two variables often depend on several other variables. These **moderator variables** may influence the correlations found in trait research. For instance, correlations between measures of risk-taking and impulsivity may be found for males but not for females; they may even be negative for one sex but positive for the other. Similarly, relations between two measures might be positive for children with low IQ but negative for highly intelligent children, or they might occur under "relaxed" testing conditions but not under "anxious" conditions.

The concept of moderator variables was introduced to trait theory to refer to the fact that the effects of any particular disposition generally are "moderated" by or dependent upon many other conditions and variables. Such variables as the person's age, sex, IQ, the experimenter's sex, and the characteristics of the situation all are common moderators of test behavior. For example, people who perceive themselves as consistent on a trait such as "friendliness" might actually be more consistent in their friendly behavior across situations than those who do not see themselves as consistent on this trait (Bem & Allen, 1974). Moderator variable effects like these may make it possible to at least predict some of the people some of the time, as Bem and Allen suggested. Evidence is found in support of the value of such moderator variables (Sarason & Sarason, 1990; Zuckerman, Koestner, DeBoy, Garcia, Maresca, & Sartoris, 1988), but by no means all of the time: The extent and importance of moderator variable effects for personality measurement is still being debated (Chaplin, 1991).

PERSONALITY SCALES: EXAMPLES

So far we have been considering tests in general, ignoring the individual person. It is time to apply those methods to individuals. Therefore, we now turn again to "Gary W.," our case history, whom we glimpsed before from a psychodynamic perspective. Here is what one of his friends says about him.

Impressions of Gary W. by a Fellow Graduate Student

From the moment I first met Gary, one year ago, he seemed likable enough, but he always seemed preoccupied. His personality had a forced quality, as though he were trying to be something he wasn't. Central to his personality is his overconcern with himself. It's not conceit, but rather continual self-observation and self-criticism. In personal relationships he seems always to be trying to figure out what the other person expects of him and seems to have no personality of his own. He can be friendly and outgoing with a shy, self-conscious person. He often displays a cynical humor and arbitrary bossiness bordering on personal insult, which seems to be his only method of feeling at ease. Feeling at ease seems to mean dominating the relationship as completely as possible. If he encounters someone more capable than he is, Gary tends to draw back within himself, too afraid of being shown up by the other person to develop any kind of close relationship. Gary is something of a "loner." He has few close friends, since his relationships are based on domination (or fear of being dominated) rather than companionship. Gary is very conscious of social standards, grades, any measure of superiority. If he doesn't reach the mark, he feels he is a failure, but even if he does, he seems not to be satisfied. An ironic feature of his personality is that though he seems to seek attention, he is uncomfortable once he gets it. When speaking to a group of people, he becomes extremely nervous and, at times, so confused that he cannot continue and starts falling apart. He wants to succeed. He is ambitious and able and very persistent. He seems really driven to do well.

The impression Gary's friend gives us, while interesting, is of uncertain value: We know neither its accuracy nor its meaning. Then how can we find out more about Gary? From the viewpoint of trait theory, we want quantitative information that reveals Gary's status on important dispositions so that we can compare him with others. One major step in that direction is provided by Gary's scores on psychometric tests. So that these data can be properly understood, they will be introduced in the context of our discussion of some major trait measures.

The MMPI

The most thoroughly studied questionnaire is the **Minnesota Multiphasic Personality Inventory (MMPI),** and it has become the basis for investigating many personality traits and types. The MMPI best illustrates the psychometric approach. This widely used, influential test contains a set of self-report scales that initially were devised to classify mental patients into types on many psychiatric dimensions (Hathaway & McKinley, 1942, 1943). In format, the MMPI comprises 550 printed statements to which one may answer "true," "false," or "cannot say" (undecided). The items range over diverse topics and differ widely in style. They inquire into attitudes, emotional reactions, psychiatric symptoms, the subject's past, and other content, with items similar to these:

> Sometimes I think I may kill myself.
> My greatest troubles are inside myself.
> I certainly have little self-assurance.
> I wish I were not so awkward.
> I am shy.

Self-report tests such as the MMPI are called "psychometric," "objective," and "standardized." These terms correctly describe the stimulus material, the scoring procedure, and the administration. The stimulus materials are objective and standardized or reproducible in the sense that they usually are presented as printed items on questionnaires, inventories, or rating scales. Likewise, the scoring procedure is objective because the respondent has to react to each question or item with one of a limited number of prescribed or "structured" choices by selecting, for example, from printed answers like "yes," "no," "strongly agree," "frequently," and "don't know."

Both the questions and the instructions on psychometric tests, however, usually require the respondent to go far beyond direct behavior observation and to supply subjective inferences about the psychological meaning of behavior. While the questions are standardized, that is, printed and always the same on each occasion, they often are vague. For example, the test asks questions like "Are you shy?" or "Do you worry a lot?" or "Is it really wise to trust other people?" Such items are ambiguous. They require one to evaluate behavior and generalize about it, rather than describe particular behaviors in particular contexts on clear dimensions.

People may not be willing or able to reveal themselves accurately in response to such items, especially when they are emotionally upset or aware that their answers may be used to make important decisions about them. Recognizing these problems (Meehl, 1945), researchers have tried to establish the meaning of particular answer patterns on the test by research (e.g., Edwards & Edwards, 1992).

The investigator starts with a pool of items and administers them to a group known to differ on an external criterion or measure (for example, males versus females or hospitalized versus nonhospitalized people). Ideally, the test scales are constructed so that ultimately only those items are retained that best discriminate among people who differ on the selected criterion. Suppose, for example, an item such as "I cry easily" tends to be answered affirmatively by people who have been hospitalized for psychiatric problems but not by those who have no history of psychiatric hospitalization. That item would be retained on a "maladjustment" scale.

The MMPI scales are administered to many groups of subjects, such as college students, medical personnel, and nonpsychiatric patients, as well as psychiatric patients who have been independently diagnosed as having symptoms of some type of schizophrenia. The items then are examined to determine the ones on which there are significant differences between the answers of particular diagnostic groups as compared with "normals." In this manner it becomes possible gradually to devise scales that discriminate among different groups of people.

MMPI items have been sorted into 10 basic scales named Hypochondriasis (Hs), Depression (D), Hysteria (Hy), Psychopathic deviate (Pd), Masculinity-femininity (Mf), Paranoia (Pa), Psychasthenia (Pt), Schizophrenia (Sc), Hypomania (Ma), and Social introversion (Si). It would be incorrect, however, to think that these scales tap what their names indicate. Instead, these labels serve as abbreviations for scales whose meanings are defined by their extensive correlations (associations) with other indices (e.g., psychiatrists' ratings of adjustment, scores on other personality questionnaires). These correlations have been amassed during decades of vigorous research with the scales, which continue to be studied and revised with sophisticated statistical methods (e.g., Tellegen & Ben-Porath, 1992).

In addition to the 10 basic scales, three "control" scales have been devised. The L or Lie scale was intended to measure the tendency to falsify about oneself by "faking good." High scores on this scale indicate that the individual has endorsed many items that suggest he does unlikely things such as daily reading of all the newspaper editorials or never telling a lie. The K scale, the second control, was intended to indicate defensiveness in the form of a tendency to present oneself in a more socially desirable way. The F scale, the third control, sought to tap the intrusive effects of answering the items carelessly and confusedly, as indicated by describing oneself as having rare and improbable characteristics.

The results of an individual's MMPI answers (or the summary of a group's average responses) may be recorded in the form of a "profile." Such a profile for our case, Gary W., is illustrated in Figure 7.7. Gary's position on each scale is summarized in terms of converted or **T scores.** These scores readily provide quantitative comparisons against norms. A T score of 50 is the average score for the particular normative reference group. Procedures have been developed to discriminate people with extreme scores for many different diagnostic and selection purposes. Collections of MMPI profiles have been "coded" in different ways and catalogued in "handbooks" or "atlases." They may be used to compare a single individual's profile to similar profiles and information collected in many cases (Gilberstadt & Duker, 1965; Marks & Seeman, 1963).

Gary's MMPI profile fits most closely a 2-8/8-2 code in the atlas developed by Marks and Seeman (1963, p. 137). We can see what types of information the atlas provides for individuals whose average MMPI profiles are most similar to Gary's. The atlas tells us that people with this type of profile are most often described with characteristics like these:

> Keeps his distance and avoids close relations with people, tends to fear emotional involvement with others, manifests his psychic conflicts with somatic symptoms, tends to be resentful, shows obsessive thinking, feels tense, jumpy, and high-strung.

The atlas also gives much other information found previously on the average for people with Gary's profile. These data are a helpful first step. How well they really fit

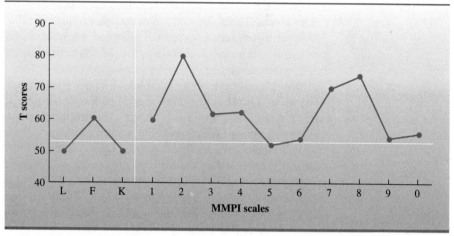

Figure 7.7
Gary's MMPI Profile

SOURCE: Marks, P. A., & Seeman, W. (1963). *Actuarial description of abnormal personality.* Baltimore: Williams & Wilkins.

Gary and how closely they match other data about him is still a question. On first impression, some of the atlas statements seem at least somewhat consistent with the impressions given by Gary's fellow graduate student, who also judged him to be "shy" and a "loner." On the other hand, the same student rated Gary as high in ambition, aspiration level, and "drive." These ratings seem to contradict parts of the atlas information. Specifically, the 2-8/8-2 atlas code lists high aspirations and ambitiousness as characteristics that are *least* descriptive of people with his profile. Who is right? Is Gary's friend inaccurate, or does this part of the atlas simply not fit Gary? To understand Gary better, we would need much more information about him.

The MMPI has become the model for dozens of other personality questionnaires. Many investigators drew on the large pool of MMPI items to create special personality scales (for example, dealing with anxiety), whose meaning they studied empirically. Popular descendants of the MMPI include the California Psychological Inventory (CPI), the Jackson Personality Inventory (1976), and the Taylor Manifest Anxiety Scale (MAS), illustrated next.

An Example: Trait Anxiety

MMPI scales and atlases have some practical value in personality assessment and clinical work. Many psychologists, however, are most interested in the search for theoretically important personality traits and have tried to use a variety of personality questionnaires for that purpose. A notable example is the measurement of an extremely significant psychological attribute, anxiety.

A classic distinction has been made between **state anxiety** and **trait anxiety** (Spielberger, 1966). State anxiety refers to a person's momentary or situational anxiety, and it varies in intensity over time and across settings. Trait anxiety, in contrast, refers to one's more stable, overall characteristic level of anxiety. Usually trait anxiety is measured by the person's self-report on questionnaires.

Anxiety inventories ask people to report the extent to which various anxiety responses generally characterize them. The MMPI is the forerunner and model for most anxiety questionnaires. For example, the most popular anxiety test, the Manifest Anxiety Scale or MAS (Taylor, 1953), borrowed from the pool of MMPI items. Construction of the scale started with selection of 200 items from the MMPI. These items were given to five clinical psychologists with instructions to identify those that seemed to tap anxiety. To facilitate judgment, the clinicians were given a lengthy description of anxiety reaction. Gradually the best items were selected and the meaning of the resulting scale was elaborated through extensive research. The items on anxiety scales like the MAS deal with various forms of anxiety such as feeling uneasy, worrying, perspiring, and experiencing unhappiness and discomfort (see Table 7.3).

Are people who feel anxious in some situations likely to feel anxious in many other situations? For instance, are people who are anxious about taking tests also likely to worry more about their health or their family? The basic question is: Does "anxiety" constitute a broadly generalized trait? To study this question, investigators assess the correlations among people's anxiety responses on diverse measures (Sarason, 1978).

Substantial correlations are often found among different self-report anxiety questionnaires that deal with topics like "test anxiety" (anxiety about taking tests) or more "general anxiety" reactions (Ruebush, 1963; Sarason et al., 1960; Sarason & Sarason, 1990). For example, the correlation between scores on the Test Anxiety Scale for Children and the General Anxiety Scale for Children tends to be highly significant. The associations become smaller, however, when anxiety is measured by diverse methods, involving response modes and formats other than questionnaires—for example, measures of physiological (autonomic) arousal and actual avoidance behavior. The correlations are highest for people who are most extreme in their self-reported anxiety (very high or very low). Especially interesting, some types of anxiety (e.g., about test taking) are debilitating because they produce excessive emotional distress and lead to avoidance and distraction, thus undermining performance. But test anxiety can also improve test scores if the person uses it to harness effort, solve problems, and prepare for the test (Rafferty, Smith, & Ptacek, 1997).

Table 7.3
Items Similar to Those on the Manifest Anxiety Scale

Item	High Anxiety Response
I rarely get really tired.	False*
I am not a worrier.	False
I cannot keep my mind focused on anything.	True
I almost never blush.	False
Often I cannot keep from crying.	True
It's hard for me to attend to a job.	True
Often I think I am no good.	True

*The person must respond "true" or "false."

The California *F* Scale

One of the most popular of these self-report measures is the **California *F* Scale** (Adorno et al., 1950). This measure was intended to assess authoritarian attitudes. It contains a set of items like these:

The most important thing to teach children is absolute obedience to their parents.

Any good leader should be strict with people under him in order to gain their respect.

Prison is too good for sex criminals. They should be publicly whipped or worse.

There are two kinds of people in the world: the weak and the strong.

No decent man can respect a woman who has had sex relations before marriage.

Strong agreement with items like these results in a high *F* Scale, or "authoritarianism," score.

Gary's score on the *F* Scale was slightly below average when compared to other college students. What does that imply about him? As with all scales, the meaning of high or low scores on this measure depends on the network of associations that have been found for the test in research.

An enormous set of correlations has emerged from more than 100 studies that have related *F* Scale scores to other variables. Correlations have been found, for example, with intelligence, family ideology, prejudice, anxiety, voting behavior, military reenlistment intent, and cooperation in psychological experiments (Titus & Hollander, 1957).

In one study among college students with high scores on the California *F* Scale (suggesting strong ideological conservatism), 76% stated they preferred the Republican party, whereas 65% of those low on the *F* Scale preferred the Democratic party (Leventhal, Jacobs, & Kurdirka, 1964). The relationships between *F* Scale scores and stated voting behavior indicated that students with high *F* Scale scores tended to choose the more conservative political candidate. Results like these are typical.

The *F* Scale is most strongly correlated with other paper-and-pencil measures, but not as closely associated with nonquestionnaire measures of interpersonal behaviors (Titus & Hollander, 1957). Correlations between the *F* Scale and other questionnaires sampling attitudes (for example, toward minority groups) sometimes are impressive. The relationships obtained between the *F* Scale and nonquestionnaire measures, on the other hand, tend to be much weaker. Scores on the *F* Scale also tend to be highly correlated with education; more highly educated people tend to respond in a much less authoritarian fashion (see *In Focus 7.2* on page 190).

The Q-Sort Technique

Another helpful way to study a person's traits is through a special rating technique. The **Q-sort** or Q technique consists of a large number of cards, each containing a printed statement (Block, 1961). The cards may contain such statements as "I am a submissive person," "I am likable," and "I am an impulsive person." Or the items might be "is a thoughtful person," "gets anxious easily," "works efficiently."

The Q-sort may be used for self-description, for describing how one would like to be (the ideal self), or even for describing a relationship. For a self-sort, clients would be instructed to sort the cards to describe themselves as they see themselves currently, placing cards in separate piles according to their applicability, ranging from those attributes that are least like them to those that are most like them. For example, the terms that Gary W. had indicated as most self-descriptive were: "haughty, determined, ambitious, critical, logical, moody, uncertain."

Or people might be instructed to use the cards to describe the person they would most like to be—their ideal person. To describe a relationship, they would sort the cards into piles ranging from those that are most characteristic of the relationship to those least characteristic. As these examples indicate, the method asks one to sort the cards into a distribution along a continuum from items that are least characteristic (or descriptive) to those that are most characteristic of what one is describing.

The items for a Q-sort may come from a variety of sources. They may stem from a particular theory of personality (Stephenson, 1953), from therapeutic protocols (Butler & Haigh, 1954), or from personality inventories (Block, 1961). It is also possible to use the Q-sort to describe the characteristics associated with successful performance in a given task. For example, one can find the profile of qualities "most characteristic" of people who succeed in a particular situation. One can then search for those individuals who best match that profile when trying to predict who will or will not do well in that type of situation (Bem & Funder, 1978). Likewise, Q-sorts are often used to characterize changes in development. For example, children who differed on certain tests in preschool may be compared in the Q-sort profiles that describe them in adolescence (Mischel, Shoda, & Peake, 1988).

Do the Measures Overlap?

Methods like those summarized in this section have many uses and often yield interesting correlations. But one must interpret the correlations found among tests carefully. For example, high correlations among paper-and-pencil inventories may partly reflect the fact that inventory constructors often borrow items from earlier inventories. Different tests actually may contain similar items presented in similar formats. Thus, Eysenck's (1952) measure for inferring neuroticism and extraversion-introversion contains such questions as: Are your feelings easily hurt? Are you rather shy? Do you find it difficult to get into conversation with strangers? Are you troubled with feelings of inferiority? Very similar items occur on such tests as the MMPI. Even within the subscales of a single test, items may overlap considerably. Shure and Rogers (1965) noted that the basic scales of the MMPI consist of items that overlap 69%, on the average, with items on one or more other scales of the test.

Campbell and Fiske (1959) analyzed many of the correlations that have been obtained among personality measures. They found that much commonality was attributable to similarity or overlap between the methods employed to elicit responses. In

IN FOCUS 7.2   *The Authoritarian Personality: The Current View*

After World War II, there was great interest in understanding what kind of persons could have submitted to authority and committed the atrocious acts of inhumanity in Nazi Germany during the Holocaust. Adorno and associates (1950) detailed such a personality type in their book, *The Authoritarian Personality*. Working within a psychodynamic framework, they portrayed this type as arising from early childhood experiences, particularly when parents forbid any unconventional behavior and harshly punish their child for it. Such experiences were believed to contribute to the development of an inadequate ego (in the psychodynamic sense of the term) that needed such defense mechanisms as projection of anger toward outgroups (rather than toward parents who were feared) in order to release the underlying aggressive and sexual impulses.

Measurement: The *F* Scale

The researchers began with in-depth interviews and projective tests and in time devised a questionnaire for the diverse aspects of authoritarianism they had identified, such as authoritarian aggression, authoritarian submission, conventionalism, and stereotyping. They labeled their questionnaire the *F* Scale, in which F stood for "Fascism"—an antidemocratic or autocratic type. Published as a 990-page book, this work was extremely influential, leading to thousands of studies examining the *F* scale and its correlations that included, for example, ethnocentrism, prejudice, trust in authorities, and dogmatism.

Scores on the scale turned out to have many interesting links to other aspects of personality, but the measure also had some serious methodological problems. For example, all the items were worded in the same direction (pro-authoritarianism), so high scores might simply reflect the person's tendency to agree ("yea-saying") rather than a tendency to fascism or an authoritarian type. High scores on the scale also were strongly related to lack of education, suggesting that a poor school background rather than a personality pattern might underlie the responses (Mischel, 1968).

other words, correlations among measures intended to tap different traits may reflect similarities between methods (Campbell, 1960; Campbell & Fiske, 1959). If, for example, three questionnaires are used to measure "dependency," the correlations obtained among them may be more due to similarity in the questionnaires than to the trait they intend to elicit. If different methods were employed (e.g., a questionnaire, a peer rating, and a Rorschach), the correlations would be substantially lower. On the basis of a review of relevant studies, Campbell and Fiske (1959) concluded that the effect of the method is usually greater than the effect of the trait measured. Applied to our case, this means that we have to be sure that the patterns of traits attributed to Gary do not merely reflect overlap among the questionnaires he has answered.

Moreover, we would want to know whether Gary's trait would test out identically if it were measured by a technique that is not a questionnaire. To be most confident of his level of authoritarianism, for example, we would want to see what he *does* with authority figures behaviorally as well as what he *says* about authority on questionnaires. To have faith that he is a "loner," fears emotional involvement, and is anxious, we would want to measure each of these attributes in several ways, not just by question-

Renewal of Interest

Interest in authoritarianism was renewed with the release of an abridged version of Adorno et al.'s book in 1982 and with new conceptualizations, in particular one offered by Altemeyer (1981, 1988, 1996). Adequately addressing previous criticisms (Christie, 1991), Altemeyer devised a reliable and valid scale. He narrowed the conception of authoritarianism into three aspects—authoritarian submission, authoritarian aggression, and conventionalism, which the scale tried to measure.

Empirical Support

Individuals identified as high on authoritarianism on Altemeyer's scale have been found (a) to be prejudiced toward a variety of groups, including homosexuals (Haddock, Zanna, & Esses, 1993) and people with AIDS (Peterson, Doty, & Winter, 1993); (b) to support conventional beliefs and issues such as religious fundamentalism (Hunsberger, 1995) and traditional gender roles (Duncan, Peterson, & Winter, 1997) and to oppose nontraditional ones such as abortion (Moghaddam & Vuksanovic, 1990) and drug use (Peterson, Doty, & Winter, 1993); and (c) to be punitive to criminals (see Altemeyer, 1996).

Why? When?

Most researchers on this topic have embraced Altemeyer's scale as well as his interpretation for the development of authoritarianism. In that view, this pattern is more likely to occur when the person is socialized in an authortitarian culture, peer group, and family in which authoritarian attitudes and behaviors are displayed by authority figures and rewarded, whereas more liberal or open-minded attitudes are punished and shunned. Although the original researchers on authoritarianism after World War II began by thinking they were describing a "German personality" type, research since then has shown that this pattern is not unique to any one country or people. It now has been found, for example, in samples in North America, Russia, South Africa, and Australia. Although much has become known about this pattern, much remains to be learned, particularly about the conditions and situations in which people with these attitudes will and will not act upon them. For example, when will authoritarians act aggressively and punitively toward other people and when will they not?

naires (West & Finch, 1997). Otherwise, how could we be sure that the impression we get of him reflects more than his manner of talking about himself on inventories?

Factor Analysis to Find Dimensions: The NEO-PI

Trait terms number in the thousands and unless simplified and organized are unmanageable as units for describing people and the patternings of their behavior. Consider, for example, the mass of data yielded by the 550 MMPI responses from each of 100 persons. To extract order from such a stack of facts, investigators searching for underlying traits try to group responses into more basic clusters. For this purpose, many trait psychologists turn to **factor analysis,** a mathematical procedure that helps to sort test responses into relatively homogeneous clusters. Working in the *psycholexical approach* discussed in the previous chapter, a number of researchers have reached reasonable agreement about the five types of dimensions or factors on which English trait terms may be clustered, often called the "Big Five Structure" (e.g., Goldberg, 1991; John, 1990).

These dimensions emerged from mathematical analyses of the responses with the method of factor analysis. Factor analysis is a very useful tool for reducing a large set of correlated measures to fewer unrelated or independent dimensions. As such, it can be a powerful aid to psychological research by clarifying which response patterns go together. Suppose, for example, that 50 students have answered 10 personality questionnaires, each of which contains 100 questions. A factor analysis of this mass of information can show which parts of the test performances go together (for example, are closely correlated with one another yet uncorrelated with other parts). Factor analysis, however, does not necessarily reveal the basic traits of persons. The results depend on the tests and the subjects selected by the researcher and on the details of his or her procedures and decisions.

As has long been recognized (Overall, 1964), factor analysis cannot establish which characteristics of persons or things being measured are "real" or "primary." The factors obtained are simply names given to the correlations found among the particular measures. In other words, factor analysis yields a greatly simplified patterning of the test data put into it, but it cannot go beyond the limitations of the original tests and depends on many decisions by the investigator (e.g., in the type of factor analysis he or she conducts). Consequently, while the factor-analytic search for hypothesized underlying traits may yield mathematically pure factors, their psychological meaningfulness and relevance for the person's actual behavior cannot be assumed and must be demonstrated.

The factor-analytic approach to describing trait dimensions is illustrated in a series of pioneering factor-analytic studies (Norman, 1961, 1963; Tupes & Christal, 1958, 1961). These studies investigated the factors obtained for diverse samples of people rated by their peers on rating scales. The scales themselves came from a condensed version of the thousands of trait names originally identified by Allport and Odbert's search for trait names in the dictionary. After much research, 20 scales were selected and many judges were asked to rate other people on them. The results were carefully factor-analyzed. The same set of five relatively independent factors appeared consistently across several studies and continues to form the basis of what has become the Big Five Structure (e.g., John, 1990; Goldberg, 1992), summarized in the previous chapter, with such dimensions as neuroticism (N), extraversion (E), and openness to experience (O). These are measured with a personality inventory called the NEO-PI (Costa & McCrae, 1997).

Links between Perceiver and Perceived: Valid Ratings

One enduring concern about these factors that emerged from trait ratings was that they may reflect the social stereotypes and concepts of the judges rather than the trait organization of the rated persons. Mulaik (1964), for example, conducted three separate factor-analytic studies, using many trait-rating scales, to determine the degree to which the method reveals personality factors in the person as opposed to in the rater's concepts. The judges in one study rated real persons on the scales, including family members, close acquaintances, and themselves. In a second study, they rated stereotypes like "suburban housewife," "mental patient," and "Air Force general." The raters in the third study rated the "meaning" of 20 trait words. There was much similarity between the factors found for ratings of real persons and those found for ratings of stereotypes and words. Results like these led many investigators to conclude that personality factors that emerge from ratings may reflect the raters' conceptual categories rather than the traits of the subjects being judged (Mischel, 1968; Peterson, 1968).

It is quite possible that raters' stereotypes and preconceptions enter into these ratings, and it is also the case that different investigators may arrive at somewhat different views of trait organization. Nevertheless, a few basic trait dimensions seem to be found over and over again and, most importantly, the characterizations of people on these dimensions, based on ratings by peers, reasonably agree with the self-ratings of the rated individuals themselves (e.g., McCrae & Costa, 1987). Thus, even if stereotypes and oversimplifications enter into these judgments, as they probably do, they are made reliably, shared widely, and seem significantly linked to qualities of the rated persons (Funder & Colvin, 1997).

In sum, although there has been extensive debate about the limitations and usefulness of trait ratings (e.g., Block, Weiss, & Thorne, 1979; Romer & Revelle, 1984; Shweder, 1975), it is clear that the descriptions of people obtained from different raters in different contexts often do agree with one another. This basic conclusion was reached more than three decades ago and still stands. To illustrate, in one classic study, agreement was found between peer judgments on dimensions of aggressive and dependent behavior and separate behavior ratings of actual aggressive and dependent behavior (Winder & Wiggins, 1964). Subjects were first classified into high, intermediate, and low groups on aggression and dependency on the basis of their peer reputations. Separate behavior ratings made later indicated that the three groups differed from one another significantly in the amount of aggression and dependency they displayed in an experimental situation. Similarly, college students were preselected as extremely high or low in aggressiveness (on the basis of ratings by their peers). They tended to be rated in similar ways by independent judges who observed their interaction (Gormly & Edelberg, 1974). Thus (see *In Focus 7.3*) there are linkages between a rater's trait constructs and the behavior of people he or she rates (e.g., Funder & Colvin, 1997; Jackson & Paunonen, 1980; Mischel, 1984; McCrae & Costa, 1987).

EVALUATING TRAIT TESTS

To evaluate trait approaches and their applications requires that we evaluate the trait tests on which they rely. In recent years there has been a loud public outcry against the widespread use of trait tests in schools, business, and government. Critics both inside and outside the psychological profession have raised grave questions about the ethics as well as the value of many personality assessment practices that are most central to the trait approach. Neither the questions nor the answers are simple.

You saw that trait-oriented research usually has assessed differences among people on paper-and-pencil inventories and questionnaires. Many problems arise in efforts to clarify the meaning of the answers. Notice that almost all the psychometric information we have about Gary W. is based on what he *says* about himself. His MMPI profile, his California *F* Scale, all rest on self-reports on questionnaires. Since we want to

IN FOCUS 7.3   *Personality Judgments to Predict Behavior*

Do trait judgments reflect the constructs of perceivers rather than the behavior of the perceived? What are the links between the perceiver's judgments of what people "are like" and the behaviors that those people actually display? Some theorists argue that personality structure exists "all in the head" of the perceiver (Shweder, 1975). Others believe it is "all in the person" perceived (Epstein, 1977; Funder & Colvin, 1997). Still others favor the view that it depends both on the beliefs of observers and on the characteristics of the observed (e.g., Cantor & Mischel, 1979; Magnusson & Endler, 1977; Mischel, 1984). They believe that ratings may be influenced by the rater's expectations but have roots in the behavior of the perceived.

Until recently, most researchers studied either the judgments of the perceiver or the behavior of the perceived; they rarely considered the fit between the two. One recent study tried to relate observers' overall judgments of children's aggressiveness (and other traits) to the children's independently coded actual behavior (Mischel, 1984; Wright & Mischel, 1987). Specifically,

their trait-related acts were recorded during repeated observation periods on 15 separate occasions distributed across three camp situations during a summer. Examples of behaviors coded as aggressive are: "I'm gonna punch your face" or "Let's go beat up . . ." or lifting a dog by its collar and choking it.

The question was: Do raters' judgments of the child's overall aggression relate to the actual frequency of the child's aggressive acts as coded by other independent observers? The results clearly answered the question: Yes. Thus children who are rated by independent observers as more aggressive actually tend to be aggressive more frequently. For instance, they yell and provoke more. These differences, however, were seen primarily only in certain situations, namely in those stressful situations that greatly taxed or strained the competencies of the children. In sum, personality judgments seem to have links to the judged person's actual behavior, although that behavior may be visible only in certain types of situations in which the relevant individual differences emerge.

know more about Gary than how he answers questionnaires, it is crucial to establish what his scores do and do not imply about him. Here we will consider only problems relevant to the interpretation of objective personality trait tests. In later chapters, the discussion will extend to many other techniques for evaluating personality.

Ethical Concerns

There have been strong objections to judging people's personalities with tests. Much of the public outrage has centered on the fear that tests are invasions of privacy, that they force people to answer questions that may be used to discriminate against them. Understandably, people are reluctant to have testers pry into their lives and extract information that may contribute to negative decisions about them.

Proper evaluation of the ethics of personality assessment and rational assessment of the testing procedures are matters of great social importance. The public and its legal representatives (in Congress, for example) have been handicapped by widespread ignorance of the tests and the techniques underlying their development. The ethical and social problems involved in the multimillion dollar personality-testing business are formidable indeed. The scope of the problem is indicated by the publication of literally thousands of personality tests, many of which are widely used throughout our society. Given the magnitude of the problem and the public's confusion about personality testing, it is especially important to consider in some depth the main problems that arise in attempts to interpret what personality tests really do and really don't permit us to say about individuals. We now have a considerable amount of data about Gary W., for example, but we are still very uncertain about how to evaluate it. How sure can we be of the impressions we have? How wise or hazardous would it be to base important decisions on this information?

Tests Can Deceive—But They Also Can Be Useful

In daily life people function like trait psychologists to the extent that they infer personality dispositions from behavioral cues. Often these impressions are formed quickly and are based on minimal information. The taxi driver who claims he can spot the main qualities of his rider's personality in ten minutes is a common example. Usually such snap diagnoses are not taken seriously and are dismissed easily as clichés. When a personality description is offered by a more creditable diagnostician, it tends to be accepted much more readily even if it is equally wrong (see *In Focus 7.4*).

IN FOCUS 7.4   *Do Psychological Tests Dupe You?*

Imagine that you have taken a large battery of psychological tests. A week later you receive a report based on the results that includes the following:

> You have a tendency to be critical of yourself. . . . You pride yourself on being an independent thinker and do not accept others' opinions without satisfactory proof. . . . At times you are extroverted, affable, sociable, while at other times you are introverted, wary, and reserved. Some of your aspirations tend to be pretty unrealistic (Ulrich et al., 1963, p. 832).

How well do these descriptions fit? Perhaps they do not seem very apt to you because you know they were not tailor-made for you individually and based on tests you actually took. However, in an actual study, a paragraph containing these excerpts was given to college students who had taken a test battery earlier (Ulrich et al., 1963). All of the students received the same report, though each one believed it was unique and that it was based on his or her own test responses. Almost all of the students felt the report captured the essence of their personalities, hailing it with such phrases as:

> For the first time things that I have been vaguely aware of have been put into concise and constructive statements which I would like to use as a plan for improving myself.
>
> I believe this interpretation applies to me individually, as there are too many facets which fit me too well to be a generalization.
>
> It appears to me that the results of this test are unbelievably close to the truth (Ulrich et al., 1963, p. 838).

People can be fooled easily into believing that psychological tests actually measure their personal qualities even when they are getting statements similar to those in fortune cookies, mass produced and therefore unrelated to the individuals they supposedly describe. What can psychological tests really tell us then? How can we evaluate their worth and their limitations? This chapter considers these questions and examines some of the problems and findings of efforts to study and compare individuals with tests. You will have to draw your own conclusions.

The ease with which students in the *In Focus 7.4* study were duped about their own personality is not at all atypical; it reflects less their gullibility than the hazards of personality impressions and everyday trait descriptions. When personality impressions are stated in broad terms they are difficult to disconfirm. The individual may readily add extra meaning to clichés and adopt them with great confidence even when they turn out to be untrue (or untestable). Thus, the naïve person may attribute profound significance to the vague comments provided by palmists and newspaper astrologers and may accept as personal revelations "insights" that could fit almost anyone.

It is therefore extremely important for psychologists to provide real support and evidence for their statements about personality and to make their statements in a form that is testable. You should approach the matters of "reliability" and "validity" in personality study (defined and discussed next) not as mere textbook terms to be memorized and not used: Instead, try to see these concepts as guides for establishing the value of psychologists' claims about the nature of personality. When tests are reliable and well-validated and take account of the issues discussed next, they can be extremely useful for all sorts of screening and personnel selection decisions, as well as for research and theory building (West & Finch, 1997).

Reliability: Are the Measurements Consistent?

A number of techniques are available for estimating the consistency or "reliability" of personality measures. When the same test is given to the same group of people on two occasions, a retest correlation or "coefficient of stability" is obtained. This measure provides an index of *temporal reliability*. Generally, the longer the time interval, the lower the coefficient of stability. If there is only a short interval between test and retest, the two occasions are not entirely independent. For example, if subjects remember some of their initial responses, the correlation is strengthened.

Other reliability estimates are more concerned with the consistency with which different parts or alternate forms of a test measure behavior. The correlation between parts of a single form gives an index of *internal consistency*. Consistency may also be measured by the intercorrelation of scores on *alternate forms* of a test administered to the same set of subjects. The alternate-form method is especially valuable for assessing the effects of an intervening procedure, such as psychotherapy or special training, on test performance, because it avoids the contaminating effects of administering the same form twice.

If subjective judgment enters into scoring decisions, a special kind of reliability check is needed. This check is called *interscorer agreement* or consistency. It is the degree to which different scorers or judges arrive at the same statements about the same test data. For example, if three judges try to infer personality traits from subjects' interview behavior and dream reports, it would be necessary to establish the degree to which the three assessors reach the same conclusions. As noted before, interscorer agreement is easiest to achieve when scoring is objective, as on highly structured tests (for example, when all answers are given as either "yes" or "no").

The reliability of a test increases when the number of items in the test is increased (Epstein, 1979). Measures that consist of single items ("Are you happy?") tend to have very low reliability and therefore do not allow any meaningful conclusions.

Validity: What Do the Measurements Mean?

A woman's self-report on a 10-item questionnaire provides her *stated* reactions to the items under the specific testing conditions. Thus, if a person reports that she is "very friendly," that is what she *says* about herself on the test. To know more than that, one needs validity research to establish the meaning and implications of the test answers. Test results may seem valid even when they are not (see *In Focus 7.4*).

Content or *face validity* is the demonstration that the items on a test adequately represent a defined broader *class* of behavior. For example, judges would have to agree that the different items on a "friendliness" questionnaire all in fact seem to deal with the class or topic of friendliness. In practice, content validity often is assumed rather than demonstrated. Even if the content validity of the items is shown acceptably, it cannot be assumed that the answers provide an index of the individual's "true" trait position. We do not know whether or not the person who says she is friendly, for example, is really friendly.

To obtain external validity one must relate scores on the measure to other measures. For example, one might relate test scores to psychiatrists' ratings about progress in therapy, teachers' ratings of school performance, and behavior on another test. Such relationships help to provide evidence for a claim of validity and provide information about what the person's test behavior does and does not allow one to predict.

Construct Validity: Elaborating the Meaning of the Construct

Personality psychologists guided by trait theory usually want to infer and describe a person's dispositions from his or her test responses. **Construct validity** is the effort to elaborate the inferred traits determining test behavior (Campbell, 1960; West & Finch, 1997). Basically, it tries to answer the question: What does this test measure? The concept of "construct validity" was introduced by trait psychologists for problems in which the assessor accepts

> no existing measure as a definitive criterion of the quality with which he is concerned. Here the traits or qualities underlying test performance are of central importance (American Psychological Association, 1966, pp. 13–14).

Investigators interested in the traits supposedly accounting for personality test responses must generate a concept or theory about the underlying traits that they believe determine responses on their test. They then can employ a variety of methods to establish a network of relationships to illuminate what is related to the trait and what is not.

Traditionally, construct validity involves the following steps. The investigator begins with a hunch about a dimension on which individuals can be compared, for example, "submissiveness." The researchers might regard submissiveness as a "tendency to yield to the will and suggestions of others" (Sarason, 1966, p. 127). To study this tendency they devise a measure of submissiveness. They have no one definite criterion, however, and instead may use diverse indices of the subject's underlying trait of submissiveness. Hypotheses then are tested about how submissiveness, as displayed on the tests, does and does not relate to the other indices of submissiveness. On the basis of their findings the construct is revised (West & Finch, 1997).

Jack Block

An Example: Construct Validity of Ego-Control and Ego-Resiliency

Ego-control refers to the degree of impulse control in such functions as delay of gratification, inhibition of aggression, and planfulness. A related construct, **ego-resiliency,** refers to the individual's ability to adapt to environmental demands by appropriately modifying his or her habitual level of ego-control. Ego-resiliency allows functioning with some "elasticity." Together, these two constructs represent the core qualities of "ego" from one theoretical perspective (Block & Block, 1980).

A number of tasks have been developed to measure these two constructs. For example, individual differences were examined in children's patterns of ego-control. The adequacy and type of ego-control were inferred from ratings of the children's tendency to inhibit impulses. Their delay behavior in experimental situations was also observed (Block & Martin, 1955). The children were exposed to a frustration in which a barrier separated the child from desired and expected toys. The "undercontrolling" children (those who had been rated as not inhibiting their impulses) reacted more violently to the frustrating barrier than did "overcontrolling," inhibited children. The undercontrolling youngsters also became less constructive in their play.

Individuals who are high (rather than low) on indices of ego-control tend to be somewhat more able to control and inhibit their motoric activity. For example, they may be able to sit still longer or draw a line more slowly without lifting their pencil. These are only a few examples from much larger, meaningful networks of correlations that have been obtained to support the ego-resiliency and ego-control constructs for many years (Block & Block, 1980; Mischel, 1984; Shoda, Mischel, & Peake, 1990).

In studies of the ego-resiliency construct, toddlers were evaluated for the degree to which they seemed secure and for their degree of competence (in a problem-solving task). The toddlers who were secure and competent also scored higher on measures of ego-resiliency when they reached the age of four to five years (Gove et al., 1979; Matas, Arend, & Sroufe, 1978). As another example, ego-resilient children at age three years are also viewed as popular, interesting, and attractive at later ages (Block & Block, 1980). A large network of associations like these, found with many measures over long periods of childhood, suggests that both the concepts of ego-control and ego-resiliency may offer useful characterizations of important individual differences. The ego-resilience concept also is related to delay of gratification and an aspect of emotional intelligence (Shoda, Mischel, & Peake, 1990). When the constructs are studied comprehensively with good measures, coherent, meaningful patterns tend to emerge. These patterns suggest that there are significant threads of continuity in personality that may be stable over many years in the course of development (e.g., Caspi, 1987; Caspi & Bem, 1990; Mischel, Shoda, & Rodriguez, 1989).

SUMMARY

1. Mental testing at the turn of the century was the forerunner of later developments in the psychometric approach to personality. The intelligence test developed by Binet early in the 20th century profoundly influenced the history of psychometric mental and personality testing.

2. A person's intelligence is the result of heredity and environment inextricably intertwined. High "intelligence" is usually related to better school grades (academic achievements). However, it is not sufficiently related to achievement outside the classroom to allow confident predictions about how well particular individuals will do beyond school.

3. In the psychometric approach to personality, the aim is to measure an individual with respect to one or more single traits, such as aggressiveness or introversion. In order to measure objectively, the psychometrician attempts to create *standardized* self-report questionnaires and rating scales that will yield results that can be *reproduced* easily by independent observers.

4. The trait approach was applied to the case of Gary W.

5. The MMPI is one of the most widely used personality tests. It contains a set of self-report scales whose meanings are defined by their correlations with other measures. MMPI "atlases" provide descriptive information for various average test profiles or code types.

6. One especially useful technique for obtaining a person's self-appraisal is the Q-sort. In this measure, the person takes a large number of cards, each containing a descriptive statement, and sorts them into a number of categories. These Q-sorts may be used for self-description, to describe the ideal self, or to describe a relationship.

7. Similarity and overlap of measurement methods often contribute to the correlations found among traits. To demonstrate that a distinctive trait is being tapped, it is helpful to study it by at least two different methods.

8. Factor analysis is a mathematical procedure that sorts test responses into homogeneous clusters. It is a useful procedure for simplifying data, but it does not automatically reveal basic traits. There is good agreement, however, about a few dimensions (the "Big Five") often found in ratings with trait terms.

9. Trait research tends to focus on correlations among what people say on paper-and-pencil inventories and questionnaires. The interpretation of these questionnaire findings poses some special problems because what a person says about her attributes does not necessarily reflect accurately either her traits or the things that she does outside the test. Self-reports thus may or may not be closely related to other indices of the person's nontest behavior.

10. The consistency (*reliability*) and meaning (*validity*) of a personality test have to be demonstrated by research. Construct validation tries to elaborate the inferred traits determining test behavior.

Genetic and Biochemical Roots of Personality

The genes dictate whether a person will be male or female, blue-eyed or brown-eyed, curly-haired or straight-haired. To some extent they also influence height and weight. But do the genes also underlie personality traits? The rapidly developing field of *behavior genetics* studies the role of inheritance in behavior and personality. In this chapter we move beyond trait measurement strategies to examine the genetic and biochemical roots of personality, including temperament and attitudes, beliefs and behavior. We then consider the role of heredity and biochemistry in major types of abnormal behavior relevant to personality and the biological therapies for behavioral change that follow within this approach.

Most of what is known about the genetic roots of personality comes from studies that compare the similarity in personality shown by individuals who vary in the degree to which they share the same genes and/or the same family environments. Therefore, the "genetic" and "environmental" influences on personality discussed here do not refer to the effects of specific genes and specific environments but rather to the overall effects of these two types of determinants on individual differences. Although geneticists are now actively trying to identify specific genes responsible for particular aspects of personality, such links are still mostly exciting items on the research agenda for the future. Still unknown at this time for the most part are the mechanisms through which genes, singly and in complex combinations of multiple genes, might contribute to personality. Nevertheless, a great deal has been discovered in recent years about the effects of heredity and environment on personality, and the results have profound implications for how one thinks about human nature.

GENETIC ROOTS OF PERSONALITY

Trait theories emphasize the stability of human qualities, not their change and potential modification, and consistent with this focus they seek evidence for the genetic bases of stable personality traits. Genetic research on personality traits has been accelerating rapidly, producing a huge and complex literature that has a clear message: Genes play a role in personality, and it appears to be a larger one than earlier research had suspected, especially when personality is assessed by self-report questionnaires (e.g., Cattell, 1982; Eaves, Eysenck, & Martin, 1989; Loehlin, 1992; Loehlin & Nichols, 1976; Plomin et al., 1997). For example, it is now widely believed that such dispositions as extraversion-introversion (Chapter 6) have a biological-genetic basis (Bouchard et al., 1990; Eysenck, 1973; Plomin et al., 1997; Tellegen et al., 1988; Zuckerman, 1991).

The Twin Method

Most often these studies use the *twin method* to assess genetic influence, comparing the degree of similarity on trait measures obtained for genetically identical **(monozygotic)** twins as opposed to twins who are fraternal **(dizygotic)** (Plomin et al., 1997). Whereas identical twins are virtually clones, that is, they are genetically identical, fraternal twins—like other siblings—are only 50% similar genetically. To the degree that genetic factors affect a trait, it follows that identical twins must be more similar than fraternal twins with regard to that trait. A number of sophisticated statistical methods are used to estimate the degree of heritability—**the heritability index**—indicated from such investigations (e.g., Goldsmith & Campos, 1982; Neale & Cardon, 1992). (See *In Focus 8.1.*)

Twin studies are a valuable first step toward answering whether genetic factors contribute to individual differences in personality. Note, however, that even when genetics importantly influence individual differences in a trait, the trait may be modified by environmental influences. For example, substantial genetic influence for height means that height differences among the sampled individuals are largely due to genetic differences. But although height is highly heritable, such environmental interventions as improving children's nutrition and health can affect it: Indeed, environmental factors seem to account for the average increase in height across generations, although within each generation individual differences in height are highly heritable.

Studies comparing identical twins and fraternal twins help specify the role of genes in personality.

IN FOCUS 8.1   *Uses and Constraints of Heritability Estimates*

Correlations like those shown in Table 8.1 are used by behavioral geneticists to estimate the percentage of the variation in scores measuring individual differences that is attributable to genetic factors. These *heritability estimates* always are limited to the specific population that was studied in the research reported and for which they were computed. This is a crucial caution that behavioral geneticists generally emphasize but that many readers often fail to appreciate.

On the one hand, results using these estimates to date do suggest that heritability plays an important role in many aspects of personality. On the other hand, and equally important to remember, is what the heritability correlations do not tell us, as biologists themselves fully recognize and warn us to understand (Goldsmith, 1991). Heritability estimates do *not* provide an index of the degree to which a given characteristic is inherited by any individual or by any group. They do *not* imply that the particular characteristic cannot be changed significantly. And they do not even address the mechanisms through which the genetic influences on personality operate and exert their effects on the individual.

Likewise, as another example, consider the role of inheritance in intelligence. Research with twins raised in various environments (either together or apart) suggests that intelligence tends to be increasingly similar to the degree that the individuals have an increasing proportion of genes in common (Cartwright, 1978; Plomin et al., 1997; Vanderberg, 1971), although the data are open also to other interpretations (Ceci, 1996). But even if a person's genetic endowment may set an upper limit or ceiling on the degree to which his or her intelligence can be developed (Royce, 1973) it is the environment that may help or hinder achievement of that ceiling.

Results of Twin Studies

A pioneering study involving nearly 800 pairs of adolescent twins and dozens of personality traits reached a conclusion that has stood the test of time (Loehlin & Nichols, 1976): Identical twin pairs are more alike than fraternal twin pairs. The resemblance within identical twin pairs tends to be strongest for general ability and is less strong for special abilities. The resemblance is somewhat lower for personality inventory scales and lowest for interests, goals, and self-concepts (see Table 8.1). For personality, twin correlations are about .50 for identical twins and .25 for fraternal twins. This same study also found that nearly all personality traits measured by self-report questionnaires show moderate genetic influence.

Genetic research on personality has focused on five broad dimensions of personality—the "Big Five" (e.g., Goldberg, 1990), discussed in Chapter 6. The most well-studied of these are extraversion and neuroticism. Extraversion includes sociability, impulsiveness, and liveliness. Neuroticism (emotional instability) includes moodiness, anxiousness, and irritability. Genetic results for extraversion and neuroticism are

Table 8.1
Resemblance of Identical and Fraternal Twin Pairs

	Typical Correlations within Pairs	
Trait Area	Identical Twins	Fraternal Twins
General ability	.86	.62
Special abilities	.74	.52
Personality scales	.50	.28
Ideals, goals, interests	.37	.20

SOURCE: Adapted from Loehlin, J. C., & Nichols, R. C. (1976). *Heredity, environment, and personality: A study of 850 sets of twins.* Austin, TX: University of Texas Press.

summarized in Table 8.2 (Loehlin, 1992). Results from five recent twin studies in five different countries, using a total of 24,000 pairs of twins, consistently indicate moderate genetic influence. Correlations are about .50 for identical twins and about .20 for fraternal twins.

The role of heritability in extraversion and neuroticism has been studied extensively but much less genetic research has been done for the other three Big Five traits, namely, agreeableness (likeability, friendliness), conscientiousness (conformity, will to achieve), and culture (openness to experience). These qualities have been investigated with diverse measures (rather than standardized tests) that also make it more difficult to compare results across different studies. Nevertheless, results of twin and adoption studies with measures related to these three traits also suggest genetic influence for agreeableness, conscientiousness, and culture at least to a moderate degree (Loehlin, 1992).

Keep in mind that results from twin studies are open to other interpretations. Take, for example, the many studies that compare the similarity of identical and fraternal twins who grow up together and that draw mostly on their answers on self-report personality questionnaires (the measure most often used). On these tests the identical twins might give more similar answers not just because they have the same genes but also because they might identify more closely with each other and emulate each other more, or they might be treated more alike by parents and other people and, therefore,

Table 8.2
Resemblance of 24,000 Pairs of Reared-Together Twins in Five Countries and Identical Twins Reared Apart

	Correlations within Twin Pairs		
	Identical Twins Reared Together	Fraternal Twins Reared Together	Identical Twins Reared Apart
Extraversion	.51	.18	.38
Neuroticism	.46	.20	.38

SOURCE: Adapted from Loehlin, J. C. (1992). *Genes and environment in personality development.* Newbury Park, CA: Sage.

become more alike in all sorts of ways, for example, often wearing more similar clothes. Just as greater similarity in dress among identical twins does not necessarily imply that clothing tastes are genetically determined, it is important also to be cautious before concluding that similarity in answers to self-report questionnaires about an attribute necessarily implies the specific genetic heritability of that attribute. Thus, the twin method provides only a rough screen for genetic influence, although many of its findings have received considerable support when carefully researched and supplemented by other methods (Plomin et al., 1997).

Twins Reared Apart: How Much Nature? How Much Nurture?

To separate the role of genetics and environment more clearly, it is especially informative to assess identical twins who have been reared apart in different families. Reports have come from two large-scale studies of twins reared apart in Minnesota (Bouchard et al., 1990; Tellegen et al., 1988) and in Sweden (Pedersen et al., 1988; Plomin et al., 1988). The results surprised even many of the researchers who have long been convinced that genes affect personality.

In this research, Bouchard, Tellegen, and their associates for more than a decade studied a sample of identical (monozygotic) twin pairs reared apart who were separated early in life (on average before the end of the second month) and grew up in different families, mostly in English-speaking countries. As adults, their responses were assessed on many medical and psychological measures, including personality questionnaire scales and intelligence tests (as seen in Table 8.3). Most had not seen each other for an average of about 30 years, although some had contact over the years. Comparisons were made with a larger sample of twin pairs who had been reared together and grew up in Minnesota.

There were strong similarities in the test results of the identical twins. Especially interesting, the similarity was almost as high for the monozygotic twins who grew up in different homes as it was for those raised within the same family (as was seen in Table

Table 8.3
Names of Personality Scales in Studies of Twins Reared Apart and Together

Well-Being	Control
Social Potency	Harm Avoidance
Achievement	Traditionalism
Social Closeness	Absorption
Stress Reaction	Positive Emotionality
Alienation	Negative Emotionality
Aggression	Constraint

NOTE: On most scales, identical twins reared apart were as similar to each other as those reared together. The main exception was "social closeness" (on which those reared together were more similar).
SOURCE: Tellegen, A., Lykken, D., Bouchard, T., Wilcox, K., Segal, N., & Rich, S. (1988). Personality similarity in twins reared apart. *Journal of Personality and Social Psychology, 54,* 1035 (Table 3).

8.2). Bouchard and colleagues (1990) attributed approximately 70% of the individual differences found in intelligence to heredity. They interpreted the effects of heredity on personality (as assessed on their questionnaires) to be approximately 50% and the effects of family environment to be trivial (Tellegen et al., 1988). Likewise, twin studies of the Big Five factors suggest "The shared genes, not the shared experiences, mainly determine the family resemblance of 'blood relatives'" (Rowe, 1997, p. 380).

There were instances of dramatic psychological similarities within the twin pairs, even for twins who grew up in radically different environments. In spite of their background differences, these twins seemed to share some quite distinctive mannerisms, postures, attitudes, and interests. For example, in some cases they posed alike for photos. The instances of similarity in the reports are striking and remarkable.

Note, however, again that even when identical twins are reared apart, their similarities on personality measures are not necessarily due to their genes for personality itself. For example, similar interests and values in identical twins may in part reflect their similar physiques and appearance, constitutions, abilities, skills, and physical characteristics rather than any genes for personality. These physical qualities may lead other people to treat them similarly even when the twins live in different environments. A shared interest in becoming a photography fashion model, for example, may say more about the inheritance of faces than of personality. Their similar physical qualities also may lead each twin to see himself or herself in a somewhat similar way, for example, as highly attractive or unattractive, or as physically strong and skilled and competent or as weak and ineffective, which in turn could influence such aspects of personality as self-concepts and self-confidence and a host of related characteristics. These hedges notwithstanding, the overall results from this type of research indicate that heredity plays an important role in personality and must be taken into account.

Temperaments

The term **temperaments** refers to heritable traits that are visible in early childhood (Buss & Plomin, 1984) and seem especially relevant to the individual's emotional life (Allport, 1961). Dispositions usually considered temperaments include the general level of emotionality, sociability, and activity.

Emotionality is defined by some researchers as the tendency to become aroused easily physiologically (by ready activation of the autonomic nervous system) and especially to experience frequent and intense negative emotions such as anger, fear, and distress (Buss & Plomin, 1984). Other researchers find that the intensity with which an individual experiences emotions is independent of how often he or she has such feelings (Larsen, Diener, & Emmons, 1986), suggesting that these two components of emotionality need to be considered separately. For example, if Jane rarely experiences fear but becomes unbearably fearful in some situations, her emotional life would be quite different from someone who is often moderately fearful but never intensely afraid.

Sociability refers to the degree to which the person seeks to interact with others and to be with people. (As such it overlaps with the concept of extraversion versus introversion introduced in Chapter 6.)

Activity may be defined with regard both to the vigor or intensity of responses and their tempo or speed, and refers to individual differences on a dimension that ranges from hyperactivity to extreme inactivity.

In these dispositions genetic endowment seems to have a significant part in studies reported for many years (Goldsmith, 1983; Plomin & Foch, 1980; Schaffer & Emerson, 1964; Thomas & Chess, 1977) and the evidence seems increasingly strong (e.g., Plomin, 1990; Rowe, 1997).

Figure 8.1 illustrates these types of results more concretely. It shows that on the dimension of emotionality, identical twins (monozygotic) are rated as much more similar by their mothers than are fraternal (dizygotic) twins. Although the results are impressive, they are not easy to interpret. Some of the greater similarity found may reflect that the mothers themselves may treat the identical twins more similarly, as might other people in the environment. The mothers also may have been influenced in their ratings not only by the twins' behavior but by their own expectations and preconceptions for identical versus fraternal twins. Nevertheless, results like these tend to be obtained so consistently that they suggest a significant genetic role in personality with regard to the temperaments of emotionality, activity, and sociability (Buss & Plomin, 1984; Plomin et al., 1997). A recent review of this research concluded that ". . . one-third to one-half of individual differences in temperamental traits can be attributed to genetic variation among children" (Rowe, 1997, p. 378).

Figure 8.1
Similarity of Emotionality: Mothers' Ratings of Monozygotic and Dizygotic Twin Pairs

SOURCE: Correlation coefficients for degree of similarity from data in Buss, A. H., Plomin, R., & Willerman, L. The inheritance of temperaments. *Journal of Personality, 41,* 513–524.

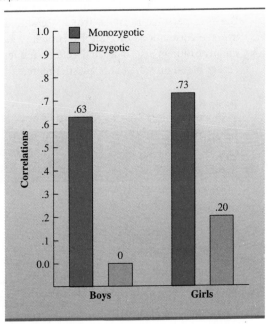

Genetic researchers investigating differences among children in temperament could not use self-report questionnaires with their young subjects and therefore were forced to use other measures, such as direct rating of the children's behavior by observers (e.g., Cherny et al., 1994; Goldsmith & Campos, 1986; Saudino et al., 1996). To illustrate, with few exceptions (confined to the first few days of life), observational studies of young twins show genetic influence for diverse characteristics in both twin and adoption studies. These characteristics include the degree to which the child's behavior is inhibited—an aspect of fearfulness (e.g., Robinson et al., 1992); shyness both when observed at home and in the laboratory (Cherny et al., 1994); activity level (Saudino & Eaton, 1991); and empathy (Zahn-Waxler, Robinson, & Emde, 1992). Findings from these studies are notable because they supplement those that rely on self-reports—which are by far the most common.

Effects beyond Self-Report Measures

One of the most surprising findings from genetic research on self-report personality questionnaires is that of the many traits that have been studied, virtually all show genetic influence. It is therefore particularly important to use measures of personality other than self-report questionnaires to investigate whether or not this result is somehow due to biases in the self-report measures themselves. To address this, in a recent relevant study, researchers gave a measure of the Big Five personality factors to almost 1,000 pairs of twins (Riemann, Angleitner, & Strelau, 1997) in Germany and Poland. They also obtained ratings of each twin's personality by two different peers (who agreed reasonably in their ratings about each twin's personality).

On average, ratings by the peers correlated .55 with the twins' self-report ratings, providing moderate validity for those ratings. Table 8.4 shows twin correlations for the Big Five personality traits, which are similar to those summarized in Table 8.2, with average correlations of .52 for identical twins and .23 for fraternal twins. The fact that the peer ratings also indicated genetic influence helps support the conclusions reached earlier based on self-report questionnaires.

Table 8.4
Twin Study Using Self-Report and Peer Ratings of Big Five Personality Traits

| | Correlations within Pairs | | | |
| | Self-Report Ratings | | Peer Ratings | |
	Identical Twins	Fraternal Twins	Identical Twins	Fraternal Twins
Extraversion	.56	.28	.40	.17
Neuroticism	.53	.13	.43	−.03
Agreeableness	.42	.19	.32	.18
Conscientiousness	.54	.18	.43	.18
Culture	.54	.35	.48	.31

SOURCE: Riemann, R., Angleitner, A., & Strelau, J. (1997). Genetic and environmental influences on personality: A study of twins reared together using the self- and peer report NEO-FFI scales. *Journal of Personality, 65,* 449–476.

Robert Plomin

Heredity *and* Environment

Debates about heredity and environment unfortunately readily turn into either/or competitions to see which one is more important. As a leader in research on the role of inheritance in behavior points out, ". . . evidence for significant genetic influence is often implicitly interpreted as if heritability were 100%, whereas heritabilities of behavior seldom exceed 50%" (Plomin, 1990, p. 187). Plomin notes that this should make it clear that "non-genetic sources of variance" are also of self-evident importance. Indeed, Bouchard and colleagues themselves acknowledge that in their own results, ". . . in individual cases environmental factors have been highly significant" (1990, p. 225), as with the case, for example, of a 29-point difference in the IQs of two identical twins.

In short, regardless of the exact percentage used to estimate the influence of genetic factors, clearly their influence is considerable, especially given that few findings in personality account for as much as 20% of the variance. Just as noteworthy, however, is the other side of that finding: namely, the fact that the same data show that at least half of the variance of personality is *not* due to genetic factors and thus also attest to the importance of the environment for personality. The recurrent theme throughout this research is clear: Unquestionably, one's genetic endowment has extensive influences on one's life and personality development, and so also does the environment. But the degree to which there are specific genes for particular personality characteristics is much less evident. The challenge will be to untangle the mechanisms through which both genes and experience interact throughout the life course to influence what we become. That will require specifying the mechanisms that produce these effects and clarifying the nature of the characteristics that are heritable and the specific aspects of the environment that are important—a topic that will be addressed in the next chapter.

Genetic Influences on Attitudes and Beliefs

Genetic influences also play a role in individual differences in attitudes and beliefs. Results come from a number of twin studies (Eaves, Eysenck, & Martin, 1989), including one of twins who were reared apart (Tellegen et al., 1988). To illustrate, a substantial genetic influence was found on *traditionalism,* a general orientation which taps conservative (as opposed to liberal) attitudes on diverse topics (Eaves et al., 1989; see Plomin et al., 1997).

The degree to which an attitude is heritable also may have an impact on how robust it is. For example, attitudes that are more heritable seem to be harder to influence and are more important for the individual. In one study the researcher separated many specific attitudes into two sets: those that twin studies had found were more heritable (such as attitudes about the death penalty and about jazz) and those that were less heritable (such as attitudes about coeducation, straightjackets, and the truth of the Bible). Then he set up experimental situations designed to change these attitudes in college students (Tesser, 1993). The more heritable attitudes were harder to influence and more important in determining the person's judgments of interpersonal attraction.

Heritability of Aggressive and Altruistic Tendencies

Research with adult twins also points to the influence of genes on other aspects of social behavior. For example, self-reports on aggressiveness questionnaires were obtained from a large number of twin pairs in England (Rushton et al., 1986). The twins answered such questions as: "I try not to give people a hard time" and "Some people think I have a violent temper." The altruism questionnaire asked for the frequency of such behaviors as "I have donated blood" and "I have given directions to a stranger." Within the identical (monozygotic) twin pairs, the answers were more similar than would be expected by chance, whereas between dizygotic twins, the correlation was merely at a chance level. These results occurred both for the males and for the females. Using sophisticated statistical techniques, the researchers estimated that genetics accounted for approximately 50% of the individual differences in test answers.

Overview

Taken collectively, findings like these consistently support the view that genetic factors play a significant role in personality traits and influence attitudes and values as well as self-esteem (e.g., McGuire, Neiderheiser, Reiss, Hetherington, & Plomin, 1994). In some cases genetic influences seem to account for as much as half of the individual differences observed, although the magnitude of these effects may be exaggerated, particularly when the findings are based on self-reports. But there are notable exceptions (see *In Focus 8.2*). Plomin and colleagues (1990), critically reviewing twin studies of personality based on self-reports, point out certain methodological problems in these studies that may systematically overestimate the role of genetics. According to these researchers, the biases can be corrected if results from adoption studies are appropriately taken into account. When corrections are made for the erroneous inflation of the heritability estimates:

> The true heritability estimate for self-reported personality is closer to the adoption study estimate of 20% than to the twin study estimate of 40% (Plomin et al., 1990, p. 233).

IN FOCUS 8.2 *Romantic Love: Beyond DNA*

Although the DNA seems to directly or indirectly influence individual differences on most measures of personality and personality traits, as well as on social attitudes (Eaves et al., 1989; Plomin et al., 1997; Tesser, 1993), including people's self-esteem (McGuire et al., 1994), one area that seems to be exempt is romantic love.

A behavior genetic twin family study focused on the genetic versus environmental influences on individual differences in adult romantic love styles. The participants were drawn from 890 adult twins and 172 spouses from the California Twin Registry, and they had been married for an average of a dozen years (Waller & Shaver, 1994). Six different love styles were measured, ranging from one that values passion, excitement, intimacy, self-disclosure, and "being in love from the start," to one that values a

relationship that is affectionate and reliable, valuing companionship and friendship (with items like "It is hard for me to say exactly when our friendship turned into love").

The findings showed that how people love is almost completely due to the environment and essentially unaffected by genetic influences. In fact, this is one domain in which it is the shared family environment—found to be largely irrelevant for most individual differences in personality—that turned out to be particularly important (Waller & Shaver, 1994). As the researchers noted, ". . . love styles may be learned during early familial or shared extrafamilial interactions and subsequently played out in romantic relationships" (pp. 272–273).

New Directions: Search for Specific Genes for Personality Components

Given the considerable evidence for genetic influence on personality traits that has been found in recent years, researchers in the vanguard of the field are now trying to become more precise and to identify specific genes that might connect to specific characteristics. Thus, they are beginning to go much beyond demonstrations that genetic influences are important for personality.

In earlier research, specific genetic defects have been linked to various abnormalities such as mental deficiencies. **PKU** is a case in point (see Table 8.5). PKU (*phenylketonuria*) disease is an inherited disorder in which a genetic abnormality

Table 8.5
Effects of Some Genetic Abnormalities: Two Examples

Name of Disorder	Description	Cause
Down's Syndrome	Severe mental retardation. Physical appearance: small skull, sparse hair, flat nose, fissured tongue, a fold over the eyelids, short neck.	A third, extra chromosome in the 21st chromosome pair. Appears to be associated with advanced age in the mother.
PKU (phenylketonuria)	Results in mental retardation if not treated soon after birth.	A gene that produces a critical enzyme is missing.

results in the lack of an enzyme necessary for normal metabolism. Because of this enzyme deficiency, a toxic chemical accumulates in the body and results in central nervous system damage and mental retardation. Diagnosis of PKU disease is now possible immediately after birth, and highly successful treatment has been devised. The child is placed on a special diet that prevents the toxic substance from building up in the bloodstream. When the biological mechanisms underlying other forms of mental deficiency are known, equally effective cures may be possible.

Some psychological characteristics are determined by an individual's genetic structure but are not inherited. For example, when the 21st chromosome in the body cell of an individual has a third member instead of occurring as a pair, the individual will have **Down's Syndrome** (mongolism), a form of mental retardation. A technique for drawing amniotic fluid from the uterus of the pregnant mother enables doctors and prospective parents to know in advance whether the developing fetus has this chromosomal abnormality. This procedure is performed routinely for pregnant women 40 years of age or older because women in this age group are more likely to give birth to children with Down's Syndrome.

In new directions to link genes to personality, promising examples include the report that a gene for a dopamine receptor was correlated with novelty seeking in two studies (Benjamin et al., 1996; Ebstein et al., 1996), with other researchers finding that the same gene was related to hyperactivity (LaHoste et al., 1996). While such findings are exciting for genetic researchers, they must be interpreted with much caution and still be treated as tentative and suggestive rather than conclusive.

These reservations are necessary because findings of associations between personality and specific genes in the past have failed to replicate. That happened, for example, for the reported correlation between neuroticism and a gene important in the functioning of the chemical neurotransmitter serotonin (Lesch et al., 1996), which two other studies could not reproduce (Ball et al., 1997; Ebstein et al., 1997). Perhaps even more important, personality traits involve extremely complex patterns of characteristics and behaviors such that an association with any specific gene probably will have only a small effect (Plomin, Owen, & McGuffin, 1994). That is, genetic influence on personality involves the action of many genes each of which has a small effect rather than the direct effect of any single major gene.

Given this great but unsurprising complexity, it can be valuable to use the sorts of promising methods for identifying genes in lower animals that cannot be employed with people (Plomin & Saudino, 1994). For example, in such animal studies it is possible to use powerful techniques that alter specific genes, called knock-outs, to test just how they influence behavior (Capecchi, 1994). In mice, for instance, several genes for fearfulness have been located (Flint et al., 1995). It was found, as predicted, that mice display greater aggression when the researchers knock out the genes for an important neurotransmitter (Saudou et al., 1994) or enzyme (Nelson et al., 1995). The limitation, of course, is that it is difficult to generalize results from studies with mice to humans. But there are exciting prospects for discoveries in molecular genetics that do speak to the human condition and will prove generalizable to personality (Hamer & Copeland, in press). However, that is the story that is not yet written but that should unfold in the next few years (see *In Focus 8.3*, page 214).

BIOCHEMISTRY, HEREDITY, AND ABNORMAL BEHAVIOR

We now turn to the role of genetic influences and biochemistry in severe forms of abnormal behavior relevant to personality. A key exemplar, **schizophrenia,** a major form of psychosis, is a complex and severe emotional and thought disorder with diverse symptoms. It provides a great challenge for researchers who try to understand its biological causes (Cohen & Servan-Schreiber, 1992). Research on the causes of schizophrenia gives important insights into both the promise and the problems of the biochemical approach applied to psychological problems and characteristics. Let us consider some highlights as illustrations.

It is difficult to interpret studies into the possible biochemical bases of schizophrenia. For example, even when distinctive chemicals are found, is schizophrenia caused by such chemicals or do schizophrenics simply produce them as part of the response to their disorder? Researchers in this area have become used to excited announcements of discoveries followed by failures to reproduce the findings. Often such "discoveries" have turned out to reflect methodological problems rather than real breakthroughs. For example, chemicals found in the urine of schizophrenics but not in control groups have sometimes turned out to be the result of the special drugs or diets given to schizophrenics in the hospital. In spite of these and related problems, many researchers are convinced that such biochemicals as dopamine in the brain will prove to have a crucial role in schizophrenia (e.g., Snyder et al., 1974). At present there are many promising leads and interesting theoretical developments (Cohen & Servan-Schreiber, 1992).

Twin Studies of Schizophrenia

For many years, the search for hereditary roots of schizophrenia was complicated by the difficulty of finding evidence that supports an interpretation of genetic determination and does not at the same time support an interpretation of environmental determination. For example, it had been shown that, in general, parents and brothers and sisters of schizophrenics are more likely to be labeled schizophrenic than are those who are not so related. Moreover, the more closely one is related to a schizophrenic, the greater the likelihood of also being labeled schizophrenic.

Specifically, identical (monozygotic) twins have been compared with fraternal (dizygotic) twins and a **concordance rate**—the percentage of pairs of twins in which the second twin is diagnosed as schizophrenic if the first twin has that diagnosis—has been computed. The concordance rate for monozygotic twins is higher than that for dizygotic twins and for siblings in all studies; careful investigations show that the concordance rate for monozygotic twins tends to range from about 25% to 40% (NIMH, 1975).

The monozygotic twin of a schizophrenic is not only more likely to be diagnosed as schizophrenic, but is also more likely to show various other forms of psychopathology or abnormal behavior even if he is not diagnosed as schizophrenic (Heston, 1970). Distant relatives of schizophrenics, such as cousins, are no more likely to be

IN FOCUS 8.3   *Sensation Seeking: A Trait with a Specific Biological Basis?*

Why do some people go parachuting and drive fast, whereas others prefer TV and rarely exceed the speed limit? According to one researcher, Marvin Zuckerman, the answer may lie in a trait called sensation seeking, and it is itself producing something of a sensation by yielding the first reports of links to a specific gene. In two studies, associations have been reported between a DNA marker (for a particular neuroreceptor gene) and measures of novelty seeking, an aspect of the broader pattern of sensation seeking (Benjamin et al., 1996; Ebstein et al., 1995). Although findings like these await further research before final conclusions can be reached, they point to the potential connections between aspects of behavior and their biological roots, which may well be found in the future, and they make sensation seeking a particularly interesting disposition.

The Nature of Sensation Seeking

Sensation seeking as a psychological pattern has a long research history (Zuckerman, Kolin, Price, & Zoob, 1964) and is measured with a Sensation Seeking Scale

(SSS) which taps into four different aspects: Thrill and Adventure Seeking (engaging in risky sports and fast driving, for example), Experience Seeking (seeking novelty), Disinhibition (seeking sensation through social stimulation and activities), and Boredom Susceptibility (lack of tolerance for repetitive events). This scale has helped to predict how individuals deal with situations in which there is a lack of stimulation: In this context, the sensation seekers get more restless and upset. It also predicts reactions to the opposite experience, as when one is placed in close confinement with another person. In that situation, those low in sensation seeking become more stressed, both in their own reports of the experience and on biochemical measures (e.g., Zuckerman, Persky, Link, & Basu, 1968).

Overall Results

Sensation seeking now has been been related to a wide range of diverse behaviors (Zuckerman, 1979, 1983, 1984, 1994), as the examples in Table 8.6 summarize.

schizophrenic (or otherwise disturbed) than anyone in the general population (Rosenthal, 1971).

These findings did not rule out an environmental or life-experience explanation. The closer the relationship between individuals, the more likely they are to interact to influence each other's environments and to model deviant behavior. The studies were needed of identical twins reared apart to compare genetic and environmental factors.

One well-known early study (Kallman, 1953) was criticized because the separation of the twins occurred late in life, after important early development had taken place. A possible solution is the study of children with schizophrenic parents who have been adopted or reared away from their parents. A study of 5,000 such children was conducted in Denmark (Kety et al., 1975). It was found that the biological relatives of schizophrenics were significantly more often schizophrenic than the biological relatives of a control group matched for age, sex, and social class. The adopted relatives of the schizophrenics showed no greater incidence of schizophrenia in spite of their close social interaction with these individuals. The findings thus support the influence of heredity in schizophrenia. In general, recent adoption studies consistently point to a

Table 8.6
Characteristics of High Sensation Seekers

Risk-Taking Behaviors

More varied sexual experience

Greater use and variety of illegal drugs

Risky driving habits

More risky sports, take risks within sports

Intellectual Preferences

Prefer complexity

Have a high tolerance for ambiguity

Are more original and creative

Rich imagery and dreams

Interests and Attitudes

Liberal, permissive, and nonconforming attitudes and choice

Prefer high-stimulation vocations (e.g., aircraft controllers; high-risk security officers, war-zone journalists, emergency room doctors)

May view love more as a game and show less commitment to their relationships

Roots of Sensation Seeking

Individual differences in sensation seeking may arise in part from physiological differences in physical arousal, such as cortical activity in reaction to novel and familiar stimuli (Zuckerman, 1990) or arousal of the catecholamine system (Zuckerman, 1994). The theory is that individuals have an *optimal level of arousal (OLA)*. Individuals with a low optimal level of arousal attempt to maintain a low level of arousal, which means that they must sometimes work toward reducing the stimulation in their environment. Those with a high OLA—the sensation seekers—must work toward increasing the stimulation they get in order to achieve and maintain their optimal level of arousal, and therefore they keep looking for change and searching for novel and complex sensations and experiences.

heritable disposition toward schizophrenia and certain other psychoses and weaken the role of the family-created environment (DeFries & Plomin, 1978; Gottesman, 1991; Rowe, 1991).

The Interaction of Factors

One extensive survey of research on schizophrenia led to the conclusion that while schizophrenia "itself is not inherited, a predisposition to it, or perhaps to psychopathology in general, almost certainly is" (NIMH, 1975, p. 30). But even in the children of parents who were both diagnosed as schizophrenic, disturbance is not inevitable. The fact that concordance rates for identical twins are far below 100% (and average about 50%) also supports the view that the explanation of schizophrenia lies in the interaction—the joint occurrence—of genetic predisposition, social stress, other conditions of life associated with social class position, and undoubtedly, other factors as well (NIMH, 1975, p. 131; Plomin et al., 1997).

In sum, schizophrenia and related forms of severe abnormality, like most complex social behaviors, are likely to be caused by the interaction of many factors. Genetics is sure to play a significant but not exclusive role, and so are biochemistry and the social environment, but the specific mix of ingredients in the interaction is still uncertain.

Trait Approach to Change: Biological Therapies

As we saw, the trait approach suggests that some psychological dispositions may have biological roots. If problematic behaviors, such as severe depression, reflect biological dispositions and biochemical problems, might they also respond to biological treatment? Researchers have actively pursued this question. If the cause is biochemical, it also makes good sense to search for the cure through biochemical means.

Biological treatments attempt to change an individual's mood or behavior by direct intervention in bodily processes. These techniques include destruction of brain tissue by surgical operation, the electrical induction of convulsions by shock treatments, and the administration of drugs that cause chemical changes in bodily processes. Some biological methods have been valuable in the treatment or prevention of certain patterns of disturbed behaviors that result from physiological disorders. For example, general paresis (an organic psychosis caused by syphilis) may be controlled with antibiotics; mental problems associated with pellagra (a disorder produced by a vitamin deficiency) have been minimized through vitamin treatment; and barbiturates have helped people who have epilepsy. In all these cases, biological therapy changes the bodily processes believed to be responsible for the troublesome behavior. In other efforts, biological methods have been tried to treat behavior disturbances that seem not to have specific physiological causes.

Pharmacotherapy, or treatment with drugs, has so far proved to be the most promising biological therapy for psychological problems. The types of drugs used for specific purposes are summarized in Table 8.7.

Table 8.7
Some Drugs Used in Pharmacotherapy

Type of Drug	Application	Therapeutic Effects
Antidepressants (cyclics, monoamine oxidase inhibitors)	Depression	Appear effective for elevating mood in some people
Antipsychotics (phenothiazines)	Schizophrenia	Well substantiated: get patients out of hospitals, have practically eliminated need for restraints in hospitals
Minor tranquilizers (benzodiazepines)	Anxiety, tension, milder forms of depression	Seem to slow down transmission of nerve impulses in the brain
Lithium	Manic behavior	Reduces mood swings
Methadone (a synthetic narcotic)	Heroin addiction	May eliminate craving for heroin; blocks "highs"

NOTE: These drugs are classified according to their effects on behavior, not according to their chemical composition. Chemically dissimilar drugs can produce similar effects.

Antidepressants.   The **antidepressants,** or psychic energizers, are used to elevate the mood of depressed individuals. Two of the largest categories are the cyclics and the monoamine oxidase inhibitors (MAOIs) (Lader, 1980). Fluoxetine (trade name Prozac) is currently one of the most favored and widely used cyclic antidepressants that increase the chemical neurotransmitter **serotonin** (Kramer, 1993). Excessively low serotonin levels seem to be related to such feelings as chronic pessimism, rejection sensitivity, and obsessive worry. Antidepressants have been shown to have varying degrees of efficacy and produce various side effects (e.g., Davis et al., 1967; Klein et al., 1980; Levine, 1991). The MAOIs, for example, appear highly effective in certain types of depressed individuals, although their side effects can include a dangerous rise in blood pressure when foods high in tyramine, such as red wine and cheese, are consumed (Howland, 1991; Kayser et al., 1988; Potter et al, 1991). Lithium, an alkali metal in a drug category of its own, is used to stabilize mood swings and occasionally to treat severe depression (Grilly, 1989).

Antipsychotics.   The **phenothiazines** (most notably chlorpromazine) have proved to be so useful in managing schizophrenic patients that they are referred to as **antipsychotic drugs.** Their use in mental hospitals has been widespread since the 1950s and has changed the character of many hospitals, eliminating the need for locked wards and straitjackets. Discharged patients are often on maintenance dosages of these drugs and must occasionally return to the hospital for dose level adjustments.

The major tranquilizers have potentially serious side effects that may include motor disturbances, low blood pressure, and jaundice. There are also unpleasant subjective effects such as fatigue, blurred vision, and mouth dryness, which may explain why patients on their own may simply stop taking these drugs and often have to return to the hospital for an extended stay.

Minor Tranquilizers.   The barbiturates were the first widely used minor tranquilizers—drugs which relieve anxiety that is not severe. However, these drugs were replaced by the **benzodiazepines,** which proved more effective with fewer side effects (Lader, 1980). For many years, the most widely used of these drugs was a synthetic chemical known by its trade name, Valium. It became the medicine most frequently prescribed in the United States for several years as Americans spent almost half a billion dollars a year on it.

Valium, like its predecessors the barbiturates, acts on the limbic system of the brain and is useful in the treatment of anxiety, panic disorder, and some convulsive disorders (Gitlin, 1990). Although Valium seemed less harmful than the barbiturates, it also proved to have side effects and to be potentially addictive. It can endanger a developing fetus and can have reverse effects of confusion and agitation, especially in the elderly. Now other benzodiazepines such as Xanax, Klonodin, and Ativan are popular alternatives, although their potentially severe side effects also require extremely cautious monitoring. The use of antidepressant medication in treatment of extreme anxiety or panic attacks also may be effective (Gitlin, 1990).

Other widely used drugs include the psychostimulants, such as *Ritalin,* which are used in treating impulse disorders and severe attention deficits. **Methadone,** a drug which blocks the craving for heroin and prevents heroin "highs," is often used to overcome heroin addiction, either by weaning the person off it or by maintaining him or her on a fixed dose; however, methadone itself is addictive, and the process can take a long time (Lawson & Cooperrider, 1988).

As this brief survey suggests, some drugs appear to be positive contributors to a treatment program for some disorders. However, no drug by itself constitutes an adequate complete treatment for psychological problems. To the extent that the person's difficulties reflect problems of living, it would be naïve to think that drugs can substitute completely for learning and practicing more effective ways to cope with the continuous challenges of life. And the fact that most drugs have negative side effects (Maricle, Kinzie, & Lewinsohn, 1988) makes it all the more important to seek psychological treatment for psychological problems whenever possible, often in conjunction with a medically supervised form of pharmacotherapy.

New Research Directions.   In spite of the formidable problems encountered by efforts to treat psychological problems chemically, there is much exciting progress in recent research, and the new field of **neuropharmacology** is thriving (e.g., Cooper, Bloom, & Roth, 1986). For example, biological responses in panic disorders are becoming better understood and, in turn, the effects of various chemicals (such as sodium-lactate) on panic states are becoming known (e.g., Hollander et al., 1989). As a result, treatments for a wide range of anxiety and mood disorders are taking account of both biochemical and psychological processes (Barlow, 1988; Klein & Klein, 1989; Simons & Thase, 1992).

SUMMARY

1. There is growing evidence for some of the biological bases of personality, encouraging efforts to study personality in genetic and biochemical terms.

2. Twin studies examine the separate role of genetics and environment. Researchers calculate the genetic heritability of traits from various twin studies and consistently find environment to be less significant than earlier theories had expected. The genetic contribution to personality seems considerable, particularly to such temperaments as emotionality, activity level, and sociability.

3. Answers on self-report personality questionnaires typically yield correlations of about .50 for the similarity of identical twins reared together and about .25 for fraternal twins reared together. When the identical twins are reared apart, correlations are only slightly lower, about .40. These correlation patterns imply that 40%–50% of the self-reported personality differences among individuals (i.e., the percentage variance) can be accounted for by their genetic differences. Adoption studies—for example, comparing birth parents and their adopted-away children—suggest much less genetic influence, however, perhaps about 20% of the variance.

4. Regardless of whether genetic factors account for about 20% or 40%, clearly their influence is significant, especially given that few findings in personality account for as much as 20% of the variance.

5. Just as noteworthy is the other side of that finding: namely, the fact that the same data show that most of the variance of personality is *not* due to genetic factors. Suppose, for example, that the heritability correlation for identical twins reared apart is .40—that is, that 40% of the variance is shared between them, attributable to their genetic relatedness. Then the same correlation also indicates that 60% is *not* shared between them. These differences between the identical twins cannot be due to genetics and thus must be attributable to environment. So the same genetic data that document the importance of genetic influences also attest to the importance of the environment for personality.

6. Most twin data on personality come from self-report personality questionnaires, and while they consistently yield evidence for moderate genetic influence, they are limited by the fact that they depend on the person's own judgments. However, in recent twin studies such measures as ratings by peers or observational measures have been employed and also indicate genetic influence.

7. The search for specific genes that contribute to genetic influence on personality is still at an early stage but provides a promising route for helping to specify the mechanisms through which heredity impacts personality.

8. Biological treatments for psychological disorders believed to have a biochemical foundation now favor pharmacotherapy, which makes use of a variety of drugs. Several drugs appear to be helpful aids in treatment. They facilitate but do not by themselves substitute for more effective coping patterns to deal with the problems of living.

CHAPTER 9

Traits: Biological Bases and Behavioral Expressions

GENE-ENVIRONMENT INTERPLAY

Given that both nature (genetics) and nurture (environment) are important influences on personality, the next step is to understand the developmental interplay between them. This interplay is seen in the course of life as the personality of the person, partly influenced by genetics, interacts with and to some degree selects and shapes the situations in his or her psychological world, just as those situations over time, in turn, exert their impact on what the person becomes. In this chapter we examine this interplay and its implications for personality. We then consider the implications of another aspect of the biological human heritage for understanding personality and social behavior. That is the process of evolution, which involves the gene-environment interplay as it unfolds over the long-term scale of time. We conclude with a discussion of how personality traits interact with situations and are expressed in behavior.

The Unique (Nonshared) Psychological Environment of Each Family Member

Twin studies have inquired into the environmental influences that make genetically identical "clones" (identical twins) different from each other. For many years it was widely thought that children growing up in the same family would be similar to one another in personality for environmental reasons because they shared the "same" family situation. Genetic researchers now believe that this assumption is false. They contend that family members resemble one another in personality largely because of genetic influences and that the environment seems to make members of a family different (e.g., Plomin et al., 1997). Their reasoning is based on two findings. First, twins reared apart are only somewhat less similar in personality than twins who grew up in the same family. In addition, in studies of adoptive families that have more than one adopted child, the genetically unrelated children show little similarity in personality even though they had the same "shared environment," that is, they were raised within the same family (Plomin, Chipuer, & Neiderhiser, 1994).

Note that the shared or "family environment" in the twin studies was treated as a global entity, as if families treat all the siblings in them the same way. The psychological environments experienced by each member of the family, however, may be quite different and each may receive distinctively different treatments within the same

221

family. Each parent may relate differently to each child. Moreover, much of the psychological environment experienced by individuals involves continuing significant encounters outside the family (with peers, school, spouse, and in the broader group and culture), the nature and effects of which may change with different phases of development.

Nonshared Environmental Influences within the Family

The *nonshared* environment or unique environment exerts its effects on each person through many routes, beginning in prenatal development and birth order effects. It includes biological events such as illness and nutrition, as well as psychosocial events such as interpersonal experiences that may range from parental reactions to peer influences and romantic partners and mates (see Table 9.1). For example, earlier-born children are larger, more powerful, and more privileged than later-born children and that, in turn, may affect their personality development (Sulloway, 1996). From the start, each child is born into a slightly different family psychologically and structurally, and parents treat siblings differently, and siblings treat one another differently.

It is understandable that most parents find it hard to admit that they treat their children differently, given the social norms that press for them to treat each one "the same." But children correctly believe that their parents do treat them differently—an impression confirmed by observational studies (Reiss, Neiderhiser, Hetherington, & Plomin, in press). So, for example, parents are likely to react differently to their first and their fifth child, perhaps hovering over their first baby and swamped by the time the fifth one arrives. On close examination, children growing up in the same family lead remarkably separate lives (Dunn & Plomin, 1990). Even such variables as parental divorce tend to affect children within the family differently, depending, for example, on the child's age and role in the family, as well as many other variables (Hetherington & Clingempeel, 1992). In short, siblings growing up in the same family experience it differently so that psychologically it is not the same.

Research that traces how differences in such experiences lead to differences in outcomes is still just beginning, but some links have already been shown (Reiss et al., in

Table 9.1
The "Nonshared Environment": Examples of Salient Environmental Influences That Siblings in the Family Do Not Share Equally

Position in the family

Parental reactions

Accidents

Prenatal events, illness

Peer group reactions and support

Other interpersonal experiences (e.g., mates)

Educational and occupational experiences

press). Most of these associations connect negative aspects of parenting (such as conflict) with such negative outcomes as antisocial behavior later in development. It is especially interesting that some associations (of modest strength) have been reported between differences in parental negativity toward identical twins and their adolescent maladjustment on such indices as depression and antisocial behavior (Reiss et al., in press). Obviously such differences cannot be due to genetic factors and thus must be due to the nonshared environment (Pike et al., 1996). Generally weaker correlations are found between positive aspects of parenting (such as affection) and positive outcomes.

The correlations between measures of the children's nonshared environment and their personality also raise the old chicken and egg question, that is, the direction of the effects: Does parental negativity cause negative outcomes in personality? Or do parents treat some of their children more negatively than others in reaction to the child's personality, responding more harshly for instance to siblings who are more difficult to deal with? If the latter holds, the differential treatment siblings receive may be due in part to each child's distinctive genetics (Plomin, 1994b). In other words, differential parental treatment of siblings may be due to genetically influenced differences among the siblings, including differences in their personality.

Nonshared Environmental Influences outside the Family

The nonshared environment includes but goes far beyond differences in siblings' unique experiences within the family (see Table 9.1). Some of the most important aspects of the nonshared environment unfold in the experiences children have outside the family as they interact with their expanding worlds. In these interactions they may form quite different relations with peers, encounter different types of social support, and build different lives with different educational, occupational, and interpersonal experiences and events along the route (Plomin, 1994b). Further, such factors as accidents and illnesses, as well as chance encounters and experiences, may initiate significant differences among siblings (Dunn & Plomin, 1990). While such events initially may be relatively minor, they can snowball and become compounded over time into large outcome differences years later.

To recapitulate, we saw that environmental influences that affect personality development do not seem to operate on a family-by-family "on the whole" basis, but rather on an individual-by-individual basis. That suggests that environmental effects on personality are specific to each child rather than general for all children in a given family. It makes the unit of analysis each child as he or she distinctively interacts with relevant specific environmental situations, including with particular family members. Environmental influences on personality development seem to operate mostly in a nonshared manner, making children growing up in the same family different from one another. As was discussed, attempts to identify specific sources of nonshared environment indicate that many sibling experiences differ. Even such seemingly shared variables as parental attitudes about childrearing and the parents' relationship might not be experienced the same way and might, in fact, be subtly different for each sibling. Some of these sibling differences in experience have already been related to psychological outcomes, but the sources of nonshared environment effects remain unclear and complex, as discussed next.

Interactions among Nature-Nurture Influences

There are continuous complex interactions between the expressions of genetic influences and the nonshared environments—the situations and events that the person experiences (e.g., Rutter et al., 1997). These interactions make it difficult and perhaps impossible to isolate the contribution of genetics versus environmental influences with precision because their interplay becomes virtually indivisible.

For example, adult twins reared apart rated the family environments in which they grew up more similarly than did fraternal twins reared apart (Rowe, 1981, 1983b). Presumably this happened for at least two possible reasons. First, identical twins even reared apart may be more alike in how they perceive and interpret their experiences, and, second, but equally important, they may have been treated more similarly due to their genetically influenced shared characteristics such as their more similar physical appearance, abilities, skills, and temperaments, for example (Plomin et al., 1988). Likewise, beyond the family environment, genetic similarity may lead to greater similarity in the experienced environments in peer groups (e.g., Manke et al., 1995), in the classroom (Jang, 1993), and in work environments (Hershberger, Lichteinstein, & Knox, 1994). It may also influence such other life events as proneness to childhood accidents or illness (Phillips & Mathews, 1995) or exposure to trauma (Lyon et al., 1993) or drugs (Tsuang et al., 1992).

Perhaps the clearest evidence for genetic effects on experience comes from observational studies that also show such genetic effects (although often of lower magnitude), making it plain that they do not just depend on self-reports and questionnaires. For example, the Home Observation for Measurement of the Environment, or HOME, is a widely used measure of the home environment that combines observations and interviews (Caldwell & Bradley, 1978). It assesses aspects of the home environment such as parental responsivity and encouragment of developmental advance. In an adoption study with this measure, the home environment of each sibling was assessed when the child was one year old and again when each child was two years old (Braungart et al., 1992). HOME correlations for genetically unrelated children adopted into the same home (adoptive siblings) were compared with those for genetically related siblings in nonadoptive homes (nonadoptive siblings). HOME scores were more similar for nonadoptive siblings than for adoptive siblings at both one and two years, suggesting genetic influence on this measure (see Table 9.2).

In another observational study, O'Connor and associates (1995) obtained videotaped observations of adolescents' interactions with their mothers or their fathers in 10-minute discussions of problems and conflicts within each parent-adolescent dyad. The adolescent participants included six groups of siblings: identical twins, fraternal twins, full siblings in nondivorced families, and full siblings, half siblings, and unrelated siblings in stepfamilies. Using sophisticated estimates of heritability the researchers found some significant genetic influences on both the positive and negative interaction with both the mothers and fathers.

Table 9.2
HOME Score Correlations for Nonadoptive and Adoptive Siblings at Ages One and Two Years

Environmental Measure	Sibling Correlations	
	Nonadoptive	Adoptive
1 year	.58	.35
2 years	.57	.40

NOTE: *Adoptive* = genetically unrelated, adopted into same home; *Nonadoptive* = genetically related in nonadoptive homes.

SOURCE: Braungart, J. M., Fulker, D. W., & Plomin, R. (1992). Genetic influence of the home environment during infancy: A sibling adoption study of the HOME. *Developmental Psychology, 28,* 1048–1055.

Influence of Genes on Environments

Genetic factors may contribute to the experienced environment in several ways (Plomin et al., 1997; Rutter et al., 1997). First, people encounter the environments that their genetic relatives in part make for them. Take activity level, for example, which seems to have a heritable component and is thus shared to some degree between the child and the parents (Saudino & Plomin, 1996). From the start, parents construct aspects of their child's early environment and tend to make it more (or less) stimulating and activity-filled in a way that is consistent with both their own and their child's genetic propensities. Thus, highly active children are likely to have active parents who model and reward high activity and who also provide them with both genes and an environment conducive to the development of high activity.

Second, the individual's genetically influenced characteristics affect how other people will react to him or her. For example, highly active children might receive more positive reactions from their peers or, in the opposite direction, more negative reactions from their school teachers.

Third, and most important, individuals actively seek and create situations and social environments in ways congruent with their genetically influenced dispositions and qualities. Whereas extremely active children are likely to create a high-energy environment by actively selecting highly active friends and activities, less active children are apt to make their environment less energy-demanding. This self-directed process of selecting and creating one's own situations is the most central for personality; it is literally the seat of the sort of dynamic *person X situation* interactions through which dispositions and the environment reciprocally influence each other. That interaction is the focus of the process-oriented approaches to personality discussed briefly at the end of this chapter and in depth in Part VI.

Given the multiple paths through which genetic influences impact the environment, it is understandable that genetic factors often contribute substantially to measures of the environment in research. But while it is clear that genetic factors influence the environments we experience and select, the effects are complex, and the direct genetic influence is only one contributor. The point that these findings make is that researchers must move away from passive models of how the environment or the genes

Michael Rutter

separately affect individuals and turn to models of person-environment interaction. These interaction models recognize the active role that persons play in selecting, modifying, and creating their own environments. In this process there is a continuous interaction between dispositions (partly influenced by genetics, partly by environmental influences) and situations as the individual deals with his or her world in the course of development. Such interaction implies that some of the most important questions in genetic research will involve the environment and some of the most important questions for environment research will involve genetics (Rutter et al., 1997).

Genetic research on personality development is sure to profit if it includes sophisticated measures of the environment, and environmental research equally should gain from the use of genetic designs. A constructive collaboration that incorporates both genetic and environmental influences and focuses on their interplay in the life course promises to clarify their interaction and at last to bury the nature versus nurture controversy (see *In Focus 9.1*).

EVOLUTIONARY PROCESSES UNDERLYING TRAITS

We next turn to the evolutionary perspective on personality traits. This perspective is distinctively different from the genetic approach, although both are attempts to link the personality dispositions that are the crux of trait psychology to their biological foundations.

In the *evolutionary approach* (Buss, 1991, 1994, 1997; Cosmides & Tooby, 1989), based on Darwin's well-established theory, major personality traits and the important differences among people in those characteristics reflect the process of *natural selection* through which change takes place in all organic forms. The processes of *adaptation* and *selection* help to explain the evolution of organisms and to understand *why* they become what they are (e.g., why kidneys, larynxes, feet, and keen sight develop). These attributes are here, in the evolutionary view, because they allowed survival and reproduction.

Applied to personality, this view also sees individual differences in traits as emerging slowly over time as humans struggled with the basic tasks of survival and

IN FOCUS 9.1

Social Environments Can Change the Expression of Genes, the Brain, and Personality

Researchers, pursuing the genetic approach to personality, readily acknowledge that even highly heritable traits can be constrained or limited in their full expression, as when the person's growth and ultimate height are affected by nutrition or disease in development. But although they refer to the "interplay" of genes and environment, they do *not* see this interplay as a two-way reciprocal or mutual influence process: Obviously, social environments and the experiences in the world (barring extreme radiation or other biochemical effects on the genes directly) cannot affect the structure of your DNA. So in that sense the interplay between genes and environment in these analyses refers to a one-way influence process from genes to environment, in which genetic influences have an impact through various routes on the environments experienced with no modification of the genetic structure itself.

But it is also the case that social-psychological environmental influences can and do affect the expression of the genes: Just by reading this paragraph you increase DNA transcription rates of certain neurotransmitters. And evironmental influences also change the hard wiring of

the brain—the neuronal structures themselves—and thus produce stable changes within the person at an organic level, even though they do not alter the structure of the DNA. This is evident, for example, in the finding that stress actually shrinks the size of the hippocampus—a brain structure basic for higher order mental functions (e.g., Sapolsky, 1996).

Sapolsky reviewed studies showing that sustained stress increases glucocorticoids (GCs), a chemical substance that at high rates can have negative effects on health (as summarized in Figure 9.1). Consistent with this finding, Sapolsky (1996) reports research with rodents showing that exposure to excessive amounts of GCs can impair the brain, with particularly unfortunate effects on the hippocampus, a brain structure crucial for learning and memory. Studies with depressed patients also showed that the volume of this brain structure was significantly reduced, and the longer the depression the greater the amount of brain atrophy (Sapolsky, 1996). Furthermore, combat veterans suffering from post-traumatic stress reactions (e.g., after terrifying war experiences) also displayed not only greater exposure to GCs but also

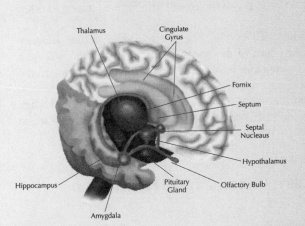

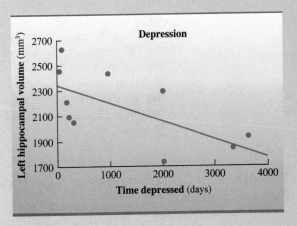

Figure 9.1
Relation between Hippocampal Volume and Duration of Depression among Individuals with a History of Major Depression

SOURCE: Sapolsky, R. M. (1996). Why stress is bad for your brain. *Science, 273,* 749–750.

substantial reduction in their hippocampi on both sides of the brain.

In short, although the social environment does not influence the structure of the genes, it can influence their expression, the brain, and the person's personality. As later sections of the text discuss, situations and environments importantly influence what people experience and do in a stable relationship to those contexts: When the situations remain stable, so does their characteristic pattern of social behavior; when the situations change, the behavior pattern also does so predictably (e.g., Mischel & Shoda, 1995, 1998). And as was just noted, such environmental events as stress levels not only dramatically impact behavior and experience, but also change the hardwiring, that is, the structures in the brain. Person-environment interactions are two-way interactions in which the person's characteristics show some change over time, just as the characteristics also in part change the environment (Rutter et al., 1997). The processes through which situations interact with the psychological characteristics and personality dispositions of the individual are addressed in detail by cognitive social approaches in the final part of the text (Part VI).

In sum, environmental, genetic, and brain influences are in continuous interaction. These interactions affect what we feel and do, which, in turn, produces further changes. The challenge in future research on the interplay of genes and environment will be to clarify the complex and dynamic processes that lie between genes, the brain, and behavior (Gazzaniga, Ivry, & Mangun, 1998).

successful reproduction. In mate selection, for example, this approach assumes that such traits as dominance, emotional stability, and sociability would have an especially significant role (e.g., Kenrick, Sadalla, Groth, & Trost, 1990). In the survival of the group itself, such traits as conscientiousness and agreeableness-friendliness likewise would be of particular value, again in terms of biological principles common to other species and not unique to humans.

Consider male sexual jealousy. From this perspective, male sexual jealousy evolved throughout the evolutionary past of the species because those who had such feelings and behaviors prevented competing males from sexual contacts that interfered with their reproductive success and paternity. Thus, the jealous males had a mechanism that allowed greater reproductive success than did those who did not interfere when their mates had sexual contact with other males (Buss, 1997), and so that mechanism survived.

Evolutionary Adaptiveness and Personality: Discriminative Facility and Flexibility in Coping

Some of the most important challenges that required adaptive solutions and that created problems for human survival came not from the physical challenges of nature but from other hostile humans. As Buss (1997) points out, this recognition comes from studies on topics that range from group warfare to the evolution of language and higher mental functions (e.g., Pinker, 1997).

David Buss

Particularly relevant for personality is the discovery of the prevalence of *domain-specific psychological mechanisms* that govern diverse aspects of human social exchange and interaction (Cosmides, 1989). This is seen in the formation of *dyadic alliances* (such as lifelong mating relationships), which pose many enduring problems that demand adaptive strategic social solutions for reproduction and survival. For example, people need to accurately assess the resources and characteristics of potential friends and enemies as they initiate efforts to develop friendships and connections that enhance their adaptation and survival. Relevant to this function, it has been suggested that humans have developed a *cheater detector*—a mechanism to detect cheaters, that is, to identify the people who seek the benefits of social exchange but refuse to reciprocate appropriately (Cosmides, 1989). This cheater detector mechanism seems to involve a mental algorithm within the human repertoire for identifying those people who will be unlikely to reciprocate social exchange efforts fairly and will prevent them from being successful (Cosmides & Tooby, 1989).

Specificity of Psychological Mechanisms Produced by Evolution: The Concept of Domain Specificity

A main point of current evolutionary thinking is that the psychological mechanisms that evolved are highly specific, rather than global, and targeted to solve quite specific evolutionary problems like mate choice and mate retention (Buss, 1997). Mate choice itself, for example, takes a somewhat different form for males and females. In turn, these psychological problem-solving mechanisms are different from those needed in social exchanges. Because humans face a host of different types of social problems, each of which requires somewhat different strategies and solutions, evolutionary theory predicts that the mechanisms that emerge will be highly *domain specific*. Such specificity appears to be a necessary requirement for achieving the enormous behavioral discriminativeness and flexibility that has been observed in domains ranging from the diversity of human motives, to the specificity of learning, to content-specific phobias or fears (Buss, 1997), to most patterns of social behavior (Cantor & Kihlstrom, 1987; Mischel, 1968, 1973; Mischel & Shoda, 1998).

Answering the question, "What psychological mechanisms could produce extreme behavioral flexibility?" Buss puts it this way:

> A carpenter's flexibility comes not from having a single domain-general "all purpose tool" that is used to cut, saw, screw, twist, wrench, plane, balance, and hammer, but rather from having many, more specialized tools each designed to perform a particular function (Buss, 1997, p. 325).

From the perspective of evolutionary theory it is the availability of many specific tools, not any single highly elastic tool, that gives the carpenter—and the human being—the flexibility required for the diverse challenges encountered. And, indeed, that also seems to be evident in the ways in which human personality characteristics are expressed in situation-specific patterns of social behavior (e.g., Mischel & Shoda, 1995, 1998).

Implications for Personality

The implications of evolutionary theory for personality are potentially great, providing provocative albeit speculative insights. In its approach to the motivations that characterize human nature, it argues that ". . . natural selection could not produce an organism with global motives like 'survive' simply because the organism would have no way of knowing how to behave when confronted with extreme cold, putrid meat, a thousand-foot cliff, or a poisonous snake" (Buss, 1997, p. 328) and thus could not survive for long. In the context of social behavior and the problems of social interaction, this implies that important individual differences will be linked to aspects of natural selection, as in the choice of mates for reproduction. That makes such characteristics as dominance, emotional stability, and friendliness—all relevant for mate selection and survival—likely to be particularly significant (Kenrick, Sadalla, Groth & Trost, 1990; McCrae & Costa, 1989, 1997; Wiggins, 1979, 1997).

In this view, such heritable characteristics as physical attractiveness and various types of abilities that are directly relevant to reproductive success also are conceptualized as ingredients of the strategic individual differences in specific coping mechanisms. These mechanisms become stable and robust because of their evolutionary value (Buss, 1997). Furthermore, in this view, personality trait terms summarize the most important features of the social terrain—the landscape—to which human beings have to adapt (Buss, 1989). They thus are used evaluatively to quickly answer questions about the status of people in the social hierarchy, their future prospects, their value for providing or sharing needed resources, their potential harmfulness or helpfulness, and so on.

These functions of trait terms make it understandable that the dimensions captured in trait taxonomies like the Big Five are both highly evaluative and interpersonal, seemingly summarizing the types of judgments people tend to make as they try to know others within their adaptive landscape. Looked at from this perspective, these dimensions provide a map plotting, for example, who to go to for advice and help (those with high intellect, the open-minded) or who to avoid (the unstable, the unconscientious, the hostile), or who to choose as a mate or partner (the stable, the dependable, the sociable). Consistent with these expectations, people do seem able to make trait judgments and evaluations quickly and on the basis of relatively limited information, and in ways that on the whole agree with the judgments made by others (Funder & Colvin, 1997).

THE EXPRESSION OF TRAITS IN INTERACTION WITH SITUATIONS

The early trait psychologists, guided by an essentially 19th-century view of science, tended to follow the example of simple physical measurement. They hoped that the measurement of traits would be basically similar to such measurements as table length with rulers or temperature with thermometers. It was assumed that broad trait structures exist and lead people to behave consistently. Consequently, trait theorists did not pay much attention to situational variables as determinants of behavior. Instead, they concentrated on standardization of measurement conditions in the hope that broad traits would emerge across many situations.

On the one hand, the existence of stable individual differences in "average levels" of different types of trait-relevant behavior and of trait ratings themselves has been widely established for many years (e.g., Epstein, 1983; Mischel, 1968, 1990; Pervin, 1990). On the other hand, the nature of the consistencies across situations or coherences in trait-relevant behavior that characterize individuals has turned out to be both complex and controversial since the start of the field (e.g., Hartshorne & May, 1928; Mischel, 1968; Mischel & Peake, 1982; Mischel & Shoda, 1995; Newcomb, 1929).

Stability of Traits over Time

Studies of individual differences on trait dimensions have produced many networks of correlations. These associations tend to be large and enduring when people rate themselves or others with broad trait terms (e.g., Block, 1971; Caspi & Bem, 1990; Costa & McCrae, 1988; E. L. Kelly, 1955). Such ratings suggest significant continuity and stability in how people are perceived over the years as well as in how they perceive themselves.

For example, long-term stability was shown using the Q-sort technique (described in Chapter 7) in some early landmark studies that closely followed children into adulthood (Block, 1971), as summarized in Table 9.3. It is also high on many personality trait inventories, with the exception of measures like the MMPI—the measure of psychopathology discussed in Chapter 7—and ranges on average from median correlations of .34 to .77 (Costa & McCrae, 1997).

In recent years, considerable stability also has been demonstrated on trait ratings and questionnaires related to the Big Five (e.g., McCrae & Costa, 1990) even for long time spans, and it tends to be particularly high during the adult years (Costa & McCrae, 1997). These authors emphasize that in spite of the many changes that often occur in life structures during adulthood over long time periods—including the

Table 9.3
Examples of Significant Stability over Time in Ratings of Personality

| | Correlations From | | |
	Junior to Senior H.S.	Senior H.S. to Adulthood	Item Rated
Males	.57	.59	Tends toward undercontrol of needs and impulses; unable to delay gratification
	.58	.53	Is a genuinely dependable and responsible person
	.50	.42	Is self-defeating
Females	.50	.46	Basically submissive
	.48	.49	Tends to be rebellious, nonconforming
	.39	.43	Emphasizes being with others, gregarious

SOURCE: Based on Block, J. (1971). *Lives through time.* Berkeley, CA: Bancroft.

changes produced by marriage, children, divorce, residential and occupational moves, and health issues—the status of most individuals on the Big Five dimensions tends to show stability (see Table 9.4).

When ongoing behavior in specific situations is sampled objectively by different, independent measures, however, the association generally tends to be more modest. Thus, while people often show consistency on questionnaires and ratings, these data may not predict their actual behavior very accurately. Therefore, one has to be cautious about generalizing from a person's personality test behavior to his or her behavior outside the test.

For example, we cannot safely conclude that Gary's lack of authoritarianism on the California *F* Scale precludes his behaving in highly arbitrary, "authoritarian" ways under certain life conditions. Perhaps, then, his friend was right when he noted that Gary could be "arbitrary" and "bossy," with an insulting cynical humor. The same friend also described Gary as "friendly and outgoing"—but only when he is "with a

Table 9.4
Stability of NEO-PI Scales (Ages 25–56)

NEO-PI Scale	Men	Women
N (Neuroticism)	.78	.85
E (Extraversion)	.84	.75
O (Open mindedness)	.87	.84
A (Agreeableness)	.64	.60
C (Conscientiousness)	.83	.84

NOTE: Retest interval is six years for N, E, and O scales, three years for short forms of A and C scales.
SOURCE: Adapted from McCrae, R. R., & Costa, P.T., Jr. (1990). *Personality in adulthood* (p. 88). New York: Guilford.

shy, self-conscious person." As these examples indicate, Gary's authoritarianism, his friendliness or hostility, and other key features of his behavior are not situation-free attributes: They depend on many modifying conditions.

The evaluation of all data on trait consistency also depends, of course, on the standards selected to evaluate them and the goals of the research. A modest consistency coefficient (of about .30, for example) can be taken as evidence either of the relative specificity of the particular behaviors or of the presence of some cross-situational generality (Burton, 1963; Epstein, 1983; Kenrick & Funder, 1988; Mischel, 1990). All individuals may be consistent in their own behavior on some traits (e.g., Bem & Allen, 1974) or in some types of situations (e.g., Wright & Mischel, 1987). But on many traits, most of us show only limited consistency from one type of situation to another (Chaplin & Goldberg, 1984; Mischel, 1968, 1990; Mischel & Peake, 1982; Mischel & Shoda, 1995), although, to reiterate, there is overall stability in trait ratings over time (Costa & McCrae, 1997).

Dispositions and Situations Interact

In this chapter we have seen that geneticists are showing the importance of genetic influences on the environments that people experience, and evolutionary theorists are underlining the domain specificity and context dependency of adaptive social behavior. At the same time, and consistent with both these developments, sophisticated trait research is taking the specific context, that is, situations (environments) into account seriously and examining how dispositions and situations interact and are connected (Mischel & Shoda, 1998).

Consistent with an interactionist view, knowledge of individual differences alone often tells us little unless it is combined with information about the conditions and situational variables that influence the behavior of interest. Conversely, the effects of conditions depend on the individuals in them. Thus, the interaction of individual differences and particular conditions, and not just the individuals or the contexts themselves, tends to be most important (Bem & Funder, 1978; Magnusson, 1980, 1990; Shoda, Mischel, & Wright, 1994; Wright & Mischel, 1987).

Consider, for example, Moos's (1968) classic studies of the reactions reported by staff and psychiatric patients to various settings in the hospital. The results revealed, first, that different individuals reacted differently to the settings. Second, a person might be high on a dimension of behavior like friendliness in the morning but not at lunch, high with another patient but not with a nurse, low in small group therapy and moderate in industrial therapy but high in individual therapy, etc. An entirely different pattern might characterize the next person. Each person's unique pattern, however, may be stable itself (Mischel, 1991; Mischel & Shoda, 1995).

We might be able to predict many of the things Gary will do simply by knowing something about the situation in which he will be: At school in an economics course Gary is likely to behave very differently than he does on a date with his girlfriend at a football game. On the other hand, our predictions in each case probably would be best if we considered Gary's relevant qualities as an individual—his academic interests and skills, his attitudes toward women, his past behavior on dates at football games—as well as the situation when we try to predict his behavior in each setting. In other words, we may predict best if we know what each situation means to the individual and consider the unique interaction of the person and the setting, rather than concentrating either on the situation itself or on the individual in an environmental and social vacuum.

Context-Specific Expressions of Traits

A great deal of research has shown that performances on trait measures are affected by the context (e.g., Mischel & Peake, 1982; Wright & Mischel, 1987) and can be modified by numerous environmental changes (Masling, 1960; Mischel, 1968; Peterson, 1968; Vernon, 1964)—a finding again consistent with the expectations of evolutionary theory with its emphasis on domain-specific adaptive behaviors designed to deal with particular types of situations and challenges. Thus, normal people tend to show considerable variability in their behavior across conditions. A person may be dependent with his wife, for example, but not with his boss, and even his dependency at home may be highly specific, varying as a result of slight situational alterations, such as subtle changes in his wife's reactions to him or the presence of other family members. Thus, behavior tends to be much more situation-specific and discriminative than early trait theorists had thought.

The significant consistency that exists is at least in part reflected in stable patterns of behavior *within* similar types of psychological situations (Mischel & Peake, 1982; Mischel & Shoda, 1995). As the similarity among situations decreases, so does the cross-situational consistency of the person's behavior (Krahe, 1990; Shoda, 1990; Shoda, Mischel, & Wright, 1994). Thus, it becomes difficult to predict from what individuals did in one type of situation to what they will do in a very different type of situation. On the other hand, within particular types of situations individuals do show characteristic stable patterns (Mischel & Shoda, 1995; Shoda, Mischel & Wright, 1994). These patterns are expressed as stable "if . . . then . . ." relationships, such that when the situation (the "if") remains stable (e.g., if "teased by peers about his glasses and appearance"), then so does the behavior (e.g., he becomes physically aggressive). So for the people we know well, we have a sense not only of what they are like in general (in trait terms) but also of what they are likely to do in particular types of situations (e.g., at the holiday dinner, in an argument about money, on a date).

An Example: Anxiety as a Person X Situation Interaction

In sum, a comprehensive approach to traits must take account of the interaction of person and situation because the expressions of a person's traits hinge on the particular psychological situation at that time (e.g., Dworkin, 1979; Magnusson, 1990; Magnusson & Endler, 1977; Mischel, 1973; Mischel & Shoda, 1995, 1998). For instance, rather than display situation-free anxiety, Gary may be anxious only under some relatively limited conditions (such as when having to speak in public) but not under many other circumstances. His anxiety may manifest itself in some ways (a subjective sense of dread, for example) but not in others (there may be no alteration in heart rate).

Norman S. Endler

To study how a person's anxiety reaction at any moment depends on the particular situation as well as on his or her disposition, Norman Endler and his colleagues led the way by developing questionnaires (see the sample item given in Table 1.2 in Chapter 1) that asked about reactions to many situations, ranging from everyday occurrences (you are undressing for bed) to highly anxiety-evoking situations (you are on a ledge high upon a mountainside). The modes of response to each situation were varied to sample many possible reactions, including the person's perception of his or her physiological reaction, such as "perspire" or "heart beats faster," and self-reported anxious feelings, such as "become immobilized" (Endler et al., 1989). The questionnaires were administered to students in many schools in order to sample a broad range of individual differences.

Statistical analyses of the results gave separate estimates of the relative effects (power) of stimulus situations, response modes, and individual differences. The results showed that anxiety is not a stimulus-free characteristic of the person, nor is it a function of the situation alone. Anxiety depends on the interaction of stimulus, person, and response mode. Thus, the occurrence of anxiety is a joint function of the individual, the particular stimulus (for example, undressing for bed), and the specific mode of response, such as "perspire" or "heart beats faster." The overall findings showed the unique patterning of anxiety in each person (see also *In Focus 9.2*).

Identifying Diagnostic Situations

One promising approach to situations attempts to characterize their personality (Bem & Funder, 1978). It tries to do so by creating a portrait of the personality traits of people who function particularly well in a given situation. Consider, for example, a situation in which children have a chance to delay taking an immediate, smaller reward in order to obtain a more preferred reward later. Bem and Funder exposed children to such a situation, measured how long they waited, and also asked the children's parents to rate their traits on a version of the Q-sort (a rating measure described in Chapter 7). The Q-sort ratings were used to make profiles of the personality of the ideal "delaying" child by simply seeing what traits had been used to characterize the children who waited the longest in that situation.

IN FOCUS 9.2   *Genetic and Environmental Influence on Person X Situation Interactions*

Person X situation interaction patterns may reflect both genetic and environmental influences, depending on the specific trait. An early study using an adult twin sample showed, for example, that the person X situation interaction patterns for anxiety were influenced significantly by genetics, whereas for dominance shared sibling-environmental influences were found (Dworkin, 1979). The results supported the general conclusion that an individual's behavior shows characteristic, meaningful patterns across situations that partly reflect genetic influences.

More recent studies with larger samples and other methods provide further and even stronger evidence for the same basic point (Cherney et al., 1994; Plomin et al.,

1997, p. 202). These are the type of context-specific relationships predicted by evolutionary theory (Buss, 1997) as well as by other interactionist approaches that emphasize the importance of flexible, discriminative coping patterns in personality (e.g., Chiu, Hong, Mischel, & Shoda, 1995; Magnusson, 1990; Mischel & Shoda, 1998). This finding is notable in illustrating that genetic influences may be expressed not simply in how much of a given trait a person "has" but in the characteristic pattern in which that behavior is typically expressed in relation to particular types of situations, as in "He always become angry if . . . but he's really friendly when . . ." (Wright & Mischel, 1987, 1989; Mischel & Shoda, 1995).

The authors also proposed that the same method could be applied to create portraits of the ideal personality in other situations that should tap the same basic disposition—in this case, the tendency to delay gratification. For example, one can create another situation in which the child has somewhat different opportunities to defer instant pleasure for the sake of better but delayed gratifications and again get the Q-sort portraits of the youngsters who wait longest.

To the degree that the portraits in the two situations overlap, one may conclude that the two situations are really psychologically similar. But to the degree that the two portraits are different, the two situations may really be tapping different personal qualities, although both situations may appear to be similar. Hopefully a search for situations that yield similar personality portraits would yield situations that are basically similar (rather than situations that merely look alike in superficial ways). After such psychologically similar situations have been identified through their common Q-sort portraits, it should be possible to demonstrate consistency in the behavior that people will display in them. That is the gist of the Bem and Funder thesis, and it has aroused much interest by suggesting a way to uncover equivalencies among situations by finding the overlapping personality characteristics that they tap.

The logic of the Bem-Funder approach is appealing. But it remains to be seen whether or not it will yield impressive cross-situational consistencies in behavior (across situations with similar Q-sort portraits). One effort tried to repeat the Bem-Funder study in the delay of gratification situation to see whether similar results would be found again (Mischel & Peake, 1982). Although the same procedures were followed as closely as possible, the findings were quite different. That is, the distinctive Q-sort trait ratings that Bem and Funder found for children who showed the greatest delay were not found again when a new sample of children was exposed to the same situation in the same preschool, thus failing to replicate the Bem-Funder results. On the other hand, and consistent with Bem and Funder's view, consistency in behavior across situations tends to be greater when the situations contain more similar psychological features. A study that intensively observed children's interpersonal behavior within a summer camp residential setting found that as situational similarity increased, so did consistency in individual differences on such dimensions as verbal aggression, friendliness, and compliance (Shoda, Mischel, & Wright, 1994).

It is also possible to specify the types of situations likely to be diagnostic of individual differences in a particular type of behavior by identifying the psychological processes that underlie that behavior. This has been shown with such behavior as the willingness and ability to delay immediate gratification in order to attain a preferred outcome later. How long preschool children were willing to delay gratification in certain laboratory situations that have been shown to tap that ability significantly predicted some of their real-life competencies, including their SAT scores, years later when they became adolescents (Shoda, Mischel, & Peake, 1990). In contrast, when the situations used to assess the preschool delay of gratification behavior did not demand the specific types of competencies necessary for effective delay of gratification, they were not diagnostic for predicting later outcomes. (These results are discussed more fully in Chapter 17.) Thus, knowledge of the processes that motivate and enable different types of behavior can be harnessed to specify the exact psychological situations needed to tap the relevant individual differences. When these processes are understood, it becomes possible to select the psychological situations in which the relevant individual differences are visible.

Aggregating across Situations

Although they acknowledge that the situation is important, many personality psychologists are convinced that past research has underestimated the personal constancies in behavior. They point out that if we want to test how well a disposition (trait) can be used to predict behavior, we have to sample adequately not only the disposition but also the behavior that we want to predict (Ajzen & Fishbein, 1977; Block, 1977; Epstein, 1979, 1983; Hogan, Johnson, & Briggs, 1997). Yet in the past, researchers often attempted to predict single acts (for example, physical aggression when insulted) from a dispositional measure (e.g., self-rated aggression). Generally, such attempts did not succeed. But while measures of traits may not be able to predict such single acts, they may do much better if one uses a *"multiple act criterion"*: a pooled combination of many behaviors that are relevant to the trait and a pooled combination of many raters (e.g., McCrae & Costa, 1985, 1987).

The methods and results of this line of research are illustrated in a study in which undergraduate women were given the "dominance scale" from two personality inventories (Jaccard, 1974). The women also were asked whether or not they had performed a set of 40 dominance-related behaviors. For example, did they initiate a discussion in class, argue with a teacher, ask a male out on a date? The dominance scales from the personality inventories did not predict the individual behaviors well. But the researcher found that when the 40 behavioral items were summed into one pooled measure, they related substantially to the personality scores. Namely, women high on the dominance scales also tended to report performing more dominant behaviors, and the reverse was also true. Thus, a longer, aggregated and therefore more reliable behavioral measure revealed associations to other measures (the self-reports on the personality tests) that would not otherwise have been seen. Similar results were found when the behaviors were measured directly by observation (e.g., Weigel & Newman, 1976).

In much the same vein, there have been a number of demonstrations to show that reliability will increase when the number of items in a test sample is increased and combined. Making this point, Epstein (1979) demonstrated that temporal stability (of, for example, self-reported emotions and experiences recorded daily, and observer judgments) becomes much larger when it is based on averages over many days than when it is based on only single items on single days. Such demonstrations also indicate that even when one cannot safely predict the individual's specific behavior in a specific situation, one may be able to predict the person's overall standing relative to other people when the behaviors are aggregated (combined) across many situations (Epstein, 1983).

Overall average differences among individuals can be construed easily and used to discriminate among them for many purposes (Funder & Colvin, 1997; Kenrick & Funder, 1988). Knowing how your friend behaved before can help you predict how he or she probably will act again in similar situations. The impact of any situation or stimulus depends on the person who experiences it, and different people differ greatly in how they cope with most stimulus conditions. It is a truism that one person's favorite "stimulus" may be the stuff of another's nightmares and that in the same "stimulus situation" one individual may react with aggression, another with love, a third with indifference. Different people act differently with some consistency in particular classes of situations, but the particular classes of conditions tend to be narrower than traditional trait theories have assumed (e.g., Cantor, 1990; Cantor & Kihlstrom, 1987; Mischel, 1990). For purposes of important individual decision making one may need highly individualized assessments of what the specific situations mean to the person (e.g., Mischel & Shoda, 1995). It also helps to take account of the person's motives and goals, which may influence how traits are expressed (Winter, John, Steward, Klohnen, & Duncan, 1998).

To apply these abstract points more concretely, think again about Gary. It is certainly possible to form some generalizations about his seemingly major qualities, strengths, and problems. Such generalizations help us to differentiate Gary from other people and to compare him with them. We learned, for example, that the MMPI indicated Gary tended to be interpersonally distant, to avoid close relations with people, and to fear emotional involvement. Such characterizations may help one to gain a quick overall impression of Gary. But in order to predict what Gary will do in specific situations or to make decisions about him (as in therapy or vocational counseling), it would be necessary to conduct a much more individually oriented study that considers the specific qualities of Gary as they relate to the specific situations of interest in his life.

Just when does Gary become more—or less—"interpersonally distant?" Under what conditions does he *not* avoid close relations with people? When does his tendency to "fear emotional involvement" increase? When does it decrease? The analysis and prediction of specific behavior requires that we ask specific questions like these to link behavior to conditions rather than to paint personality portraits with more general characterizations—although the latter can also be useful.

The utility of inferring broad traits depends on the particular purpose for which the inference is made. Inferences about global traits may have limited value for the practical prediction of a person's specific future behavior in specific situations or for the design of specific psychological treatment programs to help him. But traits have many other uses. Indeed they have value for everyday inferences about other people when we try to answer such questions as: "Is this friend reliable?" "What kind of person is my sister?" "Might this person be a good roommate?" "Do I really trust him?"

Inferences about broad traits also have value for such purposes as gross initial screening decisions (as in personnel selection), studying average differences among groups of individuals in personality research (Block & Block, 1980), or the layman's everyday perception of persons (e.g., Funder & Colvin, 1997; Schneider, 1973; Wright & Mischel, 1988). And as we have seen, when measures are combined or aggregated over a variety of situations, one can demonstrate stable differences among individuals in their relative overall standing on many dimensions of social behavior (e.g., Epstein, 1983).

SUMMARY

1. Genetic research suggests that family resemblance for personality is due to genetic resemblance, not to environmental effects shared by family members. For example, resemblance between genetically unrelated "adoptive" siblings is negligible for personality traits.

2. Nonshared (distinctive for each child) environmental influences on personality development are substantial and make children growing up in the same family different from one another.

3. Children growing up in the same family experience it differently, and these nonshared experiences may predict personality outcomes. What is cause and what is effect in these links is still unclear since there are genetic influences on the environments experienced and environmental influences on personality.

4. Individual differences in what is experienced and the environments one encounters are partly influenced by genetic factors that exert their impact through several routes. Most important, one's personality, itself influenced by genetics as well as environments, also affects the situations that one selects, influences, and creates in the course of development.

5. In the evolutionary approach, personality traits and individual differences reflect the processes of natural selection and adaptation as evolving humans struggled with the basic tasks of survival and reproduction faced by other mammals. Such traits as dominance, emotional stability, and sociability would have an especially significant role in mate selection and retention. In the survival of the group, such traits as conscientiousness and agreeableness-friendliness likewise would be of particular value, again in terms of biological principles not unique to humans. Although the evolutionary perspective is distinctively different from the genetic approach, both help to connect human

dispositions and individual differences to their biological foundations.

6. Evolutionary theory emphasizes the specificity of psychological mechanisms, allowing maximum flexibility, and generating behavior that becomes fine-tuned to solve specific types of challenges and demands. In that view, evolution results in domain-specific mechanisms that allow the person to behave discriminatingly and effectively in flexible interactions with the social environment.

7. The focus of evolutionary theory on specificity is consistent with the interactionist view of dispositions. Namely, dispositions and situations interact: The individual's characteristic behavior patterns are both stable and discriminative, taking account of the specific situation.

8. What people do depends on numerous moderating conditions. Evidence for the existence of broad traits has been questioned severely—and defended vigorously. Although specific behavior changes across situations, there is evidence for the stability and coherence of lives even over long periods of time. While measures of traits are often not able to predict single acts, they often can predict a pooled combination of many behaviors.

9. Complex interactions among dispositional and situational variables influence behavior. The relationship between any two variables—a child's dependency and his school achievements, for example—may be moderated by many other variables, such as his age, IQ, anxiety, the type of task, and the conditions of testing.

10. Recent studies of dispositions have tried to analyze the role of situations and of conditions, as well as of individual differences. They help to specify the type of situations diagnostic for identifying individual differences on particular dimensions of behavior.

11. Behavior depends both on the individual's dispositions and on the context. Personality traits are expressed in the form of patterns of person-situation interactions, as well as in overall average differences in the type of behavior displayed.

Summary Evaluation

PART III

Trait and Biological Approaches

OVERVIEW

So much has been done within trait and biological approaches that it becomes easy to lose the essential characteristics, which are summarized in the next table. The summary reminds you that the main aim of the trait approach was to provide methods to infer and quantify people's social-personal traits. These traits were assumed to be stable and broadly consistent dispositions that underlie a wide range of behaviors across a number of related situations.

Traits are inferred from questionnaires, ratings, and other reports about the subject's dispositions. Usually, the subject's self-reports are taken as direct signs of the relevant dispositions. For example, the more often you rate yourself as aggressive, the more you are assumed to have an aggressive disposition.

The focus of research is on measurement to develop quantitative ways of finding and describing important stable individual differences. Traditionally, the trait approach has recognized that behavior varies with changes in the situation but has focused on

Summary Overview of Trait and Biological Approaches

Basic units:	Inferred trait dispositions
Causes of behavior:	Generalized (consistent, stable) dispositions; biochemical (e.g., genetic) causes for some dispositions
Behavioral manifestations of personality:	Direct signs (indicators) of traits
Favored data:	Test responses (e.g., on questionnaires); trait ratings
Observed responses used as:	Direct signs (indicators) of dispositions
Research focus:	Measurement (test construction), description of individual differences and their patterning; taxonomy of traits; heritability of personality
Approach to personality change:	Not much concerned with change; search for consistent, stable characteristics; biochemical treatments for disorders
Role of situation:	Acknowledged but of secondary interest until recently

individual differences in the overall response tendency averaged across many situations. It has found evidence for the significant role of heredity and biology in personality, particularly with regard to such qualities as emotionality and activity.

Some theorists and researchers also try to take systematic account of the situation as it interacts with the individual's qualities. Individual differences on any given dimension are more visible in some situations than in others, and not all dimensions are relevant for all individuals. Some psychologists within this perspective now view traits as "act trends"—summaries of behavior—rather than as explanations or determinants of behavior. Perhaps most important, researchers continue to explore and find evidence of possible biochemical and genetic bases for aspects of personality and for some severe psychological problems.

CONTRIBUTIONS AND LIMITATIONS

It is also time to summarize the main strengths and weaknesses of these approaches. Some of the major contributions and limitations are shown in the next table. Examples and evidence for each point may be found by reviewing the previous four chapters. As suggested at the end of Part Two, it is a good review exercise to add to the table any additional strengths or weaknesses you see and to illustrate them as fully as possible with specific examples.

Summary Evaluation of the Trait and Biological Approaches

Contributions	Limitations
Objective measurement, quantification, development of tests and research tools	Lack of theoretical concepts to explain behavior psychologically
Basic methodological contributions for evaluating test results and measuring treatment effects	Does not generate treatments
Useful for summarizing and predicting broad behavioral trends, especially for large samples and groups; provides descriptive dimensions and taxonomies for classifying individuals systematically	Difficulty explaining or predicting specific behavior, especially for individual cases
Detects stable overall trends and differences	Underestimates role of situations
Calls attention to biological, genetic, and chemical bases of behavior (e.g., twin studies) and shows their importance; suggests links between evolutionary processes and personality	Underestimates role of social learning and experience

Quantification and Objective Measurement of Attributes: Identifying Average Individual Differences

Trait perspectives have made essential contributions to the quantification and objective measurement of personality. From the start of the field, this perspective has provided both concepts and methods for describing and comparing human individual differences with regard to a vast array of attributes and qualities.

Tests like the MMPI remain basic tools for the study of how individuals and groups differ. Trait measures help to describe important differences among people on dimensions relevant for everyday characterizations of abilities and personality. In psychiatric diagnostic work, they are equally relevant for describing differences among groups and types that can be distinguished in terms of the particular patterns of abnormal, maladaptive, or dysfunctional qualities that they display. Trait measures likewise are useful for assessing the effects of any treatments or life changes that individuals experience. For example, they help the researcher to see how people change or remain stable as a function of age and all sorts of life events.

Thus, the trait approach allows a great deal of information to be condensed quantitatively in the form of summary scores. These summaries in turn let us see stable trends by averaging together many observations in statistical, quantitative terms. In this way one can detect the general gist of what individuals or groups "are like" and obtain a broad overview that compresses much information. For example, one can estimate "on the average" how one person or group differs from another on whatever measures or occasions one wants to sample. For many goals, the results allow predictions of stable future trends that can be extremely useful.

While a major strength of the trait approach is that it condenses much information into averages and overall trends, for some critics that strength is also a serious liability. They see the trait approach as underestimating the role of the psychological situation and the human potential for variability and change. They also question the utility of the approach for dealing with individuals, either to predict their specific behavior in specific contexts or to design constructive psychological treatments for their unique circumstances.

Trend Summaries or Explanations?

Critics recognize that trait measures provide useful summaries of average overall differences among individuals and groups, but they question the psychological meaning of the traits that are inferred from these measures. Do they just offer summaries of overall trends? Do traits also explain behavior in ways that are psychologically interesting and useful?

The trait approach is often faulted for providing relatively little in the way of psychological theory and explanation. It says little about the underlying psychological processes needed to help us understand more about the "why" of personality and the conditions in which different kinds of people exhibit different types of social behavior. This limitation is especially serious because people are easily led to believe that by simply making a trait attribution (e.g., "he is a friendly person"), they somehow have explained adequately *why* the person behaves in the way that led them to this attribution (e.g., Mischel, 1968; Ross & Nisbett, 1991).

Meaningful Person X Situation Interactions

The trait approach focuses on the stability of human qualities expressed consistently across many kinds of situations. Some human attributes indeed show substantial stability, and there are long-term threads and patterns of coherence that characterize lives, even when studied over long periods of time (e.g., Block, 1971; Shoda, Mischel, & Peake, 1990). But there is also much variability and change as a function of the psychological situation (e.g., Mischel, 1968; Ross & Nisbett, 1991).

Situations make a difference not only in obvious ways for the types of behaviors that all people are likely to display (for example, we usually don't laugh much at funerals, but we do at parties). Situations also make subtler but important differences in the unique patterns that characterize the ways individuals consistently differ from one another in how they interact with different types of situations. Consider, for example, two adolescents who both score 80 on a measure of the degree to which they are "aggressive." Although both have the same reliable total score, 80, John may be aggressive primarily in relation to peers, while Jim's aggressive behavior may unfold mostly in relations with adult authorities (e.g., Mischel & Shoda, 1995).

To the degree that there is stability in these different patterns that characterize each person, the patterns themselves constitute meaningful *person-situation interactions* (e.g., Magnusson, 1990; Mischel, 1973, 1990). In spite of the fact that both John's and Jim's patterns of behavior produce the same total overall aggressiveness score on a summary trait measure, they require attention in their own right because each may have quite different meanings and implications. Each *pattern* may tell us different things (Mischel & Shoda, 1995, 1998), for example, about the goals and motivations that underlie them (as discussed further in the final chapter).

Such stable patterns of interaction between the person and the situation are like personal "signatures," expressed distinctively by different individuals: They are key aspects of individuality that a comprehensive approach to personality needs to incorporate. The same point is made by critics who note that the emphasis of traditional trait perspectives on overall average differences among groups and individuals (also called the *nomothetic* approach) ignores the *idiographic:* the uniqueness and organization of patterned individuality (Lamiell, 1997). As Gordon Allport (1937) noted more than 50 years ago, the study of individuality is a crucial component of trait psychology, but it has not been given the attention it deserves.

Taxonomy of Descriptive Dimensions: Structure of Traits

The psycholexical approach also has identified a set of dimensions that emerges repeatedly from factor analytic studies of natural language trait terms, now sometimes called the Big Five Structure. These dimensions provide a potentially useful systematic framework for describing and studying individual differences using natural language adjectives as the units. The growing consensus about the dimensions needed for a comprehensive classification system of traits has created fresh enthusiasm for trait perspectives in recent years. These Big Five dimensions offer a promising taxonomy of trait terms in the English language (Costa & McCrae, 1997). But the taxonomy also has substantial limitations in its present form (e. g., Block, 1995). Oliver John (1990), a major leader in current research on the Big Five, also has been one of its most perceptive critics. He recognizes the potential usefulness of comprehensive taxonomies of traits but also notes the limitations of the current Big Five taxonomy. For example, the categories are at such a broad level of abstraction that

> they are to personality what the categories "plant" and "animal" are to the world of biological objects—extremely useful for some initial rough distinctions, but of less value for predicting specific behaviors of a particular object (John, 1990, p. 93).

An ideal taxonomy, in John's view, needs to be built on causal and dynamic psychological principles and needs to be cast at different levels of abstraction from the broad to the more specific. The current structure of the Big Five is a promising step but far from this ideal:

> In contrast to the biological taxonomies, the five dimensions provide only a list of descriptive concepts specified at the highest level in the hierarchy, and a nomenclature that by no means has reached the status of a "standard." Still rooted in the "vernacular" English, the theoretical context of the Big Five is the accumulated knowledge about personality as it has been laid down over the ages in the natural language (John, 1990, p. 94).

While John and his colleagues see the limitations of the Big Five taxonomy, they also go on to explore and extend its applications vigorously (McCrae & John, 1992). As they note, an increasingly broad set of links is being found between people's positions on this taxonomy and other aspects of their behavior (e.g., Buss, 1992, 1997; Little, Lecci, & Watkinson, 1992). Further research with this taxonomy ultimately will help to clarify both its uses and its limits.

Attention to the Biological Bases of Personality

Research guided by trait perspectives also calls attention to the important role of biology and the genes in personality and social behavior as well as in human abilities. As you saw in the discussion on studies of identical twins, qualities of personality as assessed on standardized trait questionnaires are substantially influenced by genetic-biological determinants. Humans are biological creatures, importantly shaped by their genetic structures, and these biological influences extend to some aspects of personality to a significant degree.

Identifying the Mechanisms through Which Biological Influences Affect Social Behavior and Personal Qualities

The findings that genes influence personality have become sufficiently clear to avoid debates about whether or not they are important: Clearly, they are. The need now is for research that goes beyond demonstrations that genes impact personality to identify both the biochemical and the psychosocial processes that underlie these effects.

The constructive question to pursue here is not "is heredity more important than environment or vice versa?" Rather, just how do these processes interact in the course of development to influence different facets of the complex phenomena that make up personality? Valuable research into the biochemical and genetic bases of personality is now underway (e.g., Buss, 1992; Plomin et al., 1997). Ultimately, the yield from such research may help in the diagnosis and treatment of an array of human problems not yet imaginable in biochemical terms. If so, the approach also may make a great contribution to treatment and improvement of the human condition, but that possibility lies in the future.

New Directions and Challenges

Some of the challenges this perspective faces and some of the new directions to which attention is beginning to turn include

1. Further clarifying the nature of person-situation interactions theoretically and with research findings.
2. In particular, specifying the nature of the interactions of genetic influences with those coming from social-psychological and environmental sources in determining behavior.
3. Linking people's positions on descriptive taxonomies of traits to individual differences in their behavior in different types of situations.
4. Exploring the possible contributions of this orientation to issues of treatment and change.
5. Linking evolutionary processes to personality with increasing precision.

Part IV

Phenomenological Approaches

Phenomenological Conceptions

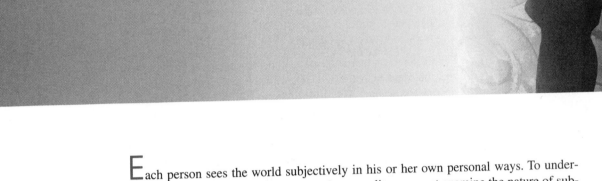

Each person sees the world subjectively in his or her own personal ways. To understand this privately experienced side of personality we must examine the nature of subjective experience; we must see how people perceive their world. For example, we cannot understand anxiety as an aspect of personality fully without understanding how the individual experiences it. We begin with a sample of such personal experience in the form of a self-description by a college student about to take a final examination:

When I think about the exam, I really feel sick . . . so much depends on it. I know I'm not prepared, at least not as much as I should be, but I keep hoping that I can sort of snow my way through it. He [the professor] said we would get to choose two of three essay questions. I've heard about his questions . . . they sort of cover the whole course, but they're still pretty general. Maybe I'll be able to mention a few of the right names and places. He can't expect us to put down everything in two hours . . . I keep trying to remember some of the things he said in class, but my mind keeps wandering. God, my folks—What will they think if I don't pass and can't graduate? Will they have a fit! Boy! I can see their faces. Worse yet, I can hear their voices: "And with all the money we spent on your education." Mom's going to be hurt. She'll let me know I let her down. She'll be a martyr: "Well, Roger, didn't you realize how this reflects on us? Didn't you know how much we worked and saved so you could get an education? . . . You were probably too busy with other things. I don't know what I'm going to tell your aunt and uncle. They were planning to come to the graduation you know." Hell! What about me? What'll I do if I don't graduate? How about the plans I made? I had a good job lined up with that company. They really sounded like they wanted me, like I was going to be somebody. . . . And what about the car? I had it all planned out. I was going to pay seventy a month and still have enough left for fun. I've got to pass. Oh hell! What about Anne [girlfriend]? She's counting on my graduating. We had plans. What will she think? She knows I'm no brain, but . . . hell, I won't be anybody. I've got to find some way to remember those names. If I can just get him to think that I really know that material, but don't have time to put it all down. If I can just . . . if . . . too goddamn many ifs. Poor Dad. He'll really be hurt. All the plans we made—all the . . . I was going to be somebody. What did he say? "People will respect you. People respect a college graduate. You'll be something more than a storekeeper." What am I going to do. God, I can't think. You know, I might just luck out. I've done it before. He could ask just the right questions. What could he ask? Boy! I feel like I want to vomit. Do you think others are as scared as I am? They probably know it all or don't give a damn. I'll bet you most of them have parents who can set them up whether they have college degrees or not. God, it means so much to me. I've got to pass. I've just got to. Dammit, what are those names? What could he ask? I can't think . . . I can't. . . . Maybe if I had a beer I'd be able to relax a little. Is there anybody around who wants to get a beer? God, I don't want to go alone. Who wants to go to the show? What the hell am I thinking about? I've got to study. . . . I can't. What's going to happen to me? . . . The whole damn world is coming apart (Fischer, 1970, pp. 121–122).

Feelings and thoughts like those reported by this student are the raw materials of theories that deal with the self and with the person's subjective, internal experiences and personal concepts. There are many complexities and variations in the orientation to personality presented in this chapter. In spite of these variations, however, a few fundamental themes emerge.

To simplify, we will call the orientation in this chapter **phenomenological,** a term that refers to the individual's experience as he or she perceives it, because that is this chapter's most basic theme. Some of the positions here have been given other labels also, such as "self" theories, "construct" theories, "humanistic" theories, "cognitive" theories, and "existential" theories. Most phenomenological theories are distinctive both in the concepts they reject and in the ones they emphasize. They tend to reject most of the dynamic and motivational concepts of psychoanalytic theories and also most of the assumptions of trait theories. Instead, they emphasize people's immediate experiences and their current relationships, perceptions, and encounters. Persons thus are viewed as experiencing beings rather than as the victims of their unconscious psychodynamics and conflicts. The focus is on the individual's subjective experience, feelings, personal view of the world and self, and private concepts. Most of the approaches discussed in this chapter also stress people's positive strivings and their tendencies toward growth and self-actualization.

Most of the theories presented here are concerned broadly with cognition—with how we know and understand the world and ourselves. An interest in cognition implies attention to the internal or mental processes through which individuals "code" and categorize information. Influenced by the Swiss psychologist Jean Piaget, cognitive theories call attention to the active ways in which the mind generates meaning and experience. Ulric Neisser, for example, puts it this way (1967, p. 3): "Whether beautiful or ugly or just conveniently at hand, the world of experience is produced by the man who experiences it." That statement, of course, does not imply that there is no "real" world of objects—houses, mountains, people, tables, books—and it does not suggest that the "environment" is a fiction that does not affect our private experience. The cognitive position stresses, however, that "we have no direct immediate access to the world, nor to any of its properties. . . . Whatever we know about reality has been *mediated,* not only by the organs of sense but by complex systems which interpret and reinterpret sensory information" (Neisser, 1967, p. 3).

Some personality psychologists concerned with cognition have tried to understand how the individual perceives, thinks, interprets, and experiences the world; that is, they have tried to grasp the individual's point of view. Their focus is on persons and events of life as seen by the perceiver. In sum, they are most interested in the person's experience as he or she perceives and categorizes it—the person's **phenomenology.** Ideally, they would like to look at the world through the "subject's" eyes and to stand in that person's shoes, to experience a bit of what it is to *be* that person. This phenomenological view is the main concern of the present chapter.

SOURCES OF PHENOMENOLOGICAL PERSPECTIVES

The orientation presented in this chapter has numerous sources. Among the many early theorists who were fascinated with the self were William James, George H. Mead, and John Dewey. Another early theorist concerned with the self was Carl Jung. As early as the start of the century, Jung called attention to the organism's strivings for self-realization and integration. He believed in creative processes that go beyond the basic instincts of Freudian psychology. Also important were Gestalt psychology and existential philosophy. Given all these contributors, it becomes a bit arbitrary to select a few for exposition, and they are merely representative. It is also noteworthy that in the psychodynamic tradition, Heinz Kohut and other "object relations" theorists (Chapter 3) more recently are also making the self a central concept.

Allport's Contribution: Functional Autonomy and the Proprium (Self)

Gordon Allport (1937) was one of the first to emphasize the *uniqueness* of the individual and of the integrated patterns that distinguish each person. He also notes the *lack of motivational continuity* during the individual's life and criticizes the Freudian emphasis on the enduring role of sexual and aggressive motives.

According to Allport, behavior is motivated originally by instincts, but later it may sustain itself indefinitely without biological reinforcement. Allport sees most normal adult motives as no longer having a functional relation to their historical roots. "Motives are contemporary. . . . Whatever drives must drive now. . . . The character of motives alters so radically from infancy to maturity that we may speak of adult motives as *supplanting* the motives of infancy" (1940, p. 545). This idea has been called "functional autonomy" to indicate that a habit, say practicing the violin at a certain hour each day, need not be tied to any basic motive of infancy. The extent to which an individual's motives are autonomous is a measure of maturity, according to Allport.

Allport thus stresses the contemporaneity of motives (1961). In his view, the past is not important unless it can be shown to be active in the present. He believes that historical facts about a person's past, while helping to reveal the total course of the individual's life, do not adequately explain the person's conduct today. In his words, "Past motives explain nothing unless they are also present motives" (1961, p. 220).

While fully recognizing the unity of growth in personality development, Allport emphasizes that later motives do not necessarily depend on earlier ones. Although the life of a plant is continuous with that of its seed, the seed no longer feeds and sustains the mature plant. In human terms, while a pianist may have been spurred to mastery of the piano through the need to overcome inferiority feelings, the later love of music is functionally autonomous from its origins.

Allport was also one of the strongest advocates of the self as a key feature of personality. To avoid a homunculus or manikin-in-the-mind conception of self, he has coined the term **proprium.** In his view, the proprium contains the root of the consistency that characterizes attitudes, goals, and values. This proprium is not innate (a

Table 10.1
Some Distinguishing Features of Individuality According to Allport (1961)

1. Motives become independent of their roots (functional autonomy).

2. A *proprium*, or self, develops, characterized by:

   bodily sense

   self-identity

   self-image

   self-esteem

   self-extension

   rational thought.

3. A *unique*, integrated pattern of adaptation marks the person as a whole.

newborn does not have a self); it develops in time. It provides a sense of self-identity, self-esteem, and self-image.

In addition to deemphasizing the person's early motivations and distant past, Allport focuses on the individual's currently perceived experiences, his or her phenomenological self and unique pattern of adaptation. He also favors a holistic view of the individual as an integrated, biosocial organism rather than as a bundle of traits and motives. Table 10.1 summarizes some of Allport's main ideas about individuality.

Lewin's Life Space

Still another important post-Freudian influence came from field theories (Lewin, 1936). These positions construed behavior as determined by the person's psychological life space—by the events that exist in the total psychological situation at the moment—rather than by past events or enduring, situation-free dispositions. The most elegant formulation of this position was Kurt Lewin's **field theory.**

The field concept of physics leading to Einstein's theory of relativity was the inspiration for Kurt Lewin's theory of personality. Einstein's concept of "fields of force" had an expression in the Gestalt movement of psychology, which asserted that each part of a whole is dependent upon every other part. The Gestaltists applied the notion of a field of interrelated components primarily to perception. They proposed that the way in which an object is perceived depends upon the total context or configuration of its surroundings. What is perceived depends on the *relationships* among components of a perceptual field, rather than on the fixed characteristics of the individual components.

Lewin defined **life space** as the totality of facts that determine the behavior (B) of an individual at a certain moment. The life space includes the person (P) and the psychological environment (E), as depicted in Figure 10.1. Thus, behavior is a function of the person and the environment, as expressed in the formula

$$B = f(P, E)$$

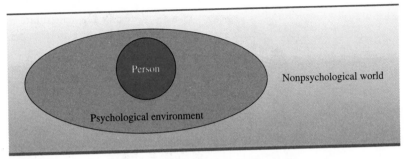

Figure 10.1
Lewin's Life Space   The life space contains the person in his or her psychological environment, which is delineated by a boundary (the ellipse) from the nonpsychological world.

Lewin also discussed the question of the temporal relationship of an event and the conditions that produce it. Generally this question concerns whether past events only, or future events also, can cause change. Ordinary cause, based on the notion of causation in classical physics, assumes that something past is the cause of present events. Teleological theories assume that future events influence present events. Lewin's thesis is that neither past nor future, by definition, exists at the present moment and therefore neither can have an effect at the present. Past events have a position in the historical causal chains whose interweavings create the present situation, but only those events that are functioning in the present situation need to be taken into account. Such events are, by definition, current or momentary. In other words, only present facts can cause present behavior.

To represent the life space, Lewin therefore took into account only that which is contemporary. He termed this the principle of *contemporaneity* (Lewin, 1936). This does not mean the field theorists are not interested in historical problems or in the effects of previous experience. As Lewin (1951) pointed out, field theorists have enlarged the psychological experiment to include situations that contain a history that is systematically created throughout hours or weeks. For example, college students in an experiment might be given repeated failure experiences (on a series of achievement tasks) during several sessions. The effects of these experiences on the students' subsequent aspirations and expectations for success might then be measured.

The boundaries between the person and the psychological environment and between the life space and the physical world are *permeable,* that is, they can be crossed easily. That makes prediction difficult because one cannot be sure beforehand when and what facts will permeate a boundary and influence a fact from another region. Lewin asserts that the psychologist might therefore concentrate on describing and explaining the concrete psychological situation in terms of field theory rather than attempt prediction.

Lewin (1935) rejected the notion of constant, entity-like personality characteristics such as unchanging traits. As a result of dynamic forces, psychological reality is always changing. The environment of the individual does not serve merely to

**Kurt Lewin
(1890–1947)**

facilitate tendencies that are permanent in the person's nature (1936). Habits are not frozen associations, but rather the result of forces in the organism and its life space.

Lewin was similarly dissatisfied with the usual concept of needs. In descriptions of psychological reality, Lewin said, the needs that are producing effects in the momentary situation are the only ones that have to be represented. A need in Lewin's theory corresponds to a tension system of the inner-person region. Lewin was also interested in reward and punishment. Instead of the hedonistic pleasure-pain formulations of early learning theorists, Lewin construed rewards as devices for controlling behavior in momentary situations by causing changes in the psychological environment and in the tension systems of the person.

For Lewin, behavior and development are functions of the same structural and dynamic factors. Both are a function of the person and the psychological environment. In general, with increasing maturity there is greater differentiation of the person and the psychological environment.

Lewin's field theory had a major impact on experimental social psychology. His students extended his ideas and pursued them through ingenious experiments designed to alter the subject's life space—by altering perceptions about the self, about other people, about events. The effects of these alterations on attitudes, aspirations, task persistence, and other indices were then examined carefully. Until recently Lewin's influence on personality psychology has been less extensive. There is now, however, an increasing recognition of the importance of the psychological situation in studies of traits and motives (e.g., Magnusson, 1980; Mischel, 1984).

Phenomenology and Existentialism: The Here and Now

Carl Rogers and George A. Kelly developed positions in which private experiences, subjective perceptions, and the self all have an important part. Somewhat similar themes emphasizing the role of higher-order "positive" motives—growth, fulfillment, and the self and its actualization—have been developed by Abraham Maslow and others. According to Maslow, for example, humans are innately good. Growth motivation moves the individual through hierarchically ordered degrees of health to ultimate self-actualization. "Every person is, in part, his own project, and makes himself" (Maslow,

1965, p. 308). Behavior is seen as goal directed, striving, purposeful, and motivated by higher actualization needs rather than by primary biological drives alone.

The ideas of most of these theorists have much in common with the existential philosophical position developed by such European thinkers and writers as Kierkegaard, Sartre, and Camus and by the Swiss psychiatrists Binswanger and Boss. The key features of their orientation are expressed by Rollo May, an American proponent of existential psychology. Thinking about a patient of his in psychotherapy, May recognizes that he has available all sorts of information about her, such as hypotheses from her Rorschach and diagnoses from her neurologist. He then comments (1961, p. 26):

> But if, as I sit here, I am chiefly thinking of these *whys* and *hows* of the way the problem came about, I will have grasped everything *except the most important thing of all, the existing person.* Indeed, I will have grasped everything except the only real source of data I have, namely, this experiencing human being, this person now emerging, becoming, "building world," as the existential psychologists put it, immediately in this room with me.

May's remarks point to the existentialist's focus on phenomenological experience, on the "here and now" rather than on distant historical causes in the person's early childhood. Furthermore, the existential orientation sees the human being as capable of choice and responsibility in the moment rather than as the victim of unconscious forces or of habits from the past.

The Swiss existential psychiatrist Binswanger commented that Freudian theory pictured human beings not yet as people in the full sense, but only as creatures buffeted about by life. Binswanger believes that for a person to be fully himself—that is, to be truly realized or actualized as a human being—he must "look fate in the face." In his view, the fact that human life is determined by forces and conditions is only one side of the truth. The other side is that we ourselves "determine these forces as our fate" (cited in May, 1961, p. 252). Thus, in the phenomenological and existential orientation, humans are seen as beings whose actualization requires much more than the fulfillment of biological needs and of sexual and aggressive instincts.

The existentialists propose that we are inevitably the builders of our own lives and, more specifically, that each person is

1. a *choosing* agent, unable to avoid choices throughout the course of life.
2. a *free* agent, who freely sets life goals.
3. a *responsible* agent, accountable personally for his or her life choices.

Our existence in life is given but our essence is what we make of life, how meaningfully and responsibly we construct it. This is an often painful, isolated, agonizing enterprise. To find satisfying values, to guide our lives accordingly, to give life meaning—these goals are all part of the existential quest, and they require the "courage to be"—the courage to break from blind conformity to the group and to strive instead for self-fulfillment by seeking greater self-definition and authenticity.

Finally, to grasp what it means to *be* also requires being in constant touch with the awareness of nonbeing, of alienation, of nothingness, and ultimately of the inevitability of death, everyone's unavoidable fate. The awareness of this inevitable fate and what that implies produces **existential anxiety.** The antidote for such anxiety is to face and live our lives responsibly, meaningfully, and with courage and awareness of our potential for continuous choice and growth.

To understand some of the main features of the existential and phenomenological orientation more closely, we shall consider the ideas of one of its most articulate proponents, Carl Rogers, in the next section.

CARL ROGERS' SELF THEORY

Unique Experience: The Subjective World

Rogers' theory of personality emphasizes the unique, subjective experience of the person. He believes that the way you see and interpret the events in your life determines how you respond to them—that is, how you behave. Each person dwells in a subjective world, and even the so-called objective world of the scientist is a product of subjective perceptions, purposes, and choices. Because no one else, no matter how hard he tries, can completely assume another person's "internal frame of reference," the person himself has the greatest potential for awareness of what reality is for him. In other words, each person potentially is the world's best expert on himself and has the best information about himself.

In Rogers' view, "behavior is typically the goal-directed attempt of the organism to satisfy its needs as experienced, in the field as perceived" (1951, p. 491). The emphasis is on the person's perceptions as the determinants of his or her actions: How one sees and interprets events determines how one reacts to them.

Carl Rogers
(1902–1987)

Self-Actualization

Like most phenomenologists, Rogers wants to abandon specific motivational constructs and views the organism as functioning as an organized whole. He maintains that "there is one central source of energy in the human organism; that it is a function of the whole organism rather than some portion of it; and that it is perhaps best conceptualized as a tendency toward fulfillment, toward actualization, toward the maintenance and enhancement of the organism" (1963, p. 6). Thus, the inherent tendency of the organism is to actualize itself. "Motivation" then becomes not a special construct but an overall characteristic of simply being alive.

In line with his essentially positive view of human nature, Rogers asserts that emotions are beneficial to adjustment. Instead of stressing the disruptive effects of anxiety, Rogers believes that "emotion accompanies and in general facilitates . . . goal-directed behavior, . . . the intensity of the emotion being related to the perceived significance of the behavior for the maintenance and enhancement of the organism" (1951, p. 493).

The organism in the course of actualizing itself engages in a valuing process. Experiences that are perceived as enhancing it are valued positively (and approached). Experiences that are perceived as negating enhancement or maintenance of the organism are valued negatively (and avoided). "The organism has one basic tendency and striving—to actualize, maintain, and enhance the experiencing organism" (Rogers, 1951, p. 487).

The Self

The self is a central concept for most phenomenological theories, especially that of Rogers. Indeed, his theory is often referred to as a self theory of personality. The self or self-concept (the two terms mean the same thing for Rogers) is an "organized, consistent, conceptual gestalt composed of perceptions of the characteristics of the 'I' or 'me' and the perceptions of the relationships of the 'I' or 'me' to others and to various aspects of life, together with the values attached to these perceptions" (Rogers, 1959, p. 200). As a result of interaction with the environment, a portion of the perceptual field gradually becomes differentiated into the self. This perceived self (self-concept) influences perception and behavior. That is, the interpretation of the self—as strong or weak, for example—affects how one perceives the rest of one's world.

The experiences of the self become invested with values. These values are the result of direct experience with the environment, or they may be introjected or taken over from others. For example, a young child finds it organismically enjoyable to relieve himself whenever he experiences physiological tension in the bowel or bladder. However, he may sometimes also experience parental words and actions indicating that such behavior is bad and that he is not lovable when he does this. A conflict then develops that may result in distortion and denial of experience. That is, the parental attitudes may be experienced as if they were based on the evidence of the child's own experience. In this example, the satisfaction of defecating may start to be experienced as bad even though a more accurate symbolization would be that it is often experienced as organismically satisfying. Rogers goes on to suggest that in bowel training, denial or distortion of experience may be avoided if the parent is able genuinely to accept the child's feelings and at the same time accept his or her own feelings.

Consistency and Positive Regard

Rogers proposes two systems: the self (self-concept) and the organism. The two systems may be in opposition or in harmony. When these systems are in opposition or incongruence, the result is maladjustment, for then the self becomes rigidly organized, losing contact with actual organismic experience and filled with tensions. Perception is selective: We try to perceive experiences in ways consistent with the self-concept. The self-concept thus serves as a frame of reference for evaluating and monitoring the actual experiences of the organism. Experiences that are inconsistent with the self may be perceived as threats, and the more threat there is, the more rigid and defensive the self structure becomes to maintain itself. At the same time, the self-concept becomes less congruent with organismic reality and loses contact with the actual experiences of the organism.

Rogers (1959) assumes a universal need for positive regard. This need develops as the awareness of the self emerges and leads the person to desire acceptance and love from the important people in his life. Sometimes they may accept him conditionally (i.e., depending on his specific behavior), or they may accept him in his own right and give him unconditional regard. The person needs positive regard not only from others but also from his self. The need for self-regard develops out of self-experiences associated with the satisfaction or frustration of the need for positive regard. If a person experiences only unconditional positive regard, his self-regard also would be unconditional. In that case the needs for positive regard and self-regard would never be at variance with "organismic evaluation." Such a state would represent genuine psychological adjustment and full functioning.

Most people do not achieve such ideal adjustment. Often a self-experience is avoided or sought only because it is less (or more) worthy of self-regard. For example, a child may experience anger toward her mother but avoid accepting that feeling because she wants to be a "good girl." When that happens, Rogers speaks of the individual's having acquired a "condition of worth." Experiences that are in accord with the individual's conditions of worth tend to be perceived accurately in awareness, but experiences that violate the conditions of worth may be denied to awareness and distorted grossly. When there is a significant amount of incongruence between the individual's self-concept and her evaluation of an experience, then defenses may become unable to work successfully. For example, if a young woman persistently experiences herself as painfully dissatisfied and "unhappy" in her efforts at schoolwork but views herself as having to "succeed at college" in order to be an adequate person, she may experience great strain in her defensive efforts.

Rogers assumed a need for unconditional positive regard not only from others but from the self.

Rogers' theory, like Freud's, posits that accurate awareness of experiences may be threatening to the self and therefore may be prevented. Anxiety in Rogers' theory might be interpreted as the tension exhibited by the organized concept of the self when it senses (without full awareness, i.e., by "subceptions") that the recognition or symbolization of certain experiences would be destructive of its organization (1951). If a person's concept of the self has been built around his "masculinity," for example, experiences that might imply that he has some unmasculine tendencies would threaten him severely. Anxiety thus involves a basic threat to the self, and defenses are erected to avoid it. Consistent with Rogers' theory, a great deal of research has demonstrated that people in fact engage in diverse strategies to protect their self-esteem when it is severely threatened. For example, they readily attribute important failures to chance rather than to themselves but see success as due to their own abilities (Snyder & Uranowitz, 1978; Weiner, 1995).

Person-Centered Therapy

Client-centered or person-centered **(Rogerian) therapy** seeks to bring about the harmonious interaction of the self and the organism. It tries to facilitate a greater congruence between the conceptual structure of the self and the phenomenal field of experience. The warm and unconditionally accepting attitude of the counselor, it is hoped, enables the client to perceive and examine experiences that are inconsistent with the current self-structure. The client can then revise this self-structure to permit it to assimilate these inconsistent experiences. According to Rogers, the client gradually reorganizes the self-concept to bring it into line with the reality of organismic experience: "He will *be*, in more unified fashion, what he organismically *is*, and this seems to be the essence of therapy" (1955, p. 269). Rogers (1980) later moved beyond individual client-centered therapy to form and lead many encounter groups intended to encourage psychological growth (see Chapter 11 and *In Focus 10.1*).

In sum, Rogers' theory highlights many of the chief points of the phenomenological and humanistic approach to personality. It emphasizes the person's perceived reality, subjective experiences, organismic striving for actualization, the potential for growth and freedom (Rowan, 1992). It rejects or deemphasizes specific biological drives. It focuses on the experienced self rather than on historical causes or stable trait structures. A unique feature of Rogers' position is his emphasis on unconditional acceptance as a requisite for self-regard.

Other phenomenological theorists have emphasized different aspects in their formulations. For example, the *gestalt* (meaning completeness or fullness) theory of Fritz Perls focuses on awareness of one's own experience in dynamic interaction with the environment (e.g., Van De Riet, Korb, & Gorrell, 1989). Although Perls' theory continues to influence many psychotherapists, perhaps the most influential phenomenological position for personality psychology is George Kelly's theory, which is discussed in the next section.

GEORGE KELLY'S PSYCHOLOGY OF PERSONAL CONSTRUCTS

To the humanist every man is a scientist by disposition as well as by right, every subject is an incipient experimenter, and every person is by daily necessity a fellow psychologist (Kelly, 1966, in B. A. Maher, 1979, p. 205).

IN FOCUS 10.1   *Rogers Reflects on His Own Work*

Looking back at the almost 50 years of his contributions to psychology, Rogers (1974) tried to pinpoint the essence of his approach. In his view, his most fundamental idea was that

> the individual has within himself vast resources for self-understanding, for altering his self-concept, his attitudes, and his self-directed behavior — and that these resources can be tapped if only a definable climate of facilitative psychological attitudes can be provided (Rogers, 1974, p. 116).

Such a climate for growth requires an atmosphere in which feelings can be confronted, expressed, and accepted fully and freely. His continued emphasis on the person's potential freedom, the hallmark of a humanistic orientation, remains unchanged:

> My experience in therapy and in groups makes it impossible for me to deny the reality and significance of human choice. To me it is not an illusion that man is

to some degree the architect of himself . . . for me the humanistic approach is the only possible one. It is for each person, however, to follow the pathway — behavioristic or humanistic — that he finds most congenial (Rogers, 1974, p. 119).

In the same humanistic vein he regrets modern technology and calls for autonomy and self-exploration:

> Our culture, increasingly based on the conquest of nature and the control of man, is in decline. Emerging through the ruins is the new person, highly aware, self-directing, an explorer of inner, perhaps more than outer, space, scornful of the conformity of institutions and the dogma of authority. He does not believe in being behaviorally shaped, or in shaping the behavior of others. He is most assuredly humanistic rather than technological. In my judgment he has a high probability of survival (Rogers, 1974, p. 119).

We all know that the map is not the terrain. Yet the two are often confused. Psychologically it is equally true that our constructs and abstractions about behavior are not the same as the behaviors that are being categorized. In addition to acting as motivated organisms, people also are perceivers and construers of behavior: They generate abstractions about themselves and others, just like psychologists do. These hypotheses and constructions have long intrigued psychologists interested in subjective states, in phenomenology, and in the experience of the self.

The Person's Constructs

In the psychodynamic approach, the motive is the chief unit, unconscious conflicts are the processes of greatest interest, and the clinical judge is the favored instrument. Kelly's (1955) personal construct theory, in contrast, seeks to illuminate the person's own constructs rather than the hypotheses of the psychologist. Its main units are personal constructs — the ways we represent or view our own experiences. Rather than seeing people as victimized by their impulses and defenses, this position views the human being as an active, ever-changing creator of hypotheses.

George A. Kelly
(1905–1967)

According to Kelly, trait psychology tries to find the subject's place on the *theorist's* personality dimension. Personal construct theory instead tries to see how the subject sees and aligns events on *his or her own* dimensions (Fransella, 1995). It is Kelly's hope to discover the nature of the subject's construct dimensions rather than to locate his position on the dimensions of the psychologist's theory. If next week's test is important to you, Kelly wants to explore how you see it, what it means to you, not what your score is on a scale of test-taking anxiety.

People as Scientists

The psychology of personal constructs explores the subjective maps that people generate in coping with the psychological terrain of their lives. Kelly emphasizes that, just like the scientist who studies them, human subjects also construe or abstract behavior, categorizing, interpreting, labeling, and judging themselves and their world. The individuals assessed by psychologists are themselves assessors who evaluate and construe their own behavior; they even assess the personality psychologists who try to assess them. Constructions and hypotheses about behavior are formulated by all persons regardless of their formal degrees and credentials as scientists. According to Kelly it is these constructions, and not merely simple physical responses, that must be studied in an adequate approach to personality. Categorizing behavior is equally evident when a psychotic patient describes his personal, private ideas in therapy and when a scientist discusses her favorite constructs and theories at a professional meeting. Both people represent the environment internally and express their representations and private experiences in their psychological constructions. Personal constructions, and not objective behavior descriptions on clear dimensions, confront the personality psychologist.

Kelly notes that most psychological scientists view themselves as motivated to achieve cognitive clarity and to understand phenomena, including their own lives. Yet the subjects of their theories, unlike the theorists themselves, are seen as unaware victims of psychic forces and traits that they can neither understand nor control. Kelly tries to remove this discrepancy between the theorist and the subject and to treat all people as if they were scientists.

Just like the scientist, subjects generate constructs and hypotheses with which they try to anticipate and control events in their lives. Therefore, to understand the subject, one has to understand his or her constructs or private personality theory. To study an individual's constructs one has to find behavioral examples or "referents" for them.

We cannot know what another person means when she says, "I have too much ego," or "I am not a friendly person," or "I may be falling in love," unless she gives us behavioral examples. Examples (referents) are required whether the construct is personal, for example the way a patient construes herself "as a woman," or theoretical, as when a psychologist talks about "introversion" or "ego defenses." Constructs can become known only through behavior.

Constructive Alternativism: Many Ways to See

If one adopts Kelly's approach to understanding people, then

> Instead of making our own sense out of what others did we would try to understand what sense they made out of what they did. Instead of putting together the events in their lives in the most scientifically parsimonious way, we would ask how they put things together, regardless of whether their schemes were parsimonious or not (Kelly, 1962, in B. A. Maher, 1979, p. 203).

The same events can be alternatively categorized. While people may not always be able to change events, they can always construe them differently (Fransella, 1995). That is what Kelly meant by **constructive alternativism.** To illustrate, consider this event: A boy drops his mother's favorite vase. What does it mean? The event is simply that the vase has been broken. Yet ask the child's psychoanalyst and he may point to the boy's unconscious hostility; ask the mother and she tells you how "mean" he is; his father says he is "spoiled"; the child's teacher may see the event as evidence of the child's "laziness" and chronic "clumsiness"; his grandmother calls it just an "accident"; and the child himself may construe the event as reflecting his "stupidity." While the event cannot be undone—the vase is broken—its interpretation is open to alternative constructions, and these may lead to different courses of action.

Kelly's theory began with this fundamental postulate: "A person's processes are psychologically channelized by the ways in which he anticipates events" (Kelly, 1955, p. 46). Phrased differently, this postulate means that a person's activities are guided (stabilized, channelized) by the constructs (ways) he or she uses to predict (anticipate) events. This postulate shares with other phenomenological theories an emphasis on the person's subjective view, but it is more specific in its focus on how the individual predicts or anticipates events. The postulate is further elaborated by a set of formal corollaries. Although the details of the theory need not concern us here, several of the main ideas require comment.

Kelly is concerned with the *convenience* of constructs rather than with their absolute truth. Rather than try to assess whether a particular construct is true, Kelly attends to its convenience or utility for the construer. For example, rather than try to assess whether or not a client is "really a latent homosexual" or "really going crazy," he tries to discover the implications for the client's life of construing himself in that way. If the construction is not convenient, then the task is to find a better alternative—that is, one that predicts better and leads to better outcomes. Just as a psychologist may get stuck with an inadequate theory, so his subjects also may impale themselves on their constructions and construe themselves into a dilemma. Individuals may torture themselves into believing that "I am not worthy enough" or "I am not successful enough," as if these verdicts were matters of indisputable fact rather than constructions and hypotheses about behavior. The job of psychotherapy is to provide the conditions in which personal constructs can be elaborated, tested for their implications, and, if necessary, modified. Just like the scientist, the subject needs the chance to test personal constructs and to validate or invalidate them, progressively modifying them in the light of new experience.

Roles: Many Ways to Be

Kelly's emphasis on roles and role enactments also merits special attention. Rather than seeing humans as possessing fairly stable, broadly generalized traits, Kelly saw them as capable of enacting many different roles and of engaging in continuous change. A role, for Kelly, is an attempt to see another person through the other's glasses—that is, to look at a person through *his or her* constructs—and to structure one's actions in that light. To enact a role requires that behavior be guided by perception of the other person's viewpoint. Thus, to "role play" your mother, for example, you would have to try to see things (including yourself) as she does, "through her eyes," and to act in light of those perceptions. You would try to behave as if you really were your mother. Kelly used the technique of role playing extensively as a therapeutic procedure designed to help persons gain new perspectives and to generate more convenient ways of living.

People Are What They Make of Themselves: Self-Determination

Like other phenomenologists, Kelly rejects the idea of specific motives. His view of human nature focuses on how people construe themselves and on what they do in the light of those constructs (Fransella, 1995). Kelly (like Rogers) believes that no special concepts are required to understand why people are motivated and active: Every person is motivated "for no other reason than that he is alive" (Kelly, 1958, p. 49). For Kelly, the concept of motivation "can appear only as a redundancy" (1958, p. 50).

He believes, like many existentialists, that the individual *is* what he *does* and comes to know his nature by seeing what he is doing. Starting from his clinical experiences with troubled college students in Fort Hays, Kansas, where he taught for many years, Kelly independently reached a position that overlaps remarkably with the views of such European existential philosophers as Sartre. In Sartre's (1956) existentialist conception, "existence precedes essence": There is no human nature—man simply *is*, and he is nothing else but what he makes of himself.

ENHANCING SELF-AWARENESS: ACCESSING ONE'S EXPERIENCES

Kelly believes that his theory, though it focuses on the person's constructs, is not purely concerned with cognitive and intellectual functions. Constructs, he says, often are not verbal, and they may have highly emotional ingredients. Nevertheless, some critics find that his view of the scientist neglects the person as an emotional being. Since Kelly's work, many phenomenologically oriented psychologists have become increasingly committed to the affective, nonverbal components of experience (e.g., Sewall, 1995). This search for feeling is seen in numerous recent psychological movements, both within psychology as a formal discipline and in the larger social scene.

The concern with feelings, the sense of being "out of touch" and isolated from emotional experiences, is illustrated poignantly in these excerpts from a troubled college student's letter:

> Long ago I lost touch with my body—my brain became separated from my body, and started commanding it. My body turned into just a machine for transporting my brain around from place to place to talk unfeelingly and analytically with other detached brains. I was glad it was a big and efficient machine—but I thought it was the inferior part of me, and that my brain should be in charge and call the tune for my feelings, letting the "positive" ones out and keeping the "negative" ones safely tucked in. . . .
>
> But now I feel lost in that head, out of phase with people—and somehow I want to reach them and my own guts—to know what I really feel, and stop all these precious intellectual games—to really live and not just to exist—So what do I do now?

The idea expressed by this distressed student is shared by many others who want "to make contact" emotionally, both with themselves and with other people.

Expanding Consciousness

Probably the most dramatic and controversial manifestation of this trend to achieve deeper feeling was the effort to expand consciousness and emotional experiences by means of psychedelic drugs. Initially, drugs such as psilocybin and LSD were advocated most energetically by Timothy Leary and Richard Alpert when they were psychologists at Harvard in 1961 and 1962. In the 1960s the "mind-expanding" movement through drug-induced "trips" or psychic "voyages" gained many enthusiastic participants. Although drawing heavily on Freudian dynamic psychology for its interpretations, this movement had a different purpose from that espoused by most neo-analytic followers of Freud. The neo-analysts emphasized "ego psychology" and the impulse-free (or "conflict-free") spheres of the ego and of rational control processes. Many advocates of consciousness expansion, instead, seemed to seek a return of the "primacy of the id"—a focus on feeling and fantasy, on "primary processes" rather than on logic and rational thought. This effort to capture pure feeling, to experience more closely one's bodily states, to escape from "ego" and "superego" and societal constraints, and to live fully in the "here and now," was seen most vividly in the "hippie" movement and the "drug culture" of the 1960s.

Such drugs as LSD undoubtedly produce major alterations in subjective experience, including the intensification of feelings (Leary, Litwin, & Metzner, 1963), but enthusiasm for them was soon tempered by the recognition that they entail serious risks. While the much less controversial drug, marijuana, received increasing acceptance, there also has been a trend to search for greater awareness without the aid of any drugs.

The peak experience is characterized by a feeling of fulfillment and joy.

Exploring Phenomenological Experience

Routes to increasing awareness that relied on psychological experiences rather than on drugs include meditation (Ornstein, 1972), encounter groups, and "marathons" of the type developed originally at the Esalen Institute in Big Sur, California (Schutz, 1967). While meditative techniques were based mainly on Eastern religious sources (Ornstein & Naranjo, 1971), the encounter or "sensitivity training" movement drew on various role-play and psychodrama techniques, on existential philosophy, and on Freudian dynamic psychology. The resulting syntheses are seen in the ideas of the **Gestalt therapy** of Fritz Perls (1969), in the efforts to expand human awareness and to achieve "joy" and true communication (Schutz, 1967), and in the pursuit of "peak experiences" and "self-actualization" (see *In Focus 10.2*). In its early versions, Gestalt therapy included confrontations and "encounters" that quickly and dramatically challenged the person's self-reported experiences, sometimes interpreting them as superficial and defensive. Often the "leader" tried rapidly and directly to stimulate and probe the deeper feelings that might underlie what the person disclosed (Polster & Polster, 1993). In more recent versions, there is less rapid and dramatic confrontation and a slower, more empathic attempt to explore the person's internal experiences in his or her own terms. The aim is to focus awareness on what is being felt fully and honestly. The process of enhancing both self-awareness and interpersonal awareness becomes the center of the therapeutic relationship, encouraging the person to be more closely in touch with what is experienced and freer to experiment interpersonally (Fodor, 1987; Wheeler, 1991). Because the implications of these positions are most relevant for psychotherapy and personality change, they will be discussed in that context in Chapter 11; also see *In Focus 10.2*.

One of the most influential spokespersons for the importance of becoming "in touch" with one's true feelings and fulfilling oneself totally was Abraham Maslow (1968, 1971). Maslow's theory overlaps considerably with that of Rogers. He also emphasized human beings' vast positive potential for growth and fulfillment. The striving toward actualization of this potential is a basic quality of being human:

> Man demonstrates *in his own nature* a pressure toward fuller and fuller Being, more and more perfect actualization of his humanness in exactly the same naturalistic, scientific sense that an acorn may be said to be "pressing toward" being an oak tree, or that a tiger can be observed to "push toward" being tigerish, or a horse toward being equine . . . (Maslow, 1968, p. 160).

Maslow's commitment was to study "optimal man" and to discover the qualities of those people who seemed to be closest to realizing all their potentialities. In his view, one has higher "growth needs"—needs for self-actualization fulfillment—that emerge when more primitive needs (*physiological needs, safety needs, needs for belongingness, and self-esteem*) are satisfied (see Figure 10.2). Maslow wanted to focus on the qualities of feeling and experience that seem to distinguish self-actualizing, fully functioning people. Therefore, he searched for the attributes that seemed to mark such people as Beethoven, Einstein, Jefferson, Lincoln, and Walt Whitman, as well as some of the individuals he knew personally and admired most. These positive qualities are elaborated as part of the humanistic view of the "healthy personality" in Chapter 11.

Self-actualization may be seen not only as a human need and as a quality of certain people, but also as a subjective experience that many of us may have, even if

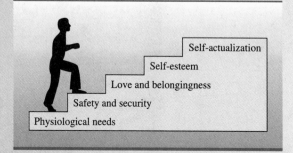

Figure 10.2
Maslow's Hierarchy of Needs   Maslow arranges motives in a hierarchy ascending from such basic physiological needs as hunger and thirst through safety and love needs to needs for esteem, (e.g., feeling competent), and, ultimately, self-actualization—the full realization of one's human potential, as in creativity. The lower needs are more powerful and demand satisfaction first. The higher needs have less influence on behavior but are more distinctly human. Generally, higher needs do not become a focus until lower ones have been at least partly satisfied.

only momentarily, at some points in life. Maslow called this special state a "peak experience," a temporary experience of fulfillment and joy in which the person loses self-centeredness and (in varying degrees of intensity) feels a nonstriving happiness, a moment of perfection. Words that may be used to describe this state include "aliveness," "beauty," "ecstasy," "effortlessness," "uniqueness," and "wholeness." Such peak experiences have been reported in many contexts, including the aesthetic appreciation of nature and beauty, worship, intimate relationships with others, and creative activities.

COMMON THEMES AND ISSUES

The approaches surveyed in this chapter are quite diverse and far more complex than a brief summary suggests. In spite of their diversity, these approaches share a focus on the self-as-experienced, on situations as perceived, on personal constructs, on feelings, and on the possibility of freedom. They search for data and methods that explore how people can disclose and reveal themselves more fully and honestly. They also see greater self-awareness, consistency, and self-acceptance as crucial aspects of personal growth and actualization (Spinelli, 1989).

Potential for Growth and Change

The existential belief that "man is what he makes of himself" and what he conceives himself to be is extremely appealing to many people. It recognizes the human potential for growth and change and for alternative ways of construing and dealing with life's challenges. It is optimistic in its belief that people do not have to be victimized by their biographies (as George Kelly put it). While emphasizing the potential for freedom and choice, it also is sensitive to the constraints and limitations of the human condition.

Psychologists who appreciate the attractiveness of these beliefs but who are committed to a deterministic view of science also have to ask, however: What are the causes that govern what individuals make of themselves and conceive themselves to be? And how do individuals come to make themselves and conceive themselves in particular ways? While philosophers may put the springs of action and cognition into the will (as Sartre does), the scientifically oriented psychologist seeks the variables that account for the phenomena of being and will itself (Mischel, Shoda, & Rodriguez, 1989). Many psychologists accept the idea that individuals are what they make of themselves, but as scientists, they want to go further and search for the conditions that make them, including those conditions that influence (or make) their self-conceptions and their ability to choose.

Are Cognitions the Causes of Behavior?

In spite of the obvious importance of personal constructs and other cognitions, one cannot assume that they are the main causes of the person's behavior. Verbal constructs and cognitions do not always cause or even influence nonverbal behavior and the things we do. The relations between personal concepts and other behaviors often are quite indirect and remote. Changes in personal constructs—or in opinions, beliefs, or values—do not always produce important behavior changes (Bargh, 1996; Gollwitzer, 1996; Festinger, 1964). Often cognitive and value changes may follow as a function of particular behavioral performances rather than serve as the causes for these performances (e.g., Bem, 1972; Festinger, 1957). That is, constructs and cognitions may be realigned to make them consistent with behavior and may be used to justify that

Hazel Markus

behavior (Chaiken, Wood, & Eagly, 1996). The issues and evidence on this topic are discussed in later chapters.

Is the Self a "Doer"?

Phenomenological accounts of the self in personality have been criticized most strongly for being descriptive rather than explanatory (see Brewster Smith's 1950 discussion). In his analysis, Smith distinguished between two different meanings of the self. One meaning of the self is as the *doer* of behavior. That meaning refers to such personality processes as self-regulation and self-control (e.g., Mischel, Cantor, & Feldman, 1996). The second meaning is the *self-as-object*. This definition refers to the person's concepts and attitudes about himself (Markus, Kitayama, & Heiman, 1996).

Smith argues that this distinction between the self-as-doer, or process, and the phenomenal construct of the self—that is, the self-as-object perceived by the individual—has been confused by phenomenologists. He notes that Rogers, for example, talks about the self this way:

> When the self is free from any threat of attack or likelihood of attack, then it is possible for the self to consider these hitherto rejected perceptions, to make new differentiations, and to reintegrate the self in such a way as to include them (Rogers, 1947, p. 365).

Smith questions these feats of the self and faults self theorists for endowing the self with all sorts of causal powers, such as the ability to evaluate itself, guard itself, and change itself. Similar criticisms have been made repeatedly (e.g., Skinner, 1964) and, for many years, have dampened enthusiasm for research on the self. More recently, researchers returned to the topic with more sophisticated methods that show the value of analyzing the diverse ways that people react to, evaluate, and regulate their own behavior and that justify the use of the self as a central construct in personality theory (e.g., Higgins & Kruglanski, 1996).

The Self as a Basic Schema (Category): New Trends

Problems with the definition of "self" should not obscure the enduring and central importance of the self as an integrative personality construct. The challenge will be to avoid endowing the self with mysterious powers without losing its subjective reality. Subjectively, there is little doubt of the "I," "me," or "self" as a basic reference point around which experiences and the sense of personal identity itself seem to be organized. There have also been some promising efforts to treat the self not as a "thing" but as a schema, cognitive category, or map that serves as a vital frame of reference for processing and evaluating experiences. In the work of Hazel Markus and others, this cognitive approach to the self has proved to be researchable as well as theoretically appealing (e.g., Baumeister, 1997; Markus, 1977; Markus & Cross, 1990; Markus et. al., 1996), as discussed in Chapter 16.

The existential idea that the person is "in possession" of himself or herself and has potential control and responsibility, and that people are what they make of themselves, has profound implications for the study of personality. Instead of a search for where the individual stands with regard to the assessor's dimensions, the assessor's task becomes the elaboration of what the individual is making of himself or herself and the "projects" and goals and plans of that person (Cantor, 1990) as they unfold in the course of life (Emmons, 1997; Mischel, Cantor, & Feldman, 1996).

In recent years, many psychologists interested in phenomenological perspectives but also committed to the scientific method have revitalized interest in the "self" as an organizing construct in personality and the individual's own perceptions and thoughts or cognition. Stimulated by the explosion of interest in cognitive approaches to personality, the self and its perceptions and cognitions are receiving unprecedented attention in personality psychology, as you will see in later chapters (Part VI).

SUMMARY

1. The diverse theories discussed in this chapter all reject specific motivational and dynamic concepts. Instead, they focus on the immediate perceived experience and concepts of individuals and on their strivings toward growth and self-actualization.

2. Allport's theory of personality stresses the functional autonomy of motives and argues that motives that are functioning currently in the mature individual may be independent of their historical roots. He gives central importance to the phenomenological or perceived self.

3. Lewin's field theory introduces the notion of life space and the importance of the psychological environment. His theory stresses the immediate relationships between person and environment and elements in the environment, rather than dealing with these as absolute entities. Contemporaneity is an important feature of this viewpoint. Lewin was dissatisfied with the usual concepts of traits and needs and saw behavior and development as functions of

dynamic changes in the psychological environment and in the tension systems of the person.

4. Many of the positions discussed in this chapter have in common an interest in subjective experience and a positive view of human nature. The human being is seen as purposeful and striving toward self-fulfillment, not simply as driven by unconscious forces and motivated by the necessity to satisfy biological needs.

5. The existentialists focus on the "here and now." They emphasize that we build our own lives and that each person is a choosing, free, responsible agent.

6. Carl Rogers' theory is illustrative of the central characteristics of the phenomenological approach to personality. The emphasis is on the person's unique experienced reality. In this theory the *self* (self-concept) is a conscious perception of self-as-object. This self-concept develops as the result of direct experience with the environment and may also

incorporate the perceptions of others. The experienced self in turn influences perception and behavior. Maladjustment occurs when the sense of self and a person's perceptions and experiences are in opposition and disharmony.

7. George Kelly's theory stresses the necessity of understanding the individual's own dimensions, categories, and hypotheses rather than viewing him or her in terms of the psychologist's constructs. It also emphasizes the convenience of the person's hypotheses and constructs for dealing with experience. Role play may help the person to select and practice more satisfactory, convenient modes of construing the world in alternative ways.

8. Meditation and encounter groups have been favored by movements that emphasize nonverbal, emotional components of experience and existence. Some of these approaches seek to explore and ex-

pand consciousness and awareness through a variety of techniques aimed at escape from the "reality-oriented ego" into more genuine feelings and enhanced sensitivity. Others search for fulfillment through self-actualization and "peak experiences," as Maslow emphasized.

9. The phenomenological emphasis has made many contributions. Nevertheless, it also has been criticized. A focus on people's subjective perceptions and cognitions does not necessarily uncover the causes of their behavior. Sometimes self theorists seem to confuse the self as an experienced phenomenon and as an agent determining behavior. Recent self theories (discussed in Part Six), building on the ideas summarized in this chapter, try to avoid these problems as they revitalize the study of the self with new methods as well as new concepts.

The Internal View

The phenomenological ideas discussed in Chapter 10 deeply influence both personality assessment and change. As we saw, the main feature of the phenomenological orientation is its emphasis on the person's experience as he or she perceives it. In Kelly's phrase, if a man's private domain is ignored "it becomes necessary to explain him as an inert object wafted about in a public domain by external forces, or as a solitary datum sitting on its own continuum" (1955, p. 39). On the other hand, if different individuals are to be construed within the same general system of laws, then commonalities and generalizations also must be discovered. To study the individual's experiences within the framework of scientific rules, methods have to be found to reach those private experiences and to bring them into view. In this chapter we will consider some of the methods intended to let us glimpse the internal view.

PEOPLE AS THEIR OWN EXPERTS

Phenomenologists like Rogers and Kelly seek to go beyond introspection and to anchor their theories to objective and scientific methods. In Rogers' view, for example, the therapist enters the internal world of the client's perceptions not by introspection but by observation and inference (1947). A concern with objectivity is reflected in Rogers' extensive efforts to study persons empirically, and these efforts are what place his work in the domain of psychology rather than philosophy. The same concern with objective measurement of subjective experience characterized Kelly's approach to assessment. This chapter considers some of the main efforts that have been made by phenomenologically oriented psychologists to study experience objectively and to provide strategies for personal growth and awareness. Although much of this work was begun almost 50 years ago, it has remained important and taken on new life (e.g., Cantor, 1990; Higgins, 1996; Lamiell, 1997).

Gary W.'s Self-Conceptualization

Phenomenological study begins with the person's own viewpoint. To approach that viewpoint one may begin with the individual's self-presentation, as expressed in the way he depicts and describes himself. Some of the raw data of phenomenology are illustrated in the following self-description recorded by Gary W. when he was asked to describe himself as a person.

I'm twenty-five years old, and a college graduate. I'm in business school working toward an MBA.

I'm an introspective sort of person—not very outgoing. Not particularly good in social situations. Though I'm not a good leader and I wouldn't be a good politician, I'm shrewd enough that I'll be a good businessman. Right now I'm being considered for an important job that means a lot to me and I'm sweating it. I know the powers at the office have their doubts about me but I'm sure I could make it—I'm positive. I can think ahead and no one will take advantage of me. I know how to work toward a goal and stick with whatever I start to the end—bitter or not.

The only thing that really gets me is speaking in a large group. Talking in front of a lot of people. I don't know what it is, but sometimes I get so nervous and confused I literally can't talk! I feel my heart is going to thump itself to death. I guess I'm afraid that they're all criticizing me. Like they're almost hoping I'll get caught with my pants down. Maybe I shouldn't care so much what other people think of me—but it does get to me, and it hurts—and I wind up sweating buckets and with my foot in my mouth.

I'm pretty good with women, but I've never found one that I want to spend the rest of my life with. Meanwhile I'm enjoying the freewheelin' life. I hope someday to find a girl who is both attractive and level-headed. A girl who is warm and good but not dominating and who'll be faithful but still lead a life of her own. Not depend on me for every little thing.

My childhood was fairly typical middle-class, uptight. I have an older brother. We used to fight with each other a lot, you know, the way kids do. Now we're not so competitive. We've grown up and made peace with each other—maybe it's just an armistice, but I think it may be a real peace—if peace ever really exists. I guess it was his accident that was the turning point. He got pretty smashed up in a car crash and I guess I thought, "There but for the grace of God. . . ." I count a lot on being physically up to par.

Dad wasn't around much when we were growing up. He was having business troubles and worried a lot. He and Mother seemed to get along in a low-key sort of way. But I guess there must have been some friction because they're splitting now—getting divorced. I guess it doesn't matter now—I mean my brother and I have been on our own for some time. Still, I feel sorry for my Dad—his life looks like a waste and he is a wreck. A walking tragedy.

My strengths are my persistence and my stamina and guts—you need them in this world. Shrewdness. My weaknesses are my feeling that when it comes to the crunch you can't really trust anybody or anything. You never know who's going to put you down or what accident of fate lies around the corner. You try and try—and in the end it's probably all in the cards.

Well, I guess that's about it. I mean, is there anything else you want to know?

The Uses of Self-Assessment

How can we begin to interpret Gary's self-portrait? It is possible to proceed in terms of one's favorite theory, construing Gary's statements as reflections of his traits, or as signs of his dynamics, or as indicative of his social learning history, or as clues to the social forces that are molding him. But can one also make Gary's comments a bridge for understanding his private viewpoint, for glimpsing his own personality theory and for seeing his self-conceptions?

Because each of us is intimately familiar with our own conscious, perceived reality, it may seem deceptively simple to reach out and see another person's subjective world. In fact, we of course cannot "crawl into another person's skin and peer out at the world through his eyes," but we can "start by making inferences based primarily upon what we see him doing rather than upon what we have seen other people doing" (Kelly, 1955, p. 42). That is, we can try to attend to him rather than to our stereotypes and theoretical constructs.

A most direct way to inquire about another person's experience is to ask him, just as Gary was asked, to depict himself. Virtually all approaches to personality have asked people for self-reports. In most orientations these reports have served primarily as cues from which to infer the individual's underlying personality structure and dynamics. Perhaps because of the assumption that people engage in extensive unconscious distortion, the subject's own reports generally have been used as a basis for the clinician (or the test) to generate inferences and predictions about her, rather than as a means of conveying the subject's view of herself.

Can people be experts about themselves? Can they assess themselves usefully? Can their reports serve as reliable and valid indices of their behavior? For example, in his self-appraisal Gary predicts that he can succeed in the job for which he is being considered. Is this self-assessment accurate, or is it a defensive hope, or an opportunistic ploy, or a belated effort at self-persuasion?

Some studies have tried to examine whether people can assess and predict their own behavior adequately. If they cannot, then the value of phenomenological inquiries would be limited severely; if they can, then it may be not only interesting but also useful to listen to their self-assessments most seriously. To establish the utility of a person's direct report about himself, you must compare it with the predictions about him that can be made from other data sources. For example, you must compare the individual's self-reports with the statements drawn from sophisticated psychometric tests or from well-trained clinical judges who use such techniques as the interview and the projective test to infer the subject's attributes.

It has been a surprise for many psychologists to learn that simple self-reports may be as valid as, and sometimes better predictors than, more sophisticated, complex, and indirect tests designed to disclose underlying personality. Thus, Marks, Stauffacher, and Lyle (1963), in a pioneering study, tried to predict future adjustment for schizophrenic patients. They found that simple self-reports on attitude scales (like the California *F* Scale, discussed in Chapter 7) may yield better predictions than did psychometrically more sophisticated scales. Simple attitude statements (on the California *F* Scale) have also been one of the best predictors of success in the Peace Corps; they have been more accurate than far more costly personality inferences. Interviews and pooled global ratings from experts did not prove nearly as accurate as self-reports did (Mischel, 1965). Another early study found that two extremely simple self-ratings (one on "adjustment" and one on "introversion–extraversion") may be as stable and useful as are inferences from factor scores based on sophisticated personality-rating schedules (Peterson, 1965). Studies designed to test the same personality characteristics by both direct and indirect measures generally found the direct measures to be better (Scott & Johnson, 1972). Contemporary research on motives, goals, and everyday life tasks that people pursue draw mostly on the person's own reports (Emmons, 1997).

At first glance evidence for the value of direct self-reports might seem more relevant to the trait approaches discussed in Chapters 6 and 7 (since many trait measures rely on self-reports) than to phenomenology. In fact, the evidence in this section does not speak to the question of the nature of personality traits; it merely shows that people can report directly about their own behavior, feelings, and attributes with as much or better accuracy than we can get from other more indirect inferences and information about them. In sum, useful information about people may be obtained most directly by simply asking them (e.g., Cantor & Kihlstrom, 1987). These conclusions seem to hold for such diverse areas as college achievement, job and professional success, treatment outcomes in psychotherapy, rehospitalization for psychiatric patients, and parole violations for delinquent children (e.g., Emmons, 1997; Merluzzi et al., 1981; Mischel, 1981; Rorer, 1990).

EXPLORING SUBJECTIVE EXPERIENCE

Thus, it seems under some conditions people may be able to report and predict their own behavior at least as accurately as experts can make inferences about them. Consequently, it often is reasonable to ask the person directly how he or she will behave, and in many instances the self-statements obtained may be as accurate as, or better than, any other data sources. Of course people do not always predict their own behavior accurately. Sometimes individuals lack either the information or the motivation to foretell their own behavior. Even if a criminal plans to steal again, we cannot expect him to say so to the examining prosecutor at his trial. Moreover, many future behaviors may be determined by variables not under the person's control (for example, other people, accidents). The obtained findings do suggest that techniques designed to obtain direct self-estimates and self-predictions merit serious attention.

One especially useful rating technique for obtaining reports about the self, the Q-technique or Q-sort, was already discussed in Chapter 7 as a tool for studying individual differences. For many phenomenologically oriented psychologists, self-statements from Q-sorts may be of interest in themselves. The phenomenologist simply wants to see the person's self-characterization for its own sake. It is possible to use techniques like the Q-sort to assess how persons describe themselves both as they really view themselves ("real self") and as they would like to be ("ideal self"). Often the difference between these two measures is especially informative.

Interviews

Most modern phenomenologists have recognized that self-reports may not reveal everything important about behavior and may not give a complete picture of personality. Persons may be conscious of the reasons for their behavior but be unable or unwilling to report them. Or they may not be conscious of all their experiences, in which case they cannot communicate them no matter how hard they try. In spite of these limitations, such phenomenologists as Rogers prefer the client's frame of reference as the vantage point for understanding. The psychologist's task, in Rogers' view, is to provide conditions that are conducive to growth and that facilitate free exploration of feelings and self.

One cannot expect people to be honest about themselves when they fear that their statements may incriminate them or lead to negative decisions about their future. In order for a person to reveal private feelings, he or she needs a nonthreatening atmosphere that allays anxieties, reduces inhibitions, and fosters self-disclosure (Jourard, 1967; Lietaer, 1993). Phenomenologically oriented psychologists therefore pay much attention to creating conditions of acceptance, warmth, and empathy in which the individual may feel more at ease for open self-exploration (Vanaerschot, 1993). These conditions of acceptance are illustrated vividly in client-centered (Rogerian) therapy, discussed later in this chapter. Rogerians have not only tried to create conditions conducive to personal growth; they also have studied those conditions in the interview.

In their earliest efforts, the approach was informal. They selected excerpts from recorded interviews in client-centered therapy mainly to document how the clients' verbalizations reflect their self-pictures and how these pictures change in the course of therapy (e.g., Rogers, 1942; Rogers & Dymond, 1954). Since these early beginnings, the content analysis of interview protocols has become a systematic research method. Going far beyond the mere tape recording of interviews, researchers have devised theory-relevant categories for reliably scoring the person's expressions. For example, many investigators have scored changes in self-references on various dimensions during therapy. They have grouped these self-references into such categories as positive or approving self-references, negative or disapproving self-references, ambivalent self-references, and ambiguous self-references. The scores obtained could then be correlated with other aspects of the therapy, such as the point in the relationship at which they occurred or the association among diverse types of changes as therapy progressed. For example, it has been possible to try to test propositions such as the idea that increasing acceptance of the self leads to increasing acceptance of others. Research in this vein has been vigorous and extensive (e.g., Chodorkoff, 1954; Marsden, 1971; Truax & Mitchell, 1971).

Rogerians have not been the only ones to attempt content analysis of verbal behavior in interviews. The technique of scoring content has been favored in descriptive studies of all sorts of psychotherapy and not just in phenomenological approaches. A typical question in psychodynamically oriented therapy, for example, might trace changes in types of conflict expressed in various phases in psychotherapy. To illustrate, Figure 11.1 depicts the percentage of total statements judged to deal with general hostility conflict as opposed to sex conflict in the course of the first 15 psychotherapy

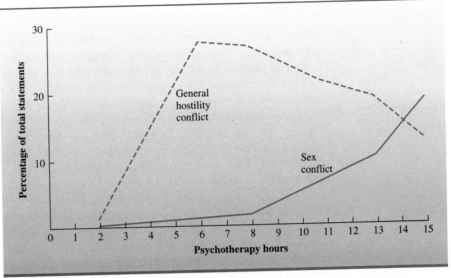

Figure 11.1
General Hostility Conflict and Sex Conflict Statements General hostility conflict statements about husband and sex conflict statements about husband in six randomly selected therapy hours with one client.
SOURCE: Murray, E. J., Auld, F., Jr., & White, A. M. (1954). A psychotherapy case showing progress but no decrease in the discomfort-relief quotient. *Journal of Consulting Psychology, 18,* 349–353.

hours (Murray, Auld, & White, 1954). As the figure suggests, sexual conflicts began to be expressed increasingly in later sessions, whereas more general conflicts were readily verbalized in earlier phases of the relationship. These content analyses, of course, depend on the clinician's inferences about the underlying meaning of the client's statements; they do not reflect the client's phenomenology directly.

As these studies indicate, phenomenological data from the interview have been objectified and investigated with diverse research strategies guided by many different theoretical viewpoints. While the interview is a favorite tool for the phenomenologist, the data from the interview can be analyzed in many different ways. In general, the interview continues to be, for most of the major theoretical orientations, a source of data for personality assessments. Its popularity probably reflects its great flexibility and the vast range of topics that it can cover rapidly.

Many phenomenologically oriented psychologists use the interview to observe how the individual interprets himself and describes his experiences. They employ the interview as a direct sample of the person's self-description (the ways he sees and presents himself), regardless of the validity of the data he provides as "signs" of his nontest behaviors or of his psychodynamics. They seek to create an atmosphere conducive to honest self-disclosure, an atmosphere in which self-revelation, self-disclosure, and honest self-report are actively encouraged (e.g., Cantor, 1990; Fodor, 1987; Jourard, 1974).

The Semantic Differential

Another route for phenomenologically oriented assessment has been developed to study meanings. This technique, the "semantic differential," yields ratings of the meaning of the persons, events, or concepts the investigator wants to study.

On the semantic differential test the meanings of diverse words, phrases, and concepts are rated on many scales (Osgood, Suci, & Tannenbaum, 1957). Raters (or subjects) are supplied with a stimulus word like "feather," or "me," or "my father," or with a phrase like "my ideal self," and are asked to rate each stimulus on a seven-point, bipolar scale. Polar adjectives like "rough–smooth" or "fair–unfair" are the extremes of each scale. Raters are instructed to mark the point that most nearly indicates the meaning of the stimulus concept for them. For example, you might be asked to rate "my ideal self" on scales like those shown in Table 11.1. To see what that is like, you should try it for yourself, both for the concepts suggested and for any others you find interesting for yourself. The technique is both objective and flexible. It permits investigation of how people describe themselves and others, as well as how special experiences (for example, psychotherapy) affect them.

A great deal of research has repeatedly indicated that three main factors tend to emerge when the results are analyzed. A primary evaluative (good-bad) factor seems to be the most important (Kim & Rosenberg, 1980). In other words, evaluations in such terms as "good-bad" enter most extensively into how people characterize themselves, their experiences, and other people (Ross & Nisbett, 1991). The two other factors are *potency*, represented by scale items like hard–soft, masculine–feminine, and strong–weak, and *activity*, tapped by scales like active–passive, excitable–calm, and hot–cold (Mulaik, 1964; Vernon, 1964).

Table 11.1

Examples of Concepts and Rating Scales from the Semantic Differential

Concepts whose meanings are rated:
- My Actual Self
- My Ideal Self
- Masculinity
- Foreigner
- Mother

Scales for rating the meaning of each concept:

strong	__:__:__:__:__:__:__	weak
pleasant	__:__:__:__:__:__:__	unpleasant
hard	__:__:__:__:__:__:__	soft
safe	__:__:__:__:__:__:__	dangerous
fair	__:__:__:__:__:__:__	unfair
active	__:__:__:__:__:__:__	passive

NOTE: As an exercise, provide these ratings yourself for each concept.

SOURCE: Based on Osgood, C. E., Suci, G. J., & Tannenbaum, P. H. (1957). *The measurement of meaning.* Urbana, IL: The University of Illinois Press.

Table 11.2
Elaboration of Personal Constructs: Examples from Gary W.

1. List the three most important people in your life:
   me   my brother   my father
   How are any two of these alike and different from the third?
   My brother and I both know how to be tough and succeed, no matter what—my father is soft, knocked out, defeated by life.

2. Think of yourself now, five years ago, and five years from now. How are any two of these alike and different from the third?
   Five years ago I was warmer, more open and responsive to others than I am now. Now I'm mostly a scheming brain. Five years from now I hope to have recaptured some of that feeling and to be more like I was five years ago.

Personal Constructs

Suppose that you see a person quietly letting herself be abused by someone else. You might conclude that the person is "submissive." Yet the same behavior might be construed by other observers as sensitive, cautious, intelligent, tactful, or polite. Recall that George Kelly (1955) emphasized that different people may construe the same event differently and that every event can be construed in alternative ways.

The personal construct is the central unit of George Kelly's theory. Kelly's operation for measuring a construct is best seen in his **Role Construct Repertory Test** or **Rep Test.** On the Rep Test subjects may list many people or things that are important to them (for example, self, mother, brother). After they list these items (or the assessor lists them), they consider them in groups of three. In each triad they have to indicate how two items are similar to each other and different from the third. In this way the subjective dimensions of similarity among events and the subjective opposites of those dimensions may be evoked systematically (Table 11.2). It is also possible to study the characteristics of the people's construct systems—for example, the number of different constructs they have in their construct repertory.

Like the semantic differential, the Rep Test is a flexible instrument that can be adapted for many different purposes, and it provides a convenient and fairly simple way to begin the exploration of personal constructs. Some examples, taken from the study of Gary W., are shown in Table 11.2 (which illustrates the general type of procedure that may be used to elaborate personal constructs).

Research on the temporal stability of personal constructs from Kelly's Rep Test indicates a good deal of consistency over time (Bonarius, 1965). For example, a high retest correlation (.79) was found for constructs after a two-week interval (Landfield, Stern, & Fjeld, 1961), and factor analyses of the Rep Test suggest that its main factor is stable (Pedersen, 1958) and thus that an individual's main constructs may be relatively permanent.

According to Kelly, the individuals' personal constructs gradually become elaborated through their answers on the Rep Test and through their behaviors in the interview and on other tests. To illustrate some features of the assessment of personal constructs, here is an analysis of our case based on how Gary spontaneously elaborates and contrasts the constructs with which he views the world. What follows are excerpts from an attempt by an assessor to summarize some of Gary's main conceptions.

A Personal Construct Conceptualization of Gary W.

Rationality—Emotionality is a construct dimension that seems to be of considerable importance for Gary. This construct is elaborated most clearly when he is discussing his interpersonal relationships. A sexual relationship with a woman is described in such terms as "spiritual," "instinctive," "sublime," and "beyond rationality." It is characterized by intense feeling and the primacy of emotions, and it is based on physical attraction. Real friendships, in contrast, are based upon verbalizable grounds— rational bases such as interests and ways of thinking that are common to both parties.

The distinction between the rational and the emotional is echoed when Gary describes his worries in terms of those that are "rational" versus those that are "immediate and threatening." In discussing anger, he says that he has learned to cover up his feelings but that his emotions sometimes "surface." He no longer gets violently angry, as he did when he was a child, but is "controlled," "stony," and "devious." He gives the most positive evaluation to reason and contrasts what is reasonable with what is "worthless."

Transposed onto a time line, his distinction between reason and emotion forms part of the contrast between adults and children. After he was about 12 years old, Gary "psyched out" his father, so the latter was no longer his "enemy" but instead became his "friendly, rational adviser." He also describes shifts in his relations with his mother and with his brother that apparently involve handling his feelings toward them in a less explosive way.

Power and control versus dependence and weakness seems to be a major dimension on which adults and children differ. Adults are the enemies of children. In his interview descriptions of his childhood experiences, what parental figures require of a child is typically the opposite of what the child wants. Gary describes life as a child as involving "denial, helplessness, nothing and nobody on my side." It was a time when he "couldn't control events," when he was being "manipulated" and "shamed." Gary contrasts foresight and events that he can plan and control with accidents, terror, and the unpredictable.

Defeat–Success is a closely related dimension around which a number of constructs are clustered. Defeat is defined in terms of lack of money, passivity, compliance, dependence, frustration, undermined masculinity, and physical pain. Success means money, activity, freedom, independence, control, and being a "real" man.

Security–Liberty is another major dimension for Gary. In describing jobs, acquaintances, and life styles, he talks in terms of "the ordinary 9 to 5 job complete with wife, kids, and mortgage" versus the "free and easy life." "Blind obedience" is contrasted to "judging the issues for oneself." Gary describes himself as being "uncertain" and contrasts being freewheeling with plodding determination. He sees himself as being currently without "acceptance" and "success" and he feels "cut off." His own "procrastination" hinders his "drive," but he hopes his "ambition will win out" and gain him both security and liberty.

As far as *role conceptions* are concerned, Gary now sees his father as "emasculated" and "knocked out," although once he saw him as "a giant" and as his "enemy." The father seems to have moved along the conceptual continuum from "power and control" to a point where he is seen as inadequate and as being competition no longer. He dislikes his father for the middle-class values that he feels he represents and for his passivity. There is also the implication that he resents his father for not comparing favorably with his mother. The turning point in Gary's feelings for his brother, whom he disliked for sharing many of their father's qualities, came when his brother was smashed up in a car crash. He now sees him as less conventional, more humorous, and self-examining.

Gary sees his mother, and ideal women in general, as "independent partners" rather than "devouring" sources of affection. Instead of making their families central in importance, they achieve success and recognition in work outside their home. They keep the male "alive" by providing stimulation through their competence, which extends even to athletics, rather than being dependent and "clinging." Gary sees himself as similar to his mother and says he loves her best, next to himself. On the more negative side, he sees his mother as frigid and incapable of expressing affection. However, in view of his own evaluation of emotionality, this criticism is a highly qualified one. He sees his mother as having in many ways been the cause of his father's defeat, but constantly adds that she did not intend this result and feels bad about it, that it was a byproduct of other admirable qualities she possesses.

His relationship with his mother is characterized by control of expression of both anger and love. He sees her dominating tendencies as dangerous, as evidenced by his childhood conception of her as omniscient and omnipotent. This fear seems to have generalized to his grandmother and to other women, as evidenced by his TAT stories.

In his relationships with women there seems to be a general distinction between sex objects and companions. In describing a sexual relationship that he felt had no potentialities for friendship, Gary says, "If we hadn't been able to 'make it' we would have stopped seeing each other." He generally prefers women who are stimulating and challenging, though he fears all forms of domination, through either authority or emotional ties.

In his relationships with men outside his family, Gary prefers distance and respect and finds that closeness leads to friction, as with his present roommate. At school he found two older men whom he could look up to: a teacher to whom he was grateful for not being "wishy-washy" and another person whom he describes as being a "real man." (Ways to obtain more information about personal constructs are discussed in *In Focus 11.1*.)

IN FOCUS   11.1   *Behavioral Referents for Personal Constructs*

Some of Gary's main constructs emerged from his self-descriptions and verbalizations. When people start to express their constructs, they usually begin with very diffuse, oversimplified, global terms. For example, Gary called himself "shrewd," "too shy," "too sharp." He also said he wanted to "feel more real," to "adjust better," and to "be happier."

What can the construct assessor do with these verbalizations? As we have seen in earlier chapters, psychodynamically oriented clinicians rely chiefly on their intuitive inferences about the symbolic and dynamic meanings of verbal behavior. Personal construct assessors recognize that talk about private experiences and feelings tends to be ambiguous. For example, statements of the kind commonly presented in clinical contexts, like "I feel so lost," generally are not clear. Instead of inquiring into why the person feels "lost," personal construct assessments try to discover referents for just what the statement means. An adequate personal construct assessment of what people say involves the analysis of what they mean. For this purpose the assessor's initial task is like the one faced when we want to understand a foreign language. Trait-oriented psychometric assessments either investigate the accuracy of the persons' statements as indices of their nontest behavior or treat their verbalizations as signs of their position on a personality dimension. A personal construct analysis of language, on the other hand, is completely different. The main aim of such an analysis is to decipher the content of what is being conveyed and to discover its behavioral referents and consequences; its aim is not to translate what is said into signs of underlying motives, of unconscious processes, or of personality dimensions.

Often it is hard to find the words for personal constructs. Just as the psychologist interested in such concepts as extraversion, identity, or anxiety must find public referents to help specify what he or she means, so must the client find public referents for his or her private concepts, difficulties, and aspirations.

In sum, Kelly urges a specific and elaborate inquiry into personal constructs by obtaining numerous behavioral examples as referents for them. Kelly has described in detail many techniques to explore the conditions under which the individual's particular constructions about emotional reactions may emerge and change (1955).

Nonverbal Communication

Techniques like the semantic differential and the Rep Test sample what people say—that is, their verbal behavior. But significant communication among people is often nonverbal—it can involve facial expressions, movements, and gestures. Nonverbal expressions have intrigued psychologists of many theoretical orientations who are interested in the subject's perceptions and inner states. Researchers explore the possible meanings and effects of such nonverbal expressions as eye contact and the stare.

It has been found, for example, that when an interviewer evaluates subjects positively, they increase eye contact with him; when he evaluates them negatively, they decrease eye contact with him (Exline & Winters, 1965). The effects of eye contact seem to interact with the verbal content conveyed in the relationship. One study varied whether an interviewer looked at the subject frequently or hardly at all and whether the conversation was positive or threatening (Ellsworth & Carlsmith, 1968). When the verbal content was positive, more frequent eye contact produced more positive evaluations of the interviewer. In contrast, when the verbal content was negative, more frequent eye contact produced more negative evaluation.

Although much is still unknown about nonverbal communication, many results have been encouraging. It has been shown, for instance, that "when people look at the faces of other people, they can obtain information about happiness, surprise, fear, anger, disgust/contempt, interest, and sadness. . . . Such information can be interpreted, without any special training, by those who see the face. . . ." (Ekman, Friesen, & Ellsworth, 1972, pp. 176–177).

Studying Lives: The Whole Person

The phenomenological approach has many of its deepest roots in the psychotherapies of theorists like Rogers and Kelly, but it also has been extended in other directions. Most notably, the approach has been adapted and combined with other methods to study lives in depth and over long periods of time (Runyan, 1997). Called **psychobiography,** the intensive study of individual lives has become a specialty area in its own right. These studies attempt to provide a comprehensive psychological understanding of one person, often selecting public figures like Adolf Hitler or Ghandi. As its advocates note, personality psychology has many sides and does not have to be confined to quantitative comparisons among people or groups (Lamiell, 1997; Runyan, 1997). Instead, the study of lives focuses on one person at a time and tries to cover the whole of his or her life in all its complexity over the life course. The methods employed borrow from biography, history, and other social sciences as well as from psychology and the phenomenological approach. As one of its most enthusiastic practitioners put it, there is a "softer human science end of psychology" whose advice to students is "Learn all you can about people and lives, including yourself" (Runyan, 1997, p. 61).

ADAPTATION, HEALTH, AND CHANGE

The phenomenological orientation also has had profound influences on applied approaches to psychological health, to problematic behavior, and to personality change.

The Healthy Personality

The phenomenological orientation implies a "humanistic" view of adaptation and deviance. There are many variations, but in general personal genuineness, honesty about one's own feelings, self-awareness, and self-acceptance are positively valued; "self-realization," the ultimate in fulfillment, involves a continuous quest to know oneself and to actualize one's potentialities for full awareness and growth as a human being. Denouncing "adjustment" to society and to other people's values as the road to dehumanization, the quest is to know oneself deeply and to be true to one's own feelings without disguise, to be oneself in the "here and now." Conversely, human problems are seen as rooted in distortions of one's own perceptions and experiences in the service of furthering the expectations of society, including the dictates of one's own self-concept with its needs for "positive regard" (Chapter 10).

A description of the "healthy" personality from a humanistic viewpoint is provided by Maslow (1968), whose characterization of the qualities of "self-actualizing" people is summarized in Table 11.3. Slightly different but overlapping perspectives come from other humanistic spokesmen (e.g., Jourard, 1974).

In sum, in spite of its many different versions, the phenomenological-humanistic orientation tends to view "healthy people" as those who

1. Become aware of themselves, their feelings, and their limits; accept themselves, their lives, and what they make of their lives as their own responsibility; have "the courage to be."
2. Experience the "here and now;" are not trapped to live in the past or to dwell in the future through anxious expectations and distorted defenses.
3. Realize their potentialities; have autonomy and are not trapped by their own self-concepts or the expectations of others and society.

To help achieve these ideals, several avenues for constructive personality change have been favored by advocates of the phenomenological approach, as discussed next.

Client-Centered Psychotherapy

One of the most influential applications of the phenomenological approach was the client-centered therapy developed by Carl Rogers (Chapter 10). Rogers rejected most of Freud's concepts regarding the nature of psychodynamics and psychosexual development. He also avoided all diagnostic terms, refusing to put any labels on the client. He maintained, however, the interview format for psychotherapy (using a face-to-face arrangement rather than the orthodox psychoanalyst's couch for the client). Rogers and his students focused on the client-clinician relationship. Usually they required fewer sessions than did psychoanalytic therapy, and they dealt more with current than with historical concerns in the client's life.

For Rogers (1959) the therapist's main task is to provide an atmosphere in which clients can be more fully open to their own "organismic" experience. To achieve a growth-conducive atmosphere, the clinician must view the client as intrinsically good and capable of self-development. The clinician's function is to be nonevaluative and to

Table 11.3
Some Qualities of Maslow's "Self-Actualizing" People

1. Able to perceive reality accurately and efficiently.

2. Accepting of self, of others, and of the world.

3. Spontaneous and natural, particularly in thought and emotion.

4. Problem-centered: concerned with problems outside themselves and capable of retaining a broad perspective.

5. Need and desire solitude and privacy; can rely on their own potentialities and resources.

6. Autonomous: relatively independent of extrinsic satisfactions, for example, acceptance or popularity.

7. Capable of a continued freshness of appreciation of even the simplest, most commonplace experiences (for example, a sunset, a flower, or another person).

8. Experience "mystic" or "oceanic" feelings in which they feel out of time and place and at one with nature.

9. Have a sense of identification with humankind as a whole.

10. Form their deepest ties with relatively few others.

11. Truly democratic; unprejudiced and respectful of all others.

12. Ethical, able to discriminate between means and ends.

13. Thoughtful, philosophical, unhostile sense of humor; laugh at the human condition, not at a particular individual.

14. Creative and inventive, not necessarily possessing great talents, but a naïve and unspoiled freshness of approach.

15. Capable of some detachment from the culture in which they live, recognizing the necessity for change and improvement.

SOURCE: Based on Maslow, A. H. (1968). *Toward a psychology of being.* New York: Van Nostrand.

convey a sense of unconditional acceptance and regard for the client (Brazier, 1993). To reach the client effectively the clinician must be "genuine" and "congruent"—an open, trustworthy, warm person without a facade (Lietaer, 1993). The congruent therapist, according to Rogers, feels free to "be himself" and to accept himself and the client fully and immediately in the therapeutic encounter, and he conveys this openness to the client by simply being himself. When a genuinely accepting, unconditional relationship is established, the client will become less afraid to face and accept her own feelings and experiences. Becoming open to the experience of herself as she is, she can reorganize her self-structure. Now, it is hoped, she will accept experiences that she had previously denied or distorted (because they did not fit her self-concept) and thus achieve greater internal congruity and self-actualization.

Rogers thus sought an empathetic, interview-based relationship therapy. He renounced the Freudian focus on psychodynamics and transference. Instead, he wanted to provide the client an unconditionally accepting relationship—an atmosphere conducive to "growth" (self-actualization). In this relationship the focus is on empathic understanding and acceptance of feelings rather than interpretation, although the latter is not excluded. The clinician is relatively "nondirective;" the objective is to let the client direct the interview while the clinician attempts to accurately reflect and clarify the feelings that emerge.

In client-centered therapy (now also called "person-centered"), permissiveness and unqualified acceptance on the part of the therapist provide an atmosphere favorable to personal honesty. Psychologists are urged to abandon their "objective" measurement orientation and their concern with tests. Instead, they should try to learn from the client how he or she thinks, understands, and feels. "The best vantage point for understanding behavior is from the internal frame of reference of the individual himself" (Rogers, 1951, p. 494). Although their focus is on empathy, the Rogerians have not neglected objective research into the relationship, as was noted earlier in this chapter in the context of interview research. As a result, Rogerians have helped to illuminate some of the processes that occur during client-centered therapy and also have provided considerable evidence concerning its effectiveness (e.g., Truax & Mitchell, 1971).

Client-centered psychotherapy has been shown to produce some significant alterations. An extensive review of outcome research indicated that some clients may improve significantly (on measures of self-concept change), while others deteriorate significantly during treatment (Bergin, 1966). Bergin's review concluded that some forms of Rogerian psychotherapy may cause clients to become either significantly better or worse than untreated controls. For example, Gendlin (1962) reported detrimental effects from client-centered relationship therapy for some people, especially those diagnosed as schizophrenic. Consequently, therapy research needs to try to identify the characteristics of clients, clinicians, and client-clinician combinations that might predispose particular forms of therapy to success or failure (e.g., Bergin, 1971). If these attributes can be isolated, it might be possible to offer particular forms of client-centered therapy only to those who can benefit from them.

It is evident that Rogers' client-centered psychotherapy differs in many ways from Freudian psychotherapy. Indeed, when Rogers first proposed his techniques they were considered revolutionary. Sometimes his approach to psychotherapy is even described as the polar opposite of Freud's. While there are major differences between Freudian and Rogerian approaches to psychotherapy, on closer inspection there also are some fundamental similarities. Both approaches retain a verbal, interview format for psychotherapy; both focus on the client-clinician relationship; both are primarily concerned with feelings; both emphasize the importance of unconscious processes (defense, repression); both consider increased awareness and acceptance of unconscious feelings to be major goals of psychotherapy.

To be sure, the two approaches differ in their focus. They differ in the specific content that they believe is repressed (for example, id impulses versus organismic experiences), in the motives they consider most important (such as sex and aggression versus self-realization), and in the specific insights they hope will be achieved in psychotherapy (the unconscious becomes conscious and conflict is resolved versus organismic experience is accepted and the self becomes congruent with it). But these differences should not obscure the fact that both approaches are forms of relationship treatment that emphasize awareness of hypothesized unconscious feelings and the need for the client to accept those feelings.

Phenomenologically Oriented Groups

As part of the search for growth and expanded awareness, in the 1960s and 1970s a variety of group treatments became popular. These group experiences go beyond the verbal exchange of the traditional client-clinician interview and seek to achieve better communication and contact among a group of people as well as to increase each individual's insight and self-awareness. This trend toward group experiences is found in diverse forms, especially in encounter groups and marathons like those developed at the Esalen Institute in California (Schutz, 1967) and in the gestalt therapy of Fritz Perls (1969).

Encounter groups have many different labels, such as human-relations training group (T-group), sensitivity training group, and personal growth group, and include many varieties of experiences, but in this discussion the focus is on their common qualities.

Schutz (1967) in his book *Joy* noted that encounter group methods involve doing something, not just talking. The aim is to help people to experience, to feel, to make life more vital. In this quest he advocated a host of group methods that include body exercises, wordless meetings, group fantasy, and physical "games." These games range from gentle face and body explorations by mutual touching and holding to physically aggressive encounters involving shoving, pushing, and hitting. In many activities the group leaders and group members interpret the meaning of the members' behavior as their encounters occur.

Elliot Aronson (1972, p. 238) described what is learned in group experiences this way: ". . . in a psychology course I learn how people behave; in a T-group I learn how I behave. But I learn much more than that: I also learn how others see me, how my behavior affects them, and how I am affected by other people." Referring to the process through which such learning occurs, Aronson (p. 239) emphasizes learning by doing; ". . . people learn by trying things out, by getting in touch with their feelings and by expressing those feelings to other people, either verbally or nonverbally." Such a process requires an atmosphere of trust so that members learn not how they are "supposed" to behave but rather what they really feel and how others view them.

At a theoretical level, the encounter group movement involves a complex synthesis of both Freudian and Rogerian concepts with a focus on nonverbal experiences and self-discovery. The psychodynamic motivational framework is largely retained and is used in many of the interpretations, but it is implemented by direct "acting-out" procedures for expressing feelings through action in the group, by body contact designed to increase awareness of body feelings, and by games to encourage the expression of affection and aggression. Thus, many of Freud's and Rogers' ideas have been transferred from the consulting room to the group encounter and from verbal expression to body awareness and physical expression. Indeed, Carl Rogers (1970) developed and extended many of his theoretical concepts to the encounter experience and has become one of its leading advocates. Rather than talking about impulses, feelings, and fantasies, the individual is encouraged to act them out in the group. For example, rather than talk about repressed feelings of anger toward his father, the individual enacts his feelings, pummeling a pillow while screaming "I hate you, Dad, I hate you."

Many of these therapies are phenomenologically oriented and seem to emphasize the achievement of greater consciousness and personal integration. The aim is to help individuals to gain awareness, self-acceptance, and spontaneity and ultimately to achieve fulfillment and joy. The objective seems to include a feeling of wholeness and of independence and autonomy.

The same philosophy has also been applied to deal with social and racial issues. For example, an encounter group was used to reduce racial tensions between black and white South Africans in Amsterdam (Saley & Holdstock, 1993). Over a period of two years, the group meetings provided the participants with an arena in which to discuss problems related to South Africa common to them and to gradually reduce or even shed their prejudices. As one white member of the encounter group described its value:

> It broke the isolation. Inevitably one feels that one represents that collective reputation of the whites. That is the main thing that I feel has gone. I can trust myself as a person and not to have to represent South Africa. I can begin to use my own mind and trust my own heart in matters. I have a lot of strength that I did not have before, and I feel that the group has done that for me. We reached a level of intimacy that was not there in the community (Saley & Holdstock, 1993, p. 214).

A factor that seemed especially valuable for breaking down the barriers between the white and black South Africans in the Amsterdam community was the opportunity to make decisions and have opinions independent of their own race and the group to which they felt allegiance. A concern with "doing your own thing" and achieving self-acceptance also characterized the gestalt therapy advocated by Fritz Perls (1969) for personal growth, and it still has strong supporters (e.g., Jacobs, 1989). The philosophy of that position is summarized in the "prayer" of gestalt therapy (Perls, 1969, p. 4):

> I do my thing, and you do your thing
> I am not in this world to live up to your expectations
> And you are not in this world to live up to mine.
> You are you and I am I
> And if by chance we find each other, it's beautiful
> If not, it can't be helped.

Group Experiences

Many people have reported positive changes as a result of group experiences. To illustrate, consider this testimonial cited by Rogers (1970, p. 129):

> I still can't believe the experience that I had during the workshop. I have come to see myself in a completely new perspective. Before I was "the handsome" but cold person insofar as personal relationships go. People wanted to approach me but I was afraid to let them come close as it might endanger me and I would have to give a little of myself. Since the

institute I have not been afraid to be human. I express myself quite well and also am likeable and also can love. I go out now and use these emotions as part of me.

While such reports are encouraging, they of course are not firm evidence, and they are offset in part by reports of negative experiences (Lieberman et al., 1973). Some behavior changes do seem to emerge, but their interpretation is beset by many methodological difficulties (Campbell & Dunnette, 1968). When careful control groups are used, some doubt is raised whether the gains from encounter experience reflect more than the enthusiastic expectancies of the group members. For example, people in weekend encounter groups showed more rated improvement than did those who remained in an at-home control group: But improvement in the encounter groups did not differ from that found in an on-site control group whose participants believed they were in an encounter group although they only had recreational activities (McCardel & Murray, 1974).

Nevertheless, a number of experimental studies indicate specific changes that may occur in some types of groups. These changes include a decrease in ethnic prejudice (Rubin, 1967; Saley & Holdstock, 1993), an increase in empathy (Dunnette, 1969) and in susceptibility to being hypnotized (Tart, 1970), and an increased belief by subjects that their behavior is under their own control (Diamond & Shapiro, 1973). This evidence is accompanied by a greater awareness on the part of therapeutic group enthusiasts that not all groups are for all people, that bad as well as good experiences may occur (Bates & Goodman, 1986), and that coerciveness in groups is a real hazard that needs to be avoided (Aronson, 1972). Particularly important is the finding that self-disclosure and sharing of stressful, traumatic experiences, either in groups or in other forms (e.g., in diaries), can have dramatically beneficial effects on well-being and health (Pennebaker, 1993, 1997).

Meditation

As Eastern cultures have long known, and as Western cultures have only recently learned, meditation can have powerful effects on subjective experience. The term *meditation* refers to a set of techniques which are the product of another type of psychology, one that aims at personal rather than intellectual knowledge. As such, the exercises are designed to produce an alteration in consciousness—a shift away from the active, outward-oriented, linear mode and toward the receptive and quiescent mode, and usually a shift from an external focus of attention to an internal one (Ornstein, 1972, p. 107).

Transcendental Meditation. Students, businessmen, athletes, ministers, senators, and secretaries are among the more than 600,000 people in the United States alone who have enthusiastically endorsed one version of meditation called **transcendental meditation (TM).** Introduced into the United States in 1959 by Maharishi Mahesh Yogi, a Hindu monk, TM in the public's mind changed over the years from counterculture fad to mainstream respectability as it became one of the largest and fastest-growing movements of the 1970s. TM is defined as a state of restful alertness from which one is said to emerge with added energy and greater mind-body

Table 11.4
The Mechanics of Meditation

1. Sit in a comfortable position in a quiet environment, eyes closed.
2. Deeply relax all muscles.
3. Concentrate on breathing in and out through your nose. As you breathe out, repeat a single syllable, sound, or word such as "one" silently to yourself.
4. Disregard other thoughts, adopt a passive attitude, and do not try to "force" anything to happen.
5. Practice twice daily for 20-minute periods at least two hours after any meal. (The digestive process seems to interfere with the elicitation of the expected changes.)

SOURCE: Adapted from Benson, H. (1975). *The relaxation response.* New York: Morrow.

coordination. It is practiced during two daily periods of 20 minutes each. The meditator sits comfortably with eyes closed and mentally repeats a Sanskrit word called a *mantra*.

Maharishi and his movement and more recent followers maintain that the technique of TM can be learned only from specially trained TM teachers, who charge a substantial fee. One of the pioneer researchers into the effects of TM, Herbert Benson, a Harvard cardiologist, disagreed (1975). He believed that the same kind of meditation can be self-taught with a one-page instruction sheet, achieving the same measurable results (see Table 11.4).

The goal of TM is to bring about greater use of an individual's full potential. Those who practice TM report that they have more physical energy, are more mentally alert, are less tense, and are better able to cope with stress. There are also reports of improved physical health as a result of regular and sustained TM practice, and variants of the technique, focusing on deep relaxation, have been incorporated into many current health-maintenance regimes.

Effects of Meditation.   Scientific research into the effects of TM indicates that there are direct physical responses to meditation (Alexander, Robinson, Orme-Johnson, & Scheneider, 1995). These changes include decreased rate of metabolism (decreased oxygen consumption) and an increase in alpha waves (slow brain-wave patterns). Although TM was initially introduced as a technique for expanding consciousness, the current emphasis is on reducing stress and achieving such special effects as lowering blood pressure, alleviating addictions (O'Connell & Alexander, 1994), and increasing energy and powers of concentration.

The research publicized by the TM movement is open to criticism. The fact that many of the researchers are dedicated meditators themselves makes it possible that their results and interpretations may be unintentionally biased. Perhaps most important, the characteristic brain-wave pattern that the TM movement claims to be a sign of the "alert reverie" produced by meditation does not appear to be unique to meditation (Pagano et al., 1976). It can occur, for example, in hypnosis when a state of deep relaxation is suggested. And Benson's (1975) relaxation technique (see Table 11.4) produces the same reductions in oxygen consumption and respiration rate that are produced during transcendental meditation without the expense and the complex rituals of meditation training. In reply, those committed to the movement argue that TM produces a wide range of more fundamental changes than relaxation, including a tremendous improvement in the quality of life. Perhaps because the subjective experience produced by meditation may appear unique to the meditators, they often continue to claim that meditation is a distinct state of consciousness in spite of the contradictory physiological evidence.

The Uses of Meditation.   Meditation has been practiced throughout the ages, usually within a religious context. It seems to have few undesirable side effects, and many subjectively positive effects have been reported by its practitioners. However, most researchers agree that meditation should not be practiced in excess (more than the prescribed two brief periods a day), that it cannot be substituted entirely for sleep, and that it should be used only with medical care and supervision in the treatment of such disorders as high blood pressure. For many meditators, the most important use of meditation is to achieve the mystical experience.

The Person's Experience and the Unconscious

For many years most psychologists slighted people's perceptions and constructs and did not consider them as phenomena of interest in their own right. They preferred, instead, to infer what dispositions and motives might underlie the person's phenomenology and behavior.

The historical neglect of the person's viewpoint probably has many reasons. One was the belief that because of unconscious distortions and defenses, people's self-appraisals were biased and inaccurate. Some psychologists thus refrained from studying the perceptions, concepts, and reasons of the individual because they felt these data were not really scientific. But it is entirely legitimate philosophically and logically to take account of individuals' reported subjective perceptions—the rules they use and the reasons they give to explain their own actions (Lamiell, 1997; T. Mischel, 1964). It is not legitimate, however, to assume that these rules and reasons are useful bases for predicting what individuals will do—their behavior—in other situations. The links between persons' reported feelings and beliefs and their other behaviors must be demonstrated empirically.

Another reason for neglecting the person's viewpoint in personality study was the difficulty of finding objective methods of studying private experiences. But while such experiences are obviously difficult to study, they demand attention and are extremely important. Objecting to the neglect of the "subject's" private experience in psychology, the phenomenological orientation in the past few decades has sought to explore the individual's perceptions and personal constructs. This movement, under the leadership of such theorists as Rogers and Kelly, has had a major impact on the study of personality.

Although the phenomenological orientation focuses on the subject's viewpoint, in some of its variations it also seeks to infer his or her unconscious characteristics and conflicts. For example, Carl Rogers in some of his formulations (1963) has emphasized integration, unity, and people's achieving congruence with their "inner organismic processes." Rogers thought that these organismic processes were often unconscious. As a result of unfortunate socialization procedures in our culture, persons often become dissociated, "consciously behaving in terms of static constructs and abstractions and unconsciously behaving in terms of the actualizing tendency" (Rogers, 1963, p. 20).

Early encounter groups (Schutz, 1967) also paid considerable attention to unconscious processes, making clinical inferences about the person's behaviors as signs whose meaning individuals themselves do not know consciously. The emphasis on interpretation of underlying meanings is implied in this excerpt from the introduction to a group session provided by the "trainer" (leader):

> . . . you, not me, decide what to do in here, such as the topic you want to talk about or the activities you try . . . but I can be counted on to ask, "What's going on?" The idea is to try to understand not only what we do or say—the content level—but also the feelings underneath, the processes going on (Lakin, 1972, p. 20).

Except for the fact that the setting is a group in which the members will be active and participate in the interpretation, this orientation may not be very different from the type supplied in more traditional psychotherapy. As such, the problems of reliability and validity found in connection with clinical judgment (Chapter 4) apply here just as strongly. It of course may be argued that group members are always entirely free to reject any interpretations they feel do not fit them. But such "resistance" may require more independence than can be expected realistically. To try to guard against poor

Family therapy analyzes the transactions in a relationship, helping each partner to see the viewpoint of the other.

group practices, many advocates of encounter experiences note the importance of the leader's competence and experience and urge that prospective members choose their groups with the greatest care, cautioning, "Let the buyer beware!"

To the extent that psychologists accept the idea that unconscious processes are key determinants and rely on clinical judgment to infer them, they face all the challenges previously discussed in the context of clinical judgment. But no methodological difficulties should deter psychologists from listening more closely to what their "subjects" can tell them; the caution applies to the interpretation process, not to the value of listening and empathizing.

Accessing Painful Emotions: Hypnotic Probing

In one promising direction, hypnosis is being used to help individuals access the painful feelings and memories that may become disassociated and difficult to recall in the aftermath of traumatic stress experiences (Spiegel et al., 1994). As discussed in Chapter 2, such disassociation and mental avoidance may follow potentially life-threatening events and losses of the sort experienced by victims of disasters or violent crimes or war, as when body parts are lost or mutilated or loved ones are murdered. But they may also occur in the course of everyday life, especially in early childhood when people have experiences and feelings that they may find traumatic and too difficult to deal with, as Freud stressed in his theory. The dissociated state itself is characterized by being out of touch with one's feelings, sometimes with amnesia, depression, a sense of numbing, detachment, and withdrawal.

In this type of therapy, hypnosis may be used within a highly supportive, structured setting to induce a trance state. While the person is in this state, memories of the painful events may be intensified and reexperienced in the safe therapeutic setting. Recall of the traumatic events is stimulated by the careful guidance and suggestions of the therapist, designed to elicit vivid images that make the memories more accessible (Spiegel, 1981, 1991). It then becomes possible for the person to try to place the traumatic experience into perspective and to bear it emotionally. In this process the person is encouraged to grieve for what has been lost rather than continue to "split off" the painful feelings and run away from them. According to this approach ". . . a loss not grieved leads to a life not lived — to a kind of numbing or withdrawal and depression. . . ." (Spiegel, 1981, p. 35).

Peering into Consciousness: Brain Images of Subjective Experiences

Interestingly, it was Freud who initially thought that hypnosis would provide a window into the unconscious but who soon decided to abandon it in favor of other techniques — a choice that, from the perspective of hindsight, now seems like a mistake to some of his critics. Especially exciting is the prospect that new functional brain imaging techniques may allow hypnosis to be used not only as a window to experiences that are difficult to access in memory but also to the working brain itself. Studies on attention that use these techniques are already helping to specify the brain locations that become activated during hypnotic concentration and that underlie different types of mental states and events (Spiegel, 1991). In future work, it may become increasingly possible not only to more fully access and experience particular life events subjectively and emotionally, but also to see the distinctive brain patterns that become activated during those experiences (e.g., Schachter, 1995).

PHENOMENOLOGICAL APPROACHES TO RELATIONSHIPS: AN ILLUSTRATION

An exciting development from a phenomenological perspective comes from the application of "family" or "systems" therapy to problems ranging from child abuse, battering, and incest to the trauma of HIV infection and AIDS (e.g., Walker, 1991; White & Epston, 1990). These applications illustrate how many key phenomenological concepts can help in understanding, analyzing, and treating some of the most difficult problems of contemporary life. They also illustrate how well the ideas of George Kelly, articulated three decades ago, have stood the test of time. Becoming increasingly popular, they now echo in different voices, from those of philosophers such as Michel Foucault (Foucault, 1980), to anthropologists such as Gregory Bateson (1979) and Clifford Geertz (1986), to modern family therapists (e.g., Minuchin, Lee, & Simon, 1996; White & Epston, 1990). For example, in cutting-edge applications of **family therapy,** the approach to the family's "problem" is cast as a search for constructing alternative stories or scripts. Like Kelly's constructive alternativism, the goal is to help the family members to see one another more constructively and conveniently. The aim is to reconstrue the "problem" to move beyond old stereotypes and essentially create or write new "narratives" that work better and fit the changing circumstances and the contexts of the family and all its members as they evolve.

In this section, the focus is on one application of family therapy: the analysis and treatment of sustained abusive relationships in which men are violent with women, as described in the work of Virginia Goldner and her colleagues (Goldner et al., 1990). We will consider this work in some depth because it shows how diverse concepts and methods may be constructively integrated within an essentially phenomenological framework. Throughout this section we draw extensively on the article by Goldner and associates. As you will see, it uses a wide range of ideas that sometimes have been described with terms like *systems theory* and *transactional analysis,* although family therapy is perhaps the simplest and most widely accepted summary label for this still-evolving theoretical and therapeutic approach.

Transactional Analysis

In their approach to violent relationships, family therapists try to integrate their humanistic perspective with their recognition of gender inequity and their feminist commitment. They believe that in a sustained, violent relationship the beaten woman is clearly the victim. The couple's reciprocal relationship is also implicated, however, in understanding how the cycle of violence is maintained.

It is assumed that although violence and victimization are psychological and require a psychological explanation, that does not explain away or excuse or forgive their moral and ethical violation. The therapeutic goal, consistent with the "here and now" emphasis of the phenomenological perspective, is "to make sense of the confusing circumstances of violence so that the parties caught in its grip can begin to stop it" (Goldner et al., 1990, p. 345). In this effort, family therapists try to construe the situation both from the male and the female perspectives and then analyze in detail sequences of transactions within the couple's relationship as the cycle of violence unfolds. Note that this approach includes both the empathic, personal construct emphasis on the individual's internal view and feelings and the relational, interpersonal focus of the phenomenological perspectives now centered on the experienced, specific meanings of the transactions that occur, as described in the previous chapter.

Analyzing the Cycle

This analysis views male violence as a powerful attempt by the male to exert control over the partner and "enforce his will" while also being, subjectively, a regressive experience, perceived internally as a feeling of "losing it." It sees the females in these relationships as typically sharing a common story. They grew up in families that did not tolerate their daughters' independence strivings and even saw them as bad, destructive, or "crazy." These women feel "they did not count unless they were tending to the needs of others" and, indeed, that "being loved was contingent upon some kind of self-abnegation" (Goldner et al., 1990, p. 358).

The violent men in many cases enter into their relationships, even as adults, with intrinsically impossible prohibitions and personal constructs: ". . . I must never feel fear, know need, respect a woman's point-of-view" (Goldner et al., 1990, p. 352). These researchers give the example of Raymond, who often asserted that he would never be "a wimp." In fact, whenever he felt himself becoming vulnerable and having the emotions he labeled as "wimpy," he tended to become most ferocious in his arguments with his wife and prone to violence.

Breaking Vicious Cycles: Changing Relationships

To break the cycle of violence, the transactions in the relationship are scrutinized, put as it were into slow motion so that the violent moment can be "deconstructed" and more constructive alternatives can be explored and developed. In this process, the triggers of the escalation are identified; the various voices in the heads of the participants are heard empathically but also challenged to examine their meaning and implications. Often these analyses reveal some of the conditions that served unwittingly to retain the abusive cycle. For example, after the violence, the man may make strong emotional bids to be forgiven and promises to reform and make amends that feed into some of the needs that keep the abused woman in the relationship.

In sum, the application of family therapy to the analysis of transactions in couples and families helps to make clear the complex paradoxes and interaction cycles that sustain relationships, even when violence and coercion are embedded in them. When these processes are analyzed in terms of the triggers and circumstances that elicit automatic reactions and that can maintain painful and even dangerous interaction patterns, the participants become free to change them or, if necessary, to leave the relationships.

THE "SUBJECT" AS PSYCHOLOGIST

Influenced by George Kelly's insistence that human beings (regardless of their formal credentials) are like scientists who generate hypotheses and theories about themselves and the world, psychologists also have begun to seriously study the "subject" as an intuitive psychologist. Questions here include the theories that even young children develop about themselves and their own abilities (e.g., Dweck, 1990; see Chapter 16) and the development of one's intuitive awareness of psychological principles needed for such basic functions as self-control and purposeful delay of gratification (Mischel & Mischel, 1983; see Chapter 17). Of particular interest to the phenomenological approach are the naïve perceiver's attempts to explain the meaning and causes of behavior, with regard to both his or her own actions and intentions and those of other people.

When you think about people you do not describe their actions objectively, nor do you analyze their specific responses in relation to particular stimuli. Instead, one forms broad impressions about their characteristics as people, evaluates their intentions, and assesses their worth.

Causal Attributions: Why Did He (She) Do It?

As a first step in judging people, we often ask ourselves why they acted as they did. Why did she not keep our appointment? Why did he seem so distant last night? Why did the professor seem to make a special effort to chat with me at the party? These questions all inquire into the causes of people's behavior: They deal with the causal attribution of behavior. They ask, what is responsible for particular actions, to what can a given pattern of behavior be attributed? In our interactions with one another, each person is both a source of behavior and an "attributor," an analyzer of the reasons underlying behavior, including his or her own. The answers to our questions about attribution—about the causes of behavior—influence our subsequent understanding of the interaction, our feelings about the other person, and our choice of further action.

In everyday relationships, judgments of a person's actions depend on the perceived intentions of the actor (Heider, 1958; Weiner, 1974, 1990). Whether the actions seem deliberate or accidental is especially important. Did the waiter spill the soup accidentally, or was he deliberately rude? If you trip over my foot, your reaction will depend on whether you think I deliberately tripped you. Similarly, a dropped plate, an error in making change at the cash register, a passing friend who does not say hello—the meaning of each of these acts, and hence their impact, depends on the observer's inferences about the intentions motivating them (Jones & Davis, 1965; Kelley, 1973).

Inferring Internal Causes

Although people can and do distinguish among different types of causes, they show systematic bias toward certain kinds of attributions. One of these biases is toward internal (dispositional) rather than external (situational) causes to explain behavior.

We readily use behavioral cues to infer purposeful dispositions and motives in others and ourselves, even when the cues are trivial and momentary. The simplest behavior may be taken as a sign of underlying motives and traits as the perceiver quickly jumps from observed acts to hypothetical dispositions (Weiner, 1995). Even moving geometric shapes may be credited with purposes and emotions ranging from anger through fear (Michotte, 1954).

When observers watch a disk, a large triangle, and a small triangle moving about, they tend to interpret the shapes as if they were people embroiled in interpersonal conflicts and competitions: The large triangle is viewed as aggressive, the small one as heroic, and the disk as timid and feminine (Heider & Simmel, 1944). Obviously, people do not really believe that such moving shapes or cartoon pictures have psychological qualities, but they do readily endow almost any agent of behavior with motives, wishes, and traits, especially when conditions are ambiguous.

Indeed, historians tell us that ancient physicists often personified inanimate objects by giving them dispositions and attributing motives and wills to them. According to Butterfield (1965), Aristotle contended that a falling body accelerated because it became more jubilant as it approached the ground. While modern man is more sophisticated, the tendency to attribute motives as causes, especially in explaining the behavior of other people, persists.

When explaining other people's behavior, we easily invoke their consistent personality dispositions as causes. Harry is the type of person who is quiet at parties; Mary had a car accident because she is careless. However, when asked to explain our own behavior, we may be more alert to specific conditions: "I was quiet because the party was boring." Jones and Nisbett (1971) believe that "actors tend to attribute the causes of their behavior to stimuli inherent in the situation while observers tend to attribute behavior to stable dispositions of the actor" (p. 58). One possible reason for this seeming paradox may be that when we try to understand ourselves, we have more information available concerning the diversity and complexity of the situations that we encounter in our lives. But because we observe others in only narrow contexts, we may tend to overgeneralize from their behavior in those few instances and treat every sample of their behavior as if it were typical.

As we become more familiar with other people, we get information that allows us to see how differently and even inconsistently they may behave in different situations and at different times in their lives. We begin to see that their behavior, like our own, also varies and depends on the particular situation. Thus, with increasing information and familiarity, our concepts about other people become more highly differentiated and situation specific. For example, when describing someone we do not know well, we may at first see her as very stable and secure, but with more experience, we begin to recognize that while she makes friends readily, she also is afraid of being alone or getting left out (Prentice, 1990). Likewise, in the course of development, with greater maturity individuals increasingly come to qualify their characterizations of people with "hedges." These hedges state or imply the particular type of situations in which a familiar other is expected to show his or her characteristic qualities. To illustrate, older children may characterize a friend as aggressive, for example, by saying that "Jim really gets mad" but then qualify it by adding "when kids tease him" (Wright & Mischel, 1988).

In sum, we tend to overattribute consistent dispositions to unfamiliar others and to minimize the role of the situation in our explanations of their behavior (Nisbett & Ross, 1980). Once these attributions have been made, we tend to stick to them even in the face of strong disconfirming evidence, sometimes believing our incorrect intuitions more than the objective data (Ross, 1977; Ross & Nisbett, 1991). But on the other hand, as seen in the previous chapter, there also is agreement among raters in dispositional judgments, both about other peoples' traits and one's own (Funder & Colvin, 1997).

The Perception of Control and Meaningfulness

There is a strong bias to see everyone's behavior as meaningful, orderly, and not the result of chance even when it is random. This common attributional bias is known to everyone who has ever watched behavior in a casino. If you watched such behavior closely, you probably noticed how often gamblers act as if they can control chance by shaking the dice just right, or waiting to approach the roulette wheel at the perfect moment, or pulling the slot machine levers with a special little ritual. Gamblers are not unique in believing they can control chance events.

Even when something is clearly the result of chance (like the cards one draws in a poker game), people may see it as potentially controllable and not just luck. There is a

Shelley Taylor

deep human tendency to see the world as predictable, orderly, and controllable rather than random and chaotic. We expect a "just world" (Heider, 1958), a world in which the things that happen to people are deserved and caused by them—even things like whether or not they win a lottery, get cancer, or are raped and murdered. Much research (reviewed by Langer, 1977) suggests that people often do not discriminate between objectively controllable and uncontrollable events. Instead, they seem to have the "illusion of control," acting as if they can even control events that actually are pure chance.

In most people, this bias is self-enhancing: We are more likely to see ourselves as causally responsible for our actions when they have positive rather than negative outcomes. When we do

IN FOCUS 11.2 *The Meaningful Life, The Healthy Self*

While to some degree biology is destiny, mind and body are closely linked, and the choices and interpretations people make can impact importantly their health. In recent years, research has discovered many of the key psychosocial ingredients that enhance well-being, summarized in Table 11.5, and the results are quite consistent with the expectations of the phenomenological approach.

Table 11.5
Some Key Ingredients for Well-being

Finding meaning in life

Optimism (versus helplessness/hopelessness)

Self-efficacy (beliefs that one can do things effectively)

Social support (e.g., groups that share experience caringly)

The findings from this research on well-being are particularly supportive of the approach discussed in this part of the text. Namely, human resilience and strength—including physical well-being and health—in dealing with serious stressors is enhanced when the individual can find meaning in the experience and in life itself. That is the case even when (or perhaps especially when) the experience is tragic, such as the loss of a life partner or the development of a life-threatening illness (O'Leary, 1997). A dramatic example is seen in how the actor Christopher Reeve, who had starred as Superman in the movies, dealt with his sudden paraplegic condition after an accident. He managed to construe this experience not as an occasion for self-pity but as an opportunity to make a contribution, becoming a dedicated spokesperson to increase research for spinal cord injury.

Beyond such vivid single cases, there is a great deal of evidence that the ingredients of well-being, summarized in Table 11.5, significantly improve the biological response to illness, for example, by acting on the immunological and neuroendocrine systems (Ickovics, 1997). To illustrate, Shelly Taylor found that HIV positive gay men who had lost a life partner but construed the experience as giving new meaning to their life maintained their level of immune functioning longer than did those who did not find meaning in the same experience (O'Leary, 1997; Taylor, 1995).

A second ingredient of resilience is an optimistic (as contrasted to a pessimistic, hopeless, helpless) orientation. Scheier and colleagues (Scheier & Carver, 1992) compared optimists and pessimists (identified through a self-report measure) on a well-researched measure of coping styles in dealing with stress, the COPE (Table 11.6). Optimists characteristically tend to use more active coping and planning, seek emotional support more, use religion, and attempt to grow constructively with the adverse experience they are having. They also are less likely than pessimists to use negative kinds of coping strategies. For example, when dealing with breast cancer, optimists are less likely to deny that they have cancer, tend to disengage less, and use generally positive ways of coping with their disease. In turn, such active coping styles and realistic acceptance of the illness tends to be predictive of survival.

Table 11.6
Illustrative Coping Approaches Measured by the COPE

Active coping and planning

Seeking social support

Religion

Humor

Denial

Mental/behavioral disengagement

Alcohol/drug use

Acceptance

Finding growth potential in adverse experience

well or win, it is to our personal credit; when we do badly or lose, we could not help it (e.g., Fitch, 1970; Urban & Witt, 1990; Wortman et al., 1973). As Shelley Taylor noted, even when outcomes are negative, as in a tragic accident, we may find it hard to cope with events unless we somehow can see them as "just," meaningful, and orderly (e.g., Taylor & Armor, 1996; Taylor & Brown, 1988) rather than meaningless (see *In Focus 11.2*). Although this finding was first seen as evidence for a simple self-enhancing bias by perceivers, more recently it has been shown to have important, potentially beneficial and therapeutic effects for personality (e.g., Seligman, 1990; Seligman, Reivich, Jaycox, & Gillham, 1995; see review in Taylor & Armor, 1996). Indeed, it has become a focus for new cognitive social theories about personality and effective coping, discussed in Part VI (Chapter 16).

SUMMARY

1. The assessment techniques discussed in this chapter represent attempts to study the person's subjective experience within the framework of scientific rules. Most phenomenologically oriented personality psychologists try to bring the individual's private experiences into the public domain by studying subjective experiences with objective techniques. This chapter has shown that the phenomenological orientation to personality has available a variety of methods for studying personal meanings and experiences objectively. The phenomenological approach hence is not merely a point of view about personality; it also offers distinctive techniques for studying persons.

2. Gary W.'s self-conceptualization serves as an example of the raw data of phenomenology. In the phenomenological view, the person may be his or her own best assessor. Research indicates that self-assessment has yielded predictions as accurate as those from more sophisticated personality tests, from combinations of tests, from clinical judgments, and from complex statistical analyses. Thus, the person may be a good predictor of his or her own behavior for such diverse outcomes as success in college, in jobs, and in psychotherapy.

3. One especially useful technique for obtaining a person's self-appraisal is the Q-sort. These Q-sorts may be used for self-description, to describe the ideal self, or to describe a relationship.

4. The interview has been favored by phenomenologically oriented psychologists. Through empathy the interviewer tries to explore the person's feelings and self-concepts and to see the world from his or her framework and viewpoint. Content analysis has been used by Carl Rogers and others in research on processes in the interview.

5. The "semantic differential" is a rating technique that permits the objective assessment of the meaning of the rater's words and concepts. Research with these scales reveals an evaluative, a potency, and an activity factor. These three factors are similar to those found often in trait ratings of persons.

6. The Role Construct Repertory (Rep) Test was devised by George Kelly to systematically study personal constructs. The test tries to explore the subjective dimensions of similarity among events (people or things) and the subjective opposites of those dimensions as the individual construes them. Interviews and other techniques (such as the TAT) also may be used to elaborate personal constructs more fully. A personal construct conceptualization of Gary W. illustrates some of the main features of the personal construct approach to phenomenology.

7. Recently attention has been given to the importance of nonverbal expressions, movements, and gestures.

8. The phenomenological orientation also has influenced views of what constitutes healthy personality and it has significant practical applications for personality change. Most influential have been Rogers' client-centered therapy and a variety of encounter group experiences. These methods offer potential gains for some people but may be hazardous under certain conditions.

9. In other directions, efforts have been made to explore the use of meditation to change consciousness and to increase personal awareness.

10. Usually phenomenological analyses focus on experience and perceptions. Sometimes, however, extensive inferences are made about unconscious problems and conflicts beyond the individual's awareness. Then the psychologist faces all the problems encountered in psychodynamic efforts to make clinical inferences. It is necessary to demonstrate the reliability and validity of the clinician's inferences, regardless of his or her particular theoretical orientation.

11. In treatment of psychological problems, "family" or "systems" therapy has recently become a promising approach. Family therapy for couples in abusive relationships illustrates the method. The focus is on analyzing the circumstances and transactions of the cycle of violence so that the abuse can be halted. The family-systems approach includes both a personal construct and a phenomenological emphasis.

12. People are intuitive psychologists who try to explain and interpret behavior. There is a bias to explain behavior (particularly others' behavior) in terms of internal dispositions rather than external or situational causes. This bias decreases as more information becomes available about the person one is trying to understand. We also tend to see events as controllable and meaningful, even when they are objectively the result of chance. Usually people see positive outcomes as more under their personal control than negative outcomes. This tendency can be beneficial: Individuals who view tragic accidents as unavoidable or as meaningful in some way cope better than those who see the accident as a chance occurrence or who blame others for its happening.

Summary Evaluation

Phenomenological Approaches

As Part IV, Phenomenological Approaches, concludes, this section summarizes its main strengths and weaknesses and its basic features. Chapters 10 and 11 showed that these approaches include a wide range of theories and research. They also have been undergoing an important evolution.

OVERVIEW

In sum, many psychologists welcome the emphasis on the person's cognitions, feelings, and personal interpretations of experience stressed by the theories discussed in Part IV. This concern with how individuals construe events and see themselves and the world has been a most influential force, and it has generated a great deal of research. The resulting contributions are widely acknowledged. Some of the main features of phenomenological approaches are summarized in the next table, which shows some of their shared characteristics.

As the table indicates, the basic unit of personality is the experienced self and the personal concepts and feelings of the individual. These feelings and concepts and the conflicts experienced about them are seen as basic causes of behavior.

Individuals are believed to have freedom in their choices and the potential for self-directed change. The favored data are people's reports and self-disclosures about their personal feelings and constructs. They provide the assessor with a glimpse of the person's inner states, perceptions, and emotions, an empathic sense of what it is like to view the world through that person's eyes. The goal of research is to explore the individual's private feelings and concepts and examine their implications and consequences for him or her. It is assumed that by increasing self-awareness and "being in touch with" one's genuine experienced feelings, persons will enhance their perceived coherence, realize their potential for growth, and self-actualize. The effect of situations can be substantial but always depends on how they are perceived subjectively by the person.

CONTRIBUTIONS AND LIMITATIONS

These approaches continue to focus on important, previously neglected topics: The self, emotions, current subjective experience, and social perceptions are still its princi-

Summary Overview of Phenomenological Approaches

Basic units:	The experienced self; personal constructs and self-concepts; subjective feeling and perceptions; attributions
Causes of behavior:	Self-concepts, feelings and conflicts, attributions; free choices
Behavioral manifestations of personality:	Private experience, perceptions, and interpretations
Favored data:	Self-disclosure and personal constructs (about self and others); self-reports
Observed responses used as:	Signs (of the person's inner states, perceptions, or emotions)
Research focus:	Self-concepts; self-awareness and expression; human potential and self-actualization; emotion; attribution
Approach to personality change:	By increased awareness, personal honesty, internal consistency, and self-acceptance; by modifying constructs; by alternative construals
Role of situation:	As the context for experience and choice; focus on the situation as perceived

pal concerns (see the Summary Evaluation table). As such, the phenomenological approaches in their modern versions remain an appealing alternative to excessively narrow, mechanistic views of personality.

The phenomenological focus on the present and on the future, on the "here and now" as experienced as well as on the future as anticipated, is seen by many psychologists as a strength. Historically, this focus came as a welcome correction to an excessive emphasis in previous approaches on the individual's history and early roots. Of course, every advantage also has a possible disadvantage. For some personality psychologists, the phenomenologists neglect the past and fail to provide an adequate account of personality development, stability, and change.

The original phenomenological theorists, like Rogers and Kelly, writing more than 40 years ago, were lone voices calling for a new kind of personality psychology.

Summary Evaluation of Phenomenological Approaches

Contributions	Limitations
Focus on previously neglected topics: person's subjective current experiences, emotions, and perceptions; the self studied scientifically	Difficulty relating perceptions and personal experiences to objective conditions and external causes
Focus on present and future	Neglect of history and past development
View of persons as scientists and potential experts—but capable of systematic errors and distortions	Persons may be biased perceivers and reporters; difficult to objectify personal experiences
Focus on healthy personality and positive strivings	Excessive reliance on personal growth; less applicable to severely disturbed, poorly functioning, or nonverbal persons

They wanted to make central such topics as the person's subjective perceptions in the "here and now," personal feelings and emotions, and the importance of the self. At the time, little formal research was available on these topics. Therefore, many of the original theoretical statements were more an inspired call for a new focus than a building of a science with systematic observations.

It is a great tribute to the early theorists in these approaches that many of the topics they championed are being investigated decades later with fresh and intense new interest (e.g., Gergen, 1984; Harter, 1983; Higgins & Kruglanski, 1996; Kihlstrom & Cantor, 1984; Markus, 1996; Mischel, Cantor, & Feldman, 1996; Zajonc, 1980). These topics include the role of the person's concepts and constructs (e.g., about the self, about other people) and the individual's subjective internal states, moods, feelings, and thoughts as discussed in Part VI.

An earlier criticism of phenomenological approaches was the fact that people are sometimes biased in their perceptions and therefore may be inaccurate sources of information. In recent years this recognition has been turned into an exciting research problem rather than a handicap of the approaches. The possible biases and cognitive strategies of the perceiver, rather than being dismissed as merely unreliable, have become major topics of scientific interest in their own right, stimulating the study of "social cognition," that is, the thought processes in social perception and judgment (e.g., Kahneman & Tversky, 1984; Ross & Nisbett, 1991). For example, the topic of how the self knows itself and others is getting the attention it deserves (e.g., Berkowitz, 1984; Gergen, 1984; Higgins, 1990; Higgins & Kruglanski, 1996; Markus & Kitayama, 1991), as will be seen in Part VI.

The evolution of phenomenological approaches owes much to a growing link between the ideas of personality theorists such as George Kelly and cognitive psychology more generally. In the past few decades cognitive psychology has become a central area of the field of psychology, especially important to both social and personality psychologists. This new interest in cognition reflects the realization that how people perceive themselves and their experiences crucially influences their behavior (e.g., Cantor, 1990).

The phenomenological orientation discussed in Part IV is not only cognitive, it also began with a humanistic focus. Theorists such as Maslow called attention to higher-order human needs, such as self-actualization. For Carl Rogers, the conditions under which organismic experiences and genuineness were possible were of great importance. The humanistic commitment to enhance personal growth and the human potential has in part been absorbed into some forms of psychotherapy. Encounter groups, family and systems therapy, and various forms of counseling and community service all show the influence of the humanistic movement.

Critics of the phenomenological orientation raise questions about the usefulness of concepts like self-actualization both as explanations and for designing treatments to help severely disturbed people. They point out that Rogers and Kelly both built their theories with healthy college students as their clients in therapy. The ideas of these theorists may have had their greatest appeal and relevance to young, well-functioning people in search of personal growth. The applications of these ideas may be less clear for the severely malfunctioning and the severely disadvantaged socially, culturally, and economically.

Part **V**

Behavioral Approaches

Behavioral Conceptions

Within the broad boundaries set by human genes, what people become is influenced importantly by learning. Through learning, things that attract one person may come to repel another, just as one individual's passions may become another's nightmares. There is a substantial amount of knowledge about human learning, and it can be harnessed to influence human behavior for good or for ill.

In this chapter and in Chapters 13 and 14, you will find some approaches to personality that utilize the principles of learning to analyze and change behavior and to understand personality. These approaches are called **behavioral theories** or **learning theories,** and several different varieties have been formulated. In this chapter, we will consider some of the original concepts of this approach; in later chapters, we will examine its more recent developments, modifications, transformations, and applications.

THE EARLY BEHAVIORAL APPROACH TO PSYCHODYNAMICS: DOLLARD AND MILLER

In one important early direction, some American psychologists committed to the scientific, experimental study of behavior were also heavily influenced by Freud and developed his ideas in new ways. While they were intrigued by the insights of Freud and his followers, these behaviorally oriented psychologists were primarily dedicated to the scientific, rigorous study of psychology. Working more than 50 years ago, they devoted themselves to the development of an experimental methodology through which precise and reliable research might be possible. Heavily influenced by strategies in other natural sciences, early workers in this field began with careful study of lower animals in highly controlled laboratory situations. While some were fascinated by Freud's bold speculations about the mind, most were skeptical about his informal clinical methods. Rather than probe the dreams and free associations of neurotic patients or theorize broadly about human nature and society, these researchers sought a system that would be objectively testable, preferably by laboratory techniques.

Psychologists in this tradition focused on the basic processes of learning through which an organism in interaction with its environment acquires and performs a repertoire of responses. They studied the learning mechanisms through which certain events—"stimuli"—become associated with particular behaviors or responses. Like all scientific theorists, their objective was to understand causes—in this case, learning or the ways in which stimuli become associated with responses.

In this section we will concentrate on the theory developed in the late 1940s by John Dollard and Neal Miller at Yale University. We will call their orientation **psychodynamic behavior theory** because it is the major effort to integrate some of the fundamental ideas of Freudian psychodynamic theory with the concepts, language, and methods of experimental laboratory research on behavior and learning.

Primary Needs and Learning

The newborn infant begins life with a set of *innate* or *primary* biological needs, such as the need for food and water, oxygen, and warmth. Satisfaction of these needs to some minimal degree is essential for the organism's survival. But although these needs are innate, the behaviors required to satisfy them involve learning.

For example, sucking is an innate response that is readily elicited in the newborn when a nipple stimulates its mouth. But although the sucking response itself may be innate, its efficiency increases with practice. Thus, even the seemingly elementary response patterns required to satisfy primary needs depend on learning processes for their efficient execution. The most casual observation of other cultures quickly reveals that there are almost endless ways to fulfill even such primary needs as hunger and thirst. Through learning great variability develops in the ways in which needs are fulfilled. Consider, for example, food preferences: The gourmet dishes of one culture may be the causes of nausea in another. The same learned variability seen in food preferences is also found in standards of shelter, clothing, aesthetics, and values when one compares different cultures.

Most human behaviors involve goals and incentives whose relations to innate needs are extremely remote. People seem to strive for such exceedingly diverse goals as money, status, power, love, charity, competence, mastery, creativity, self-realization, and so on. These and many more strivings have been characterized and classified as human motives. Neal Miller and John Dollard have deeply explored the learning processes through which such motives may evolve from primary needs.

Starting with the basic assumption that behavior is learned, Dollard and Miller (1950) have constructed a learning theory to explain the wide range of behavior involved in normal personality, neurosis, and psychotherapy. In their view, the four important factors in the learning process are **drive** (motivation), **cue** (stimulus), **response** (act or thought), and **reinforcement** (reward). In its simplest form, their idea is that

> in order to learn one must want something, notice something, do something, and get something (Miller & Dollard, 1941, p. 2).

These four events correspond respectively to "drive," "cue," "response," and "reward." Learning, in their view, is the process through which a particular response and a cue stimulus become connected.

Think of an animal in the psychologist's laboratory. Motivated by the *drive* of hunger, the animal engages in diffuse activity. At one point he happens to see a lever (*cue*). His *response,* at first accidental, is to press the lever, and this action releases food into his cup. The animal eats the food at once, thereby reducing the tension of his hunger drive (reward or reinforcement). Now in the future when he is hungry, he is more likely to press the lever again: The association between the cue stimulus (the lever) and the response (pressing it) has been strengthened. On subsequent trials the hungry animal will press the lever sooner. Let us consider each of the four components of learning separately.

Drive

According to Dollard and Miller (1950), any strong stimuli (internal or external) may impel action and thus serve as drives. The stronger the stimulus, the greater its drive function. A mild stimulus (such as the faint sound of a distant horn) does not motivate behavior as much as a strong stimulus (the blare of the horn near one's ear). Examples of strong stimuli are hunger pangs and pain-inducing noise—they motivate behavior. While any stimulus may become strong enough to act as a drive, certain classes of stimuli (such as hunger, thirst, fatigue, pain, and sex) are the primary basis for most motivation. These stimuli are primary or innate drives. The strength of the primary drives varies with the conditions of deprivation: The greater the deprivation, the stronger the drive.

Often the operation of primary drives is not easy to observe directly. Society generally protects its members from the unpleasant force of strong primary drives by providing for their reduction before they become overwhelming. In instances when this is not true—for example, conditions of prolonged famine in India—psychologists usually are not present to study behavior systematically. Moreover, social inhibitions—for example, in the area of sex—may further prevent the direct or complete public expression of primary drives. Consequently, much visible behavior is motivated by already altered secondary or learned drives. It is these transformed motives that are most evident under conditions of modern society and that are important in civilized human behavior.

Dollard and Miller believed that these learned drives are acquired on the basis of the primary (unlearned, innate) drives and are elaborations of them. The acquisition of fear as a learned drive has been studied carefully. (Some of the specific mechanisms of such learning are discussed in detail in the next chapter.) A fear is learned if it occurs in response to previously neutral cues (e.g., a white room). A learned fear is also a drive in the sense that it motivates behavior (e.g., escape from the room) and its reduction is reinforcing.

In one study, rats were exposed to electric shock in a white compartment and were permitted to escape to a black compartment where there was no shock (Miller, 1948). Eventually the rats responded with fear to the white compartment alone (that is, without shock). Even when the shock (primary drive stimulus) was no longer present, the animals learned new responses, such as pressing a lever or turning a wheel, in order to escape from the harmless white compartment. In common sense terms, they behaved as if they were afraid of an objectively harmless stimulus. The motivation for this new learning lies, according to Miller and Dollard, in the reduction of the learned fear of the white compartment. Thus, fear is conceptualized as both a learned response and a learned drive, and its reduction is considered to be a reinforcement.

Dollard and Miller's emphasis on drives, both "primary" and "secondary," is reminiscent of the Freudian emphasis on motives and impulses as the forces underlying behavior. While Freud's conceptualization stresses instinctual wishes, however, Dollard and Miller's makes room for many learned motives, whose roots are in primary drives.

Cue

"The drive impels a person to respond. Cues determine when he will respond, where he will respond and which response he will make" (Dollard & Miller, 1950, p. 32). The lunch bell, for example, functions as a cue for hungry schoolchildren to put away their books and get their lunchboxes. Cues may be auditory, visual, olfactory, and so on. They may vary in intensity, and various combinations of stimuli may function as cues. Changes, differences, and the direction and size of differences may be more distinctive cues than is an isolated stimulus. For example, a person may not know the absolute length of an unmarked line but yet be able to tell which of two lines is the longer.

In Dollard and Miller's formulation a very intense stimulus may become a drive. A stimulus thus may serve as both a drive and a cue, motivating behavior and directing it as well.

Response

Before a response to a cue can be rewarded and learned, it must of course occur. Dollard and Miller suggest ranking the organism's responses according to their probability of occurrence. They call this order the initial hierarchy. Learning changes the order of responses in the hierarchy. An initially weak response, if properly rewarded, may come to occupy the dominant position. The new hierarchy produced by learning is termed the resultant hierarchy. With learning and development, the hierarchy of responses becomes linked to language, and it is heavily influenced by the culture in which social learning has occurred.

Reinforcement

A reinforcement is a specific event that strengthens the tendency for a response to be repeated. A reduction in the strength of a drive reinforces any immediately preceding response. In other words, drive reduction serves as a reinforcement (or reward). This is true for both primary and secondary, or acquired, drives. The reduction or avoidance of painful stimulation and of learned fears or anxieties associated with pain and punishment also may function as a reinforcement. We saw earlier that rats seemed to work hard to escape from the white, fear-inducing compartment (Miller, 1948).

Miller and Dollard's concept of reinforcement as drive reducing or tension reducing has some similarity to Freud's pleasure principle. Both concepts view need states as states of high tension and construe the reduction of tension and the attainment of equilibrium as the organism's goals.

Reinforcement is essential to the maintenance of a habit as well as to its learning. Extinction is the gradual elimination of a tendency to perform a response; it occurs when that response is repeated without reinforcement. The time required to extinguish a habit depends on the habit's initial strength and on the conditions of the extinction situation. Conditions of weak drive, effortful responses, short time between extinction trials, and strong alternative responses influence extinction.

According to Dollard and Miller, extinction merely inhibits the old habit; it does not destroy it. If new responses performed during extinction are rewarded, they may be strengthened to the point where they supersede the old habit. For example, if a child is praised and rewarded for independent, autonomous play but consistently nonrewarded (extinguished) when he or she dependently seeks help, the independent pattern will become predominant over the dependent one.

Miller (1963) also speculated about possible alternatives to his drive-reduction concept of reinforcement learning. His hypothesis of an alternative to drive reduction includes the tentative assumption of "activating" or "go" mechanisms in the brain. These "go" mechanisms, Miller conjectured, could be activated in a variety of ways (such as by thinking), not merely by the reduction of drives or noxious stimulation.

Conflict

Individuals may experience conflict when they want to pursue two or more goals that are mutually exclusive. For example, a person may want to spend the evening with a friend but thinks he should prepare for an examination facing him the next morning; or she may want to express her anger at her parents but also does not want to hurt them. When an individual must choose among incompatible alternatives, he or she may undergo conflict.

Neal Miller's (1959) conceptualization of conflict, which is influenced by Lewin (1935), hypothesizes *approach* and *avoidance* tendencies. For example, in an **approach-approach conflict** the person is torn, at least momentarily, between two desirable goals. Conversely, people often face avoidance-avoidance conflicts between two undesirable alternatives: to study tediously for a dull subject or flunk the examination, for example. The individual may wish to avoid both of these aversive events, but each time he starts to move away from his desk he reminds himself how awful it would be to fail the test.

Some of the most difficult conflicts involve goals or incentives that are both positive and negative in valence. These are the goals toward which we have "mixed feelings" or ambivalent attitudes. For example, we may want the pleasure of a gourmet treat but not the calories, or we may desire the fun of a vacation spree but not the expense, or we may love certain aspects of a parent but hate others.

Recall that **approach-avoidance conflicts** had a predominant place in Freud's hypotheses regarding intrapsychic clashes—for example, between id impulses and inhibitory anxieties. Just as conflict is central to Freud's conception of personality dynamics, so it is the core of Dollard and Miller's theory. But whereas Freud developed his ideas about conflict from inferences regarding id-ego-superego clashes in his neurotic patients, Dollard and Miller tested their ideas in careful experiments with rats (Brown, 1942, 1948; Miller, 1959).

Neurotic Conflict

Like Freud, Dollard and Miller conceptualized conflict and anxiety as the core ingredients of neurotic behavior. In Freud's formulation, neurotic conflict involves a clash between id impulses seeking expression and internalized inhibitions that censor and restrain the expression of those impulses in accord with the culture's taboos. Dollard and Miller state the same basic ideas in the language of learning theory.

In Dollard and Miller's view of neurosis, strong fear (anxiety) is a learned drive that motivates a conflict concerning "goal responses" for other strong drives, such as sex or aggression. Specifically, when the neurotic person begins to approach goals that might reduce such drives as sex or aggression, strong fear is elicited in him or her. Such fear may be elicited by thoughts relevant to the drive goals, as well as by any overt approach attempts. For example, sexual wishes or hostile feelings toward a parent may be frightening; hence, a conflict ensues between the wishes and the fear triggered by their expression. These inhibitory fearful responses further prevent drive reduction, so that the blocked drives (such as sex and aggression) continue to "build up" to a higher level. The person is thus trapped in an unbearable conflict between frustrated, pent-up drives and the fear connected with approach responses relevant to their release.

The neurotic person in this dilemma may be stimulated simultaneously by the frustrated drives and by the fear that they evoke. The high drive state connected with this conflict produces "misery" and interferes with clear thinking, discrimination, and effective problem solving. The "symptoms" shown by the neurotic arise from the build up of the drives and of the fear that inhibits their release.

Anxiety and Repression

Like Freud, Dollard and Miller accept unconscious factors as critically important determinants of behavior, and, again like Freud, they give anxiety (or learned fear) a central place in dynamics. In their view, repression involves the learned response of *not-thinking* of something, and it is motivated by the secondary drive of fear. That is, due to past experiences certain thoughts may have come to arouse fear as a result of their associations with pain or punishment. By not thinking these thoughts, the fear stimuli are reduced and the response (of not-thinking) is further reinforced. Eventually, "not-thinking" (inhibiting, stopping, repressing) becomes anticipatory, in the sense that the individual avoids particular thoughts before they can lead to painful outcomes. This formulation is similar to Freud's idea that repression is the result of anxiety and functions to reduce the anxiety caused when unacceptable material starts to emerge from the unconscious to the conscious.

Dollard and Miller's account thus serves as a clear translation of the psychodynamic formulation of anxiety, repression, and defense into the terms of reinforcement learning theory. Defenses and symptoms (e.g., phobias, hysterical blindness) are reinforced by the immediate reduction of the fear drive. While the temporary effect of the symptom is drive reduction and momentary relief, its long-range effects may be debilitating. For example, a phobic symptom may prevent a person from working effectively and, hence, create new dilemmas, fear, guilt, and other conditions of high drive conflict.

Reactions against Psychodynamic Behavior Theory

As was noted earlier (Chapter 2), Freud constructed a theory of development without the benefit of learning concepts. He adopted a body language and invented new terms such as "fixation" that made it difficult to coordinate his theory with experimental psychology. Dollard and Miller demonstrated that this coordination could be achieved. They drew on laboratory research with animals to devise a personality theory in learning terms that closely paralleled and, in many respects, translated, Freudian theory. The psychodynamic emphasis on motives, on unconscious processes, on internal conflicts and defenses, such as repression, remained largely unchanged. Many psychologists found Freud's basic ideas more congenial and easier to adopt when they were put into the language of learning and experimental psychology. Consequently, these concepts stimulated much research.

But other strong voices in the early behavioral tradition rejected psychodynamic and motivational constructs in any form, whether or not they were put in the language of learning. Instead, they tried to understand complex human problems, such as irrational fears and anxiety, in simple conditioning terms.

CLASSICAL CONDITIONING: LEARNED ANXIETY

Classical conditioning (conditioned-response learning) is a type of learning (emphasized by Pavlov) in which a neutral stimulus (for example, a bell) becomes conditioned by being paired or associated with an unconditioned stimulus (one that is naturally powerful).

How Classical Conditioning Works

A dog automatically salivates when food is in its mouth. The response of salivation is a **reflex** or **unconditioned response** (UCR): It is natural and does not have to be learned. Like most other reflexes, in humans and in animals alike, salivation helps the organism adjust or adapt: The saliva aids in digesting the food. Stimuli that elicit unconditioned responses are called **unconditioned stimuli** (UCS). The unconditioned stimulus (food in this example) can elicit behavior without any prior learning.

Any dog owner knows that a hungry dog may salivate at the mere sight of food, before it gets any in its mouth. The dog may even begin to salivate at the sight of the empty dish in which the food is usually served. Salivating to the sight of the empty dish that has been associated with food is an example of a learned or **conditioned response** (CR). The stimulus that elicits a conditioned response is called a **conditioned** (learned) **stimulus** (CS): Its impact on behavior is not automatic but depends on learning.

Ivan Pavlov
(1849–1936)

Pavlov discovered some of the ways in which such neutral stimuli as lights and metronome clicks could become conditioned stimuli capable of eliciting responses like salivating. His pioneering experiments with dogs began with his repeatedly making a certain sound whenever he gave his dogs their food. After a while he found that the dogs salivated to the sound even when it was no longer followed by food: **Conditioning** had occurred. This type of learning is what we now call classical conditioning.

To sum up, in classical conditioning the subject is repeatedly exposed to a neutral stimulus (that is, one that elicits no special response) together with an unconditioned stimulus that elicits an unconditioned response. When this association becomes strong enough, the neutral stimulus by itself may begin to elicit a response similar to the one produced by the unconditioned stimulus. (See Tables 12.1 and 12.2 for basic definitions and examples.)

Most experiments in classical conditioning are performed in the laboratory, but the knowledge they have generated may help us to understand many things that hap-

Table 12.1
The Language of Classical Conditioning

Term	Definition
Unconditioned stimulus (UCS)	A stimulus to which one automatically, naturally responds without learning to do so.
Unconditioned response (UCR)	The unlearned response one naturally makes to an unconditioned stimulus. The response may be positive or negative (for example, salivating when food is placed in the mouth; jerking one's hand away from a hot stove).
Conditioned stimulus (CS)	A previously neutral stimulus to which one learns to respond after it has been paired or associated with an unconditioned stimulus.
Conditioned response (CR)	The learned response to a conditioned stimulus. This response was previously made only to an unconditioned stimulus, but now it is made to a conditioned stimulus as a result of the pairing of the two stimuli.

Table 12.2
Examples of Possible Effects of Classical Conditioning

Before Conditioning	After Conditioning
Dog knocks child over. (UCS) Child cries. (UCR)	Dog approaches. (CS) Child cries. (CR)
Mother feeds and cuddles baby. (UCS) Baby relaxes. (UCR)	Baby smells mother's perfume. (CS) Baby relaxes. (CR)
Car accident injures woman. (UCS) Woman is afraid. (UCR)	Woman thinks about getting in car. (CS) Woman is afraid. (CR)
Man drives across a swaying bridge. (UCS) Man is afraid. (UCR)	Man approaches another bridge. (CS) He is afraid and avoids bridge. (CR)
Mother discovers her daughter masturbating, scolds her, slaps her hands. (UCS) Daughter is hurt and afraid. (UCR)	Daughter looks at her nude body. (CS) Daughter feels anxious and negative about her body, particularly her genitals. (CR)

pen outside the laboratory, such as the development of affections and attractions (Byrne, 1969; Lott & Lott, 1968). For example, a liking for particular people and things may depend on the degree to which they have been associated with positive or pleasant experiences (Griffitt & Guay, 1969). If so, one's affection for a friend may be directly related to the degree to which he or she has been associated with gratifications for oneself.

Now consider the development of fear. How do initially neutral (or even positive) stimuli acquire the power to evoke fear? Suppose for example, a person repeatedly sees a light and experiences an electric shock simultaneously. In time, the light by itself may come to evoke some of the emotional reaction produced by the shock. Neutral stimuli that are closely associated in time with any pain-producing stimulus then become conditioned stimuli that may elicit fear and avoidance reactions. Thus, the seemingly irrational fears that some people have may reflect a conditioned association between previously neutral stimuli and painful events.

Classical conditioning may influence development throughout a person's life. If, for example, sexual curiosity and fear-producing experiences (such as severe punishment) are closely associated for a child, fear may be generated by various aspects of the individual's sexual behavior even after there is no longer any danger of punishment. And conditioning can spread as well as persist: The child who is made to feel bad about touching the genitals may also become anxious about other forms of sexual expression and may even develop broader fears.

In a classic study, following a strategy that would not be tolerated now because of the ethical issues it raises, Watson and Rayner (1920) induced a severe fear of rats in a little boy named Albert, who had not been afraid of rats before. This was done by classical conditioning: Just as Albert would reach for the rat, the experimenters would make a loud noise that frightened him. After he had experienced the rat and the aversive noise several times in close association, he developed a strong fear of the rat.

How much we like a person may depend on the degree to which he or she has been associated with gratification.

Albert's fear generalized so that later, when shown a variety of new furry stimuli such as cats, cotton, fur coats, human hair, and wool, he responded with obvious fear to them as well. His fear had spread to these new objects even though they had never been paired with the noise. This is a human example of the kind of learning found when rats who were shocked in a white compartment began to respond fearfully to the compartment itself even when the shock no longer occurred (Miller, 1948). The case of Little Albert has become one of the first bases for applications of classical conditioning to the analysis and treatment of human problems.

A Behavioral Challenge to the Psychodynamic Theory of Neurosis

Differences among theoretical approaches are seen most clearly when applied to the same case. Behavior theorists have strongly challenged Freud's theory of neurosis by reanalyzing in learning terms a case that he presented. Recall that Freud's view of how neuroses develop begins with the child's aggressive or sexual impulses, which seek direct, immediate release. Because expression of these impulses may be punished severely, the child may become anxious about his own impulses and try to repress them. But the impulses continue to seek release and become increasingly pent up. Eventually they may be impossible to repress, and components of them may break through, creating further anxiety. To reduce this anxiety, the person may attempt a variety of defense mechanisms. In neurosis, these defenses begin to break down: The unacceptable impulses start to express themselves indirectly and symbolically in various disguised forms, such as in phobias or obsessive-compulsive thoughts and actions. The roots of neurosis, in Freud's view, are always in childhood:

> It seems that neuroses are acquired only in early childhood (up to the age of six), even though their symptoms may not make their appearance till much later. The childhood neurosis may become manifest for a short time or may even be overlooked. In every case the later neurotic illness links up with the prelude in childhood (Freud, 1933, pp. 41–42).

An example from Freud's (1963) theory is his published case of Little Hans. Hans was a five-year-old boy who developed a horse phobia. He was afraid of being bitten by a horse and, after seeing a horse hitched to a wagon slip and fall on a street near his home, began to dread going out. Freud interpreted the phobia as an expression of the child's psychodynamic conflicts. These conflicts included his desires to seduce his mother and replace his father. These desires, in turn, made him fear castration by the father; symbolically, the horse came to represent the dreaded father.

A behavioral analysis of this case, however, explains Hans's phobia without invoking any internal conflicts or symbolism (Wolpe, 1997; Wolpe & Rachman, 1960). Namely, the scene Hans witnessed of a horse falling down and bleeding on the street was sufficiently frightening to the young child to produce fear. In turn, the fear generalized to all horses and resulted in Hans's avoidance behavior. Thus, a simple conditioning process might explain a phobia: Since the horse was part of an intensely frightening experience, it became a conditioned stimulus for anxiety, and the anxiety generalized to other horses.

As this example illustrates, the behavioral view of neurosis is concerned with anxiety and avoidance no less than the psychodynamic view, but it tries to link them to external circumstances rather than to internal conflicts (Redd, 1995; Redd et al., 1978). Through direct or vicarious frightening experiences, people often develop anxiety in response to particular objects, persons, or situations. Not only encountering these events in reality but even just thinking about them may be upsetting. These emotional reactions may generalize and take many forms. Common examples include muscle tensions and fatigue and intense fear reactions to seemingly neutral stimuli.

Psychodynamic and behavioral theorists do agree that the neurotic individual may make all sorts of efforts to escape and avoid painful feelings. Many of his avoidance attempts may be maintained persistently because they serve to terminate the pain. For example, such elaborate avoidance defenses as obsessive-compulsive rituals, in the form of handwashing for many hours, may be maintained because they reduce the person's anxiety (Wolpe, 1963). In addition, attention and sympathy from relatives and friends for being sick or relief from pressures and obligations can also serve to maintain the anxious person's avoidance patterns by providing reinforcement for them.

From Trauma to Anxiety

As the reanalysis of Little Hans suggested, some of the clearest examples of anxiety reactions occur after the individual has experienced a threatening danger or trauma. A near-fatal automobile accident, an almost catastrophic combat experience, an airplane crash—such intense episodes of stress are often followed by anxiety. After the actual dangers have passed, stimuli that remind the individual of those dangers, or signs that lead him or her to expect new dangers, may reactivate anxiety that may persist and distort perceptions (e.g., Chapita & Barlow, 1998; Rachman & Cuk, 1992).

After severe trauma, the victim is more likely to respond anxiously to other stress stimuli that occur later in life (Archibald & Tuddenham, 1965; Milgram, 1993). Surviving victims of Nazi concentration camps, for example, sometimes continued for years to be hypersensitive to threat stimuli and to react to stress readily with anxiety and sleep disturbances (Chodoff, 1963). These observations support the idea that anxiety involves a learned fear reaction that is highly resistant to extinction and that may be evoked by diverse stimuli similar to those that originally were traumatic. That is, the fear evoked by the traumatic stimuli may be reactivated and also may *generalize* to stimuli associated with the traumatic episode. For example, after a child has been attacked and bitten by a dog, her fear reaction may generalize to other dogs, animals, fur, places similar to the one in which the attack occurred, and so on (Figure 12.1). Moreover, if the generalization stimuli are very remote from the original traumatic stimulus, the person may be unable to see the connection between the two and the anxiety may appear (even to her) particularly irrational. Suppose, for example, that the child becomes afraid of the room in which the dog bit her and of similar rooms. If the connection between her new fear of rooms and the dog's attack is not recognized, the fear of rooms now may seem especially bizarre.

From a learning point of view, anxieties after traumas, like other learned fears, may be acquired through simple association or conditioning principles. If neutral stimuli have been associated with aversive events or outcomes, then they also may come to

Figure 12.1
From Trauma to Anxiety

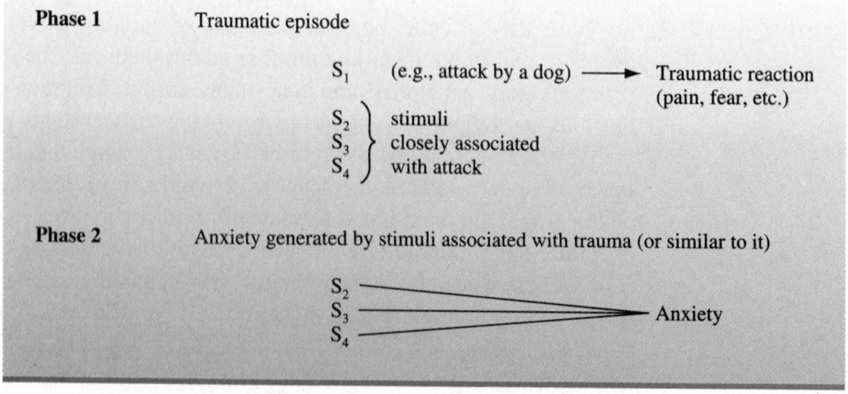

elicit anxiety in their own right. Such aversively conditioned emotional reactions may also generalize extensively to new stimuli (Figure 12.1). Clinical examples of aversive arousal and avoidance include many phobic and anxious reactions to objects, as we saw with Little Hans, people, and social and interpersonal situations. Not only external events, but also their symbolic representations in the form of words or of thoughts and fantasies, may create painful emotions. In our example of the child traumatized by the dog, even thinking about the incident, or the room in which it occurred, or similar rooms may terrify the youngster.

Stimuli closer or more relevant to those associated with emotional arousal tend to elicit stronger reactions. In one study, novice sports parachutists and control participants were administered a specially constructed word association test (Epstein & Fenz, 1962; Fenz, 1964). The words contained four levels of relevance to parachuting. Throughout the word association tests, participants' physiological reactions (*galvanic skin response,* or GSR, which is a change in electrical activity of the skin due to sweating) were recorded to measure their emotional arousal in response to the various stimulus words. One testing occurred two weeks before the scheduled jump, another testing was done the day before the jump, and a final test was on the day of the parachute jump.

The results showed more arousal in parachutists for parachute-relevant words. The effect was greatest for the words most relevant to parachuting, and the gradient of arousal was highest and steepest when the testing time was closer to the emotion-arousing parachute jump itself.

Traumas often may lead to anxiety, but many other effects are also possible. One study examined differences between children in Israeli settlements subjected to frequent artillery shellings during Arab-Israeli conflicts and those from comparable settlements that were not shelled (Milgram, 1993; Ziv, Kruglanski, & Shulman, 1974). The children in the shelled settlements appeared to cope actively with the stress and did so in ways that were supported by the social norms in their community. Specifically, they developed greater patriotism for the settlement in which they resided, showed more externally oriented aggressiveness, and became more appreciative of courage as a personality trait.

Anxiety, Avoidance, and Conflict

Because anxiety is aversive, we usually try to reduce or avoid it. When the dangerous event is external—like an attacker—anxiety may be reduced by physical escape from the threatening situation or by other forms of problem solving (such as calling for help). The reduction of the anxiety state in turn reinforces the behaviors that led to the relief. Consequently, the person's successful escape or avoidance behaviors become strengthened.

The strengthening of successful escape behaviors may be adaptive to the extent that one can then more readily avoid similar future dangers. On the other hand, because the escape pattern was effective, the person may continue to avoid similar situations in the future when in fact they are no longer dangerous. That is, previously reinforced quick escape and avoidance maneuvers may prevent the person from learning that the danger feared is no longer there or that its aversive effects can be mastered. The child who was bitten by a dog and then runs away from all dogs has no chance to learn that most dogs are friendly. In that case the fearful person continues to defensively avoid similar or related situations instead of unlearning his or her fear of them. Hence, avoidance reactions may be highly persistent (Chapita & Barlow, 1998; Peterson, Maier, & Seligman, 1993; Seligman, 1975).

Reinforced escape and avoidance patterns, if widely generalized, may have debilitating consequences. As an example, consider the case of a little girl who has been sexually molested by an intruder at home. As a result of this traumatic experience, the child may acquire a phobic reaction, not just to the painful encounter and the man who terrified her, but also to other men and to many aspects of sexual experience and intimacy. Her subsequent refusal of dates and her generalized avoidance of closeness with men would make it increasingly difficult for her to overcome her anxieties and to develop satisfying heterosexual relationships.

Avoidance reactions may become most problematic when the threat stimuli persist and cannot be escaped by moving away from them physically. Often individuals cannot escape from the sources of possible anxiety around them by simply avoiding them. This is true when they depend upon and love the very people who threaten them.

In the course of socialization, the same significant persons who nurture and care for the child and to whom the child becomes most deeply attached are also the ones who discipline and punish him or her. For example, the same mother who gives the child her attention and social approval may cause pain and anxiety. Thus, the same social stimulus—the mother, in this example—that has been associated with positive rewards and gratification is also connected with pain because of the punishments she dispenses and the rewards that she withholds from the child. The phenomena of "ambivalence" and "conflict" may result whenever the same persons or objects who evoke positive feelings and approach tendencies are also the sources for negative emotions and avoidance reactions. This duality is common in life and it does not end with childhood. In an adult's life, for example, the same spouse who gives love may also be the source of many bitter frustrations. Hence, mixed feelings develop.

Just how the individual will feel and react in relation to these ambivalence-producing stimuli depends on many considerations. For example, a child may be harshly punished by his father when he is physically aggressive to his baby sister but may be warmly praised by his father when he is physically self-assertive with peers. If that happens consistently, he soon may learn to expect positive gratification from his father in one context but punishment and aversive consequences in the other context. Thus, in one situation he will expect praise and love from the same father who is the source of his anxiety in the second situation. These situations will be discriminated clearly, and anxiety associated with uncertainty and conflict, therefore, will probably be minimal.

Anxiety may be much higher, however, when the child is uncertain about the behaviors that will lead to punishment and those that will not, and when she does not feel that she can control the important aversive outcomes in her life. It may be especially difficult for a child to cope adequately if punishment from the parent (and other important people) is unpredictable and inconsistent so that she is unsure of what to expect.

A fear may generalize to stimuli similar to the one that initially produced it.

In that case the child may experience a more generalized dread because threat and punishment are possible at almost any time and place.

Higher-Order Conditioning

When a previously neutral stimulus, such as a light, a bell, or a face, has become a conditioned stimulus through its association with an unconditioned stimulus, such as food or pain, it can in turn modify one's reactions to another neutral stimulus by being associated with it. This process is called **higher-order conditioning.** It was demonstrated when Pavlov found that after a metronome sound had become a conditioned stimulus (by being paired with food), it could itself be paired with a neutral stimulus (such as a black triangle) and, as a result of that association, the neutral stimulus would also elicit the unconditioned response of salivation. In people, words and other complex symbols can be powerful conditioned stimuli capable of evoking emotional responses through higher-order conditioning.

A wide variety of stimuli, including activities, individuals, groups, and events, are valued according to their associations with positive or negative outcomes and even mere labels. For example, when neutral items are paired with words like "dirty" and "ugly," they take on negative valuations, but the same items become positively evaluated when they have been associated with words like "beautiful" and "happy" (Staats & Staats, 1957). Likewise, the names of countries and political parties and the sight of national flags can come to arouse intense positive or negative feelings depending on their earlier associations. The Russian patriot who feels deep emotion at the playing of "The Internationale" is unlikely to have similar feelings for "The Star-Spangled Banner."

B. F. SKINNER'S OPERANT CONDITIONING

We can know people only by examining their behavior—the things they say and do. Thus, all psychological approaches are based on the study of behavior, but they differ in how the behavior is used. Both the trait approach and the psychodynamic approach use behaviors as signs, inferring attributes or motives from the observable things the individual does. In the behavioral approach favored by B. F. Skinner and many of his students, however, the observed behavior is the basic unit, and the interest is in specifying the conditions that "control" it.

In this tradition, behaviorists tried to sample the individual's behaviors directly but generally were reluctant to interpret them as signs (indicators) of the person's motives or other attributes. For example, from this perspective one might try to sample Gary's behaviors to find out just what he does before speeches, without drawing any inferences from them about his underlying anxiety, insecurity, or other personal qualities. To the degree that theorists limit themselves to behavior, their definition of personality itself becomes equated with the whole of an individual's behaviors: The person "is" what the person "does."

Rejection of Inferred Motives

To explain behavior, many earlier theorists hypothesized a wide range of human motives. Theories concerning motivation have helped to reveal the variety and complexity of human strivings and also have contributed to the development of research about their causes. Investigators of motives originally were inspired by the model of experimental research on biological drives in animals. In animal studies of motivation, the hypothesized need of the animal (its hunger or sex drive, for example) has been linked clearly to observable conditions manipulated in the laboratory. For example, the strength of the hunger drive may be inferred in part from the amount of time that the animal has been deprived of food. When a dog has not been fed for two days, we may safely say that it has a high hunger drive. In such cases, references to drives and motives are straightforward. Likewise, some careful investigations of hypothesized higher-order motives in people have specified clearly the objective conditions that define the motive (e.g., Emmons, 1997; McClelland, 1992; McClelland et al., 1953).

Less rigorous applications of motivational theory to personality, however, may use motives loosely (for example, as "wishes" and "desires"), and their value as explanations of behavior is open to question. The tendency to invoke motives as explanations of why people behave as they do is understandable because that is how we "explain" behavior in commonsense terms. To explain why a child spent an unusual amount of time cleaning and grooming himself neatly, we easily might say "because he had strong cleanliness needs" or "because he had a compulsive desire for order."

Such hypotheses about motives may sound like explanations, but they tell us little unless the motive is defined objectively and unless the causes of the motive itself are established. What makes the child have "cleanliness needs"? What determines his

**B. F. Skinner
(1904–1990)**

"compulsive desires"? Why does he "wish" to be clean? These are the kinds of questions raised by the internationally influential American psychologist B. F. Skinner, who worked for many years at Harvard University.

A pioneer in the behavioral approach, Skinner criticized many concepts regarding human needs as being no more than motivational labels attached to human activities. Thus, orderly behavior may be attributed to a motive for orderliness, submissive behavior to submissiveness needs, exploratory behavior to the need to explore, and so on. To avoid such circular reasoning and to untangle explaining from naming, behaviorally oriented psychologists like Skinner prefer to analyze behaviors in terms of the observable events and conditions that seem to vary with them. Hence, they refuse to posit specific motivations for behavior. Rather, they try to discover the external events that strengthen its future likelihood and that maintain or change it. This approach leads to questions like: When does that child's cleaning activity increase, and when does it decrease in relation to observable changes in the environment? For example, how do the reactions of the parents influence the behavior?

For Skinner, psychology is the science of behavior: Inferences about unobservable states and motives are not adequate explanations, and they add nothing to a scientific account of the conditions controlling behavior. "Motivation" is simply the result of depriving or satiating an organism of some substance such as water or food for a given period of time. Thus, a "drive" is just a convenient way of referring to the observable effects of such deprivation or satiation. Likewise, Skinner avoids any inferences about internal "conflicts," preferring an experimental analysis of the stimulus conditions that seem to control the particular behavior in the situation. In his words:

> Man, we once believed, was free to express himself in art, music, and literature, to inquire into nature, to seek salvation in his own way. He could initiate action and make spontaneous and capricious changes of course. . . . But science insists that action is initiated by forces impinging upon the individual, and that caprice is only another name for behavior for which we have not yet found a cause (Skinner, 1955, pp. 52–53).

The essence of Skinner's behavioristic view is the belief that our behavior is shaped by the external environment, not by motives, dispositions, or "selves" that are "in" the person.

Basic Strategy

Skinner's work is based on the premise that a genuine science of human behavior is not only possible but desirable. In his view, science should try to predict and determine experimentally the behavior of the individual organism (Skinner, 1974).

Skinner proposed a "functional analysis" of the organism as a behaving system. Such an analysis tries to link the organism's behavior to the precise conditions that control or determine it. Skinner's approach, therefore, concentrates on the observable covariations between "independent variables" (stimulus events) and "dependent variables" (response patterns). The variables in a functional analysis, according to Skinner, must be external, observable, and described in physical and quantitative terms. It will not do to say that a child becomes concerned with cleanliness when she "fears her father's disapproval;" one must specify the exact ways that changes in the father's specific behavior (e.g., his praise) are related to specific changes in what the child does (e.g., how much she washes her hands per hour).

Skinner contends that the laboratory offers the best chance of obtaining a scientific analysis of behavior; in it, variables can be brought under the control of experimental manipulation. Furthermore, the experimental study of behavior has much to gain from dealing with the behavior of animals below the complex human level. Science, Skinner points out, advances from the simple to the complex and is constantly concerned with whether the processes and laws discovered at one stage are adequate for the next.

Skinner incorporated into his position many concepts regarding classical conditioning, but he concentrated on another kind of learning that is different in some ways from classical conditioning. He contends (1953) that most human social behavior consists of freely emitted response patterns, or operants. Even a little baby shows much spontaneous behavior: It reaches up to a mobile, turns its head, looks at objects, cries and gurgles, and moves its arms and legs. Through such operants the organism operates on its environment, changing it and, in turn, being changed by it.

How Operant Conditioning Works

Operant behavior is modified by its consequences: The outcome of any operant response (or pattern of responses) determines how likely it is that the subject will perform similar responses in the future. If a response has favorable (reinforcing) consequences, the subject is more likely to perform it again in similar situations. Contrary to some widespread misconceptions, "reinforcers" or favorable outcomes are not restricted to such primitive rewards as food pellets or sexual satisfactions. Almost all events may serve as reinforcers, including such cognitive gratifications as information (Jones, 1966) or the achievement of competence. Such learning, based on the consequences produced by responses, is called **operant conditioning** (or, in earlier usage, trial-and-error or instrumental learning).

When the consequences of a response pattern change, the probability of it and of similar response patterns occurring again also changes (Nemeroff & Karoly, 1991). If a little boy whines and clings to his mother and she drops everything in an attempt to

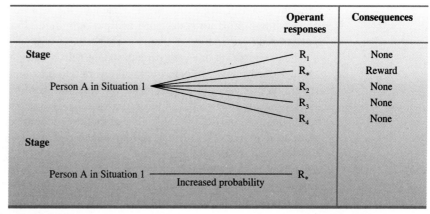

Figure 12.2
Operant Conditioning A person performs (emits) many operant responses in any given situation. If one operant is followed by a favorable outcome (reward) in that situation, the person will be more likely to perform that operant again in a similar situation.

appease him, the chances increase that he will behave in this way in the future. If she systematically ignores the behavior, however, and consistently fails to react to it, the chances decrease that the child will continue to behave this way.

In Skinner's research on operant conditioning, the typical experiment involves an animal or a person freely performing (emitting) operant responses. The experimenter has preselected a particular class of responses to reinforce (for example, a young child successfully using a potty-training chair or an adult using personal pronouns in an interview). When the selected operant response is made (the child urinates in the potty or the adult says, "I," "you," "she," and so on), the reinforcement occurs: The child gets a small toy; the interviewer nods or murmurs "good." Figure 12.2 illustrates what happens in operant conditioning.

The outcomes a person obtains for a particular behavior influence his or her future behavior. A child's refusal to eat may gain attention from a father usually too busy to pay the child much attention. Since the child's behavior is reinforced by the attention, she may refuse to eat again. If she is offered special treat foods in an effort to tempt her, she may quickly turn into a finicky eater with limited food preferences. By changing the outcomes of responses, reinforcing previously unreinforced behaviors or discontinuing reinforcement for other behaviors, even behavior patterns that seem deeply ingrained may be changed.

Influenced by Skinner, many psychologists have tried to modify maladaptive behavior by altering the consequences to which it leads. Working with people who have severe behavioral problems, they attempt to remove reinforcement for disadvantageous behavior and to make attention, praise, or other reinforcement contingent on the occurrence of more adaptive advantageous behavior. Learning programs of this type follow a set of definite steps. First, the problem behaviors are carefully defined and their frequency in a naturalistic context is measured. Next, one observes and records the reinforcing consequences that seem to maintain the behaviors. Guided by this analysis, the relearning program is designed and put into effect. Finally, the resulting changes are assessed over a period of time.

For example, in one case parents sought help because their three-year-old daughter developed regressive behaviors and reverted to crawling rather than walking. This regression produced serious problems for the child and the family. An analysis of the girl's behavior suggested that her regressive, babyish actions were being encouraged and maintained unwittingly by the attention they brought her. Therefore, an effort was made to rearrange the response-reinforcement patterns so that crawling and infantile acts were not rewarded by the attention of worried adults. Instead, attention and other rewards were made contingent on more adaptive and age-appropriate behaviors, such as jumping, running, and walking, thereby increasing these desirable behaviors while the infantile ones decreased (Harris et al., 1964).

Conditioned Generalized Reinforcers

As noted before, neutral stimuli may acquire value and become conditioned reinforcers when they become associated with other stimuli that already have reinforcing powers and emotion-arousing properties. Conditioned reinforcers become *generalized* when they are paired with more than one primary reinforcer. A good example of a conditioned generalized reinforcer is money because it can provide so many different primary gratifications (food, shelter, comfort, medical help, and alleviation of pain). Gradually generalized reinforcers may become quite potent even when the primary reinforcers upon which they were initially based do not accompany them anymore. Some people, for example, seem to learn to love money for its own sake and work to amass "paper profits" that they never trade in for primary rewards.

Some generalized reinforcers are obvious—like money—but others are subtle and involve complex social relationships. Attention and social approval from people who are likely to supply reinforcement—such as parents, a loved one, or a teacher— often are especially strong generalized reinforcers.

Discrimination and Generalization in Everyday Life

Discriminative stimuli indicate when an operant response will or will not have favorable consequences. Without such signals we would not know in advance the outcomes to which different behaviors are likely to lead, and life would be chaotic. With the help of discriminative stimuli, we learn to stop the car when coming to a railroad crossing; to eat certain foods with forks and spoons and to continue to eat others with our fingers; to shout and cheer at football games but not at course examinations; to wear warmer clothes when the temperature starts to drop and to shed them when it becomes hot; to stop at red traffic lights and to go when they turn green.

When a particular response or pattern of responses is reinforced in the presence of one stimulus but not in the presence of others, discrimination occurs. It may be all right to belch in your own room when alone or with close friends but less acceptable to do so when talking to a faculty advisor in her office. Discrimination results from the

"Generalized reinforcers" often are subtle and involve complex human relationships.

reinforcement or condoning of behavior in some situations but not in others. The individual is more likely to display the behavior in those situations in which it will probably be reinforced than in those in which it is unlikely to be reinforced.

If a response pattern is uniformly rewarded in many conditions or situations, **generalization** occurs. For example, a child is likely to develop generalized aggressive patterns if he is encouraged or allowed to behave aggressively with his parents and teachers as well as with his siblings and classmates both when he is at school and at home. Generalization depends on the similarity among stimulus situations. Stimuli that are physically similar or that have similar meanings result in the greatest generalization.

From the behavioral perspective, the socialization of children is based on discrimination training. For example, children must learn to control their bowel and bladder functions so that defecation and urination occur only in some situations and not in others. Active exploration of the toy box or the sandbox is permitted and encouraged, while forays into the medicine chest or mother's jewel box have quite different outcomes. As a result of such "discrimination" training, the child's behavior begins to depend on the specific conditions in which it unfolds.

When behavior yields similar consequences in a broad variety of settings, it can be expected to generalize from one situation to another. For example, if a little girl easily gets help in solving problems at home, at school, with parents, teachers, and siblings, she may develop widespread dependency. In contrast, when certain behaviors, such as curiosity, are punished in some situations but not in others, consistencies across the different situations should not be expected. A child becomes increasingly

For many years, psychologists who studied learning searched for general laws of learning which they assumed would hold for all species and for all types of responses and stimuli. The "laws" of conditioning should be universal, they thought, and would apply broadly. This assumption has been seriously challenged (Seligman, 1971) and by now is difficult to maintain given the evidence (Marks, 1987; Marks & Nesse, 1994; Pinker, 1997). Nature seems to prepare organisms to learn some associations much more easily than others.

Instinctive Drift

Many amusement centers feature exhibits that show what odd things animals can be taught to do—demonstrations to which behaviorists point as evidence for the power of conditioning. Hungry chickens, for example, can be trained through standard techniques of operant conditioning to do things that are very unusual for chickens: For instance, they can be trained to deliver plastic capsules to outstretched human hands. Similarly, hungry pigs can be trained to put coins in "piggy" banks (Breland & Breland, 1966). But animal trainers also report that after a while the chickens begin to throw the capsules on the ground and peck at them and the pigs

pause to "root" the coins (manipulate them with their snouts). Note that the animals do this in spite of the fact that through these behaviors the rewards given for the learned responses are postponed or even forfeited. In fact, the tendencies to peck and root grow stronger and stronger with more time. This gradual shift away from a conditioned response toward one that is made naturally by the animal in its usual environment (even though it means giving up rewards) is called *instinctive drift*. Findings like these first suggested that innate predispositions limit what organisms can learn.

Biological "Preparedness"

It is now clear that not all associations between stimuli are formed with equal ease. For example, rats fed a distinctively flavored new food and then made sick to their stomachs will avoid that food even if their illness does not occur until 12 hours later. If the same food is followed by electric shock, however, the rat does not learn to avoid eating it, even when the shock is delivered immediately (Garcia, McGowan, & Green, 1972). These variations in the ease of associating different types of events suggest selective *biological preparedness*. Organisms seem biologically prepared to learn some

discriminating as the various roles of sibling, student, lover, and many more are learned. Each of these roles implies its own distinct set of appropriate behaviors in particular situations.

Shaping Behavior by Successive Approximations

Before a response can be reinforced, it must occur. Extremely complex responses, such as saying new words in a foreign language, are unlikely ever to be performed spontaneously by the learner. If you do not know how to say "How do you do?" in Greek, you are unlikely ever to come out with the right phrase spontaneously, no matter how many sounds you utter. To try to overcome this problem, and to help an organism form new responses, Skinnerians often use a procedure called shaping.

   Shaping is a technique for producing successively closer approximations to a particular desired behavior. It consists of carefully observing and immediately rewarding associations or pairings more readily than others. Social evolutionary theory holds that the differences found among species in the types of associations learned readily may reflect differences in what it is necessary to learn in the evolutionary struggle for survival (Buss, 1996, 1997; Seligman, 1971; Seligman & Hager, 1972).

On the other hand, evidence that learning in animals, especially lower animals, is constrained by their biological capacities does not necessarily mean that humans are innately programmed in favor of specific associations (Bandura, 1977, 1986). Indeed, such preprogramming in humans might be very disadvantageous in evolution because of our need to adapt to more complex and rapidly changing circumstances— circumstances that we ourselves often create. The human ability to symbolize experience allows enormous potential for learning. The extraordinary variety of human behaviors is well documented both by formal evidence and by casual observation. While chickens and pigs may have serious biological learning constraints, people are generally not so prewired, according to the counterargument (Bandura, 1986).

Some stimulus relationships may be more readily learned by both humans and by lower organisms because the events covary in ways that make it easier to recognize their covariation in the environment. A rat can be taught in one trial to avoid shock from a grid floor if it can escape to a compartment with a smooth black floor. It takes close to 10 trials to learn to avoid the shock when

the escape compartment has a grid floor continuous with that of a shock compartment (Testa, 1974). Little Albert was conditioned by Watson and Rayner to fear rats by pairing the appearance of the animal with a loud noise. But a student of Watson's was unable to produce fears when either a block of wood or a dark curtain was paired with the noise.

The argument that people are disposed biologically to fear things that have threatened human survival throughout evolution is intriguing (Buss, 1997; Seligman, 1971). For example, there are only a small number of common human fears and they seem to be virtually universal. Fears of snakes and spiders, of blood, of storms and heights and darkness, and of strangers are typical, and they share a common theme; they endangered our evolutionary ancestors and now we seem to be prewired to have them. As Pinker (1997, p. 387) puts it: "Children are nervous about rats, and rats are nervous about bright rooms, before any conditioning begins, and they easily associate them with danger." These findings are only small examples of a wide range of data that in recent years increasingly point to prewired dispositions in the brain. And these dispositions seem to make humans distinctively prepared not only for some fears rather than for others but also for all sorts of high-level mental activities, from language acquisition to mathematical skills, to music appreciation, to space perception (Pinker, 1997).

any small variations of the behavior in the desired direction as they are spontaneously performed by the organism. At first, a large class of responses is reinforced; then gradually the class is narrowed, and reinforcement is given only for closer approximations to the final form of the desired behavior. For example, when teaching a pigeon to stand only in the center of a large bull's-eye target painted on the floor, one might reward the bird for standing increasingly close to the center. (For possible biological limits on such learning, see *In Focus 12.1*.)

The Patterning of Outcomes: Schedules of Reinforcement

The patterning or sequencing ("scheduling") of reinforcement affects the future occurrence and strength of the reinforced behavior (Ferster & Skinner, 1957). Sometimes the scheduling of reinforcement may be even more important than the nature of the reinforcer (Morse & Kelleher, 1966). Continuous reinforcement usually increases the speed with which responses are learned. Intermittent reinforcement tends to produce more stable behavior that is more persistently maintained when reinforcement stops. For example, rewarding temper tantrums intermittently (by occasionally attending to them in an irregular pattern) may make them very durable. Since many potentially maladaptive behaviors, such as physical aggression and immature dependency, are rewarded intermittently, they can become very hard to eliminate (Plaud & Gaither, 1996).

Different schedules have different influences on operant responses. Operant strength is measured by the *rate of responses:* the more frequently a response is made in a given period of time, the greater its rate (and inferred strength).

Continuous reinforcement (CRF) is a schedule on which a behavior is reinforced every time it occurs. Responses are usually learned most quickly with continuous reinforcement. A child would become toilet trained more quickly if he were praised and rewarded for each successful attempt. While continuous reinforcement is easy to create in a laboratory, in life it is a rare experience; a partial reinforcement or intermittent schedule, in which a response is reinforced only some of the time, is much more common. We see partial reinforcement when a child's bids for attention succeed only occasionally in getting the parent to attend, or when the same sales pitch produces a sale once in a while, or when the gambler hits the jackpot but only in between many losing bets.

Behavior that has received partial reinforcement often becomes hard to eliminate even when reinforcement is withdrawn altogether. A mother who intermittently and irregularly gives in to her child's nighttime bids for attention (crying, calling for a drink of water or for just one more story) may find the child's behavior very durable and unresponsive to her attempts to stop it by ignoring it. Many potentially maladaptive behaviors (facial tics, physical aggression, immature dependency) are hard to eliminate because they are rewarded intermittently.

The child with a speck of grit in her eye who successfully follows her father's instruction to blink to get it out may keep on blinking periodically long after the eye is clear of irritation. If her blinks are further reinforced by her parents' occasional attention (whether troubled concern or agitated pleas to "stop doing that!"), she may develop an unattractive facial tic that is extremely resistant to extinction. Likewise, as has often been noted, the gambler who hit a jackpot once may persist for a long time even when the payoff becomes zero. The persistence of behavior after partial reinforcement suggests that when one has experienced only occasional, irregular, and unpredictable reinforcement for a response, one continues to expect possible rewards for a long time after the rewards have totally stopped.

Superstitions: Getting Reinforced into Irrationality

The relationship between the occurrence of an operant response and the reinforcement that follows it is often causal. For example, turn the door knob and the door opens, the outcome reinforcing the action. Consequently, in the future we are likely to turn door knobs to enter and leave rooms, and our behavior at the door seems rational. Often, however, the response-reinforcement relationship may be quite accidental, and then bizarre and seemingly superstitious behavior and false beliefs may be produced

(Matute, 1994). For example, a primitive tribe may persist in offering human sacrifices to the gods to end severe droughts because occasionally a sacrifice has been followed by rain.

The development of superstition, according to Skinner, may be demonstrated by giving a pigeon a bit of food at regular intervals—say every 15 seconds—regardless of what it is doing. Skinner (1953, p. 85) describes the strange rituals that may be conditioned in this way:

> When food is first given, the pigeon will be behaving in some way—if only standing still—and conditioning will take place. It is then more probable that the same behavior will be in progress when food is given again. If this proves to be the case, the "operant" will be further strengthened. If not, some other behavior will be strengthened. Eventually a given bit of behavior reaches a frequency at which it is often reinforced. It then becomes a permanent part of the repertoire of the bird, even though the food has been given by a clock which is unrelated to the bird's behavior. Conspicuous responses which have been established in this way include turning sharply to one side, hopping from one foot to the other and back, bowing and scraping, turning around, strutting, and raising the head. The topography of the behavior may continue to drift with further reinforcements, since slight modifications in the form of response may coincide with the receipt of food.

Punishment

Skinner focused on the role of rewards, but punishment or "aversive stimulation" is also important. In laboratory studies of anxiety the unconditioned stimulus is usually a painful electric shock and the stimulus to be conditioned is a discrete event such as a distinctive neutral tone or a buzzer. Generally, human life is not that simple and neat. Often "aversive stimuli" involve punishments that are administered in less obvious and less controlled ways. These punishments may be conveyed subtly, by facial expressions and words rather than by brute force, and in extremely complicated patterns, by the same individuals who also nurture the child, giving love and other positive reinforcement. Moreover, the events that are punished often involve more than specific responses; they sometimes entail long sequences of overt and covert behavior (Aronfreed, 1994).

The behaviors that are considered inappropriate and punishable depend on such variables as the child's age and sex as well as the situation. Obviously, the helplessness and passivity that are acceptable in a young child may be maladaptive in an older one, and the traits valued in a girl may not be valued in a boy. While the mother may deliberately encourage her son's dependency and discourage his aggressiveness, his school peers may do the reverse, ridiculing dependency at school and modeling and rewarding aggression and self-assertion. Given this, the influence of punishment on personality development is, not surprisingly, both important and complex (Aronfreed, 1968, 1994; Walters & Grusec, 1977).

A careful review of research on the effects of punishment upon children's behavior concluded, in part, that

> aversive stimulation, if well timed, consistent, and sufficiently intense, may create conditions that accelerate the socialization process, provided that the socialization agents also provide information concerning alternative prosocial behavior and positively reinforce any such behavior that occurs (Walters & Parke, 1967, p. 218).

The important point to remember here is that when punishment is speedy and specific it may suppress undesirable behavior, but it cannot teach the child desirable alternatives. Therefore, parents should use positive techniques to show and reinforce appropriate behavior that the child can employ in place of the unacceptable response that has to be suppressed (Walters & Parke, 1967). In that way the learner will develop a new response that can be made without getting punished. Without such a positive alternative, the child faces a dilemma in which total avoidance may seem the only possible route. Punishment may have very unfortunate effects when the child believes there is no way in which he or she can prevent further punishment and cope (Linscheid & Meinhold, 1990). If you become convinced that no potentially successful actions are open to you, that you can do nothing right, depression, hopelessness, and negative thinking may follow (Nolen-Hoeksema, 1997; Seligman, 1975).

Criticisms of Behaviorism: Anti-Humanistic/Simplistic?

We have seen that radical behaviorists refuse to invoke qualities of the person as causes of his behavior and attribute causal control instead to the environment. "Whatever we do," Skinner asserts (1971, p. 188), "and hence however we perceive it, the fact remains that it is the environment which acts upon the perceiving person, not the perceiving person who acts upon the environment." Such assertions have led to charges that behaviorally oriented psychologists overemphasize the environment and the situation while "losing the person" (Bowers, 1973; Carlson, 1971). Closely related to these criticisms is the protest against the behavioral approach in general developed by humanistic psychologists like Carl Rogers (Chapter 10). From the humanistic perspective, behaviorism is said to dehumanize the person, to neglect his potential for freedom, and to overlook his consciousness while focusing on observable behavior and environmental conditions. Some humanistic psychologists believe behaviorists may have literally "lost man's mind."

We are all familiar with the image of the white-coated behaviorist scheming to manipulate society into creating robotlike creatures whose buttons are controlled by laboratory assistants trained to condition people into puppets. Fears of behaviorism are not limited to the popular mass media. Sidney Jourard, a humanistic psychologist, says:

> I have always been uneasy about the behavioristic approach to man, because it appeals to the power motive in the behavior scientist. Moreover, research in behaviorism is frequently funded by agencies interested in controlling the behavior and experience of others, not necessarily with their knowledge or consent nor always with the best interest of the controllees at heart (1974, pp. 20–21).

This comment is representative of the humanistic distrust of behaviorism. The heart of the humanistic protest is the belief that behaviorally oriented psychologists treat and manipulate people as if they were externally controlled rather than free, self-determining beings responsible for their own growth and actions.

Behaviorists have their own counterarguments (Baum & Heath, 1992). They realize that it may seem amusing to watch pigeons generate elaborate superstitious rituals and bizarre behaviors as a result of accidental reinforcement contingencies. They argue, however, that understanding such behavior also helps us to see that people can inadvertently become bizarre and develop neurotic symptom patterns in fundamentally similar ways. According to many Skinnerians, there is much overlap between the ways in which pigeons become victimized by the scheduling of reinforcement and the manner in which people may become twisted by the response-reinforcement arrangements in their lives. These ideas have been widely applied in both analyses and modifications of human problems (Chapters 13 and 14). They also have been severely criticized not only by humanists but also by cognitive scientists who view them as naïve and simplistic and believe that behaviorists bypass the richness and complexity of the human mind (e.g., Pinker, 1997).

OBSERVATIONAL LEARNING (MODELING): ALBERT BANDURA

Reinforcement has powerful influences on behavior in a great variety of situations. But people also learn a great deal by observing others, not merely by experiencing rewards for what they do themselves. Much social learning occurs through observation without any direct rewards or reinforcement administered to the learner. Classical and operant conditioning are important types of learning, but it is now also clear that some of the most important human learning occurs through observation and involves more than the simpler learning conceptions of earlier behavioral approaches.

Learning through Observation

Learning without direct reinforcement is sometimes called modeling, sometimes cognitive or observational learning. All these terms refer to the acquisition of knowledge and potential behavior without the learner's receiving direct external reinforcement for that behavior. In fact, observational learning can occur without the person's ever performing the learned response at all. You can learn a lot about travel to the moon, for example, without ever going there yourself.

Observational learning occurs when people watch others or when they attend to their surroundings, to physical events, or to symbols such as words or pictures. Albert Bandura (1969, 1986) for the past three decades has led the way in the analysis of observational learning and its relevance for personality. Much human learning, from table manners and interpersonal relations to school and work, depends on observation of this kind rather than on direct reinforcement for a particular action. Nor is the observation itself always direct.

Albert Bandura

Children learn partly through observation and imitation.

We learn much from what others observe and then tell us about. The mass media, which are highly effective means of communicating experiences and observations, contribute heavily to the enormous amount we learn about the environment and the behavior of others.

The influence of observational learning through the mass media is seen in the contagion of aggression that has spread through the United States as a result of so many people's watching television violence. Although the television networks deny it, watching violence on television can have definite negative effects on viewers (Liebert, 1986; Murray, 1973). For example, after observing segments of aggressive films (from "The Untouchables"), children were more willing to hurt others than after viewing a neutral program that featured a track race (Liebert & Baron, 1972). Similarly, after watching violent cartoons for some time, children became more assaultive toward their peers than other youngsters who had viewed nonviolent cartoons for the same period of time (Steuer, Applefield, & Smith, 1971).

Completely new response patterns can be learned simply by observation of others performing them. Observation is of especially great importance for learning a language. Bandura (1977) emphasizes the advantages of observation for language learning compared with direct reinforcement for uttering the right sounds. He notes that exposure to models who speak the language leads to relatively rapid acquisition, while shaping would take much longer.

Effects of Models: An Illustration

Laboratory experiments studied the determinants of preferences for immediate, less valuable outcomes, as opposed to more desirable but delayed outcomes. Bandura and Mischel (1965) hypothesized that self-imposed delay of reward would be determined in part by the delay patterns displayed by social models. In the initial phase of this experiment, many children were administered a series of paired rewards. In each of these pairs they were asked to select either a small reward that could be obtained immediately or a more valued item contingent on a delay period ranging from one to four weeks. For example, children chose between a smaller, immediately available candy bar and a larger one that required waiting. From the total pool of subjects those falling in the extreme upper and lower 25% of scores were selected for the succeeding phases of the experiment.

Children from each of these extreme groups (who exhibited predominantly either delayed-reward or immediate-reward patterns of behavior) were then assigned to treatment conditions. In one treatment children observed a live adult model who exhibited delay-of-reward responses counter to their own self-gratification pattern. For example, if the child was initially high in delay preferences, the adult model consistently chose immediate rewards. (He selected, for instance, a cheaper set of plastic chess figures immediately instead of a more attractive set available a week later.) The model also explained his choices. For example, he said: "Chess figures are chess figures. I can get much use out of the plastic ones right away." Or he commented: "You probably have noticed that I am a person who likes things now. One can spend so much time in life waiting that one never gets around to really living. . . ." Conversely, children who initially displayed strong immediate reward preferences were exposed to models who chose delayed, costlier rewards. In other treatment groups children were similarly exposed to a model displaying delay-of-reward behavior opposite to their own, with the exception that the model's responses were presented only in written form rather than "live." In a final condition children had no exposure to any models.

Right after the experimental procedure the children's delay-of-reward responses were measured. To test the generality and stability of changes in delay behavior, they were reassessed by a different experimenter in a different social setting approximately one month later. The overall results revealed strong effects. Figure 12.3, for example, shows the mean percentage of immediate-reward responses produced by the high-delay children in each of the test periods as a function of treatment conditions. Children who had shown a predominantly delayed-reward pattern displayed an increased preference for immediate and less valuable rewards after observing models favoring immediate gratification; conversely, those who had exhibited a marked preference for immediate rewards increased and maintained their willingness to wait for more valuable but delayed reinforcers following exposure to models displaying high-delay behavior. The effects of seeing the models' written responses were similar to those of watching live models, although less pronounced and less generalized.

Similar effects occurred when similar procedures were extended to a population of young prison inmates. Specifically, exposure to high-delay peer models substantially increased delay of gratification in 18- to 20-year-old inmates who initially had displayed an extreme preference for immediate rewards (Stumphauzer, 1972). The effects showed some generalization and were maintained in a follow-up one month later.

Acquisition versus Performance: Knowing versus Doing

What a person is able to do in any given situation is often very different from what he actually does. No one does everything he has learned and is capable of doing. Many 12-year-old children know how to suck their thumbs as well as three-year-olds, but few do. Even among three-year-olds there are striking individual differences in the

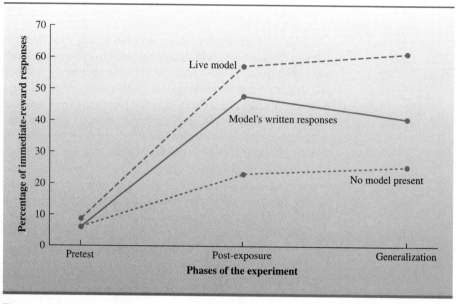

Figure 12.3

Effects of Modeling on Delay of Gratification   Mean percentage of immediate-reward responses by high-delay children on each of three test periods for each of three experimental conditions.

SOURCE: Adapted from Bandura, A., & Mischel, W. (1965). Modification of self-imposed delay of reward through exposure to live and symbolic models. *Journal of Personality and Social Psychology, 2,* 702.

amount of time they spend sucking their thumbs, though they are all equally able to do it. Likewise, men and women in our culture are equally capable of using eggbeaters and driving racing cars, but the sexes have differed markedly in how often they engage in these activities. In each of these instances we are distinguishing between the learning or *acquisition* of behaviors and their *performance* or enactment.

Human learning (acquisition) of new behavior is not dependent on reinforcement (Bandura, 1986). Learning (acquisition) is mainly regulated by what we observe, perceive, and know rather than by conditioning and direct reinforcement. What a person can do, thus, depends on acquired knowledge and skills rather than on incentives or reinforcement. However, incentives, values, and expected outcomes are crucial for performance—that is, for what the person actually does. A person's choice of what to do in a particular situation thus depends on such considerations as the outcomes expected for the different choices available in the particular context and their subjective values.

It is often difficult to discover a person's potential (previously learned) response patterns. We can only observe the person's performance. If one does not, for example, swear, play aggressively, cook, or fondle kittens, it may be because that individual never learned these behaviors. On the other hand, these responses may be potentially available, but the incentives provided in the situation may not elicit them. The introduction of a more potent incentive may readily produce the behavior, revealing that it has been learned but was not performed because the rewards offered were not powerful enough.

Observing Other People's Outcomes: What Happens to Them Might Happen to You

Valuable information about the possible consequences of various behaviors is gained from observing what happens to others when they engage in similar behaviors. Your expectations about the outcomes of a particular course of action depend not only on what has happened to you in the past when you behaved similarly in a similar situation, but also on what you have observed happening to others.

We are more likely to do something if we have observed another person (model) obtain positive consequences for a similar response. Seeing other children praised for cooperative play, for example, makes a child more likely to behave cooperatively in similar situations. If, on the other hand, models are punished for a particular pattern of behavior such as cooperation, observers are less likely to display similar behavior.

In one study, young children in a preschool watched a film of an adult hitting and kicking a Bobo doll and displaying other novel aggressive responses (Bandura, 1965). (See Figure 12.4). The consequences to the adult of behaving aggressively varied for different groups of children. One group saw a film strip in which the adult's aggressive behavior was punished, a second saw it rewarded, and a third group saw no consequences of any kind for the model. A fourth group saw no film at all. The children were then presented with the Bobo doll and their behavior was observed and recorded. Those who had observed aggressive behaviors modeled and rewarded imitated them most; those who saw no aggressive model showed the least aggression.

When the children who had seen the film were told they would receive a small prize if they could reproduce all the modeled behaviors, the differences between the group that had watched different films (with different consequences to the model) were wiped out. All the children seem to have learned the model's behavior equally well, regardless of the reinforcing consequences. The observation of different consequences for the model's aggressive behavior increased or decreased the children's spontaneous performance of such behavior but not their knowledge of what the model had done.

Although laboratory studies offer clear demonstrations of the importance of expected consequences, examples from life are more dramatic. Consider, for instance, the role of modeling in airline hijackings (Bandura, 1973). Air piracy was unknown in the United States until 1961. At that time some successful hijackings of Cuban airliners to Miami were followed by a wave of hijackings, reaching a crest of 87 airplane piracies in 1969. Fresh impetus came from news of a hijacker who successfully parachuted from an airliner with a huge sum of extorted money. Finally, hijackings were seemingly extinguished in the United States when new security procedures greatly decreased the chances of success and stern sanctions punished the offenders.

An equally dramatic modeling effect on a worldwide scale was the rash of kidnappings following the well-publicized abduction of Patricia Hearst in 1974. Within less than a month an unprecedented outbreak of kidnappings followed in the United States

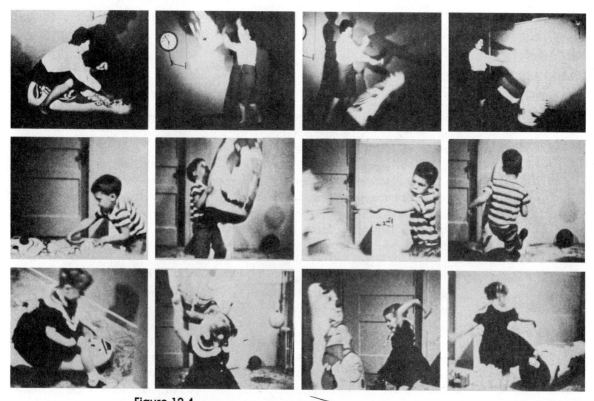

Figure 12.4
After Watching Films of an Aggressive Model Who Punched, Pummeled, and Hurled a Bobo Doll, These Children Spontaneously Imitated the Model's Aggressiveness When Put in a Similar Situation

SOURCE: Bandura, A. (1965). Vicarious processes: A case of no-trial learning. In L. Berkowitz (Ed.), *Advances in experimental social psychology* (Vol. 2, pp. 1–55). New York: Academic Press.

and in Europe and Latin America as well. Ransom demands ranged from $1 million to more than $20 million. In addition to the many actual kidnappings, kidnap threats escalated. The kidnappers seemed to have little in common, and their motives ranged from political revolution to cash.

In sum, you do not have to perform particular actions yourself in order to learn about them and their consequences; the observed as well as the directly experienced consequences of performances influence subsequent behavior. You do not have to rob a bank to learn that it is punishable; you do not have to be arrested for hijacking to learn about its consequences; and you do not have to rescue a burning child from a fire or return found money to discover that such acts are considered good. Information that alters the person's anticipations of the probable outcomes to which a behavior will lead changes the probability that he will perform that behavior. Models inform us of the probable consequences of particular behaviors and thus affect the likelihood that we will perform them.

Observation also influences the emotions we experience. A person does not need to have a direct experience with a stimulus to learn an emotional response to it. By observing the emotional reactions of others to a stimulus, it is possible vicariously to learn an intense emotional response to that stimulus. You may become "vicariously conditioned" when you observe repeated contiguity (association) between a stimulus and an emotional response exhibited by another person without receiving any direct positive or aversive stimulation yourself.

In one study adults observed another person making fear responses in reaction to the sound of a buzzer supposedly associated with the onset of an electric shock. (Actually the person was a confederate of the experimenter and only feigned fear without getting any shocks.) Gradually, after repeatedly watching the pairing of the buzzer and the fear responses made by the confederate, the observers themselves developed a measurable physiological fear response to the sound of the buzzer alone (Berger, 1962).

Vicarious conditioning can help explain the development of emotional behavior and anxiety — for example, fear of dogs or snakes — in people who have had no direct experiences with the emotion-provoking stimuli (Mineka & Zinbarg, 1996). A person may come to fear the animal just from observing the emotional reaction of another person to the same animal or even from reading about it. Likewise, a girl whose mother repeatedly reveals inhibited attitudes toward men and sex might adopt some of her mother's attitudes without ever having a traumatic sexual experience herself. Thus, previously neutral stimuli may come to elicit strong emotional responses by merely being observed under appropriate conditions (Venn & Short, 1973).

Observational learning can help remove fears and other strong emotional reactions as well as teach them. A group of preschool children who were intensely afraid of dogs watched from a safe distance while a fearless model (another preschool child) played with a dog (Bandura, Grusec, & Menlove, 1967). The model began by briefly petting the dog through the bars of a playpen in which the animal was confined and became progressively bolder over a series of eight short sessions. In the final session the child model joined the dog inside the playpen, fed it wieners and milk from a baby bottle, and hugged it joyfully. Fearful children who observed the model later showed less fear and approached dogs more than did equally fearful children who had not had the opportunity to observe the model.

Summary of Three Types of Learning

Table 12.3 summarizes the three types of learning discussed so far: classical conditioning, operant conditioning, and observational learning. There is much overlap among these types of learning, but each has some relatively distinct features, as indicated in the table, and each has a place within current social learning theory.

Theoretical Implications of Observational Learning

The studies of observational learning by Albert Bandura (1969, 1986) demonstrated as you saw that learning occurs even when there is no direct external reinforcement to the

Table 12.3
Summary of Three Types of Learning

Type	Arrangement	Effect	Example	Interpretation
Classical conditioning	A neutral stimulus (e.g., a bell) repeatedly and closely precedes a powerful unconditoined stimulus (e.g., food).	The originally neutral stimulus becomes a conditioned stimulus—that is, acquires some of the impact of the powerful unconditioned stimulus.	Bell begins to elicit a salivary response, even when not paired with food.	Organism learns that the conditioned stimulus (bell) signals (predicts) the occurrence of the unconditioned stimulus (food).
Operant conditioning	A freely emitted response (operant) is repeatedly followed by a favorable outcome (reinforcement).	The operant increases in frequency. particular	If crying is followed by attention, its frequency is increased.	Organism learns that this response will produce that particular outcome.
Observational learning	Observer attends to a modeled sequence of novel behavior.	Observer becomes capable of enacting the sequence. The frequency of performing it and related behaviors may change.	Watching unusual forms of violence on TV.	Through observation the ability to reconstruct the behavior is acquired; its enactment depends on expected outcomes.

learner and indeed when there are no overt learning trials, for example, when people watch others or when they attend to their surroundings, to physical events, or to symbols such as words or pictures. Bandura clearly showed that people can learn completely new response patterns simply by observing others performing them. The theoretical importance of observational learning became especially evident, as Bandura (1977) noted, when he compared it with language learning through direct reinforcement for uttering the right sounds. Exposure to models who speak an unfamiliar language leads to relatively rapid acquisition, whereas, in contrast, "shaping" a native English speaker to say "good morning" in Chinese when the correct sounds are uttered spontaneously could take forever.

Observational learning also makes it plain that people acquire rules that can be applied to many new instances, permitting them to generate adaptive new behaviors that go far beyond simple mimicry or rote repetition of what was previously observed. Thus, observational learning reflects a type of cognitive activity, not explicable in sim-

Even the young child is an attentive perceiver and thinker, not a passive learner.

ple stimulus-response terms, requiring cognitive constructs in any theory that tries to understand it. Now consider briefly the basic processes that occur in observational learning. These processes have four components: attention, retention, reproduction, and motivation (Bandura, 1977).

To learn from observation, it is obviously essential to attend to the distinctive features of the modeled behavior. Models would have little long-term impact if we did not remember (retain) their behavior after watching it. Consequently, organizing and rehearsing mentally what was observed are important ingredients of learning from models. Especially when the behavior involves complex motor activities (as in swimming, driving, or tennis), the observer also must be able to organize and put together physically the components of the action. Such motor reproduction requires accurate self-observation and feedback during rehearsal. For example, it is essential to observe the consequences of particular movements on the steering wheel and on the gas and brake pedals of the car when learning to park. It suggests that self-observation or self-monitoring and complex self-regulatory processes "in the head" are human phenomena that a comprehensive theory has to take into account, again in cognitive social terms. Finally, to go from knowledge to performance the observer must have the motivation to enact the behaviors that he or she has learned (Bandura, 1986).

SUMMARY

1. Dollard and Miller's behavior theory represents a fusion of psychoanalytic concepts with the more objective language and methods of laboratory studies of animal learning. Their theory emphasizes drive, cue, response, and reinforcement as the basic components of learning. Drives are strong stimuli that impel action. Primary or innate drives (such as hunger, pain, sex) are the basis of motivation. Many other drives or motives may be learned from their association with primary drive reduction. Cues direct behavior, determining when, where, and how the response (behavior) will occur. A reinforcement is any specific event that strengthens the likelihood of a response. Reinforcement is essential to the learning and to the maintenance of a response. Events that reduce a drive serve as reinforcements.

2. Dollard and Miller translate such Freudian dynamic concepts as internal conflict and repression into the terms of learning theory. They interpret conflict in terms of the simultaneous existence of approach and avoidance tendencies. Moreover, they saw repression as a learned response of "not-thinking" that reduces the learned drive of fear.

3. In classical conditioning, a potent and a neutral stimulus event have been paired together so that eventually the previously neutral event alone evokes portions of the same response that the potent one did initially. Classical conditioning principles have been extended to explain some complex social phenomena and neurotic or abnormal behaviors, such as irrational fears.

4. Life-threatening dangers or "traumas" result in the clearest examples of intense anxiety reactions. Moreover, a person's traumatic fear may generalize so that events and cognitions closely associated with the original traumatic experiences may later evoke anxiety even after the objective danger is gone. If the anxiety spreads to stimuli remote from the traumatic stimulus, the connection may not be apparent and the anxiety may seem particularly irrational. Under some conditions, however, traumas

may lead to active coping rather than to generalized anxiety.

5. Avoidance or escape behaviors performed in a state of anxiety become strengthened when they are successful in reducing the anxiety state. Ambivalence and conflict may result when the same persons (or events) are associated with both positive and aversive experience, as happens commonly in life. The very people the child loves and depends upon also may threaten and punish him or her. Different types of conflict were described.

6. In B. F. Skinner's approach, one refuses to infer drives or other internal motivational forces or traits. Analysis of the stimulus conditions controlling behavior replaces inferences about internal conflicts and underlying motives. Skinner's conceptualization leads to the analysis of behavior in terms of conditioning processes.

7. In operant conditioning, behavior patterns may be modified by changing the consequences (reinforcements) to which they lead. Information and attention, as well as food and sexual gratification, are among the many outcomes that can serve as reinforcers and increase the probability of a particular behavior in operant conditioning.

8. Discrimination in learning is fundamental in the socialization process. In almost every culture, growing up requires learning numerous behaviors that are acceptable and expected under some circumstances but prohibited or punished under others, producing many discriminations. When behavior yields similar consequences under many conditions, generalization occurs and the individual may display similar behavior patterns across diverse settings. Similarity in meaning as well as in physical characteristics results in increased generalization.

9. The patterning or sequencing of the outcomes produced by a particular behavior can be even more important than the type of outcome itself. While continuous reward or reinforcement for behavior may result in faster learning, irregular or intermittent reinforcement often produces more stable behavior that persists even when reinforcement is withdrawn. In life situations, many potentially maladaptive behaviors are rewarded irregularly and may, therefore, become very resistant to change.

10. The influence of punishment is complex and depends on many conditions, such as its timing. Unlike conditions in laboratory studies of punishment, in the child's life punishment is often subtle and indirect. Punishment in socialization depends on many contingencies, such as the child's age and sex as well as the type of behavior and the setting.

11. Modern social learning theories emphasize observational learning. Complex and important potential behavior can be acquired without external reinforcement to the learner. Observational learning without direct reinforcement may account for the learning of many novel responses. Studies of observational learning make it clear that much of what we know and learn involves cognitive and attentional processes. Outcomes, incentives, and reinforcements are important, however, as determinants of what the person does in a particular situation, that is, which response one selects from the repertoire of alternatives available.

CHAPTER 13

Analyzing Behavior

CHARACTERISTICS OF BEHAVIORAL ASSESSMENTS

Behavioral assessments emphasize stimulus conditions as regulators of behavior (Cone & Hoier, 1986). Rather than seeking behavioral signs of the individual's general traits and motives, behavioral approaches focus on the specific conditions and processes — both "inside" and "outside" the person — that might govern his or her behavior. For this purpose behaviorally oriented psychologists often followed an experimental strategy in which stimulus conditions are varied so that one can observe systematically any changes in the behavior of interest in relation to the changing conditions.

In one sense, all psychological approaches are based on behavioral observation: Check marks on MMPI answer sheets and stories in response to inkblots obviously are behaviors just as much as crying or running or fighting. Moreover, we saw that the psychodynamic approach also samples such lifelike behaviors as bridge building under stress. The difference between approaches depends on how these behaviors are used. As we saw, in the dynamic orientation the observed behaviors serve as highly indirect *signs* (symptoms) of the dispositions and motives that might underlie them. In contrast, in behavior assessments the observed behavior is treated as a *sample,* and interest is focused on how the specific sampled behavior is affected by alterations and conditions (Mischel, 1968). Most behavioral approaches thus seek to directly assess covariations between conditions (situations) and behavioral responses (Skinner, 1990).

Case Example: Conditions "Controlling" Gary's Anxiety

The general strategy of behavior assessment can be illustrated by once again considering the case of Gary W. An assessment of Gary in the framework of a behavioral orientation obviously would focus on his behavior in relation to stimulus conditions. But what behaviors, and in relation to which conditions? Rather than seek a portrait of Gary's personality and behavior "in general" or an estimate of his "average" or dominant attributes, a behavioral perspective dictates a much more specific focus.

The particular behavior patterns selected for study depend on the particular problem that requires investigation. In clinical situations, priorities are indicated by the client; in research contexts, they are selected by the investigator.

During his first term of graduate school, Gary found himself troubled enough to seek help at the school's counseling center. As part of the behavioral assessment that followed, Gary was asked to list and rank in order of importance the three problems that he found most distressing in himself and that he wanted to change if possible. He listed "feeling anxious and losing my grip" as his greatest problem. To assess the behavioral referents for his felt "anxiety," Gary was asked to specify in more detail just what changes in himself indicated to him that he was or was not anxious and "losing his grip."

He indicated that when he became anxious he felt changes in his heart rate, became tense, perspired, and found it most difficult to speak coherently. Next, to explore the covariation between increases and decreases in this state and changes in stimulus conditions, Gary was asked to keep an hour-by-hour diary sampling most of the waking hours during the daytime for a period of two weeks and indicating the type of activity that occurred during each hour. Discussion with him of this record suggested that anxiety tended to occur primarily in connection with public speaking occasions—specifically, in classroom situations in which he was required to speak before a group. As indicated by the summary shown in Table 13.1, only on one occasion that was not close in time to public speaking did Gary find himself highly anxious. That occasion turned out to be one in which he was brooding in his room, thinking about his public speaking failures in the classroom.

Table 13.1
Occurrence of Gary's Self-Reported Anxiety Attacks in Relation to Public Speaking

Occurrence of Anxiety	Hours with Anxiety (10)	Hours without Anxiety (10)
Within 1 hour of public speaking	9 (90%)	0 (0%)
No public speaking within 1 hour	1 (10%)	80 (100%)

Having established a covariation between the occurrence of anxiety and public speaking in the social-evaluative conditions of the classroom, his assessors identified the specific components of the public speaking situation that led to relatively more and less anxiety. The purpose here was to establish a hierarchy of anxiety-evoking stimuli ranging from the mild to the exceedingly severe. This hierarchy then was used in a treatment designed to gradually desensitize Gary to these fear stimuli.

Note that this behavioral assessment of Gary is quite specific: It is not an effort to characterize his whole personality, to describe "what he is like," or to infer his motives and dynamics. Instead, the assessment restricts itself to some clearly described problems and tries to analyze them in objective terms without going beyond the observed relations. Moreover, the analysis focuses on the *conditions* in which Gary's behavior occurs and on the covariation between those conditions and his problem. Behavior assessment tends to be focused assessment, usually concentrating on those aspects of behavior that can be changed and that require change. Indeed, as you will see often in this chapter, behavior assessment and behavior change (treatment) are closely connected.

The assessment of Gary's anxiety illustrates one rather crude way to study stimulus-response covariations. Of course there are many different ways in which these covariations can be sampled (see *In Focus 13.1*). This chapter illustrates some of the main tactics developed for the direct measurement of human behavior within the framework of the social behavior orientation.

DIRECT BEHAVIOR MEASUREMENT

For many purposes in personality study it is important to sample and observe behavior in carefully structured, lifelike situations. In clinical applications, direct observation may give both client and assessor an opportunity to assess life problems and to select treatment objectives. Direct observation of behavior samples also may be used to assess the relative efficacy of various treatment procedures. Finally, behavior sampling has an important part in experimental research on personality.

The types of data collected in the behavioral approach include situational samples of both nonverbal and verbal behavior, as well as physiological measurements of emotional reactions. In addition, a comprehensive assessment often includes an analysis of effective rewards or reinforcing stimuli in the person's life. Examples of all of these measures are given in the following sections.

Situational Behavior Sampling

Lovaas and his associates (1965b) wanted a comprehensive description that would contain not only the behaviors the subject performed but also the duration and the specific time of onset of each type of behavior. Such detailed information is needed if one wants to determine the covariations among an individual's specific behaviors or their

IN FOCUS 13.1   *Two Views of the Same Case: Pearson Brack Reanalyzed*

Different approaches to personality can lead to quite different interpretations of the same case. This point is illustrated in the case of "Pearson Brack" (Grinker & Spiegel, 1945, pp. 197–207; Mischel, 1968).

Pearson Brack was a bombardier in the Tunisian theater of operations during World War II. During Brack's ninth mission, his airplane was severely damaged by flak. It suddenly jolted and rolled and then began to dive. The pilot regained control of the plane just in time to avoid crashing. During the plane's fall, however, Brack was hurled violently against the bombsight and was seriously injured. After his return from this mission, he was hospitalized for a month and then, seemingly recovered, was returned to flight duty. On his next two missions, the 10th and 11th, he fainted, and gradually his problem was brought to the attention of a psychodynamically oriented psychiatrist. Direct observations revealed that Brack's tendency to faint seemed specifically linked to being at an altitude of about 10,000 feet.

After intensive interviews, the psychiatrist concluded that Brack's fainting was connected to deep, underlying anxieties rooted in his childhood experiences. Brack was viewed as a basically immature person with long-standing insecurity who had inadequately identified with his father. The near-fatal plane incident was seen as essentially trivial, except in so far as it precipitated anxiety in an already insecure and immature individual.

In contrast, a behavioral analysis of the same case (Mischel, 1968) emphasized the severe emotional trauma that might have been conditioned to altitude cues during the mishap. That is, if Brack's injury occurred at about 10,000 feet, then any altitude cues present at that time might have become conditioned stimuli capable of eliciting a traumatic reaction (such as fainting). In that case, every time Brack later reexperienced cues connected with the accident (such as being in a plane at a comparable altitude), he would again become emotionally debilitated. In fact, when Brack was taken up in an airplane for further assessments, it was found that his emotional upset and fear occurred only around that altitude.

From the viewpoint of behavior theory, the relevant causes of Brack's problem were the conditions that seemed to control its occurrence, in this instance altitude cues that may have been associated with the trauma. But from the perspective of psychodynamic theory, the causes were Brack's inferred underlying anxiety and its antecedents in childhood. The key point is that different approaches to personality and assessment can lead to quite different interpretations of the same case.

---

alterations in relation to various changes in the environment and in the behavior of other people.

Lovaas and his collaborators devised an apparatus that consists of a panel of buttons that are pressed by the observer. Each button represents a category of behavior (for example, "talking," "running," "sitting alone") and is attached to an automatic pen-recorder. Whenever a button is pressed, the corresponding pen on the recorder is activated. A continuous record is thus provided.

The observer presses the button when the subject starts the specific behavior designated by that button and does not release the button until that behavior stops. The observer after a little practice can devote his whole attention to watching what the subject is doing and yet record up to 12 different categories of behavior without looking at the button panel. The apparatus permits a record that is precise enough to include duration and the specific time of onset of each behavior. The method, or its computer-assisted variations, can then be applied to discover covariations among the individual's different behaviors and between his behavior and that of other people in the situation.

Even without the aid of such apparatus, there have been many attempts to measure important interpersonal and emotional behaviors precisely. Some impressive examples come from assessments of the intensity or magnitude of such emotional behaviors as seemingly irrational fears and anxiety (e.g., Barlow, 1988).

The strength of diverse avoidance behaviors has been assessed reliably in clinical situations by exposing fearful individuals to a series of real or symbolic fear-inducing stimuli. For example, fear of heights was assessed by measuring the distance that the phobic person could climb on a metal fire escape (Lazarus, 1961). The same people were assessed again after receiving therapy to reduce their fears. In this phase, the subjects were invited to ascend eight stories by elevator to a roof garden and to count the passing cars below for 2 minutes. Claustrophobic behavior—fear of closed spaces— was measured by asking each person to sit in a cubicle containing large French windows opening onto a balcony. The assessor shut the windows and slowly moved a large screen nearer and nearer to the client, thus gradually constricting her space. Of course each client was free to open the windows and thereby to terminate the procedure whenever she wished, although she was instructed to persevere as long as possible. The measure of claustrophobia was the least distance at which the person could tolerate the screen. As another example, Table 13.2 shows a checklist for performance anxieties before making a public speech.

Another study assessed nursery-school children's fear of dogs (Bandura, Grusec, & Menlove, 1966). Each child was led into a room containing, in the far corner, a playpen in which a dog was enclosed. The children's approach behavior was scaled objectively according to how near they ventured toward the animal. To get the highest scores, the child had to climb into the playpen and sit in it while playing with the dog.

Direct behavior sampling has also been tried extensively in the analysis of psychotic behavior. One study, for instance, employed a time-sampling technique. At regular, 30-minute intervals, psychiatric nurses sought out and observed each hospitalized patient for periods of 1 to 3 minutes without directly interacting with him (Ayllon & Haughton, 1964). The behavior observed in each sample was classified for the occurrence of three previously defined behaviors (for example, psychotic talk), and the time-check recordings were used to compute the relative frequency of the various behaviors. This time-sampling technique was supplemented by recordings of all the interactions between the patient and nurses (such as each time the patient entered the nursing office). The resulting data served as a basis for designing and evaluating a treatment program. Similar ways of sampling and recording family interactions that occur naturally in the home have been developed by others (Patterson, 1976; Ramsey et al., 1990). They studied highly aggressive children in the contexts of everyday family life, for example, at dinner. The attempt was to analyze the exact conditions under which aggression would occur more or less.

Verbal Behavior

What people say—their "verbal behavior"—may be just as important as what they do nonverbally. Most personality assessors, guided by trait and psychodynamic theories, have focused on verbalizations as signs of personality rather than as descriptions of reactions to stimulus conditions. In behavior assessment, on the other hand, what the

Table 13.2
Timed Behavioral Checklist for Performance Anxiety

Behavior Observed	Time Period							
	1	2	3	4	5	6	7	8
1. Paces								
2. Sways								
3. Shuffles feet								
4. Knees tremble								
5. Extraneous arm and hand movement (swings, scratches, toys, etc.)								
6. Arms rigid								
7. Hands restrained (in pockets, behind back, clasped)								
8. Hand tremors								
9. No eye contact								
10. Face muscles tense (drawn, tics, grimaces)								
11. Face "deadpan"								
12. Face pale								
13. Face flushed (blushes)								
14. Moistens lips								
15. Swallows								
16. Clears throat								
17. Breathes heavily								
18. Perspires (face, hands, armpits)								
19. Voice quivers								
20. Speech blocks or stammers								

SOURCE: Paul, G. L. (1966). *Insight vs. desensitization in psychotherapy.* Stanford, CA: Stanford University Press.

person says is intended to help define the relevant stimuli and the response patterns that they have come to evoke and to specify the covariations between them. For example, a number of self-report techniques have been used to sample specific self-reported fears (Geer, 1965; Lang & Lazovik, 1963). These schedules list many items that were found to elicit frequent anxiety in patients. The respondent indicates on scales the degree of disturbance provoked by such items as strangers, bats, ugly people, mice, making mistakes, and looking foolish.

As was illustrated in the assessment of Gary's public speaking anxieties, a daily record may provide another valuable first step in the identification of problem-producing stimuli. Many behaviorally oriented clinicians routinely ask their clients to keep specific records listing the exact conditions under which their anxieties and problems seem to increase or decrease (Wolpe & Lazarus, 1966). The person may be asked to prepare by himself lists of all the stimulus conditions or events that create discomfort, distress, or other painful emotional reactions.

Finding Effective Rewards

So far we have considered the direct measurement of various responses. Behavior assessments, however, analyze not just what people do (and say and feel), but also the conditions that regulate or determine what they do. For that reason, behavior assessments have to find the rewards or reinforcers that may be influencing a person's behavior. If discovered, these reinforcers also can serve as incentives in therapy programs to help modify behavior in more positive or advantageous directions. Psychologists who emphasize the role of reinforcement in human behavior have devoted much attention to discovering and measuring effective reinforcers. People's actual choices in lifelike situations, as well as their verbal preferences or ratings, reveal some of the potent reinforcers that influence them. The reinforcement value of particular stimuli also may be assessed directly by observing their effects on the individual's performance (Daniels, 1994; Weir, 1965).

Primary reinforcers, like food, and generalized conditioned reinforcers, such as praise, social approval, and money, are effective for most people. For example, in one case study, researchers and teachers attempted to reduce the disruptive behaviors of a blind, learning-disabled boy (Heitzman & Alimena, 1991). His behaviors were problematic because they disrupted the class and also prevented the boy from achieving optimal academic success. Differential reinforcement was used to reduce the level of inappropriate behaviors to a socially acceptable level. In this procedure, the boy could not exceed a certain number of disruptive or inappropriate behaviors in one day if he wanted to be rewarded. Examples of rewards were listening to a favorite tape, free time to talk to friends, and sitting in the teacher's car (he liked the feel of velour seats). After 26 days, there was an 88% reduction in target behaviors.

Sometimes, however, it is difficult to find potent reinforcers that would be feasible to manipulate. With disturbed groups (such as hospitalized schizophrenic patients), for example, many of the usual reinforcers prove to be ineffective, especially with people who have spent many years living in the back wards of a mental hospital. Ayllon and Azrin (1965) have shown how effective reinforcers can be discovered even for seemingly unmotivated psychotic patients. These reinforcers then can serve to motivate the patients to engage in more adaptive behavior.

As a first step, the patients were observed directly in the ward to discover their most frequent behaviors in situations that permitted them freedom to do what they wished. Throughout the day observers carefully recorded the things the patients did, or tried to do, without pressures from the staff. The frequency of these activities provided an index of their potential values as reinforcers.

Six categories of reinforcers were established on the basis of extensive observation. These categories were: privacy, leave from the ward, social interactions with the staff, devotional opportunities, recreational opportunities, and items from the hospital canteen. Privacy, for example, included such freedoms as choice of bedroom or of eating group and getting a personal cabinet, a room-divider screen, or other means of

Table 13.3
Mean Tokens Exchanged for Various Available Reinforcers
(by 8 Patients During 42 Days)

Reinforcers	Mean Tokens Paid	Number of Patients Paying Any Tokens
Privacy	1352.25	8
Commissary items	969.62	8
Leave from ward	616.37	8
Social interaction with staff	3.75	3
Recreational opportunities	2.37	5
Devotional opportunities	.62	3

SOURCE: Based on Ayllon, T., & Azrin, N. H. (1965). The measurement and reinforcement of behavior of psychotics. *Journal of the Experimental Analysis of Behavior, 8,* 357–383.

preserving autonomy. Recreational opportunities included exclusive use of a radio or television set, attending movies and dances, and similar entertainment.

The patients could obtain each of the reinforcers with a specific number of tokens, which they earned by participating in such rehabilitative functions as self-care and job training. A sensitive index of the subjective reinforcement value of the available activities is obtained by considering the outcomes for which the patients later chose to exchange most of their tokens. Over 42 days the mean tokens exchanged by eight patients for the available reinforcers are shown in Table 13.3. Note that chances to interact socially with the staff and opportunity for recreation and spiritual devotion are most unpopular. These results suggest that, with chronic hospitalized patients such as these, therapy programs that rely primarily on social motivations would not fare well. Instead, such reinforcers as privacy, autonomy, and freedom might be the most effective incentives.

Measurement of Bodily Changes

Measures of bodily changes in response to stimulation also provide important information, especially when the stimuli are stressful or arousing. Various indirect measures of bodily reactions during emotional activity have been developed. One of the most convenient methods is the polygraph recording of some of the critical effects produced by the bodily activity involved in the reactions of the autonomic nervous system. The polygraph apparatus contains a series of devices that translate indices of body changes into a visual record by deflecting a pen across a moving paper chart.

One popular component of polygraphic measurement is the electrocardiogram (EKG). As the heart beats, its muscular contractions produce patterns of electrical activity that may be detected by electrodes placed near the heart on the body surface. Figure 13.1 shows a record of heartbeats monitored by the polygraph, the area from one peak to another on the record representing one beat of the heart. An especially useful index of heart activity is based on the *rate* at which the person's heart is beating: It is measured in terms of the time between each beat on the electrocardiogram.

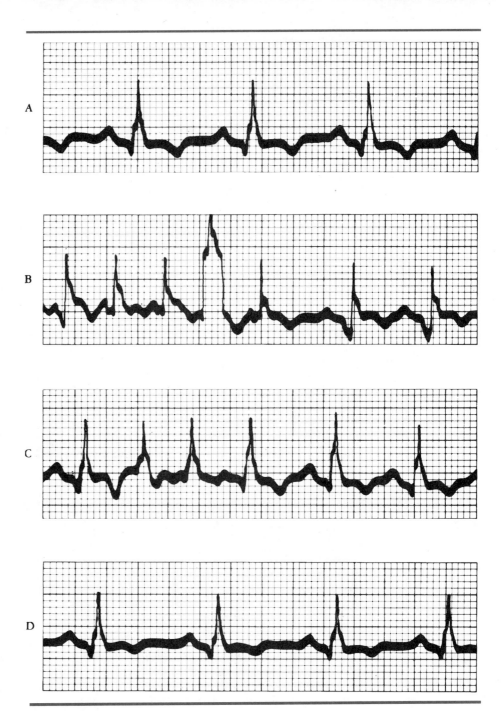

Figure 13.1

Heart Rhythm in an Elderly Subject   A: Normal heart rhythm (control level, rate 80). B and C: Initial beats show an abnormally irregular heartbeat during extreme emotional arousal. Last two beats show the heart rate has increased to 115. D: Following the end of arousal, heart rate returns to control level; abnormal beating is no longer present.

SOURCE: Courtesy of George Prozan, M.D.

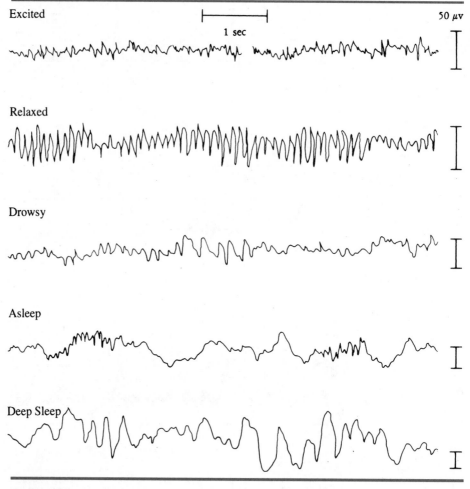

Figure 13.2
Various Human EEG Patterns under Several Arousal States

SOURCE: Jasper, H. (1941). In Penfield & Erickson (Eds.), *Epilepsy and cerebral localization*. Courtesy of Charles C. Thomas, Publisher, Springfield, IL.

In a basically similar manner, changes in blood volume may be recorded by means of a **plethysmograph.** Other examples of valuable indices include changes in the electrical activity of the skin due to sweating (recorded by a galvanometer and called the **galvanic skin response** or GSR), changes in blood pressure, and changes in muscular activity (Cacioppo, Berntson, & Crites, 1996; Geen, 1997).

Intense emotional arousal is generally accompanied by high levels of "activation" (Malmo, 1959; Birbaumer, 1993). That is shown by increases in the activity of the cerebral cortex, increases in muscle tension, and, at the behavioral level, increasingly vigorous activity and excitement. The degree of activation in the cerebral cortex may be inferred from "brain waves" recorded by the electroencephalograph (EEG), as illustrated in the records shown in Figure 13.2. As the EEG patterns in this figure indicate,

IN FOCUS 13.2 *Windows on the Brain: Beyond Behaviorism*

Technological advances in brain imaging now allow researchers to use methods like the MRI and CAT scan to observe areas within the brain that become activated in response to different stimuli or in the course of mental activities. These methods, however, are being used mostly by cognitive neuroscientists rather than by behaviorists given the latter's reluctance to deal with what goes on "inside the head."

To illustrate, one new wave of research seeks to identify the brain areas that are needed for different types of learning. The goal is to clarify the role of two different brain structures, the *amygdala* and the *hippocampus* (shown in Chapter 9, p. 227), in learning and memory. On the basis of past research (e.g., Ledoux, 1996) it is predicted that

1. The amygdala is crucial for the emotional conditioning of fears and for the fear reaction itself.
2. It is, however, the hippocampus that is essential for the person to have a memory of the event ("episodic memory").

In one study examining this hypothesis, the MRI was used to diagnose and select three patients. One had a damaged amygdala but an intact hippocampus; the second had an intact amygdala but hippocampal damage; the third had damage to both of these brain structures

(Bechara, Tranel, Damasio, Adolphs, Rockland, & Damasio, 1995). The patients were exposed to conditioning experiments designed to create an emotional response (fear) to previously neutral stimuli (slides of the color blue) by pairing the slides with a startlingly loud boat horn blast (the unconditioned stimulus). The patients' emotional reactions were recorded by monitoring their GSR (galvanic skin responses), and they also were questioned extensively about their experience.

Consistent with other findings, it was shown that the patient who only had damage to the amygdala could identify that the blue slides were followed by the horn blast and thus had clear memory of the event but did not develop an emotional conditioned response to those slides. In contrast, the patient with hippocampal damage developed the fear reaction to the blue slides but could not relay the facts regarding the associations involved. The patient with damage to both brain structures did not develop the fear response and did not indicate memory for the event. Studies like these promise to provide an increasingly precise understanding of how the brain works and underlies behavior. At the same time, they make clear that it is possible to systematically and scientifically study such mental events as emotions and memories, going far beyond the early behaviorism that confined itself to overt behavior (Gazzaniga, Mangun, & Ivey, 1998).

the frequency, amplitude, and other characteristics of brain waves vary according to the subject's degree of behavioral arousal and excitement. More recent technology goes much beyond the EEG (see *In Focus 13.2*).

ASSESSING CONDITIONS CONTROLLING BEHAVIOR

To assess behavior fully, behavior theorists believe that we have to identify the conditions that control it. But how do we know whether or not a response pattern is really controlled or caused by a particular set of conditions? Behaviorally oriented psychologists test the conditions by introducing a change and observing whether or not it produces the expected modification in behavior. They ask: Does a systematic change in stimulus conditions (a "treatment") in fact change the particular response pattern that it supposedly controls? If we hypothesize that a child's reading problem is caused by poor vision, we would expect appropriate treatment (such as corrective eyeglasses or corrective surgery) to be followed by a change in the behavior (that is, an improvement in reading). The same should be true for psychological causes. For example, if we believe that the child's reading difficulty is caused by an emotional problem in her relation to her mother, we should try to show that the appropriate change in that relationship will yield the expected improvement in reading. That is, to understand behavior fully we need to know the conditions that cause it. We can be most confident that we understand those conditions when we can show that a change in them yields the predicted change in the response pattern.

A rigid distinction between behavior assessment and treatment (i.e., behavior change) thus is neither meaningful nor possible. Indeed, some of the most important innovations in behavior assessment have grown out of therapeutic efforts to modify problematic behavior (discussed in Chapter 14). A main characteristic of these assessment methods is that they are linked closely to behavior change and cannot really be separated from it.

Functional Analyses: Basic Method

The close connection between behavior assessment and behavior change is most evident in "functional analyses"—that is, analyses of the precise covariations between changes in stimulus conditions and changes in a selected behavior pattern. Such functional analyses are the foundations of behavior assessments, and they are illustrated most clearly in studies that try to change behavior systematically. The basic steps may be seen in a study that was designed to help a girl in nursery school.

Functional Analyses: Case Examples

Ann was a bright four-year-old from an upper-middle-class background who increasingly isolated herself from children in her nursery school (Allen et al., 1964). At the same time, she developed various ingenious techniques to gain prolonged attention from the adults around her. She successfully coerced attention from her teachers, who found her many mental and physical skills highly attractive. Gradually, however, her efforts to maintain adult attention led her to become extremely isolated from other children.

Soon Ann was isolating herself most of the time from other youngsters. This seemed to be happening because most of the attention that adults were giving her was contingent, quite unintentionally, upon behaviors that were incompatible with Ann's relating to other children. Precisely those activities that led Ann away from play with her own peers were being unwittingly reinforced by the attention that her teachers showered on her. The more distressing and problematic Ann's behavior became, the more it elicited interest and close attention from her deeply concerned teachers.

Ann was slipping into a vicious cycle that had to be interrupted. A therapeutic plan was formed where Ann no longer received adult attention for her withdrawal from peers and her attempts at solitary interactions with adults. At the same time, the adults

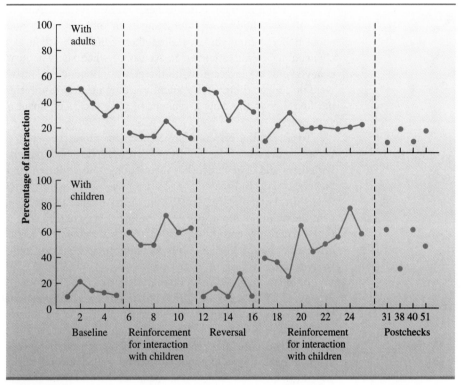

Figure 13.3

Percentages of Time Spent by Ann in Social Interaction During Approximately Two Hours of Each Morning Session

SOURCE: Allen, E. K., Hart, B., Buell, J. S., Harris, F. R., & Wolf, M. M. (1964). Effects of social reinforcement on isolate behavior of a nursery school child. *Child Development, 35,* 310.

gave her attention only when she played with other children. That is, attention from adults became contingent on her playing with her peers.

As part of the assessment, two observers continuously sampled and recorded Ann's proximity to and interactions with adults and children in school at regular 10-second intervals. The therapeutic plan was instituted after five days of baseline data had been recorded. Now whenever Ann started to interact with children an adult quickly attended to her, rewarding her participation in the group's play activities. Even approximations to social play, such as standing or playing near another child, were followed promptly by attention from a teacher. This attention was designed to further encourage Ann's interactions with other children. For example: "You three girls have a cozy house. Here are some more cups, Ann, for your tea party." Whenever Ann began to leave the group or attempted to make solitary contacts with adults, the teachers stopped attending to her.

Figure 13.3 summarizes the effects of the change in the consequences to Ann for isolate behavior with her peers. Notice that in the baseline period before the new response-reinforcement contingencies were instituted, Ann was spending only about 10% of her school time interacting with other children and 40% with adults. For about half the time she was altogether solitary. As soon as the contingencies were changed and adults attended to Ann only when she was near children, her behavior changed quickly in accord with the new contingencies. When adult-child interactions were no longer followed by attention, they quickly diminished to less than 20%. On the first day of this new arrangement (day six), Ann spent almost 60% of her time with peers.

To assess the effects of reinforcement more precisely, the procedures were reversed on days 12 to 16. Adults again rewarded Ann with their attention for interacting with them and disregarded her interactions with children. Under these conditions (the "reversal" days in Figure 13.3), Ann's previous behavior reappeared immediately. In a final shift (beginning on day 17), in which attention from adults again became contingent upon Ann's interacting with children, her contact with peers increased to about 60%. After the end of the special reinforcement procedures (day 25), periodic postchecks indicated that Ann's increased play behavior with peers tended to remain fairly stable.

Another example of functional analysis comes from a series of studies (Lovaas, Freitag, Gold, & Kassorla, 1965a) assessing the conditions controlling self-destructive behavior in a psychotic nine-year-old girl. This child was extensively and severely self-destructive, tormenting herself violently. Her tragic repertoire included banging her head and arms and pinching and slapping herself repeatedly. Her intensely maladaptive behaviors dated back at least to her third year of life, and currently she engaged in almost no appropriate social activities. Her self-destructive tortures included sticking her head in an electric wall heater, thus setting her hair on fire. She spent much time in repetitive and stereotyped physical self-stimulation, and her interactions with others were minimal.

To explore the possible conditions controlling the child's self-destructiveness, the investigators studied how changes in selected variables affected the child's objectively measured self-destructive behavior. These assessments were made over a period of many sessions. One of the most important parts of the study investigated systematically any changes in the girl's self-destructive behavior following withdrawal of reinforcement (in the form of attention) for previously rewarded behavior.

The child's self-destructiveness seemed to increase most when attention was withdrawn from response patterns for which she previously had been reinforced. Thus, the withdrawal of attention (reinforcement) from a previously reinforced response appeared to be the critical stimulus for her self-destructive behavior. The assessors interpreted their results to suggest that whenever her previously reinforced responses began to be unattended by others (extinguished), the girl could consistently reinstate the reinforcement (attention) by hurting herself.

Hurting oneself is painful, but sometimes it may be the only way to obtain such valued outcomes as parental attention. Experimenting with matches and stoves may be dangerous and potentially painful, but it also attracts Mother's interest quickly. Thus, the same stimulus that supplies pain can also lead to positive consequences and hence may serve to support seemingly bizarre behaviors—such as self-destructive acts. A complete analysis must deal with all the acquired meanings of a stimulus for the individual—not just the normative ones (e.g., MacLeod & Rutherford, 1992).

A complete analysis also must consider the total relations among stimulus conditions rather than focus on single aspects of reinforcement in isolation. These assessments showed, for example, that this child was highly discriminating in the very particular times and circumstances during which she became self-destructive. For example, massive withdrawal of attention—as when the experimenter withheld attention for an entire session—did not affect her self-destructive behavior. In contrast, the removal of smiles and attention only for previously reinforced responses changed her behavior (also see Smith et al., 1992). Note that in this approach, assessment and behavior change become inextricably fused: The assessments guide the therapeutic program, and the efficacy of the treatment program is in turn continuously assessed (e.g., Frank & Hudson, 1990).

Predicting from Situations

The emphasis in this approach on conditions and stimuli as determinants of behavior also has important implications for efforts to predict behavior. Psychologists guided by this approach point out that often behavior may be predicted simply from knowledge about relevant conditions. Consider, for example, studies that tried to predict the posthospital adjustment of mental patients. Accurate predictions of posthospital adjustment required knowledge of the environment in which the ex-patient would be living in the community—such as the availability of jobs and family support—rather than any measures of person variables or in-hospital behavior (e.g., Fairweather, 1967; Fairweather et al., 1969; Holahan & Moos, 1990).

Likewise, to predict intellectual achievement it helps to take account of the degree to which the child's environment supports (models and reinforces) intellectual development (Wolf, 1966). And to predict whether or not people respond to stress with illness, it helps to know the degree to which they have social supports (e.g., spouse, family) in their environments (Holahan & Moos, 1990; Nilson et al., 1981). Finally, when powerful treatments are developed, predictions about outcomes may be useful when based simply on knowing the treatment to which the individual is assigned (e.g., Bandura, Blanchard, & Ritter, 1969; Bandura, 1986).

BEHAVIORAL CONCEPTION OF ADAPTATION AND DEVIANCE

Behavioral theories influenced radically how one thinks about adaptation and deviance, as this section shows. They also greatly affected the approach to treatment, as will be seen in this and later chapters.

Evaluating the Consequences of Behavior, Not the Person

The behavioral approach avoids evaluating the health, adequacy, or abnormality of the person or personality as a whole. Instead, when judgments must be made, they focus

Social judgments and evaluations about deviance and adaptation depend on the values of the community.

on evaluation of the individual's specific behaviors. Behaviors are evaluated on the basis of the kinds of consequences that they produce for the person who generates them and for other people who are affected by them. "Advantageous" (adaptive, constructive) behaviors are those whose consequences are judged to be favorable; conversely, "disadvantageous" (problematic, maladaptive, destructive) behaviors are those that yield negative effects.

Evaluations about the positive or negative consequences of behavior are social and ethical judgments that depend on the values and standards of the community that makes them. Advantageous behaviors are those judged to have positive personal and interpersonal consequences (for example, helping people "feel good" or increasing constructive, creative outcomes) without any aversive impact on others. Behaviors that have negative, life-threatening, destructive consequences or those that endanger the full potentialities of the person or other people (for example, debilitating fears, homicidal attempts) would be considered maladaptive.

The behavioral approach also implies a high value for the development of the individual's total competencies and skills so that he or she can maximize opportunities and options. Similarly, the person must be able to discern the important contingencies and rules of reinforcement in his or her life in order to maximize satisfactions and minimize aversive, disadvantageous outcomes. To be able to overcome unfavorable environments and life conditions, a high premium is also put on the development of effective strategies for self-control and for modifying the impact of the environment itself to make it more favorable.

Beyond these generalizations, the behavioral approach to deviance has sharply attacked the traditional "disease" models that view problematic (deviant, disadvantageous) behaviors as symptoms of an underlying mental illness, as discussed next.

Disease Models

Historically, with the growth of modern biology and medicine, disease explanations of abnormal behavior became especially favored. At the turn of this century the discovery and cure of a psychotic disorder stemming from syphilis ("general paresis") greatly reinforced the belief that deviant behavior might be a sign of organic disease. Similarly, more recent findings concerning biochemical and genetic antecedents in certain forms of mental deficiency (discussed in Chapter 8) bolstered the biological approach to psychological problems.

In the biological view, deviant behaviors are construed as symptoms of underlying organic pathology. Different types or patterns of deviant behavior (for example, delusions, depression) presumably might be linked to different types of pathology (such as brain infections, tumors), just as different symptoms of physical disease may be attributed to particular underlying organic causes. As noted previously (Chapter 8), research continues in the search for organic causes of psychological problems, but at present most difficulties in social behavior appear to be "functional" (nonorganic). Nevertheless, the disease view is still widely used as an *analogy* for conceptualizing psychological problems even when no physical disease has been implicated. In this quasi-disease approach the person is seen as a "patient" whose deviant behaviors are considered "symptoms" of underlying *mental* or emotional pathology comparable to a physical disease like influenza or cancer. The patient's disturbed behavior is not the focus of interest because it is seen as merely symptomatic of underlying pathology, as was illustrated in the psychodynamic approach to problematic behaviors.

Criticisms of Disease Models

Some behaviorally oriented critics have argued that while the disease model may be appropriate for the analysis and treatment of physical illness in medicine, it is not useful for conceptualizing psychological problems (Bandura, 1969; Krasner & Ullmann, 1973). When there are no identified discrete organic causes (like germs) that can be tied clearly to social behavior, speculations about hypothesized pathology cannot help the troubled person. On the contrary, conceptualizing behavior in terms of diseases whose properties and physiological bases are not established can divert the assessor from the psychological and life conditions that influence the maladaptive behavior. The disease model may also lead to an unfortunate emphasis on psychiatric hospitalization, rather than on new learning experiences in life settings and on social education.

IN FOCUS   13.3   *Mental Illnesses or Problems of Living?*

The medical model or disease approach to psychological problems has had a complex history. Some have considered it misguided because they believe psychological problems, unlike physical illnesses, are not caused by underlying agents such as germs that can be closely tied to a pattern of symptoms (Szasz, 1970; Ullmann & Krasner, 1969). Moreover, while it may appear to be more humane to consider troubled people ill than to consider them evil or possessed, the people who have been labeled mentally ill may lose many of their human rights and responsibilities and may be stigmatized and victimized by society in many ways, such as job and social discrimination.

In one study normal individuals (doctors, psychologists, and graduate students) participated in a research project in which they admitted themselves to psychiatric hospitals and then, during their confinement, proceeded to behave rationally. What happened to them dramatically illustrates some of the hazards of the diagnostic system and the medical model or disease approach (Rosenhan, 1973). These individuals were consistently treated by the hospital staff (who did not know their true identity) as if they were insane as soon as they were admitted to the hospital and labeled psychotic. Even when their behavior was completely rational and normal, they were still treated as insane by the staff, although some of the other patients suspected that they did not really belong there.

Thomas S. Szasz, himself a psychiatrist, became the most controversial and outspoken challenger of the tendency to view deviant behavior as a sign of mental illness. He wrote:

My aim is to suggest that the phenomena now called mental illness be looked at afresh . . . that they be removed from the category of illnesses . . . and

regarded as the expressions of man's struggle with the problem of how he should live (Szasz, 1989, p. 116).

An emphasis on treating psychiatric problems as problems of living can have many beneficial effects. For example, it can help reduce the tendency to stigmatize people as ill or crazy whenever their behavior upsets us or is socially deviant. As many anthropologists have pointed out often, what seems normal in one culture may seem bizarre or abnormal in another. However, a closer look at diverse cultures yields some surprising results. A careful analysis of the Eskimos on an Alaskan island and a Yoruba group in Nigeria, for example, indicated that they both have a word translatable as "insanity" (Murphy, 1976). The word is used to label conduct consistent with the Western definition of schizophrenia, such as hearing voices, talking to oneself, and having outbreaks of violence. In both cultures, people who consistently show such conduct are considered ill and seek the help of native healers. In the words of the anthropologist who studied them, in both the Eskimo and Yoruba cultures, the labels for insanity

refer to beliefs, feelings, and actions that are thought to emanate from the mind or inner state of an individual and to be essentially beyond his control; the afflicted persons seek the aid of healers; the afflictions bear strong resemblance to what we call schizophrenia. Of signal importance is the fact that the labels of insanity refer not to single specific attributes but to a pattern of several interlinked phenomena. Almost everywhere a pattern composed of hallucinations, delusions, disorientations, and behavioral aberrations appears to identify the idea of "losing one's mind," even though the content of these manifestations is colored by cultural beliefs (Murphy, 1976, p. 1027).

Szasz (1960, 1989) has been a foremost critic of the "disease approach" to psychological problems. He believes that to speak of "mental illness" as if it were a disease-like sickness is to subscribe to a myth. He contends that the so-called sick person has problems of living and is not a victim of "demons, witches, fate, or mental illness" (Szasz, 1960, p. 118). The term *mental illness* may have had some value initially in that

In sum, at least certain human problems—subsumed in our culture under the broad label "schizophrenia"—involve more than specific violations of the social norms of the particular society: They appear widely enough to indicate a type of affliction that may be shared "by virtually all mankind" (Murphy, 1976, p. 1,027). Such findings strengthen the view that many "problems of living" seem to have a genetic basis and "diseaselike" character (Kety et al., 1975; Plomin et al., 1997). The degree to which that is true and the types of problems for which it holds is likely to be hotly disputed for many years (see Chapter 8). The truth, as usual, is likely to support elements from both positions, namely, that severe problems often reflect interactions of biochemical, genetic, and social-cognitive-environmental process.

The Rights of Mental Patients

Although many experts saw Szasz's strong attacks on psychiatry (1960, 1970, 1989) as too extreme, he has made important points and championed some worthy causes. His basic concern is with individual freedom, including the person's right to be grossly deviant from the prevailing conventions of society. But rather than urge that people be held less responsible for their actions, he insists that legal responsibility should apply to everyone, even those who defy conventions. And with legal responsibility come legal rights, requiring the protection of the civil liberties of people judged mentally ill. Szasz's goals include the abolition of involuntary hospitalization, the retention of civil rights as a citizen even when one is hospitalized, and the abolition of the insanity plea in criminal cases except when even laypeople would agree that the criminal was wildly insane, a "raving maniac."

While Szasz's position seemed radical when first proposed, in the 1970s it gained increasing acceptance in social policy. There has been a growing awareness that the rights of hospitalized mental patients may be jeopardized. In a landmark decision, the United States Supreme Court ruled in 1975 that "mental illness alone is not a sufficient basis for denying an individual his fundamental right to liberty." Specifically, an involuntarily hospitalized patient who is not dangerous to himself or others has a right to be released (see Figure 13.4).

NOTICE TO PATIENTS

The United States Supreme Court recently ruled that a mental patient who has been involuntarily hospitalized, who is not dangerous to himself or to others, who is receiving only custodial care, and who is capable of lively safely in the community has a constitutional right to liberty—that is, has a right to be released from the hospital. The Supreme Court's opinion is available for patients to read.

If you think that the Supreme Court ruling may have a bearing on your present status, please feel free to discuss the matter with the hospital staff. In addition, if you wish to talk with an attorney about the meaning of the Supreme Court decision and how it may apply to you, the Superintendent has a list of legal organizations that may be of assistance. The staff will be glad to aid anyone who wishes to contact a lawyer.

Figure 13.4
Notice on the Legal Rights of Patients Following the 1975 Supreme Court Decision
SOURCE: Rep. of the Research Task Force of the NIMH. (1975). Research in the service of mental health (DHEW Publication No. 75-236). Washington, DC: Author.

---

it permitted troubled and unusual individuals to be considered "sick" rather than morally tainted. But while shielding individuals from social criticism, the concept of mental illness also divests them of the privileges and human rights that are part of responsibility. Szasz maintains that hospitalized, legally committed mental patients in fact lose their basic freedoms and are victimized by society rather than by a disease.

Moreover, the widespread practice of construing the whole person as either "sick" or "healthy" is often unjust because a person may function perfectly well in many aspects of life and be incompetent or deficient only in some domains. In fact, most "mentally ill" individuals are capable of much adequate and responsible behavior and show impairments that are relatively specific rather than generalized (Fairweather, Sanders, Cressler, & Maynard, 1969). Therefore, many therapists bemoan the "common tendency to classify people as either sick or well, even though a person's social status *should* primarily be determined by his or her ability to assume particular rights and duties" (Fairweather et al., 1969, p. 18).

Some of the essentials of the criticisms of the disease model were put this way: "A child who strangles kittens or spits at his mother does not have a disease although he does have something that somebody judges to be a problem" (Peterson, 1968, p. 5). But no matter how deserved some of the criticisms of the disease model may seem to be, it is essential to keep an open mind. Research increasingly reveals distinctive pathology, genetic patterns, or brain or hormonal problems correlated with at least some patterns of deviant behavior that not long ago we considered to be of psychological origin (for further discussion, see *In Focus 13.3*). Indeed research in recent years has clearly indicated that there are major disease-like mental conditions that have biochemical and genetic roots, as discussed in Chapter 8.

Deviance as Problematic Behavior

Even severe critics of the disease model generally recognize that at least some patterns of behavior may exist in many cultures or even everywhere. But they still insist that the vast bulk of human problems reflect unfortunate social histories and environments. They therefore focus their attention on the disadvantageous behaviors themselves. Rather than viewing maladaptive patterns as merely symptoms or signs of underlying diseases or dynamics, this view rejects the symptom-disease distinction and concentrates on the individual's problematic behaviors. For example, rather than seeing an individual's fear of snakes as possibly symbolic of unconscious sexual conflicts, the behavior therapist deals with the snake phobia itself and attempts to treat it in its own right. Thus, in the behavioral approach, the focus shifts from hypothesized but unobservable physical or mental disorders in the person to problematic behaviors. The focus on behavior was illustrated in the assessment of Gary in this chapter. Rather than infer Gary's traits and motives or try to reconstruct his history, the troublesome behaviors (for example, anxiety related to public speaking) were identified so that they could be modified directly.

The behavior orientation to deviance usually assumes a fundamental *continuity between normal and abnormal behavior* (Bandura, 1977, 1986; Kanfer & Phillips, 1970; Ullmann & Krasner, 1969). Rather than attributing deviance to distinct pathology or basically different conditions, one sees it as governed by the same laws that might (under other specific circumstances) lead to adequate or even creative behavior. That is, normal and abnormal behavior are not viewed as distinctly separate entities; instead, all behavior—regardless of its social value—is analyzed in the same terms.

Table 13.4
Arguments for and against Disease Models of "Mental Illness"

Against	For
Many human difficulties are problems of living and coping effectively and appropriately. Even severe problems reflect unfortunate social histories and environments.	Many human difficulties are illnesses. They often reflect unfortunate biochemistry and genetic predispositions.
Coping is the person's own responsibility.	Coping problems may be like physical illnesses.
Mental illness is a myth that strips the "ill" of their rights and responsibilities.	Mental illness is a tragic reality and its victims are sick.
Behavioral and cognitive interventions can help.	Medication and medical interventions can help.

For example, observational learning processes are basically the same regardless of whether a child's parental models are criminals or pillars of social virtue: The behaviors the child learns will be different in these two cases but the learning principles will be the same. Similarly, reinforcement principles presumably are the same regardless of whether incompetent behaviors or creative ones are reinforced. Thus, disadvantageous interpersonal behaviors and deviance may result from inadequate or inappropriate social learning in regard to any (or all) aspects of personal adaptation. Examples of disadvantageous behaviors include antisocial reactions to frustration, excessive avoidance patterns in the face of stress and threat, unduly severe self-evaluations, and negative self-concepts. Belief in the continuity of normal and abnormal behavior also implies that the same basic strategies may be used to understand and study disadvantageous behaviors and more normative behaviors. Arguments for and against the view of "mental illness" as behavioral problems of living versus diseases are summarized in Table 13.4 and discussed further in *In Focus 13.3.*

The emphasis on the specificity of behavior implies that an individual may engage in deviant or disadvantageous behaviors only under some conditions and not under others. A boy may be hyperaggressive at school but not at home, failing in schoolwork but excelling in sports, popular with boys but terrified of girls. Gary may be anxious about public speaking but quite calm when facing sports competitions and even when climbing hazardous mountain peaks. In the behavioral orientation, therefore, one does not characterize the person as normal or deviant and concentrates instead on identifying specific problematic behaviors and the situations in which they occur.

Finally, attention is devoted to the *current,* immediate causes of behaviors rather than to their historical development in early childhood. This focus on current causes implies a belief that behavior change techniques can be used to modify problems regardless of their historical beginnings in the individual's past. Regardless of *why* Gary developed public speaking anxiety, behavior therapists want to modify the fears that trouble him now.

SUMMARY

1. Although there are various behavioral approaches to personality, their methods have in common the careful measurement of behavior in relation to specific stimulus conditions. Behavioral observation is common to all psychological approaches: It is the use that is made of the data obtained that distinguishes among approaches. In the psychodynamic orientation behaviors serve as indirect signs of hypothesized underlying dispositions and motives. Behavioral approaches treat observed behavior as a sample, and the focus is on how the specific sample is affected by variations in the stimulus conditions.

2. Analysis of the case of Gary W. illustrates the behavioral assessment of anxiety: Rather than attempting to make statements concerning underlying motives and conflicts, the search is for how changes in stimulus conditions produce changes in the response patterns of interest.

3. Ways in which behavior may be measured directly include situational behavior sampling, both verbal and nonverbal, and the physiological measurement of emotional reactions. In behavior sampling, the emphasis is on detailed information concerning the onset, magnitude, and duration of the behaviors of interest and the circumstances of their occurrence. The subject may supply this information through various self-report techniques such as daily records, lists of problematic situations, or responses on preset survey scales (schedules). Polygraphic measurement of bodily changes includes indices of heart rate, changes in blood volume and blood pressure, and changes in muscular activity and in sweat gland activity. Brain waves also provide clues about changes in activity level. Most dramatic are such advances in technology as the MRI and CAT scan that now make it possible to see the areas of the brain that become activated in response to various stimuli.

4. The assessment of the reinforcing value of stimuli may be made from an individual's choices in lifelike situations, verbal preferences and ratings, or the observed effects of various stimuli on actual behavior. In clinical work it may be especially important to discover rewards that are effective for the individual concerned. Sometimes the usual reinforcers are not effective and new ones must be sought to facilitate therapeutic progress.

5. Functional analyses, the foundations of behavior assessments, are illustrated by studies of single cases. Careful observation of the behavior in question as it naturally occurs suggests which specific conditions maintain this behavior. Then systematic changes are made in those conditions until the problem behavior no longer occurs and more satisfying behaviors are substituted.

6. Behaviorally oriented approaches to adaptation and deviance propose an alternative to both psychiatric diseases and inferred psychodynamics. They suggest, instead, a focus directly on the behaviors themselves and on what the person does rather than his or her hypothesized underlying mental diseases or dynamics.

Behavior Change

The most important applications of behavioral approaches have been their innovations for producing change. Traditional approaches to personality change emphasized insight, awareness, and the acceptance of feelings. In contrast, behavior theories led to new methods of behavior change based on specific learning experiences. These learning forms of therapy have three main common features:

1. They attempt to modify the problematic behavior itself and address it directly; therefore, they are called **behavior therapies.**
2. Like the behavior theories and assessments that guide them, behavior therapies emphasize the individual's current behaviors rather than the historical origins of his or her problems.
3. Most behavior therapists assume that disadvantageous or "deviant" behavior can be understood and changed by the same learning principles that govern normal behavior.

Traditionally, "normal" personality psychology was sharply distinguished from the study of abnormal personality. Recently this distinction became blurred. Behavior therapists try to show that they can use the same psychological principles to modify all sorts of human problems, regardless of the specific type of problem or its severity. Indeed they prefer to treat severely disturbed human behaviors — such as long-standing, bizarre difficulties that have been highly resistant to other forms of treatment — to demonstrate the power of their methods.

The methods and findings of behavior therapy challenged traditional concepts about normal and abnormal personality and the conditions necessary for personality change in highly disturbed as well as in more adaptive people. Finally, behavior therapies had an important impact not only on techniques for treating people but also on theories about the basic nature of personality. In the rest of this chapter, you will learn about basic strategies of behavior therapy and their implications for this approach to personality.

CHANGING EMOTIONAL REACTIONS

Next we will consider some of the main techniques and findings of behavior therapy based on the concepts of learning theories. First we focus on methods designed to change previously learned disadvantageous emotional reactions, such as anxiety.

Systematic desensitization has been used effectively to treat anxiety about public speaking and many other fears.

Desensitization: Overcoming Anxiety

Learning principles for therapeutic behavior change have been available for more than 50 years, but until recently they were only rarely applied because most therapists were afraid that "symptom substitution" would occur. They believed that the removal of problematic behaviors would be followed by other symptoms that might be even worse than the original ones. Joseph Wolpe, a psychiatrist who became skeptical about psychoanalytic theory, took the risk of attempting direct behavior modification with many of his patients. In 1958 he published a book describing a method of **systematic desensitization** based on the principle of classical conditioning.

Wolpe was impressed by the work of such early learning theorists as Pavlov and believed that neurosis involves maladaptive learned habits, especially anxiety (fear) responses. In neurotic behavior, he hypothesized, anxiety has become the conditioned response to stimuli that are not anxiety-provoking for other people. He reasoned that therapy might help the neurotic individual to inhibit anxiety by **counterconditioning** him to make a competing (antagonistic) response to anxiety-eliciting stimuli. In his words, "If a response antagonistic to anxiety can be made to occur in the presence of anxiety-evoking stimuli so that it is accompanied by a complete or partial suppression of the

Table 14.1
Three Basic Steps in the Desensitization of Anxiety

Step	Example
1. Establishing the anxiety stimulus hierarchy: anxiety-evoking situations ranked from least to most severe	Low anxiety: reading about speeches alone in your room
	Intermediate anxiety: getting dressed in the morning on which you are to give a speech
	High anxiety: presenting a speech before an audience
2. Learning an incompatible response	Learning deep muscle relaxation by tensing and relaxing various muscle groups (head, shoulders, arms), deep breathing techniques, and similar methods
3. Counterconditioning: learning to make the incompatible response to items in the hierarchy	Practicing relaxation responses to the lowest item on the hierarchy and moving gradually to higher items

anxiety responses, the bond between these stimuli and the anxiety response will be weakened" (Wolpe, 1958, p. 71). His attempt to desensitize the individual to anxiety-evoking stimuli includes three steps (summarized in Table 14.1):

1. *Establishing the anxiety stimulus hierarchy.* First the situations that evoke distressing emotional arousal and avoidance are identified. That is done with a detailed assessment usually conducted through interviews. Sometimes a person has many areas of anxiety, such as fear of failure, self-doubts, dating, guilt about sex, and so on. Regardless of how many areas or "themes" there are, each is treated separately. For each theme the person grades or ranks the component stimuli on a hierarchy of severity ranging from the most to the least intensely anxiety-provoking events (see Table 14.2). For example, a person who is terrified of public speaking might consider "reading about speeches while alone in my room" a mildly anxiety-provoking stimulus, while "walking up before the audience to present the speech" might create severe anxiety in him (Paul, 1966). In Gary's case, "the minute before starting a formal speech" was the most anxiety-provoking, while "watching a friend practice a speech" and "taking notes in the library for a speech" were only moderately disturbing. As another example, a woman who sought treatment for sexual dysfunction indicated that "being kissed on cheeks and forehead" evoked merely mild anxiety but thinking about items like "having intercourse in the nude while sitting on husband's lap" produced the most intense anxiety in her (Lazarus, 1963).

2. *Training the incompatible response (relaxation).* After identifying and grading the stimuli that evoke anxiety, the person needs to learn responses that can be

Table 14.2
Items of Different Severity from Four Anxiety Hierarchies*

Severity (Degree of Anxiety)	Anxiety Hierarchies (Themes)			
	1 Interpersonal Rejection	2 Guilt about Work	3 Test Taking	4 Expressing Anger
Low	Thinking about calling Mary (a new girlfriend) tonight	Thinking "I still haven't answered all my mail"	Getting the reading list for the course	Watching strangers quarrel in street
Intermediate	Asking for a date on the telephone	Taking off an hour for lunch	Studying at my desk the night before the final	My brother shouting at his best friend
High	Trying a first kiss	Going to a movie instead of working	Sitting in the examination room waiting for the test to be handed out	Saying "No! I don't want to!" to mother

*These items are examples from much longer hierarchies.

used later to inhibit anxiety. Wolpe prefers to use relaxation responses because they can be taught easily and are always inherently incompatible with anxiety: No one can be relaxed and anxious simultaneously. The therapist helps the client to learn to relax by elaborate instructions that teach first to tense and then to relax parts of the body (arms, shoulders, neck, head) until gradually an almost hypnotic state of total calm and deep muscle relaxation is achieved (see *In Focus 14.1*). Most people can learn how to relax within a few sessions. The critical problem is to learn to relax to anxiety-evoking stimuli, and that task is attempted in the next phase.

3. *Associating anxiety stimuli and incompatible responses.* In the critical phase, counterconditioning, the client is helped to relax deeply while presented with the least anxiety-arousing stimulus from the previously established hierarchy. The stimulus event usually is described verbally or presented symbolically (in a picture) while the client is deeply relaxed and calm. As the therapist says the words for the item, the client tries to generate the most vivid image of it that his or her imagination can form. As soon as the client can concentrate on this item while remaining calm, the next, more severe item from the hierarchy is introduced until, step by step, the entire hierarchy is mastered.

If at any point in the procedure the client begins to become anxious while presented with an anxiety stimulus, he or she signals the therapist. The client is promptly instructed to discontinue the image of the stimulus until calm again. Then a somewhat less severe item from the hierarchy is presented so that he or she can concentrate on it without anxiety. After that, the client is ready to advance to the next item in the anxiety hierarchy and the step-by-step progress up the list can be resumed.

IN FOCUS 14.1   *Combining Relaxation and Biofeedback to Treat Asthma*

The technique of desensitization is used most often to reduce anxiety as, for example, in phobias, compulsions, and various patterns of general apprehension and avoidance. As a first step, the fearful person is taught to relax deeply. While reclining comfortably he gets instructions like these:

> Your whole body is becoming heavier . . . all your muscles are relaxing more and more. Your arms are becoming very relaxed. (*Pause*) Your shoulders. (*Pause*) Your neck. (*Pause*) Now the muscles of your jaws . . . your tongue . . . (*Pause*) and your eyes . . . very relaxed. Your forehead . . . very relaxed . . . noticing that as you become more relaxed you're feeling more and more calm. (*Pause*) Very relaxed . . . relaxing any parts of your face which feel the least bit tense. (*Pause*) Now, back down to your neck . . . your shoulders . . . your chest . . . your buttocks . . . your thighs . . . your legs . . . your feet . . . very, very relaxed. (*Pause*) Feeling very at ease and very comfortable (Morris, 1975, p. 244).

An exciting program at a special research and treatment center for children with asthma combined training in relaxation with **biofeedback** techniques. This combination was used to teach the children how they can control their respiratory disorder themselves rather than relying solely on medication or on the help of doctors and nurses (Creer, 1974).

The children are first taught a sequence of steps toward deep relaxation. As they are practicing these relaxation techniques, they are given feedback through earphones that deliver a clicking sound in proportion to the child's muscular tension: The less tension, the fewer the clicks. The relaxation is combined in a standard desensitization procedure with stimuli that the child has identified as anxiety arousing (for example, waking in the night and having to come to the hospital for treatment). Immediate improvement was observed in these children after they used the relaxation and biofeedback techniques. The children seemed to be increasing their capacities and learning new skills (such as more efficient expiratory flow) for relieving their distress whenever and wherever an asthma attack might occur. Note that this therapy program combined the procedure of substituting relaxation for anxious responses with the technique of providing feedback to reinforce the child for relaxing.

In sum, the **desensitization** (counterconditioning) procedure attempts to make responses strongly antagonistic to anxiety (such as relaxation) occur in the presence of mildly anxiety-evoking stimuli. The incompatible response then will at least partially prevent the anxiety response. In that way, the association between the aversive stimulus and anxiety becomes reduced, while the association of the stimulus with the relaxation reaction becomes strengthened (Guthrie, 1935; Wolpe, 1958).

Desensitization has been used to modify diverse avoidance patterns and problematic behaviors as well as specific fears. McClanahan (1995), for example, treated a woman who suffered from severe habitual nail biting. McClanahan noted that the nail biting was almost always precipitated by anxiety which included feeling overwhelmed, apprehensive, nervous, and worried. The desensitization techniques used were deep muscle relaxation and transcendental meditation. Systematic desensitization reduced anxiety and decreased the frequency and duration of nail biting significantly.

Clinical reports of successful desensitization may be encouraging, but they do not prove that the clinical procedure, rather than other things in the client's life, was responsible for the observed improvement. More conclusive evidence has come from controlled experiments. The findings from these studies generally indicate that desensitization is a valuable method for modifying phobias and reducing anxiety (Kazdin & Wilson, 1978; Wilson & O'Leary, 1980).

One careful experiment, for example, studied the efficacy of desensitization for treating intense public-speaking anxieties (Paul, 1966). Students who had severe anxieties about speaking in public were assigned to one of four conditions. In one group they received Wolpe's desensitization treatment, learning to relax to progressively more threatening imagined situations connected with public speaking. Students in a second condition received brief traditional, insight-oriented psychotherapy from an expert clinician. In a third condition the students served as control subjects, obtaining only placebo "tranquilizers" and bogus training allegedly designed to help them "handle stress." Thus, these subjects were given attention but received no specific treatment. In each of the above conditions the students had five contact hours over a six-week period for their treatments, so that all were given the same amount of time. A fourth group was used as a no-treatment control, taking a pre- and post-treatment assessment battery of tests but receiving no special treatment.

Before and after treatment all students were assessed by tests, ratings, and observations of their behavior. Public-speaking anxiety was measured through self-report, physiologically and behaviorally (by observations of actual public-speaking behavior under stress). As Figure 14.1 indicates, systematic desensitization was consistently the best treatment. Brief insight-oriented psychotherapy did not differ from attention-placebo, although people in both these conditions obtained greater anxiety reduction (on some measures) than did the untreated controls. On the physiological measures, only the desensitization group showed a significant reduction in anxiety when compared to the no-treatment controls. A follow-up on the test battery six weeks later, and another one two years later, found that improvement was maintained (Paul, 1966, 1967). There were no indications of "symptom substitution." On the contrary, students who had received the counterconditioning treatment in addition to becoming desensitized to public-speaking anxiety also improved in overall college grades when compared with students in the other conditions (Paul & Shannon, 1966).

Observational Learning (Modeling)

In treatment by observational learning, or modeling, the individual observes another (the model) who displays more appropriate or adaptive behavior sequences (Bandura, 1969, 1986). The model may be observed live or, in some cases, on film. Modeling techniques have been used to modify fears and other strong emotional reactions with dramatic success. For example, an important experiment compared the effects of modeling and desensitization treatments in removing phobic behavior (Bandura, Blanchard, & Ritter, 1969). Teenage and adult volunteers with intense fear of snakes were assigned to three treatment groups and a nontreated control group.

One group was trained to relax while visualizing progressively stronger fear-arousing scenes involving snakes (systematic desensitization treatment). A second group of fearful people saw films in which fearless children and adults interacted in a

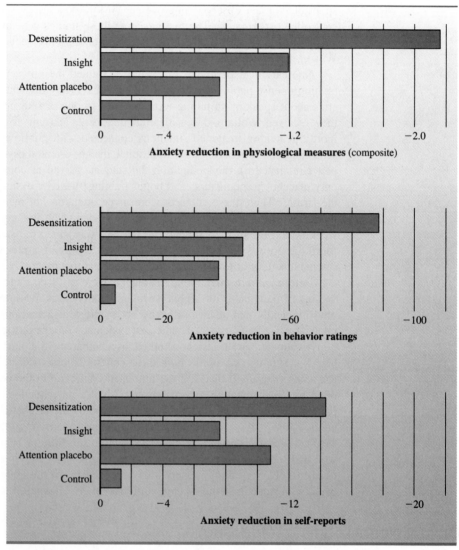

Figure 14.1
Mean Reduction in Anxiety (from Pretest to Posttest) in Each of Three Measures

SOURCE: Adapted from Paul, G. L. (1966). *Insight vs. desensitization in psychotherapy.* Stanford, CA: Stanford University Press.

progressively bold fashion with a snake (symbolic modeling treatment). In early scenes the models handled only plastic snakes. Later scenes showed models touching, holding, and allowing a large snake to crawl freely over them (see Figure 14.2). Participants were instructed in relaxation techniques to use during the showing of the film and were able to regulate the film presentation, stopping the film and reversing it back

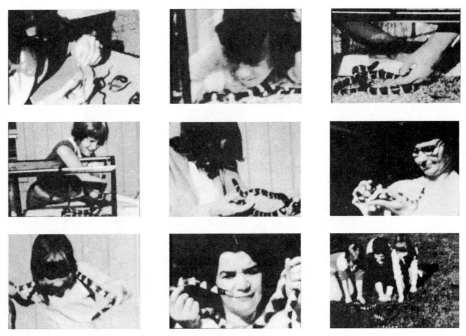

Figure 14.2
Photographs of Children and Adults Modeling Progressively Bolder Interactions with a King Snake

SOURCE: Bandura, A., Blanchard, E. B., & Ritter, B. (1969). Relative efficacy of desensitization and modeling approaches for inducing behavioral, affective, and attitudinal changes. *Journal of Personality and Social Psychology, 13,* 179.

to an earlier, less threatening scene if they became too anxious. When they were able to stay relaxed during the previously threatening scene, they moved on to the next scene.

The third group received a treatment that combined live modeling with guided participation. They watched live models boldly handling the snake, at first through an observation window; later the model handled the snake directly in front of them. The model then gradually led the participants into handling the snake at first with gloves and then with bare hands. The model's physical guidance was gradually reduced until everyone was able to perform all the prescribed activities with the snake. It was found that modeling with guided participation was the most powerful of the three methods, almost completely removing the fearful behavior in everyone who received this treatment. In this group the participants tended to be amazed at how quickly and thoroughly they had been able to overcome their deep fear.

The volunteers in all groups were tested for the strength of their fear and avoidance of snakes before and after completion of their respective treatments. They also completed an extensive fear inventory. Some of the main results are shown in Figures 14.3 and 14.4. Of the three methods, modeling with guided participation was

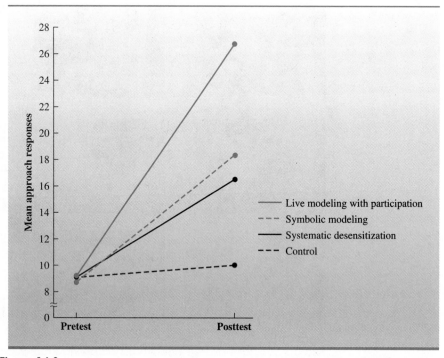

Figure 14.3
Effects of Modeling and Desensitization on the Development of Approach Responses to Previously Feared Stimuli Mean number of approach responses performed by participants before and after receiving their respective treatments.

SOURCE: Bandura, A., Blanchard, E. B., & Ritter, B. (1969). Relative efficacy of desensitization and modeling approaches for inducing behavioral, affective, and attitudinal changes. *Journal of Personality and Social Psychology, 13*, 183.

most powerful; it produced virtually complete removal of phobic behavior in every participant.

Snake fears have received much attention because of the symbolic sexual significance attributed to them by psychoanalytic theory (Brill, 1949). If such phobias are symbolic of an underlying psychodynamic problem (as is postulated by psychoanalytic theory), then a genuine cure of the phobia cannot be achieved without first modifying the unconscious conflicts supposedly symbolized by the phobic symptom. Many behavior therapists have eliminated these phobias directly without any exploration of their possible unconscious meanings and historical etiology to obtain enduring improvement (Lang & Lazovik, 1963). The success of such direct methods (Bandura, 1977, 1986) contradicts predictions of psychoanalytic theorists and is of considerable theoretical and practical significance (e.g., Zimmerman, 1983).

Modeling also has been used to help people overcome shyness and assert themselves more effectively when they feel they should. Assertive skills may be sought by

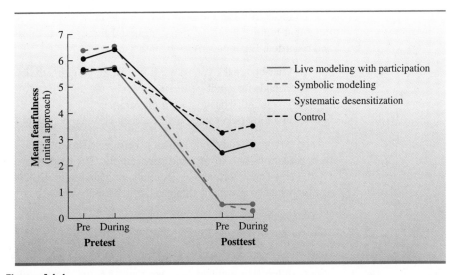

Figure 14.4
Reduction in Fear Levels after Modeling and Desensitization Treatments   Mean level of fear arousal associated with the approach responses performed before treatment and the fear levels reported in the post-treatment period for the same subset of approach responses. (*Pre* refers to the intensity of fear experienced when each snake approach response was described to participants, and *During* signifies the fear level they reported while actually performing the corresponding behavior.)

SOURCE: Bandura, A., Blanchard, E. B., & Ritter, B. (1969). Relative efficacy of desensitization and modeling approaches for inducing behavioral, affective, and attitudinal changes. *Journal of Personality and Social Psychology, 13,* 183.

anyone who wishes to be more effective with other people, whether roommates, a boss, a spouse, or a parent. People who are unable to be assertive, who cannot stand up for their rights, may not only be exploited and deprived by others but feel ineffective and incompetent and lack self-esteem. Thus, **assertiveness training** may have many positive effects on one's life. The procedure may include observation of models who assert themselves effectively. This step may be followed by role playing with the therapist and by rehearsing more assertive responses, first in safe situations and ultimately in real life when the assertive responses are needed.

Improvement in assertive behavior may be achieved by **covert modeling** as well as by observation of live models who display assertiveness. In covert modeling, unassertive individuals imagine scenes in which a model performs assertively when it is appropriate. Here is a typical scene:

> The person (model) is dining with friends in a restaurant. He (she) orders a steak, instructing the waiter that it be rare. The steak arrives and as the person cuts into it, it is apparent that something is wrong. He (she) signals the waiter, who comes to the table. The person says, "This steak is medium; I ordered it rare. Please take this back and bring me a rare one" (Adapted from Kazdin, 1974, p. 242).

To measure assertive behavior, people may be presented with interpersonal situations that require assertive responses, and their assertiveness or lack of it is observed and recorded. Examples of such situations are:

1. Your boss asks you to work late when you already have plans.
2. Friends interrupt your studying.
3. The laundry has lost your cleaning.
4. In a long ticket line outside a theater, two people cut in directly in front of you.

In a typical study, participants were asked to imagine that they were actually in these situations and to respond accordingly. The responses were recorded and judges rated them for assertiveness (McFall & Marston, 1970), thus providing a measure against which subsequent changes could be compared.

Conditioned Aversion: Making Stimuli Unattractive

While some people suffer because they have learned to react negatively to certain situations, others are plagued because they become pleasurably aroused by, or even addicted to, stimuli that most people in the culture find neutral or even aversive. One example of this problem is fetishistic behavior, in which the person may become sexually excited by such objects as undergarments. In these cases, things that are neutral or even disgusting for most people have acquired the power to produce pleasurable emotional arousal. Another example is drug addiction for which the arousal may have a significant and necessary physiological component to it. While such reactions may provide the person with some immediate pleasure, they often are severely disadvantageous in their long-term consequences for the individual. They may, for example, provoke severe guilt, negative self-reactions, and/or physical harm, as well as scorn and punishment from others, and therefore treatment is needed if the person desires change.

A positively valued stimulus may be neutralized by counterconditioning if it is presented with stimuli that evoke extremely unpleasant reactions. Gradually, as a result of repeated pairings, the previously positive stimulus acquires some of the aversive emotional properties evoked by the noxious events with which it has been associated (e.g., Okifuji et al., 1990).

An Example: Treating Cocaine Dependency

Chemical aversion therapy was used to treat cocaine addicts who volunteered to participate in a two-week study (Frawley & Smith, 1990). The stimulus used to represent cocaine was a mixture of chemicals which tasted and smelled like "street cocaine." In the treatment room, there were pictures of paraphernalia for cocaine use, as well as the utensils used to snort cocaine. The patients were instructed to "snort" the "cocaine" in their normal fashion. They then were given an injection of nausea-inducing drugs and were instructed to continue to "snort" the "cocaine." Afterwards, the patients were encouraged to focus on paraphernalia and pictures of cocaine, and to pair the cocaine use with negative consequences, all while experiencing nausea.

At six months posttreatment, more than half of the cocaine addicts had totally abstained from cocaine since the treatment. As predicted, the pairing of the nausea with the cocaine use produced a conditioned aversion for the recovering addicts and helped them break their habit. Systematic counterconditioning has also been attempted with other addictions such as alcoholism (Bandura, 1969, 1986).

Psychologists are reluctant to use **aversion therapies** like this one because they inflict aversive experiences on a troubled person. However, aversion therapies usually are attempted only after other forms of help (such as interview therapies) have been tried unsuccessfully. In some cases aversion treatments have come as a last resort in lieu of more drastic treatments, such as long imprisonment or irreversible brain surgery (Rachman & Hodgeson, 1980; Raymond, 1956). And usually they are not imposed on the client: They are voluntary and the person submits to them with full knowledge and consent.

Indeed it is this very dependence on the client's cooperation that limits the efficacy of the treatment. That is, after the initial counterconditioning trials the client often may revert to the fetish without submitting voluntarily to further treatment. Since it becomes impractical to hospitalize such people continuously or remove them from exposure to the problematic stimuli, they must learn to administer aversive stimulation to themselves whenever necessary. For example, they may be taught to administer electric shock to themselves from a small portable, battery-operated apparatus concealed in their clothing, or to induce aversive thoughts or imagery whenever the problematic urges are experienced. Thus, counterconditioning procedures ultimately provide the individual with a form of *self*-control. Whether or not people continue to practice and seek this self-control is up to them. And whether or not they practice self-control determines how effectively their new behavior will be maintained.

CHANGING BEHAVIOR BY MODIFYING THE CONSEQUENCES

Many psychologists have tried to modify maladaptive behaviors by changing the consequences to which those behaviors lead. Guided to a large extent by B. F. Skinner's ideas about learning, they try to withdraw reinforcement for undesired behavior and to make attention, approval, or other reinforcement contingent on the occurrence of more appropriate, advantageous behavior (e.g., Haring & Breen, 1992). Their basic procedure (discussed in Chapter 12 as it bears on assessment) is well illustrated in the work of Hawkins and his colleagues (1966).

Case Example: Hyperactivity

Hawkins' case was Peter, a young child of low intelligence. Peter was brought to a clinic by his mother because he was "hyperactive" and "unmanageable." Because the problems seemed to involve the relations between Peter and his mother, he was assessed and treated directly in his home. His mother served as a therapist under the guidance of the professional workers.

A first task was to specify the problematic behaviors. Direct observations of Peter in the home revealed the following problems to be among the most common and disturbing ones:

1. Biting his shirt or arm.
2. Sticking out his tongue.
3. Hitting and kicking himself, other people, or objects.
4. Using derogatory names.
5. Removing his clothing or threatening to remove it.

The frequency of these and similar behaviors was carefully recorded at 10-second intervals during one-hour observation sessions in the home. After the first assessments were completed, the mother was helped to recognize the occurrence of Peter's nine most objectionable behaviors. Whenever these occurred during subsequent one-hour sessions at home, she was taught to respond to them with definite steps. These steps involved signaling to Peter when his behavior became disruptive and, if a verbal warning failed, isolating him briefly in a separated, locked "time out" room without toys and other attractions. Release from the room (and reinstatement of play, attention, and nurturance) was contingent on Peter's terminating the tantrum and showing more reasonable, less destructive behavior. This arrangement was opposite to the one the mother may have inadvertently used in the past, when she became increasingly concerned and attentive (even if distressed) as Peter became increasingly wild. Subsequent assessment revealed that the new regimen was effective in minimizing Peter's outbursts. While apparently helpful to Peter's development, however, the modification of his tantrums may have been just one step toward the more extensive help he needed.

Using a combination of modeling and reinforcement procedures, Lovaas and his coworkers (Lovaas, Berberich, Perloff, & Schaeffer, 1966, 1991) modified the deficient speech and social behaviors of severely disturbed ("autistic") children who were unable to talk. First the therapist modeled the sounds himself. He rewarded the child only for vocalizing the modeled sounds within a specified time interval. As the child's proficiency increased the therapist proceeded to utter more complicated verbal units. Gradually training progressed from sounds to words and phrases. As the training continued, rewards from the therapist became contingent on the child's reproducing increasingly more elaborate verbalizations more skillfully (i.e., more quickly and accurately). The combination of modeling and reinforcement procedures gradually helped the child to learn more complex meanings and complicated speech. Research like this shows the value of wisely used reinforcement, but rewards also may be hazardous, as discussed in *In Focus 14.2.*

People often are judged maladjusted mainly because they have not learned how to perform the behavior patterns necessary to effectively meet the social or vocational demands they encounter. They cannot behave appropriately because they lack the skills required for successful functioning. For example, the socially deprived, economically underprivileged person may suffer because he or she never has acquired the response patterns and competencies needed to obtain success and avoid failure in school and in vocational and interpersonal situations. Similarly, the high school dropout in our culture does indeed carry an enduring handicap. Behavioral inadequacies, if widespread, may

IN FOCUS 14.2   *Rewards May Backfire*

Rewards are important for effective behavior, but they can be used unwisely. A major purpose of effective therapy (and socialization) is to wean the individual away from external controls and rewards so that his behavior becomes increasingly guided and supported by intrinsic gratifications—that is, satisfactions closely connected with the activity itself. Therefore, it is essential to use rewards or incentives only to the extent necessary to initiate and sustain prosocial (adaptive, desirable) behavior.

External incentives may be important in order to encourage a person to try activities that have not yet become attractive for him or her. When rewards are used to call attention to a good job or to an individual's competence at an activity, they may actually bolster interest. They provide positive performance feedback and supply tangible evidence of excellence (Harackiewicz, Manderlink, & Sansone, 1984). Approval and praise from parents for trying to play a violin, for example, may be helpful first steps in encouraging the child's earliest musical interest. But when the youngster begins to experience activity-generated satisfactions (for example, from playing the music itself), it becomes important to avoid excessive external rewards. Too much reward would

be unnecessary and possibly harmful, leading the child to play for the wrong reasons and making him or her prone to lose interest easily when the external rewards are reduced or stopped altogether (Lepper, Greene, & Nisbett, 1973). The same consideration would apply to the encouragement of such prosocial activities as concern for fairness, empathy, helpfulness, responsiveness to the needs of other people, and attention to the long-term consequences of one's behavior and not just to its immediate payoffs. While such sensitivities would initially be encouraged by external rewards, ultimately they should be sustained by gratification from the activities themselves.

In sum, "overjustification" of an activity by excessive external reward may interfere with the satisfactions (intrinsic interests) that would otherwise be generated by the activity itself. Excessive external rewards may even have boomerang effects and lead the recipient to devalue and resist the rewarded activity. Such resistance is especially likely in a culture that values autonomy and freedom, for any seemingly undue or exaggerated external rewards may be seen as pressures and may lead to intense, though possibly covert, resistance (Brehm, 1968).

lead to many other problems, including severe emotional distress and avoidance patterns to escape the unhappy consequences of failure and incompetence. Many special learning programs have been designed to teach people a variety of problem-solving strategies and cognitive skills (Bijou, 1965), to help rehabilitate psychotic children (Ferster & DeMyer, 1961), to assist families to cope with serious conduct disorders displayed by their children (Patterson, 1976), and to help achieve many other changes in behavior (e.g., Kamps et al., 1992; Karoly, 1980).

Stimulus Control: The Insomnia Problem

An effective way to improve performance is to bring it under **stimulus control**; that is, allow the behavior only under certain restricted conditions. The stimulus control strategy is illustrated in a treatment to help people who suffer from insomnia (Bootzin, 1973).

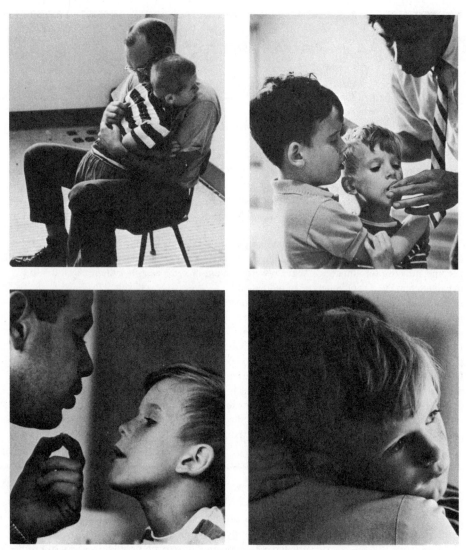

Food treats and physical comfort and affection have been used as rewards to help severely disturbed children to improve their verbal and social skills.

SOURCE: Photos courtesy of Dr. Ivor Lovaas, UCLA.

The basic reasoning was simple. Many people find it hard to sleep because the bed and bedtime have become associated for them with all sorts of activities that are incompatible with falling asleep. For example, they use bedtime to rehash the day's happenings and worry about the next day and its problems. Therefore, treatment should separate cues for such extraneous activities from cues for going to sleep. To achieve that aim, the patients were advised to follow these instructions (Bootzin, 1973; Bootzin, Epstein, & Wood, 1991):

1. Lie down intending to go to sleep only when you are sleepy.
2. Do not use your bed for anything except sleep; that is, do not read, watch television, or eat in bed. Sexual activity is the only exception to this rule. On such occasions, the instructions are to be followed afterward when you intend to go to sleep.
3. If you find yourself unable to fall asleep, get up and go into another room. Stay up as long as you wish and then return to the bedroom to sleep. Although we do not want you to watch the clock, we want you to get out of bed if you do not fall asleep immediately. Remember the goal is to associate your bed with falling asleep quickly! If you are in bed more than about ten minutes without falling asleep and have not gotten up, you are not following this instruction.
4. If you still cannot fall asleep, repeat step 3. Do this as often as is necessary throughout the night.
5. Set your alarm and get up at the same time every morning no matter how much sleep you got during the night. This will help your body acquire a consistent sleep rhythm.
6. Do not nap during the day.

These stimulus control instructions proved to be highly effective. Patients in this treatment learned to fall asleep sooner and sleep longer; they also reported feeling better on awakening (compared with a no-treatment group). Similar procedures have been applied successfully to bring many other problem behaviors under stimulus control.

Control of Internal States through Biofeedback

The work discussed so far in this chapter merely provided some selected examples from a huge area of research. In another direction are the efforts to achieve control of internal bodily responses through biofeedback and operant conditioning. Inside our bodies a multitude of internal or **visceral responses** occur without our thinking about them, including changes in the secretions of the glands, the pumping action of the heart, and the electrical waves of the brain during emotional arousal. While Western scientists were labeling the system responsible for the control of this internal environment "automatic" or "autonomic" because of its seemingly involuntary character, Eastern mystics and yogis were demonstrating a remarkable degree of control over it in their own bodies. At the start of the 20th century, British colonists reported that yogis could reduce their own metabolism while being buried alive for days and could even reduce their pulse to such an extent that their hearts seemed to have stopped. Today, instead of dismissing such reports as exaggerations or chicanery, researchers are investigating how voluntary control of visceral responses can be achieved.

One important clue came from the use of **biofeedback** techniques for the control of such voluntary activity as the practice of motor skills. In daily life, learning often is speeded and improved by feedback. After rolling a bowling ball down the alley we observe the consequences of the movements we made a moment ago. The consequences, whether a strike or a gutter ball, provide information regarding the effectiveness of our movements, and we adjust our behavior in an attempt to make a strike more likely next time. Similarly, the cook who tastes the soup and then adds some salt and the guitarist who refingers a chord to achieve the desired sound are using feedback to achieve the consequences that they desire.

What is distinctive about biofeedback is that it provides feedback from such internal sources as one's own glands, heart, blood vessels, and bioelectric brain rhythms,

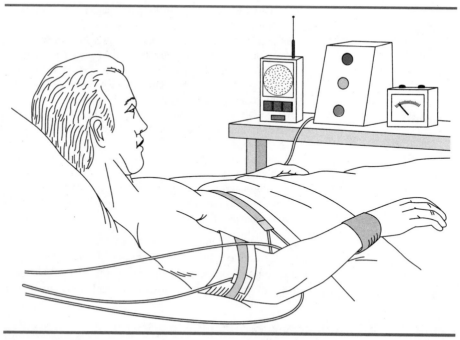

Figure 14.5
Biofeedback to Train a Patient to Control His Heart Rate   The patient watches a "traffic sign" on which red, yellow, and green lights signal how he is doing continuously as he tries to control his heart rate. On the left side of the table an intercom allows communication with the doctor. A meter (at right) shows the percentage of time the patient is mastering the task.

which we are ordinarily not aware of. We can then use this information to modify activity in the body parts themselves. The use of biofeedback in muscle relaxation provides an illustration. The activity of muscles controlled by the somatic, or voluntary, nervous system is detected, amplified, and presented through a loudspeaker. This feedback permits the individual to be aware of even the most minute tension in those muscles. When she gets such feedback information, the person can use various techniques to reduce the muscular tension. Such relaxation has proved to be useful clinically for the treatment of headaches and insomnia (Budzynski, Stoyva, & Adler, 1970; Schwartz, 1987). But this example involves muscles that are controlled by the voluntary nervous system. Can the same strategy also influence activities controlled by the autonomic nervous system, which has traditionally been assumed to be involuntary and automatic? Pioneering studies by Neal Miller (1974) and others suggest an affirmative answer.

In one study baboons were rewarded with food for increasing their blood pressure and were punished with electric shock when they failed to do so. Under these conditions the baboons were able to maintain significant elevation in their blood pressure for periods of up to 12 hours (Harris et al., 1973). Similarly, in a striking experiment with humans, six patients suffering from high blood pressure were able to reduce it when decreases in blood pressure were rewarded by money or presentations of slides of

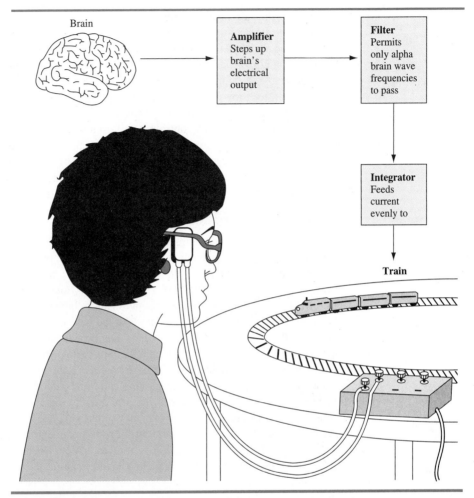

Figure 14.6
Brain Waves Control a Train: Alpha Waves for Go, Beta Waves for Stop
SOURCE: Based on Brown, B. (1975). *New mind, new body.* New York: Harper.

scenes from around the world (Schwartz, 1973). The general procedure is shown in Figure 14.5. To demonstrate that brain waves can also be controlled, a person's amplified brain wave output was hooked up to a small electric train (Brown, 1975) (see Figure 14.6). The system was designed so that alpha waves (the rhythms associated with restful, pleasant feelings) would make the train run, and beta waves (a higher-frequency, lower-amplitude pattern associated with problem solving) would bring the train to a stop. When the person is made so vividly aware of which type of brain wave he is producing, he learns to produce more alpha to keep the train running.

Visceral training has been used successfully to treat patients with abnormal heart rhythms of a type associated with sudden death (Engel & Bleecker, 1974; Weiss & Engel, 1971). In the training situation, the patient sits in front of three colored lights: green, red, and yellow. When the green light flashes, it is a signal for the patient to try to speed up the rate of his heartbeat. Red means to slow down heart rate and yellow means heart rate is in the desirable range.

First the patient learns to speed up and slow down his heart rate by a few beats per minute. This convinces him that he can actually control his heart. Next he learns to hold his heart rate within a narrow range. Heart rates that are too fast cause the red light to flash; too slow heart rates (which typically follow a too rapid rate) activate the green light. The patient learns to identify these abnormal heart rhythm sequences and to suppress them. When his control is well established, the feedback from the lights is gradually phased out by omitting it on an increasing number of trials. This procedure helps the patient to determine by himself whether or not his heart rate is correct and enables him to transfer his control from the laboratory to everyday life. Follow-up studies, which measured the patients' heart rates while they performed their normal activities, suggested that most of the nine patients who were studied retained good control of their heart rhythms even after many months.

Such results are encouraging, but whether or not the learned modifications in visceral activity can be made large enough to be valuable for the practical treatment of many serious medical disorders remains debatable. Most of the effects reported so far have been limited in magnitude and duration. The means by which the obtained modifications are achieved also remain uncertain. Some investigators believe that a learned modification of the voluntary (somatic) nervous system is at the base of all so-called autonomic learning effects. In their view, the obtained findings may be achieved in the same way that you can increase your heart rate by running up a flight of stairs or by imagining that you are about to take an important examination. Other researchers hold that such deliberate intervention is not required and that autonomic learning can occur directly. At present, various experiments can be cited to support either view. Of greatest significance is the finding that visceral responses can be changed by operant conditioning and it is hoped that such learning can be harnessed effectively in the future for the treatment of a variety of disorders. As Neal Miller (1974), a leader in this area of investigation, has urged, researchers should be bold in what they attempt but cautious in what they claim.

Finally, there are interesting and surprising parallels between the methods of biofeedback on the one hand and, on the other hand, the attempts of mystics (including those influenced by Zen, Yoga, and other "esoteric" traditions) to get into closer contact with their bodily states and internal "signals." Both strategies involve observing (monitoring) one's own inner states and changing them through some internal, and perhaps indescribable, effort. Ornstein (1972, pp. 195–196) compares the two strategies this way:

> There are, now, two major procedures available for contacting the weak signals within. In the esoteric traditions, one tries to turn off the competing activity, to turn day into night, so that the subtle signals are perceptible. In the newly developed feedback system, the "stars" are brought to consciousness by another method. The faint signals *themselves* are amplified, to make them perceptible even in the brilliance of the daylight. In the esoteric traditions, the "noise" is lessened; in biofeedback research, the "signal" is strengthened. In both cases, when these normally unconscious processes enter consciousness, we can receive this subtle information, and can learn to control what was previously an "unconscious" or "autonomic" process.

The Control of Weight

Human obesity may have biological roots that make it especially difficult for the overweight to achieve better control of their weight. While weight loss is often obtained in response to crash diets and other dietary regimes, a common problem appears to be that the weight loss is difficult to maintain: Often the dieter seems to lose much weight quickly, but six months later is back to the pre-diet weight. Regardless of the possible roots of obesity, ways are needed to help people control their own weight enduringly.

Many investigators have been searching for better techniques to help people sustain desired weight. Prospects seem best for programs that make it possible for the dieter to eat nutritious and palatable foods while gradually losing weight and maintaining the losses. Listed below are the main steps of these programs.

1. The dieter practices **self-observation,** keeping careful records and monitoring his or her own weight regularly. Daily records of the type and amount of food eaten and the events surrounding eating are important for establishing a baseline and sometimes promote weight loss just by themselves (Mahoney, 1974).
2. The dieter establishes reasonable *specific goals* for weight loss. Usually a weekly goal of between 1 and 2 pounds is realistic. The total number of pounds to be lost should also be specific. Crash diets are to be avoided because they may be harmful to health, are often unpleasant, and do not ensure that the weight will not be regained quickly.
3. The dieter practices *stimulus control,* eating in only one place and doing nothing else while eating. For example, the dieter does not watch television or read when eating (Stuart, 1967).
4. **Self-reinforcement:** The dieter rewards himself for improving eating behavior and losing weight. Friends and relatives may help by providing social reinforcement for improvement (Mahoney, 1974).
5. *Incompatible responses:* One does things that prevent inappropriate eating. When tempted to eat, for example, the dieter may go for a walk, drink water, eat only in the presence of someone who will make it embarrassing to overeat, look at the diet plan or weight charts, or think about wanting to be more attractive and not wanting to stay overweight (Rimm & Masters, 1974).
6. The dieter can reduce the attractiveness of especially troublesome foods by **self-instructions** or by imagining a scene combining the problem food with aversive images that induce nausea (Stuart, 1967).

Weight control programs of this sort have yielded some positive results, not just for immediate weight loss but for a loss (averaging about 20 pounds) sustained after a one-year follow-up (Craighead, Stunkard, & O'Brien, 1981). These investigators compared the five groups shown in Table 14.3. Subjects in all three treatment groups also received nutritional counseling (including low-calorie diets) and information about exercise.

Interestingly, the best long-term results were obtained for the group that received behavior modification only, unassisted by any appetite-suppressant drug (fenfluramine). In contrast, the group that combined the appetite-suppressant drug with

Table 14.3
Effects of Treatment on Weight Loss

Group	Weight Loss (in pounds)	
	After Treatment	After One Year
Treatments		
Behavior modification only	24.0	19.8
Drug therapy only	31.9	13.8
Combined	33.7	10.1
Controls		
Waiting list	2.9 gain	_____
Physician office visits for weight control	14.2	_____

SOURCE: Adapted from Craighead, L. W., Stunkard, A. J., & O'Brien, R. M. (1981). Behavior therapy and pharmacotherapy for obesity. *Archives of General Psychiatry, 38,* 763–768.

behavior modification lost more weight initially (almost 34 pounds), but had regained more weight after one year (see Table 14.3).

Why did those who received behavior modification without drugs maintain their weight loss best? It is plausible that these individuals attributed their weight loss more to their own efforts (compared with those who were also aided with the drug). As a result they may have developed a greater sense of self-efficacy that helped them to more enduringly withstand temptations and avoid a return to old eating habits. The people in the drug-assisted group, on the other hand, may have seen their initial weight loss as due to the medication, and when it was withdrawn, they gave in more to their renewed hunger.

More recently, weight control treatments have addressed the influence of people's thoughts and social factors on weight control. This new direction has been stimulated, in part, by research which shows that dieters relapse most often when experiencing negative emotions and/or when in interpersonal situations such as parties when the pressure to eat is high (Sperry, 1994). One successful 10-session treatment program designed by Fremoux and Heyneman (1984) incorporates the teaching of coping strategies as well as discussion of effects of mood on eating.

Therapeutic Communities

There also have been efforts to modify the behavior problems of groups of people by altering the reinforcement they get in their environment. Much of this work was conducted with hospitalized adult patients diagnosed as chronic schizophrenics (Atthowe & Krasner, 1968). Many of the patients treated in these studies were hospitalized in the first place because of severe behavioral inadequacies. Moreover, their initial inadequacy and dependency problems usually became much worse as a result of the mental hospital regime in which they lived. The hospital routine tends to "institutionalize" the patient, discouraging individuality and fostering dependency by removal of privacy, fixed daily routines for eating, medication, and cleaning, and reinforcement (by privileges and praise) for passive, docile conformity. After being institutionalized for many years under such a regime, patients tend to become progressively more deficient in interpersonal and vocational skills and increasingly dependent upon the hospital. With passing years they lose whatever contacts with family and relatives they may have had in the "outside world," and their prospects of ever achieving a life beyond the institutional shelter approach zero. Here is one comment on the typical plight of the long-term mental hospital patient:

> The great majority of patients still remain untreated. Recent statistics indicate that the median age of state mental hospital patients is approximately 65 years. This means that half of all patients in state mental hospitals are at such an advanced age that vocational opportunities are almost totally lacking and family ties have usually been broken. Even if there were nothing wrong with them, it would be difficult to discharge them into the outside world, since the outside world has no place for them. The longer these patients remain in the mental hospital, the more severe their behavioral problems seem to grow. One currently hears the phrases "hospitalism" and "institutionalization," which describe a state of apathy and lack of motivation that is acquired by a stay at a mental hospital. The hospital community is usually geared to providing the biological necessities of life, and perhaps some minimal level of recreational opportunities, but the overall relationship is a parasitic dependency in which the patient need not function in order to obtain most, if not all, of the activities or privileges that might still be of interest to him (Ayllon & Azrin, 1968, p. 3).

To help overcome this grim situation, programs with these patients have attempted to increase their independence and to help them achieve more adequate self-care and autonomy by creating a more appropriately motivating environment. Reinforcement is made contingent on their becoming more independent, first in the simplest functions, such as grooming and self-feeding and then, gradually, in more complex and interpersonal areas such as work and social relations (Ayllon & Azrin, 1965; Kennard, 1983).

Some behavior change programs minimize the role of the professional therapeutic agent as a controller of the client's behaviors. They try to transfer responsibility to the client and his or her peer group as rapidly as possible. An outstanding example is the therapeutic community designed by Fairweather to rehabilitate chronic psychotics who had been hospitalized for years. This program tried to move long-term schizophrenics out of the hospital and into a specially designed patient lodge located in the larger community as quickly as it could. Fairweather recognized that many psychotic patients who have undergone more than two years of hospitalization become "marginal men" who continue to remain in the hospital and, if discharged, are returned to the hospital within a few months (Fairweather, 1964). Therefore, he tried to develop small social systems that could function in the community itself and provide these individuals with more autonomy. He tried to organize this social system so that the members would regulate and discipline one another and share all responsibility for the step-by-step progress of their community.

To start, a group of patients was organized in the hospital and lived and worked together in a special ward. The patients were given the greatest autonomy possible over their own behavior throughout the program. They had to make increasingly complex and difficult decisions about their collective behavior, beginning with the simplest functions (for example, self-care, dressing). The entire group was held responsible for the behavior of all its members at each stage of the program and advanced through a carefully graded series of steps; each new step required new responsibilities but also

IN FOCUS 14.3   *Depression: More Than Insufficient Reinforcement*

According to one influential behavioral theory, depression may be understood as a result of a persistent lack of gratification or positive outcomes (reinforcement) for the person's own behavior (Lewinsohn, 1975; Lewinsohn, Clarke, Hops, & Andrew, 1990). That is, depressed persons feel bad and withdraw from life because their environments are consistently unresponsive to them and fail to provide enough positive consequences for what they are doing. The situation is analogous to an extinction schedule in which reinforcement for a behavior is withdrawn until gradually the behavior itself stops. In the case of the depressed person, the only reinforcement that does continue tends to be in the form of attention and sympathy from relatives and friends for the very behaviors that are maladaptive: weeping, complaining, talking about suicide. These depressive behaviors are so unpleasant that they soon alienate most people in the depressed person's environment, thus producing further isolation, lack of reinforcement, and unhappiness in a vicious cycle of increasing misery and increasing withdrawal.

Behavioral View of Depression

Depressed people, according to this theory, may suffer from three basic problems. First, they tend to find relatively few events and activities gratifying. Second, they tend to live in environments in which reinforcement is not readily available for their adaptive behaviors. For example, they may live highly isolated lives, as often happens with older people living alone, or with younger people in large universities that make them feel lost. Third, they lack the skills and are deficient in the behaviors that are needed to elicit positive reactions from other people. For example, they may be shy and socially

awkward, making gratifying relationships with others very difficult. It follows that they in turn develop feelings such as "I'm not likable," or even "I'm no good." The essentials of the theory are shown schematically in Figure 14.7.

Although the theory has not been tested conclusively, a good deal of evidence is consistent with it. For example, depressed people do seem to elicit fewer behaviors from other people and thus presumably get less social reinforcement from them. Depressed people also tend to engage in fewer pleasant activities and enjoy such events less than do nondepressed individuals (Lewinsohn, 1975).

This concept of depression immediately suggests a treatment strategy (Lewinsohn et al., 1990): Increase the rate of positive reinforcement for the depressed person's adaptive efforts. Note that such a plan would require increasing the rate of positive outcomes received by depressed people contingent on their own behavior; it does not mean simply giving more rewards regardless of what the individual does.

Role of Biochemistry and Cognition

A criticism of this theory—and of virtually all behavioral theories—is that while it makes useful points, it is incomplete. A comprehensive theory of depression needs to consider the fact that at least some types of clinical depression appear to have a biochemical and genetic basis (Klein et al., 1980; Plomin et al., 1997).

Depression, once it develops, may be maintained by different mechanisms. Research has shown that to fight depression it is important to increase depressed people's expectations that their own efforts and actions will yield positive consequences for them, thereby enhancing their involvement in life and reducing their **sense of helplessness** as well as their feelings of hopelessness

provided more privileges (such as weekend passes). Reinforcement (progress to the next step) was always contingent upon success at the earlier, prerequisite step.

Soon the group moved from the hospital to the lodge, and after a month there they began to function as a basically independent, self-sufficient organization. For example, they organized and maintained a commercial and residential janitorial and yard service

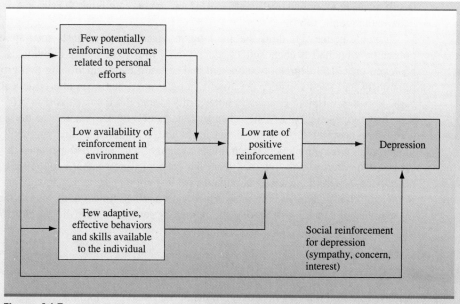

Figure 14.7
Schematic Representation of Lewinsohn's Theory of Depression
SOURCE: Based on Lewinsohn, P. M. (1975). The behavioral study and treatment of depression. In M. Hersen (Ed.), *Progress in behavior modification.* New York: Academic Press.

(Seligman et al., 1979). Once depression develops it may be maintained by different mechanisms, such as **rumination** (Nolen-Hoeksema, 1991, 1996). In a ruminative style of dealing with depression, the person focuses on the fact that he or she is depressed, on the symptoms (like fatigue and disinterest) that are experienced, and on negative consequences ("I might lose my job").

While rumination tends to amplify depression, creating even more negative thoughts and feelings, distraction from the depressed state has been shown to relieve it. Such distraction requires a "purposeful turning of one's attention away from one's symptoms of

depression and its possible causes and consequences to pleasant and neutral activities" (Nolen-Hoeksema, 1991, p. 570). These findings help to spell out some of the mechanisms through which depression may be sustained, increased, or reduced. On the whole, they are consistent with Lewinsohn's theory in focusing on the importance of increasing the person's pleasant and positive experiences. They take an important new step, however, in showing that **cognitions,** that is, what the person *thinks*, and not just what he *does*, influence what is experienced and the behaviors that follow.

employing their own members, took care of their own records, arranged their transportation, and assumed responsibility for their own living, working, and health arrangements. Consultants to the lodge were gradually replaced by nonprofessional volunteers and then slowly were withdrawn completely. In time the patients themselves fully assumed such responsible roles as nurse and work manager. Within three years all external help was withdrawn, and the ex-patients then remained together freely as an autonomous, self-sufficient group in the community (Fairweather, 1967; Fairweather et al., 1969).

It would be naïve to think that the lodge program quickly transformed these schizophrenics who had been hospitalized for years into totally new individuals. It did, however, provide a degree of competent and self-sufficient functioning to a group that previously had been considered virtually hopeless and had been utterly dependent on caretakers in a hospital. Especially noteworthy is that it did so at a cost in professional time and money that was vastly cheaper than confining the patients to the custodial care of the hospital. Ex-patients living in the lodge remained in the community much longer and were employed much more steadily than matched patients in control groups, who were simply released from the hospital (Fairweather et al., 1969). On the other hand, when the discharged patients are left without an adequate support system in the community, they often remain adrift and unable to function, as seen in the growing number of mentally ill among the homeless persons wandering on city streets in the 1990s.

Contingency Contracting

A move to enroll the person actively in his or her own behavior change program whenever possible is reflected in the use of "contingency contracting" (Rimm & Masters, 1974; Thoresen & Mahoney, 1974). An example was the treatment of "Miss X" for drug abuse as described by Boudin (1972). Miss X, a heavy user of amphetamines, made a contingency contract with her therapist. She gave him $500 (all of her money) in 10 signed checks of $50 each and committed him to send a check to the Ku Klux Klan (her least favorite organization) whenever she violated any step in a series of mutually agreed upon specific actions for curbing her drug use. After applying the contract for three months, a follow-up for a two-year period indicated that Miss X did not return to amphetamine use. The principle of contingency contracting can be extended to a wide variety of commitments in which the client explicitly authorizes the therapist to use rewards and punishments to encourage more advantageous behaviors in ways formally agreed upon in advance. While reinforcement can be used strategically in change efforts, it also has its limits (see *In Focus 14.3*).

Contracts for self-reward in which one gives oneself money for the purchase of special items and entertainment when certain goals are reached also may be used to lose weight (Mahoney, 1974; Mahoney, Moura, & Wade, 1973). A typical behavioral contract is shown in Figure 14.8. Behavior contracts can also be drawn up between the individual and persons other than the therapist.

For example, such contracts between children and parents have been effective in improving homework performance in grade school (Howard, Sweeney, & McLaughlin, 1993; Kahle & Kelley, 1994). They have also been used effectively to help delinquents and their families improve their relationships (Stuart, 1971). The responsibilities that must be fulfilled and the privileges that will be gained on fulfillment are clearly stated in the contracts (see Table 14.4). Penalties for failing to comply are determined in

Name _____ Date _____
Agreement: During the next _____ days, if I
successfully (specify desired behavior)

_____

_____

then I will reward myself with (specify reward) _____

_____.

I will be consistent in rewarding myself if I perform the
above specified behaviors and I will not reward myself
if I don't perform them. If earned, my self-reward will
be received before (date) _____.

Signature _____
Witness _____
Witness: Please contact the above person on or before
         the self-reward date to determine whether (a)
         the desired behavior was successfully
         performed, and (b) the self-reward was
         appropriately administered. Your
         encouragement of consistency and persistence
         will be appreciated.

Figure 14.8
An Example of a Behavioral Contract
SOURCE: From Mahoney, M. J., & Mahoney, K. (1976). *Weight control as a personal science.* New York: Norton.

Table 14.4
Typical Responsibilities and Privileges Used in Behavioral Contracts with Juvenile Delinquents and Their Families

Responsibilities	Privileges
School attendance	Free time
Grades	Spending money
Curfew hours	Choice of hair and dress styles
Household chores	Use of the family car
Informing parents of whereabouts	

advance and bonuses are provided for extended periods of fulfilling all responsibilities. These penalties and bonuses help to assure the child's or the adolescent's sustained participation and the family's faithfulness in keeping its promises.

TRENDS AND ISSUES

Combining Principles

In contemporary applications relevant for personality psychology, behavior therapists generally combine diverse social influence and learning methods, rather than favoring only one (e.g., Bandura, 1986). For example, to treat alcohol abuse, ingenious combinations of cognitive-behavioral therapy, social skills training, aversion therapies, covert aversion, stress management, and relaxation techniques have been developed (Ritson, 1992). Innovative treatment strategies also have been developed for social action programs and educational problems in the classroom (O'Leary & Kent, 1973). Combinations of modeling and direct reinforcement tactics have been devised for the treatment of severely disturbed autistic children (Epstein, Taubaum, & Lovaas, 1985). To treat social phobic people, a combination of modeling, desensitization, and cognitive-behavioral therapy has proven to be successful in reducing self-focused attention and consequently alleviating social phobia (Woody, Chambless, & Glass, 1997). In a similar vein, a number of learning-based methods have been synthesized in a step-by-step program of arousing experiences designed to increase sexual responsivity in nonorgasmic women (LoPicolo & Lobitz, 1972). The use of learning principles was also evident in the well-publicized program of Masters and Johnson (1970) for the treatment of sexual inadequacy in both sexes. The hallmark of all these programs is that they search for the most effective combinations of treatments possible and do not confine themselves to a single method, while still adhering to the general orientation of the behavioral approach (Kanfer & Goldstein, 1991). Table 14.5 summarizes some of the major methods that may be used in various combinations to fit the particular problem.

Community Health: Behavioral Medicine

An especially exciting direction for the combination of influence procedures is in the application of behavioral approaches to health. In particular, psychological principles are applied to improve and maintain health and well-being and to prevent disease, for example, by reducing the use of tobacco and alcohol (Taylor, Repetti, & Seeman, 1997). This approach is based on the premise that behavior and physical health are closely connected. Table 14.6 summarizes three ways in which behavior and physical disease may be linked. The specific mechanisms through which stress and illness may be linked are a special topic in their own right (discussed in Chapter 16). Examples of how health-impairing behaviors and poor reactions to illness can be improved through behavioral intervention are considered next. These efforts combine various social influence procedures to change behaviors that affect health (Krantz, Grunberg, & Baum, 1985). The new field that devotes itself to such efforts is called "behavioral medicine" or health psychology (e.g., Taylor & Brown, 1988).

Table 14.5
Summary of Some Techniques Used in Behavioral Treatment

Technique	Method	Application
Counterconditioning: desensitization and aversive conditioning	Stimuli that evoke problem responses are paired with incompatible responses.	Treatment of phobias by pairing feared stimuli (snakes, heights) with relaxation. Treatment of addictions, for example, pairing alcohol with nausea or cigarettes with thoughts of cancer.
Modeling (observation)	The client observes an individual (model) engage in the desirable behavior successfully. In participant modeling the client attempts the behavior under the guidance of the model.	For acquiring complex, novel responses in a relatively short time (as in assertiveness training) and for overcoming fear. Symbolic presentations of the model (on film) also may be useful.
Contingency management	New consequences for behavior are introduced. Reinforcement for maladaptive behavior is withdrawn and approval and other rewards are made contingent on more advantageous behavior.	Used with children and hard-to-reach hospitalized patients. Often combined with modeling in the teaching of new skills.
Self-management	Evaluative and reinforcing functions are transferred from change agents (therapists, parent, teacher) to the individual.	Enables the individual to control his own behavior with minimum external constraints and artificial inducements.

The acid test of social influence procedures is their ability to change important attitudes and behavior in real-life situations, not just in momentary laboratory demonstrations. The combination of diverse change principles is seen clearly in the new field of **behavioral medicine,** aimed at improving health self-care. One large-scale effort is trying to apply the principles of social influence for community betterment.

Table 14.6
Three Mechanisms Linking Behavior to Physical Disease

Mechanism	Examples
Direct physiological effects	Changes in body functioning due to psychological stimuli such as stress
Health-impairing habits and behavior	Smoking, excessive alcohol use, poor diet, lack of exercise, and poor hygienic habits
Reactions to illness and the sick role	Delay in seeking medical care, failure to comply with treatment or rehabilitation regimen

SOURCE: Based on Krantz, D. S., Grunberg, N. E., & Baum, A. (1985). Health psychology. *Annual Review of Psychology, 36,* 352–353.

Specifically, in 1972 a pioneering long-term field experiment intended to reduce the risk of cardiovascular disease was launched in three northern California communities (Farquhar et al., 1977). In two of these communities there were extensive mass-media campaigns using standard social influence procedures (such as giving information to change attitudes and exposure to models). In one community, face-to-face counseling was also provided for a small sample of individuals judged to be at high risk of coronary disease. Both mass-media and face-to-face instruction were aimed at modifying four of the important risk factors for cardiovascular disease: cigarette smoking, obesity, high blood pressure, and high levels of cholesterol in the blood. A third community served as a control, receiving no educational campaign.

Among the unusual aspects of the study were:

1. Participants were randomly selected from open communities, providing a better basis for generalizations about future public health education efforts.
2. The mass-media materials attempted to teach specific necessary behaviors and skills (for example, food selection and preparation) in addition to providing information aimed at changing attitudes and motives relevant to reducing the four risk factors. The mass-media campaign included about 50 television spots; over 100 radio spots; hours of television and radio programming; regular newspaper columns; advertisements; and stories, community posters, billboards, and printed matter mailed to the participants.
3. Diverse methods of social influence, attitude and behavior change, and self-control training were used in both the face-to-face instruction and the mass-media approaches.
4. Before the campaign began, participants were interviewed to determine their knowledge about the probable causes of coronary disease and the specific measures that may reduce risk (e.g., reduction of saturated fat in the diet, exercise, avoidance of cigarette smoking). The campaign was then designed to provide the specific knowledge and skills necessary to accomplish and maintain the necessary behavior changes (e.g., caloric reduction in the daily diet, reduced alcohol intake and smoking, increased physical activity).

At the end of the two years, the risk of cardiovascular disease increased in the community which had not received the educational campaign. In the two treatment communities there was a substantial and sustained decrease in risk as measured by risk-factor knowledge, saturated fat intake, cigarette use, blood pressure, and blood cholesterol levels. In the community where there was some face-to-face counseling with high-risk individuals, there was a greater increase in knowledge about coronary disease and a reduction of smoking and weight after one year. By the end of the second year, however, the decrease was similar in both treatment communities. The authors concluded, "These results strongly suggest that mass-media educational campaigns directed at entire communities may be very effective in reducing the risk of cardiovascular disease" (Farquhar et al., 1977, p. 1,192). The results also show that social influence procedures may be effectively employed for the good of the community in life-enhancing and even lifesaving ways.

Behavior therapies try to avert the need for hospitalization and the alienation it can create.

More recently, psychological principles are being used to help prevent HIV (human immunodeficiency virus) infection among college students (Fisher, Fisher, Misovich, Kimble, & Malloy, 1996). In one study, half of the participants were assigned to a control group while the other half received no intervention. The experimental intervention involved informational, motivational, and behavioral components. These included activities such as role-playing safer sex communication, learning how to put on a condom, and watching a video designed to make students aware of their personal vulnerability to HIV. Reports from the participants at least two months after the intervention indicated a significant increase in AIDS risk reduction information, relevant motivation and behavioral skills, and sustained increases in AIDS preventive behavior, such as condom use. Findings like these have served as a foundation for the growth of the field of behavioral medicine or health psychology (Taylor et al., 1997), which is devoted to applying psychology's findings and principles to improve and maintain human health and well-being.

A Caution

Behavior therapies have been criticized on many grounds for many years. It has been noted, for example, that some therapies that are at best loosely connected with learning theory claim to be derived from it, that the actual practice of behavior therapy may include many uncontrolled and unreported factors, and that learning theory itself often may be inadequate to deal with complex life phenomena (Breger & McGaugh, 1965). Moreover, the efficacy—and limitations—of particular forms of behavior modification for particular types of problems still need much more research. Too many claims for the value of behavior change strategies rest on case studies rather than on large-scale comparisons among different methods. In addition to asking, "Does it work?" about each type of change strategy, one must ask, "Does it work better than other available alternatives, how does it work, and why does it work?" (e.g., Meichenbaum, 1995).

Behavior Therapy and Ethics: Toward Self-Direction

Due to misrepresentation in the media, for many people behavior therapy or **behavior modification** has come to stand for the sinister brainwashing portrayed in fiction and movies. Behavior modification should mean no more and no less than the application of psychological principles to produce a desired change in behavior. Such applications are found in routine educational efforts of the sort common in school systems and in every attempt, explicit or implicit, to exert an influence on behavior, including in our daily relations. When you smile at some of your friend's comments and ignore or frown at others, you are modifying your friend's behavior. Obviously, psychological principles can be used ethically or unethically, effectively or absurdly, wisely or foolishly.

In addition to becoming increasingly sensitive to ethical issues, perhaps the best way for behavior therapists to avoid abuses is to emphasize *self*-control by the client rather than external control by the therapist. A focus on "power to the person" (Mahoney, 1974; Meichenbaum, 1992, 1995) means that the client chooses the therapeutic objectives and voluntarily implements the methods for achieving them. (For example, clients select their dieting goals, record their weight, and reward themselves for pounds lost.) A vital goal of behavior change methods should be to increase the individual's competence and independence as quickly as possible so that any external control by the therapist can be eliminated rapidly. Individuals who have learned to regulate and direct their own behavior will also be better equipped to resist the pressures of the environment and to pursue their desired goals even when circumstances are difficult.

In sum, probably the best way to assure that behavior therapies will not be abusive is to enroll the client actively in every step of the procedures, from the selection of goals to the implementation of each therapeutic step. The client's voluntary participation in behavior therapies may not only be ethically desirable; it may also be important for effective behavior change to be achieved at all. People who do not want their behavior changed generally can and do subvert the efforts of others who are trying to change them involuntarily.

Ideally, behavior change programs are designed to increase individuals' independence and competence as rapidly as possible so that external control of their behavior by the therapeutic regime can be reduced and ended quickly. Many techniques can help to achieve that objective and increase the person's autonomy (Bandura, 1986; Meichenbaum, 1992, 1995).

Is There Transfer? Moving into Life

Critics recognize that behavior therapy may produce alterations in the individual's specific behavior, but they question the genuineness and "depth" of such behavior modification. Their doubts seem to center on several points.

Will beneficial effects achieved in behavior therapy *transfer* or generalize to the life situations in which people must actually function on their own? Will timid persons who have practiced more assertive behaviors in the safety of the therapist's office really become more masterful on the job? Will they become more confident with the headwaiter who snubs them? Will persons who have learned to think calmly about taking tests during desensitization in the therapist's office also become calm when they must actually take examinations?

Generalization is helped to the degree that the stimulus conditions sampled in treatment are similar to those in the life situation in which the new behaviors will be used. Therefore, behavior therapists try to introduce into treatment situations that closely approximate the life situations in which behavior change is desired. For example, if a person can think calmly about public speaking but becomes upset when he tries it, treatment might teach him to speak calmly in public rather than to think about it in private. Similarly, if a person is able to take examinations effectively but devalues and derogates her own achievements, an appropriate treatment might help her to reevaluate her performance rather than to change her test-taking skills. In other words, treatment should be directed as closely and specifically as possible to the intended terminal behaviors or objectives.

Toward Community Psychology

To facilitate generalization many therapists also believe it is best if the treatment occurs in the relevant life setting rather than in an artificial one like a laboratory or a clinic. Therefore, they are bringing their treatment services into the community rather than waiting for people to be brought to mental hospitals or other institutions. (This trend has even become part of a new field within psychology called **community psychology.**) For example, just as academic learning programs for children are conducted in schools, so may social learning programs for youngsters with interpersonal problems be located in the school system itself. Similarly, if parent-child relations are problematic, it may be better to have consultants observe and help to modify the problems where they occur—in the home—rather than transport the family to a clinic. Moreover, in these settings, teachers, parents, friends, and other professionals may be enrolled to help in the treatment process (e.g., Patterson, 1976). To help a married couple, it may be more appropriate to work with their relationship directly, treating the couple together rather than each mate in isolation. There is a trend now to engage in the treatment process the people with whom the client has important daily relations, rather than rely on repeated contacts with clinics, hospitals, special agencies, and professional personnel.

A concern with community-oriented action programs and with "preventive health" of course has not been limited to advocates of behavior modification. In recent years an increasing number of psychologists, guided by many different theoretical orientations, have noted that effective programs to deal with the enormous problems of people in our society will have to go beyond the "patching and healing" of psychologically wrecked individuals. Like the individual's biological health, psychological adaptation hinges on the condition of one's personal environment. There is a psychological as well as a biological ecology, an intimate, continuous interplay of people and environment. A destructive psychological environment that submits people to excessive stress, insufficient gratification, confusing and conflicting demands, or frustrating routines can create havoc in human lives more quickly than any therapy can repair them. A satisfying life requires a satisfying environment. An adequate approach to psychological welfare will have to be concerned with prevention of problems before they become too difficult to handle and with the construction of a psychological environment in which people can live without debilitatingly twisting themselves and one another.

Symptom Substitution?

Do behavior therapies neglect the causes of the person's problematic behavior and thus leave the "roots" unchanged while modifying only the "superficial" or "symptomatic" behaviors? It is often charged that behavior therapists ignore the basic or underlying causes of problems. Advocates of behavior therapy insist that they do seek causes but that they search for *observable* causes controlling the current problem, not its historically distant antecedents nor its hypothesized but unobservable psychodynamic mechanisms. This search for observable variables and conditions controlling the behavior of interest was demonstrated most clearly in the functional analyses discussed in Chapter 13. Traditional, insight-oriented approaches have looked, instead, for historical roots in the person's past and for theoretical mechanisms in the form of psychodynamics. The difference between these two approaches thus is not that one looks for causes whereas the other does not: Both approaches search for causes but they disagree about what those causes really are.

> All analyses of behavior seek causes; the difference between social behavior and [psychodynamic] analyses is in whether current controlling causes or historically distant antecedents are invoked. Behavioral analyses seek the current variables and conditions controlling the behavior of interest. Traditional [psychodynamic] theories have looked, instead, for historical roots and developmental etiology (Mischel, 1968, p. 264).

Traditional approaches ask about their patient, "Why did she become this kind of person?" Behavioral approaches ask, "What is now causing her to behave as she does and what would have to be modified to change her behavior?"

Does a neglect in treatment of the psychodynamics hypothesized by traditional therapies produce **symptom substitution?** In spite of many initial fears about possible symptom substitution, behavior change programs of the kind discussed in the preceding sections tend to be the most effective methods presently available; the changed behaviors are not automatically replaced by other problematic ones (Bandura, 1986; Kazdin & Wilson, 1978; Lang & Lazovik, 1963; Paul, 1966; Rachman, 1967; Rachman & Wilson,

1980). On the contrary, when people are liberated from debilitating emotional reactions and defensive avoidance patterns, they generally tend to become able to function more effectively in other areas as well. As was noted years ago:

> Unfortunately, psychotherapists seem to have stressed the hypothetical dangers of only curing the symptoms, while ignoring the very real dangers of the harm that is done by not curing them (Grossberg, 1964, p. 83).

On the other hand, some enthusiastic proponents of behavior modification overlook the complexity of the client's problems. They may oversimplify the difficulties into one or two discrete phobias, when in fact the client may have many other difficulties. In that case, it would not be surprising to find that even after removal of the initial problem the individual still is beset with such other psychological troubles as self-doubts, feelings of worthlessness, and so on. Such a condition of course would imply that the person had an incomplete treatment rather than that symptom substitution had occurred. It would be extremely naïve to think that reducing Gary's public speaking anxiety, for example, would make his life free of all other problems. Whatever other difficulties he might have would still require attention in their own right.

In sum, to avoid the emergence of disadvantageous behaviors, a comprehensive program must provide the person with more adaptive ways of dealing with life; such a program may have to go beyond merely reducing the most obvious problems. Behavior modification does not automatically produce generalized positive effects that remove all the person's troubles.

Behavior Change and Self-Concept Change

Often when competence improves, so do self-reactions. Self-concepts tend to reflect the individual's actual competencies: Self-perceptions include the information that we get about the adequacy of our own behaviors. The individual who learns to perform more competently achieves more gratification and is also likely to develop more positive attitudes toward himself or herself. As a result of being able to overcome fears and anxieties, one should also become more confident. Reducing Gary's fears of public speaking would not be a cure-all, but it might certainly help him to feel more positively about himself and would open alternatives (for example, in his career opportunities) otherwise closed to him. But while this is often true, it does not always happen. Indeed critics of behavior therapy note that people may suffer not because their behavior is inadequate but because they evaluate it improperly. That is, some people have problems with distorted self-concepts more than with performance.

Behavior theorists consider such self-concept problems to be just as much behavior problems as any other difficulties; in these cases, the behaviors are self-evaluation and self-labeling. Often a person labels himself and reacts to his own behaviors very differently than do the people around him and the rest of society. An esteemed financier, for example, may receive the rewards and praise of society while he is privately unhappy enough to commit suicide. Or a popular student who is the prom queen of her school might have secret doubts about her sexual adequacy and femininity and might be torturing herself with these fears.

Thus, many personal problems involve inappropriate self-evaluations and self-reactions. In these cases the difficulty often may be the person's appraisal of his or her performances and attributes rather than their actual quality and competence level. For example, a student may react self-punitively to his scholastic achievements even when their objective quality is high. The student who is badly upset with himself for an occasional "low A" may need help with self-assessment rather than with school work. From the viewpoint of behavior theory, such problems should be treatable by the same learning principles used to change any other type of behavior.

The Trend to Cognitive Behavior Therapies

A clear trend has occurred in behavioral approaches designed to change people's problematic behavior: During the 1980s many behavior therapies became more cognitive.

Dissatisfactions with Behavior Modification.

Although behavior therapists wanted to treat specific, clearly definable behaviors, such as concrete fears, fetishes, speech problems, sexual handicaps, and motivational deficits, they were soon confronted with the fact that many people suffer from much more diffuse problems.

A person may complain, for example, of an "identity crisis," "feeling miserable," "wasting my life," or may even say, "I hate my personality" or "I am lost—I just don't know what's wrong." People tend to conceptualize themselves in psychological terms rather than in highly specific behavioral descriptions. When a person begins to describe herself, she may say, "I am too timid" or "I'm scared of meeting people"; she probably will not say, "My heart rate seems to increase sharply and I feel dizzy and start to stutter when I have to address a group of strangers in a new situation, especially in a social setting." Thus, while in some cases specific treatment objectives are evident (as when a person is terrified of flying), in many cases it is difficult to specify just what requires treatment, and one must look beyond concrete behavioral difficulties (Mahoney, 1974) to more complex concepts and mental activities (e.g., Meichenbaum, 1995; Rachman, 1996).

In their early efforts to treat complex problems, behaviorally oriented therapists tried to keep the focus directly on specific behavior. If a person described himself as, for example, "depressed," the clinician would explore with him just when he felt depression and when he did not. To specify examples or behavioral referents for depression, the clinician inquired into just what happened when the client felt more depressed and less depressed and the changes that occurred when he experienced the depression. This specific assessment focus was an extremely important step because it allowed a much clearer definition of the problems experienced in their contexts.

With increasing therapy experience, however, even behaviorally oriented clinicians began to suggest specific behaviors, such as not doing enough pleasurable activities to allow positive feelings to occur. In addition, they also tended to employ dysfunctional cognitive strategies for interpreting and explaining their experience, for example, blaming themselves for the bad events that befell them but not crediting themselves with the good events and with their own achievements (Beck, 1976; Seligman, 1990). These poor cognitive strategies call for cognitive therapies that help the person to interpret experiences differently (Meichenbaum, 1995), as discussed in Chapter 16.

The Role of Cognition in Behavior Therapy.

Behavior therapists began to become more cognitive—that is, to pay attention to how people process information, think, and interpret their experience—when they saw that these cognitive processes seriously influenced their therapeutic efforts. For example, they found that patients with panic disorders could control their panic attacks more effectively when their treatment went beyond systematic muscle relaxation and included cognitive therapy to alter how they think about the problem (Craske, Brown, & Barlow, 1991). Likewise, the types of thinking in which people engage habitually (for example, whether they tend to think in extremes) is related to indices of their health (e.g., Pennebaker et al., 1990). Behavior therapists also have included the self-expression of thoughts and feelings in their therapies for such problems as traumatic anxiety after such experiences as rape. For example, they learned that the opportunity to self-disclose deeply troubling thoughts and feelings helped victims of traumas (such as Holocaust survivors) to enjoy better long-term health (Pennebaker, Barger, & Tiebout, 1989).

Theoretically, it also became clear that behavior change itself can produce insight. Thus, when people's behavior changes significantly and they become capable of new ways of relating, they also may think differently about themselves and see themselves in new ways (Arkowitz, 1989). Changes in behavior can generate new insights, feelings, and perceptions which in turn lead to new behavior in a cycle of therapeutic effects that the treatment program needs to consider and harness effectively.

Behavior Therapies Become Cognitive.

The shift in behavior therapies to emphasize cognitive processes is seen in the development of highly influential forms of behaviorally oriented treatment that are explicitly cognitive in their approach both conceptually and technically. The cognitive trend is reflected even in their labels, for example, Aaron Beck's "cognitive restructuring" and Albert Ellis's "rational emotive therapy" (see Chapter 16).

Because so many current behavioral approaches in clinical psychology and therapy have become cognitive, their more accurate new name within the profession is **cognitive behavioral therapy,** or CBT. Donald Meichenbaum (1995, p. 141), a CBT leader, describes how cognitive-behavioral therapists challenged the earlier behaviorists this way:

Donald
Meichenbaum

> They [cognitive-behavioral therapists] questioned the tenets of classical learning theories and psychoanalytic formulations, and caused the field to question how best to conceptualize the clients' thoughts and feelings. Moreover, they raised questions of how the clients' thoughts influence and, in turn, are

Table 14.7
Some Reasons for the Growth of Cognitive Behavior Therapy

Recognition of problems that go beyond specific behaviors (e.g., career conflict, depression).

Need to help people interpret and construe experiences constructively.

Need to address affect (feelings and emotions) as well as action.

Need to deal with interactions between thoughts, feelings, and action.

Need to use and combine diverse methods and concepts that prove useful.

influenced by their feelings, behaviors, resultant consequences, and physiological processes. They emphasized that individuals not only respond to their environments but are also the architects of those environments.

Within the past four decades, the cognitive-behavioral model has evolved into a prominent force in psychology (Dobson & Craig, 1996). CBT is currently used to treat conditions such as depression, anxiety, phobias, obsessional disorders, aggression, and hypochondriasis (Kendall & Panichelli-Mindel, 1995; Rachman, 1996). Its growth reflects many changes and has many reasons, as summarized in Table 14.7.

Although conceptually and historically CBT is rooted deeply within behavioral approaches, it also was influenced importantly by other contributions and has taken on a distinctive quality. In this book, therefore, it is elaborated further within Part VI, "Social Cognitive-Affective Approaches." There you will see its links both to its behavioral roots and to other developments that seem to be transforming the field of personality psychology (e.g., Chapter 16).

SUMMARY

1. Behavior therapies attempt to modify disadvantageous behavior directly by planned relearning experiences and by rearranging stimulus conditions.

2. Systematic desensitization is used to help people overcome fears or anxieties. In this procedure, the individual is exposed cognitively (i.e., in imagination) to increasingly severe samples of aversive or fear-arousing stimuli; simultaneously she is helped to make responses incompatible with anxiety, such as muscle relaxation. Gradually the anxiety evoked by the aversive stimulus is reduced and the stimulus is neutralized.

3. Just as strong emotional reactions may be acquired by observing the reactions of models, so may

they be modified by observing models who display more appropriate reactions. In addition to modeling fearless behavior, the model also may guide the phobic person directly to behave more bravely when faced with the anxiety-producing stimulus.

4. It is possible to neutralize a positive arousing stimulus (for example, cocaine for a cocaine addict) by repeatedly pairing it with one that is very aversive (for example, chemically induced nausea). Periodic follow-up treatments help to sustain the new emotional reactions.

5. Maladaptive behaviors also may be modified by changing the consequences to which they lead. The basic procedure is to withdraw attention, approval, or other positive consequences from the maladaptive behavior and to make rewards contingent instead on the occurrence of more advantageous behavior. First, the naturally occurring response-reinforcement contingencies are identified, then new and more advantageous response-reinforcement relations are instituted.

6. In some of the newest behavior change programs, responsibility is transferred as quickly as possible from the therapist to the client and his peer group. In one therapeutic community, chronic psychotics who had been hospitalized for many years were organized on a special ward. Their autonomy was gradually increased, and their rewards were made contingent on their increasingly responsible self-management as a group.

7. A promising theory of depression suggests that the misery of depressed people reflects insufficient gratification from the environment for their own behavior. Depressed people are caught in a vicious cycle of lack of reinforcement for their own efforts, leading to greater withdrawal from other people and, in turn, increased depression.

8. In everyday life, as well as in psychotherapy, several different forms of behavior therapy may occur simultaneously. Current behavior therapies often combine several learning strategies, such as modeling, desensitization, and direct reward, rather than confining themselves to one.

9. There is much controversy with regard to the depth and endurance of behavior change. Some of the most important questions concern transfer of gains to life situations, the capacity of the individual for self-control independent of the therapeutic regime, the possibility of symptom substitution, and the adequacy of behavior change techniques to deal with a person's self-concepts. Basically, these questions ask whether behavior change entails genuine, durable change—that is, basic personality change—or whether it is restricted to relatively minor, specific behaviors that have limited applicability to major life problems.

10. To facilitate transfer from treatment to life, one introduces into treatment stimulus conditions that are as similar as possible to the life situations in which the new behaviors will be used. Treatment samples the relevant situations and occurs in the same life setting in which improvement is desired. New behavior change methods encourage self-management so that individuals may gain relative independence and control of their own behavior as rapidly as possible.

11. Many learning programs to eliminate maladaptive behaviors have shown promising results. The modified behaviors are not automatically replaced by other problematic ones; there is more evidence for positive generalization than for symptom substitution, although the theoretical issues are complex. Behavior theories contend that people are what they do. Therefore, behavior change is the prerequisite for any alteration in personality.

12. Many behavior therapies are becoming more cognitive and pay greater attention to how clients think, interpret, and perceive. These cognitive behavioral therapies are discussed further in Part VI.

Summary Evaluation

PART V

Behavioral Approaches

It is time to pause to summarize and evaluate the main ideas that have been discussed in the chapters devoted to the behavioral approaches.

OVERVIEW

The next table summarizes the main characteristics of the behavioral approaches. The table condenses points from both the more traditional behavioral and the newer, more cognitive social learning versions of these approaches.

As the table indicates, the approaches focus on the individual's behavior in its context. Prior learning, expectations, and cues in the situation are seen as important determinants of behavior. Preferred data consist of direct observations of behavior as it changes in relation to changing situations. Responses are used as samples of behavior, not as indirect indicators of hypothesized but not directly observable inner states, motives, or traits. Research seeks to analyze the conditions that influence or control the behavior of interest, including the conditions that allow persons to enhance their "self-control" (for example, by rearranging their environments).

To change the person's behavior, therapy is directed at identifying and modifying the consequences behavior produces or the expected outcomes associated with it. The situation is treated as an integral aspect of behavior; it provides cues and outcomes that impact the maintenance and modification of behavior.

CONTRIBUTIONS AND LIMITATIONS

Early efforts to apply concepts from learning theories to personality relied on "stimulus-response" formulations that came from laboratory research on simple learning with animals. These efforts drew mostly on the principles of classical and operant conditioning, discussed in Chapter 12. Many psychologists recognized that these principles might be useful for treatment of at least some human behavioral problems, such as specific fears. Most psychologists, however, were concerned that the early behavioral work was based largely on studies with animals constrained in artificial laboratory situations. Elegant experiments were done on the behavior of rats running in mazes and of pigeons pecking on levers as food pellets dropped down. But how could one extend the results from

Summary Overview of Behavioral Approaches

Basic units:	Behavior-in-situation
Causes of behavior:	Prior learning, expectations, and cues in situation (including the behavior of others)
Behavioral manifestations of personality:	Stable behavior equated with personality
Favored data:	Direct observations of behavior in the target situation
Observed responses used as:	Behavior samples
Research focus:	Behavior change; analysis of conditions controlling behavior; self-control
Approach to personality change:	By changing conditions; by experiences that modify behavior
Role of situation:	Extremely important; regulates much behavior

these studies meaningfully to the complex lives of people under the often unpredictable social conditions of real life?

Critics severely attacked early behaviorism as far too simplistic to permit a reasonable account of such everyday human behavior as language (e.g., Chomsky, 1965; Neisser, 1976). If the early behavioral conceptions could not deal adequately with how people talked and thought—and they could not—then how could they possibly address the complex phenomena of personality?

At the same time (before the 1970s), most clinicians saw behavioral concepts as too superficial and even dangerous to be applied usefully to troubled people. Partially in response to these challenges, behaviorally oriented workers attempted some applications of their ideas and methods with human subjects. They began in the past two decades to treat some of the most difficult behavioral problems that had resisted other forms of therapy. For example, they were allowed to try to treat hospitalized people who were so severely disturbed that there was little to lose by attempting experimental

Summary Evaluation of Behavioral Approaches

Contributions	Limitations
Concepts based on principles of general psychology; benefits from basic research on learning and conditioning	Concepts not integrated into a distinctive, comprehensive, systematic theory of personality
Methods based on experimental psychology and behavior analysis; allow rigorous testing of concepts and the efficacy of treatments	Neglect of problems that do not lend themselves to study by available methods
Systematic development of principles for behavior change; useful for behavior change	Insufficient attention to stable characteristics that resist change
Focus on observable behavior and the psychological environment	Insufficient attention to genetic and biochemical causes

innovations with them after other available methods had proved to be unsuccessful. You saw many examples of these applications in the treatment and assessment of disturbed mental patients in Chapters 13 and 14. Some impressive studies of effective human behavior change emerged and gained some credibility as possible treatment methods (e.g., Krasner & Ullmann, 1973; Ullmann & Krasner, 1969). The systematic rigor of the work was widely appreciated, but severe doubts remained about the relevance of the approach for understanding personality and complex social behavior (e.g., Pinker, 1997).

Some critics appreciate the contributions of behavioral approaches for applied purposes but still fault them for overemphasizing the "stimulus" or "situation." They view this overemphasis as part of a "situationism in psychology" that erroneously minimizes the importance of dispositional or intrapsychic determinants such as traits (Bowers, 1973; Carlson, 1971). On the other hand, a great deal of research in recent years has again demonstrated the power of stimuli to trigger automatically all sorts of cognitive, emotional, and behavioral reactions and has questioned the importance of the person's consciousness or internal thought processes (e.g., Bargh, 1996).

One of the persistent concerns about behavioral approaches is whether they really contribute to an understanding of the phenomena of interest to personality psychologists. Do they merely translate those phenomena into the language of learning, cognition, and general psychology, or do they help clarify and explain them? Do they even deal with them? An early worry about behavioral approaches was that they did not even try to study complex and distinctively human qualities. Indeed some critics charged that behavioral psychologists only study what is easy to study with available methods rather than turn to study what is worth studying.

Sharing these same concerns, a number of theorists began to make learning and behavior theories more "social." They preferred to study complex social learning rather than simple animal response (e.g., Bandura, 1986, 1969; Bandura & Walters, 1963; Mischel, 1968; Rotter, 1954). They drew on a wide range of phenomena and principles. Although they remained committed to the understanding and analysis of behavior from the perspective of learning theory, they tried to develop a more comprehensive, yet rigorous approach to personality.

They did not limit themselves to simple reinforcement principles and increasingly relied on mental or "cognitive" processes in their account of the development of all complex social behaviors (e.g., Bandura, 1977; Mischel, 1973). They increasingly used such cognitive concepts as "observational learning," expectancies, values, and even "self" in their theorizing, their research, and their applications to the point where they became part of a broader, new approach, which is the focus of Part VI. The early forms of behavioral approaches were criticized as too narrow; the later forms tend to seek greater breadth and to integrate a variety of concepts from many areas of psychology into a larger framework (e.g., Bandura, 1986), as will be seen in Part VI.

Behavior Theory and Existentialism: Unexpected Similarities

Psychological theories sometimes have unexpected similarities. The behavioral approaches involve a focus on what the person is doing in the here and now, rather than on reconstructions of personal history and a reluctance to hypothesize drives, forces, motives, and other psychic dispositions as explanations. All these features, surprisingly, are not unique to a behavioral position. They just as fully seem to describe the platform of some existentially oriented and phenomenological psychologists (Chapter 10). Thus, the behavioral focus on what the person is doing, rather than on attributes or motives, also fits the existential doctrine. As Sartre put it, "existence precedes essence." He meant by that phrase that

> . . . man first of all exists, encounters himself, surges up in the world—and defines himself afterwards. If man as the existentialist sees him is not definable, it is because to begin with he is nothing. He will not be anything until later, and then he will be what he makes of himself. Thus, there is no human nature. . . . Man simply is (Sartre, 1965, p. 28).

A rejection of preconceptions about motives, traits, and the content of human nature is hardly unique to behavior theorists. George Kelly in his personal construct theory (Chapter 10) meant something similar when he said, "I am what I do," and urged that to know what one is one must look at what one does.

Behavior theories also share with phenomenological theories the belief that it is impossible to conceptualize people apart from the context or environment (the "field") in which they exist. The possible compatibility between modern behavior theory and the existential-phenomenological orientation seems to hinge on several common qualities. Both share a focus on the here and now and a reluctance to posit specific motivational and trait constructs. Both emphasize what the person is doing—"where he is at"—rather than the constructs of the psychologist who studies him. Both share a lack of interest in distant historical reconstruction and a concern with new action possibilities for the individual. These commonalities are impressive.

The overlap between the behavioral and existential-phenomenological orientation seems intriguing, especially because historically the latter developed in part as a protest against early behavioral approaches. However, the two positions may have one critical incompatibility. The existentialist takes the philosophical position that the individual is responsible and attributes to him or her the ultimate causes of behavior. In Sartre's phrase, a person "is what he wills to be" (1956, p. 291). Though a behavior theorist may share Sartre's desire to put "every man in possession of himself," rather than allow him to be possessed by psychic forces, a behavioral analysis of causation cannot begin with the person's will as the fundamental cause of what he does, nor can it end with his constructs as a final explanation of his behavior.

George Kelly (personal communication, 1965) once emphasized his belief that personal constructs are the basic units and that it is personal constructs, rather than stimuli, that determine behavior. He recalled vividly from his Navy experience during World War II how very differently he related to the same officer on different occasions depending on how, at the time, he construed that officer. He remembered that the captain seemed different to him in an informal role, chatting with his jacket off, from the way he seemed when he wore his officer's coat. "You see," Kelly said, "it is not the stimulus—the captain—but how I construed him that channelized my reactions to him."

But a behavior theorist would find this story an excellent example not of "construct control," but of "stimulus control": With his four stripes on, you see the captain one way; without his four stripes, you see him differently. To understand the construct change, in the behavioral view, you have to include in your understanding how those four stripes came to control it.

The phenomenological and behavioral positions differ in their focus of attention: The former seeks to know and understand the person's experience; the behaviorally oriented psychologist wants to clarify the conditions that control the ultimate behavior, including the events that control constructs, cognitions, and feelings.

The Trend to Cognitive Therapies and Cognitive Behavior Theories

One step in this direction is the gradual but unmistakable growth of behaviorally oriented therapies that take account of the client's cognitive processes. These "cognitive behavioral therapies" or, simply, "cognitive therapies" (see Chapter 16) focus on the client's personal constructs, assumptions, expectancies, and perceptions, on how experiences are anticipated, interpreted, and explained, and on the impact of these cognitions on behavior and personal coping strategies (e.g., Meichenbaum 1993, 1995). In the 1980s these developments in therapy methods and theories also were accompanied by greater reliance on cognitive processes in behavior theories concerned with the development and modification of complex social behavior (e.g., Bandura, 1986). These theories became cognitive in their orientation to the extent that they now best fit in the context of the "cognitive social approaches" which are the subject of Part VI, considered next.

Is a reasonable synthesis of phenomenological psychology and social learning theory possible? Perhaps. Such a synthesis would require the ability to view people both as active construers who perceive, interpret, and influence the environment and themselves and continuously respond to the conditions of their lives.

Part **VI**

Social Cognitive-Affective Approaches

Social Cognitive-Affective Conceptions

A new perspective on personality has emerged in the past two decades under the label **social cognitive theories** (Bandura, 1986; Cantor, 1990; Cantor & Kihlstrom, 1987; Dweck, 1990; Higgins, 1990; Markus, 1977; Mischel, 1973, 1990). These authors all use the terms *cognitive* and *social,* although some reverse the sequence of the two terms while others include either *learning* or *motivational* as a third word in the phrase. But they are united in their belief that conceptions of personality must view persons both as cognitive and as social beings. They all try to understand the cognitive processes and mental structures that underlie individual differences. And they define individual differences in terms of meaningful, personally relevant patterns of thought, judgment, emotion, and social behavior. This still-evolving approach seeks an increasingly comprehensive account of diverse findings from research on personality and social behavior accumulating for many years (Bandura, 1969; Mischel, 1968, 1973, 1990; Neisser, 1967).

This chapter discusses the development and emergence of this approach. It then provides an overview of its most recent and systematic version, a **Cognitive-Affective Personality System (CAPS)** theory (Mischel & Shoda, 1995, 1998). CAPS theory extends the social cognitive approach to encompass affect and emotion. Its goal is to understand both the nature of individual differences and the social cognitive and affective (emotional) processes or dynamics that underlie them. Thus, it addresses within one framework both the dynamic processes that characterize a given person and the personality dispositions on which individuals differ distinctively in stable ways.

The aim of CAPS theory is to help make personality psychology a genuinely **cumulative science** that builds on its best findings and concepts and integrates them into a unifying general framework. It therefore deliberately is not limited to the insights of any one theory or approach but instead draws on the most solid findings and concepts available from a century of personality theory building and research—findings and concepts reviewed in all the preceding chapters. Later chapters in this part of the text illustrate the basic principles and methods of this approach with research and case study examples.

DEVELOPMENT OF THE SOCIAL COGNITIVE-AFFECTIVE PERSPECTIVE

For more than three decades, psychology has experienced a cognitive revolution that has made the mind and how it works the focus of the field (Bruner, 1957; Chomsky,

1965; Neisser, 1967; Piaget, 1932). Discoveries about how people think and how they selectively attend to, manipulate, store, and generate information have made it clear that any comprehensive psychological theory of complex human behavior must give cognition a central role. The cognitive revolution also has spread to increasingly influence the conceptualizations and strategies of personality psychologists (Bandura, 1986; Mischel, 1973, 1990), clinical psychologists (Arkowitz, 1989; Beck, 1976; Seligman, 1990), and social psychologists (Flavell & Ross, 1981; Higgins, 1987; Higgins & Kruglanski, 1996; Ross & Nisbett, 1991).

Historical Roots

The social cognitive approach to personality began in the late 1960s and was conceived by many psychologists who were in rebellion, frustrated by the limitations of earlier theories when they tried to use them to understand and study personality. At that time the field of personality was divided into three theoretical camps. In one were enthusiastic Freudians guarding Freud's original work against anyone who sought to revise or criticize it. In a second camp were students of individual differences searching for broad personality trait dimensions. In the third camp were radical behaviorists concerned only with stimuli and responses, not with the internal ways an organism mediates between them. This third camp opposed any constructs that invoked the mind or mental activity in any form that could not be directly or simply measured, as in a count of how often a specific motor act occurred. Except for occasional exchanges to attack each others' work, there was little communication among the camps. It was a milieu unresponsive to any "constructive alternatives."

You have already seen one protest movement in response to this state of affairs in the humanistically oriented ideas developed within the phenomenological approach by psychologists such as Carl Rogers and George Kelly. But these voices were treated more as a sideline protest movement than as a route for redirecting mainstream theory and research. Major disturbances were needed in that mainstream before serious attention would be paid to possible alternatives, and they occurred in the late 1960s.

The 1968 Challenge

Personality psychologists for many years had searched for evidence to document the breadth and power of global personality traits and psychodynamics. In the late 1960s, a number of them began to recognize that these efforts consistently yielded disappointing results (Mischel, 1968; Peterson, 1968; Vernon, 1964). Mischel (1968) in particular reviewed research that showed that what people do depends to a surprising degree on the particular situation and context. For example, the person who seems conscientious about work may show a very different pattern with family, as was discussed in Part III. Thus, Mischel and his colleagues sharply questioned the value of broad trait scores for predicting what a given person will do in different kinds of situations and for explaining the seeming inconsistency or variability that was observed across those situations.

Mischel (1968) also reviewed research that led to equally skeptical conclusions about the usefulness of the traditional trait and psychodynamic perspectives for assessing and treating troubled individuals. These methods simply did not seem effective or efficient for dealing with the formidable psychological problems that millions of people faced daily—problems with which they seemed unable to cope without more efficacious and readily available forms of help (Bandura, 1969; Mischel, 1968, 1990).

Cognitive Processes Underlying Behavior: Limitations of the Behavioral Perspective

To try to overcome these problems, some personality psychologists committed themselves to modernizing and reinvigorating trait psychology (e.g., Funder, 1991), as reviewed in earlier chapters. Others, however, were drawn to the behavioral perspective, attracted by its rigorous scientific emphasis (Bandura, 1969; Mischel, 1968; Rotter, 1954), as discussed in Part V. In their theorizing, they drew heavily on principles of learning established originally in experimental work with animals, as in the operant and classical conditioning studies (reviewed in Chapter 13). Nevertheless, much as they tried to stretch existing behavioral concepts, these personality psychologists encountered more and more new research findings that forced a change in their view and required moving beyond behaviorism.

The Role of Awareness and Information in Learning and Conditioning

Evidence accumulated that often the person's private expectations and hypotheses about what is happening turned out to influence his or her actions much more than did the external reinforcements in the situation. For example, if you are aware of the consequences to which your responses will lead, you learn better and faster (Bandura, 1969). (See *In Focus 15.1*.)

Cognition plays a role even in classical conditioning. Suppose, for example, that a person has been conditioned in an experiment to fear a light because it is repeatedly paired with electric shock. Now if the experimenter simply informs her that the light (the conditioned stimulus) will not be connected again with the electric shock, her emotional reactions to it can quickly extinguish (Bandura, 1969). On later trials, she can see the light without becoming aroused. Findings like these forced both researchers and behavior therapists to pay more attention to the individual's mental processes, understanding, and knowledge. In the development of therapeutic methods to change behavior, they began to more directly engage the person's thought processes and mental activities for therapeutic ends (Davison & Neale, 1990).

Cognitive Transformations: Changing the Impact of the Stimulus through Mental Operations

Although behavioral approaches assert that stimuli control behavior, in fact the perceiver's mental representations and **cognitive transformations** of the stimuli can

IN FOCUS 15.1   *Rethinking Conditioning*

Operant Conditioning and "Shaping" Re-examined

In behavioristic research on verbal operant conditioning, an experimenter typically would give "social reinforcement" (saying "Mmm-hmm") to college students for certain utterances, for example, when they said human nouns (i.e., "girl") in a word-naming task, in order to condition them to say more human nouns. The goal was to demonstrate the power of conditioning without the person's awareness. In time it was found that the so-called conditioning effect actually depended on the subject's awareness of what the experimenter was trying to do. Those people who became aware of the contingency (i.e., guessed correctly that sounds of approval from the experimenter depended on their saying human nouns) greatly increased their use of these words (DeNike, 1964), whereas those who remained unaware of the contingency showed no more conditioning than those in a control group who were given "Mmm-hmms" randomly for 10% of their responses. Most interesting, the students showed no appreciable improvement in their performance until they correctly discerned the contingency for reinforcement; as soon as they became aware of the contingency, they gave dramatically more human nouns. Results like these suggested that the reinforcers may have

been providing little more than information to tell subjects what they are supposed to do in an ambiguous situation and pointed to the importance of cognition in human learning.

Rules and Symbolic Processes

Thus, people did not seem to need trial-by-trial "shaping" but rather seemed to be helped most by the rules and self-instructions they used to link discrete bits of information meaningfully to learn and remember materials (Anderson & Bower, 1973). Likewise, studies with children indicated that it helps not only to reward appropriate behavior but also to specify the relevant underlying rules and principles so that children can more readily learn the standards that they are supposed to adopt (Aronfreed, 1966). When children understand that particular performance patterns are considered good and that others are unsatisfactory, they adopt the appropriate standards more easily than when there are no clear verbal rules (Liebert & Allen, 1967). Beginning early in life, the young child is an active thinker and perceiver who forms theories about the world, not a passive learner shaped by external rewards (Bruner, 1957; Flavell & Ross, 1981).

determine and even reverse their impact. Such transformations were illustrated in research on the determinants of how long preschool children will actually sit still alone in a chair waiting for a preferred but delayed outcome that they face (e.g., tempting pretzels or marshmallows) before they signal with a bell to terminate the waiting period and settle for a less preferred but immediately available gratification (Mischel, Ebbesen, & Zeiss, 1972). How long children voluntarily continue to delay depends importantly on how they represent the rewards mentally and selectively attend to different features of the situation (Mischel, 1974; Mischel et al., 1989; Mischel et al., 1996).

For example, if the young child is left during the waiting period with the actual desired objects—the pretzels, for example—in front of him, it becomes extremely difficult for him to wait for more than a few moments. If the child focuses cognitively on the consummatory qualities of the reward objects, such as their salty, crunchy taste, he tends to be able to wait only a short time. But through self-instructions he can cognitively transform the objects in ways that permit him to wait for long periods of time. If he cognitively transforms the stimulus, for example, by thinking about the stick pretzels he wants now as little logs or by thinking about the marshmallows as round white clouds or as cotton balls, he may wait much longer than the graduate student experimenters who test him. Through self-instructions the children can easily transform the real objects in front of them into a "color picture in your head," or they can transform the picture of the objects (presented on a slide projected on a screen in front of them) into the "real" objects by imagining that they are actually there on a plate in front of them (Mischel, 1974; Mischel et al., 1989).

The results indicated that what is in the children's heads—not what is physically in front of them—determines their ability to delay. Through self-instructions (cued before the child begins to wait) about what to imagine during the delay period, it is possible to completely alter (indeed, to reverse) the effects of the physically present temptations in the situation. Thus, children can cognitively control their delay behavior, purposefully transforming the meaning and impact of stimuli in the situation (for example, by self-instruction) to overcome the "pull" of temptations.

New Directions

These sorts of findings suggested that a more cognitive approach to personality was required that takes into account how the individual characteristically deals mentally and emotionally with experiences (see Cervone, 1991; Higgins & Kruglanski, 1996; Pervin, 1990). The search began for a theory of the cognitive-emotional-motivational processes that underlie the person's characteristic behavior—a theory that respects the complexity of the human mind and its often contrary, conflictful behavioral expressions. As such, these efforts are in the tradition pioneered by Sigmund Freud and George Kelly, advanced over the century by many theorists reviewed in earlier chapters. Growing out of these contributions, a unifying framework has emerged (articulated in Mischel & Shoda, 1995, 1998), called the Cognitive-Affective Personality System (CAPS) theory.

COGNITIVE-AFFECTIVE UNITS (PERSON VARIABLES)

The first assumption of CAPS theory is that individuals differ in the **chronic accessibility,** that is, the ease with which particular cognitive-affective units or internal mental representations become activated or "come to mind." These **cognitive-affective units (CAUs)** refer to the mental-emotional representations—the cognitions and affects or feelings—that are available to the person. Such units were conceptualized initially in terms of five relatively stable **person variables** on which individuals differ (Mischel, 1973). Over the years, these units have been modified and refined by research (reviewed in Mischel & Shoda, 1995; Mischel et al., 1996) and are summarized in Table 15.1.

Table 15.1
Types of Cognitive-Affective Units in the Personality System

1. ENCODINGS: Categories (constructs) for the self, people, events, and the situations (external and internal experience)

2. EXPECTANCIES AND BELIEFS: About the social world, about outcomes for behavior in particular situations, about self-efficacy, about the self

3. AFFECTS: Feelings, emotions, and affective responses (including physiological reactions)

4. GOALS AND VALUES: Desirable outcomes and affective states; aversive outcomes and affective states; goals, values, and life projects

5. COMPETENCIES AND SELF-REGULATORY PLANS: Potential behaviors and scripts that one can do, and plans and strategies for organizing action and for affecting outcomes and one's own behavior and internal states.

SOURCE: Mischel, W., & Shoda, Y. (1995). A cognitive-affective system theory of personality: Reconceptualizing situations, dispositions, dynamics, and invariance in personality structure. *Psychological Review, 102,* 253.

As the table shows, the mediating units within the CAPS system include encodings, expectancies and beliefs, affects (feeling states and emotions), subjective values and goals, as well as competencies and self-regulatory strategies. While these units (mental representations) obviously overlap and interact, each provides distinctive information about the individual, and each may be measured objectively and studied systematically, as discussed next.

Walter Mischel

Encodings: How Do You See It?

People differ greatly in how they encode (represent, construe, interpret) themselves, other people and events, and their experiences. The same hot weather that upsets one person may be a joy for another who views it as a chance to go to the beach. The same stranger in the elevator who is perceived as dangerous by one person may be seen as interesting by another. Individuals differ stably in how they encode and categorize people and events, and these interpretations influence their subsequent reactions to them.

Suppose Mark, a teenager, tends to encode (construe, perceive) peers in terms of their hostile threats and is

Different individuals may encode the same situation in different ways.

highly sensitive to their possible attempts to challenge, manipulate, and control him. If he cognitively represents his world in such terms, Mark will be vigilant to threats and primed to defend himself. He therefore may see an innocent accident, such as having someone push against him in the crowded staircase, as a deliberate affront or violation (Cantor & Mischel, 1979; Dodge, 1986).

Different persons group and encode the same events and behaviors in different ways (Argyle & Little, 1972), developing distinctive encoding strategies as they selectively attend to and seek out different kinds of information (Bower, 1981; Miller, 1987). Such differences are seen, for example, in the finding that some individuals tend to encode ambiguous negative events as instances of personal rejection (e.g., Downey & Feldman, 1996), whereas others may easily feel angry even when they hear a mumbled greeting (e.g., Dodge, 1993), while others characteristically feel irritable and distressed (e.g., Eysenck & Eysenck, 1985). How people encode and selectively attend to observed behavioral sequences also greatly influences what they learn and how they subsequently act, and it relates meaningfully to other aspects of personality. For example, people who have poor social skills tend to encode situations in terms of the degree to which they might feel self-conscious versus self-confident in them. In contrast, more socially skilled individuals encode the same situations in terms of such other dimensions as how interesting or pleasant they might be (Forgas, 1983).

Expectancies and Beliefs: What Will Happen? What Do You Think?

The CAPS analysis of personality does not stop with a description of what people know and how they interpret events. It also seeks to predict and understand actual performance in specific situations. This goal requires attention to the determinants of *performance* which in part depends on the individual's expectancies and beliefs within the situation.

A particularly important type of expectancy consists of **self-efficacy expectations:** the person's belief that he or she *can* perform a particular behavior, like handling a snake or taking an exam. Measures of these expectations predict with considerable accuracy the person's actual ability to perform the relevant acts. And therapeutic improvement of efficacy expectancies in turn allows the person to function more effectively

(Bandura, 1986). People differ dramatically in how effective they expect themselves to be in different situations (Bandura, 1986) as well as in their more general sense of optimism versus helplessness and pessimism (Carver & Scheier, 1981; Scheier & Carver, 1992; Seligman, 1990), and these expectations have profound consequences for them. To predict specific behavior in a particular situation, one has to consider the individual's specific expectancies about the consequences of different behavioral possibilities in that situation. These expectancies guide the person's selection of behaviors from among the many which he or she is capable of constructing within any situation.

We generate behavior in light of our expectancies even when they are not in line with the objective conditions in the situation. If you expect to be attacked, you become vigilant even if your fears later turn out to have been unjustified. If you expect to succeed, you behave quite differently than if you are convinced you will fail. Indeed, we sometimes behave in ways that directly help to confirm our expectations, thus enacting self-fulfilling prophecies (Buss, 1987). The person who is easily suspicious, angry, and ready to aggress is likely to extract reciprocal hostility and defensiveness from others that in turn will confirm his beliefs about them.

One type of expectancy concerns **behavior-outcome relations.** These behavior-outcome expectancies (hypotheses, contingency rules) represent the expected *if* . . . *then* . . . relations between behavioral alternatives and expected probable outcomes in particular situations. In any given situation, we generate the response pattern that we expect is most likely to lead to the most subjectively valuable outcomes in that situation (Bandura, 1986; Mischel, 1973; Rotter, 1954). In the absence of new information about the behavior-outcome expectancies in any situation, behavior will depend on one's previous behavior-outcome expectancies in similar situations (Mischel & Staub, 1965). That is, if you do not know exactly what to expect in a new situation (a first job interview, for example), you are guided by your previous expectancies based on experiences in similar past situations.

Affects: Feelings, Emotions, and "Hot" Reactions

What we feel—our affects and emotions—profoundly influence other aspects of behavior (e.g., Bower, 1981; Contrada et al., 1990; Foa & Kozak, 1986; Smith & Lazarus, 1990; Zajonc, 1980). They also have an impact on the person's efforts at self-regulation and the pursuit of goals (e.g., Mischel et al., 1989; Mischel, Cantor, & Feldman, 1996). It has long been known that such cognitions as beliefs about the self and one's personal future are themselves "hot" and emotional (Mischel, 1973). As Smith & Lazarus (1990) noted, anything that implies important consequences, harmful or beneficial, for the individual can trigger an emotional reaction. For example, when one is feeling bad or sad—that is, experiencing a negative affective state—and gets negative feedback about performance (e.g., a disappointing test score), it is easy to become demoralized and to overinterpret the feedback, resulting in depression (Wright & Mischel, 1982).

Affective reactions to situation features (such as faces) may occur immediately and automatically (e.g., Murphy & Zajonc, 1993; Niedenthal, 1990), outside of awareness (Gollwitzer & Bargh, 1996; Zajonc, 1980). These emotional reactions in turn can trigger closely associated cognitions and behaviors (Chaiken & Bargh, 1993). The affective states and moods experienced are easily influenced by situational factors even by such simple events as finding a coin on the street (e.g., Isen, Niedenthal, & Cantor, 1992; Schwarz, 1990). But what we feel also reflects stable individual differences (e.g., Fazio, Sanbonmatsu, Powell, & Kardes, 1986), which may be related to temperament and biological variables (Metcalfe & Mischel, 1998; Rothbart et al., 1994).

Goals and Values: What Do You Want? What Is It Worth?

Goals and values drive and guide the long-term projects people pursue, the situations and outcomes they seek, and their reactions to them (e.g., Cantor, 1994; Dweck, 1991; Gollwitzer, 1993; Higgins, 1996; Higgins & Kruglanski, 1996; Linville & Carlston, 1994; Markus, 1977; Martin & Tesser, 1989; Pervin, 1989, 1990). They serve to organize and motivate the person's efforts, providing the direction and structure for the life tasks and projects selected and pursued (Grant & Dweck, 1999).

Goals also influence what is valued, and values also influence performance. Even if two individuals have similar expectancies, for example, they may act differently if the outcomes they expect have different personal values for them (Rotter, 1954, 1972) or if they are pursuing different goals (e.g., Cantor, 1990). If everyone in a group expects that approval from a teacher depends on saying certain things the teacher wants to hear, there may be differences in how often they are said due to differences in the perceived value of obtaining the teacher's approval. Praise from the teacher may be important for a student striving for grades, but not for a rebellious adolescent who rejects school. What delights one person may repel his or her neighbor, making it necessary to consider the individual's goals and the subjective (perceived) value of particular classes of events, that is, his or her preferences and aversions, likes and dislikes, positive and negative values. These goals and values are particularly important because much human behavior is driven by **intrinsic motivation:** the gratification the individual receives from the activity or task itself, that is, by "doing it" (Cantor, 1990; Deci & Ryan, 1987; Harakiewitz, Abrahams, & Wageman, 1987).

Self-Regulation: Overcoming Stimulus Control

People regulate their own behavior by self-imposed goals and self-produced consequences. Even in the absence of external constraints and social monitors, we set performance goals for ourselves. We react with self-criticism or self-satisfaction to our behavior depending on how well it matches our expectations and standards (Bandura, 1986; Higgins, 1990; Mischel, 1990; Mischel et al., 1996). The expert sprinter who falls below his past record may condemn himself bitterly; the same performance by a less experienced runner who has lower standards may produce self-congratulation and joy. To predict Mark's reaction to being pushed, for example, it helps to know the personal standards he uses to evaluate when and how to react aggressively. Will he react aggressively even if the peer who pushed him is much younger? Likewise, can he regulate his own response strategically, or will he react explosively and automatically?

People also differ in the types of plans that guide their behavior in the absence of, and sometimes in spite of, immediate external situational pressures. Such plans specify

Self-observation plays an important role in the acquisition of skills and competencies.

the kinds of behavior appropriate (expected) under particular conditions, the performance levels (standards, goals) which the behavior must achieve, and the consequences (positive and negative) of attaining or failing to reach those standards (Mischel, Cantor, & Feldman, 1996). Plans also specify the sequence and organization of behavior patterns (Gollwitzer & Moskowitz, 1996; Miller, Galanter, & Pribram, 1960; Schank & Abelson, 1977). Individuals may differ with respect to each of the components of self-regulation (e.g., Baumeister & Heatherton, 1996).

Self-regulation provides a route through which we can influence our environment substantially, overcoming "stimulus control" (the power of the situation). We can actively *select* many of the situations to which we expose ourselves, in a sense creating our own environment, entering some settings but not others (Buss, 1987; Ross & Nisbett, 1991). Such active choice, rather than automatic responding, may be facilitated by thinking and planning and by rearranging the environment itself to make it more favorable for one's objectives (e.g., Gollwitzer & Markowitz, 1996). Even when the environment cannot be changed physically (by rearranging it or by leaving it altogether and entering another setting), it may be possible to *transform* it psychologically by self-instructions and ideation as in mental self-distractions (Baumeister & Heatherton, 1996; Mischel, 1990).

Through direct and observational learning, each individual acquires information and understanding about the world and his or her relationship to it. Each one develops competencies to construct (create, generate) many cognitions and behaviors that may be conceptualized in terms of the constructs known as social and emotional intelligence, as was discussed in Chapter 7 (Cantor & Kihlstrom, 1987). These competencies include such knowledge as the rules that guide conduct, the concepts generated about self and others and a host of social, interpersonal, and physical skills, and cognitive social strategies for solving problems (Cantor, 1990).

Each individual acquires the capacity to actively construct a multitude of potential behaviors with the knowledge and skills available to him or her. Great differences among persons exist in the range and quality of the cognitive and behavioral patterns that they can generate and in their social problem-solving strategies. That becomes obvious from even casual comparison of the different competencies, for example, of a used car salesman, a politician, or a psychotherapist. The subtle psychological differences in the social problem-solving strategies employed by people of similar overall intelligence are receiving increasing attention (Cantor, 1990; Mischel et al., 1996; Kuhl, 1985; Sternberg & Kolligian, 1990). For a history of the development of person variables, see *In Focus 15.2*.

IN FOCUS 15.2 *On the History of Person Variables*

The development of person variables has a long history. They reflect an attempt to integrate contributions from two quite different, at first seemingly opposing, theoretical perspectives: the personal construct theory of George Kelly (discussed in Chapter 10) and the social learning theory developed by Julian B. Rotter (1954). Both Rotter and Kelly were professors in the graduate training program in clinical psychology at Ohio State University in the early 1950s. Although their offices were across the hall, the men were as different as their theories, and they had little influence on each other.

The person variable of "encoding strategies" explicitly reflected George Kelly's core emphasis—the importance of how individuals construe their experience and themselves. This construal characterizes the first phase of how individuals make sense of incoming social information and interpret its personal meaning. The reconceptualization of personality in cognitive social terms, however, sought a personality theory that includes not only how people perceive, construe, and interpret but also what they actually choose and do (Mischel 1973). For that purpose, it explicitly drew on expectancy-value concepts which had been given a central place by Rotter (1954). In Rotter's early social learning theory, the probability that a particular pattern of behavior would occur was a joint function of the individual's outcome expectancies and the subjective value of those outcomes.

In the late 1940s and early 1950s, Rotter introduced the expectancy construct to personality psychology and made it a centerpiece of his version of social learning. He had argued convincingly for the importance of both expectancies and values as basic building blocks for a

Julian B. Rotter

theory of social learning that he wanted to speak more directly to the assessment and treatment of clinical problems. While his theory was extremely elegant, it was, like his colleague George Kelly's theory of personal constructs, apparently ahead of its time: The impact of both these theorists seems to be felt more decades later in indirect forms than when Rotter and Kelly first advanced their ideas.

PERSONALITY STRUCTURE, DYNAMICS, AND DISPOSITIONS (CAPS)

Recall that the first assumption of CAPS theory is that there are stable individual differences in how easily each of the CAUs or person variables is activated within a given person, that is, in their degree of chronic accessibility. Equally important is the second assumption of CAPS theory, namely, that individuals differ in the stable organization of relations (the interconnections) among the CAUs.

It is this organization that constitutes the basic stable structure of the personality system (shown schematically in Figure 15.1 on page 425): It underlies and reflects the person's characteristic distinctiveness. It is the result of the individual's experience and history in interaction with temperamental and genetic-biochemical determinants (e.g., Plomin et al., 1994; Posner, 1997; Rothbart et al., 1994; Wachs & King, 1994). This stable structure of personality, which emerges in the course of development, thus reflects both experience and genetics. In turn it generates the distinctive patterns of behavior, including cognitions and affects, that characterize the person (Mischel & Shoda, 1995).

Dynamic, Transactional System

In CAPS theory, the personality system interacts continuously and dynamically with the social world in which it functions (Mischel et al., 1996; Shoda & Mischel, 1997). The interactions with the external world involve a two-way reciprocal process: The behaviors that the personality system generates impact the social world, partly shaping and selecting the interpersonal situations the person subsequently faces. In turn, these situations influence the person (e.g., Bandura, 1986; Buss, 1987).

Figure 15.1 shows that this personality system is characterized by the available cognitive and affective units (Table 15.1), organized in a distinctive network of interrelations. When a person experiences certain features of a situation, a characteristic pattern of cognitions and affects (shown schematically as circles) becomes activated through this distinctive network of connections. The personality structure—the person's stable system of interconnections among the cognitive and affective units—guides and constrains further activation of other units throughout the network, ultimately activating plans, strategies, and potential behaviors. These stable distinctive patterns of thoughts, feelings, and behaviors, activated by particular types of situations, constitute the personality dynamics (also called "processing dynamics"). The personality system, with its distinctive dynamics, changes situations as well as reacting to them. It is active and indeed proactive: It does not just respond to the environment but generates, selects, modifies, and shapes situations in reciprocal transactions (see Dodge, 1997a, b; Mischel & Shoda, 1995, Figure 5, p. 264).

Illustrative Dynamics and Dispositions: Rejection Sensitivity

Individuals differ characteristically in types of situational features that activate their distinctive cognitive-affective personality dynamics—their characteristic pattern of

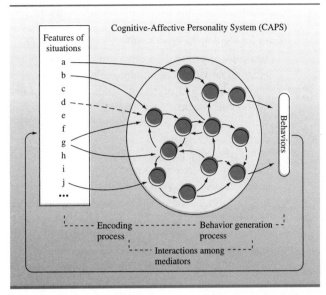

Figure 15.1
CAPS Model

SOURCE: Mischel, W., & Shoda, Y. (1995). A cognitive-affective system theory of personality: Reconceptualizing situations, dispositions, dynamics, and invariance in personality structure. *Psychological Review, 102,* p. 254.

thoughts, feelings, and behavioral reactions to those situations (Mischel & Shoda, 1995).

To illustrate such a system in action, consider a person who is especially sensitive to rejection and is disposed to expect it with a romantic partner, to look for it, and to emotionally overreact to it (Downey & Feldman, 1996). Many of these individuals have histories of exposure to family violence and rejection (Downey, Feldman, Khuri, & Friedman, in press; Feldman & Downey, 1994). Such a person may see even innocent or ambiguous behavior from the partner as rejection, triggering such thoughts as "She doesn't love me," which activate further thoughts and feelings of rejection, abandonment, and betrayal. In turn, the person is likely to become angry and hostile (Ayduk et al., 1997), activating scripts for coercive and controlling behaviors. Men may see such strong control and rage responses as justified if they are to be a "real man." In a study of these types of individuals, for example, one participant insisted he would never be a "wimp," which for him meant feeling that he needed his wife: When he felt "wimpy" he became most furious and violent with his wife (Goldner, Penn, Sheinberg, & Walker, 1990, p. 352). Over time such hostility is likely to lead to actual rejection even when there was none before, making the person's worst fears come true (Downey et al., 1997).

Dynamics like these are both stable and specific and they produce dispositions to react in consistent ways, but only in relation to particular types of situations or conditions. The rejection sensitive person becomes hostile not in general but specifically in relation to potential rejection from a romantic partner. In other situations (such as early in the relationship), the same person may behave most caringly. Thus, a defining situation-behavior profile for this disposition—its behavioral signature—may include both being more prone than others to anger, disapproval, and coercive behaviors in certain types of situations in intimate relationships and being more supportive, caring, and romantic than most people in other situations. For example, these people tend to be exceptionally warm and engaging in initial encounters with potential partners who are not yet committed to them, or later in the relationship when they are about to lose the partner.

The profile analysis of these individuals suggests that the same rejection sensitive man who coerces and abuses his partner also can behave in exceedingly tender and loving ways (e.g., Walker, 1979). In semantic terms, he is both hurtful and kind, caring and uncaring, violent and gentle. Traditional analyses of such seeming inconsistencies in personality lead to the questions: "Which one of these two people is the real one? What is simply the effect of the situation?" In CAPS theory, both aspects are equally real. They become comprehensible if one understands their dynamics.

In CAPS theory, **personality dispositions** like rejection sensitivity are defined in terms of their characteristic cognitive-affective processing dynamics. The processing dynamics of the disposition refer to the interactions among the cognitive-affective units that unfold when these individuals encounter the relevant situations (e.g., when they feel rejected). These situations may be external, or they may be internally generated. For example, people can activate their own dynamics by thinking about situations (such as being rejected), by ruminating about them (e.g., Nolen-Hoeksema et al., 1994), or through selective recall and re-experiences of past events and feelings (e.g., Bandura, 1986; Mischel, Ebbesen, & Zeiss, 1973, 1976; Norem & Cantor, 1986). They also may be activated in daydreaming, fantasies, and scenarios that are planned or imagined (e.g., Taylor & Schneider, 1989), as when the rejection-sensitive person imagines that the partner is betraying him.

Situation-Behavior Personality Signature: Stable *If . . . Then . . .* Relations

In the CAPS model, the underlying structure of the personality system remains stable, although the surface behaviors it generates change in relation to changing situations (see also Larsen, 1992). As in a musical piece, the notes played at any moment change, but they do so in an organized pattern that reflects the structure of the composition. Specifically, CAPS theory predicts that individuals will be characterized by distinctive *if . . . then . . .* situation-behavior profiles of characteristic elevation and shape like those illustrated in Figure 15.2. These profiles provide a kind of behavioral **personality signature.**

Intra-Individual Consistency.   Suppose, for example, that in situation A people rarely initiate personal interactions while in situation B they are common. Suppose also that Mark tends to become irritated when he thinks he is being ignored, whereas April is happier when she is left alone and even becomes irritated when people tell her personal stories about themselves. Mark will then become irritated in situation A but not

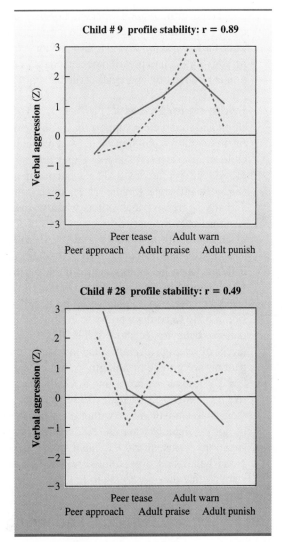

Figure 15.2
Individual *If . . . Then . . .* **Situation-Behavior Profiles**

SOURCE: Shoda, Y., Mischel, W., & Wright, J. C. (1994). Intra-individual stability in the organization and patterning of behavior: Incorporating psychological situations into the idiographic analysis of personality.
Journal of Personality and Social Psychology, 67, 678.

in situation B, and April will show the opposite *if . . . then . . .* pattern, annoyed if B
but not if A. These feelings further activate other cognitions and feelings in each situation in a characteristic pattern for each individual. So even if both people have similar
overall levels of irritability they will generate distinctive, predictable *if . . . then . . .*
signatures.

Thus, an individual's personality may be seen not only in its overall average frequency of different types of behavior but also in when and where the behavior occurs. The stable patterns of situation-behavior relationships that unfold provide a key to the personality—an expression of personality coherence that is eliminated when the situation is removed by aggregating the behavior across different situations.

Evidence for Stable *If . . . Then . . . Profiles.* Researchers have tested this proposition and found clear support for it (Shoda, Mischel, & Wright, 1989, 1993a, b, 1994). In these studies children were systematically observed for more than 150 hours per child in a residential summer camp setting (e.g., Shoda et al., 1993a, 1994). As predicted, children tended to display stable, distinctive patterns of *if . . . then . . .* relationships. To illustrate (Figure 15.2), some children were found to be consistently more verbally aggressive than others when warned by an adult but were much less aggressive than most when their peers approached them positively. In contrast, another group of children with a similar overall average level of aggression was distinguished by a striking and opposite *if . . . then . . .* pattern: They were more aggressive than any other children when peers approached them positively but were exceptionally unaggressive when warned by an adult (Shoda et al., 1994). A child who regularly becomes aggressive when peers try to play with him is quite different from one who expresses aggression mostly to adults who try to control him, even if both are equal in their overall aggressive behavior. In short, stable *if . . . then . . .* personality signatures, not just stable levels of average overall behavior, were found to characterize individuals, and their patterns seem to be meaningful reflections of the personality system.

To summarize, according to CAPS theory, individuals differ stably in their distinctive *if . . . then . . .* strategies and behavior patterns. Consequently, they will behave in their characteristic ways within a given type of situation, but they will vary their behavior predictably when the "if" changes, thus producing behavioral variability across situations. Consequently, by aggregating behavior across situations in their search for broad behavioral dispositions, researchers eliminate the distinctive individuality and stability that they are trying to find.

Demystifying the Personality Paradox: Redefining Consistency

The types of *if . . . then . . .* situation-behavior relations that a personality system like CAPS necessarily generates has important implications for resolving the classic "personality paradox" (Bem & Allen, 1974). Bem and Allen called attention to this paradox decades ago. They noted that, on the one hand, the person's behavior across situations yields only modest correlations from situation to situation (Hartshorne & May, 1928; Newcomb, 1929), but on the other hand, personality theory's fundamental assumption, and our intuition, insists that personality surely is stable (e.g., Bem & Allen, 1974; Krahe, 1990; Heatherton & Weinberger, 1994; Mischel, 1968; Moskowitz, 1982, 1994). The controversy on this topic has been intense (e.g., Epstein, 1983; Mischel & Peake, 1982).

CAPS theory dissolves this paradox, however, by conceptualizing the variability of the person's behavior across different situations as an expression of the stable personality system and its dynamics in interaction with those situations (Mischel & Shoda, 1995). CAPS theory expects that the person's behaviors in a domain will necessarily change from one type of situation to another because when the *if* changes, so will the *then,* although the personality structure and dynamics remain stable.

Thus, the theory resolves the person-situation debate not just by recognizing that the person and the situation are both important—a fact that has long been acknowledged. Rather, it conceptualizes the personality system in ways that make variability of behavior across situations an essential aspect of its behavioral expression. To the degree that people are characterized by stable and distinctive patterns of variations in their behavior across situations, their level of cross-situational consistency cannot be very high (Shoda, 1990), and there is no reason to expect it to be. It likewise follows that the "situation," in this view, is not a source of error to be removed in the search for personality but the locus in which it is expressed.

COMMON THEMES

The perspective that is illustrated by CAPS includes many different themes and variations (Bandura, 1986; Cantor, 1990; Dodge, 1986; Higgins, 1990; Mischel, 1990; Mischel & Shoda, 1998). Some of the main shared features of this still-evolving approach are summarized next and will be elaborated throughout Part VI.

Social Cognitive-Affective Focus

The approach is social in its concern with patterns of social behavior and the interpersonal aspects of life. The approach is **cognitive** in its emphasis on mental processes and on understanding how different people process incoming information that is personally relevant (Higgins & Kruglanski, 1996). It examines how people process and use information about themselves and their social worlds and studies the cognitive strategies they develop for coping with important life challenges and stressors. It explores differences among individuals in cognitive problem-solving strategies and styles, such as their constructs for interpreting and understanding experience, their goals, and their expectations. The approach is also increasingly concerned with **affect**—with feelings and emotions—emphasizing the close interconnections between cognition and affect and the need to include them both within a comprehensive approach to personality (Mischel & Shoda, 1995).

Thus, what constitutes a situation in part depends on the perceiver's constructs and subjective maps, that is, on the acquired meaning of situational features for that person, rather than being defined exclusively by the observing scientist (e.g., Kelly, 1955; Medin, 1989; Mischel, 1973). In the CAPS theory, individuals differ in how they selectively focus on different features of situations, how they categorize and encode them cognitively and emotionally, and how those encodings activate and interact with other cognitions and affects in the personality system. The theory views the person not as reacting passively to situations, nor as generating behavior impervious to their subtle features, but as active and goal-directed, constructing plans and self-generated changes, and in part creating the situations themselves. While the organization of cognitions and affects in the system reflects the individuals' total experience, and hence their cognitive social learning history, it also reflects genetic and constitutional influences such as temperament (e.g., Plomin, Owen, & McGuffin, 1994; Rothbart, Derryberry, & Posner, 1994; Wachs & King, 1994).

Focus on Internal Dynamics

The models within this perspective tend to focus on the social-cognitive-emotional mediating processes—the internal dynamics—that motivate and guide behavior. Many draw on social, cognitive, and social learning theories and concepts, as well as on self theories and research (e.g., Bandura, 1986; Baumeister & Heatherton, 1996; Cantor, 1990, 1994; Dodge, 1986, 1993; Dweck & Leggett, 1988; Fiske & Taylor, 1991; Higgins, 1987, 1996b, c; Markus & Kitayama, 1991; Scheier & Carver, 1988a, b). They also recognize automatic and unconscious processing (e.g., Kihlstrom, 1987, 1990; Uleman & Bargh, 1989) and try to take into account the person's goals and motivations (e.g., Gollwitzer & Bargh, 1996; Grant & Dweck, 1999; Pervin, 1989; Read & Miller, 1989a, b; Westen, 1990). And they emphasize that what emerges in behavior reflects the interaction between internal processes—such as the goals that motivate the person—and the particular situation.

Focus on Information Processing: From Computers to Neural Networks

These approaches are all influenced by information processing models. Although at first based on simple computer systems, these models in recent years have gained more of the depth and complexity essential for a dynamic conception of personality. First, modern information processing models are more like biological and cognitive neuroscience models of how the brain works in terms of **neural networks** through which the neurons in the brain are interconnected and interact when processing information (e.g., Anderson, 1996; Churchland & Sejnowski, 1992; Crick & Koch, 1990; Edelman, 1987; Kandel & Hawkins, 1992; Rumelhart & McClelland, 1986; Shoda & Mischel, 1998). Their focus now is not just on how much of a particular quality (e.g., of self-efficacy expectations) a person has. Rather, most important is the way the person's internal mental representations—the specific cognitions and feelings that become activated—are related to each other and interconnected.

This type of processing system operates rapidly and functions at multiple levels often outside conscious awareness (Kihlstrom, 1990). It is able to deal with the fact that personally important information processing is emotional and goes beyond merely "cool" cognitions to "hot" affect-laden representations and feeling states (e.g., Metcalfe & Mischel, in press; Smith & Lazarus, 1990; Kahneman & Snell, 1990) that profoundly influence what we decide and do (e.g., Mischel & Shoda, 1995; Wright & Mischel, 1982).

Focus on Human Potential

Many researchers in this perspective also hope that their ideas and work will help people to enhance their options and possibilities. In other words, they would like their work to ultimately help optimize human freedom and choice. Often they study such real-life problems as overcoming anxious, depressive, and health-threatening mental states and self-handicapping or debilitating cognitive-behavioral styles and strategies (Aspinwall & Taylor, 1997; Cantor, 1990; Cantor & Kihlstrom, 1987; Taylor & Armor, 1996; Taylor, Repetti, & Seeman, 1997). Much of this work tries to improve people's sense of mastery and competence so that they can better fulfill their potential. The commitment to enhancing the human potential for alternative, more constructive ways of coping seems directly responsive to such concepts as "constructive alternativism" and the "potential for change," which we saw in the phenomenological perspectives of such earlier theorists as George Kelly. Furthermore, it has implications for the psychological treatment of a wide range of human problems.

The Active Organism: Reciprocal Interactionism

The emphasis on the role of stimulus conditions in early behavioral approaches often implies a passive view of people—an image of organisms that are empty except for some psychological glue that cements or bonds a bundle of responses automatically to impinging external stimuli. In contrast, social cognitive-affective approaches emphasize that humans actively "shape" their world as much as they are shaped by it (Bandura, 1986). The relations between the individual and the social environment may be described as a mutual continuous interaction process (Magnusson, 1990; Mischel, 1973). Sometimes this process is called **reciprocal interactionism** (Bandura, 1977) to refer to the chain of determinants in which the qualities of a person (including all cognitive social person variables), the behaviors generated by the person, and the environment all interact with one another. People do not function in isolation: Judgments and actions occur in social contexts and interact with them (Chapter 18).

Focus on Self-Regulation: The Self as Agent

Social behavior is guided with reference to the massive social knowledge one acquires about the world and particularly about the behavior of other people (Cantor & Kihlstrom, 1987). Individuals compare themselves and their anticipated performance with that of important relevant others. "Success" and "failure" thus are not objective facts but self-defined in terms of the judgment criteria one applies to oneself (Bandura, 1986). In this analysis, the continuing internal self-evaluations that flow from these comparison processes affect the individual's perceived self-efficacy and in this way powerfully influence his or her behavior.

We interpret ourselves and our behavior—we evaluate, judge, and regulate our own performance. Thus, in addition to being rewarded and punished by the external environment, people monitor and evaluate their own behavior and reward and punish themselves, modifying their own behavior and influencing their environment (Bandura, 1971, 1986; Mischel, 1973, 1984). The principles that govern whether we applaud or condemn our own behavior have been given much attention in this perspective (e.g., Mischel, Cantor, & Feldman, 1996), as will be discussed in later chapters.

Coherence and Discriminativeness in Personality: Focus on the Individual's Uniqueness

Recall that trait theories hypothesize broad dispositions and cross-situational consistencies as the basic units of personality (Chapter 6). In contrast, cognitive social theory suggests that a person will behave consistently across situations to the extent that similar behavior leads, or is expected to lead, to similar consequences across those conditions (Mischel, 1968), and the situations are perceived (encoded) as functionally equivalent (Bandura, 1986; Mischel, 1973, 1990). Most social behaviors do not yield uniform outcomes across different settings or situations. For example, while physical aggression is encouraged among boys sparring in the gym, it is not supported when the boys aggress toward their fathers or their younger siblings. Consequently, sharp discriminations develop, the individual becoming aggressive in one context and not in the other (Bandura, 1973). Such discriminitiveness often is highly adaptive, protecting the person from potentially negative consequences (Chiu, Hong, Mischel, & Shoda, 1995).

Moreover, many of these patterns are unique to the individual. Jack and Bill may both have the same total "aggressiveness" score when averaged across many situations, but each one has a distinctively different *pattern* that characterizes where and when he is more and less aggressive in a stable, predictable way (Mischel, 1991; Shoda, 1990). These patterns reflect the uniqueness of the individual in his or her social world, and that uniqueness is emphasized in the social cognitive perspective.

Guided by the idea that behavior depends on its probable outcomes, one should anticipate both "behavioral specificity" and unique but stable person-situation interactions rather than broad consistency across conditions that are encoded differently and that lead to different outcomes. On the other hand, if similar behaviors are perceived as uniformly effective across diverse conditions, "generalization" occurs, and the person will show similar behaviors across many situations.

Consider a woman who seems hostile and fiercely independent some of the time but passive and dependent on other occasions. What is she really like? Which one of these two patterns reflects the woman that she really is? Must she be a really aggressive person with a facade of passivity—or is she a warm, passive-dependent woman with a surface defense of aggressiveness? CAPS theory suggests that it is possible for her to be all of these: a hostile, fiercely independent, passive, dependent, aggressive, warm person all in one (Mischel, 1969). Indeed, each of these aspects may constitute a different "possible self" (Markus & Cross, 1990). Of course, which of these she is at any particular moment would not be random and capricious; it would depend on who she is with, when, and why, and most importantly on how she construes and interprets the situation, that is, its meaning to her. But each of these aspects of her self may be a quite genuine and real aspect of her total being, part of her own unique but stable patterning of person variables.

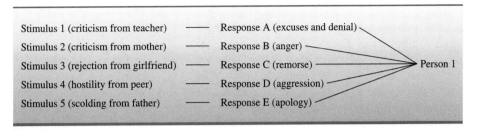

Figure 15.3
The Same Person Behaves in Distinctive but Stable Ways in Response to Various Psychological Situations

Focus on Doing: From Cognition and Motivation to Action

This perspective is also "behavioral" to the degree that it also asks: Why and when will individuals *do* what they do? That is, it goes from social cognition and feelings and motivation to human action (e.g., Gollwitzer & Bargh, 1996). But although the approach includes a focus on studying behavior, its primary goal is to clarify the psychological processes that underlie the behavior.

Assessment in this approach includes exploration of how the person's thoughts, feelings, and actions change in response to changes in the situation. For example, one wants to know not only a person's "general self-esteem" but also how the different self-efficacy beliefs hold with regard to diverse possibilities and domains (e.g., social, academic, athletic).

Recall that trait theories emphasize differences *among* people in their response to the same situation or even regardless of the situation. In contrast, cognitive social theories also emphasize differences in the behavior of the same person as a result of even slight changes in conditions, indicated in Figure 15.3. They focus on these *within-individual* differences (*intra-individual* stability) as well as on the differences among individuals. Understanding the psychological impact or meaning of particular events and conditions in the person's life requires observing how changes in those conditions alter what he or she expects, thinks, and feels. In turn, the influence of these expectations, cognitions, and affects on subsequent action also needs to be understood (Cantor, 1990; Cantor & Kihlstrom, 1987; Merluzzi et al., 1981).

SUMMARY

1. In the past two decades, a new approach to the study of personality has developed, influenced both by behavior theory and by the cognitive revolution in psychology. Called the social cognitive (or cognitive social) perspective to personality, it seeks to understand the cognitive, affective, and social processes that characterize an individual distinctively.

2. This approach began to develop at a time when the field of personality was divided into three camps—disciples of Freud, seekers of broad personality trait dimensions, and strict behaviorists. By 1968 serious questions arose about the efficacy of traditional trait and psychodynamic perspectives for understanding and treating individuals and for predicting their behavior. While the strict behavioral approach provided a more rigorous alternative, it soon also proved to have severe limitations.

3. Many findings pointed to the need for a more cognitive approach to personality. For example, it became clear that human performance is dramatically improved by awareness of the rules or principles that influence the outcomes for behavior. From early childhood on, individuals seem to actively form their own personal theories about themselves and their surroundings, and these theories influence their behavior. Other studies showed that even young children can significantly affect their own reactions to stimuli by altering how they perceive them and cognitively transform them. All these findings pointed to the importance of cognition for understanding both social learning and individual differences in personality. Also, new information on how the brain and its neural networks operate have allowed researchers to better understand and incorporate information processing into current personality theory.

4. In the reconceptualization of personality in cognitive-affective terms, a set of *person variables* (CAUs) was identified to explain individual differences (Mischel, 1973; Mischel & Shoda, 1995). These consist of *encoding strategies* (how an individual appraises a situation); *expectancies and beliefs* of various types; *affects* (the feelings and emotions experienced); the goals and values that motivate the person; and the *self-regulatory strategies* and *competencies* that allow the person to overcome stimulus control through self-control.

5. The Cognitive-Affective Personality System (CAPS) theory conceptualizes individual differences as reflecting differences (1) in the chronic accessibility of the cognitive-affective units (the person variables) and (2) in their interconnections or organization. It is a dynamic system in which the person and the situation are in continuous interaction, reciprocally influencing each other. The system's structure is seen in the person's stable patterns of *if . . . then . . .* relationships which form a distinctive behavioral signature. Such a system produces behaviors that are stable over time but predictably variable across different situations. It offers a resolution of the so-called personality paradox by providing a different perspective on the nature of personality consistency.

6. The approaches reviewed have several common themes. These include a focus on how individuals select, attend to, and process information about the self and the world and react to it cognitively and emotionally; an effort to understand the "why" and the "when" of the person's actions; a concern with the mental-emotional processes or dynamics that underlie individual differences in social behavior across different situations or contexts; and a focus on how people can use their potential more effectively and creatively in coping with their personal environment. The focus on *reciprocal interactionism* refers to the fact that people's attributes and the actions they generate interact with the social environment continuously in a reciprocal process, each influencing the other. The focus on *self-regulation* reflects the belief that individuals at least sometimes can control and guide their own behavior, actively shaping their environments as well as being shaped by them, in a continuing dynamic transaction.

Cognitive-Affective Processes

In the first paragraph of this book, two students, Charles and Jane, both received a D in the same course but reacted in sharply different ways, an example intended to challenge the reader not only to recognize the large differences among people in reaction to the same objective event, but to join in the search for their psychological explanation. From the social cognitive-affective perspective and in CAPS theory, the explanation begins by seeing how the two individuals themselves encode and explain the same event, how they interpret and appraise the meaning and significance of the D for them, and the different expectations, cognitions, and affects that become activated in them.

How individuals encode and what they expect importantly influence the emotions that become triggered and the reactions that unfold. Encodings and expectancies impact how one feels and self-evaluates and how one copes with life tasks and challenges, all of which can influence physical health and psychological well-being. In this chapter we discuss encoding and expectancies, first with reference to the self and then with regard to situations and other people.

In our culture, a major dimension of encoding used by most people (Osgood et al., 1957) concerns evaluation (good-bad, able-unable, success-failure). Unsurprisingly, this dimension is also the one on which individual differences and relevant expectancies have been most thoroughly researched. It turns out to have strong implications for personality, as the examples throughout this chapter will illustrate, including in the concepts people form about themselves (Baumeister, 1996).

A second common dimension for encoding social experience concerns perceived causation: Did I do it? Was it my fault? Did I really deserve it? Or was it just luck? Such questions often are aimed at explaining events that we also evaluate in positive and negative terms (i.e., the good and bad things that happen). The different ways in which individuals answer these kinds of questions are the bases of some extremely interesting individual differences among them that also influence what they feel, do, and become.

SELF-PERCEPTIONS: SEEING AND EVALUATING OURSELVES

In the course of development, the child acquires an increasingly rich concept of himself or herself as an active agent, an "I" separate from other people and objects. A sense also develops of a "me" that has defining features and qualities. In time the child identifies the network of characteristics that define his or her self and comes even to recognize how the "me" changes with age and how it might evolve and become different in the future.

The "I" and the "Me"

This distinction between two different aspects of the self was originally made a century ago by America's pioneering psychologist William James (1890). The self as an "I" is an *agent,* actor or doer, an executive who conducts basic psychological functions. The "I" as an agent engages in such functions as self-regulation (as in impulse control and planning for the future), self-monitoring to evaluate the individual's own progress along the way, and self-presentation, which manages the ways in which the self is shown or presented to others.

The self has another important aspect that William James also recognized: the "me" that is observed and perceived. It is the "me" that one sees when attention is focused on the self, the "me" as an *object,* represented in self-concepts, in how we see ourselves. Each person develops a self-theory about his or her "me." This theory is a construction, a set of concepts about the self. It is created by the child from experience, but it in turn affects future experience (Harter, 1983; Higgins, 1996; Epstein, 1973, 1983; Wiley, 1979).

The individual's self-concepts are not a simple mirrorlike reflection of some absolute reality. Self-concepts, like impressions of other people and of the world, involve an integration and organization of a tremendous amount of information (Harter, 1983; Higgins, 1990; Higgins & Kruglanski, 1996). Although self-concepts are not a mirror of reality, they are correlated with the outcomes that the person has obtained throughout the past and expects to obtain in the future (Wiley, 1979), and they influence what that future becomes (Markus & Cross, 1990; Markus, Kitayama, & Herman, 1996). The roots of our self-concepts are the impressions and evaluations that other people have of us in their responses to us as we interact with them. Although the concepts continue to change over time, their foundations form early in life.

Self-Schemata

Self-concepts, also called **self-schemata** (Markus, 1977), include generalizations about oneself, such as "I am an independent person" or "I tend to lean on people." These cognitions arise from past experiences and, once formed, guide how we deal with new information related to the self. To illustrate, if you have strong self-schemata about being extremely dependent, passive, and conforming, you would process and remember information relevant to those schemata more quickly and effectively than do people for whom those schemata are not personally relevant (Markus, 1977). People have better recall for information about traits that they believe describe them than for traits that are not self-descriptive (Rogers, 1977; Rogers, Kuiper, & Kirker, 1977). Thus, we give information relevant to the self special cognitive treatment, for example, by being more oriented and attentive toward it.

Self-schemata are examples of the most accessible personal constructs that a person is ready to use for encoding information. As CAPS theory assumes, people differ stably in the schemata and constructs they have "at the ready" (i.e., that are highly accessible) for encoding new events relevant to themselves and their world (Higgins, 1996; Higgins, King, & Mavin, 1982). These self-concepts also have motivational implications. For example, most people desire to maintain positive views of themselves (Baumeister, 1996) and are motivated to pursue self-knowledge and to enhance and improve themselves (Baumeister & Prentice, 1994).

Perceived Stability of Self and Potential for Change

When all of an individual's self-conceptions are combined, perhaps the most compelling quality of the self-perceived or phenomenological self is its continuity and consistency. The experience of subjective continuity in ourselves—of basic oneness and durability in the self—seems to be a fundamental feature of personality. Indeed, the loss of a feeling of consistency and identity may be a chief characteristic of personality disorganization, as is seen in schizophrenic patients who sometimes report vividly experiencing two distinct selves, one of them disembodied (Laing, 1965).

Each of us normally manages to reconcile seemingly diverse behaviors into one self-consistent whole. A man may steal on one occasion, lie on another, donate generously to charity on a third, cheat on a fourth, and still readily construe himself as "basically honest and moral." People often seem to be able to transform their seemingly discrepant behaviors into a constructed continuity, making unified wholes out of diverse actions. How does this integration work?

Many complex factors are involved (Cantor & Kihlstrom, 1987; Harter, 1983; Markus & Cross, 1990). One answer to this question may be that people tend to reduce cognitive inconsistencies and, in general, to simplify and integrate information so that they can deal with it (Nisbett & Ross, 1980; Ross & Nisbett, 1991; Tversky & Kahneman, 1974). The human mind may function like an extraordinarily effective reducing valve that creates and maintains the perception of continuity even in the face of perpetual observed changes in actual behavior (Mischel, 1973). The striving for self-consistency that the phenomenologists emphasize (Rogers, 1951) has received support in the work of other researchers working on related topics (Aronson & Mettee, 1968; Cooper & Fazio, 1984; Festinger, 1957).

Another basis for perceived consistency is that people often know a good deal about their own characteristic *if . . . then . . .* situation-behavior patterns. There is a strong relationship between the intra-individual stability of those patterns and the person's self-perception of consistency. Thus, college students who perceived themselves as consistent with regard to their "conscientiousness" had much more stable patterns of situation-behavior relations in their conscientious behavior than did those who saw themselves as not highly consistent. To illustrate, students who always conscientiously prepared for tests but were not conscientious about keeping appointments on time would see themselves as consistent. Note that their consistency was in their stable pattern, rather than from one type of situation (test preparation) to another (punctuality). These results are shown in Figure 16.1.

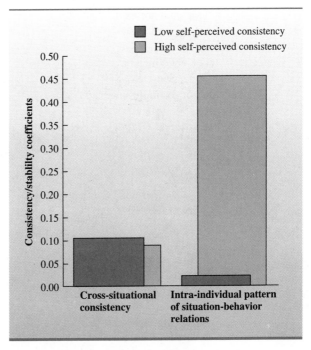

Figure 16.1
Self-Perceived Consistency and the Organization of Behavior Cross-situational consistency and the stability of person-situation profiles for people high versus low in perceived consistency in conscientiousness.

SOURCE: Based on data from Mischel, W., & Shoda, Y. (1995). A cognitive-affective system theory of personality: Reconceptualizing situations, dispositions, dynamics, and invariance in personality structure. *Psychological Review, 102,* 246–268.

In general, the self-concepts and personal constructs that people have seem to show a good deal of stability (Byrne, 1966; Gough, 1957; Mischel, 1968). Thus, our cognitive constructions about ourselves and the world—our personal theories about ourselves and those around us—tend to be relatively stable and resistant to change (Nisbett & Ross, 1980), as are our attitudes and values (E. L. Kelly, 1955). This perceived stability, however, coexists with the equally compelling fact that throughout the life course, people modify and transform their self-concepts as they envisage and construct "alternative future selves" (Cantor, 1990, p. 735) and strategically adapt to diverse life challenges.

Multiple Self-Concepts: Possible Selves

The self traditionally has been viewed as unitary: a single self that is relatively consistent (Allport, 1955; Snygg & Combs, 1949). More recently, it is increasingly common to characterize the self as a multifaceted, dynamic set of concepts consisting of multiple selves. These different perceived selves reflect different aspects of an individual's total personality.

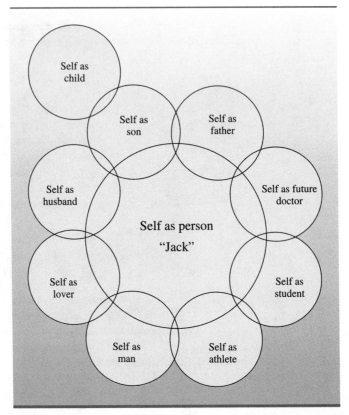

Figure 16.2

Schematic Representation of a Working Self-Concept The working self-concept
contains mental representations of diverse aspects of the self, from the present
and the past, as well as imagined possible future selves.

The self-concepts that encode different aspects of the person vary, depending on
particular contexts, on the type of behaviors that are self-assessed, and on the culture
(Markus & Kitayama, 1991; Markus, Kitayama, & Herman, 1996). The beliefs and
values of their culture and group profoundly influence how individuals construe themselves and their future possibilities (e.g., Stigler, Shweder, & Herdt, 1990), and even
the conception and definition of the self varies greatly across cultures. Thus, the self
may be a more central concept for individualistic societies like ours than for collec-
tivist societies like the Japanese in which importance is placed on the relations between the person and other people rather than on self-enhancement and the self as an
entity (e.g., Markus & Kitayama, 1991; Markus, Kitayama, & Herman, 1996).

The salient concepts of the self that the person can access comprise what has been
called the **working self-concept** (Markus & Nurius, 1986), which derives from various self-conceptions that are present in thought and memory. According to Markus and
her colleagues, this working self-concept includes ever-changing combinations of *past
selves* and *current selves,* as well as the imagined *possible selves* that we hope to be-

come or are afraid of becoming. These possible selves serve as guides for behavior and can have a significant impact on one's emotional and motivational states. A schematic representation of some components of a working self-concept is shown in Figure 16.2.

Self-Discrepancies and Their Emotional Consequences

Sometimes discrepancies exist among various mental (cognitive) representations of the self, as Carl Rogers first noted (Chapter 10). For example, your actual self (that is, the representation of yourself as you are) may be discrepant with your ideal self (the representation of who you would like to be). Likewise, the actual self may be discrepant with the ought self (the representation of who you believe you should be). According to Higgins (1987), such discrepancies may be experienced not only from one's own vantage point, but also from that of significant others, such as a parent or an older sibling (see Table 16.1). For example, there may be a discrepancy between the self you believe yourself to be and the ought self that you perceive your father thinks you should be.

Higgins proposed that particular discrepancies give rise to specific feelings (see Table 16.2). For example, a perceived discrepancy between the actual self and ideal self makes an individual more vulnerable to feelings of dejection, such as disappointment and dissatisfaction. In contrast, a discrepancy between the actual self and ought self can lead to feelings of agitation, such as fear and worry. If the discomfort associated with these negative feelings becomes too great, people may try to reduce or eliminate it in various ways. For example, they may eliminate a discrepancy between their perceived actual self and their own ideal self by re-evaluating their negative interpretation of past events. This is illustrated by the high school student who feels rejected by others ("nobody likes me") because he was not elected class president. He reduces the experience of negative feelings by thinking about the many close friends he has.

Alternatively, individuals may remove discrepancies by changing their actual behavior to match an important standard. For example, suppose an undergraduate studies very little for a midterm and receives a low grade on the exam. For the final, she may study very hard. In doing so, she relieves her guilt (discomfort) for not living up to what she herself perceives to be her responsibility to work diligently in college and receive exemplary grades. In this approach, regardless of the form the change actually takes, the

E. Tory Higgins

Table 16.1
Types of Concepts about the Self

Self-Concept	Definition	Example
Actual	One's representation of oneself: the belief about the attributes one actually has	I am a caring and warm person, athletic and attractive.
Ideal	One's representation of who one would hope, wish, or like to be: the beliefs about the attributes one would like to have ideally	I would love to be generous and giving, successful, popular, brilliant, and loved.
Ought	One's representation of who one should be, or feels obligated to be: the beliefs about the attributes one is obligated to have, i.e., that are one's duty to possess	I should be more ambitious and tough, hardworking and disciplined.

NOTE: In addition to one's own standpoint, each concept also can be represented from the viewpoint of a significant other. For example, your perception of who your father thinks you should be (e.g., strong-willed instead of caring) is an "ought/other" representation of the self.

SOURCE: Based on Higgins, E. T. (1987). Self-discrepancy: A theory relating self and affect. *Psychological Review, 94,* 319–340.

motivation for the change arises from the conflicts each individual feels among his or her various representations of the self. These discrepancies, Higgins argues, cause specific types of emotional discomfort that individuals are motivated to reduce as best they can.

The relevance of this analysis for the social cognitive-affective perspective is that it helps to specify in cognitive terms how individuals may encode or represent different facets of themselves and their experience. It makes these cognitive representations

Table 16.2
Illustrative Self-Discrepancies

Types of Self-Discrepancies	Induced Feelings	Example
Actual/Own: Ideal/Own	Disappointment and dissatisfaction	I'm dejected because I'm not as attractive as I would like to be.
Actual/Own: Ideal/Other	Shame and embarrassment	I'm ashamed because I fail to be as kind a person as my parents wished me to be.
Actual/Own: Ought/Own	Guilt and self-contempt	I hate myself because I should have more willpower.
Actual/Own: Ought/Other	Fear or feeling threatened	I'm afraid my father will be angry with me because I didn't work as hard as he believes I should.

SOURCE: Based on Higgins, E. T. (1987). Self-discrepancy: A theory relating self and affect. *Psychological Review, 94,* 319–340.

basic components in the study of personality. It goes on to analyze how and when individuals cognitively access or activate these different representations and examines their emotional and motivational consequences as the person interacts with psychological situations (Higgins, 1990, 1996).

Self-Esteem and Self-Evaluation

One of the most critical aspects of the self-concept is **self-esteem** (Harter, 1983). Self-esteem refers to the individual's personal judgment of his or her own worth (Coopersmith, 1967; Epstein, 1973, 1990). Self-esteem is such an important aspect of the self-concept that the two terms are often used as if they were the same. Although "self-esteem" is sometimes discussed as if it were a single entity, persons evaluate their functioning in different areas of life discriminatively. These self-evaluations reflect in part the feedback that they continuously get from the environment as they learn about themselves.

Self-evaluations partly reflect the individual's performance and the outcomes achieved objectively, but that is only one ingredient in a complex process of self-appraisal. In their self-appraisal, individuals also are guided by their memories and interpretations of earlier experiences. They are influenced by the frameworks of self-concepts, self-standards, and self-perceptions through which they view and filter their experiences as they compare themselves with their own standards, as well as with their perceptions of the performance of relevant others (Bandura, 1986; Higgins, 1996; Mischel, 1974; Norem & Cantor, 1986).

These self-evaluation processes are central for understanding how people see themselves and respond to their own experiences and to what they label as "achievements" or "failures." They reflect each person's compromises between the need for accurate perception of his or her performance in the real world and the self-protective desire to maintain a favorable self-image. Personality theorists have long recognized that in this self-evaluation process, we generally manage to combine a mix of "thorough realism" and "protective maneuvering" (Cantor & Kihlstrom, 1987, p. 152).

Expectancies for Success

Self-concepts about one's adequacy may be thought of as consisting of both highly situation-specific, self-relevant performance expectancies and more generalized expectancies as reflected in self-esteem. According to Rotter (1954), *specific expectancies* refer to the individual's expectancies that a particular set of behaviors on his or her part will lead to particular outcomes (reinforcements) in the specific situation. *Generalized expectancies* refer to broader expectations regarding the probable outcomes of the person's behavior based on past experiences and total history in similar situations. Both kinds of expectancies regarding future performance depend on information about past performance. The precise relationships among performance, performance feedback, and changes in the person's expectancies about herself or himself have been studied extensively (e.g., Ainslie, 1992; Bandura, 1986; Weiner, 1972).

While self-concept changes are related to the feedback that individuals get about themselves, the relationship may be influenced by many important variables (Markus & Cross, 1990; Wiley, 1979), including the person's subjective values and goals. For example, people who greatly value achievement and who are motivated to achieve tend to react quite differently to failure experiences than do people who are low in achievement striving (Heckhausen, 1969; Koestner & McClelland, 1990). The same outcome that is a discouraging "wipe out" for one may be a motivating challenge for the other. Depending on such moderating variables as the value of achievement striving or the degree of fear of failure, the person may adopt many different strategies to cope with performance feedback. Again self-concept changes are not a direct reflection of performance feedback; they are influenced by many other factors that combine to affect how one interprets and reacts to the experience, which in turn influences subsequent performance.

Self-Efficacy

Self-efficacy, a more specific concept than self-esteem, refers to the individual's belief that he or she can successfully execute the behaviors required by a particular situation. Perceptions of one's own efficacy importantly guide and direct one's behavior. The close connection between high self-efficacy expectations and effective performance is illustrated in studies of people who received various treatments to help reduce specific fears. A consistently high association was found between the degree to which persons improved from treatment (becoming able to handle snakes fearlessly) and their perceived self-efficacy (Bandura, 1977). If we assess perceived self-efficacy (asking people to specifically predict their ability to do a given act successfully), we can predict the relevant behavior (Bandura & Adams, 1977). Results of this kind suggest some clear links between self-perceptions of one's competence and the ability to actually behave competently.

Perceived self-efficacy influences the goals people set for themselves and the risks that they are willing to take: The greater their perceived self-efficacy, the higher the goals they choose and the stronger their commitment and perseverance in pursuing them (Bandura, 1989). Conversely, people who view themselves as lacking efficacy for coping with life tasks are vulnerable to anxiety and may develop avoidance patterns designed to reduce their fears. People who see themselves as lacking in essential efficacy also may become prone to depression. They may even show impairments in their immune system when coping with stressors that they believe they cannot control (Wiedenfeld et al., 1990).

Self-efficacy is Bandura's most basic construct for understanding human motivations and emotional reactions. People with a sense of self-efficacy about their intended actions are more able to carry them out. High efficacy expectations thus help the individual to persist in the pursuit of goals, even in the face of adversities that would derail or depress persons who are less sure of their relevant personal competencies.

The Role of Self-Efficacy.   Although many different therapy techniques may produce changes in behavior, might they all work through the same basic mechanism? Bandura (1978, 1982) has proposed that there is such a common mechanism: people's

The development of self-efficacy takes many forms.

expectations of self-efficacy; their belief that they can personally master the previously problematic behavior. Behavior therapy works, according to Bandura, by increasing efficacy expectations and thus leading people to believe that they can cope with the difficult situations that threatened them before. In this view, individuals will try to overcome a particular fear to the extent that they expect they can do so successfully. Any methods that strengthen expectancies of personal efficacy will, therefore, help the person perform the relevant behavior. The best methods will be the ones that give the person the most direct, compelling success experiences in performing the particular behavior, thereby increasing efficacy expectancies most. For example, actually climbing a fire escape successfully is a better way to overcome a fear of heights than just thinking about it, because it provides a more complete success experience and a stronger expectation for future mastery.

In sum, diverse processes of behavior therapy in Bandura's view exert their beneficial effects mainly by enhancing the individual's sense of self-efficacy. Thus, he sees each of the major behavioral strategies for inducing change as sharing one crucial ingredient: They improve perceived self-efficacy, thereby freeing the individual to perform actions that previously were not possible.

Table 16.3
Measuring Self-Efficacy Expectancies

Listed below are situations that can arouse anxiety, annoyance, and anger. Imagine the feelings you might have in each situation, such as your heart beats faster and your muscles tense. Indicate whether you could tolerate now the emotional strain caused by each of the situations.

Under the column marked *Can Do,* check (✓) the tasks or activities you expect you could do *now.*

For the tasks you check under *Can Do,* indicate in the column marked *Confidence* how confident you are that you could do the tasks. Rate your degree of confidence using a number from 10 to 100 on the scale below.

	10	20	30	40	50	60	70	80	90	100	
Quite Uncertain					Moderately Certain						Certain

	Can Do	Confidence
Attend a social gathering at which there is no one you know.	_____	_____
At a social gathering, approach a group of strangers, introduce yourself, and join in the conversation.	_____	_____
At a social gathering, discuss a controversial topic (politics, religion, philosophy of life, etc.) with people whose views differ greatly from yours.	_____	_____
Be served by a salesperson, receptionist, or waiter whose behavior you find irritating.	_____	_____
Complain about poor service to an unsympathetic sales or repair person.	_____	_____
When complaining about bad service, insist on seeing the manager if you are not satisfied.	_____	_____
In a public place, ask a stranger to stop doing something that annoys you, such as cutting in line, talking in a movie, or smoking in a no-smoking area.	_____	_____
Ask neighbors to correct a problem for which they are responsible, such as making noise at night or not controlling children or pets.	_____	_____
At work, reprimand an uncooperative subordinate.	_____	_____

SOURCE: Examples selected from Bandura, A., Taylor, C. B., Ewart, C. K., Miller, N. M., & Debusk, R. F. (1985). Exercise testing to enhance wives' confidence in their husbands' cardiac capability soon after clinically uncomplicated acute myocardial infarction. *American Journal of Cardiology, 55,* 635–638.

Measuring Expectancies.   As part of their increasing use of cognitive constructs, personality psychologists have paid more attention to the measurement of people's cognitive activities, especially their expectancies (Bandura, 1978, 1986; Merluzzi et al., 1981). Self-efficacy is assessed by asking the person to indicate the degree of confidence that he or she can do a particular task. For example, Bandura and associates (1985) wanted to assess the recovery of patients who had suffered heart attacks. Many tasks were described to the patients. These included such potentially stressful things as driving a few blocks in the neighborhood, driving on a freeway, and driving on a narrow mountain road. They also included situations that would induce other kinds of emotional strain, as illustrated in Table 16.3. For each item the respondent indicated the confidence level for being able to do the task.

As noted earlier, self-efficacy measures seem to predict the relevant behaviors at high levels of accuracy. For example, a consistently strong association was found between rated self-efficacy and the degree to which people showed increased approach behavior toward previously feared objects after they had received treatment for their fears (Bandura, Adams, & Beyer, 1977).

PERCEIVED HELPLESSNESS, MASTERY, AND STYLES OF EXPLANATION

Beyond specific efficacy expectations, people also develop more general concepts about their ability to behave effectively and control events. On the negative end of a dimension of perceived self-efficacy is perceived helplessness.

Learned Helplessness and Apathy

When people believe that there is nothing they can do to control negative or painful outcomes, they may come to expect that they are helpless (Seligman, 1975) and encode themselves in helpless terms. They expect that the aversive outcomes are uncontrollable and that there is nothing they can do. In that state, called **learned helplessness,** they also may become apathetic and despondent. They now may be slow to learn that they actually can control the outcomes, even when in fact they do become potentially controllable. Such states of helplessness may generalize, persist, and involve feelings of depression or sadness.

The concept of learned helplessness originally was based on findings from some experiments with animals exposed to extreme frustration. Consider, for example, a dog who first is placed in a situation where he can do nothing to end or escape an electric shock delivered to his feet through an electrified grid on the floor. Later he may sit passively and endure the shocks even though he can escape them now by jumping to a nearby compartment. This is the state called learned helplessness (Seligman, 1975, 1978). These findings also were consistent with less rigorous observations of humans forced to face extreme and persistent frustration. Such reactions as withdrawal, listlessness, and seeming emotional indifference are often found among war prisoners and inmates of concentration camps, for example. The victims seem to have given up totally, presumably overwhelmed by their inability to do anything that will change their desperate lot.

Dramatic examples of learned helplessness may be found among the children of America's migrant families whose plight was described by Coles (1970). He notes that unlike typical children in the middle class, migrant children soon discover that their shouts and screams will not necessarily bring any relief from their pains and frustrations. Consider this description by a migrant mother of her own helpless feelings in the face of her children's suffering:

> My children, they suffer, I know. They hurts, and I can't stop it. I just have to pray that they'll stay alive, somehow. They gets the colic, and I don't know what to do. One of them, he can't breathe right and his chest, it's in trouble. I can hear the noise inside when he takes his breaths. The worst thing, if you ask me, is the bites they get. It makes them unhappy, real unhappy. They itches and scratches and bleeds, and oh, it's the worst. They must want to tear all their skin off, but you can't do that. There'd still be mosquitoes and ants and rats and like that around and they'd be after your insides then, if the skin was all gone. That's what would happen then. But I say to myself it's life, the way living is, and there's not much to do but accept what happens. Do you have a choice but to accept? That's what I'd like to ask you, yes sir. Once, when I was little, I seem to recall asking my uncle if there wasn't something you could do, but he said no, there wasn't, and to hush up. So I did. Now I have to tell my kids the same, that you don't go around complaining—you just don't (Coles, 1970, pp. 9–10).

Indeed, a good deal of research with humans now suggests that when people believe they cannot control events and outcomes, they gradually do develop a sense of helplessness (Wortman & Brehm, 1975; Seligman, 1990) and even severe depression. In the extreme, when people feel they cannot tolerate the frustrations in their lives, they may lose interest in all activities and virtually stop behaving, often spending a great deal of time in bed. They tend to become very sad and are filled with feelings of worthlessness and physical complaints.

There is general agreement that the behaviors listed in Table 16.4 characterize depressed people as a group. Each depressed individual displays his or her own combination of any of these behaviors, often including deep unhappiness, emotional numbness and loss of interest, withdrawal from normal activities, and profoundly negative feelings about oneself and life. In contrast, when people believe that they can make an impact on their environment, that they can influence and control events, they become more alert, happier—and may even live longer (Seligman, 1990).

Causal Attributions: Explanations Influence Emotions and Outcomes

The close links between cognitive encoding and subsequent emotional and behavioral reactions are also seen if we examine how causal attributions—our explanations of the causes of events—influence our emotions (Weiner, 1990). For example, we may see the same event—say, getting an A on an exam—as due to *internal causes* (such as high ability or hard work) or as due to *external causes* (such as the ease of the task or good luck). How we feel about the grade depends on whether we see it as due to internal or external causes (Phares, 1976; Rotter, 1966).

Pride and Shame.   Generally, "pride and shame are maximized when achievement outcomes are ascribed internally, and minimized when success and failure are attributed to external causes" (Weiner, 1974, p. 11). In other words, a success that is per-

Table 16.4
Some Indicators of Depression

Mood
Feel sad and blue most of the time
No longer enjoy things they used to
General loss of feeling
Fatigue, apathy, boredom
Loss of interest in eating, sex, and other activities

Physical Symptoms
Headaches
Difficulty sleeping
Gastrointestinal symptoms (indigestion, constipation)
Weight loss—loss of appetite
Vague physical complaints

Behaviors
Unsociable—often alone
Unable to work, less sexual activity
Complaining, worrying, weeping
Neglect appearance
Speak little (speech is slow, monotonous, soft)

Ideation
Low self-esteem ("I'm no good")
Pessimism ("Things will always be bad for me")
Guilt, failure, self-blame, self-criticism
Feel isolated, powerless, helpless
Suicidal wishes ("I wish I were dead." "I want to kill myself.")

SOURCE: Based on Lewinsohn, P. M. (1975). The behavioral study and treatment of depression. In M. Hersen (Ed.), *Progress in behavior modification* (pp. 19-64). New York: Academic Press.

ceived to be the result of one's ability or effort (internal causes) produces more positive feelings about oneself than does the same success when it is viewed as merely reflecting luck or an easy task (external causes). Conversely, we feel worse (for example, experience "shame") when we perceive our failure as reflecting low ability or insufficient effort than when it is seen as due to bad luck or the difficulty of the particular task. For example, being fired from a job for one's incompetence has a different emotional impact than does being fired because the firm went bankrupt.

Self-Enhancing Bias.   In most people, perceptions of these causes may be biased in self-enhancing ways (Greenwald, 1980; Harter, 1983). For example, we are more likely to see ourselves as responsible for our actions when they have positive rather than negative outcomes. When we do well or succeed, it is to our personal credit; when we do badly or fail, it is because we could not help it (Schneider, Hastorf, & Ellsworth, 1979). To be less self-protective may risk developing a depressive orientation (Lewinsohn, Mischel, Chaplin, & Barton, 1980).

Reinterpreting Helplessness: Pessimistic Explanatory Styles

Perceived helplessness has been reinterpreted as reflecting a distinctive, essentially pessimistic explanatory style. In that view, persons are most vulnerable to self-perceived helplessness when they see the bad things that happen in life as due to their own enduring, widespread internal qualities (for example, "I'm incompetent") rather than to more momentary, external, or situational considerations (Abramson, Seligman, & Teasdale, 1978). Thus, the person's attributions about the causes and reasons for events have an important part in determining their emotional impact.

People differ greatly in their **explanatory styles**—how they interpret the reasons or causes for what happens in life. **Pessimism** involves an explanatory style of seeing bad events as enduring, widespread, and due to oneself.

Pessimism at an early age can be a predictor of poor health for the future (Peterson, Seligman, & Valliant, 1988). In one study, a group of healthy 25-year-old college graduates filled out questionnaires asking them to tell about difficult personal experiences in their lives. Researchers then analyzed the way the students explained the bad events that had occurred to determine whether or not their explanatory styles were generally pessimistic. Judges rated the explanations according to three criteria: the level of **stability** (seeing an event as having no end in sight; for example, "It won't ever be over for me"), **globality** (generalizing the event to many aspects of one's life), and **internality** (accepting one's self as causing or central to the problem rather than attributing it to some external factor or just plain circumstances). The more consistently stable, global, and internal the explanations, the higher the "pessimistic" style score.

Over a span of 35 years, the group was followed up with health examinations, and measures of illnesses were recorded. For about 20 years after college, there were no significant differences in the health of the participants. By the time they reached the ages of 45 through 60, however, those who at age 25 had been more pessimistic in their responses were more likely to be suffering from illness.

Researchers of optimistic-pessimistic explanatory styles also studied newspaper interviews with ballplayers from the Baseball Hall of Fame, published throughout the first half of the century. The interviews quoted the players' explanations of good and bad events as they discussed how and why they won or lost games. Players who attributed their losses to their own personal, stable qualities and thus saw them as their own fault, but saw their wins as due to momentary external causes (e.g., "the wind was right that afternoon") tended to live less long than those who used more optimistic explanatory styles to construe their good and bad experiences (Peterson & Seligman, 1987).

Learned Optimism

A pattern of experience and thinking called **learned optimism** is the opposite of the learned helplessness pattern (Seligman, 1990). Seligman suggests more benign ways of encoding the daily hassles and setbacks in life by deliberately using an explanatory style that is self-enhancing and avoids the self-perception of helplessness. The essence of this effort to increase optimism and perceived efficacy is to encourage explanations that are the opposite of the pessimistic style. This way of interpreting experience seems to be associated with a wide range of positive outcomes, from self-reports of feeling happier to more effective functioning and work success (also see *In Focus 16.1*).

Similar results were found with different measures based on self-reported optimism in one's orientation to and interpretation of life events. For example, the degree of optimism in the person's orientation to life predicts recovery from coronary bypass surgery in patients; it also predicts fewer physical symptoms in college students (Scheier & Carver, 1987). People with a more optimistic orientation to life seem to face stressful situations and try to reinterpret the problem constructively so that it can be resolved. In contrast, the pessimistic orientation is associated with withdrawal,

IN FOCUS 16.1　*The Illusory Warm Glow of Optimism*

Traditionally, psychologists have considered an accurate perception of self as essential for mental health (Jahoda, 1958). Recent studies, however, have found that most psychologically healthy people have somewhat unrealistically positive illusory self-views, whereas those who perceive themselves more accurately tend to be the less mentally healthy (Taylor & Brown, 1988). For example, people with realistic self-perceptions are more likely to experience low self-esteem and depression, while more stable individuals tend to see positive personality traits as being most descriptive of themselves (Alicke, 1985; Brown, 1986).

The exaggeratedly positive self-perceptions that most people have became apparent in a study comparing depressed patients with nondepressed psychiatric and normal controls (Lewinsohn, Mischel, Chaplin, & Barton, 1980). Patients who had interacted in small group situations were asked to rate both themselves and one another with regard to personality characteristics. Nondepressed individuals' self-ratings were considerably more favorable than the ratings others had given them. Self-ratings of depressed individuals were consistent with the ratings given them by others, suggesting that the nondepressed people had unrealistically positive self-views, seeing themselves through rose-colored glasses.

Individuals biased by such self-enhancing illusions also tend to feel they have an unrealistically large amount of control in pure chance situations, where in fact they cannot influence the outcome (Langer, 1975). In a study involving dice throwing, for example, nondepressed subjects felt that they would have greater control when throwing the dice themselves than when someone else did it for them (Fleming & Darley, 1986). The opposite state is found in depressed persons, who are likely to have a more realistic perception of the amount of control they have in chance situations—which in the case of dice throwing is zero. Likewise, people in a depressed state tend to be reasonably accurate when predicting the future, while the nondepressed display an unrealistic optimism (Alloy & Ahrens, 1987; Pyszczynski, Holt, & Greenberg, 1987). These results are clear, interesting, and consistent but, of course, they should not be misread as suggesting that gross distortions of reality characterize nondepressed individuals.

which automatically prevents problem solutions or constructive reinterpretation (Scheier, Weintraub, & Carver, 1986).

Helpless versus Mastery-Oriented Children

Following failure on a task, some individuals seem to fall apart and their performance deteriorates. But other people actually improve. What causes these two different types of responses to failure? The answer to this question again requires understanding how the person construes or interprets the reasons for the experience. Consistent with the work on learned helplessness, children who believe their failure is due to lack of ability (called *helpless children*) were found to perform more poorly after they experienced failure than did those who see their failure as due to lack of effort (called *mastery-oriented children*). Indeed, the mastery-oriented children often actually performed better after failure. Most encouraging, training the helpless children to view outcomes as the result of their own effort resulted in their improved performance after a failure experience (Dweck, 1975).

When faced with failure, helpless children seem to have self-defeating thoughts that virtually guarantee further failure. This became clear when groups of helpless and mastery-oriented fifth-graders were instructed "to think out loud" while solving problems. When children in the two groups began to experience failure, they soon said very

The depressed may perceive themselves *more* accurately than the nondepressed perceive themselves.

Table 16.5
Coping Strategies of Helpless and Mastery-Oriented Children

Helpless Children	Mastery-Oriented Children
Attributions for failure to self	*Self-instructions to improve performance*
"I'm getting confused"	"The harder it gets, the harder I need to try"
"I'm not smart"	
Solution irrelevant statements	*Self-monitoring statements*
"There's a talent show this weekend, and I am going to be Shirley Temple"	"I'm really concentrating now"
	Positive prognosis statements
	"I've almost got it"
Statements of negative affect	*Statements of positive affect*
"This isn't fun anymore"	"I love a challenge"

SOURCE: Based on Diener, C. I., & Dweck, C. S. (1978). An analysis of learned helplessness: Continuous changes in performance, strategy, and achievement cognitions following failure. *Journal of Personality and Social Psychology, 36,* 451–462.

different things to themselves. The helpless children made statements reflecting their loss or lack of ability, such as "I'm getting confused" and "I never did have a good memory" (Diener & Dweck, 1978, p. 458). None of the mastery-oriented children made lack-of-ability statements. Instead, these children seemed to search for a remedy rather than for a cause for their failure. They gave themselves instructions that could improve their performance, such as "I should slow down and try to figure this out" and "The harder it gets, the harder I need to try."

The helpless children made many statements that were irrelevant to the solution and that usually were ineffective strategies for problem solving (see Table 16.5). For example, one helpless male repeatedly chose the brown-colored shape, saying "chocolate cake" in spite of the experimenter's repeated feedback of "wrong." Finally, the attitudes of the two groups toward the task differed markedly. Even after several failures, mastery-oriented children remained positive and optimistic about the possibility of success, while helpless children expressed negative feelings and resignation, declaring, for example, "I give up."

Impact of Incremental versus Entity Theories

Helpless children also tend to differ from those who are mastery-oriented in their theory of intelligence (Dweck & Leggett, 1988). Children who display the helpless pattern see their intelligence as a fixed trait or static entity that they cannot change or control. In contrast to such an entity interpretation, youngsters who are mastery-oriented tend to view their intelligence more flexibly as something they can increase and develop. These different views or theories about intelligence also orient them toward different types of goals. The **entity theorists** seem to choose goals motivated by the desire to avoid unfavorable judgments and to gain approval about their competence. The **incremental theorists** choose goals motivated by the desire to increase their competence, for example, seeking opportunities to learn new things and enhance their mastery.

Carol Dweck

Interestingly, these differences in children's theories about their intelligence also predict important real-life outcomes in their development. Children were tracked from sixth to seventh grade in their transition to junior high school (Henderson & Dweck, 1990). The most impressive gains in grades during this transition were found for the incremental theorists. In sharp contrast, children who saw their intelligence as fixed tended to remain low achievers if they had been low achievers before and, most distressing, among these entity theorists ". . . many of those who had been high achievers in sixth grade were now among the lowest achievers" (Dweck, 1990, p. 211). Clearly our self-concepts and theories about our important qualities, our way of "encoding" or construing ourselves, impact our subsequent development and potential (see *In Focus 16.2*).

The Dynamics of Effective Coping

Personality psychologists correctly emphasize that there are many alternative ways to cope with the challenges, tasks, and setbacks of daily life and that each person develops his or her own distinctive patterns for doing so in their own way (e.g., Cantor, 1990). In other words, there are always many different routes for dealing well with the projects and demands within one's life. Nevertheless, as the research reviewed in the preceding sections suggests, certain types of cognitive-affective dynamics tend to seriously undermine effective goal pursuit and to perpetuate self-defeating patterns, leading to such unfortunate outcomes as depression. In contrast, the psychological opposite of such a self-defeating dynamic can serve to enhance persistence and mastery in the coping process and to nurture positive affect.

We next consider examples of these two types of processing dynamics, using the achievement domain for the illustrations. The cognitive-affective processes likely to enhance persistence and mastery are shown in Figure 16.3, (page 456), and those likely to undermine it are shown in Figure 16.4 (page 456). In reading the figures, keep in mind that the task in this example involves achievement challenges—as in dealing with a poor exam grade in a valued course. The figures show the type of ability theory and task encoding, the expectations and beliefs, the affects, the goals and values, and the strategies whose activation is likely to help or hurt subsequent performance and feelings. (As an exercise you can construct analogous dynamics and examples for dealing effectively and ineffectively with challenges in the social-interpersonal domain, as when a friend criticizes you severely.)

IN FOCUS 16.2   *Effect of Implicit Theories on Judgments and Attitudes*

Theories, even if not spelled out and only implicit, are held not just by psychologists but by everyone, and they can have profound effects on daily life.

Carol Dweck and colleagues find that people's implicit theories or beliefs about the malleability or fixedness of personality and character predict many of their own reactions to others. Recall that entity theorists believe that personality is fixed, whereas incremental theorists believe it is malleable.

Erdley and Dweck (1993) divided late grade school children into those who held entity versus incremental theories and showed them slides depicting some negative behaviors of a "new boy at school." For example, he lied about his family background, cheated from a classmate's paper, and stole a classmate's leftover art materials. They also received information about situational factors (the boy had moved in the middle of the school year to the new school) and about possible psychological mediators (the boy was nervous about making a good impression). As predicted, entity theorists made significantly stronger judgments about the boy's global moral traits (e.g., bad, mean, nasty) than did incremental theorists.

Furthermore, entity theorists did not revise their trait judgments of the boy when positive information was provided, whereas incremental theorists responded to the inconsistent information. Entity theorists also expected their first impression of the boy to remain valid forever, whereas incremental theorists predicted that the boy might act differently in the future.

Once they have rendered a negative moral judgment, entity theorists generally recommend punishment for the transgressor (Chiu, Dweck, Tong, & Fu, in press; Erdley & Dweck, 1993), whereas incremental theorists recommend education or rehabilitation, consistent with their belief in the possibility of personality change even in wrongdoers.

The implications of these two types of theories for other attitudes and behaviors also have been explored across different cultures. For example, although Hong Kong college students were significantly more "collectivistic" than U.S. students, the entity theorists in both cultures made stronger dispositional inferences than did incremental theorists, apparently assuming that what people do even in a single instance reflects their stable, fixed traits (Chiu, Hong, & Dweck, 1997). Likewise, entity theorists, in another study, endorsed both positive and negative stereotypes about ethnic groups (African Americans, Asians, Latinos) and occupational groups (lawyers, politicians) more strongly than did incremental theorists in studies with college students (Levy, Stroessner, Dweck, in press). In short, one's implicit personality theory shows itself in many forms, influencing how one judges people and interprets behavior.

Is the entity theory or the incremental theory better? Although an entity view has so far been linked with more maladaptive outcomes, neither view necessarily reflects the truth. Indeed, these alternative approaches to human nature are roughly represented in the two alternative conceptions of personality offered in the trait versus the social cognitive approaches within personality psychology today. And each theory has advocates convinced of its greater value.

ENCODING EMOTIONAL EXPERIENCES AND SITUATIONS

Cognitive encoding and expectancies also influence the subjective experience of emotions. We are aware of these feelings and of our many different emotional states, and they matter greatly to us and our sense of being alive. This subjective impression—of fear, joy, anger, pride, shame—is a distinctive aspect of self-perception, and it has

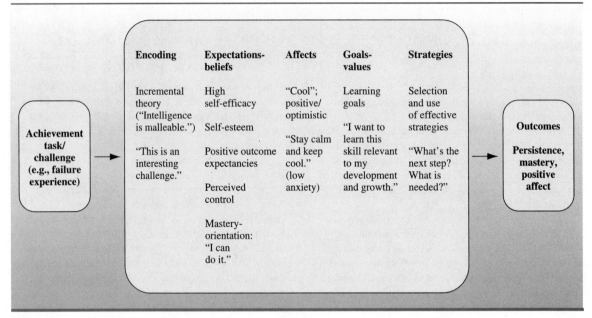

Figure 16.3
Cognitive-Affective Dynamics for Enhancing Goal Pursuit (Achievement Domain)

Figure 16.4
Cognitive-Affective Dynamics for Undermining Goal Pursuit (Achievement Domain)

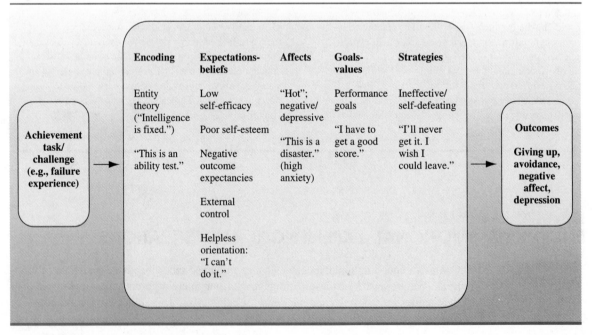

important implications not only for what individuals experience but also for how they subsequently act.

Emotions seem to range from the mildest inclinations to the most profound passions and from the most positive to the most negative feelings. The English vocabulary gives us names for this vast range, from subtle sensations such as pleasure or annoyance to intense emotions such as ecstasy, misery, joy, and loathing. Some studies suggest that the diverse emotions people self-report on questionnaires may be grouped on a dimension of positive versus negative affect. Both types, positive and negative, also vary in intensity from high to low (Watson & Tellegen, 1985). Nevertheless, the particular emotions experienced in different contexts are dramatically different. How does that happen?

The emotion that one experiences depends on how the state of arousal is interpreted.

Stanley Schachter

How Do You Know What You Feel?

An individual's emotional experience at any given moment depends importantly on how he or she cognitively encodes or interprets the general state of physiological arousal in the body. In Stanley Schachter's theory (1964), emotions one experiences depend on two factors: first, the level of physiological arousal in the body, and second, the cognitive interpretations by the individual of the arousing situation. On the basis of situational cues, the individual may label his or her state cognitively, assigning a name to the arousal, encoding it, and giving it psychological meaning. Let us consider each component.

Bodily Changes in Emotion

Visceral or physiological reactions in the body are an important part of emotional experience (Geen, 1997). Such phrases as "took my breath away," "makes my heart race," and "choked up with emotion" suggest that emotional states involve bodily changes. In fact, the activation of the sympathetic division of the autonomic nervous system produces many of the physiological changes that we experience in intense emotional states. These bodily changes include:

1. Channeling of the blood supply to the muscles and brain.
2. Slowing down of stomach and intestinal activity.
3. Increase in heart rate and blood pressure.
4. Widening of the pupils of the eyes.
5. Increase in rates of metabolism and respiration.
6. Increase in sugar content of the blood.
7. Decrease in electrical resistance of the skin.
8. Increase in speed of the blood's ability to clot.
9. "Goose pimples" resulting from the erection of hairs on the skin.

These changes are sometimes referred to as the "fight or flight" reaction because they are considered to be the body's emergency reaction system to threat and danger. They enable the organism to cope rapidly and effectively with environmental dangers, in part by providing the alertness and energy necessary for survival in the face of attack. In humans the arousal pattern can lead to a wide variety of behaviors and can be elicited in response to situations that do not objectively endanger survival, as when you face a French examination or walk into the boss's office to ask for a raise. Bodily changes play a role in emotion, but they are only one part of a two-part process, according to Schachter.

Interpreting the Situation

Often the source of emotional arousal is easy to identify. When faced by an attacking animal or by an impending car crash, the source of excitement is self-evident. The label attached to the experience in these cases depends on the source—the stimulus producing the arousal. Thus, the emotional response to an attacking animal is probably fear, identified by the fact that a dangerous animal is approaching. Identification of the emotion also depends on the person's goal-directed response when confronted by the stimulus. For example, attempted escape from the animal also leads to calling the emotion fear. As another example, suppose that the arousal source is an insult. The resulting emotion is probably "anger," especially if the insulted person responds aggressively; but it might be "fear" if the insulted person views the insult as a prelude to greater attack. These examples illustrate that the interpretation and encoding (in this case the actual labeling) of the emotion depend in part on the source of arousal and in part on the response to it.

The emotional meaning attributed to arousing stimuli and response patterns depends on previous experience and expectations. This point becomes most evident from anthropological reports of differences among cultures in the ways in which feelings are expressed. Visitors to a strange culture would make many mistakes if they tried to assess the meaning of emotional expressions in terms of their own social learning history. A Masai warrior honors a young man who looks promising by spitting in his face, an Andaman Islander greets a visitor by sitting down on his lap and sobbing his salutation tearfully, a scolded Chinese schoolboy takes a reprimand with cheerful grinning as a sign of his respect, and to show anger, the Navajo and Apache tribes lower the voice instead of raising it (Opler, 1967). Within each culture, people reach good agreement about the meaning of emotional cues. But these observations of the importance of culture coexist with the possibility that certain facial expressions seem to have a universal meaning. The emotions of anger, happiness, disgust, sadness, fear, and surprise, shown in photographs of faces, tended to be correctly identified in a variety of extremely different cultures (Ekman, 1982).

Often persons cannot completely identify the source of their own arousal and are uncertain about their response to it. Under these ambiguous conditions, person variables play an especially dominant part in determining the experience. Depending on the cognitive encoding, the context, and social cues from other people, the individual might experience the same physiological arousal pattern in alternative ways, as discussed in *In Focus 16.3*.

The Cognitive Appraisal of Stress

The fact that the psychological impact of events depends on the way in which individuals encode or interpret them has been well-documented in studies of "stress." This term, pervasive in descriptions for what ails modern life, has been the label used to

IN FOCUS 16.3   *Experiments on Cognitive Appraisal in Emotion*

How we know what we feel under ambiguous conditions was explored in several classic experiments by Stanley Schachter (1964). In one study, supposedly attempting to investigate the effects of vitamins on visual skills, college students received an injection of epinephrine, a drug that increases heart rate and raises blood sugar levels, thus producing physiological arousal (Schachter & Singer, 1962). Some students were told what to expect from the injections, others were told nothing, and a third group was misinformed—that is, they were told that their hands and feet would feel numb and that they would have an itch and a slight headache, none of which would actually be a result of the epinephrine injection. A control group received a saline injection that has no physiological effect.

Next, each student was left alone in a waiting room with a person who appeared to be another subject but who actually served as the experimenter's confederate. In one condition the confederate behaved in an angry, aggressive, and insulting fashion; in another condition he was wild and euphoric, laughing, throwing paper airplanes, and playing games. Those students who had been given the arousing drug and had been uninformed or misinformed concerning its effects were most susceptible to the cues provided by the confederate. More than the other groups, they reported feeling angry if the confederate in their case displayed angry behavior and euphoric if the confederate was euphoric. (see Figure 16.5).

The emotional experiences of aroused participants who had been given an appropriate explanation for their bodily arousal, on the other hand, were influenced very little by the confederate. This finding supported the hypothesis that an individual who has a plausible explanation for his state of arousal does not depend on momentary situational cues to evaluate and label his experiences. But a person who cannot plausibly explain his aroused state must label his emotions on the basis of whatever cues the environment provides.

This led Schachter in his **cognitive-physiological theory** to suggest that emotions may depend on two factors: (1) a state of physiological arousal and (2) an interpretation of the causes responsible for the arousal. When we do not have an explanation for a state of arousal, we become dependent on situational cues to understand what we are feeling. But if the arousal is

completely explained—if one knows it is caused by an injection, for example—one does not have to use the present situation to interpret it.

Schachter's work helps us to understand behavior in everyday situations when individuals are unsure about the sources of their own arousal and uncertain about what is making them emotional. In such cases, the same pattern of physiological arousal (such as increased heart rate and blood pressure) may be experienced as anything from euphoria to anger, depending on the context in which it occurs and the way it is interpreted. Of course, in many life situations the source of the emotional arousal is easy to identify, and the emotion is readily labeled. An approaching grizzly bear or a car coming head-on would result in an emotional response labeled fear with little hesitation. In sum, the subjective experience of emotion often seems to be labeled from contextual cues, and we know what we feel partly by seeing where we are and what is happening. To understand another person's emotional experiences fully, we have to consider the person in the context and the complex relations between the contextual variations and subjective experience; to understand our own feelings, we may have to do the same.

Schachter also has applied his theory to try to understand the effects of smoking marijuana. In his view, labels are attached to the physiological changes accompanying marijuana intoxication. The smoker must decide whether dizziness, misjudgments of time and distance, and the other effects of the drug are pleasant or not. Situational cues enter into these judgments. For example, if the setting is pleasant and includes warm, supportive models who enjoy smoking, one is likely to have a positive experience, but under different circumstances or expectations, the same physical arousal pattern may be labeled very differently.

The Schachter and Singer (1962) experiment has been challenged by research that questions their conclusions (Reisenzein, 1983). Schachter and Singer (1979), however, continue to maintain their interpretation and rebuke their sharp critics with equal vigor. What shall we conclude? A good deal of evidence indicates that we often do use external information to judge and encode our inner states. But there are also many different types of information that influence how we experience, judge, and

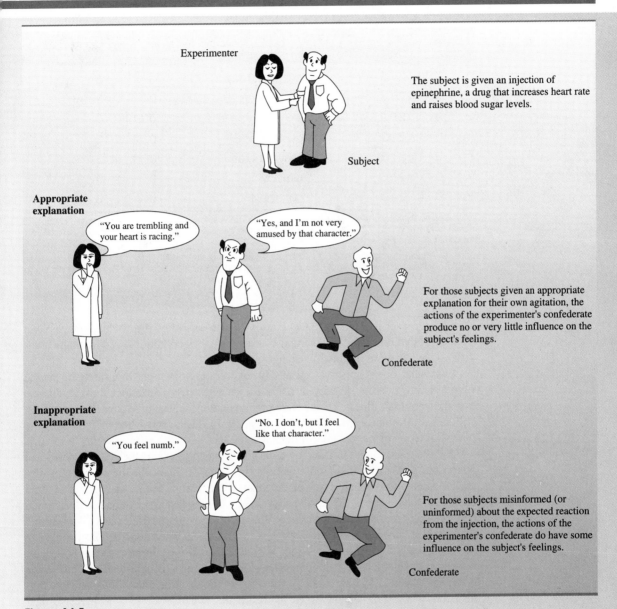

Figure 16.5
The Schachter Experiments

SOURCE: Mandler, G. (1962). Association to structure. *Psychological Review, 66,* 415–427.

label our inner states (Leventhal, 1984; Schneider, Hastorf, & Ellsworth, 1979). Human emotions remain as complex and intriguing to understand scientifically as they are to deal with in life. But the research has made one point clear: How an ambiguous situation is encoded or appraised affects what is felt and helps us to understand individual differences in emotions and the behavioral reactions that follow.

Table 16.6
Measuring Stress as Perceived Hassles versus Uplifts: Illustrative Questions

How much of a hassle was this today?		How much of an uplift was this today?
0 1 2 3	Your child(ren)	0 1 2 3
0 1 2 3	Your parents	0 1 2 3
0 1 2 3	Sex	0 1 2 3
0 1 2 3	Your friends	0 1 2 3
0 1 2 3	Fellow workers	0 1 2 3
0 1 2 3	Intimacy	0 1 2 3
0 1 2 3	Your smoking	0 1 2 3

NOTE: For each entry, the subject is asked to circle the number on the left to indicate the degree of hassle and the number on the right to indicate the degree of uplift (how glad, joyful, or satisfied it made you).

SOURCE: Adapted from DeLongis, A., Folkman, S., & Lazarus, R. S. (1988). The impact of daily stress on health and mood: Psychological and social resources as mediators. *Journal of Personality and Social Psychology, 54,* 486–495.

classify a host of potentially unpleasant or dangerous events that include unavoidable pain, excessive noise and fatigue under strenuous work conditions, and traumatic dangers, as well as more routine life changes.

Just what is a "stressful" event? To answer this question, thousands of people were asked to rate the severity of many life changes (from vacations through divorce and the terminal illness of a loved one), yielding scales of Social Readjustment (Holmes & Masuda, 1974; Holmes & Rahe, 1967). The events listed in Table 16.6 are ranked in terms of the amount of readjustment that each life change seems to require.

People respond on this scale by indicating which life events they have experienced within the past year. Their score reflects their degree of recent life change (in life-change units). This score serves as the measure of current degree of stress: The more change, the more stress. Generally, a significant but modest association has been found between degree of stress and physical illness. More stressful life events take a somewhat greater physical and emotional toll on most—but not all—people (Rabkin & Struening, 1976). Most important, the cognitive appraisal of the stressfulness of events influences their impact on the perceiver (Lazarus, 1981). People who perceive more stress (on scales of "hassles and uplifts" such as the one illustrated in Table 16.6) thus also feel worse later on measures of well-being, whereas those who perceive their lives as less hassled tend to have better outcomes on later measures of well-being (DeLongis, Folkman, & Lazarus, 1988; Lazarus, 1990).

Some people may be more psychologically hardy than others; they resist illness even when faced with highly stressful life events. For example, business executives who express attitudes of vigorousness about life, of being more oriented to challenge, also may experience less illness than do those who express opposite attitudes while encountering similarly high levels of stress (Kobasa, 1979). The people who face stress but remain healthy thus seem to perceive change not as a threat but as a challenge and an opportunity (Kobasa, Maddi, & Kahn, 1982). For example, rather than seeing a job loss as a terrible setback, they view it as a chance for a more challenging new career.

In sum, these results again underline that the cognitive appraisal—how a stressor is viewed by the person—may be more important than the amount of stress (change) that actually occurs in the environment. Likewise, whether or not one believes that one can cope with the stress, for example, influences how one reacts to it predictably. This point has been made most consistently by R. S. Lazarus (1990) and colleagues in research to show that the way in which stress is cognitively appraised influences how one experiences it and copes with it (e.g., Folkman et al., 1986; Lazarus & Folkman, 1984).

Encoding Threatening Experiences Adaptively: How Victims Cope

The remarkable resilience of personality can be glimpsed when we observe how people reinterpret and constructively encode such crises as grave illness or the death of a family member in ways that allow them to adapt constructively (Taylor, 1983, 1996, 1997). Studies by Shelley Taylor and her colleagues with cardiac, cancer, and HIV patients and loved ones have helped to illuminate the impressive adaptive value of interpreting one's problems in ways that make them personally meaningful. An essential element in this adaptation process is to construct a way to make what happened personally significant and positive. The resulting interpretations to endow the tragedy with special meaning and significance, sometimes religious or spiritual, may seem like transparent illusions to the skeptical observer, but as long as they are self-persuasive for the afflicted person, they serve as a buffer against the threat.

In addition to giving the event a meaning and significance that changes its emotional impact, individuals often find new areas on which to focus in an effort to regain a sense of control or mastery (Aspinwall & Taylor, 1997). For example, they take "active steps" (Taylor, 1983, p. 1164) to enhance their sense of control by focusing on special diets, medications, or other self-management regimes. Cognitively, they often try to gain mastery over their condition and its side effects through various mental exercises and cognitive transformation (Taylor & Armor, 1996). Undergoing radiation, one woman imagined a protective shield that kept her body safe from being burned by the radiation, while another patient visualized her chemotherapy ". . . as powerful cannons which blasted away pieces of the dragon, cancer" (p. 1164).

CHANGING DYSFUNCTIONAL COGNITIONS AND EMOTIONS

In social cognitive-affective theory, cognitions and emotions, even when chronic, can be changed and it is important to devise methods that make it possible to do so when the individual is distressed by them. Two well-known approaches are described next.

Beck's Cognitive Therapy for Depression

Aaron T. Beck has developed a form of **cognitive behavior therapy** directed at changing how people encode their experiences and themselves that he has applied systematically to the treatment of depression. He defines cognitive therapy this way:

Cognitive therapy is an active, directive, time-limited, structured approach used to treat a variety of psychiatric disorders (for example, depression, anxiety, phobias, pain problems, etc.). It is based on an underlying theoretical rationale that an individual's affect and behavior are largely determined by the way in which he structures the world. . . . His cognitions (verbal or pictorial "events" in his stream of consciousness) are based on attitudes or assumptions (schemas), developed from previous experiences. For example, if a person interprets all his experiences in terms of whether he is competent and adequate, his thinking may be dominated by the schema, "Unless I do everything perfectly, I'm a failure." Consequently, he reacts to situations in terms of adequacy even when they are unrelated to whether or not he is personally competent (Beck, Rush, Shaw, & Emery, 1979, p. 3).

There are five basic steps in Beck's version of cognitive therapy:

1. Patients first learn to recognize and monitor their negative, automatic thoughts. These thoughts are "dysfunctional," that is, ineffective, and lead to serious dilemmas.
2. They are taught to recognize the connections among these negative thoughts (cognitions), the emotions they create, and their own actions. (See Figure 16.6 for examples of connections between thoughts and emotions.)
3. They learn to examine the evidence for and against their distorted automatic thoughts.
4. They substitute for these distorted negative thoughts more realistic interpretations.
5. They are taught to identify and change the inappropriate assumptions that predisposed them to distort their experiences. Examples of such assumptions are shown in Figure 16.7.

A variety of ingenious techniques have been developed to encourage people to undertake these five basic steps and to use them effectively to alter their actions,

Figure 16.6
Examples of Connections between Negative Automatic Thoughts and Emotion

SOURCE: Adapted from Beck, A. T., Rush, A. J., Shaw, B. F., & Emery, G. (1979). *Cognitive therapy of depression* (p. 250). New York: Guilford Press.

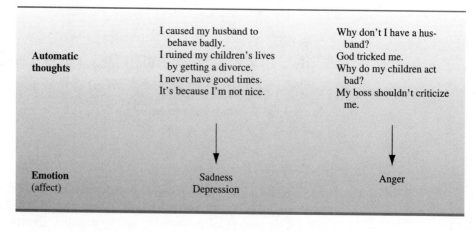

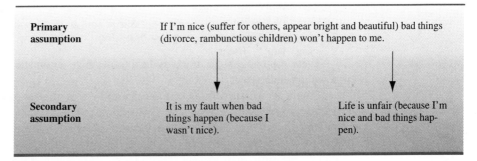

Primary assumption	If I'm nice (suffer for others, appear bright and beautiful) bad things (divorce, rambunctious children) won't happen to me.	
Secondary assumption	It is my fault when bad things happen (because I wasn't nice).	Life is unfair (because I'm nice and bad things happen).

Figure 16.7
Examples of Assumptions That Encourage Depression
SOURCE: Adapted from Beck, A. T., Rush, A. J., Shaw, B. F., & Emery, G. (1979). *Cognitive therapy of depression* (p. 250). New York: Guilford Press.

thoughts, and feelings. The following excerpt from Beck's therapy illustrates how patients can be helped to change dysfunctional beliefs. The intent is to help the patient see how the unfortunate assumption or belief becomes a self-fulfilling prophecy: It traps the believer into the very same dilemma that the belief was designed to avoid in the first place. The therapist in this excerpt tries to illuminate these self-fulfilling assumptions.

PATIENT: Not being loved leads automatically to unhappiness.

THERAPIST: Not being loved is a "nonevent." How can a nonevent lead automatically to something?

P: I just don't believe anyone could be happy without being loved.

T: This is your belief. If you believe something, this belief will dictate your emotional reactions.

P: I don't understand that.

T: If you believe something, you're going to act and feel as if it were true, whether it is or not.

P: You mean if I believe I'll be unhappy without love, it's only my belief causing my unhappiness?

T: And when you feel unhappy, you probably say to yourself, "See, I was right. If I don't have love, I am bound to be unhappy."

P: How can I get out of this trap?

T: You could experiment with your belief about having to be loved. Force yourself to suspend this belief and see what happens. Pay attention to the natural consequences of not being loved, not the consequences created by your belief. For example, can you picture yourself on a tropical island with all the delicious fruits and other food available?

P: Yes, it looks pretty good.

T: Now, imagine that there are primitive people on the island. They are friendly and helpful, but they do not love you. None of them loves you.

P: I can picture that.

T: How do you feel in your fantasy?

P: Relaxed and comfortable.

T: So you can see that it does not necessarily follow that if you aren't loved, you will be unhappy (Beck et al., 1979, p. 260).

These assumptions in turn may lead to negative automatic thoughts and emotions shown in Figure 16.7.

Cognitive therapy of this sort appears to be a promising part of treatment for depression and related emotional and behavioral problems. Its value has been explored in a large number of studies with subjects ranging from those with mild problems to hospitalized, severely depressive patients. The results seem to be consistently encouraging, indicating improvement from treatment greater than that found for individuals who remain in no-treatment control or other comparison conditions (Beck et al., 1979).

Ellis's Cognitive Restructuring

Other cognitive methods of therapy include helping clients to talk to themselves differently (Meichenbaum, 1977, 1995) and to constructively solve personal problems mentally (Goldfried & Goldfried, 1980; Mahoney, 1974).

An important example is **cognitive restructuring:** ways to view problems differently by thinking about them more constructively and less irrationally. One of the most

Table 16.7
Some Widespread Irrational Beliefs

1. An adult human must be loved or approved by almost everyone.
2. In order to feel worthwhile, a person must be competent in all possible respects.
3. When things are not the way you want them to be, it is a catastrophe.
4. People have little or no control over the external causes of the bad things that happen to them.
5. The best way to handle a dangerous or fear-producing event is to worry about it and dwell on it.
6. It is easier to avoid certain life difficulties and responsibilities than it is to face them.
7. One needs to depend on others and to rely on someone stronger than oneself.
8. One's present behavior is determined primarily by one's past history.
9. One should be upset by the problems of others.
10. There is always a perfect solution to a human problem, and it is essential to find it.

SOURCE: Based on Ellis, A. (1962). *Reason and emotion in psychotherapy.* New York: Lyle Stuart; and on Ellis, A., Sichel, J. L., Yeager, R. J., DiMattia, D. J., & DiGiuseppe, D. (1989). *Rational-emotive couples therapy.* Elmsford, NY: Pergamon.

influential forms of cognitive restructuring is Albert Ellis's (1962, 1977) **rational emotive therapy.** This approach is based on the idea that irrational beliefs produce irrational behaviors (Ellis et al., 1989). It follows that if people are taught to think more rationally, their behavior will become less irrational and their emotional problems will be reduced.

Some common irrational beliefs, according to Ellis, include the ones summarized in Table 16.7. These beliefs are irrational in the sense that they do not accurately represent the individual's real world. Reacting to situations on the basis of such irrational beliefs will produce ineffective behavior and such maladaptive emotions as anxiety and depression. Irrational beliefs may be revised by rational restructuring, as when a person who believes she must be loved by everybody rethinks this potentially debilitating attitude and realizes its impossibility.

Some evidence supports the value of rational emotive therapy. For instance, self-verbalizations (how one talks to oneself) can affect emotional arousal (Russell & Brandsma, 1974). Irrational self-statements do seem to be associated with maladaptive emotional reactions (Goldfried & Sobocinski, 1975) and many problem behaviors may be reduced by teaching clients to restructure (revise) their irrational self-statements. Some of Ellis's techniques and concepts are therefore now being used by other therapists. While the approach seems promising, the relations between attitudes and actions are more complex than Ellis's theory suggests, and his position tends to oversimplify the complex and multiple determinants of behavior. Rational restructuring may help some people with some problems, but it is only one cognitive technique among many potentially fruitful alternatives. Its value still has to be tested further, and although the evidence to favor it so far is encouraging, it is not conclusive (Davison & Neale, 1990; Rachman & Wilson, 1980; Wilson & O'Leary, 1980).

SUMMARY

1. Encoding and expectancies are two person variables that significantly affect the inner thought processes and external actions of individuals. Two forms of encoding on which individuals differ importantly are *evaluation* of performance and *attribution* of the causes of events.

2. The "self" is a concept used in different ways by different theorists. William James distinguished between two aspects of the self: the "I," which executes the basic psychological functions of the individual, and the "me," which is a creation of the self-perceptions of the individual. Self-schemata is a more modern term that refers to the self-relevant cognitions which form the "me." They develop from the person's perceived life experiences, and they in-

fluence how new information relevant to the self will be processed.

3. The perception of a stable overall self develops despite the many diverse self-concepts that are modified throughout life and the variety of seemingly discrepant behaviors that may characterize an individual in different life contexts. In some current theories, a person has diverse concepts about the self or multiple perceived selves. The working self-concept refers to the combination of *past, current,* and *possible* selves accessible at a given time. In one theory, people also may see discrepancies between their perceived actual self and their desired selves. When those discrepancies produce negative feelings, individuals may alter thought processes and

behaviors to reduce them. Typically, a person's self-esteem seems to combine a mix of "thorough realism" on the one hand with "protective maneuvering" for self-enhancement on the other.

4. *Specific expectancies* are an individual's expectations that his or her specific behaviors will produce specific results in particular contexts. *Generalized expectancies* reflect past experiences with behaviors and situations, which then serve to predict present and future outcomes. Changes in self-concept are affected both by self-relevant expectancies and by the person's subjective values and goals. Self-efficacy, a person's belief in his or her ability to act effectively in a specific situation and perform the relevant behavior competently, often helps to predict the person's level of motivation and quality of performance. Albert Bandura also explains the effectiveness of behavior therapies as due to their ability to improve self-efficacy for mastering the primary problematic behavior.

5. People in a state of learned helplessness believe they have no control over negative outcomes and may become apathetic and depressed. They tend to become more alert and happy as they feel more able to control their environment. The emotions people experience are affected by the causal attributions they make. Events (such as test results) that we attribute to *internal causes* are more likely to produce pride or shame than are results attributed to *external causes*. For self-protection against depression, we generally perceive causes in ways that are *self-enhancing*. Learned optimism is a self-enhancing explanatory style that has positive effects for most individuals. Pessimism is an explanatory style that attributes high levels of *stability, globality,* and *internality* to negative life events (for example, "bad things are always my fault"). This style of explaining may predict future poor health in individuals who display it consistently.

6. *Helpless children,* who perceive their intelligence as an unchanging entity, tend to perform poorly after experiencing failure, which they construe as due to lack of ability. Conversely, *mastery-oriented children,* who feel they can control and improve their intelligence and see failure as lack of effort, can cope better with failure. Entity theorists choose goals to avoid negative outcomes and ensure approval; incremental theorists prefer goals that will enhance their knowledge and competence.

7. Stanley Schachter's cognitive-physiological theory posits that emotion is a product both of physiological response and cognitive perception of the situation. In physiological arousal, the sympathetic division of the autonomic nervous system is activated. The emotional response one experiences subjectively depends on the perceived source of the physiological arousal and the interpretation of the situation.

8. The way an individual is affected by a potentially stressful event depends importantly on how it is cognitively appraised. Through constructive encoding, individuals are able to cope more effectively with stressful or threatening experiences. For example, they may endow tragic events, such as victimization by disease or accidents, with personal significance; even if the meaning is illusory, its effect can be beneficial.

9. Aaron Beck's cognitive therapy is founded on the premise that the way the individual structures his or her world cognitively influences behavior and affect (emotion). It treats psychiatric disorders by changing the way people encode (construe) themselves and their experiences, focusing on more constructive ways of thinking to help them to overcome their dysfunctional beliefs. In a similar direction, Albert Ellis's rational emotive therapy aims at cognitive restructuring to reduce irrational behavior and emotional problems by teaching more rational thinking.

Self-Regulation and Control

Self-regulation may sound like a highly abstract concept, but it is not. We see it in the differences among people in how they formulate and pursue their New Year's resolutions. We see it not only in the goals they set (to diet, to stop smoking, to save more money), but in their strategies for pursuing them in the face of the temptations and frustrations that arise along the route in daily life. The ways in which an individual characteristically self-regulates in dealing with life goals and tasks is a distinguishing central aspect of personality and of the self, and it is this chapter's concern.

THE SELF-REGULATORY PROCESS

A century ago Freud conceptualized the infant as an impulse-driven creature, ruled by a pleasure principle that demands immediate gratification here and now. The challenge ever since has been to understand how people, while remaining capable of great impulsivity, also become able to regulate themselves effectively, to purposefully delay gratification, and to exercise self-control for the sake of later consequences and goals. The question is: What are the processes that make this possible?

As indicated in Table 17.1, within the present framework, self-regulation is influenced by all the person variables discussed in Chapter 15. It involves the organized interplay of every aspect of the Cognitive-Affective Personality System (CAPS). Self-regulation depends on the ways in which the individual *encodes* or construes the situation in which self-regulation is attempted, the *expectancies* and *beliefs* that become activated, the feelings experienced, the *goals* and *values* engaged, and the *skills* and *competencies* that are employed to try to pursue them strategically. This process is especially important to understand because through effective self-regulation the person can actively influence and partially shape his or her own life course and future. Conversely, ineffective self-regulation, beginning in the early years of life, is associated with such adverse outcomes as subsequent school failure, poor academic and social competence, conduct disorders, and many addictive and antisocial behavior patterns (Bandura, 1986; Mischel et al., 1996; Rutter, 1987).

Individual differences in self-regulation are dramatic. While some people adhere to stringent diets, give up cigarettes after years of smoking them addictively, or continue to struggle and wait for distant goals even when tempted to quit, others fail in spite of affirming the same initial good intentions. The ancient Greeks considered a lack or weak-

Table 17.1
Aspects of Self-Regulation: Overview

Encoding (Construal)	Expectancies/ Beliefs	Affects	Goals/Values	Regulatory Competencies
Self-relevance (personal meaningfulness)	Perceived control/ helplessness	Emotional arousal, fears and desires	Self-standards	Control strategies (distraction/ "cooling")
Automaticity (trigger reactions)	Self-efficacy/ expected outcomes	Feeling states/ "hot" (impulsive) automatic responses	Self-evaluation	Planning/self-instruction/self-monitoring

SOURCE: Based in part on material in Mischel, W., Cantor, N., & Feldman, S. (1996). Principles of self-regulation: The nature of will-power and self-control. In E. T. Higgins & A. W. Kruglanski (Eds.), *Social Psychology: Handbook of Basic Principles* (pp. 329–360). New York: Guilford.

ness of the will as a character trait and called it *akrasia*—the deficiency of the will. To this day, this type of trait remains important in personality theories, as seen in the dimensions of "ego resilience" and "ego strength" (e.g., Block & Block, 1980) or the factor of "conscientiousness" within the Big Five (Chapter 6). A major aim of CAPS theory is to understand the processes that underlie such differences among people and the reasons that their efforts succeed or fail. Let us consider each of the contributing influences shown in Table 17.1 and their interplay in the self-regulatory process.

Encoding and Construal

Self-Relevance.　　The motivation to try to self-regulate tends to increase to the extent that the activity or situation is encoded as personally meaningfully and **self-relevant** (Bandura, 1986; Cantor, 1990). New mothers, for example, cope better with the often exhausting and sometimes anxiety-provoking or boring chores and routines of parenting an infant when they view those tasks as fulfilling important self-obligations rather than as taking time away from other modes of self-fulfillment, such as a career (Alexander & Higgins, 1993).

Automaticity.　　Even if events and situations are perceived as highly self-relevant, however, the person does not necessarily consciously attempt to self-regulate. On the contrary, such situations easily automatically trigger the enduring behavior patterns that characterize an individual's personality. These are exactly the reaction patterns that have become well-established and then are enacted with little or no control, thought, or awareness. Examples of this **automaticity** (Bargh & Gollwitzer, 1994) are the angry and violent reactions of rejection sensitive men who are quick to perceive rejection from a romantic partner even when it does not occur (Chapter 15). Their maladaptive reaction pattern of uncontrolled hostility may be essentially reflexive, bypassing conscious control and preventing purposeful self-intervention efforts. In these cases, the person applies encodings even when they do not fit and maintains them regardless of contradictory evidence.

Expectancies and Control Beliefs

Self-Efficacy.   Expectancies and beliefs that one will be able to exert control and successfully execute necessary actions are essential for self-regulation. They support one's efforts and guide whether, where, when, and how one attempts to self-regulate (Mischel et al., 1996). To even try purposeful self-regulation requires a representation of the self "as a causal agent of the intended action" (Kuhl, 1984, p. 127). As discussed in the previous chapter, **perceived self-efficacy** — the belief that "I can do it" — is a foundation for the successful pursuit of a difficult goal or for changing and improving one's situation or oneself. Its psychological opposite, perceived helplessness, is the route to giving up, apathy, and depression.

Perceived Control and Predictability.   Even when the self-regulatory task is something aversive that has to be endured and cannot be controlled — like a painful dental procedure — the belief that one can predict or control the stress is an important ingredient for coping. For example, in a classic study, college women were exposed to an aversive noise that occurred either at a predictable time or unpredictably and then had to work on a task (Glass et al., 1969). Their tolerance for frustration and the quality of their performance on the task were impaired only when the noise was unpredictable. Equally interesting, the negative effects could be reduced considerably if during the stress period the subjects believed they could do something to control the end of the stress. Generally, most people tend to become less upset when they think they can predict and control stressful or painful events (Staub et al., 1971), even if the perception is illusory (Taylor & Brown, 1988).

Outcome Expectancies.   Goal striving is also bolstered — or undermined — by **outcome expectancies** about the likelihood that time and energy spent on the task will actually result (or not result) in the desired outcome (Brunstein, 1993; Carver & Scheier, 1982; Klinger, 1975). When and where and what we choose to wait or work for depends in part on the anticipated consequences. To the extent that an effort to self-regulate has a relatively high perceived likelihood of leading to desirable consequences, the person will be more likely to choose to perform it (Carver & Scheier, 1982; Feather, 1990; Klinger, 1975; Mischel, 1973; Rotter, 1954).

People base these outcome expectations both on information in the current situation and on expectations generalized from previous similar situations. Such expectancies strongly influence whether people will try to perform a task that is a prerequisite for attaining a larger reward, such as completing a boring work assignment, or instead settle for a smaller reward that is available noncontingently and immediately: Those who expect to succeed on the task are more willing to try to perform it (e.g., Mischel & Staub, 1965). In sum, expectancies have a substantial impact on self-regulatory choices: People are more likely to choose to perform an action that requires effort if they believe that they can perform the action (i.e., have high self-efficacy expectancies) and expect that it will lead to favorable consequences (e.g. Bandura, 1986; Mischel, 1973).

The role of efficacy and outcome expectancies for helping important self-regulatory efforts in daily life is demonstrated, for example, in studies designed to increase commitments to condom use among inner-city African-American adolescents (e.g., Jemmott, Jemmott, Spears, & Hewitt, 1992). A key component for achieving this goal required raising the participants' self-efficacy beliefs and their outcome expectancies about the positive hedonistic consequences of using condoms.

Affects: "Hot" Reactions and the Emotional Brain

The situations in which people most need and want to self-regulate and control their impulses often are those in which it is most difficult for them to do so. These tend to be the situations that elicit "hot" emotional reactions such as intense fear and anxiety or strong appetites and cravings. In these situations, the person may be subject to what the behaviorists call "stimulus control" in which the stimulus virtually triggers the response (Chapter 14). The challenge for efforts at self-regulation is how to overcome such reflexive, automatic stimulus control with more reflective self-control.

Consider, for example, the student with public-speaking anxiety who panics at the prospect of having to make a presentation to a group. Or think of the dilemma of the addict who is trying to quit but is tempted with heroin, or the starving dieter faced with the ultimate chocolate cake. These kinds of hot situations and stimuli tend to automatically trigger hot reactions, rapidly generating the associated feelings of fear or desire and the urge to respond impulsively, bypassing self-regulatory controls just when they are most important to have. Such hot reflexive reactions may be part of the overall arousal state that helps initiate quick adaptive action, as in an emergency response to sudden dangers that mobilize the body's resources like a fire alarm. However, it makes thoughtful self-regulation and planful action and reflection most difficult (Metcalfe & Mischel, 1998).

Role of the Amygdala.　As was noted in Chapter 13, a small almond-shaped region in the forebrain, called the **amygdala** (which means *almond* in Latin), is crucially important in emotional reactions, particularly fear (LeDoux, 1996). The central nucleus of this brain structure reacts almost instantly to signals that warn of danger, immediately sending out behavioral, physiological (autonomic), and endocrine responses. It mobilizes the body for action, readying it to flee or fight. This reflexive emergency reaction is useful for adaptation: It has evolutionary survival value to react automatically to the snake in the grass without having to reflect about it slowly, or to fight the opponent who is ready to strike when flight is not possible.

But as LeDoux (1996, p. 176) says, these automatic reactions are only a "quick fix." Unlike lower animals in the evolutionary ladder, human beings have the capacity to eventually take control with higher level brain centers (the prefrontal cortex) and to start thinking and planning their way through the problem that the amygdala has already begun to respond to automatically and emotionally. The trick in achieving effective self-regulation is to move from the automatic hot emotional responses that can quickly become maladaptive to cool, reasoned, reflective reactions that make use of the vast cognitive resources that give humans their advantage (Metcalfe & Jacobs, 1998; Metcalfe & Mischel, 1998).

Effects of Anxiety.   The ability to self-regulate and pursue goals effectively is particularly undermined by anxious feelings and self-preoccupying thoughts, for example, the thoughts, "I'm no good at this—I'll never be able to do it" in the test-anxious person. These thoughts compete and interfere with task-relevant thoughts (such as, "Now I have to recheck my answers"). The result is that performance (as well as the subject) suffers (Sarason, 1979). The interference from self-preoccupying thoughts tends to be greatest when the task to be done is complex and requires many competing responses (Metcalfe & Mischel, in press). One just cannot be full of negative feelings and thoughts about oneself and simultaneously concentrate effectively on difficult work. Likewise, as the motivation to do well increases (as when success on the task is especially important), the highly anxious person may become particularly handicapped. The reason for this is that under such highly motivating conditions, test-anxious people tend to catastrophize and become even more negatively self-preoccupied, dwelling on how poorly they are doing. In contrast, the less anxious pay attention to the task and concentrate on how to master it effectively (e.g., Bandura, 1986; Dweck, 1989).

Values, Goals, and Self-Standards

Self-regulatory efforts are generally greater to the degree that they are highly valued and relevant to one's goals (Mischel et al., 1996). They also depend on the self-regulatory standards used to evaluate and monitor one's own progress toward these goals, for example, as the sprinter tries to improve performance or the student tries to study longer (e.g., Bandura, 1989; Carver & Scheier, 1990). People compare their current state of performance with those standards. If they perceive a discrepancy, they tend to be motivated to reduce it or to reset their standards to a lower level (e.g. Carver & Scheier, 1981, 1990). As Bandura explained: "When people make self-satisfaction or tangible gratifications conditional upon certain accomplishments, they motivate themselves to expend the effort needed to attain the requisite performance" (Bandura, 1986, p. 350). By generating consequences for their own actions, individuals can bring them into line with their higher order values and goals.

Acquisition of Standards.   The standards and goals people observe in the behavior of the important models they value quide their self-regulatory efforts. In a pioneering series of studies on the acquisition of self-regulatory standards, Bandura and Kupers (1964) examined young children's patterns of self-reward during a rigged bowling game. They found that children who observed adults reward themselves for low levels of performance (i.e. low-standard models) subsequently treated themselves to available rewards after achieving low or moderate scores. In contrast, those who had been exposed to high-standard models adopted a stricter criterion for self-reward, making it contingent on high levels of performance.

Social comparisons with peers also influence adult standards and self-regulation. For example, the levels of drinking that college students consider acceptable depend on their perceptions of the drinking behavior and values that are characteristic of a typical member of their group (Prentice & Miller, 1993). When these perceived norms turn out to be inaccurate and exaggerated, they can encourage the perceiver to drink excessively, that is, even more than most of the other group members (Miller & Prentice, 1994). The effects can be enduring if students who conform to these misperceived group norms then drink more than they themselves believed to be appropriate and subsequently revise their personal standards to become consistent with their new behavior (Abrams, 1994).

Practicing and Preaching.   How do the standards that socialization agents practice and those that they "preach" to the child impact the child's subsequent self-control? Given that the two are often discrepant in the course of rearing children, this question needs to be addressed. Research supports the belief that what they practice matters much more than what they preach, and when their own behavior violates what they advocate, they seem to discredit themselves. If adult models impose the same standards on their own performance as they demand of the child, the child is likely to adopt and maintain these standards, however stringent (Mischel & Liebert, 1966).

Activation of Self-Standards: From Mindlessness to Self-Focus.   Much of what we do as we pursue goals is **mindless** (Langer, 1978), guided by more-or-less automatic behavioral routines or scripts that are familiar and require little active attention or self-regulatory effort (Abelson, 1976). In a fast-food restaurant or at a football game, for example, we tend to act out more or less automatic routines. Under such

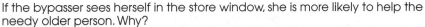
If the bypasser sees herself in the store window, she is more likely to help the needy older person. Why?

conditions, active, conscious self-regulation plays little role and we do not experience self-awareness; that is, we do not focus on ourselves and our self-standards but behave more or less as if on automatic pilot.

Self-regulation is more likely to be attempted when attention is focused on the self. That happens, for example, when one is observed, or sees oneself in a mirror. Under such self-focus, people become more conscious of their behavior and how it compares with their standards. In turn, awareness of any discrepancies motivates them to modify their actions in order to bring them more into line with their standards and ideals. Thus, a focus of attention on the self motivates the person to try to reduce perceived discrepancies between what he or she is doing and the relevant standards for comparison (Carver & Scheier, 1981; Duval et al., 1992; Scheier & Carver, 1988). For example, a self-perceived "caring" person who sees herself reflected in a store window about to pass a sick old man sprawled on a city sidewalk is more likely to bring herself in line with her own standards and pause to try to help. (Also see *In Focus 17.1.*)

Bypassing Self-Standards

Self-standards may be bypassed easily, however, under various pressures of the moment (Carver & Scheier, 1978, 1992; Higgins, 1990; Wright & Mischel, 1987). Just as looking at yourself in the mirror makes it harder to bypass your "conscience" (that is, the personal standards and values to which you strive to adhere), listening to the "leader," the "authority," or the "group" can make it easy to forget those standards. Films about lynch mobs, gang rapes, wartime atrocities, the Holocaust, and urban riots document what can happen when personal responsibility is forsaken. Although we become desensitized easily by viewing them repeatedly in the media, they illustrate some of the many life situations in which self-standards and careful self-examination are forgotten, often with terrible consequences both to the victim and to the perpetrator. Research also has shown how easily people can be urged by authority figures into acts of aggression, failing to access their own self-standards and readily doing to others what they would consider unthinkable for themselves (Milgram, 1974).

On the other hand, when self-regulatory scripts and plans for self-control are activated, the person may be able to overcome such pressures. The purposeful activation of self-regulatory competencies and skills is discussed next.

DEMYSTIFYING WILLPOWER: STRATEGIES OF SELF-CONTROL

Even when perceived self-efficacy and control are high, the person is motivated to self-regulate, and self-standards are activated, the effective pursuit and attainment of difficult but desired goals can collapse easily. That happens when the necessary self-regulatory competencies and skills are not available to the person or are not accessed when needed. We can see this most clearly when the goal lies in the future (think of your favorite, still unfulfilled New Year's resolution) and thus requires deliberate delay of gratification (such as forgoing the dessert now for the sake of the desired shape or healthy heart much later) in the face of the temptations of the moment (the dessert looks wonderful).

IN FOCUS 17.1 *Self-Evaluation, Perceived Self-Discrepancies, and Eating Disorders*

Alarmed by the growing number of cases of eating disorders especially among adolescents and young adult women, researchers and clinical psychologists have been trying to understand this self-destructive, potentially fatal behavior. Explanations offered for eating disorders range from maladaptive interactions among family members to perceptual distortions in the way victims actually see their own bodies. Eating disorders also may reflect discrepancies among the individual's self-concepts, which impact on his or her self-evaluation and can disturb self-regulation (Strauman et al., 1991). This explanation stems from self-discrepancy theory (Higgins, 1987), in which different kinds of negative feelings typically are associated with particular kinds of perceived self-discrepancies. Discrepancies between the "actual" self one perceives oneself to be and the "ideal" self that one wants to be are called **actual/ideal discrepancies** (also see Chapter 16). According to the theory, they make one vulnerable to feelings of dejection. In contrast, discrepancies between one's "actual" self and the "ought" self one feels one should be (called **actual/ought discrepancies**) make an individual susceptible to feelings of agitation.

In Higgins' (1987) theory, the person's **self-evaluative standards** (self-guides) are represented by the ideal self and the ought self. When the actual self falls short of these self guides, the individual becomes prone to negative emotions and motivational states. These negative feelings, in turn, can produce distress and maladaptive behavior (Strauman et al., 1991). Some of the negative effects may be seen in eating disorders.

Thus, anorexic behavior (self-starvation) has been linked to actual/ought discrepancies (Strauman et al., 1991). According to these researchers, anorexic behaviors

tend to be more characteristic of individuals whose actual self-concepts are discrepant from their representations of how significant others believe they ought to be. The anorexic behaviors seem to be part of a pattern of self-punitive, self-critical efforts to meet what these individuals see as the demands and expectations of significant others. In contrast, bulimic eating problems, such as binging, tend to be more associated with discrepancies between the person's actual self-concept and their own ideal self-concepts. Emotionally, those suffering from bulimia experience dejection and related feelings as a reflection of the discrepancy between the body types they perceive themselves to have and their ideals. Interestingly, this seems to be the case irrespective of the person's actual body mass.

Self-discrepancy theory also suggests another insight into eating disorders. The fact that eating disorders are much more prevalent among adolescent girls than boys has led to speculation that women are more commonly socialized to derive feelings of self-worth from their physical appearance. Because modern society mainly considers thin women to be beautiful, many women feel compelled to constantly monitor their body weight and thus are more prone to eating disorders. An alternative explanation, however, is that girls typically are more restricted and controlled than boys. Consequently, prior to adolescence they develop more rigid self-guides, that is, more clearly defined ideal and ought selves. The stronger the self-guides, the more vulnerable the individual is to experience self-discrepancy and negative feelings (Strauman et al., 1991, p. 947). According to the theory, then, women are more likely than men to develop disordered eating habits.

The dilemma and frustrations that may occur when it becomes difficult to delay gratification are familiar to everyone, beginning in earliest childhood. They have been debated and analyzed ever since the ancient Greek philosophers discussed the concept of willpower, and they have been the subject of stories about internal human conflict since the earliest legends. Within psychology, the problem was labeled the puzzle of "voluntary delay of gratification," and it began to be addressed with the birth of the field a century ago.

From the start, Freud's (1911) original theory provided one of the few theoretical discussions of how delay of gratification may be bridged. According to the psychoanalytic formulation, ideation (cognition) arises initially when there is a block or delay in the process of direct gratification (Rapaport, 1967). During such externally imposed delay, according to Freud, the child constructs a "hallucinatory image" of the physically absent, need-satisfying object. This mental image provides fantasy satisfactions (Freud, 1911; Singer, 1955). But in spite of much psychoanalytic theorizing and speculation about the role of the mental representation of blocked gratifications in the development of delaying capacity, the exact process remains far from clear (Kopp, 1982).

Delay of Gratification as a Basic Human Task

The ability to voluntarily refuse immediate gratification, to tolerate self-imposed delays of reward, is at the core of most concepts of willpower and ego strength. It is hard to imagine civilization without such self-imposed delays. Learning to wait for desired outcomes and to behave in the light of expected future consequences is essential for the successful achievement of long-term, distant goals. Every person must learn to defer impulses and to express them only under special conditions of time and place, as seen in toilet training. Similarly, enormously complex patterns of deferred gratification are required for people to achieve the delayed rewards provided by our culture's social system and institutions.

To achieve educational and occupational objectives, such as a college degree or a career in medicine or science, the route requires a continuous series of delays of gratification, as seen in the progression from one grade to the next and from one barrier to another in the long course from occupational choice to occupational success. In social relationships the culture also requires delays, as seen in the expectation that people should postpone sexual relations, marriage, and children until they are "ready for them." Although judgments of what constitutes such readiness differ greatly across cultures and among different people, some norms concerning appropriate timing are found in every society.

The importance of self-control patterns that require delay of gratification has been widely recognized by theorists from Freud to the present. The concept of voluntary postponement of gratifications for the sake of more distant, long-term gains is fundamental for many conceptualizations of complex human behavior and personality development (Harter, 1983; Kanfer & Karoly, 1972; Kopp, 1982; Mischel et al., 1989, 1996). Given that one has chosen to wait for a larger deferred goal or gratification, how can the delay period be managed?

Frustration Tolerance

Recall that in the delay of gratification situation described previously (Chapters 7, 15, and 16), the child is shown two objects (for example, food treats like marshmallows or pretzels), one of which he or she clearly prefers (as determined by pretesting). To at-

Figure 17.1
Waiting for Delayed Gratification

SOURCE: Based on Mischel, W., Ebbesen, E. B., & Zeiss, A. R. (1972). Cognitive and attentional mechanisms in delay of gratification. *Journal of Personality and Social Psychology, 21,* 204–218.

tain the preferred object, the child has to wait for it until the experimenter returns "by himself," but could signal at any time for him to return and then would get only the less preferred object. Because the research results proved to have important value for predicting long-term outcomes such as school success, the media publicized the method, naming it the "marshmallow test" (Goleman, 1995), as discussed in Chapter 7.

In this type of situation (shown in Figure 17.1), more than 500 preschoolers were studied systematically through observation and experiments (e.g., Mischel, 1974; Mischel et al., 1989; Mischel, Ebbesen, & Zeiss, 1970, 1972). One of the most striking delay strategies used by some youngsters was as simple as it was effective. These children seemed to manage to wait for the preferred reward for long periods apparently by converting the aversive waiting situation into a more pleasant, nonwaiting one. They seemed to do this by elaborate self-distraction techniques through which they spent their time psychologically doing something (almost anything) other than waiting. Rather than focusing prolonged attention on the objects for which they were waiting, they avoided looking at them. Some of these children covered their eyes with their hands, rested their heads on their arms, or found other similar techniques for averting their eyes from the reward objects. Others seemed to try to reduce the frustration of delay of reward by generating their own diversions: They talked to themselves, sang, invented games with their hands and feet, and when all other distractions seemed exhausted, even tried to fall asleep during the waiting situation—as one child successfully did.

These observations suggested that diverting yourself from attention to the delayed reward stimulus (while maintaining behavior directed toward its ultimate attainment) may be a key step for effective delay of reward. That is, learning *not* to attend to or think about what you are awaiting may enhance effective delay of gratification much more than does focusing attention on the outcomes. When hungry, for example, it seems easier to wait for supper if one is not confronted with the sight and smell of food.

The idea that directing attention away from the rewards is a major strategy for self-control also was tested more rigorously with experiments. For example, Figure

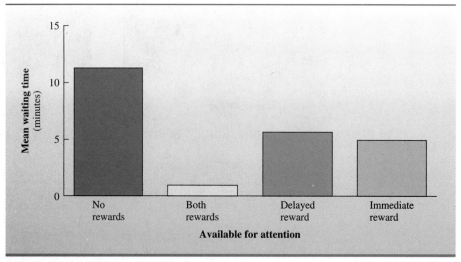

Figure 17.2
Effects of Attention on Delay of Gratification

SOURCE: Based on data from Mischel, W., & Ebbesen, E. B. (1970). Attention in delay of gratification. *Journal of Personality and Social Psychology, 16*, 239–337.

17.2 shows results of an experiment that manipulated the extent to which children could attend to the reward objects while they were waiting (Mischel, Ebbesen, & Zeiss, 1972). As shown in Figure 17.2, in one condition, the children waited with both the immediate (less preferred) and the delayed (more preferred) reward facing them in the experimental room so that they could attend to both outcomes. In another group neither reward was available for the child's attention, both having been removed from sight. In the remaining two groups either the delayed reward only or the immediate reward only was available for attention while the child waited. The measure was the length of time before each child voluntarily stopped waiting. Note that the child waited much longer when the rewards were not available for attention, supporting the observations and hypotheses discussed above.

Self-Distraction to Cope with Frustration

Delay of gratification and frustration tolerance is enhanced when the person can transform the aversive waiting period into a more pleasant, nonwaiting situation. This can be done by diverting attention and thoughts away from the frustrative components of delay of gratification and thinking instead about other things. Such distractions can be achieved if one can engage in activities, overtly or mentally, during the delay period that help to suppress or decrease the aversiveness of waiting for the desired outcome.

Thus, voluntary delay of reward can be aided by any overt or covert activities that serve as distracters from the rewards and thus from the aversiveness of wanting them but not having them. Through such distraction it is possible to convert the frustrative delay-of-reward situation into a psychologically less aversive condition. For example, children waited much longer for a preferred reward when they were distracted cognitively from the goal objects than when they directly attended to them (Mischel, Ebbesen, & Zeiss, 1972; Mischel, Shoda, & Rodriguez, 1989). Thus, cognitions directed toward the rewards while the children waited greatly reduced, rather than enhanced, the length of time that the children were able to delay gratification. In contrast, distracting oneself from the rewards, overtly or cognitively, (e.g., by thinking of "fun things") made it possible to wait longer for them.

These results contradicted the notion that "willpower" requires one to maintain directed attention to things that are aversive, difficult, or boring. Rather than trying to maintain aversive activities such as delay of reward through "acts of will" and focused attention, effective self-control is helped by *transforming* the difficult into the easy, the aversive into the pleasant, and the boring into the interesting, while still maintaining the task-required activity on which the ultimate reward depends. You can create such transformations either by engaging in the appropriate overt distracting activity or changing your own mental content and ideation. A good way to master the difficult or aversive thus may be to think or do something pleasant while doing the task (for example, waiting, working). Rather than "willing" oneself to heroic bravery, one needs to enact the necessary "difficult" response while engaging in another one cognitively (Mischel, 1984; Mischel et al., 1996). To do this effectively, when the task is complex, may require extensive rehearsal and planning for implementing the necessary actions when they are needed (Gollwitzer & Moskowitz, 1996).

Cool versus Hot Encoding

The outcomes or rewards in this type of situation may be encoded in terms of their "hot," consummatory properties or in terms of their "cool," informative properties. A "hot" representation of a rewarding stimulus such as a desired treat activates the behaviors associated with experiencing or consuming it. When young children look at the actual rewards or think about them, they may focus spontaneously on these hot, arousing qualities, thereby increasing their own frustration and arousal, making it more difficult to continue to wait (e.g., Mischel & Ebbesen, 1970; Mischel, Ebbesen, & Zeiss, 1972; Mischel, Shoda, & Rodriguez, 1989; Toner, 1981).

In contrast, a cool, abstract representation of the rewards has the opposite effect on self-regulation, enhancing goal-directed waiting. Thus, presenting children with abstract representations of the rewards (e.g., slide-projected images) or instructing them to cognitively transform the rewards to focus on their "cool," abstract properties (e.g., by transforming pretzels into thin, brown logs in their imagination) actually facilitates waiting (Mischel & Moore, 1973; Moore, Mischel, & Zeiss, 1976; Mischel & Baker, 1975). In short, just how one thinks about (encodes) the rewards in the contingency crucially influences how long one can wait to attain them (Metcalfe & Mischel, in press; Mischel et. al., 1996).

Observations of children's behavior during the delay period (Mischel & Ebbesen, 1970) suggested how "cool" ideation supports self-control. At points throughout the waiting period, most of the children's spontaneous attempts at self-distraction wavered.

Those children who were successful in reorienting themselves to self-distraction, rather than succumbing to the frustrativeness of the situation and terminating the waiting period, used strategies such as verbalizing self-instructions to remind themselves of the contingency (e.g., "If I wait I get [the preferred reward] but if I ring the bell I get [the less preferred reward]") or otherwise reestablish the goal of obtaining the delayed reward. Correspondingly, instructing children to verbalize about "the goodness of waiting" or the consequences of so doing during the delay period leads to longer waiting times (Toner, 1981; Toner & Smith, 1977). Thus, in effective delay of gratification the child tunes out the hot properties of the reward stimulus while (at least periodically) concentrating on its cool, abstract properties and the contingency in order to direct and sustain her waiting behavior.

Strategies like these also help one to self-regulate in other potentially stressful situations. Self-distraction (e.g., watching travel slides or recalling pleasant memories) increases tolerance of experimentally induced physical pain (e.g., Berntzen, 1987; Chaves & Barber, 1974; Kanfer & Seidner, 1973; Rosenbaum, 1980). Similarly, distracting and relaxation-induced activities such as listening to music reduce anxiety in the face of uncontrollable shocks (Miller, 1979, 1996) and help people cope with the daily pain of rheumatoid arthritis (Affleck et al., 1992) and even with severe life crises (e.g., Taylor & Brown, 1988). "Cooling" strategies generally can help one to transform potentially stressful situations to make them less aversive. For example, if surgical patients are encouraged to reconstrue their hospital stay as a vacation from the stresses of daily life, they show better postoperative adjustment (Langer, Janis, & Wolfer, 1975), just as chronically ill patients who reinterpret their conditions more positively also show better adjustment (Carver et al., 1993).

Summary

Taken collectively, research on delay of gratification and tolerance for self-imposed frustration suggests a two-part process. First, consider the determinants of the *choice* to undergo frustrative delay for the sake of preferred delayed outcomes. This choice is influenced mainly by expectations concerning the probable consequences of the choice. These consequences include the relative subjective values of the immediate and delayed outcomes themselves as well as other probable gratifying outcomes associated with each alternative. Expectancies about these outcomes depend on direct and vicarious past experiences and trust relationships, modeling cues, the specific contingencies in the choice, and so on. So if you really expect to get the delayed reward and want it, you are more likely to wait for it.

Second, once the choice to self-impose delay of gratification has been made, effective delay depends on cognitive and overt self-distractions to reduce the aversiveness of the self-imposed frustration. For this purpose, the person needs to avoid the goal objects, generating his or her own distractions while maintaining the necessary behavior on which goal-attainment is contingent. An effective way of coping with the frustrations imposed by delay in many life situations is to transform the aversive delay period cognitively into a more positive or interesting experience. This can be achieved by doing something else, overtly or internally, while continuing to wait for the desired goal or by cognitively transforming the desired goal objects to reduce their excessively

IN FOCUS 17.2   *The Growth of Self-Control Knowledge*

Much is now known about what makes it harder or easier for young children to delay gratification. But when and how do the children themselves acquire knowledge of the "delay rules" that make waiting less frustrating? For example, does the preschool child know that thinking about the arousing, desirable qualities of the rewards (the pretzel's crunchy taste, for instance) will make self-imposed delay more difficult? Questions of this sort have been explored (e.g., Yates & Mischel, 1979) and the results suggest that children's understanding and knowledge of effective delay rules show a clear progression in the course of development (Mischel & Mischel, 1983).

Most children below the age of about four years do not seem to generate clear or effective strategies for delay; indeed they sometimes even make waiting more difficult for themselves by focusing on what they want but cannot

have (Mischel, 1981). By the age of five to six years they know that covering the rewards will help them wait for them while looking at the rewards or thinking about them will make it difficult. By third grade, children spontaneously generate and reasonably justify a number of potentially viable strategies and clearly understand the basic principles of resistance to temptation. For example, they avoid looking at the rewards because: "If I'm looking at them all the time, it will make me hungry . . . and I'd want to ring the bell." Often they also indicate the value of distraction from the rewards or of negative ideation designed to make them less tempting ("Think about gum stuck all over them"). And by the time they reach sixth grade, children show considerable sophistication, utilizing ideal strategies that allow them to delay gratification with relative ease.

arousing qualities. So if you can make the waiting easier for yourself, you are more likely to wait successfully (see also *In Focus 17.2*).

Early Delay Predicts Later Personality and SAT Scores: Long-Term Coherence

We saw before that a child's momentary mental representation of the outcomes in the delay situation influences his or her waiting time. Indeed it is possible to predict how long children will tend to wait from knowledge of the psychological conditions in which they are waiting. But individual differences in waiting time in the delay situation, regardless of condition, are not trivial matters. They are, instead, robust features of an important and enduring **cognitive social competence,** a basic person variable (Chapter 15). For example, there is significant continuity between how long preschoolers delay while waiting for a couple of pretzels or marshmallows in the appropriate laboratory situations and independent ratings of their perceived cognitive and social competence made by their parents a dozen years later (Mischel et al., 1989). In some conditions, how long four-year-olds wait can even significantly predict their SAT scores when applying to college (Shoda, Mischel, & Peake, 1990). Results like these suggest that this measure taps an important aspect of social/emotional competence or intelligence (as noted in Chapter 7).

A clear picture has emerged of adolescent correlates significantly associated with preschool delay in the experimental situation years earlier. Table 17.2 illustrates

Table 17.2

Characteristics Associated with Delay of Gratification

As adolescents, children who delayed gratification longer in preschool were described by parents as:
Less likely to be sidetracked by minor setbacks.
More likely to exhibit self-control in frustrating situations.
Coping well with important problems.
Capable of doing well academically when motivated.
Less likely to yield to temptations.
When faced with a choice, less likely to settle for an immediate but less desirable choice.
More able to pursue goals when motivated.
Intelligent.
When motivated, capable of exhibiting self-control in tempting situations.
Skilled in maintaining friendships and getting along with peers.
Not distractible when trying to concentrate.
Capable of exhibiting self-control when frustrated.
Able to effectively pursue goals.
Capable of diverting attention from the frustration of having to postpone a desired gratification while continuing to pursue it.

SOURCE: Based on delay time in diagnostic conditions from Shoda, Y., Mischel, W., & Peake, P. K. (1990). Predicting adolescent cognitive and self-regulatory competencies from preschool delay of gratification: Identifying diagnostic conditions. *Developmental Psychology, 26,* 978–986.

significant relations between the child's preschool delay time and parental ratings years later. The children's mean age at first delay was about four years and about 17 years at the time of the parental ratings. The results are based on the most diagnostic delay condition, in which children waited with the reward exposed in front of them without being given any special strategies for coping with the delay.

These results (and those reported in Mischel et al., 1988) give a general picture of the child who delayed in preschool developing into an adolescent who is seen as attentive, able to concentrate, able to express ideas well, responsive to reason, competent, skillful, planful, able to think ahead, and able to cope and deal with stress maturely. These relations seem impressive given that they span a lengthy period of development and are based on the child's preschool behavior objectively assessed in seconds of delay time. Perhaps most important, the attributes suggested by the adolescent ratings are consistent with the cognitive competencies essential for delay revealed by the experimental research, namely the ability to divert and control attention strategically in the pursuit of one's goal. These qualities are likely to be major ingredients of the "cognitive social competence" considered to be a basic person variable in the social cognitive-affective approach (Chapter 15). They also seem to relate to the "ego resiliency" construct suggested in other investigations of child development and personality coherence (Block & Block, 1980).

STRATEGIES TO ENHANCE CONTROL

Taken collectively, research on self-regulation points to a variety of strategies that can enhance coping with life challenges and pursuing personal goals effectively. These are reviewed next.

Making the Difficult Easier

Many methods can help empower individuals to improve their efficacy themselves and persist with self-control efforts in the pursuit of difficult goals they desire. Such methods have made it easier for people to diet, to give up smoking, and to overcome fears and insomnia (Mahoney, 1974; Meichenbaum, 1995; Yates, 1985). Examples of these methods (summarized in Table 17.3) include self-observation, which involves carefully monitoring one's own behavior, such as when a dieter records the time and place of everything he or she eats. In stimulus control, one learns to do certain things only in certain places and at certain times, for example, studying only at one desk at fixed hours. You already saw the applications of the stimulus control method to treat insomnia (Chapter 14).

Self-reward and self-contracting consist of making desired outcomes contingent on first reaching specific goals, such as when one postpones a coffee break until half the reading assignment has been completed. Self-instruction involves explicit self-directions so that individuals can help themselves to resist the pressures of the situation and pursue, instead, more difficult but desired objectives. People can use self-instruction to help sustain their own continued work and effort even under difficult conditions (Bandura, 1986; Kanfer & Zich, 1974; Meichenbaum & Goodman, 1971; Meichenbaum 1995). To illustrate, young children can resist transgression better if they are first given a plan they can verbalize ("I must not turn around and look at the toy") to repeat to themselves later when they are alone and tempted (Hartig & Kanfer,

Table 17.3
Some Methods to Increase Self-Control

Method	Definition	Example
Self-observation	Systematic observation of one's own behavior	A dieter records everything he eats.
Stimulus control	The performance of certain behaviors only in the presence of certain cues	A person studies only in a special place at special times.
Self-reward and self-contracting	Providing positive consequences to oneself, contingent on desired behavior	A student rewards herself (e.g., with new clothes) for achieving specified grades.
Self-instruction	Talking to oneself to control one's behavior on a difficult task	An impulsive child is taught to think: "Go slow," "Work carefully."

SOURCE: Based on Kazdin, A. E. (1975). Effects of covert modeling and model reinforcement on assertive behavior. *Journal of Abnormal Psychology, 83,* 194.

Table 17.4

Examples of Self-Statements Used to Increase Creativity

Be creative, be unique.
Break away from the obvious, the commonplace.
Think of something no one else will think of.
Just be free-wheeling.
If you push yourself you can be creative.
Quantity helps breed quality.

Size up the problem; what is it you have to do?
You have to put elements together differently.
Use different analogies.
You're in a rut—okay, try something new.
Take a rest now; who knows when the ideas will visit again.

Release controls; let your mind wander.
Free-associate; let ideas flow.
Relax—just let it happen.
Let your ideas play.
Ideas will be a surprise.
Refer to your experience; just view it differently.

SOURCE: Meichenbaum, D. H. (1974). *Cognitive-behavior modification* (p. 15). Morristown, NJ: General Learning Press.

1973; Mischel & Patterson, 1976; Patterson & Mischel, 1975). Similarly, fearful people may be able to cope better if they learn and practice calming, problem-solving self-instructions which they can say to themselves when they must actually face the stressful situations (Meichenbaum, 1974, 1992, 1995).

Self-instructions also have been applied to help increase creativity. For this purpose one researcher urged college students to modify what they say to themselves. Statements like those in Table 17.4 were modeled by the psychologist and then practiced by the students. The groups given self-instructional training showed increased creativity (compared with control groups) on some measures and reported that their training generalized to help them take a more creative approach to their academic and personal problems (Meichenbaum, 1974). The approach appears to have promise in helping people overcome the rigidity that often blocks creative solutions (Meichenbaum, 1992).

A critical aspect of self-regulation stems from the fact that people assess and monitor themselves. Self-praise and censure, self-imposed treats and punishments, self-indulgence and self-laceration are signs of this pervasive human tendency to congratulate and condemn oneself. People learn to set their own performance standards and to make their own self-reward contingent upon their achieving these self-prescribed criteria (Bandura, 1986; Higgins, 1990). To adequately understand personality, we must know how people self-administer and regulate rewards and punishments that are in their own control and how this self-regulation develops and grows, allowing them to achieve increasing mastery in the pursuit of their goals.

Enhancing Perceived Efficacy and Coping

In part, anxiety sabotages performance by creating negative expectancies: People who expect failure are likely to fulfill their prophecy. But if they are led to think they can do better, will their performance actually improve? One study of academically borderline college freshmen examined just this question (Meichenbaum & Smart, 1971) and, as was discussed in Chapter 1, concluded that students who were led to expect success in fact became more successful in their school work.

The power of positive thinking is shown even more dramatically through "mental practice." In one experiment, subjects were instructed to imagine throwing darts at a target (Powell, 1973). Half the subjects were asked to imagine that their darts were hitting near the target's center; the other half imagined that their darts were striking outside the target area. Dart throwing improved significantly for people who had imagined successful performances during mental practice but not for those who had imagined poor performances. Numerous studies to increase self-efficacy have shown similar effects (Bandura, 1986). The moral is plain: Think success!

Planning and Future Orientation

As people develop, they become increasingly able to think of the future, using rules and plans to guide their behavior and cope with situational pressures and frustrations (Cantor, 1990; Kopp, 1982). Such rules and plans help a person organize complex behavior patterns into orderly, effective sequences over long time periods (e.g., Cantor & Kihlstrom, 1987) and thus achieve life goals more effectively.

Through plans and other forms of self-regulation, we can influence the environment's effect on us and exert control over it (e.g., Patterson & Mischel, 1976). We can actively choose the situations to which we expose ourselves, in a sense creating our

Self-regulation and planning require monitoring and coordination of many concurrent processes.

own environment, entering some settings but not others, anticipating different possibilities, and deciding what to do and what not to do. We can plan for the winter, for example, long before the storm hits by preparing snow tires and chains to avoid getting stuck. Although we cannot change the weather itself, we can plan vacations that will remove us from a harsh environment, at least for a while, or we can even move permanently.

Life Tasks, Personal Plans, and Projects

The individual's thoughts, plans, theories, and personal problem-solving styles have become the focus of increasing interest to psychologists guided by the social cognitive perspectives (Cantor & Kihlstrom, 1987; Cantor, 1990; Zirkel, 1992). One aim of this more recent work is to clarify the ways in which people formulate and pursue their own long-term goals and personal projects.

Current life tasks are defined as those central projects to which individuals perceive themselves as being committed during particular periods in their lives, such as in the transition from high school to college (Cantor & Kihlstrom, 1987, p. 168). These self-created tasks help to give meaning to the individual's life and provide organization and direction for many more specific activities that are in their service.

Examples of common life tasks include "getting promoted," "finding the right person and getting married," "making myself more fit and getting my figure back," and "taking off a couple of years to do something meaningful for needier people." Life tasks thus constitute significant long-term goals that are meaningful for the individual at some point in his or her life. While they are typically experienced as personally urgent, they are also often ill-defined and loosely formulated.

Certain types of life tasks are shared by many people in the same phase of life. For example, first-year students in an honors college at the University of Michigan often had life tasks like the following ones in common: "Being on my own," "making friends," "establishing an identity," "getting good grades," and "establishing a future direction" (Cantor & Kihlstrom, 1987, p. 172). When the students were encouraged to elaborate their plans, feelings, and specific strategies, some common themes emerged concerning achievement, intimacy, and gaining better self-control. Each student, however, also uniquely construed

Nancy Cantor

his or her tasks and focused on somewhat different aspects of the same common themes. For example, while "being on my own" meant learning to cope with personal failures without the help of parental hugs for one student, for another it meant working on how to manage money responsibly.

Investigations of this type are helping to provide systematic methods for accessing these personally significant, often unique aspects of experience. They draw on the individual's own expertise to articulate his or her personal constructs, plans, and problem-solving strategies for dealing with everyday real-life challenges.

Intrinsic Motivation in Self-Regulation

Intrinsic motivation is inferred when individuals engage in a task and enjoy and are interested in the activity for its own sake, not because of any external rewards. Although its exact origins are uncertain, there is little doubt that much human behavior is sustained by the satisfaction of "doing it." Intrinsic motivation seems to promote behaviors whose main rewards are that they allow the person to experience efficacy and autonomy (Deci & Ryan, 1985, 1987).

Intrinsic motivation is enhanced by the opportunity to make choices (Zuckerman et al., 1978), while rewards, deadlines, and surveillance tend to diminish it (Amabile et al., 1976; Deci, 1971; Lepper & Greene, 1975). For example, external rewards for playing with a puzzle of course can induce children to play with it. A long-term effect, however, may be that after the rewards are no longer offered these children lose interest in the puzzle itself more than does a control group for whom external rewards were never introduced (Lepper & Greene, 1975).

Extrinsic motivation is inferred when motivation seems only motivated by external rewards. Unlike intrinsic motivation, extrinsic motivation tends to be outcome-oriented and driven by social reactions (Koestner & McClelland, 1990). Extrinsically motivated behavior also can be promoted by different types of feedback on one's performance. Feedback that is perceived as controlling (for example, "You must do the puzzle this way") tends to result in extrinsically motivated behavior. Feedback that is perceived as informational, however, (for example, "Some people do the puzzle this way") encourages behavior that is more intrinsically motivated. In general, events that enable an individual to feel efficacious and in control will increase intrinsic motivation, while those that cause an individual to feel incompetent or controlled undermine intrinsic motivation (Deci, 1975). Although people differ in their levels of intrinsic motivation, behavior also can be affected by characteristics of a situation that change the motivation. Intrinsic motivation is influenced by many variables, including the structure of the situation, the other motives that are activated (for example, anxiety), and the outcomes that are expected and obtained (Harackiewicz, Abrahams, & Wageman, 1987).

Performance Goals and Learning Goals

In a related direction, Dweck and Leggett (1988) outlined two types of goals that affect the way individuals address an activity. **Performance goals** are aimed toward earning positive judgments of one's skill. **Learning goals** are oriented toward mastery or learning something new. Performance goals have been associated with a variety of

IN FOCUS 17.3 *Dealing with Anxiety: How to Talk to Yourself Better*

To perform more competently in the face of stress, it may help to "inoculate" oneself to it. One successful training program aims to modify both one's appraisal of the fearful situation and one's expectancies about being able to cope with it. To accomplish these aims, anxious people may be taught better ways to talk to themselves while anticipating and handling stressful situations. The idea is simply that if you improve your internal monologue, if you talk to yourself better, you will be able to cope more effectively. Examples of potentially useful self-statements are shown in Table 17.5. Since failure often occurs because people become upset by their own thoughts and fears of failure, it follows that a more positive monologue increases the chances for more competent performance. Whether or not you can perform effectively and fearlessly (and calmly drape a 6-foot king snake around your neck, for example) may depend most importantly on whether or not you expect that you can do it (Bandura, 1978). And such expectations of competence, in turn, depend on exactly what you say to yourself before and during the effort.

Table 17.5
Examples of Coping Self-Statements

Preparing for a Stressor
What is it I have to do?
I can develop a plan to deal with it.
Just think about what I can do about it. That's better than getting anxious.
No negative self-statements, just think rationally.
Don't worry. Worry won't help anything.
Maybe what I think is anxiety is eagerness to confront it.

Confronting and Handling a Stressor
I can meet this challenge.
One step at a time, I can handle the situation.
Don't think about fear—just about what I have to do. Stay relevant.

maladaptive behaviors in children, especially in approaching challenging material. Specifically, when faced with failure, children who emphasize performance goals exhibit negative affect and negative self-attributions while their strategies for coping tend to deteriorate (Elliot & Dweck, 1988). In contrast, children who possess learning goals do not exhibit negative affect when confronted with a task that is too difficult for them. They do not change their self-attributions, and they either maintain or improve their problem-solving strategies.

Note that children's behavior in such situations is independent of their actual ability level. If they have performance goals, even children with high ability tend to view themselves negatively and avoid the chance to learn something new when there is a possibility of experiencing difficulty or making mistakes. Thus, children with performance goals, regardless of actual skill, perceive exertion of effort as evidence of low ability, while children with learning goals see their effort as a tool to catalyze their ability. Performance goals make one more vulnerable to becoming dejected by failure experiences and giving up. Learning goals, in contrast, orient one to the challenge of the task and to devising strategies for mastering it and persisting (Grant & Dweck, 1999).

This anxiety is what the doctor said I would feel. It's a reminder to use my coping exercises.

This tenseness can be an ally, a cue to cope.

Relax; I'm in control. Take a slow, deep breath. Ah, good.

Coping with the Feeling of Being Overwhelmed

When fear comes, just pause.

Keep focus on the present; what is it I have to do?

Let me label my fear from 0 to 10 and watch it change.

I was supposed to expect my fear to rise.

Don't try to eliminate fear totally; just keep it manageable.

I can convince myself to do it. I can reason my fear away.

It will be over shortly.

It's not the worst thing that can happen.

Just think about something else.

Do something that will prevent me from thinking about fear.

Just describe what is around me. That way I won't think about worrying.

Reinforcing Self-Statements

It worked; I was able to do it.

Wait until I tell my therapist about this.

It wasn't as bad as I expected.

I made more out of the fear than it was worth.

My damn ideas—that's the problem. When I control them, I control my fear.

It's getting better each time I use the procedures.

I'm really pleased with the progress I'm making.

I did it!

SOURCE: Meichenbaum, D. H., & Cameron, R. (1974). The clinical potential of modifying what clients say to themselves. In M. J. Mahoney & C. E. Thoresen (Eds.), *Self-control: Power to person.* Monterey, CA: Brooks-Cole.

In sum, learning goals (rather than performance goals) and intrinsic motivation (rather than extrinsic motivation) seem to enhance effective and creative problem solving (Amabile, 1985). They reflect less sensitivity to the evaluation and judgments of others and a greater focus on satisfactions and opportunities derived from the activity.

Toward Self-Management: From External to Internal

Ideally, therapeutic and educational change programs are designed to increase individuals' independence and competence as rapidly as possible so that external control of their behavior can be reduced and ended quickly. Many techniques in education, therapy, and child-rearing can help to achieve that objective (Bandura, 1969, 1986; Kanfer, 1980; Kazdin & Wilson, 1978; Rachman & Wilson, 1980). Carefully dispensed external reinforcement (like tokens or praise) may be necessary at first to help a disturbed child learn to speak, read, and write, for example. But the satisfactions derived from these new activities, once they begin to be mastered, will help maintain and develop them further in their own right, even when the therapist's help is gradually withdrawn.

The young child who is learning to play the piano may at first be highly dependent on praise, attention, treats, and parental guidance to induce him or her to practice. However, to the extent that the learning program is structured effectively, piano practice will be increasingly supported by the pleasure of the activity (for example, the sounds produced and the satisfactions and "sense of competence" from playing). If the learning experience is successful, in time the child "wants to play" and "loves the piano." There is a shift from performing to please others to performing to please oneself, a transition from behavior for the sake of the "extrinsic" rewards it yields to behavior for "its own sake"—that is, for "intrinsic rewards." The behavior that offers the intrinsic rewards for which people strive may range from painting miniatures to racing sports cars, from playing the flute to wrestling, from climbing rocks to yoga exercises, from lifting weights to gourmet cooking.

Whether or not an activity becomes intrinsically rewarding may have less to do with the activity than with how it was learned and the conditions influencing its performance. Often in the course of socialization the conditions of learning inadvertently are poorly arranged. We see that when activities like piano practice or schoolwork become occasions for tension and family quarrels rather than for satisfaction and personal achievement. But often even under difficult conditions a variety of "self-management" strategies allow people to master all sorts of achievements and skills that characterize human accomplishments. The processes involved in this "mastery" have become a major topic in their own right, as discussed throughout this chapter.

Coping with Unavoidable Stress

So far, the discussion of self-regulation has focused on ways to gain control to enhance one's pursuit of important but difficult goals. Often, however, people have to face stressful situations that they cannot avoid or change. In that case, a strategy of detachment or "tuning out" to reduce personal involvement can be effective (Miller, 1996). Examples come from interviews with medical students witnessing a medical autopsy for the first time (Lief & Fox, 1963). The many aspects of the autopsy procedure that appear to have been designed as an institutionalized ritual to make detachment easier may help students cope with their distress. The autopsy room itself is arranged to provide a sterile, clinical, impersonal atmosphere. The face and genitalia of the corpse are kept covered, and after the vital organs have been removed, the body is taken out of the room. A detached, scientific, professional stance further helps to keep the whole procedure distant and impersonal.

Experimental research confirms that an attitude of detachment helps people react more calmly when exposed to gory scenes portraying bloody accidents and death (Koriat et al., 1972) or when expecting electric shock (Holmes & Houston, 1974). These results are consistent with reports showing that soldiers may immunize themselves against emotion by distancing themselves psychologically from their victims, for example, by labeling them as subhumans. While highly effective for reducing feeling, a detachment strategy to reduce emotionality can easily be misused, producing callous, insensitive attitudes and cold-bloodedness toward others.

Table 17.6
Summary of Some Major Influences Related to Coping Responses

Cognitive appraisal

Perception of control and competence

Predictability of stress

Availability of social supports and sharing

The type of cognitive strategy that helps one to deal best with stress depends on the individual (Miller, 1987, 1996; Miller, Shoda, & Hurley, 1996). Recall, for example, the individual differences in the tendency to use distraction and to "blunt" rather than to sensitize or "monitor," discussed in the chapter on repression as a mechanism of defense (Chapter 5). The point to remember is that such preferences in the type of information sought for dealing with stress affect how the person copes best with stress; while one strategy helps some people, the opposite strategy may help others.

Effective coping also depends on the individual's psychological environment. For example, people generally deal better with stress (and are less likely to respond to it with illness) when they have social ties and supports, such as spouses, relatives, close friends, and groups to which they belong (Antonovsky, 1979; Holahan & Moos, 1990; Spiegel, 1996). Coping is also better when people can share their stressful experience with others (Nilson et al., 1981). When people work together in response to a common stress, such as an earthquake disaster or the bombing raids of war, they seem to focus less on their personal problems and more on the common goal of survival. When people are members of a group to which they "belong," they can receive emotional support, help with problems, a boost in self-esteem (Cobb, 1976; Cohen & McKay, 1984), and even better health (Pennebaker, 1996; Spiegel, 1994, 1996).

Although social support may help buffer many daily life stresses, the effects depend not just on having other people available (e.g., a spouse, a partner, a family), but on the quality of support. For example, while being married slightly reduces the chance for becoming severely depressed, having a spouse to whom one feels unable to talk makes the risk of depression considerably greater (Coyne & Downey, 1991). Table 17.6 summarizes some of the variables that influence the individual's coping attempts.

SUMMARY

1. Self-regulation depends on the ways in which the individual *encodes* or construes the situation in which self-regulation is attempted, the *expectancies* and *beliefs* that become activated, the feelings experienced, the *goals* and *values* engaged, and the *skills* and *competencies* that are employed to try to pursue them strategically. This process was discussed and illustrated. Self-regulation may be needed when hot emotional reactions and overlearned maladaptive patterns are easily triggered. Overcoming such automatic hot reactions requires "cooling."

2. In the course of development, people learn to set their own performance standards and to make their self-reward contingent upon achievement of the self-prescribed criteria. Children's patterns of

self-reward are influenced by the models whom they have observed, as well as by standards imposed on them through direct training. At the core of a self-regulatory system are the contingency rules that guide both a child's and an adult's behavior in different types of situations.

3. The theory of self-awareness posits that attention can be "self-focused" (directed inward toward the self) or directed outward toward the environment. Both public and private types of self-consciousness, or self-focus, can be measured to show individual differences. The degree of self-consciousness is apt to affect self-evaluation; the more closely individuals examine themselves, the more aware they are of actual/ought self discrepancies and the more diligently they seek to reduce them.

4. Self-discrepancy theory cites discrepancies between "actual" self and "ideal" or "ought" self (which determine a person's self-evaluative standards) as a factor in producing negative feelings. In this theory, anorexic and bulimic behavior may stem from discrepancies between the actual self and the ought self or the ideal self, respectively.

5. To understand willpower in psychological terms requires analyzing voluntary delay of gratification and the processes that make self-regulation possible. In self-regulation, people evaluate and control their own behavior, trying to act in the light of future-oriented considerations as well as the pressures of the moment. One approach to understand these processes explored children's willingness to delay immediate, smaller gratification for the sake of delayed but larger rewards and goals.

6. People's subjective expectations concerning the outcome of their choice influence their willingness to select delayed rather than immediate gratification. Will the delayed rewards for which one postpones immediate satisfaction actually materialize? Will they be worthwhile? Will one be able to earn them? A person's answers to these questions depend partly on his or her past history and on relevant social models. For example, after children were exposed to the patterns of delayed or immediate gratification displayed by social models, their own choices changed in accord with the preferences they had observed.

7. How can people delay gratification for the sake of preferred but delayed outcomes? When young children attended to the available outcomes while waiting, they were less able to wait for them. Thus, under some conditions, *not* thinking about the desired outcomes seems to enhance effective delay behavior. Delay of gratification may be helped by cognitive and overt self-distractions to reduce the aversiveness of waiting.

8. In the course of development, children acquire knowledge of effective rules for delay of gratification so that they can increasingly engage in the self-distractions and cognitive activities that make waiting less frustrating. Early delay behavior has also been related to aspects of personality years later, and this indicates a pattern of stable individual difference.

9. It is possible to reduce stress through cognitive transformation of unpleasant situations or through the belief that one can predict and control the stressful situation. When a situation is unquestionably beyond a person's control, the strategy of "tuning out" can be an effective coping mechanism. Mental practice can influence outcomes; the expectation of failure often leads to failure, just as the expectation of success makes a successful result more likely. Effective performance is threatened, however, by self-preoccupying, negative thoughts that can loom large under stressful conditions.

10. Individuals use rules and plans to regulate their environment and guide their behavior in anticipation of the future. They adopt life tasks to which they devote themselves during specific periods of their lives. Intrinsic motivation implies interest in a task for its own sake; it is increased by allowance of choice and informational feedback but reduced by awareness of rewards, deadlines, and surveillance. Extrinsic motivation stems from external encouragements such as rewards, social reactions, or controlling feedback; unlike intrinsic motivation, it seems to diminish the behavior itself and makes it less enjoyable. Regardless of actual ability, failure tends to burden individuals with negative emotions if they are motivated by performance goals and seek approval for their performance. Individuals who possess learning goals, however, are less likely to be daunted by failure and even use it to enhance their coping strategies.

11. Effective self-regulation is made easier through the application of plans for coping with especially difficult stressful situations. Methods found useful include self-observation of one's behavior; stimulus control (which involves regulating one's environment); self-contracting in which self-reward is made contingent on completion of specified behaviors (such as finishing an assignment) toward desired outcomes; and self-instruction to help oneself to persist in the pursuit of desired but more difficult and/or distant objectives while resisting the temptations and distractions of the moment. Coping also can be enhanced by appropriate social support from the individual's environment.

Person-Situation Interaction

This chapter begins by applying the social cognitive-affective approach to the life of one individual, Gary W. With that example, we will consider how the psychological variables within the person interact to determine his or her characteristic behavior patterns in relation to situations. To understand that interaction requires attention both to characteristics of the individual and to the relevant social environments.

The View of the Individual: Gary W.

Assessing Person Variables and CAPS Dynamics

The assessments of Gary on each of the person variables used many sources: his own self-reports, diary notes that he was asked to keep based on daily self-observations, and interviews that focused on each of the person variables and on the situations in which they were expressed. Specially designed measures, including questionnaires, were devised to sample a wide range of information about Gary and his personal world.

These measures drew on recent research which has provided relevant strategies for such assessments of experiences and behaviors that take account of the situations in which they occur (Cervone & Williams, 1982; Mischel, 1993; Mischel et al., 1996; Mischel & Shoda, 1998). The methods include time sampling of tasks, behavior and perceptions at the moment they occur in the everyday course of life (e.g., Cantor et al., 1991; Moskowitz et al., 1994), self-reports of reactions to daily stressors (e.g., Bolger & Schilling, 1991), as well as sampling of physical symptoms and emotional reactions to them (Larsen & Kasimatis, 1991). They also include records of personal strivings and well-being (Emmons, 1991). All these methods allow systematic analyses of the types of *ifs* and *thens* significant in the lives of individuals in which their characteristic behavioral patterns unfold.

The assessments of Gary were intended to obtain answers to questions such as the following:

1. *Encodings:* What are Gary's enduring views of himself (self-concepts) and of his relations to the significant people in his life that are most important for him? In which of these is he particularly vulnerable? How does he assign causal responsibility for the positive and negative events and outcomes experienced in different domains (e.g., work, interpersonal)?

2. *Expectancies and Beliefs:* What are Gary's self-efficacy beliefs and expectations in the domains that matter most to him? What are the major anticipated consequences (outcomes) of different alternative courses of action that he is considering for dealing with his current life tasks and challenges?

3. *Affects:* What are his characteristic "hot" reaction patterns? What triggers them? What consequences does he anticipate for them?

4. *Goals and Values:* What values seem to be guiding his behavior? What life goals motivate Gary and shape the direction of his efforts? What are his main personal projects and life tasks, both currently and long-term?

5. *Competencies and Self-regulatory Strategies:* What strategies and competencies are available and readily activated by him to sustain long-term effort and self-control in the pursuit of his personal projects and goals? What cognitive and social skills, social knowledge, and competencies are available as resources for generating and realizing alternative possible courses of action and purposeful change and growth? What standards does he use in self-evaluation?

Note that the assessment of Gary in this approach does not address each person variable in isolation. Rather, it seeks to clarify how they interact, i.e., their organization. For example, how do Gary's expectations affect his mood, and how does his mood, in turn, influence the self-regulatory strategies that are activated? It is these interactions that generate the distinctive stable patterns of situation-behavior relations—the *if . . . thens . . .*—that characterize the person.

The following excerpts from the assessment of Gary illustrate the CAPS theory approach.

Gary's Ways of Encoding and Explaining Experience and Himself

Gary tends to encode situations on the basis of their potential threat for him. He views himself as a person who needs and wants a warm and caring relationship with a woman but he also sees women as a source of threat and provocation who "can't really be trusted."

For example, he views his new girlfriend's bids for "more emotional space"—"I feel like you're strangling me"—as "cold" and "rejecting." He becomes quickly infuriated when she expresses her feelings of anger and frustration with his demands and expectations and feels it means "she doesn't really love me." He says he tries to control himself on such occasions but in fact he quickly loses his temper. He then becomes enraged, although he claims to have overcome his childhood tendency toward emotional outbursts. He justifies and dismisses this behavior as an inevitable result of his girlfriend's lack of understanding and sympathy for him. Thus, he sees his explosions of anger as not in his control, attributes them to her "cold and rejecting style" and his "temper"—"I got it from my dad"—and exempts himself from responsibility.

Gary sees himself as shrewd and analytic, able to persist tenaciously in pursuit of a work goal. He seems to be exceptionally sensitive to the reactions of other people. Although Gary often seems to devalue many of his work achievements, particularly those that are in a verbal form, he actually has high regard for his quantitative abilities and work (for example, priding himself on an innovative financial software program he developed). In the quantitative domain, he takes appropriate credit for his achievements ("with numbers I have a mind like a sharp razor"). Here he accurately evaluates himself as exceptionally talented and sometimes even inflates the magnitude of his contribution (when compared with its assessment by his peers).

Gary tends to categorize experiences into two basic types: those in which he fears he may be "caught with my pants down" and those in which he feels he could succeed. The former tend to dominate, and he sees much of his life currently as threatening and upsetting. The prototype for these anxiety-filled situations is speaking in a large group, in which he feels he will embarrass himself, "sweating and with my foot in my mouth." His implicit personality theory seems to be an entity theory, in which he views people, particularly women, as unchangeable: "People are what they are—you can't change personality."

Affective (Hot) Reaction Patterns

When dealing with public speaking situations, Gary is prone to becoming swamped with debilitating anxiety, followed by some depressive feelings. Most important, Gary becomes easily upset by any feedback short of complete approval and applause, especially in close romantic relationships. Unless he gets rapt attention and praise from his girlfriend, he feels she is rejecting him. He then becomes angry and hostile. After only several months, his relationship with his new girlfriend is in danger of being soured by the same conflicts that ended his relationship with his former girlfriend.

Gary's Rejection Sensitivity Dynamics.   Figure 18.1 shows these dynamics, which are typical of rejection sensitivity in the domain of interpersonal relations. Although it occurs mostly in relations with the romantic partner, Gary's sensitivity to rejection sometimes is also visible in the domain of work and relations with authority. For example, he can suddenly become angry, impulsive, and hostile when he believes his work, especially quantitative, is not sufficiently respected and appreciated, once even starting a physical scuffle that later embarrassed him greatly.

As seen in Figure 18.1, Gary anxiously expects and vigilantly looks for signs that he is being criticized, "violated," ignored, or rejected. He easily interprets even ambiguous events, like the partner's momentary wandering attention or preoccupation with other concerns, as if they were intended to hurt him deliberately. His anger and even rage become easily and automatically activated. In this pattern he bypasses serious efforts at self-control, rapidly enacting hostile behavior. Such behavior (i.e., throwing things against the wall) in turn impacts the partner negatively and the relationship progressively deteriorates.

Figure 18.1
Gary's Rejection Sensitivity Dynamics

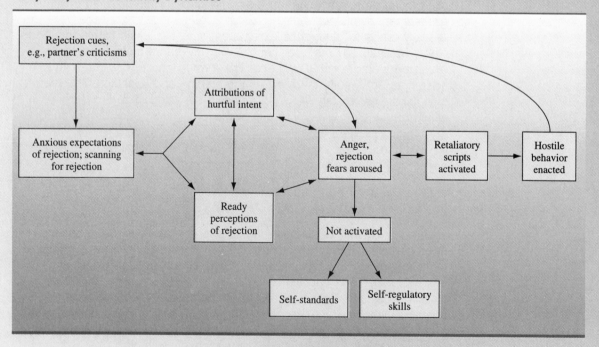

Expectancies, Values, and Goals

At first Gary tries to present the self-confidence expected of an ambitious business student; on closer examination he has many self-doubts. An important exception to these self-doubts is his genuine high self-efficacy expectations in the quantitative domain.

To a large degree Gary's goals, even in business school, seem to be directed at avoiding negative reactions from other people. Rather than being characterized by learning goals and motivated by the intrinsic satisfaction of mastering a given activity itself, Gary seems driven by concerns about the evaluative reactions of other people, particularly male peers, and is oriented to preventing himself from getting hurt.

He becomes especially anxious and even depressed at the prospect of intimate relations with women. This is conflictful for him because he values and seeks such intimacy. Unfortunately at present he does not seem to see clearly how his behavior, specifically his temper outbursts, impacts his closest relationships and he assumes no responsibility for it.

Self-Regulatory System

Although Gary is strongly motivated by concerns about how other people—particularly romantic partners—will see him and treat him, he does not seem to acknowledge approval or praise from others. He undermines his own hopes and potential with a pessimistic explanatory style. Privately, he tends to dismiss and trivialize his successes and to magnify his perceived shortcomings, on which he focuses much of his attention, ruminating about them obsessively. But he can also flip and present a glowing picture of his abilities in his self-presentation.

At work or in school, he drives himself harshly. He holds himself to rigid goals for perfectionist performance, setting standards so high they virtually guarantee self-perceived failure, for which he criticizes himself severely.

A notable exception to this pattern of stringent self-evaluation is in the domain of aggressive behavior. When he feels highly frustrated and stressed (which is not infrequent), he still becomes capable of angry outbursts of temper and rage with no apparent negative self-reactions for his lack of control. As was discussed above and shown in Figure 18.1, he expresses this particularly in his relations with his current girlfriend but sometimes also when frustrated in work situations with people he sees as less competent or senior.

Gary lacks understanding of how his behavior undermines his ability to achieve the caring interpersonal relations he desires. He seems especially immature and vulnerable in this domain and flounders between bursts of anger and a sense of uncontrolled helplessness. He feels unable to influence his relationship or himself in directions that allow effective communication with a partner, a feeling that only furthers his frustration and anger and erodes his relationships.

Potential Change and Treatment

In the social cognitive-affective approach, assessments identify the person's problematic situation-behavior patterns and are closely linked to therapeutic efforts and plans. In Gary's case, rather than merely characterizing his overall stress level and negative affect, the assessments specify the particular types of psychological conditions in which he runs into difficulties and toward which improvement efforts need to be directed.

Gary has excellent academic and cognitive skills. However, there is an obvious and urgent need to assess his social, interpersonal, and self-regulatory competencies, as well as his personal theories about relationships and his ways of thinking about himself and other people. While many of his problems may reflect disadvantageous styles of encoding, interpreting, and explaining experiences, events, and people, they also may involve insufficient interpersonal skills. He may benefit from role play and practice with alternative ways of construing and solving conflicts in close relationships when he feels threatened.

Self-improvement efforts for Gary need to be directed at identifying and controlling social and internal cues that signal eruptions of his anger. The focus should be on ways in which he can more effectively regulate those emotions without eruptive anger and hostility that jeopardizes relationships he cares most about. He needs to develop less rigid and obsessive control patterns for coping with anxiety, particularly in public speaking contexts. At the same time, Gary needs to reexamine and rethink his interpersonal assumptions and personal theories. It will be especially important for him to probe alternative ways of construing criticism when he feels provoked in order to find more effective ways of coping.

Thus, Gary needs to identify the interpersonal situations in which he feels provoked. He then can explore how his perceptions of rejection in those situations make him vulnerable to eruptions and automatic reactions that ultimately destroy the relations and intimacy that he is trying to build. Likewise, he can be helped to see the consequences to which his assumptions and habitual reactions lead in his close relations with women. Alternative ways of thinking likely to generate better outcomes then can be explored and practiced (Meichenbaum, 1995).

After recognizing and understanding the situations he finds most provoking and in which he feels violated, he then can try to reconstrue or reframe them in alternative, more constructive ways that make them less threatening and/or modify his own reactions to them. For example, by understanding the interpersonal situations in which he feels especially vulnerable he can reconstrue them and activate his own self-regulatory controls. He can then begin to respond with appropriate assertiveness rather than with massive anxiety or uncontrolled rage. He also can learn to communicate more effectively about his feelings and needs. Developing more adaptive ways of thinking constructively about his relationships can make it easier to stop being destructive with the women he cares about and allow him to get what he wants more effectively.

Personality Coherence

As indicated in the excerpts from the interpretation of Gary summarized above, in this perspective Gary's personality consists of a configuration of cognitive-affective person variables, each of which contains many components, and all of which interact. For example, his self-efficacy expectancies cannot be summarized by a single phrase such as "high self-esteem"; they include a multiplicity of context-specific efficacy expectancies that depend on the type of behavior and the conditions in which it occurs.

The expression of these person variables in Gary's behavior depends on the psychological situation as well as on the type of behavior involved. For example, while he may respond pessimistically and with defensive withdrawal in many interpersonal situations, when tasks call for quantitative skills he is self-confident and optimistic. And while on average Gary is not a "generally aggressive person," he does have disruptive outbursts of anger, especially when he feels ignored or rejected. As was emphasized, *if* Gary feels provoked or threatened in an intimate relationship with a woman, *then* he becomes vulnerable to outbursts of rage. On the other hand, *if* he feels secure, *then* he can be extremely caring. Such *if . . . then . . .* relationships provide a window for seeing Gary's unique but stable patterns, the "signature" of his personality. In short, this perspective emphasizes that both the person and the situation need to be considered when trying to predict and understand individuals and the important ways they differ from one another.

Consider the differences between Gary W. (green line) and Charles W., his older brother (black line). Figure 18.2 illustrates their self-reported (in daily diaries) emotional states (from extremely stressed, upset, and negative affect at the top of the scale to extremely pleased and positive at the bottom). As the figure shows, Gary and Charles are similar in becoming very upset in situation 1. This is when they feel "provoked or threatened" in close personal relations with women. They differ, however, in the other events that upset them most. In situation 2, public speaking (for example, in seminar presentations), Gary becomes distressed;

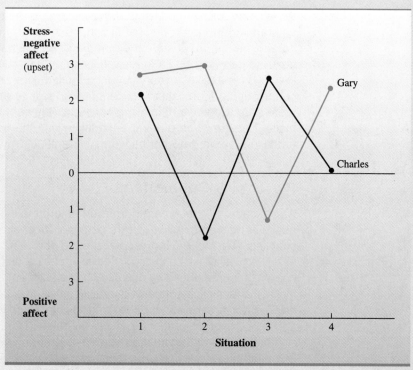

Figure 18.2

Illustrative Person-Situation Interaction Patterns   Self-reported stress and emotion, for Gary and Charles, in four situations (sampled repeatedly in daily diaries for three months).

Charles enjoys those occasions and looks forward to them. Likewise while Gary becomes extremely unhappy and "mad" when he gets negative feedback about his work (situation 4), Charles readily dismisses complaints from unhappy patients or colleagues as "part of the grumbling you have to expect. . . . There are always people you can't please." Interestingly, the pattern reverses when the brothers must deal with quantitative work problems (situation 3), for example, when writing research reports in their technical specialties. Gary finds those tasks a "real high—a challenge"; Charles experiences them as anxiety-provoking, fearing that his inadequate grasp of the quantitative method he uses in his medical research will be revealed.

Recall that in the classic trait view (Chapter 6) the observed variability within each person on a dimension as shown in these profiles is simply averaged out to get the best approximation of each person's overall level ("true score") aggregated across the various situations. The goal is a single summary score of the average amount of the attribute or quality that each person has. The present approach takes another step, as was discussed in Chapter 15. It also obtains profile information about where and when and why Gary behaves as he does with regard to the particular dimension of behavior. That is the essence of an **interactional analysis** (e.g., Magnusson & Endler, 1977; Mischel, 1973, 1991): The focus is on how the expressions of the stable personality system are visible in the person's unique *patterns* of *if . . . then . . .* situation-behavior relationships (Mischel & Shoda, 1995, 1998).

THE PSYCHOLOGY OF SITUATIONS

For many years personality psychologists have minimized the role of situations, but as you saw throughout this section of the text, the present approach views them as an essential part of how personality is expressed. In recent years, personality research is starting to take situations into account (Bolger & Schilling, 1991; Bornstein, 1992; Buss, 1987; Krahe, 1990; Mischel & Shoda, 1998), as discussed next.

Environments as Situations

At one level, situations have been conceptualized as the environments in which social interactions occur. The study of human behavior in relation to the environment from a psychological perspective has become a field in its own right called **environmental psychology** (Craik, 1990; Mischel, 1995; Stokols, 1978, 1990). Environmental psychology includes explorations of the specific effects of noise, temperature, and space on behavior. It also includes broader analyses of the interrelations among individuals and their social and physical environments (Proshansky, 1976; Proshansky et al., 1983).

Environmental psychologists use scientific strategies to help solve community problems such as urban stress, the perceived quality of the environment, and the conservation of natural resources. They study "the impact that physical and social environments have on human beings" (Moos & Insel, 1974, p. ix) and are concerned with "human problems in relation to an environment in which man is both victim and conqueror" (Proshansky et al., 1970, p. 4). The psychological study of the environment shows the close links between human experiences and the world in which those experiences occur. Hopefully, the findings of environmental psychology research will help people to optimize the human environment and to design environments that fulfill the needs and goals of those who live in them.

Table 18.1
Some Dimensions of Human Environments

Dimensions	Examples
1. Ecological	Climate and geographical qualities; architectural and physical use of space and constraints (e.g., the walls of a prison)
2. Behavior settings	School, drugstore, football game, church
3. Organizational	Size and type of staff in a hospital; student/teacher ratio in a school; population density
4. Characteristics of inhabitants	Age, sex, abilities, status of members
5. Perceived social climate (psychosocial characteristics)	Nature and intensity of personal relations
6. Functional properties	Reinforcement consequences for particular behaviors in that situation

SOURCE: Based on Moos, R. H. (1973). Conceptualizations of human environment. *American Psychologist, 28,* 652–665.

Classifying Situations

One influential attempt to describe some of the many dimensions of environments was proposed originally by Moos (1973, 1974) and is summarized in Table 18.1. The classification in Table 18.1 makes it clear that environments are complex and that they can be characterized in many ways, from the weather, to the buildings and settings, to the perceived social climates and the outcomes (reinforcements) that behaviors in that situation yield. Other schemes have tried to classify situations on the basis of their perceived similarity, emerging with such dimensions as "positive," "negative," "passive," "social," and "active" (Magnusson & Ekehammar, 1973), or on the basis of the types of psychological demands they make and the competencies they require (Shoda & Mischel, 1993; Wright & Mischel, 1987). Of course, many different classifications are possible, depending on one's purpose, and there probably is no single universal taxonomy of situations: We can categorize situations in many different ways, focusing on many different features, from physical characteristics (for example, heat, density) to perceived psychological qualities, such as the degree to which a psychiatric hospital ward has a "democratic atmosphere" in the eyes of its patients or staff or the degree to which the situation requires self-control.

Psychological Features of Situations

In any given ecological setting or environment, such as a hospital ward or a school classroom, situations may be conceptualized at two levels, as illustrated in Table 18.2. First are the **nominal situations,** which are the routine activities and places within the setting, such as "math class" and "study period" and "group therapy." Such nominal situations have been studied in research (e.g., Hartshorne & May, 1928; Mischel &

Table 18.2
Illustrative Environmental Settings, Nominal Situations, and Psychological Features

Setting	Nominal Situation	Psychological Features
Mental hospital	Ward dayroom	When peer approached for positive contact When peer teased When speaking in therapy group When feeling frustrated
Home	Mealtime	When teased by siblings When praised by mother When warned by father When required to wait
	Watching TV	When teased by siblings When praised by mother When warned by father When required to wait
School	Playground	When peer approached for positive contact When peer teased When praised by teacher When punished by teacher
	Math classroom	When peer teased When praised by teacher When warned by teacher When taking test

Peake, 1982; Newcomb, 1929) and consist of the environments sampled in the setting, regardless of their psychological meaning for the individual.

Environments, however, also may be conceptualized in terms of the **psychological features** contained within the larger nominal situations (Shoda, Mischel, & Wright, 1994). "Mealtime" in a summer camp (Newcomb, 1929) for example, may include such diverse psychological features or events as being teased by peers in a food fight, becoming frustrated by the demands of a counselor, or getting ignored by everyone in spite of pleas for attention (Shoda, Mischel, & Wright, 1994). Examples are given in Table 18.2.

Finding Psychological Features

To some degree, all individuals within a culture have a shared understanding of the meaning of common situations. A college instructor does not have to explain what she means when she announces a math quiz next week. But of course, as emphasized throughout this book, individuals also differ greatly in the personal meaning and significance they assign to the same situation: Is the quiz a challenge to be mastered? Or an anxiety-provoking stress to be avoided until the last moment? Or just another minor hurdle to be taken in stride? The same party for one person is a "fun time for mixing it up with old friends," but for another it is "an embarrassing endless evening for trying to make small talk with people in a tight little in-group who are great at making you feel

Psychological situations include social interactions such as friendly peers talking or peers teasing and provoking aggressively.

like an awkward outsider no matter what you do." In sum, the psychological impact of a situation depends on how it is interpreted or construed by the perceiver, and there are important individual differences in these interpretations (Dunning, Perie, & Story, 1991; Griffin & Ross, 1991; Mischel, 1973; Shoda, Mischel, & Wright, 1993, 1994).

The case of Gary also illustrates the unique interpretations that people give to situations and their impact for the individual. As previously noted, he maps situations on a dimension that has special significance for him: Are they places in which, in his words, he may be "caught with my pants down"? Or are they situations which he sees as relevant for "making it" and "proving" himself? Are they situations in which he is being "provoked" or "rejected"? Further assessments of Gary revealed more about the psychological features of situations he viewed as most dangerous: They proved to be those in which he felt himself being socially evaluated by male peers whom he respected. In interviews, Gary indicated that the people he respects most tend to be "strong, autonomous, tough, and not needy—that is, really independent." He saw himself as "making it" in contexts in which he could work and be by himself, setting his own standards, not open to peer scrutiny about his personal qualities, and in which he could excel in what he valued highly, namely "analytic mental work."

In the study of persons, the selection of the psychological features of situations depends on many considerations, particularly on the specific goals of the assessment

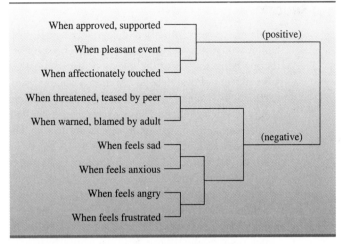

Figure 18.3
Illustrative Clusters of Psychological Features of Situations

SOURCE: Adapted from Wright, J. C., & Mischel, W. (1988). Conditional hedges and the intuitive psychology of traits. *Journal of Personality and Social Psychology, 55,* 454–469.

and the behavior one is trying to understand (Hoffman, Mischel, & Baer, 1984; Neuringer, 1996). Such features also can be selected by asking the participants themselves about the important psychological events or situations that matter to them. This is illustrated in a study in which children and staff in a camp setting were asked to characterize selected youngsters: "Tell me everything about Jim [for example], so I will know him as well as you do." Their descriptions were tape-recorded and coded. It was found that even children included references to the conditions in which an individual's behavior varied predictably, as in "Joe always gets mad . . . when teased" (Wright & Mischel, 1988).

With increasing age, people used more of these situational hedges or qualifiers. Thus, younger children hedged by indicating, for example, that Jim sometimes hits, but Joe hits more. Older participants described behavioral tendencies with greater certainty but qualified them by indicating the relevant features of psychological situations in which these occurred (see Figure 18.3 for examples). The lesson from this study is that people intuitively recognize and include the psychological features of situations as important qualifiers in their characterizations of the traits people display. Personality psychologists can enrich their assessments by taking these features into account more fully. These psychological features are the "active ingredients" in which the person's relevant behavior occurs predictably: Joe is aggressive when teased, but Bill is aggressive when depressed.

THE PERSON X SITUATION INTERACTION PROCESS

Throughout this book you have seen examples of person-situation interactions. Granted that both situations and individual differences are important and interact, how can this interaction be conceptualized?

Persons *and* Situations

Some researchers initially had hoped that studies of persons, situations, and their inter-action would answer the question "Are persons or situations more important for pre-dicting behavior?" But the question served mostly to stimulate futile debates. The an-swer must always depend on the particular situations and the particular persons sampled. The question of whether individual differences or situations are more impor-tant is an empty one that has no general answer. While some situations may be power-ful determinants of behavior, others are trivial. The relative importance of individual differences and situations will depend on the situation selected, the type of behavior assessed, the particular individual differences sampled, and the purpose of the assess-ment (Magnusson & Allen, 1983; Magnusson & Endler, 1977; Mischel, 1973, 1984; Wright & Mischel, 1987).

Recognizing that the question "Are persons or situations more important?" is mis-leading and unanswerable, one can now turn to the more interesting issue: *When* are situations most likely to exert powerful effects and, conversely, *when* are person vari-ables likely to be most influential?

Response Freedom

Psychological "situations" ("stimuli," "treatments") exert uniform effects to the degree that they lead everyone to construe the particular events the same way, induce uniform expectancies regarding the most appropriate response pattern, provide adequate incen-tives for the performance of that response pattern, and require skills that everyone has to the same extent. A good example of such a stimulus is a red traffic light; it exerts the same effects on the behavior of most motorists because they all know what it means, are motivated to obey it, and are capable of stopping when they see it. Therefore, it would be easier to predict drivers' behavior at stop lights from knowing the color of the light than from making inferences about the "conformity," "cautiousness," or other traits of the drivers.

Conversely, situations allow **response freedom** and the display of individual dif-ferences to the degree that they are not uniformly encoded, do not generate uniform expectancies concerning the desired behavior, do not offer sufficient incentives for its performance, or fail to provide the learning conditions required for successful gene-sis of the behavior. An extreme example of such a "weak stimulus" is the blank card used on a projective test (Chapter 4) with the instructions to create a story about what might be happening; clearly the answers will depend more on the storytellers than on the card.

On the other hand, even when the stimulus is relatively unambiguous—as when one child spills milk on another in the cafeteria line—there often is response freedom, allow-ing the expression of individual differences. One child may interpret the spilled milk as accidental and cheerfully wipe it off, but another sees it as a purposeful aggression and reciprocates in kind (Dodge, 1986, 1993; Downey & Walker, 1989). This example reflects differences in how the same event was encoded. But even if the event is encoded the same way (everyone agrees the milk was spilled on purpose), individuals may react differently,

The range of individual differences in behavior can be constrained by the situation.

for example, to the degree that they have different expectancies and values about responding aggressively in that type of situation.

In sum, individual differences will be visible in a given situation strongly when the situation allows a wide range of possible responses. In that case, each person can construe the situation in his or her own terms and act in light of his or her expectancies, goals and values, feelings, and self-regulatory system. Conversely, suppose everyone expects that only one response will be appropriate (for example, only one "right" answer on an achievement test, only one correct response for the driver when the traffic light turns red). Suppose also that no other responses are equally good, and all people are motivated and capable of making the appropriate response. Under those conditions individual differences become minimal and situational effects dominate. (Also see *In Focus 18.1.*)

Diagnostic Situations

The types of situations likely to be "diagnostic" for different aspects of personality are beginning to be specified. For example, individual differences in children's level of aggressive behavior were visible primarily in demanding, aversive situations when the individuals became stressed, but not in many other contexts (Wright & Mischel, 1987).

Kenrick and associates (1990) asked undergraduates to describe the settings in which they last displayed behaviors relevant to each of a number of dimensions such as likeability, adjustment, self-control, and "intellectance." To illustrate, "likeability" was defined by phrases such as "polite, trusting, frequently praising others." On each dimension, they also rated themselves and indicated how frequently they displayed each behavior in different settings.

The results were analyzed to determine the types of settings in which different types of behavior were most likely. Students reported behaviors indicative of different dimensions, often in some settings but rarely in others. For example, dominance was displayed strongly in

athletic settings but not in religious contexts, while behaviors relevant to intelligence were most visible in academic situations. Likewise, while self-control was evoked in academic and business settings, it had little visibility in religious and athletic settings. The results were similar when the students were asked to indicate the settings in which someone else would be most likely to see them displaying various characteristics. People agreed about the situations in which individual differences in particular qualities are likely to be seen most clearly. They also agreed about the settings they considered most appropriate for the display of individual differences in various types of behavior (Schutte, Kenrick, & Sadalla, 1985).

In this study, it was anticipated that a child's typical coping behavior will occur in situations in which cognitive, social, and self-regulatory competency requirements strain his or her available competencies (Wright & Mischel, 1987). When such competency requirements are relatively low, the predictability of the child's behavior from dispositional judgments by observers who are familiar with the child will be modest. Predictability should be greater when competency requirements (for the situationally expected or appropriate behavior) are higher and make stressful demands on the subjects, activating dispositional coping strategies (for example, aggressive, withdrawn). It was hypothesized that coping strategies for dealing with stress—either by becoming aggressive or by becoming withdrawn—occur in those conditions that "primed" or "activated" them by being demanding (stressful).

This **competency demand hypothesis** was tested in a summer residential facility with children characterized by problems relevant to aggression and withdrawal. As expected, ". . . children judged to be good examples of two dispositional categories—aggressive and withdrawn—diverged into what might be characterized as relatively stable aggressive versus withdrawn 'coping strategies' in those situations that were sufficiently demanding of cognitive, self-regulatory, and social skills" (Wright & Mischel, 1987, pp. 1171–1172).

Situational Similarity: Local Consistency

If situations are similar in the psychological features they share, for example in terms of the demands they make, individuals tend to respond more consistently across them (Shoda, Mischel, & Wright, 1993). Of course individuals differ not only in their overall vulnerability to demands but also in the types of demands (e.g., social, cognitive, self-regulatory) that are particularly problematic for them. The situations likely to be difficult or demanding for a particular person depend on the match, or mismatch, between the types of competency they demand and the individual's ability and motivation to meet those types of demands.

Shoda and associates specified similarity among situations in terms of the particular types of demands they make. As they expected, across those situations that make similar types of demands, the researchers found higher cross-situational consistency in aggressiveness with children in the same camp setting (Shoda, Mischel, & Wright, 1993). Thus, an individual's level of aggressiveness was more predictable from one situation to another if the two situations made similar types of competency demands. An aggressive individual for whom cognitive demands were stressful but athletic demands were not stressful would thus tend to become aggressive in situations that required cognitive competence but not in those that demanded athletic skill.

Conditions Diagnostic for Long-Term Outcomes

The research on delay of gratification in young children reviewed in the previous chapters also made it possible to specify the types of preschool delay conditions in which the child's behavior will be diagnostic for predicting relevant long-term developmental outcomes (Shoda, Mischel, & Peake, 1990). These are the highly demanding conditions in which it is difficult to delay and in which the child's self-regulatory competencies are challenged.

These expectations were supported in a follow-up study of the Stanford preschool children whose delay behavior had been assessed when they were four years old (Shoda, Mischel, & Peake, 1990). It was found that when the tempting rewards were exposed (making it difficult for them to wait for them), preschoolers who delayed longer were rated in adolescence as significantly more attentive and able to concentrate, competent, planful, and intelligent. In high school they were seen by their parents as more able to pursue goals and to delay gratification, better in self-control, and more able to resist temptation, to tolerate frustration, and to cope maturely with stress. Beyond parental ratings, both verbal and quantitative SAT scores were significantly related to the number of seconds the children delayed in the preschool test in the condition in which the rewards were exposed. In contrast, individual differences in delay behavior when the rewards were obscured (making delay not particularly difficult) did not reliably predict either parental ratings or SAT performance. By knowing the situations that would be diagnostic it was possible to predict—and find—important long-term outcomes that would otherwise have been obscured.

THE MULTIPLE DETERMINANTS OF PERSONALITY

One of the main goals of personality theories is to understand the causes of personality. The present approach views personality as determined by a large number of environmental, biological, psychological, psychosocial, and cultural influences that interact throughout the life course.

Nature *and* Nurture

For more than a century, **nature-nurture** has been the slogan for a controversy about the relative importance of inheritance and environment as determinants of individual differences in personality. As was seen in Chapters 8 and 9, the more that has been learned both about the genetics of personality and about the social and psychological and biological influences that affect personality, the more clear it has become that the hyphen in nature-nurture which has so long implied *versus* must be replaced with the word *and* (Plomin et al., 1990, p. 225): Nature *and* nurture interact and are complex partners in the genesis of individual differences, and it is inappropriate to pit them against each other. This insight is similar to what was learned from the debate about the importance of persons compared with situations: Of course, persons and situations both are crucial and interact in their effects. Likewise, as more is learned about genetics they become another basic source of influence that must be incorporated into understanding individual differences in personality in all its forms.

The interplay of biological and psychological processes is evident at every level of analysis. It is apparent even at the molecular level as cognitive neuroscientists can "see the synapses in the brain change physically on the basis of experience, hinting at a microscopic place where biology and personal history intersect" (Hall, 1998, p. 28). In this intersection, genes are switched on to make new proteins which are crucial in long-term memory, wherein the person's history resides, making ideas about nature versus nurture seem outdated at best.

Interaction of Biological and Psychological Influences

The challenge is to clarify how the multiple determinants from both biological and psychological sources exert their effects and interact. While genetics surely are significant for personality, they leave ample room for questions that require psychological answers. Indeed ". . . behavior genetic data provide the best available evidence for the importance of nongenetic factors in the etiology of individual differences in personality" (Plomin et al., 1990, p. 225).

The Role of Temperament. As the chapters on genetic influences illustrated, years of behavior genetics work, including studies of twins reared apart, show that genes play a significant part in the development of many individual differences in social behavior, from extroversion and cognitive-intellectual abilities and intelligence to social behavior tendencies that may range from aggression to altruism, and from mood disorders, including depression, to diverse other psychiatric disorders (Chapters 8 and 9). It is therefore possible, for example, that Gary's depressive tendencies may be genetically related to those of his father (who was twice hospitalized for clinical "biological" depression), although there is no way to be sure at this time about the nature or strength of the genetic link.

As seen in Chapter 9, biological and psychological processes interact in the expression of genes as individual differences in social behavior (e.g., Contrada, Leventhal, & O'Leary, 1990; Miller & O'Leary, 1993). Even relatively small heritable differences in qualities of temperament, such as activity and energy levels, emotionality, and sociability, which appear to be visible in early childhood (Buss & Plomin, 1984), can be biological foundations for diverse enduring behavioral tendencies that may develop from these roots. For example, if temperamentally more active, energetic children explore and interact more vigorously and forcefully with their environments (rapidly encountering its challenges and gratifications as well as its dangers and frustrations), in time they also may become more aggressive than children who are temperamentally inhibited from exploring the unfamiliar and thus inclined toward shyness (e.g., Daniels et al., 1985). Heritable variations in arousal thresholds in certain loci of the brain also could influence such behaviors as shyness (e.g., Kagan, Reznick, & Snidman, 1988). Heritable differences in sensitivity and physiological reactivity in response to sensory stimulation partly predispose people to become introverted rather than extroverted (Stelmack, 1990). In turn, introverts may be more disposed to avoid the types of social stimulation that extroverts desire and actively select for themselves (Plomin et al., 1996).

Genetic Influences on the Cognitive-Affective Personality System. Taking account of these findings, CAPS theory assumes that the individual's cognitive-affective processing system develops from a foundation that is both biochemical and psychosocial; it is genetically guided, as well as shaped by experience and learning and by social and cultural influences, and these processes interact in the course of development (Mischel & Shoda, 1995). Thus, CAPS theory views personality structure and dynamics as based on biochemical-genetic foundations. These influence such person variables as how the person construes or encodes—and shapes—his or her environments and experiences, which in turn produce important person-context interactions throughout the life course (Mischel & Shoda, 1998; Saudino & Plomin, 1996; Plomin, 1994).

Although the study of the biochemical foundations of dispositions is still at an early phase, it already indicates some of the temperamental characteristics that seem particularly significant for the personality system. Such large heritable characteristics as activity level, visible early in development, seem especially basic for the person's emotional life (e.g., Bates & Wachs, 1994; Buss & Plomin, 1984; Plomin et al., 1990) and probably relate to emotional-attentional-self-regulatory processes (e.g., Posner, 1997; Rothbart et al., 1994).

Gene-Person-Environment Interplay: The Case of Aggression. Assuming that there is some heritability in such individual differences as the tendency to be aggressive, for example, how might the influence of genes and environment interact in the genesis of stable personality differences? At present, answers to questions like this necessarily still lack precision, but it is possible to speculate about some of the outlines as discussed in Chapters 8 and 9. As one example, if more aggressive parents tend to have offspring with temperaments that dispose them toward more vigorous, forceful, aggressive behavior, the effects could be cumulative: Aggressive parents are more likely to model and reinforce aggressive behavior, which their more aggressively disposed children would themselves tend to evoke more.

Because behavior tends to beget reciprocal reactions from the social environment, aggressive actions typically get aggressive reactions. (In the same vein, sociable behavior gets friendly responses, and kind acts beget gratitude.) The result is a continuing reciprocal influence process in which aggressive parents and their aggressive children escalate and reinforce each other's aggressive tendencies. On the other hand, more empathic parents would model, encourage, and reinforce more empathic reactions from their more empathetically sensitive children, thereby enhancing altruistic rather than aggressive patterns of behavior (Bandura, 1986; Patterson, 1976).

In each life, there are many possible biological and psychological sources of important influence early in development. In Gary's case, aggressiveness was not strongly modeled or rewarded by the parents, although his father sometimes lost his temper in family arguments. However, a specific pattern of verbal and occasional physical abusiveness was characteristic of his older brother, Charles, particularly in his relations with women. Gary was aware of this pattern, witnessed it, and may have adopted it as part of his desire to be like his brother, "strong" and "manly." Since Gary and Charles share genes as well as social experiences, it is of course not possible to separate the potential contributions of these different components.

In sum, these early behavioral tendencies in the person interact with the psychological environment to forge the emerging personality in relatively stable ways (e.g., Contrada, Leventhal, & O'Leary, 1990). This entails a process of long-term interactions among biological foundations, the emerging personality system, and the social environment. In this process, individuals with early dispositions toward aggressiveness may become relatively consistent in their aggressive behavior, while those inclined toward other types of behavior, such as sociability and altruism, would develop more consistent patterns in those directions.

Cognitive-Affective Dynamics: The CAPS Level.   In CAPS theory, these interactions are mediated by changes in the relevant person variables and their interconnections within the personality system (e.g., Miller & O'Leary, 1993; Mischel & Shoda, 1995; Contrada, Leventhal, & O'Leary, 1990). For example, if individuals are genetically and temperamentally disposed toward greater aggressiveness, they soon become more likely to interpret the motives of other people as aggressive and to anticipate aggression from others (Dodge, 1986). They also may confirm these expectations and beliefs by behaving more aggressively, thus evoking more aggressive reactions from their social environments. Likewise, as aggressiveness becomes an established pattern, it also may be incorporated into the values and self-standards and goals of the individual. Increasingly the person may seek out peers and groups likely to further support this type of behavior and to strengthen it as a source both for self-esteem and peer approval.

Selecting and Creating One's Own Psychological Environment

People not only impose their own meanings on situations but also select and create them through their own behavior (e.g., Kenrick & Funder, 1988; Pervin, 1977; Snyder, 1983; Swann, 1983). Specifically they tend to choose and generate environments likely to further reinforce and encourage their existing behavioral propensities, for example, by selecting marriage partners who are similar to themselves (e.g., Buss, 1984a, 1987, 1996).

Gary's case also illustrates this process of shaping one's own situations. Since he dreads social-evaluative situations (he sees them as exposing him to being "caught with his pants down"), he avoids them whenever he can, preferring to isolate himself. His inclination to withdraw and be "a loner" is thereby further strengthened, and isolation increasingly becomes his refuge and comfort zone. A side effect is that he never learns to confront and cope more effectively with the social encounters he fears most. This is painfully evident in public speaking situations that he simply cannot avoid and in which he easily panics, especially when he feels himself being evaluated by respected male peers in business contexts. His panic response further elicits what he perceives as the disrespect and "snickers" of his peers, thereby intensifying his dread and avoidance pattern in a vicious cycle.

Gary's preference for isolation and withdrawal has by now become a well-established pattern. He even announces to acquaintances that he prefers his own company to meeting other people, which they perceive as a rejection by him or an expression of aloofness, and then they reciprocate by avoiding him, which in turn further isolates him and fuels his sense of alienation and distrust.

Consistent with such clinical data, it has been shown that personality variables influence the choice of types of situations to which people expose themselves (e.g., Bolger & Schilling, 1991; Buss, 1987). "Neuroticism" (a sensitivity to negative, aversive experiences and emotions) as a personality characteristic, for example, may produce distress in daily life both by influencing the stressors to which people become exposed and their sensitivity to them.

Personality impacts not only the social environments the individual selects, but also how those environments and the people in them react to that individual: *"Charming, provocative, honored, trusted, and fearsome are dispositional terms that describe not so much the actions that persons perform, but rather the reactions that such persons typically elicit from others"* (Buss, 1987, p. 1,217). Thus, people differ in how they perceive given situations, and these perceptions influence the strategies they select, which in turn rapidly alter the consequences they experience from the environment. For example, individuals who cooperate tend to elicit reciprocal cooperation from their partners on a task, which in turn confirms and strengthens their choice of a cooperative rather than a competitive strategy (Kelley & Stahelski, 1970).

The analysis of complex social interactions (e.g., Patterson & Cobb, 1971; Patterson, 1976) shows how each of us continuously selects, changes, and generates conditions just as much as we are affected by them. Some classic studies of the interactions between husbands and wives illustrate this point (Raush et al., 1974). In these studies, husband-wife interactions were observed as the couples coped with such conflicts as how to celebrate their first wedding anniversary when each had made different plans. For example, Bob had arranged and paid in advance for dinner at a restaurant, but Sue had spent half the day preparing for a special dinner at home. As the couple realized their conflict and tried to resolve it, their interactions continuously revealed that each antecedent act (what Sue had just said to Bob) constrained each consequent act (how Bob responded).

In such interactions, the interpersonal strategy characteristically selected depends both on the type of person and the type of situation. For example, in the context of getting along with a peer, a "dependent person" is likely to use a self-denigrating strategy; on the other hand, when the situation focuses on pleasing an authority, the dependent person is apt to use a self-promoting strategy (Bornstein, Riggs, Hill, & Calabrese, 1996). Once more, we see the effects of "person X situation" interactions.

THE PERSON OVER TIME

Long-Term Life Course Stability

Are a person's qualities stable? Do early characteristics predict later qualities? When parents say, "Fred was always so friendly, even as a little baby," are their comments justified? Can we predict the six-year-old's behavior from responses in the first year of life? Is there much continuity in the qualities and behaviors of the child throughout childhood? Research has made it clear that although behavior depends on context and the same person may be quite different in very different contexts, there also is significant stability over time, particularly after the first few years of life.

Many important connections have been found over time in the life course. For example, babies who make certain responses with lower intensity at birth tend to show some positive qualities later in life (see Figure 18.4). Such newborn behaviors as lower sensitivity to touch on the skin, for example, in the newborn predicted more mature communication and coping at age two and one-half and at age seven and one-half. High touch sensitivity and high respiration rates at birth were related to low interest, low participation, lower assertiveness, and less communicativeness in later years (Bell et al., 1971; Halverson, 1971a, 1971b). But these links between newborn and later behaviors were exceptions. Most of the relations that were examined turned out to be nonexistent, and the associations that were found generally were not strong. So there are some connections between a newborn's qualities and characteristics later in life, but in the individual case one could not predict confidently from responses at birth any later characteristics:

> To use an analogy, newborn behavior is more like a preface to a book than a table of its contents yet to be unfolded. Further, the preface is itself merely a rough draft undergoing rapid revision. There are some clues to the nature of the book in the preface, but these are in code form and taking them as literally prophetic is likely to lead to disappointment (Bell et al., 1971, p. 132).

As one progresses beyond the "preface of the book" to the first few chapters (to the early years of life), continuities in development do become increasingly evident (Block & Block, 1980; McCrae & Costa, 1996; Mischel et al., 1989). Children who are seen as more active, assertive, aggressive, competitive, outgoing, and so on at age three years are also more likely to be described as having more of those qualities later in development, for example. In sum, the specific links between qualities of the child, say in the fourth year and in the eighth year, may be complex and indirect. But a thorough analysis of the patterns indicates that significant threads of continuity do emerge over time (Caspi, 1987, 1998). Thus, childhood characteristics may be connected co-

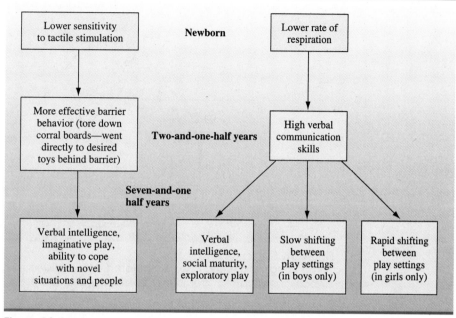

Figure 18.4

Examples of Relationships between Children's Behavior at Different Ages. The Relationship Holds for Both Sexes Unless Otherwise Indicated in the Chart

SOURCE: Based on data from Bell, R. Q., Weller, G., & Waldrop, M. (1971). Newborn and preschooler: Organization of behavior and relations between periods. *Monographs of the Society for Research in Child Development, 36;* Halverson, C. (1971). Longitudinal relations between newborn tactile threshold, preschool barrier behaviors, and early school-age imagination and verbal development. *Monographs of the Society for Research in Child Development, 36;* Halverson, C. (1971). Relation of preschool verbal communication to later verbal intelligence, social maturity, and distribution of play bouts. Paper presented at the meeting of the American Psychological Association; Halverson, C. F., Jr., & Waldrop, M. R. (1974). Relations between preschool barrier behaviors and early school-age measures of coping, imagination, and verbal development. *Developmental Psychology, 10,* 716–720.

herently to later behavior and attributes at least to some degree (Arend, Gove, & Sroufe, 1979; Block, 1971; Mischel et al., 1989). Experiences in the early pages of the book do affect what happens in the later pages, although these early experiences do not prevent the possibility of genuine changes later. The amount of stability or change over time varies for different types of characteristics and different types of experiences at different points in development (Caspi, 1998; Caspi & Bem, 1990).

To illustrate with one concrete example, studies of lives over many years indicate that "ill-tempered boys become ill-tempered men" (Caspi & Bem, 1990, p. 568). These continuities in development reflect the fact that stable qualities of the individual, whether adaptive (such as the ability and willingness to delay gratification) or aversive and maladaptive (such as inappropriate displays of temper), can have profound "chain effects" that quickly accelerate. Beginning early in life, they can trigger long

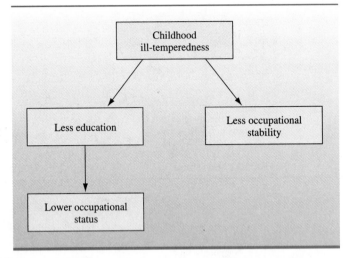

Figure 18.5
Some Long-Term Outcomes Associated with Childhood Ill-Temperedness Statistically significant correlations are shown. Data are for 45 men from middle-class origins.

SOURCE: Figure and data adapted from Caspi, A., Elder, G. H., Jr., & Bem, D. J. (1987). Moving against the world: Life-course patterns of explosive children. *Developmental Psychology, 23,* 308–313.

sequences of interconnected events that impact the person's subsequent opportunities and options, often greatly limiting them. As Caspi and Bem note, a child's ill temper rapidly produces trouble in school, which in turn makes school a negative experience, which provokes the school authorities and can lead to expulsion, which permanently limits occupational opportunities and constrains the future. The unhappy network of consequences is illustrated in Figure 18.5.

The network of outcomes associated with early ill-temperedness is broader than just school and career. For example, Bem and Caspi reported that almost half of the men (46%) with a history of ill-tempered behavior as children were divorced by age 40 while only 22% of the other men studied were divorced at that age.

Long-Term Life Tasks and Personal Projects: Happiness and Meaning

Long-term continuities also are maintained by the major life tasks, goals, and personal projects to which individuals commit themselves and which have important value for them (e.g., Cantor et al., 1991; Cantor & Harlow, 1994). These tasks vary, of course, depending on one's developmental phase and context. Research on personal projects suggests that people are more emotionally involved with those tasks that they see as personally relevant to their own goals. While most individuals in a subculture see many similar tasks as personally relevant, there are substantial individual differences in the relative importance they place on different tasks, and these unique appraisals influence their involvement with them.

Furthermore, different personal projects and tasks may have different functions, be in the service of different goals, and lead to different emotional experiences. For example, people evaluate many of the tasks they take on in terms of how well they do on them, that is, their efficacy. Generally, the better they do on these tasks, the happier they feel (McGregor & Little, 1998). But efficacy and happiness are not necessarily the only — or even the most important — components of well-being and of full and healthy psychological functioning. Researchers are calling increasing attention to the limitations of equating "doing well" (and thus feeling happy) with being well and feeling self-fulfilled. They suggest that efficacy and happiness are not necessarily the gold standard of well-being: as wise people have long known, a life that focuses on personal identity and integrity may be at least as meaningful and worth living as one defined in terms of doing well and feeling happy. These authors illustrate their point with Arthur Miller's play *Death of a Salesman,* noting that its main character ". . . neglects integrity in favor of being well-liked and successful, but as his life progresses his dissonant self begins to protrude from beneath his thinning veneer of accomplishments, causing him confusion and despair" (McGregor & Little, 1998, p. 508).

Other illustrations of the distinction between happiness and meaning are seen in the so-called parental paradox: Raising children and living with them tends to decrease the parents' level of perceived happiness but to increase their sense that their life is meaningful (Baumeister, 1992, p. 214). And as the same author notes, dedicated guerrilla revolutionaries may live in wretched conditions that make them unhappy but be sustained by the feeling that their struggle gives meaning to their lives. Finally, note that although life projects that provide meaning do not necessarily make people happy, the two are not necessarily in conflict. The same life project can lead to both types of feelings.

Stable Patterns of Change over Time.

Stability may occur not only in the *if . . . then . . .* situation-behavior relation, but also in the patterning of change. Evidence for this comes from studies of the frequency and regularity of daily mood changes over time when individuals are assessed repeatedly (Larsen, 1987, 1992). For example, some college students reliably exhibit a pronounced weekly pattern of change in their affects, while others do not (Larsen & Kasimatis, 1990). And for some individuals, different affects covary over time so that on some days they might experience most of the negative affects, while on others the positive affects occur. Other individuals, on the other hand, are characterized by the fact that their affects do not covary to a high degree, so that on some days they may be happy but not necessarily contented, and on other days they are sad but not angry. Such differences in the degree to which distinct affects covary in turn have been related to emotional reactivity and among men to psychosomatic complaints (Larsen & Cutler, 1996).

Continuity and coherence in the course of personal development partly reflect individual differences in the life goals that are formed and in the degree of commitment and motivation with which persons pursue and maintain these goals throughout the life span. After the school years, individuals often retain the same occupation and interpersonal family goals for most of life. As careers and occupations are formed and individuals create and establish their own families, new roots are grown. In time stable social systems at work and home also tend to develop which further support the maintenance of the long-term goals themselves.

A variety of rapid political, social, and structural changes in modern society often create conditions of "anomie" and "alienation" in which stable and meaningful support systems may be difficult to find. The result may be to undermine traditional types of coherence and stability of the sort represented by the extended family rooted in the same town or farm for generations. On the other hand, the greater the freedom provided by the loosening of traditional structures and roles, the more individuals can find and create their own selves, identities, and life goals by pursuing projects of their own making.

Constraints and Opportunities for Constructing One's Future

Social cognitive-affective approaches to personality emphasize the individual's potential for change. They recognize, however, that the findings of behavior geneticists underline the role of genes (Wright, 1998). For example, identical twins reared apart often display amazing similarities in what they do and value and become. But as a counterexample, you may recall that mate choice, for instance, seems exempt from genetic influences (Chapter 9). As one writer put it: "If one's love life and mate choices are not under some degree of genetic control, then how can we confidently declare that we don't 'become' but 'are'? Are we not defined in a profound sense by the relationships we forge with others. . . ?" (Angier, 1998, p. 9).

The CAPS perspective focuses on the fact that individuals can construe and interpret themselves and their experiences and explain events in ways that help to empower them, even when their lives are exceedingly troubled. Throughout Part VI we saw evidence that if people believe that they can control their fates and influence important events in their lives, if they believe their own attributes and intelligence are open to growth, then they can partly shape their own futures; they can be instrumental in realizing many of their hopes and goals. In Chapter 16, for example, we saw that optimistic explanatory styles and positive self-efficacy expectations may allow people not only to lead happier lives but to be healthier and live longer. In the same vein, we saw that the concept of "possible selves" focuses on the potential of human beings to actively transform themselves and actualize a diverse range of lives, roles, and identities.

Nevertheless, the exciting possibilities for freedom and growth that each person has are constrained: People may reconstrue their possible selves and expand their efficacy to a great degree, but our DNA also enacts its messages. Likewise, cultural and social forces in part influence and limit both the events that people can control and their perceptions of their own possibilities (e.g., Ross & Nisbett, 1991; Stigler, Shweder, & Herdt, 1990). Within these substantial boundaries, social cognitive-affective approaches emphasize people's potential to gain control over their own lives, shaping their futures in ways whose limits remain to be seen.

SUMMARY

1. The case of Gary W. illustrated personality assessments from a social cognitive perspective. The goal is to take account of both psychological situations and the individual's strategies of encoding (construing) these situations and coping with them in terms of his or her expectancies, values, goals, self-regulatory system, and competencies.

2. It is difficult to predict an individual's behavior from one situation to another, but when behaviors are averaged across many situations individual differences emerge. These analyses "average out" the effects of situations rather than take the specific situation into account.

3. Stability *within* individuals can be found in the distinctive behaviors a person shows predictably in relation to given types of situations. For example, although Gary copes well with situations that challenge his quantitative skills, he predictably loses his temper when frustrated in certain situations with women. The social cognitive-affective approach focuses on such intra-individual consistency within the person's patterns of behavior in relation to particular types of situations. In this view, these distinctive, stable patterns of person-situation interaction are the behavioral reflections of the individual's unique configuration of underlying person variables.

4. The psychological impact of a situation depends on the individual's perception and interpretation of it. People differ not only in their perceptions of situations, but in their choice of the situations they select and create, for example, choosing those they like, avoiding those they fear. The situations people select can tell much about their personalities. Often they will choose situations in which behaviors to which they are inclined will be approved, which in turn encourages them to further use these behaviors, thus increasing their consistency.

5. Environmental psychology relates the study of human behavior to the individual's environment. There have been numerous efforts to classify these environments on dimensions. Within any setting or environment one can distinguish nominal situations (routine activities and places) from psychological situations—the stimuli or events in the environment that affect behavior psychologically. Psychological situations impact person variables, thereby influencing behavior.

6. The greater the amount of response freedom in a particular situation, the more individual differences can influence how a person will behave in that situation. The competency demand hypothesis suggests that individual differences in coping strategies become increasingly visible as the competency requirements of a situation increase. A person's coping behavior is likely to be more consistent across situations that make similar types of competency demands.

7. Just as persons and situations interact to determine individual behavior, so do nature and nurture interact to create an individual's personality. Early individual differences (for example, in aggression) may have biological bases which interact with psychological influences, such as selective modeling and encouragement by parents and preferences for interaction with others who are similar. These interactions may further increase long-term coherence and stability. The reciprocal influence process also can be seen in everyday social interaction among individuals.

8. Some personal qualities are relatively stable over the course of the person's life and may be seen in the life tasks and goals selected by the individual for long-term commitments. Individual differences can be perceived in the different life goals formed and in the degree of motivation with which they are pursued. Support systems, such as the family, can help people perpetuate these continuities; conditions of *anomie* and *alienation* will often undermine stability, yet they can also at times be liberating and enable expression of unique personal qualities and the creation of new opportunities and challenges.

Summary Evaluation

Social Cognitive-Affective Approaches

OVERVIEW

The next table summarizes the main characteristics of the approaches discussed in Part VI.

Summary Overview of Social Cognitive-Affective Approaches

Basic units of personality:	Underlying person variables and processes: encoding (construing, including self-concepts and explanatory styles), expectancies and beliefs, affects, values and goals, self-regulatory competencies
Behavioral manifestations of personality:	Stable patterns of person-situation interactions; distinctive configurations of *if . . . then . . .* relationships (she does *X* when *Y*, but she does *A* when *B*)
Causes of behavior:	Reciprocal interaction between person and situation, mediated by the social cognitive-affective person variables interacting within the personality system
Favored data:	Self-reports, diaries, ratings, and behavior samplings relevant to person variables; outcome information (such as symptoms, later school grades) within specific situations
Observed responses used to:	Infer underlying person variables and cognitive, emotional, motivational processes; assess and predict behavior and outcomes (such as proneness to disease, well-being)
Research focus:	Refining theories about underlying processes, discovering practical implications (for health, for risk prevention in vulnerable individuals, for therapeutic applications, such as overcoming depression and perceived helplessness by enhancing self-efficacy)
Approach to personality change:	By changing person variables and mediating processes (dynamics) (e.g., focusing on alternative possible selves; modify-ing efficacy and outcome expectations, developing effective self-regulatory strategies and plans for attaining important goals); also by restructuring situations in light of person variables
Role of situation:	Provides psychological cues and information that activate person variables and interact with them reciprocally

As the overview table indicates, these approaches focus on the person variables that underlie the differences among individuals in their cognitions, emotions, and actions. For that purpose, psychologists study such variables as the person's self-concepts and encoding of the self and of situations, stable expectations, values and goals, self-regulatory standards and strategies, and cognitive social competencies. They see these variables as basic units of personality and as important—but not exclusive—determinants of the patterns of behavior that characterize individuals distinctively and enduringly. They try to understand (1) the processes through which the variables operate and exert their effects and (2) the unique patterns through which different persons manifest these variables in their behavior. These behavioral expressions of personality are found in stable patterns of *if . . . then . . .* person-situation interaction.

THE COGNITIVE AFFECTIVE PERSONALITY SYSTEM (CAPS)

The most recent attempt to build a unifying theoretical framework within this approach, CAPS theory, is summarized in the figure. The figure gives an overview of the

The Cognitive-Affective Personality System (CAPS) in Relation to Concurrent Interactions and Development Influences

SOURCE: Mischel, W., & Shoda, Y. (1995). A cognitive-affective system theory of personality: Reconceptualizing situations, dispositions, dynamics, and invariance in personality structure. *Psychological Review, 102* (2), 246–268 (Figure 5).

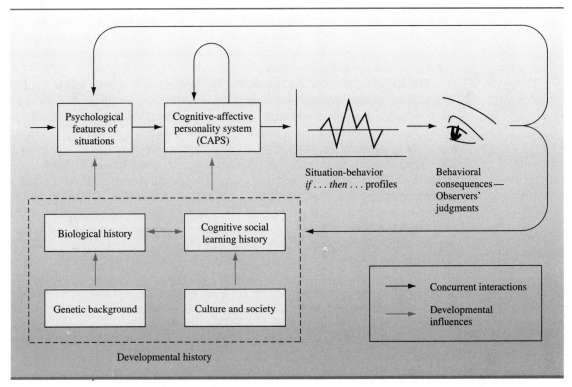

personality system in its interactions with situations and its links to social, cultural, and biological influences and antecedents (Mischel & Shoda, 1995, Figure 5).

In CAPS theory, the personality system generates—and is expressed through — characteristic, predictable patterns of variation—the situation-behavior, *if . . . then . . .* profiles that distinguish the individual and that tend to be relatively stable. The characteristic behavior patterns that the system generates also tend to have a stable overall average level that can be seen when the person's behavior within a particular domain is averaged over many different situations (e.g., the overall mean level of aggression). Taken together, the *if . . . then . . .* profiles and the mean levels provide the behavioral signatures of the personality system.

As the figure shows, the personality system is activated in part in relation to psychological features of situations that are experienced at a given time. In part, it is continuously activated by its own internal feedback system (the arched arrow shown above "CAPS" in the figure). Such internal activation happens, for example, in long-term planning and sustained goal pursuit as well as in such activities as fantasy, ruminations, and daydreams. The stable dispositional qualities of individuals are characterized in terms of the enduring structure of the organization among cognitive-affective mediating units—the person variables—interacting within the personality system.

The figure also indicates that the individuals' behaviors generate consequences that in turn affect the psychological features of situations that are subsequently encountered. They are seen and encoded (as symbolized by the eye) both by the person in self-observation and by other people in social interactions and direct observations as the behaviors unfold. Such encodings often take the form of personality judgments in terms of traits and types. The evaluations and reactions that they trigger in turn may influence the situations to which the individual is subsequently exposed (e.g., by changing the feelings and behaviors of the interactants).

The stable structure of the personality system and its dynamics reflect the individual's social, cognitive, and emotional history in interaction with the biological history, including temperamental and genetic-biochemical factors. (These antecedents are shown in the lower left-hand box in the figure). They make it clear that CAPS theory seeks to take account of findings and contributions coming from diverse theoretical orientations. These include the contributions of trait and biological-behavior genetics research (Part III), of self and phenomenological theorists (Part IV), and of behavioral approaches (Part V). CAPS theory also draws on the insights of the psychodynamic approach (Part II), particularly in its emphasis on processing of information concurrently at multiple levels of awareness and beyond awareness. It is also receptive to the psychodynamic contribution in its focus on the individual motives and goals and the frequent conflicts and discrepancies produced by competing motivations and goals. The theory in its most recent form thus attempts to build a cumulative science of personality on a base of the most solid empirical and theoretical contributions available to date. It seeks a unifying framework that encompasses the many different goals and perspectives of personality psychology within one coherent field, devoted to understanding individuals with the depth and complexity that this most formidable task demands.

APPLICATIONS

Personality assessors in this approach seek to identify the underlying person variables and processes that seem to account for the individual's stable behavior patterns. They tend to conceptualize these underlying variables in relatively specific (rather than global) terms. Recall, for example, that self-efficacy refers to individuals' beliefs that they can do what is required in a particular type of situation or task, not their overall efficacy expectations in general. Researchers, therefore, obtain self-reports, ratings, and other data to infer the particular person variable as directly and specifically as possible within these contexts. Some also try to sample and observe behavior as it occurs naturally. For example, they ask people to provide daily diary reports of what they actually did and experienced within specific situations (such as in family arguments or when asking for a pay raise).

Many psychologists who work in this orientation explore practical applications, for example by seeking links between personality and health (e.g., Miller, Shoda, & Hurley, 1996). In recent years they have been exploring the individual differences in vulnerability to severe psychological disorders, such as depression, as well as to physical diseases, such as cancer and coronary-pulmonic disease. The approach is also being applied to understanding social and cultural differences (Mendoza-Denton, Ayduk, Shoda, & Mischel, 1997).

Therapists within this approach try to help clients to identify their disadvantageous ways of thinking about themselves, other people, and their problems. In the safety of the therapy situation, therapist and client interact to experiment and explore ways of reconstruing and modifying basic assumptions in thinking and the automatic emotional reactions that are not working well for the client. A fundamental aim is to increase the client's perceived and real freedom to change in desired directions. One route is to provide experiences that enhance efficacy expectations. When clients begin to expect that they really can cope more effectively and that they can face previously terrifying situations more calmly, for example, change becomes easier. Therapy includes a wide range of actual and imagined (symbolic) experiences designed to develop more effective strategies and plans for setting and achieving desired goals, for functioning more comfortably and effectively interpersonally, and for reducing anxiety, depression, and perceived stress.

CONTRIBUTIONS AND LIMITATIONS

The Summary Evaluation table summarizes some of the major contributions and limitations of these approaches.

A Cumulative Theory

As the Summary Evaluation table suggests, social cognitive-affective approaches are unique in that collectively they offer a reconceptualization of personality that

Summary Evaluation of Social Cognitive-Affective Approaches

Contributions	Limitations
Integrate concepts, insights, findings, and methods that proved useful in earlier approaches into a larger, comprehensive framework; promise a cumulative science of personality that builds progressively on foundations of earlier valid work.	Critics may note that these approaches do not provide a completely original, unique view developed by any single theorist; by trying to incorporate the "best" of what seems to be established as valid, it may lack the distinctiveness of a unique conception.
Employ well-established psychological variables, such as efficacy expectancies, goals, and self-standards, as the underlying units of personality. Much is already understood about psychological development and determinants of many of these variables, the processes that influence them, and their implications for the individual's future behavior.	These units of personality seem unfamiliar and even counterintuitive given the long tradition and spontaneous preference for using trait constructs based on everyday adjectives (e.g., friendly, shy, hostile, cold).
Use the same psychological concepts and principles to understand psychological processes (cognition, social learning, emotion) and to characterize individual differences.	Need to demonstrate utility for conceptualizing individual differences usefully.
Demonstrated links between person variables and health outcomes; potentially valuable for reducing health risks and vulnerabilities.	Need to pay greater attention to genetic and biological determinants of personality and behavior.
Development of effective cognitive therapies.	Need to combine with appropriate medications.

incorporates concepts and findings from earlier approaches which historically were considered incompatible and integrates them into a larger framework. For example, they draw extensively on the work of theorists in the phenomenological approach like Kurt Lewin and George Kelly. They also adapt concepts and findings from behavioral approaches, especially early social learning theories (e.g., Bandura, 1969; Mischel, 1968; Rotter, 1954). Likewise, they incorporate tests and measurement methods from earlier trait approaches, as well as adapting psychodynamic concepts such as the focus on ego-enhancing selective attention and on the processing of information at levels often below awareness.

In sum, a common theme here is that these approaches build a cumulative theory based on promising ideas, findings, and methods from all areas of social, behavioral, cognitive, and personality psychology. In contrast, earlier theorists, like Freud, insisted on using only their own unique constructs and drew firm boundaries that separated them from other conceptions: To cross those boundaries was considered a theoretical (and political) violation. This tendency to build on earlier work has advantages but also can be criticized, as discussed next.

The Hazards of Breadth

On the negative side, increasing breadth and integration may be seen as decreasing a theory's distinctiveness and incisiveness. It allows many alternative explanations and interpretations: The cost of breadth may be an increase in looseness and a loss of uniqueness. It can lead to a conglomeration of concepts and findings with no clear criteria for inclusion or exclusion. It risks losing the distinctive specific focus of each of the earlier approaches on which it builds.

For example, the focus on the psychological variables and processes within the person contrasts with earlier behavioral approaches which refused to make such inferences about internal qualities and considered only the behavior itself in relation to external conditions. It thus risks using concepts loosely without connecting them to observable behavior—a trap that behavioral approaches deliberately avoided. Defenders of the newer approaches note, however, that although they make inferences about person variables, their inferences tend to be relatively direct and do not rely on complex clinical judgments. Thus, in comparison with classic psychodynamic theory, the steps used to measure and infer person variables usually are objective and easy to follow reliably. In comparison with trait inferences, person variables tend to be more specifically linked to particular situations and thus are less global, as in the example of task-specific efficacy expectations rather than global self-esteem. These differences between approaches, however, are primarily matters of degree.

The Value of Breadth

On the positive side, a cumulative science develops by gathering and integrating the best available concepts supported by the best available research. A theory of personality gains breadth by including useful concepts from all areas of the field rather than limiting itself to a few favorite ideas by a given theorist and his or her circle of followers.

To illustrate, the present approaches have built on and revitalized the contributions of phenomenological approaches and self-theorists (Part IV), and reopened many of the topics they pioneered more than 30 years ago (e.g., Cantor, 1990; Contrada, Leventhal, & O'Leary, 1990; Higgins, 1990; Kihlstrom & Cantor, 1984). This renewal has already proved to be fruitful. Decades ago phenomenological approaches were criticized because they relied heavily on people's perceptions, which are subject to all sorts of biases and, therefore, are potentially inaccurate sources of information. Researchers within the social cognitive-affective approach in recent years have turned this so-called problem into an exciting research topic. Instead of dismissing the individual's perceptions because of their possible biases, they have made those biases major topics in the study of social cognition, investigating how they influence social judgment and decisions (e.g., Kahneman & Tversky, 1984; Ross & Nisbett, 1991).

The increased awareness of the crucial roles of cognition and emotion in personality also has reopened such classic topics as how the self knows itself and the implications for personality of the many possible selves on which an individual can focus (e.g., Berkowitz, 1984; Gergen, 1984; Higgins, 1990; Higgins & Kruglanski, 1996; Markus & Kitayama, 1991). Thus, the realization that how people perceive themselves and their experiences crucially influences their behavior, previously the distinctive hallmark of phenomenological approaches, is now also a central assumption within social cognitive-affective approaches (e.g., Cantor, 1990).

From Perception to Action

Because researchers now use more sophisticated methods, difficult topics that previously resisted objective research are being opened, as you saw throughout Part VI. For example, the "self" in personality psychology has gone from an abstract concept about which theorists speculated to become an active research topic about which much has been learned. The same can be said for emotions, whose nature has become much clearer (Chapter 15). Thus, researchers in the social cognitive-affective approach have found ways to link social cognition and social perception to other aspects of personality and social behavior. We saw, for example, some of the determinants of perceptions of personal control and that changes in those perceptions can influence behavior for good or ill. The results ultimately should help clarify the relations between what people perceive and think and what they feel and do.

The classic humanistic commitment to enhance personal growth and the human potential has long been a key feature of phenomenological approaches. Now it also seems to be absorbed increasingly into some forms of cognitive behavior therapy. Personality psychologists within this framework devote much attention to the therapeutic implications of their work for both psychological and physical health and well-being (e.g., Contrada et al., 1990).

Focus on Behavior

Social cognitive-affective approaches to personality also have built on the foundations provided by earlier behaviorally oriented theorists, particularly social learning theory (e.g., Bandura, 1969; Rotter, 1954). Going beyond the "stimulus-response" concepts developed in simple learning studies with animals, these theorists investigated more complex social learning and expanded their theories of personality to include the role of both cognitive and social variables (e.g., Bandura, 1969, 1986; Mischel, 1973, 1990; Rotter, 1954). They moved away from a focus on external stimuli and reinforcers and have explicitly rejected the idea that situations are the only (or even the main) determinants of behavior. Instead they try to apply cognitive and social variables, conceptualized as internal psychological qualities, to understand individual differences in behavior. They emphasize the reciprocal (mutual) interaction between the person and the situation, noting that people select, create, and change situations actively and are not merely passively "shaped" by them (Bandura, 1977, 1986; Mischel, 1973, 1984). They also insist that a full account of behavior must pay attention to the person's "self-system": the standards and rules used in self-control and the expectations and plans about what one can and cannot do successfully in the future.

Thus, in the past two decades, earlier behavioral and social learning theories have evolved into social cognitive-affective theories (e.g., Mischel, 1973, 1990) or social cognitive theories (e.g., Bandura, 1986). While these conceptions still include principles of social learning as a centerpiece for understanding many aspects of personality and social behavior, they now give an even greater role to cognition, emotion, and motivation and address an increasingly wide range of personality phenomena, as you saw throughout Part VI.

Just Another Approach?

Traditionally, most approaches to personality have proposed certain basic assumptions about the nature and causes of personality (e.g., in terms of unconscious psychodynamics and motives): Their proponents have devoted themselves to trying to prove the truth and importance of those assumptions, usually ignoring findings from other approaches. As a science progresses, however, it tends to develop a more cumulative strategy in which concepts are modified, deleted, and incorporated in light of new research findings, regardless of the theoretical orientation that guided the original researchers. The field then matures into one in which the contributions of individual theorists become moments in a larger history of continuous change and evolution: In time, the best of what proves useful and valid is retained; the rest is left behind.

The ultimate question about the social cognitive-affective perspective is: Will it provide just another view of personality or will it become a foundation for a cumulative science of individuals? Reviewing much of this work, the emerging "convergence and complementarity of theoretical conceptions and empirical findings" may be seen as a basic indicator of the field's progress (Cervone, 1991, p. 371). Whether this convergence proves to be a sign of good health in the development of a cumulative science, or whether this perspective becomes merely another viewpoint, remains to be seen.

Epilogue and Perspective

Personality in Perspective: Toward a Cumulative Science and Theory of Personality?

SUMMARY OVERVIEW OF APPROACHES

As the student of personality reviews and concludes this book and forms an image of the field of personality psychology as a whole, it is easy to become lost in details, to "miss the forest for the trees." To capture the main features of the five approaches reviewed, the next table summarizes them in a final overview that allows you to compare them.

Summary Overview of Approaches to Personality

Causes of Behavior	
Psychodynamic	Underlying stable motives and their unconscious transformations and conflicts
Trait and Biological	Generalized (consistent, stable) dispositions; biochemical (genetic) causes for some (most) dispositions
Phenomenological	Self-concepts, feelings and conflicts, attributions, free choices (not mechanistically determined)
Behavioral	Prior learning and cues in situation (including the behavior of others)
Social Cognitive-Affective	Reciprocal interaction between person and situation, mediated by the person variables interacting within the Cognitive-Affective Personality System (CAPS)

Behavioral Manifestations of Personality	
Psychodynamic	Symptoms, "mistakes," dreams, fantasies
Trait and Biological	Direct signs of traits
Phenomenological	Private experiences, perceptions, and interpretations
Behavioral	Stable behavior equated with personality
Social Cognitive-Affective	Stable patterns of person-situation interactions; distinctive configurations of *if . . . then . . .* relationships (i.e., she does *X* when *Y*; but she does *A* when *B*)

Preferred Data Sources

Psychodynamic	Interpretations by expert judges (clinicians)
Trait and Biological	Test responses (on questionnaires); trait ratings, behavior genetics research, twin studies
Phenomenological	Self-disclosure and personal constructs (about self and others); self-reports
Behavioral	Direct observations of behavior in the target situation
Social Cognitive-Affective	Measures of person variables in interaction with one another and relevant situations

Research Focus

Psychodynamic	Personality dynamics and psychopathology; unconscious processes; defense mechanisms; the fragmented self
Trait and Biological	Measurement (test construction), description of individual differences and their patterning; taxonomy of traits; heritability of personality
Phenomenological	Self-concepts; self-awareness and expression; human potential and self-actualization; emotion; attribution
Behavioral	Behavior change; analysis of conditions controlling behavior
Social Cognitive-Affective	Refining theories about underlying processes and discovering practical implications (for health, for risk prevention in vulnerable individuals)

Approach to Personality Change

Psychodynamic	By insight into motives and conflicts underlying behavior
Trait and Biological	Not much concerned with change; search for consistent, stable characteristics; biochemical treatments for disorders
Phenomenological	By increased awareness, personal honesty, internal consistency, and self-acceptance; by modifying constructs; by alternative construals
Behavioral	By changing conditions; by experiences that modify behavior
Social Cognitive-Affective	By changing underlying person variables (e.g., focusing on alternative possible selves; modifying efficacy and outcome expectations and processing dynamics)

Role of Situation

Psychodynamic	Deliberately minimized or ambiguous
Trait and Biological	Acknowledged but of secondary interest until recently
Phenomenological	As the context for experience and choice; focus on the situation-as-perceived
Behavioral	Extremely important; regulates much behavior
Social Cognitive-Affective	Provides psychological cues and information that activate CAPS dynamics and dispositions

As the table indicates, each approach suggests different "truths," each proposes different routes, each yields different insights.

INCONSISTENCIES OR COEXISTING TRUTHS?

Throughout this text, the study of personality emerged with many themes that may seem to be mutually contradictory and confusing. Let us briefly consider some of the main themes from the study of personality that may appear especially paradoxical because, as the following list of examples shows, for each theme a seemingly contrary one also emerges:

Personality is stable. Personality is capable of change.

Dispositions are important. Situations are important.

Behavior depends on the social environment. Genetic and biological factors are foundations of social behavior.

People are consistent. People are inconsistent.

Humans are cognitive beings. Humans are emotional beings.

Behavior is rational. Behavior is irrational.

On close analysis such apparent inconsistencies dissolve. Personality is both stable and capable of change, for example, and the two statements do not necessarily conflict: Both are true. The questions, rather, are when and how we find stability, and when and how we find change, and how we can best understand each phenomenon. The same holds for each of the other seeming contradictions listed above: Each has some validity.

COMPETING OR COMPLEMENTARY APPROACHES?

Traditionally, the field of personality has been characterized by alternative approaches and conceptions of personality which competed against one another. Each approach and each theorist claimed to offer a comprehensive view of personality, with the implication that if a given approach proved to be "right" and useful, the other approaches were bound to be "wrong" and useless. However, the different approaches at least in part ask different questions and address different phenomena, usually dealing only with selected aspects of the diverse phenomena subsumed under the construct of personality. Rather than perpetuating a competition between views, personality psychologists may be reaching a new stage in the development of their science. In this stage, insights and knowledge become increasingly precise and cumulative, culled from the work of many researchers guided by diverse approaches as they pursue different specific goals with different methods. As a science becomes genuinely cumulative, it allows researchers to distill the findings that prove to be valid, reliable, and useful, regardless of the theoretical convictions, passions, and arguments that motivate the search and chart the course.

RECONCILING ALTERNATIVE APPROACHES?

The largest barrier to the growth of such a cumulative science currently seems to be the split that has occurred between the two main approaches to personality that have emerged after a century of personality psychology from the array of alternatives reviewed above (Mischel & Shoda, 1998; Pervin, 1994).

On the one hand are the trait approaches, which emphasize the existence of broad stable behavioral dispositions or traits, most notably The Big Five, and identify individual differences with regard to them. On the other hand are the social cognitive-affective processing approaches, which focus on the individual's characteristic internal mental and emotional processes—the dynamics—activated in his or her interactions with different types of situations. It is these two—the dispositional (trait) and the **processing** (social cognitive-affective) approaches—that currently are defining most of the field's agenda in both theory and research.

The field seems to be at a choice point: Will these two approaches continue in their separate paths, each pursuing its own goals with its own focus and methods, leading to two fields of personality psychology, each with its own goals and agendas (Cervone, 1991)? Or can—and should—the two pursuits be reconciled within some unifying larger framework within a single unitary field?

Each of these approaches has been criticized for neglecting the aspects of personality on which the other one focuses. Processing approaches often have been faulted for neglecting the stable dispositional differences among individuals—the broad traits—and thus bypassing a core aspect of the personality construct. Processing approaches in the past often tended to focus on the effects of situational characteristics of people *in general.* Consequently, they are often viewed as underemphasizing the role of individual differences or even as losing the person and personality itself in their focus on processes (Funder, 1991, 1994).

On the other hand, dispositional approaches have been criticized for neglecting the intra-individual dynamics and psychological processes that underlie the consistencies and behavioral dispositions that characterize the person. As Seymour Epstein (1994) said, "If one wishes to understand what makes people tick, and what to do about their off-beat ticking, a more dynamic interactive approach capable of elucidating cause-and-effect relations is necessary" (p. 121).

The question that faces the field as the century ends is: Can these competing approaches be constructively reconciled within one unifying framework and pursued within a unitary field? There seem to be some signs that such a trend toward unification is already underway (Mischel & Shoda, 1998).

On the one hand, processing approaches seem to be taking increasing account of the enduring important differences among individuals in such qualities as temperament, chronic mood and affective states, and skills. Processing approaches are incorporating the substantial genetic contributions to personality into the same framework used to understand their internal social cognitive-affective processes that characterize the individual (Mischel & Shoda, 1995, 1998). Likewise, rather than denying the importance of individual differences in personality and behavior, they are identifying diagnostic situations in which such differences can be found (e.g., Baumeister et al., 1993; Cantor, 1990; Mischel & Shoda, 1995; Shoda et al., 1990, 1993, 1994; Wright & Mischel, 1987).

On the other hand, moves towards integration also are visible from dispositional theorists who increasingly seem to allow room for the contextualized, situation-bound expressions of traits. Researchers are specifying the boundary conditions within which traits will be selectively activated (e.g., Stemmler, 1997) and are trying to incorporate motivational and processing-dynamic concepts into dispositional models (e.g., Revelle, 1995). If these trends continue, personality psychology may evolve into a more unified field that encompasses both dispositions and processing dynamics, identifying the distinctive characteristics that people have and the psychological processes that underlie them, conceptualized within one overarching theoretical framework.

ability traits   Cattell's term for traits concerned with effectiveness in achieving a goal.

actual/ideal discrepancies   The differences between the self one perceives oneself to be and the self one would like to be.

actual/ought discrepancies   The differences between the self one perceives oneself to be and the self one thinks one should be.

affect   Feelings and emotions.

amygdala   A small, almond-shaped region in the forebrain that is crucially important in emotional reactions, particularly fear.

anaclitic identification   Hypothesized by Freud as the earliest form of identification based on the infant's intense dependency on the mother.

anal stage   The second of Freud's psychosexual stages, it occurs during the child's second year. Pleasure is focused on the anus and on the retention and expulsion of feces.

analytical psychology   Carl Jung's theory of personality. Humans are viewed as purposive and striving toward self-actualization. The unconscious includes a collective as well as a personal unconscious and is a healthy force.

anima   In Jung's theory, the feminine, passive element in the unconscious of every male.

animus   In Jung's theory, the masculine, assertive element in the unconscious of every female.

anorexia nervosa   A disorder in which the individual (usually an adolescent female) refuses to eat, without any apparent cause, sometimes starving to death.

antidepressants   Drugs used to elevate the mood of depressed individuals.

antipsychotic drugs   Drugs used in the treatment of major psychosis, notably schizophrenia.

anxiety   A state of emotional arousal which may be experienced as a diffuse fear. In Freud's theory, the result of the struggle between an impulse and an inhibition.

approach-approach conflict   A conflict that occurs when a person must choose one of several desirable alternatives (see approach-avoidance conflict).

approach-avoidance conflict   A conflict that occurs when a person confronts an object or situation that has both positive and negative elements (see approach-approach conflict).

archetypes   Jung's term for the contents of the collective unconscious—images or symbols expressing the inherited patterns for the organization of experience (e.g., mother archetype).

assertiveness training   Training usually involving modeling and practice in developing and using effective assertive skills; a type of behavior therapy.

automaticity   Responses made automatically with little or no control, thought, or awareness.

availability heuristic   A cognitive rule or principle suggesting that the more easily we can think of something, the more likely we are to believe it to be in reality.

aversion therapy   Procedures that pair attractive, arousing, but problem-producing stimuli with another stimulus that evokes extremely negative reactions. The positive stimulus comes to evoke some of the negative or aversive reactions or is at least neutralized. For example, alcohol may be paired with nausea-producing drugs.

behavioral medicine   An interdisciplinary field that focuses on the influence of social and psychological factors on health.

behavioral theories (approaches)   Approach to psychology emphasizing observable, objectively measurable behaviors and the relationships between these behaviors and specific events or stimuli in the environment.

behavior modification   Techniques used in behavior therapy which are derived from learning principles and intended to change behavior predictably for therapeutic goals.

behavior-outcome relations   The relationship between possible behavior patterns and expected outcomes in particular situations; an aspect of the expectancies that constitute one of the cognitive social person variables in the cognitive social approach to personality.

behavior therapy   Therapy that tries to change problem behaviors directly with techniques based on the concepts of learning theories.

benzodiazepines   Minor tranquilizers that replaced the barbiturates as primary pharmacologic treatment for anxiety; an example is Valium.

Big Five Structure   A popular taxonomy for characterizing individuals in terms of five major traits based on factor analysis of bipolar trait ratings and questionnaires.

biofeedback   Use of equipment to provide immediate feedback about the activities of the autonomic and somatic systems; for example, giving information about heart rate or brain waves to the person in whom they occur, at the time they occur.

bipolar representations   According to object relations theorists, the combination of an individual's perception of self, his or her perception of another individual significant to him or her, and the emotions produced in him or her as a result of interaction between them. They become the templates through which the individual perceives ensuing relationships.

blunting Ignoring anxiety-arousing stimuli as a means of coping with them; a style of information processing designed for dealing with stress.

California *F* Scale A self-report measure designed to identify authoritarian attitudes and tendencies.

cardinal trait Allport's term for a highly generalized disposition or characteristic that influences most aspects of an individual's behavior throughout life.

castration anxiety A male's fear of losing his penis. Freud believed this anxiety was central in the resolution of the Oedipus complex and in the boy's identification with his father.

catharsis The belief that the verbal or fantasy expression of an impulse leads to its reduction; a key concept in psychoanalytic theory.

causal attribution Perception (judgment) of the causes of behavior, either to internal or to external causes.

central traits Allport's term for a trait that is less important and pervasive than a cardinal trait but that still influences much of a person's behavior.

chronic accessibility The ease with which particular cognitive-affective units or internal mental representations become activated or "come to mind."

classical conditioning (conditioned-response learning) A type of learning, emphasized by Pavlov, in which the response to an unconditioned stimulus (e.g., food) becomes conditioned to a neutral stimulus (e.g., a bell) by being paired or associated with it.

client-centered (Rogerian) therapy Approach to therapy developed by Carl Rogers. Emphasizes a nonevaluative, accepting atmosphere conducive to honesty and concentrates on present relationships and feelings.

cognition Thought; mental activity.

cognitive Pertaining to thoughts; mental.

Cognitive-Affective Personality System (CAPS) The personality system as conceptualized within a social-cognitive framework (see Mischel & Shoda, 1995).

cognitive-affective units Mental-emotional representations—the cognitions and affects or feelings—that are available to the person.

cognitive behavior therapy Therapy aimed at changing problematic behavior by thinking about one's problems and oneself more constructively and less irrationally (e.g., by modifying one's assumptions).

cognitive learning *See* modeling and observational learning.

cognitive-physiological theory Theory of emotion developed by Stanley Schachter, stating that our experience of an emotion depends on the cognitive interpretation of physiological arousal. The same state of physiological arousal may be labeled differently under different circumstances. Also known as the two-factor theory of emotions.

cognitive restructuring Therapeutic technique aimed at learning to think about one's problems more constructively and less irrationally. Albert Ellis's rational emotive therapy is a form of cognitive restructuring.

cognitive social competence (social and cognitive competencies) Person variable referring to an individual's abilities to cognitively process and use social information (see social and cognitive competencies).

cognitive social theories (approaches) An approach to personality that focuses on the cognitive processes and structures underlying personal differences.

cognitive transformations (of stimuli) Cognitively changing the mental representation of a stimulus by focusing on selected aspects of it or imagining it differently.

collective unconscious Inherited portion of the unconscious, as postulated by Jung. Consists of ancestral memories and archetypes that are part of each person's unconscious.

common trait According to Allport, a trait that is shared in different degrees by many people.

community psychology Treating individuals by practicing behavior modification within their environments, not in a mental hospital or therapeutic setting.

competence motivation Desire to acquire mastery of a task for its own sake; "higher-order" motivational needs.

competency demand hypothesis The theory that an individual's characteristic coping behavior will tend to be manifested in situations that put greater demand on the individual's competencies.

concordance rate (in schizophrenia) Percentage of pairs of twins in which the second twin is diagnosed as schizophrenic if the first twin has been diagnosed as schizophrenic. Higher for monozygotic twins.

conditioned response A learned response to a conditioned stimulus. A response previously made to an unconditioned stimulus is now made to a conditioned stimulus as the result of the pairing of the two stimuli.

conditioned stimulus A previously neutral stimulus to which one begins to respond distinctively after it has been paired with an unconditioned stimulus.

conditioning A basic form of learning (*see also* classical conditioning; operant conditioning).

constitutional traits Those source traits that reflect constitutional factors.

constructivist view of science Theory of science that there is no single, absolute Truth awaiting discovery, merely different ways of viewing and conceptualizing phenomena that are useful and valid for particular purposes and contexts.

contingency rules Self-imposed regulations that guide a person's behavior in the absence of immediate external pressures.

construct validity The process of establishing that the theory about what accounts for behaviors on a particular test is valid; it involves validation of both the test and the theory that underlies it.

constructive alternativism Recategorization of individuals or events to facilitate problem solving; a concept in George Kelly's theory.

continuous reinforcement Schedule of reinforcement in which a response is reinforced every time it occurs.

control group A group that does not receive the experimental treatment but is otherwise comparable to the experimental group. Responses by this group can be compared with those by the experimental group to measure any differences.

correlation The relationship between two variables or sets of measures. May be either positive or negative, and is expressed quantitatively in a coefficient of correlation.

correlation coefficient Quantitative expression of correlation. Ranges from 0 to +1 or −1.

counterconditioning Replacement of a response to a stimulus by a new response in behavior therapy.

covert modeling A type of behavior therapy in which the individual imagines a model performing the desirable behavior in an appropriate situation (*see also* modeling).

cue Stimulus that directs behavior, determining when, where, and how the response (behavior) will occur.

cumulative science A science that builds over time on its best findings and concepts and integrates them into a unifying general framework.

current life tasks Long-term projects to which individuals commit themselves during designated periods of their lives.

defense mechanisms According to Freud, ways in which the ego unconsciously tries to cope with unacceptable id impulses or frightening or stressful situations, as in repression, projection, reaction formation, sublimation, or rationalization.

denial In Freudian theory, a primitive defense mechanism in which a person denies a threatening impulse or event even though reality confirms it; the basis for development of repression.

dependent variable Aspect of the person's behavior that is measured after the independent variable has been manipulated.

desensitization Method of eliminating anxiety or fear responses to a stimulus in which the individual learns to make an incompatible response, such as relaxation, to a series of increasingly anxiety-evoking stimuli.

discriminative stimuli Stimuli that indicate when a response will or will not have favorable consequences.

dizygotic twins Fraternal twins; two organisms that develop in the uterus at the same time but from two egg and two sperm cells; not genetically identical.

domain specific knowledge and expertise The group of competencies essential for everyday problem-solving and coping behaviors.

double-blind method Experimental procedure in which neither participants nor experimenters know whether participants are in experimental or control conditions in order to preclude bias.

Down's syndrome ("mongolism") Genetic abnormality consisting of a third chromosome in the 21st chromosome pair. Causes severe mental retardation and a distinctive appearance.

dream interpretation A method used in psychoanalysis to better understand the unconscious fears and desires of the patient through an analysis of the patient's dreams.

drives Any strong stimuli (internal or external) that impel action.

dynamic traits Cattell's term for traits that are relevant to the individual's being "set into action" with respect to some goal.

ego In Freudian theory, the conscious part of the personality that mediates between the demands of the id and of the world. Operates on the reality principle.

ego-control Degree of impulse control; important in delay of gratification, planfulness, and aggression inhibition (*see also* ego-resiliency).

ego psychology The variety of psychoanalytic theory that stresses ego functions and de-emphasizes instinctual drives.

ego-resiliency Refers to the individual's ability to adapt to environmental demands by appropriately modifying his or her habitual level of ego-control, thus functioning with some flexibility.

emotional stability   The opposite of neuroticism, according to Eysenck, who viewed emotional stability–neuroticism as an important trait dimension.

empathic mirroring   Learning emotions and behaviors from the examples of others.

encoding   A cognitive social person variable that includes the individual's personal constructs and units for categorizing people, events, and experiences.

entity theorists   Those who see abilities and traits as fixed, unchangeable characteristics; they tend to choose goals that will assure them favorable judgment and approval.

environmental-mold traits   Those source traits (according to Cattell) that reflect environmental conditions.

environmental psychology   A field of study that applies psychology to understanding human behavior in relation to the person's environment.

Eros   One of two sides of the personality, as seen by early psychoanalysts, that represented sexuality and love (*see also* Thanatos).

existential anxiety   An awareness of the nothingness and death that necessarily accompanies being and that must be resolved by enhanced attention to how we choose to lead our lives.

expectancies   A person variable that includes behavior-outcome and stimulus-outcome expectancies and guides an individual's choices.

experiment   Attempt to manipulate a variable of interest while controlling all other conditions so that their influence can be discounted and the effects of the variable measured.

experimental group   The group in an experiment into which the independent variable is introduced. In order to determine the effects of the independent variable, the results from this group are compared with those from the control group.

explanatory styles   The way in which people interpret and construe the reasons for different events and outcomes.

external control   When an individual believes that positive and/or negative events are a result of factors outside of one's control.

extinction   The decrease in frequency of a response that follows the repetition of the response (or in classical conditioning, the repetition of the conditioned stimulus) in the absence of the unconditioned stimulus.

extraversion–introversion   According to Eysenck, a basic dimension of personality along which all individuals can be placed at some point.

extravert   According to Jung, an individual who is conventional, sociable, and outgoing and who reacts to stress by trying to lose himself or herself among people.

extrinsic motivation   Motivation inferred when a person engages in a task for the sake of the expected outcome, not out of enjoyment of the task itself.

factor analysis   A mathematical procedure for sorting trait terms or test responses into clusters or factors; used in the development of tests designed to discover basic personality traits. It identifies items that are homogeneous or internally consistent and independent of others.

family therapy   A therapeutic approach based on the premise that the roots of problems lie within the family system and therefore must be treated by improving family dynamics and relations.

field theory   Position that construes behavior as determined by the person's psychological life space—by the events in his or her total psychological situation at the moment—rather than by past events or by enduring, situation-free dispositions.

fixation   A psychodynamic term referring to a process by which a person remains attached to a person or symbol appropriate to an earlier stage of development and fails to progress satisfactorily through the stages of development.

free association   A technique used in psychoanalytic therapy in which the patient is instructed to report whatever comes to mind, no matter how irrational it may seem.

galvanic skin response (GSR)   Changes in the electrical activity of the skin due to sweating, as recorded by a galvanometer, and used as an index of emotional state, for example, in a lie detector test.

generalization   Responding in the same way to similar stimuli, for example, when a child who has been bitten by a dog becomes afraid of all dogs.

genital stage   Last of Freud's psychosexual stages, in which the individual becomes capable of love and of adult sexual satisfaction.

Gestalt therapy   An approach developed by F. Perls that aims at expanding the awareness of self and putting the person in touch with his or her own feelings and creative potential. Often practiced in groups, use is made of body exercises and the venting of emotions.

globality Generalizing an event to pertain to many aspects of one's life.

Harvard personologists A group of psychologists in the 1940s and 1950s whose study of personality was strongly influenced by the work of Freud and by biosocial, organismic theory stressing the integrated, whole aspect of personality.

heritability index A measure used in behavior genetic research to try to assess the degree to which a trait or attribute is due to inheritance.

hermaphrodite A person who is born with both male and female sex organs.

higher-order conditioning Process that occurs when a conditioned stimulus modifies the response to a neutral stimulus with which it has become associated.

higher-order motive A hypothesized motive that, unlike thirst or hunger, does not involve specific physiological changes.

hostile attribution bias Tendency to perceive others who are implicated in, though not necessarily responsible for, negative events as being driven by hostile intentions.

hysteria A neurotic condition consisting of two subcategories: conversion reaction (physical symptoms such as paralysis or loss of sensation without organic cause) and dissociative reaction (disruption of a consistent unitary sense of self that may include amnesia, fugue, and/or multiple personality).

id In Freudian theory, the foundation of the personality and a basic component of the psyche, consisting of unconscious instincts and inherited biological drives; it operates on the pleasure principle.

identity crisis According to Erikson, a point in psychological development when the adolescent or young adult defines his or her identity.

I-E Scale Trait dimension that reflects whether a person's perceived locus of control is internal (I) or external (E).

incremental theorists Those who view abilities and traits as open to change; they tend to choose goals that will enhance their competence, though not necessarily guarantee success.

independent variable Stimulus or condition that the investigator systematically varies in an experiment.

inferiority complex According to Adler, feelings of inferiority in the individual that stem from the experience of helplessness and organ inferiority in infancy. It results from a failure to compensate for early weakness through mastery in life tasks.

interactional analysis An analysis of the ways in which the individual's behavior varies predictably across different situations (e.g., she does A when X but B when Y).

interjudge reliability Degree of consistency among different judges scoring or interpreting the same information. If scoring decisions are subjective, then it becomes especially necessary to demonstrate interscorer agreement.

internal control An individual's beliefs that positive and/or negative events are a result of his or her own behavior.

internality Tendency to perceive oneself, and not external circumstances, as responsible for a problem.

internalized Aspects of the personality that were acquired from external sources (e.g., parents) but become part of oneself.

internal working models Mental representations of the others or self, or of relationships, that guide subsequent experiences and behavior.

interview A verbal method in which a person interacts directly with an interviewer in a one-on-one situation (e.g., to study personality; to survey beliefs).

intrinsic motivation Motivation (e.g., curiosity, achievement, affiliation, identity, stimulation, and social approval) that does not depend on the reduction of primary drives (such as hunger and sex) and does not have specific physiological correlates.

introversion–extraversion Trait dimension based on Jung's typology, researched by Eysenck. The introvert is characterized as quiet and introspective, while the extravert is active and sociable (*see also* introvert, extravert).

introvert According to Jung's typology, the introvert is shy and withdrawn, and prefers to be alone (*see also* extravert).

IQ (Intelligence Quotient) Concept formulated by Binet to summarize an individual's mental level based on test scores. IQ means "mental age" divided by chronological age $\times$ 100. The average IQ at any given chronological age is set to be 100.

latency period In Freud's theory of psychosexual stages, the period between the phallic stage and the mature, genital stage, during which the child represses memories of infant sexuality.

learned helplessness A condition in animals and humans that results from exposure to inescapable painful experiences in which passive endurance persists even when escape becomes possible; it can lead to hopelessness and depression.

learned optimism Believing that one can induce positive outcomes and is not responsible for negative events.

learning goals Goals that are directed toward gaining new skills or competencies.

learning theories Theories that seek to identify how and when new behaviors are acquired, performed, and modified.

libido In Freudian theory, psychic energy that may be attached to different objects (e.g., to the mouth in the oral stage of psychosexual development).

life space Lewin's term for the determinants of an individual's behavior at a certain moment; it includes the person and his or her psychological environment.

machismo Pride in male physical and sexual prowess.

mandala One of Jung's archetypes, a circle symbolizing the self's search for wholeness and containing designs often divided into four parts.

Miller Behavioral Style Scale (MBSS) Measure of monitoring-blunting tendencies.

methadone A drug that appears promising in the treatment of heroin addiction. Blocks the craving for heroin and prevents "highs" if heroin is taken.

mindless Guided by automatic behavioral routines or scripts that are familiar and require little active attention or self-regulatory effort.

MMPI (Minnesota Multiphasic Personality Inventory) Most popular and influential personality questionnaire, consisting of more than 500 statements to which the person responds "true," "false," or "cannot say." Items cover a wide range of topics and have been grouped into nine clinical and three control scales. Scores are summarized in a profile.

modeling A technique used in behavior therapy in which the client observes the successful performance of the desirable behaviors by a live or symbolic model. Effective in teaching complex, novel responses in short time periods and in overcoming fears (*see* observational learning, covert modeling).

moderator variables Variables such as gender and age that influence the relationship and possible correlations between any two variables.

monitoring A cognitive coping mechanism or style of information processing in which people attend to anxiety-arousing stimuli, often in the hope of controlling them.

monozygotic twins Identical twins; two organisms that develop from a single fertilized egg cell and share identical genes.

moral anxiety In Freud's theory, guilt about one's unacceptable feelings, thoughts, or deeds (*see also* neurotic anxiety, reality anxiety).

motivational determinism Freud's belief that everything a person does may be determined by his or her pervasive, but unconscious, motives.

multiple act criterion A criterion measure consisting of a combination of many acts or behaviors that are expected to be interrelated; combining these components increases the reliability of the measure.

n Ach Need for achievement (in the theory of achievement motivation).

nature–nurture Phrase delineating the long-standing controversy in psychology over inheritance versus environment as significant determinants of individual differences in personality. Nature *and* nurture are important, and their interaction may be of greatest interest.

neo-Freudians Post-Freudian innovators in the field of psychology who expanded on Freud's original work, putting less emphasis on the significance of the id and paying greater attention to the ego and the self.

neural networks Interconnection of neurons in the brain that are activated during information processing and mental activities.

neuropharmacology The use of chemicals in treating problems with psychological symptoms and disorders of the nervous system.

neurotic anxiety In Freud's theory, fear that one's own impulses will go out of control and lead to punishment (*see also* moral anxiety, reality anxiety).

neuroticism The opposite of emotional stability, according to Eysenck, who viewed neuroticism–emotional stability as an important trait dimension.

nominal situations The routine activities and places that exist within a given environment.

object relations theory An approach to psychoanalysis that stresses study of the interactions between individuals, especially in childhood.

observational learning The process of learning through observation of a live or symbolic model. Requires no direct reinforcement.

Oedipus complex According to Freud, the love for the opposite-sex parent during the phallic stage of psychosexual development, particularly the son's love for the mother and hostility toward the father.

operant conditioning The increase in frequency of an operant response after it has been followed by favorable outcome (reinforced).

operants Freely emitted response patterns that operate on the environment; their future strength depends on their consequences.

oral stage First of Freud's psychosexual stages, when pleasure is focused on the mouth and on the satisfactions of sucking and eating, as during the first year of life.

outcome expectancies Belief that a particular behavior will lead to the anticipated outcome (e.g., that waiting for the promised dessert will actually lead to getting it).

parapraxes In psychoanalytic theory, slips of the tongue that express unconscious thoughts.

partial reinforcement Reinforcement in which a response is sometimes reinforced, sometimes not reinforced.

penis envy Envy of the male sex organ. Believed by Freud to be universal in women, to be responsible for women's castration complex, and to be central to the psychology of women.

perceived self-efficacy The belief that one is capable of performing or achieving the relevant task or goal (e.g., "If I jump into that pool, I can swim to the other side.")

perceptual defense Unconscious repressive mechanisms that screen and block threatening visual and auditory inputs.

performance goals Goals that are directed toward earning acclaim for one's actions and skills.

personality dispositions Behavioral tendencies or patterns that characterize individuals or types distinctively in relatively stable ways.

personality signature Distinctive *if . . . then . . .* situation-behavior profiles that characterize individuals.

personologists Psychologists who study personality; phrase used by the "Harvard personologists" for their style of personality research.

person-situation interaction The idea that individual differences in behavior are reflected in the way each person responds to a particular situation and that the way a particular situation will affect behavior depends on the individual.

person variables Relatively stable social, cognitive, and emotional variables on which individuals differ (e.g.,

expectations, goals, values, and competencies). Sometimes these are called cognitive social person variables.

pessimism An explanatory style in which the individual sees negative events as being widespread and largely a result of his or her own doing, while failing to take credit for positive events.

phallic stage Third of Freud's psychosexual stages (at about age five), when pleasure is focused on the genitals and both males and females experience the "Oedipus complex."

pharmacotherapy The use of drugs to treat psychological disorders or psychological symptoms.

phenomenological approach Theory that emphasizes the person's experience as he or she perceives it.

phenomenology The study of an individual's experience as he or she perceives and categorizes it, with emphasis on the self and interactions with other people and the environment.

phenothiazines Major tranquilizer drugs useful in controlling schizophrenia (also called "antipsychotic drugs").

physiological measures Measures of how a person responds physiologically (e.g., change in heart rate, degree of arousal) to different events.

PKU (phenylketonuria) A genetic abnormality in which the gene that produces a critical enzyme is missing. It results in mental retardation if not treated soon after birth.

placebo An inert substance administered to someone who believes it is an active drug.

pleasure principle In Freud's theory, the basis for id functioning. Irrational, seeks immediate satisfaction of instinctual impulses.

plethysmograph An instrument that records changes in blood volume.

practical intelligence The competencies, skills, and knowledge (expertise) essential for everyday problem-solving and coping behaviors.

pragmatics The aspects of a person's intelligence that make allowances in order to maintain realistic problem solving and goal seeking. It is a measure of social or practical intelligence that takes into account environmental factors.

preconscious Thoughts, experiences, and memories not in a person's immediate attention but that can be called into awareness at any moment.

primary process thinking Freud's term for the id's direct, reality-ignoring attempts to satisfy needs irrationally.

processing (approaches) Theoretical approaches that focus on the mental and emotional (psychological) processes or determinants that underlie behavior.

processing dynamics Characteristic pattern of thoughts, feelings, and behavioral reactions activated in relation to situations.

projection A defense mechanism by which one attributes one's own unacceptable aspects or impulses to someone else.

projective methods Tests (such as the Rorschach or TAT) that present the individual with materials open to a wide variety of interpretations based on the belief that responses reveal important aspects of the respondent's personality central in psychodynamic assessment.

proprium Allport's term for the region of personality that contains the root of the consistency that characterizes attitudes, goals, and values. Not innate, it develops in time.

prosocial aggression Verbal threats and statements about the goodness or badness of behavior.

prototypicality The degree to which the member of a category is representative of that category or exemplifies it.

psychoanalysis A form of psychotherapy developed by Freud that aims at relieving neurotic conflict and anxiety by airing repressed, unconscious impulses over the course of regular meetings between patient and analyst.

psychobiography The intensive study of individual lives using narrative methods.

psychodynamic behavior theory Developed by John Dollard and Neal Miller in the late 1940s to integrate some of the fundamental ideas of psychoanalytic theory with the concepts and methods of experimental research on behavior and learning.

psychodynamics In psychoanalytic theory, the processes through which personality is regulated. It is predicated on the concept of repressed, unconscious impulses and the significance of early childhood experience.

psycholexical approach A research strategy that seeks to classify people into different trait groups by identifying differences among individuals on the basis of ratings with natural language terms (adjectives) that then are factor analyzed.

psychological features The aspects or ingredients of situations that activate the person's characteristic reaction patterns (e.g., being rejected by peers in a social situation).

psychological situation The circumstances and events within a nominal situation that affect behavior.

psychometric trait approach Approach that emphasizes quantitative measurement of psychological qualities, comparing the responses of large groups of people under standard conditions, often by means of paper-and-pencil tests.

psychosexual stages According to Freudian theory, development occurs in a series of psychosexual stages. In each stage (oral, anal, phallic, and genital) pleasure is focused on a different part of the body.

psychosocial stages Erikson's eight stages of development; extending throughout life, each stage centers around a "crisis" or set of problems and the individual's attempts to solve it.

Q-sort A method of obtaining trait ratings; consists of many cards, on each of which is printed a trait description. The rater groups the cards in a series of piles ranging from those that are least characteristic to those that are most characteristic of the rated person.

randomization The assignment of research participants to different conditions on the basis of chance. If many participants are used, differences should average out except for the effects produced by the experiment itself.

rational emotive therapy Albert Ellis's approach based on the idea that if people learn to think more rationally, their behavior will become more rational and their emotional problems will be reduced.

rationalization A defense mechanism that occurs when one makes something more acceptable by attributing it to more acceptable causes (*see* defense mechanisms).

reaction formation A defense mechanism that occurs when an anxiety-producing impulse is replaced in consciousness by its opposite.

reality anxiety In Freud's theory, the fear of real dangers in the external world (*see also* moral anxiety, neurotic anxiety).

reality principle In Freud's theory, the basis for ego functioning. Rational; dictates delay in the discharge of tension until environmental conditions are appropriate.

reciprocal interactionism The interaction of a person's qualities and behaviors with the environment to produce a particular outcome.

reflex An instinctive, unlearned response to a particular stimulus.

regression In psychodynamic theory, reversion to an earlier stage; the return of the libido to its former halting places in development.

reinforcement Any consequence that increases the likelihood that a response will be repeated.

relational self   The self perceived not as a single entity but as an object in relation to other objects, as in Kohut's object relations theory.

relational therapy   A therapeutic approach that emphasizes the role of early, current, and analyst–patient relationships in the development and resolution of personality problems.

repression   According to psychoanalytic theory, an unconscious defense mechanism through which unacceptable (ego-threatening) material is kept from awareness. The repressed motives, ideas, conflicts, memories, etc. continue to influence behavior.

repression–sensitization   A dimension of differences in defensive patterns of perception, ranging from avoiding the anxiety-arousing stimuli to approaching them more readily and being extravigilant or supersensitized.

resistance   Difficulties in achieving progress in psychotherapy due to unconscious defenses as anxiety-producing material emerges during the treatment.

response   Any observable, identifiable activity of an organism.

response freedom   The condition in a situation that does not produce a similar reaction in all individuals but that allows individual differences in the behaviors of each person to become visible.

Role Construct Repertory Test   A technique for measuring personal constructs developed by Kelly.

Rorschach test   Projective test consisting of 10 symmetrical inkblots to which the person describes his or her reactions, stating what each blot looks like or might be.

rumination   Dwelling on particular types of cognitions and emotions, usually negative. In a ruminative style of dealing with depression, the person focuses on the fact that he or she is depressed, on the symptoms (like fatigue and disinterest) that are experienced, and on their negative consequences ("I might lose my job").

schizophrenia   Most common form of psychosis. Prominent symptoms may include thought disorder, delusions, highly inappropriate or bizarre emotions, and hallucinations, all without known organic cause.

Scholastic Aptitude Test (SAT)   A standardized measure of verbal and quantitative skills given routinely to high school seniors before entrance into college.

secondary dispositions   The most specific, defined traits, or "attitudes," that influence an individual's behavior.

self-consciousness   Attention directed toward the self.

self-efficacy (expectations)   The person's confidence that he or she can perform a particular behavior, like handling a snake or making a public speech.

self-esteem   Refers to the individual's personal judgment of his or her own worth.

self-evaluative standards   Standards for assessing oneself.

self-instruction   Talking to oneself to control one's behavior; an aspect of some types of control training.

self-observation   Systematic observation of one's own behavior; an important step in some types of behavior therapy.

self-regulatory systems   A person variable that includes the individual's rules, plans, and self-reactions for performance and for the organization of complex behavior sequences (*see* person variables).

self-reinforcement   The process of providing positive consequences to oneself contingent upon enacting certain desired behaviors or achieving specific performance criteria (e.g., an A on an exam).

self-relevant   Meaningful to the self.

self-schemata   Cognitions about the self that arise from past experience and guide the processing of new information.

sensate focus   A method for overcoming sexual-performance fears in which the couple concentrates on sensual pleasures without engaging in sexual intercourse.

sense of helplessness   Feeling that one's efforts and actions are not effective.

sensory anesthesia   Loss of sensory ability (e.g., blindness, deafness) or loss of feeling in a body part.

serotonin   A neurotransmitter associated with depression when available in excess amounts in the body.

sex-role identity   The degree to which an individual regards himself or herself as masculine or feminine.

sex-typing   The process whereby the individual comes to acquire, to value, and to practice (perform) sex-typed behaviors.

shadow   According to Jung, the unconscious part of the psyche that must be absorbed into the personality to achieve full emotional growth.

shaping   Technique for producing successively better approximations of a behavior by reinforcing small variations in behavior in the desired direction and by reinforcing only increasingly close approximations to the desired behavior.

sibling rivalry   Competition between the siblings of a family that, according to Adler, plays a major role in development.

single-blind method   An experimental procedure in which participants do not know whether they are in experimental or control conditions.

social cognitive theory A type of theoretical framework that focuses on the social and cognitive meanings of events or situations.

social intelligence The competencies, skills, and knowledge needed to generate the person's cognitions and behavior patterns.

sociobiology An approach to explain social behavior in terms of evolutionary theories.

source traits In R. B. Cattell's theory, the traits that constitute personality structure and determine surface traits and behavior.

stability The durability of aspects of personality over time.

state anxiety A person's momentary or situational anxiety; it varies in intensity over time and across settings.

stimulus control Behavior that is expressed stably but only under specific, predictable conditions.

stimulus-outcome relations Stable links between stimuli and other events that allow one to predict the outcomes from the stimuli.

subjective values and goals The particular outcomes and goals to which an individual assigns greatest import; a cognitive social person variable.

sublimation A process through which socially unacceptable impulses are expressed in socially acceptable ways.

subliminally (subliminal) Occurring outside of a person's consciousness or awareness.

superego In Freud's theory, the conscience, made up of the internalized values of the parents; strives for self-control and perfection, and is both unconscious and conscious.

suppression Occurs when one voluntarily and consciously withholds a response or turns attention away from something (*see also* repression).

surface traits R. B. Cattell's term for clusters of observable trait elements (responses) that seem to go together; the manifestations of source traits.

symptom substitution The controversial psychoanalytic belief that new symptoms will automatically replace problematic behaviors that are removed directly (e.g., by behavior therapy) unless their underlying unconscious emotional causes also have been removed.

systematic desensitization A behavior therapy procedure designed to reduce incapacitating anxiety; an incompatible response (usually relaxation) is paired with progressively more anxiety-arousing situations until the individual is able to imagine or be in these situations without becoming anxious.

systems theory The analysis of units like the family as a system of relationships.

T scores Scores on the MMPI converted in terms of a standard average norm to facilitate comparisons.

tachistoscope A machine (used in studies of perceptual defense) that projects words onto a screen at different speeds.

temperament Characteristic individual differences relevant to emotional expression, often visible early in life.

temperament traits R. B. Cattell's term for traits that determine emotional reactivity.

test A means of obtaining information about a person through standardized measures of behavior and personal qualities.

Thanatos One of two aspects of the personality considered by early psychoanalysts to represent destruction and aggression; the darker side of human nature (*see also* Eros).

Thematic Apperception Test (TAT) Projective test consisting of a set of ambiguous pictures about which the person being tested is asked to make up an interesting story.

trait A persistent (enduring) characteristic or dimension of individual differences. Defined by Allport as a generalized "neuropsychic system," distinctive to each person, that serves to unify many different stimuli by leading the person to generate consistent responses to them.

trait anxiety A person's stable, characteristic overall level of anxiety.

trait approach An approach to personality that categorizes individuals in terms of traits.

trait theorists Psychologists who study personality in terms of the different trait dimensions that characterize each individual.

transactional analysis *See* systems theory, family therapy.

Transcendental Meditation (TM) A form of deep meditation in which the meditator sits comfortably with eyes closed and repeats a special Sanskrit word called a "mantra."

transference In psychoanalysis, the patient's response to the therapist as though the therapist were a parent or some other important figure from childhood. Considered an essential aspect of psychoanalytic therapy.

traumatic experiences Experiences that abruptly and severely disrupt a person's life.

unconditioned response The unlearned response one naturally makes to an unconditioned stimulus (e.g., withdrawing the hand from a hot object).

unconditioned stimuli Stimuli to which one automatically, naturally responds without learning to do so (e.g., food, electric shock).

unconscious In psychoanalytic theory, the part of the personality of which the ego is unaware but that profoundly affects actions and behaviors.

unique traits In Allport's theory, a trait that exists in only one individual and cannot be found in another in exactly the same form.

value The subjective importance of an outcome or event for an individual.

variable An attribute, quality, or characteristic that may be given two or more values and measured or systematically varied.

vicarious conditioning Conditioning of a response to a stimulus through observation.

visceral responses Internal bodily responses to external events that occur without our willing them or even thinking about them (e.g., increased heart rate, changes in gland secretion).

willpower The ability to voluntarily self-control for desired but difficult goals, for example, delay of gratification in anticipation of achieving a more far-reaching but distant goal.

working self-concept The prominent concepts of the self that are foremost in an individual's thought and memory and that can be easily accessed.

working through Process that occurs in psychoanalytic therapy when the patient, in the context of the transference relationship, re-examines his or her basic problems until their emotional roots are understood and learns to handle them more appropriately.

REFERENCES

Abelson, R. P. (1976). A script theory of understanding, attitude, and behavior. In J. Carroll & T. Payne (Eds.), *Cognition and social behavior.* Hillsdale, NJ: Erlbaum.

Abrams, D. (1994). Social self-regulation. *Personality and Social Psychology Bulletin, 20,* 473–483.

Abramson, L. Y., Seligman, M. E. P., & Teasdale, J. D. (1978). Learned helplessness in humans: Critique and reformation. *Journal of Abnormal Psychology, 87,* 49–74.

Adorno, I. W., Frenkel-Brunswik, E., Levinson, D. J., & Sanford, R. N. (1950). *The authoritarian personality.* New York: Harper & Row.

Affleck, G., Urrows, S., Tennen, H., Higgins, P. (1992). Daily coping with pain from rheumatoid arthritis: Patterns and correlates. *Pain, 51,* 221–229.

Ainslie, G. (1992). *Picoeconomics: The strategic interaction of successive motivational states within the person.,* New York: Cambridge University Press.

Ainsworth, M. D. S., & Bowlby, J. (1991). An ethological approach to personality development. *American Psychologist, 46,* 331–341.

Ainsworth, M. D., Blehar, M. C., Waters, E., & Wall, S. (1978). *Patterns of attachment.* Hillsdale, NJ: Erlbaum.

Ainsworth, M. S., & Bowlby, J. (1991). An ethological approach to personality development. 98th Annual Convention of the American Psychological Association Distinguished Scientific Contributions Award Address (1990, Boston, Massachusetts). *American Psychologist, 46,* 333–341.

Ainsworth, M. S., Blehar, M. C., Waters, E. C., & Wall, S. (1978). *Patterns of attachment.* Hillsdale, NJ: Erlbaum.

Ajzen, I., & Fishbein, M. (1977). Attitude-behavior relations: A theoretical analysis and review of empirical research. *Psychological Bulletin, 84,* 888–918.

Alexander, M. J., & Higgins, E. T. (1993). Emotional trade-offs of becoming a parent: How social roles influence self-discrepancy effects. *Journal of Personality and Social Psychology, 651,* 259–269.

Alicke, M. D. (1985). Global self-evaluation as determined by the desirability and controllability of trait adjectives. *Journal of Personality and Social Psychology, 49,* 1621–1630.

Allen, E. K., Hart, B. M., Buell, J. S., Harris, F. R., & Wolf, M. M. (1964). Effects of social reinforcement on isolate behavior of a nursery school child. *Child Development, 35,* 511–518.

Alloy, L. B., & Ahrens, A. H., (1987). Depression and pessimism for the future: Biased use of statistically relevant information in predictions for self versus others. *Journal of Personality and Social Psychology, 52,* 366–378.

Allport, G. W. (1937). *Personality: A psychological interpretation.* New York: Holt, Rinehart and Winston.

Allport, G. W. (1940). Motivation in personality: Reply to Mr. Bertocci. *Psychological Review, 47,* 533–554.

Allport, G. W. (1955). *Becoming.* New Haven, CT: Yale University Press.

Allport, G. W. (1961). *Pattern and growth in personality.* New York: Holt, Rinehart and Winston.

Altemeyer, B. (1981). *Right-wing authoritarianism.* Winnipeg: University of Manitoba Press.

Altemeyer, B. (1988). *Enemies of freedom: Understanding right-wing authoritarianism.* San Francisco, CA: Jossey-Bass.

Altemeyer, B. (1996). *The authoritarian specter.* Cambridge, MA: Harvard University Press.

Amabile, T. M. (1985). Motivation and creativity: Effects of motivational orientation on creative writers. *Journal of Personality and Social Psychology, 48,* 393–399.

Amabile, T. M., DeJong, W., & Lepper, M. R. (1976). Effects of externally imposed deadlines on subsequent intrinsic motivation. *Journal of Personality and Social Psychology, 34,* 92–98.

American Psychological Association. (1966). *Standards for educational and psychological tests and manuals.* Washington, DC: American Psychological Association.

Andersen, S. (1997). The self in relation to others: Conceptualizing personality in terms of transference. Invited address at the 9th Annual Convention of the American Psychological Society. (May 24, 1997: Washington, DC).

Andersen, S. M., & Chen, S. (1998). Measuring transference in everyday social relations: Theory and evidence using an experimental social-cognitive paradigm. In H. Kurtzman (Ed.), *Cognition and Pychodynamics.* New York: Oxford University Press.

Andersen, S. M., Reznik, I., & Chen, S. (1997). The self in relation to others: Cognitive and motivational underpinnings. In J. G. Snodgrass & R. L. Thompson (Eds.), *The self across psychology: Self-recognition, self-awareness, and the self-concept* (pp. 233–275). New York: New York Academy of Science.

Anderson, J. R. (1983). *The architecture of cognition.* Cambridge, MA: Harvard University Press.

Anderson, J. R. (1996). ACT: A simple theory of complex cognition. *American Psychologist, 51,* 355–365.

Anderson, J. R., & Bower, G. H. (1973). *Human associative memory.* New York: Wiley.

Anderson, N. H. (1965). Primacy effects in personality impression formation using a generalized order effect paradigm. *Journal of Personality and Social Psychology, 2,* 1–9.

Anderson, N. H. (1974). Information integration theory: A brief survey. In D. H. Krautz, R. C. Atkinson, R. D. Luce, & P. Suppes (Eds.), *Contemporary developments in mathematical psychology.* San Francisco: W. H. Freeman.

Angier, N. (1998). Separated by birth? *New York Times Book Review.* Feb. 8, p. 9.

Antonovsky, A. (1979). *Health, stress and coping.* San Francisco: Jossey-Bass.

Antrobus, J. (1991). Dreaming: Cognitive processes during critical activation and high afferent thresholds. *Psychology Review, 98,* 96–121.

Archibald, H. C., & Tuddenham, R. D. (1965). Persistent stress reaction after combat. *Archives of General Psychiatry, 12,* 475–481.

Arend, R., Gove, F. L., & Sroufe, L. A. (1979). Continuity of individual adaptation from infancy to kindergarten: A predictive study of ego-resiliency and curiosity in preschoolers. *Child Development, 50,* 950–959.

Argyle, M., & Little, B. R. (1972). Do personality traits apply to social behavior? *Journal of Theory of Social Behavior (Great Britain), 2,* 1–35.

Ariam, S., & Siller, J. (1982). Effects of subliminal oneness stimuli in Hebrew on academic performance of Israeli high school students: Further evidence of the adaptation-enhancing effects of symbiotic fantasies in another culture using another language. *Journal of Abnormal Psychology, 91,* 343–349.

Arkowitz, H. (1989). From behavior change to insight. *Journal of Integrative and Eclectic Psychotherapy, 8,* 222–232.

Aronfreed, J. (1966). The internalization of social control through punishment: Experimental studies of the role of conditioning and the second signal system in the development of conscience. *Proceedings of the XVIIIth International Congress of Psychology.* Moscow, USSR, August, 35, 219–230.

Aronfreed, J. (1968). *Conduct and conscience: The socialization of internalized control over behavior.* New York: Academic Press.

Aronfreed, J. (1994). Moral development from the standpoint of a general psychological theory. In B. Puka (Ed.), *Defining perspectives in moral development. Moral development: A compendium, Vol. 1* (pp. 170–185). New York: Garland Publishing.

Aronson, E. (1972). *The social animal.* San Francisco: W. H. Freeman.

Aronson, E., & Mettee, D. (1968). Dishonest behavior as a function of differential levels of induced self-esteem. *Journal of Personality and Social Psychology, 9,* 121–127.

Aspinwall, L. G., & Taylor, S. E. (1997). A stitch in time: Self-regulation and proactive coping. *Psychological Bulletin, 121,* 417–436.

Atkinson, J. W. (Ed.). (1958). *Motives in fantasy, action and society.* Princeton, NJ: Van Nostrand.

Atthowe, J. M., Jr., & Krasner, L. (1968). A preliminary report on the application of contingent reinforcement procedures (token economy) on a "chronic" psychiatric ward. *Journal of Abnormal Psychology, 73,* 37–43.

Ayduk, O. N., Downey, G., Testa, S., Yin, Y., & Shoda, Y. (1998). Does rejection elicit hostility in rejection sensitive women? *Social Cognition.*

Ayllon, T., & Azrin, N. H. (1965). The measurement and reinforcement of behavior of psychotics. *Journal of the Experimental Analysis of Behavior, 8,* 357–383.

Ayllon, T., & Azrin, N. H. (1968). *The token economy.* New York: Appleton.

Ayllon, T., & Haughton, E. (1964). Modification of symptomatic verbal behaviour of mental patients. *Behaviour Research and Therapy, 2,* 87–97.

Balay, J., & Shevrin, W. (1988). The subliminal psychodynamic activation method: A critical review. *American Psychologist, 43,* 161–174.

Ball, D., Hill, L., Freeman, B., Eley, T. C., Strelau, J., Riemann, R., Sinath, F. M., Angleitner, A., & Plomin, R. (1997). The serotonin transporter gene and peer-rated neuroticism. *NeuroReport, 8* (5), 1301–1304.

Baltes, P. B., & Baltes, M. M. (Eds.). (1990). *Successful aging: Perspectives from the behavioral sciences.* New York: Cambridge University Press.

Bandura, A. (1965). Vicarious processes: A case of no-trial learning. In L. Berkowitz (Ed.), *Advances in experimental social psychology* (Vol. 2, pp. 1–55). New York: Academic Press.

Bandura, A. (1969). *Principles of behavior modification.* New York: Holt, Rinehart and Winston.

Bandura, A. (1971). *Social learning theory.* Morristown, NJ: General Learning Press.

Bandura, A. (1973). *Aggression: A social learning analysis.* Englewood Cliffs, NJ: Prentice-Hall.

Bandura, A. (1977). *Social learning theory.* Englewood Cliffs, NJ: Prentice-Hall.

Bandura, A. (1978). Reflections on self-efficacy. In S. Rachman (Ed.), *Advances in behaviour research and therapy* (Vol. 1). Elmsford, NY: Pergamon.

Bandura, A. (1982). Self-efficacy mechanisms in human agency. *American Psychologist, 37,* 122–147.

Bandura, A. (1986). *Social foundations of thought and action: A social cognitive theory.* Englewood Cliffs, NJ: Prentice-Hall.

Bandura, A. (1989). Human agency in social cognitive theory. *American Psychologist, 44,* 1175–1184.

Bandura, A. (1989). Perceived self-efficacy in the exercise of control over AIDS infection. In V. M. Mays, G. W. Albee, & S. F. Schneider (Eds.), *Primary prevention of AIDS: Psychological approaches* (pp. 128–141). Newbury Park, CA: Sage Publications.

Bandura, A., & Adams, N. E. (1977). Analysis of self-efficacy theory of behavioral change. *Cognitive Therapy and Research, 1,* 287–310.

Bandura, A., & Kupers, C. J. (1964). Transmission of patterns of self-reinforcement through modeling. *Journal of Abnormal and Social Psychology, 69,* 1–9.

Bandura, A., & Mischel, W. (1965). Modification of self-imposed delay of reward through exposure to live and symbolic models. *Journal of Personality and Social Psychology, 2,* 698–705.

Bandura, A., Adams, N. E., & Beyer, J. (1977). Cognitive processes mediating behavioral change. *Journal of Personality and Social Psychology, 35,* 125–139.

Bandura, A., Blanchard, E. B., & Ritter, B. (1969). Relative efficacy of desensitization and modeling approaches for inducing behavioral, affective, and attitudinal changes. *Journal of Personality and Social Psychology, 13,* 173–199.

Bandura, A., Grusec, J. E., & Menlove, F. L. (1966). Observational learning as a function of symbolization and incentive set. *Child Development, 37,* 499–506.

Bandura, A., Grusec, J. E., & Menlove, F. L. (1967). Vicarious extinction of avoidance behavior. *Journal of Personality and Social Psychology, 5,* 16–23.

Bandura, A., Taylor, C. B., Ewart, C. K., Miller, N. M., & Debusk, R. F. (1985). Exercise testing to enhance wives' confidence in their husbands' cardiac capability soon after clinically uncomplicated acute myocardial infarction. *American Journal of Cardiology, 55,* 635–638.

Bargh, J. A. (1996). Automaticity in social psychology. In E. T. Higgins & A. W. Kruglanski (Eds.), *Social psychology: Handbook of basic principles* (pp. 169–183). New York: Guilford Press.

Bargh, J. A. (1997). The automaticity of everyday life. In R. S. Wyer, Jr. (Ed.), *The automaticity of everyday life: Advances in social cognition, Vol. 10* (pp. 1–61). Mahwah, NJ: Erlbaum.

Bargh, J. A., & Gollwitzer, P. (1994). Environmental control of goal directed action: Automatic and strategic contingencies between situations and behavior. In *Nebraska symposium on motivation: Vol. 41* (pp. 71–124). Lincoln: University of Nebraska Press.

Barlow, D. H. (1988). *Anxiety and its disorders: The nature and treatment of anxiety and panic.* New York: Guilford Press.

Bartholomew, K., & Horowitz, L. (1991). Attachment styles among young adults: A test of a four-category model. *Journal of Personality and Social Psychology, 61,* 226–244.

Bartussek, D., Diedrich, O., Naumann, E., & Collet, W. (1993). Introversion-extraversion and event-related potential (ERP): A test of J. A. Gray's theory. *Personality and Individual Differences, 14,* 565–574.

Bates, B., & Goodman, A. (1986). The effectiveness of encounter groups: Implications of research for counseling practice. *British Journal of Guidance and Counseling, 14,* 240–251.

Bates, J. E., & Wachs, T. D. (1994). *Temperament: Individual differences at the interface of biology and behavior.* Washington, DC: American Psychological Association.

Bateson, G. (1979). *Mind and nature: A necessary unit.* New York: Dutton.

Baum, W. H., & Heath, J. L. (1992). Behavioral explanations and intentional explanations in psychology. *American Psychologist, 47,* 1312–1317.

Baumeister, R. F. (1992). *Meanings of life.* Hillsdale, NJ: Erlbaum.

Baumeister, R. F. (1996). Self-regulation and ego threat: Motivated cognition, self deception, and destructive goal setting. In P. M. Gollwitzer & J. A. Bargh (Eds.), *The psychology of action: Linking cognition and motivation to behavior* (pp. 27–47). New York: Guilford Press.

Baumeister, R. F. (1997). Identity, self-concept, and self-esteem: The self lost and found. In R. Hogan, J. Johnson, & S. Briggs (Eds.), *Handbook of personality psychology* (pp. 681–710). San Diego, CA: Academic Press.

Baumeister, R. F., & Cairns, K. H. (1992). Repression and self-presentation: When audiences interfere with self-deceptive strategies. *Journal of Personality and Social Psychology, 62,* 851–862.

Baumeister, R. F., & Heatherton, T. F. (1996). Self-regulation failure: An overview. *Psychological Inquiry, 7,* 1–15.

Bavelas, J. B. (1978). *Personality: Current theory and research.* Monterey, CA: Brooks-Cole.

Bechara, A., Tranel, D., Damasio, H., Adolphs, R., Rockland, C., & Damasio, A. R. (1995). Double dissociation of conditioning and declarative knowledge relative to the amygdala and hippocampus in humans. *Science, 269,* 1115–1118.

Beck, A. T. (1976). *Cognitive therapy and the emotional disorders.* New York: International Universities Press.

Beck, A. T., Rush, A. J., Shaw, B. F., & Emery, G. (1979). *Cognitive therapy of depression.* New York: Guilford Press.

Bell, J. E. (1948). *Projective techniques.* New York: Longmans, Green.

Bell, R. Q., Weller, G., & Waldrop, M. (1971). Newborn and preschooler: Organization of behavior and relations between periods. *Monographs of the Society for Research in Child Development, 36* (1, 2).

Bellak, L., & Abrams, D. M. (1997). *The Thematic Apperception Test, the Children's Apperception Test, and the Senior Apperception Technique in clinical use* (6th ed.). Boston: Allyn & Bacon.

Bem, D. J. (1972). Self-perception theory. In L. Berkowitz (Ed.), *Advances in experimental social psychology* (Vol. 6, pp. 1–62). New York: Academic Press.

Bem, D. J., & Allen, A. (1974). On predicting some of the people some of the time: The search for cross-situational consistencies in behavior. *Psychological Review, 81,* 506–520.

Bem, D. J., & Funder, D. C. (1978). Predicting more of the people more of the time: Assessing the personality of situations. *Psychological Review, 85,* 485–501.

Benjamin, J., Li, L., Patterson, C., Greenberg, B. D., Murphy, D. L., & Hamer, D. H. (1996). Population and familial association between the D4 dopamine receptor gene and measures of novelty seeking. *Nature Genetics, 12,* 81–84.

Benson, H. (1975). *The relaxation response.* New York: Morrow.

Bergeman, C. S., Plomin, R., Pedersen, N. L., McClearn, G. E., & Nesselroade, J. R. (1990). Genetic and environmental influences on social support: The Swedish Adoption/ Twin Study of Aging (SATSA). *Journals of Gerontology: Psychological Sciences,* P101–P106.

Berger, S. M. (1962). Conditioning through vicarious instigation. *Psychological Review, 69,* 450–466.

Bergin, A. E. (1966). Some implications of psychotherapy research for therapeutic practice. *Journal of Abnormal Psychology, 71,* 235–246.

Bergin, A. E. (1971). The evaluation of therapeutic outcomes. In A. E. Bergin & S. I. Garfield (Eds.), *Handbook of psychotherapy and behavior change* (pp. 217–270). New York: Wiley.

Berntzen, D. (1987). Effects of multiple cognitive coping strategies on laboratory pain. *Cognitive Therapy and Research, 11,* 613–623.

Bijou, S. W. (1965). Experimental studies of child behavior, normal and deviant. In L. Krasner & L. P. Ullmann (Eds.), *Research in behavior modification* (pp. 56–81). New York: Holt, Rinehart and Winston.

Billig, J. P., Hershberger, S. L., Icono, G., & McGue, M. (1996). Life events and personality in late adolescence: Genetic and environmental relations. *Behavior Genetics, 26,* 543–551.

Birbaumer, N., & Ohman, A. (1993). *The structure of emotion: Psychophysiological, cognitive and clinical aspects.* Seattle: Hogrefe & Huber.

Block, J. (1961). *The Q-sort method in personality assessment and psychiatric research.* Springfield, IL: Charles C. Thomas.

Block, J. (1971). *Lives through time.* Berkeley, CA: Bancroft.

Block, J. (1977). Advancing the psychology of personality: Paradigmatic shift or improving the quality of research. In D. Magnusson & N. S. Endler (Eds.), *Personality at the crossroads: Current issues in interactional psychology.* Hillsdale, NJ: Erlbaum.

Block, J. H., & Martin, B. (1955). Predicting the behavior of children under frustration. *Journal of Abnormal and Social Psychology, 51,* 281–285.

Block, J., & Block, J. H. (1980). The role of ego-control and ego resiliency in the organization of behavior. In W. A. Collins (Ed.), *The Minnesota symposium on child psychology* (Vol. 13). Hillsdale, NJ: Erlbaum.

Block, J., Weiss, D. S., & Thorne, A. (1979). How relevant is a semantic similarity interpretation of personality ratings? *Journal of Personality and Social Psychology, 37,* 1055–1074.

Blum, G. S. (1955). Perceptual defense revisited. *Journal of Abnormal and Social Psychology, 51,* 24–29.

Bolger, N., & Schilling, E. A. (1991). Personality and the problems of everyday life: The role of neuroticism in exposure and reactivity to daily stressors. *Journal of Personality, 59,* 355–386.

Bonarius, J. C. J. (1965). Research in the personal construct theory of George A. Kelly: Role construct repertory test and basic theory. In B. A. Maher (Ed.), *Progress in experimental personality research* (pp. 1–46). New York: Academic Press.

Bootzin, R. (1973). Stimulus control of insomnia (summary). Remarks in The Treatment of Sleep Disorders. Symposium presented at the meeting of the American Psychological Association, Montreal.

Bootzin, R. P., Epstein, D., & Wood, J. M. (1991). Stimulus control instructions. In P. Hauri (Ed.), *Case studies in insomnia* (pp. 19–28). New York: Plenum.

Bornstein, R. F. (1992). The dependent personality: Developmental, social, and clinical perspectives. *Psychological Bulletin, 112,* 3–23.

Bornstein, R. F., Leone, D. R., & Galley, D. J. (1987). The generalizability of subliminal mere exposure effects: Influence of stimuli perceived without awareness on social behavior. *Journal of Personality and Social Psychology, 53,* 1070–1079.

Bornstein, R. F., Riggs, J. M., Hill, E. L., & Calabrese, C. (1996). Activity, passivity, self-denigration, and self-promotion: Toward an interactionist model of interpersonal dependency. *Journal of Personality, 64,* 637–673.

Bouchard, T. J., Lykken, D. T., McGue, M., Segal, N. L., & Tellegen, A. (1990). Sources of human psychological differences: The Minnesota study of twins reared apart. *Science, 250,* 223–228.

Boudin, H. M. (1972). Contingency contracting as a therapeutic tool in the deceleration of amphetamine use. *Behavior Therapy, 3,* 604–608.

Bower, G. H. (1981). Mood and memory. *American Psychologist, 36,* 129–148.

Bowers, K. (1973). Situationism in psychology: An analysis and a critique. *Psychological Review, 80,* 307–336.

Bowlby, J. (1982). Attachment and loss: Retrospect and prospect. *American Journal of Orthopsychiatry, 52,* 664–678.

Braungart, J. M., Fulker, D. W., & Plomin, R. (1992). Genetic influence of the home environment during infancy: A sibling adoption study of the home. *Developmental Psychology, 28,* 1048–1055.

Brazier, D. (1993). The necessary condition is love: Going beyond self in the person-centered approach. In D. Brazier (Ed.), *Beyond Carl Rogers* (pp. 72–91). London, England: Constable.

Breger, L., & McGaugh, J. L. (1965). Critique and reformulation of "learning theory" approaches to psychotherapy and neurosis. *Psychological Bulletin, 63,* 338–358.

Brehm, J. W. (1968). *A theory of psychological reactance.* New York: Academic Press.

Breland, H. M. (1974). Birth order, family configuration, and verbal achievement. *Child Development, 45,* 1011–1019.

Breland, K., & Breland, M. (1966). *Animal behavior.* New York: Macmillan.

Brill, A. A. (1949). *Basic principles of psychoanalysis.* Garden City, NY: Doubleday.

Broadbent, D. E. (1977). The hidden preattentive processes. *American Psychologist, 32,* 109–118.

Brown, B. (1975). *New mind, new body.* New York: Harper.

Brown, J. D. (1986). Evaluations of self and others: Self-enhancement biases in social judgment. *Social Cognition, 4,* 353–376.

Brown, J. S. (1942). The generalization of approach responses as a function of stimulus intensity and strength of motivation. *Journal of Comparative Psychology, 33,* 209–226.

Brown, J. S. (1948). Gradients of approach and avoidance responses and their relation to level of motivation. *Journal of Comparative and Physiological Psychology, 41,* 450–465.

Bruner, J. (1992). Another look at New Look 1. *American Psychologist, 47,* 780–783.

Bruner, J. S. (1957). Going beyond the information given. In H. Gruber et al. (Eds.), *Contemporary approaches to cognition.* Cambridge, MA: Harvard University Press.

Bruner, J. S., & Postman, L. (1947). Emotional selectivity in perception and reaction. *Journal of Personality, 16,* 69–77.

Brunstein, J. (1993). Personal goals and subjective well-being: A longitudinal study. *Journal of Personality and Social Psychology, 65,* 1061–1070.

Budzynski, T., Stoyva, J., & Adler, C. (1970). Feedback-induced muscle relaxation. In T. Barber, L. DiCara, J. Kamiya, W. Miller, D. Shapiro, & J. Stoyva (Eds.), *Biofeedback and self-control.* Chicago: Aldine-Atherton.

Burton, R. V. (1963). Generality of honesty reconsidered. *Psychological Review, 70,* 481–499.

Buss, A. H., Plomin, R., & Willerman, L. (1973). The inheritance of temperaments. *Journal of Personality, 41,* 513–524.

Buss, A. H. (1989). Personality as traits. *American Psychologist, 44,* 1378–1388.

Buss, A. H., & Plomin, R. (1984). *Temperament: Early developing personality traits.* Hillsdale, NJ: Erlbaum.

Buss, D. M. (1984). Toward a psychology of person-environment (PE) correlation: The role of spouse selection. *Journal of Personality and Social Psychology, 47,* 361–377.

Buss, D. M. (1987). Selection, evocation, and manipulation. *Journal of Personality and Social Psychology, 53,* 1214–1221.

Buss, D. M. (1991). Evolutionary personality psychology. *Annual Review of Psychology, 42,* 459–491.

Buss, D. M. (1994). Personality evoked: The evolutionary psychology of stability and change. In T. F. Heatherton & J. L. Weinberger (Eds.), *Can personality change?* (pp. 41–57). Washington, DC: American Psychological Association.

Buss, D. M. (1996). The evolutionary psychology of human social strategies. In E. T. Higgins & A. W. Kruglanski (Eds.), *Social psychology: Handbook of basic principles* (pp. 3–38). New York: Guilford Press.

Buss, D. M. (1997). Evolutionary foundations of personality. In R. Hogan, J. A. Johnson, & S. R. Briggs (Eds.), *Handbook of personality psychology* (pp. 317–344). San Diego, CA: Academic Press.

Buss, D. M., & Craik, K. H. (1983). The act frequency approach to personality. *Psychological Review, 90,* 105–126.

Buss, D. M., Gomes, M., Higgins, D., & Lauterbach, K. (1987). Tactics of manipulation. *Journal of Personality and Social Psychology, 52,* 1219–1229.

Butler, J. M., & Haigh, G. V. (1954). Changes in the relation between self-concepts and ideal concepts consequent upon client-centered counseling. In C. R. Rogers & R. F. Dymond (Eds.), *Psychotherapy and personality change: Co-ordinated studies in the client-centered approach* (pp. 55–76). Chicago: University of Chicago Press.

Butterfield, H. (1965). *The origins of modern science.* New York: Free Press.

Byrne, D. (1964). Repression-sensitization as a dimension of personality. In B. A. Maher (Ed.), *Progress in experimental personality research* (Vol. 1). New York: Academic Press.

Byrne, D. (1966). *An introduction to personality.* Englewood Cliffs, NJ: Prentice-Hall.

Byrne, D. (1969). Attitudes and attraction. In L. Berkowitz (Ed.), *Advances in experimental social psychology* (Vol. 1). New York: Academic Press.

Cacioppo, J. T., & Petty, R. E. (1982). The need for cognition. *Journal of Personality and Social Psychology, 42,* 116–131.

Cacioppo, J. T., Berntson, G. G., & Crites, S. L., Jr. (1996). Social neuroscience: Principles of psychophysiological arousal and response. In E. T. Higgins & A. W. Kruglanski (Eds.), *Social psychology: Handbook of basic principles* (pp. 72–101). New York: Guilford Press.

Caldwell, B. M., & Bradley, R. H. (1978). *Home observation for measurement of the environment.* Little Rock: University of Arkansas.

Campbell, D. T. (1960). Recommendations for APA Test Standards regarding construct, trait, or discriminant validity. *American Psychologist, 15,* 546–553.

Campbell, D. T., & Fiske, D. W. (1959). Convergent and discriminant validation. *Psychological Bulletin, 56,* 81–105.

Campbell, J., & Dunnette, M. (1968). Effectiveness of T-group experiences in managerial training and development. *Psychological Bulletin, 70,* 73–104.

Cantor, N. (1990). From thought to behavior: "Having" and "doing" in the study of personality and cognition. *American Psychologist, 45,* 735–750.

Cantor, N. (1994). Life task problem-solving: situational affordances and personal needs. Presidential address of the society for personality and social psychology (Division 8 of the American Psychological Association, 1993, Toronto, Canada), *Personality and Social Psychology Bulletin, 20,* 235–243.

Cantor, N., & Harlow, R. E. (1994). Social intelligence and personality: Flexible life task pursuit. In R. J. Sternberg and P. Ruzgis (Eds.), *Personality and intelligence* (pp. 137–168). New York: Cambridge University Press.

Cantor, N., & Kihlstrom, J. F. (1987). *Personality and social intelligence.* Hillsdale, NJ: Erlbaum.

Cantor, N., & Mischel, W. (1979). Prototypes in person perception. In L. Berkowitz (Ed.), *Advances in experimental social psychology* (Vol. 12). New York: Academic Press.

Cantor, N., Mischel, W., & Schwartz, J. (1982). A prototype analysis of psychological situations. *Cognitive Psychology, 14,* 45–77.

Cantor, N., Norem, J., Langston, C., Zirkel, S., Fleeson W., & Cook-Flannagan, C. (1991). Life tasks and daily life experience. *Journal of Personality, 59,* 425–451.

Capecchi, M. R. (1994). Targeted gene replacement. *Scientific American, 270* (3), 52–59.

Carlson, C., Kula, M. L., & St. Laurent, C. M. (1997). Rorschach revised DEPI and CDI with inpatient major depressives and borderline personality disorder with major depression: Validity issues. *Journal of Clinical Psychology, 53,* 51–58.

Carlson, R. (1971). Where is the personality research? *Psychological Bulletin, 75,* 203–219.

Cartwright, D. S. (1978). *Introduction to personality.* Chicago: Rand McNally.

Carver, C. S., Coleman, A. E., & Glass, D. C. (1996). The coronary-prone behavior pattern and the suppression of fatigue on a treadmill test. *Journal of Personality and Social Psychology, 33,* 460–466.

Carver, C. S., Pozo, C., Harris, S. D., Noriega, V., Scheier, M. F., Robinson, D. S:, Ketchem, A. S., Moffat, F. L., Jr., & Clark, K. C. (1993). How coping mediates the effects of optimism on stress: A study of women with early stage breast cancer. *Journal of Personality and Social Psychology, 65,* 375–391.

Carver, C. S., & Scheier, M. F. (1978). Self-focusing effects of dispositional self-consciousness, mirror presence, and audience presence. *Journal of Personality and Social Psychology, 36,* 322–324.

Carver, C. S., & Scheier, M. F. (1981). *Attention and self-regulation: A control theory approach to human behavior.* New York: Springer-Verlag.

Carver, C. S., & Scheier, M. F. (1982). Control theory: A useful conceptual framework for personality-social, clinical, and health psychology. *Psychological Bulletin, 92,* 111–135.

Carver, C. S., & Scheier, M. F. (1990). Principles of self-regulation: Action and emotion. In E. T. Higgins & R. M. Sorrentino (Eds.), *Handbook of motivation and cognition* (Vol. 2, pp. 3–52). New York: Guilford Press.

Carver, C. S., & Scheier, M. F. (1992). Confidence, doubt, and coping with anxiety. In D. G. Forgays, T. Sosnowski, & K. Wrzesniewski (Eds.), *Anxiety: Recent developments in cognitive, psychophysiological, and health research* (pp. 13–22). Washington, DC: Hemisphere.

Cashdan, S. (1988). *Object relations theory: Using the relationship*. New York: Norton.

Caspi, A. (1987). Personality in the life course. *Journal of Personality and Social Psychology, 53,* 1203–1213.

Caspi, A., & Bem, D. J. (1990). Personality continuity and change across the life course. In L. A. Pervin (Ed.), *Handbook of personality: Theory and research* (pp. 549–575). New York: Guilford Press.

Caspi, A., Elder, G. H., Jr., & Bem, D. J. (1987). Moving against the world: Life-course patterns of explosive children. *Developmental Psychology, 23,* 308–313.

Cattell, R. B. (1950). *A systematic theoretical and factual study.* New York: McGraw-Hill.

Cattell, R. B. (1965). *The scientific analysis of personality.* Baltimore: Penguin.

Cattell, R. B. (1982). *The inheritance of personality and ability.* New York: Academic Press.

Ceci, S. J. (1996). *On intelligence: A bioecological treatise on intellectual development.* Cambridge, MA: Harvard University Press.

Cervone, D. (1991). The two disciplines of personality psychology [Review of the book *Handbook of personality: Theory and research*]. *Psychological Science, 2,* 371–376.

Cervone, D., & Williams, S. L. (1982). Social cognitive theory and personality. In G. V. Caprara & G. L. Van Heck (Eds.), *Modern personality psychology: Critical reviews and new directions* (pp. 200–252). New York: Harvester Wheatsheaf/ Simon & Schuster.

Chaiken, S., Wood, W., & Eagly, A. H. (1996). Principles of persuasion. In E. T. Higgins & A. W. Kruglanski (Eds.), *Social psychology: Handbook of basic principles* (pp. 702–742). New York: Guilford Press.

Chaiken, S., & Bargh, J. A. (1993). Occurrence versus moderation of the automatic attitude activation effect: Reply to Fazio. *Journal of Personality and Social Psychology, 64,* 759–765.

Chapita, B. F., & Barlow, D. H. (1998). The development of anxiety: The role of control in the early environment. *Psychological Bulletin, 124,* 3–21.

Chaplin, W. F. (1991). The next generation of moderator research in personality psychology. *Journal of Personality, 59,* 143–178.

Chaplin, W. F., & Goldberg, L. R. (1984). A failure to replicate the Bem and Allen study of individual differences in cross-situational consistency. *Journal of Personality and Social Psychology, 47,* 1074–1090.

Chaplin, W. F., John, O. P., & Goldberg, L. R. (1988). Conceptions of states and traits: Dimensional attributes with ideals as prototypes. *Journal of Personality and Social Psychology, 54,* 541–557.

Chapman, L. J., & Chapman, J. P. (1969). Illusory correlations as an obstacle to the use of valid psychodiagnostic signs. *Journal of Abnormal Psychology, 74,* 271–280.

Chaves, J. F., & Barber, T. X. (1974). Acupuncture analgesia: A six-factor theory. *Psychoenergetic Systems, 1,* 11–20.

Cherney, S. S., Fulker, D. W., Emde, R. N., Robinson, J., Corley, R. P., Reznick, J. S., Plomin, R., & Defries, J. C. (1994). Continuity and change in infant shyness from 14 to 20 months. *Behavior Genetics, 24,* 365–379.

Chipuer, H. M., Plomin, R., Pedersen, N. L., McClearn, G. E., & Nesselroade, J. R. (1992). Genetic influence on family environment: The role of personality. *Developmental Psychology, 29,* 110–118.

Chiu, C., Dweck, C. S., Tong, J. Y., & Fu, J. H. (1997). Implicit theories and conceptions of morality. *Journal of Personality and Social Psychology, 73,* 923–940.

Chiu, C., Hong, Y., & Dweck, C. S. (1997). Lay dispositionism and implicit theories of personality. *Journal of Personality and Social Psychology, 73,* 19–30.

Chiu, C., Hong, Y., Mischel, W., & Shoda, Y. (1995). Discriminative facility in social competence: Conditional versus dispositional encoding and monitoring-blunting of information. *Social Cognition, 13,* 49–70.

Chodoff, P. (1963). Late effects of concentration camp syndrome. *Archives of General Psychiatry, 8,* 323–333.

Chodorkoff, B. (1954). Self-perception, perceptual defense, and adjustment. *Journal of Abnormal and Social Psychology, 49,* 508–512.

Chomsky, N. (1965). *Aspects of the theory of syntax.* Cambridge, MA: MIT Press.

Christie, R. (1991). Authoritarianism and related constructs. In J. P. Robinson, P. R. Shaver, & L. S. Wrightsman (Eds.), *Measures of personality and social psychological attitudes* (pp. 501–570). New York: Academic Press.

Churchland, P. S., & Sejnowski, T. J. (1992). *The computational brain.* Cambridge, MA: MIT Press.

Cobb, S. (1976). Social support as moderator of life stress. *Psychosomatic Medicine, 38,* 300–314.

Cohen, J. D., & Servan-Schreiber, D. (1992). Context, cortex, and dopamine: A connectionist approach to behavior and biology in schizophrenia. *Psychological Review, 99,* 45–77.

Cohen, S., & McKay, G. (1984). Social support, stress, and the buffering hypothesis: A theoretical analysis. In A. Baum, J. E. Singer, & S. E. Taylor (Eds.), *Handbook of psychology and health, Vol. 4. Social psychological aspects of health.* Hillsdale, NJ: Erlbaum.

Colby, K. M. (1951). *A primer for psychotherapists.* New York: Ronald.

Coles, R. (1970). *Uprooted children.* New York: Harper & Row.

Cone, J. D., & Hoier, T. S. (1986). Assessing children: The radical behavior perspective. *Advances in Behavior Assessment of Children and Families, 2,* 1–27.

Contrada, R. J., Leventhal, H., & O'Leary, A. (1990). Personality and health. In L. A. Pervin (Ed.), *Handbook of personality: Theory and research* (pp. 638–669). New York: Guilford Press.

Cooper, J. R., Bloom, F. E., & Roth, R. H. (1986). *The biochemical basis of neuropharmacology* (5th ed.). New York: Oxford University Press.

Cooper, J., & Fazio, R. H. (1984). A new look at dissonance theory. In L. Berkowitz (Ed.), *Advances in experimental social psychology, Vol. 17. Theorizing in social psychology: Special topics* (pp. 229–262). New York: Academic Press.

Coopersmith, S. (1967). *The antecedents of self-esteem.* San Francisco: W. H. Freeman.

Cosmides, L. (1989). The logic of social exchange: Has natural selection shaped how humans reason? Studies with the Wason selection task. *Cognition, 31,* 187–276.

Cosmides, L., & Tooby, J. (1989). Evolutionary psychology and the generation of culture: II. Case study: A computational theory of social exchange. *Ethology and Sociobiology, 10,* 51–97.

Costa, P. T., Jr., & McCrae, R. R. (1988). Personality in adulthood: A six-year longitudinal study of self-reports and spouse ratings on the NEO personality inventory. *Journal of Personality and Social Psychology, 54,* 853–863.

Costa, P. T., Jr., & McCrae, R. R. (1992). Normal personality assessment in clinical practice: The NEO personality inventory. *Psychological Assessment, 4,* 5–13.

Costa, P. T., Jr., & McCrae, R. R. (1997). Longitudinal stability of adult personality. In R. Hogan, J. Johnson, & S. Briggs (Eds.), *Handbook of personality psychology* (pp. 269–291). San Diego, CA: Academic Press.

Costa, P. T., Jr., McCrae, R. R., & Dye, D. A. (1991). Facet scales for agreeableness and conscientiousness: A revision of the neo-personality inventory. *Personality and Individual Differences, 12,* 887–898.

Coyne, J. C., & Downey, G. (1991). Social factors and psychopathology: Stress, social support, and coping process. *Annual Review of Psychology, 42,* 401–425.

Craighead, L. W., Stunkard, A. J., & O'Brien, R. M. (1981). Behavior therapy and pharmacotherapy for obesity. *Archives of General Psychiatry, 38,* 763–768.

Craik, K. H. (1990). Environmental and personality psychology: Two collective narratives and four individual story lines. *Human Behavior and Environment Advances in Theory and Research, 11,* 141–168.

Craske, M. G., Brown, T. A., & Barlow, D. H. (1991). Behavior treatment for panic disorder: A two-year follow-up. *Behavior Therapy, 22,* 289–304.

Creer, T. (1974). Biofeedback and asthma. *Advances in Asthma and Allergy, 1,* 6–12.

Crick, F., & Koch, C. (1990). Towards a neurobiological theory of consciousness. *Seminars in Neuroscience, 2,* 263–275.

Cronbach, L. J. (1970). *Essentials of psychological testing.* New York: Harper.

D'Zurilla, T. (1965). Recall efficiency and mediating cognitive events in "experimental repression." *Journal of Personality and Social Psychology, 1,* 253–257.

Daniels, A. C. (1994). *Bringing out the best in people: How to apply the astonishing power of reinforcement.* New York: McGraw-Hill.

Daniels, D., Dunn, J. F., Furstenberg, F. F., Jr., & Plomin, R. (1985). Environmental differences within the family and adjustment differences within pairs of adolescent siblings. *Child Development, 56,* 764–774.

David, J. P., Green, P. J., Martin, R., & Suls, J. (1997). Differential roles of neuroticism, extraversion, and event desirability for mood in daily life: An integrative model of top-down and bottom-up influences. *Journal of Personality and Social Psychology, 73,* 149–159.

Davis, J. M., Klerman, G., & Schildkraut, J. (1967). Drugs used in the treatment of depression. In L. Efron, J. O. Cole, D. Levine, & J. R. Wittenborn (Eds.), *Psychopharmacology: A review of progress.* Washington, DC: United States Clearing-House of Mental Health Information.

Davison, G. C., & Neale, J. M. (1990). *Abnormal psychology: An experimental clinical approach* (5th ed.). New York: Wiley.

Davison, K. P., & Pennebaker, J. W. (1996). Social psychosomatics. In E. T. Higgins & A. W. Kruglanski (Eds.), *Social psychology: Handbook of basic principles* (pp. 102–132). New York: Guilford Press.

Deci, E. L. (1971). Effects of externally mediated rewards on intrinsic motivation. *Journal of Personality and Social Psychology, 18,* 105–115.

Deci, E. L. (1975). *Intrinsic motivation.* New York: Plenum.

Deci, E. L., & Ryan, R. M. (1987). The support of autonomy and the control of behavior. *Journal of Personality and Social Psychology, 53,* 1024–1037.

Deci, E. L., & Ryan, R. M. (1985). *Intrinsic motivation and self-determination in human behavior.* New York: Plenum Press.

Decker, H. S. (1990). *Freud, Dora and Vienna, 1900.* New York: Free Press.

DeFries, J. C., & Plomin, R. (1978). Behavioral genetics. *Annual Review of Psychology, 29,* 473–515.

DeLongis, A., Folkman, S., & Lazarus, R. S. (1988). The impact of daily stress on health and mood: Psychological and social resources as mediators. *Journal of Personality and Social Psychology, 54,* 486–495.

DeNike, L. D. (1964). The temporal relationship between awareness and performance in verbal conditioning. *Journal of Experimental Psychology, 68,* 521–529.

DeWitt, K. N., Kaltreider, N. B., Weiss, D. S., & Horowitz, M. J. (1983). Judging change in psychotherapy. *Archives of General Psychiatry, 40,* 1121–1128.

Diamond, M. J., & Shapiro, J. L. (1973). Changes in locus of control as a function of encounter group experiences: A study and replication. *Journal of Abnormal Psychology, 82,* 514–518.

Dickson, D., Saunders, C., & Stringer, M. (1993). *Rewarding people: The skill of responding positively.* New York: Routledge.

Diener, C. I., & Dweck, C. S. (1978). An analysis of learned helplessness: Continuous changes in performance, strategy, and achievement cognitions following failure. *Journal of Personality and Social Psychology, 36,* 451–462.

Diener, E., Smith, H., & Fujita, F. (1995). The personality structure of affect. *Journal of Personality and Social Psychology, 69,* 130–141.

Dixon, N. F. (1981). *Preconscious processing.* New York: Wiley.

Dobson, K. S., & Craig, K. D. (1996). *Advances in cognitive-behavioral therapy.* Thousand Oaks, CA: Sage Publications.

Dodge, K. A. (1997a, April). *Testing developmental theory through prevention trials.* Presented at Biennial Meeting for the Society for Research in Child Development, Washington, DC.

Dodge, K. A. (1997b, April). *Early peer social rejection and acquired autonomic sensitivity to peer conflicts: Conduct problems in adolescence.* Presented at Biennial Meeting for the Society for Research in Child Development, Washington, DC.

Dodge, K. A. (1986). A social information processing model of social competence in children. *Cognitive perspectives on children's social behavioral development. The Minnesota symposium on child psychology, 18,* 77–125.

Dodge, K. A. (1993). New wrinkles in the person-versus-situation debate. *Psychological Inquiry, 4,* 284–286.

Dollard, J., & Miller, N. E. (1950). *Personality and psychotherapy: An analysis in terms of learning, thinking, and culture.* New York: McGraw-Hill.

Downey, G., Freitas, A., Michaelis, B., & Khouri, H. (1997). The self-fulfilling prophecy in close relationships: Do rejection sensitive women get rejected by their partners? Department of Psychology, Columbia University, New York. Unpublished manuscript.

Downey, G., & Feldman, S. I. (1996). Implications of rejection sensitivity for intimate relationships. *Journal of Personality and Social Psychology, 70,* 1327–1343.

Downey, G., & Walker, E. (1989). Social cognition and adjustment in children at risk for psychopathology. *Developmental Psychology, 25,* 835–845.

Downey, G., Feldman, S., Khuri, J., & Friedman, S. (in press). Maltreatment and childhood depression. In W. M. Reynolds & H. F. Johnston (Eds.), *Handbook of depression in children and adolescents: Issues in clinical child psychology* (pp. 481–508). New York: Plenum Press.

Dulany, D. E., Jr. (1962). The place of hypotheses and intentions: An analysis of verbal control in verbal conditioning. In C. W. Eriksen (Ed.), *Behavior and awareness* (pp. 102–129). Durham, NC: Duke University Press.

Duncan, L. E., Peterson, B. E., & Winter, D. G. (1997). Authoritarianism and gender roles: Towards a psychological analysis of hegemonic relationships. *Personality and Social Psychology Bulletin, 23,* 41–49.

Dunn, J., & Plomin, R. (1986). Determinants of maternal behavior toward three-year-old siblings. *British Journal of Developmental Psychology, 4,* 127–137.

Dunn, J., & Plomin, R. (1990). *Separate lives: Why siblings are so different.* New York: Basic Books.

Dunnette, M. D. (1969). People feeling: Joy, more joy, and the "slough of despond." *Journal of Applied Behavioral Science, 5,* 25–44.

Dunning, D., Perie, M., & Story, A. L. (1991). Self-serving prototypes of social categories. *Journal of Personality and Social Psychology, 61,* 957–968.

Duval, T. S., Duval, V. H., & Mulilis, J. (1992). Effects of self-focus, discrepancy between self and standard, and outcome expectancy favorability on the tendency to match self to standard or to withdraw. *Journal of Personality and Social Psychology, 62,* 340–348.

Dweck, C. S. (1975). The role of expectations and attributions in the alleviation of learned helplessness. *Journal of Personality and Social Psychology, 31,* 674–685.

Dweck, C. S. (1989). Motivation. In A. Lesgold & R. Glaser (Eds.), *Foundations for a psychology of education* (pp. 87–136). Hillsdale, NJ: Erlbaum.

Dweck, C. S. (1991). Self-theories and goals: Their role in motivation, personality, and development. In R. A. Dienstbier (Ed.), *Nebraska symposium on motivation* (Vol. 38, pp. 19–235). Lincoln: University of Nebraska Press.

Dweck, C. S., & Leggett, E. L. (1988). A social-cognitive approach to personality and motivation. *Psychological Review, 95,* 256–273.

Dworkin, R. H. (1979). Genetic and environmental influences on person-situation interactions. *Journal of Research in Personality, 13,* 279–293.

Eaves, L. J., Eysenck, H. J., & Martin, N. G. (1989). *Genes, culture, and personality: An empirical approach.* London: Academic Press.

Ebstein, R. P., Gritsenko, I., Nemanov, L., Frisch, A., Osher, Y., & Belmaker, R. H. (1997). No association between the serotonin transporter gene regulatory region polymorphism and the Tridimensional Personality Questionnaire (TPQ) temperament of harm avoidance. *Molecular Psychiatry, 2,* 224–226.

Ebstein, R. P., Novick, O., Umansky, R., Priel, B., Osher, Y., Blaine, D., Bennett, E. R., Nemanov, L., Katz, M., & Belmaker, R. H. (1996). Dopamine D4 receptor (D4DR) exon III polymorphism associated with human personality trait of novelty seeking. *Nature Genetics, 12,* 78–80.

Edelman, G. M. (1987). *Neural darwinism: The theory of neuronal group selection.* New York: Basic Books.

Edwards, A. L., & Edwards, L. K. (1992). Social desirability and Wiggins's MMPI content scales. *Journal of Personality and Social Psychology, 62,* 147–153.

Ekman, P. (Ed.). (1982). *Emotion in the human face* (2nd ed.). New York: Cambridge University Press.

Ekman, P., Friesen, W. V., & Ellsworth, P. (1972). *Emotion in the human face.* Elmsford, NY: Pergamon.

Elliot, E. S., & Dweck, C. S. (1988). Goals: An approach to motivation and achievement. *Journal of Personality and Social Psychology, 54,* 5–12.

Ellis, A. (1962). *Reason and emotion in psychotherapy.* New York: Lyle Stuart.

Ellis, A. (1977). Rational-emotive therapy: Research data that support the clinical and personality hypothesis of RET and other modes of cognitive behavior therapy. *The Counseling Psychologist, 7,* 2–42.

Ellis, A., Sichel, J. L., Yeager, R. J., DiMattia, D. J., & DiGiuseppe, D. (1989). *Rational-emotive couples therapy.* Elmsford, NY: Pergamon.

Ellsworth, P. C., & Carlsmith, J. M. (1968). Effects of eye contact and verbal content on affective response to a dyadic interaction. *Journal of Personality and Social Psychology, 10,* 15–20.

Emmons, R. A. (1991). Personal strivings, daily life events, and psychological and physical well-being. *Journal of Personality, 59,* 453–472.

Emmons, R. A. (1997). Motives and goals. In R. Hogan, J. A. Johnson, & S. R. Briggs (Eds.), *Handbook of personality psychology* (pp. 485–512). San Diego, CA: Academic Press.

Endler, N. S., & Hunt, J. McV. (1969). Generalizability of contributions from sources of variance in the S-R inventories of anxiousness. *Journal of Personality, 37,* 1–24.

Endler, N. S., & Okada, M. (1975). A multidimensional measure of trait anxiety: The S-R inventory of general trait anxiousness. *Journal of Consulting and Clinical Psychology, 43,* 319–329.

Endler, N.S., Hunt, J. M., & Rosenstein, A. J. (1962). An S-R inventory of anxiousness. *Psychological Monographs, 76,* No. 536.

Engel, B. T., & Bleecker, E. R. (1974). Application of operant conditioning techniques to the control of the cardiac arrhythmias. In P. A. Obrist, et al. (Eds.), *Cardiovascular psychophysiology.* Chicago: Aldine.

Epstein, S. (1994). Trait theory as personality theory: Can a part be as great as the whole? *Psychological Inquiry, 5* (2), 120–122.

Epstein, L. J., Taubman, M. T., & Lovaas, O. I. (1985). Changes in self-stimulatory behaviors with treatment. *Journal of Abnormal Child Psychology, 13,* 281–293.

Epstein, S. (1973). The self-concept revisited or a theory of a theory. *American Psychologist, 28,* 405–416.

Epstein, S. (1977). Traits are alive and well. In D. Magnusson & N. Endler (Eds.), *Personality at the crossroads: Current issues in interactional psychology* (pp. 83–98). Hillsdale, NJ: Erlbaum.

Epstein, S. (1979). The stability of behavior: I. On predicting most of the people much of the time. *Journal of Personality and Social Psychology, 37,* 1097–1126.

Epstein, S. (1983). Aggregation and beyond: Some basic issues on the prediction of behavior. *Journal of Personality, 51,* 360–392.

Epstein, S. (1990). Cognitive-experimental self-theory. In L. A. Pervin (Ed.), *Handbook of personality: Theory and research* (pp. 165–192). New York: Guilford Press.

Epstein, S., & Fenz, W. D. (1962). Theory and experiment on the measurement of approach-avoidance conflict. *Journal of Abnormal and Social Psychology, 64,* 97–112.

Erdelyi, M. H. (1974). A new look at the new look: Perceptual defense and vigilance. *Psychological Review, 81,* 1–25.

Erdelyi, M. H. (1985). *Psychoanalysis: Freud's cognitive psychology.* New York: W. H. Freeman.

Erdelyi, M. H. (1992). Psychodynamics and the unconscious. *American Psychologist, 47,* 784–787.

Erdelyi, M. H. (1993). Repression: The mechanism and the defense. In D. M. Wegner & J. W. Pennebaker (Eds.), *Handbook of mental control. Century psychology series* (pp. 126–148). Englewood Cliffs, NJ: Prentice-Hall.

Erdelyi, M. H., & Goldberg, B. (1979). Let's not sweep repression under the rug: Towards a cognitive psychology of repression. In J. F. Kihlstrom & F. J. Evans (Eds.), *Functional disorders of memory.* Hillsdale, NJ: Erlbaum.

Erdley, C. A., & Dweck, C. S. (1993). Children's implicit personality theories as predictors of their social judgments. *Child Development, 64,* 863–878.

Ericsson, K. A., & Simon, H. A. (1980). Verbal reports as data. *Psychological Review, 87,* 215–251.

Eriksen, C. W. (1952). Individual differences in defensive forgetting. *Journal of Experimental Psychology, 44,* 442–446.

Eriksen, C. W. (1960). Discrimination and learning without awareness: A methodological survey and evaluation. *Psychological Review, 67,* 279–300.

Eriksen, C. W. (1966). Cognitive responses to internally cued anxiety. In C. D. Spielberger (Ed.), *Anxiety and behavior* (pp. 327–360). New York: Academic Press.

Eriksen, C. W., & Kuethe, J. L. (1956). Avoidance conditioning of verbal behavior without awareness: A paradigm of repression. *Journal of Abnormal and Social Psychology, 53,* 203–209.

Erikson, E. (1963). *Childhood and society.* New York: Norton.

Erikson, E. (1968). *Identity: Youth and crisis.* New York: Norton.

Exline, R., & Winters, L. C. (1965). Affective relations and mutual glances in dyads. In S. Tomkins & C. Izard (Eds.), *Affect, cognition, and personality.* New York: Springer.

Exner, J. E. (1986). *The Rorschach: A comprehensive system, Vol. 1. Basic foundations* (2nd ed.). New York: Wiley.

Exner, J. E. (1989). Searching for projection in the Rorschach. *Journal of Personality Assessment, 53,* 520–536.

Exner, J. E. (1993). *The Rorschach: A comprehensive system, Vol. 1: Basic foundations* (3rd ed.). New York: Wiley.

Exner, J. E. (1996). A comment on "The comprehensive system for the Rorschach: A critical examination." *Psychological Science, 7,* 11–13.

Eysenck, H. J. (1983). Cicero and the state-trait theory of anxiety: Another case of delayed recognition. *American Psychologist, 38,* 114–115.

Eysenck, H. J. (1952). The effects of psychotherapy: An evaluation. *Journal of Consulting Psychology, 16,* 319–324.

Eysenck, H. J. (1961). The effects of psychotherapy. In H. J. Eysenck (Ed.), *Handbook of abnormal psychology: An experimental approach* (pp. 697–725). New York: Basic Books.

Eysenck, H. J. (1973). Personality and the law of effect. In D. E. Berlyne & K. B. Madsen (Eds.), *Pleasure, reward, preference.* New York: Academic Press.

Eysenck, H. J. (1990). Biological dimensions of personality. In L. A. Pervin (Ed.), *Handbook of personality: Theory and research* (pp. 244–276). New York: Guilford Press.

Eysenck, H. J. (1991). Personality, stress, and disease: An interactionist perspective. *Psychological Inquiry, 2,* 221–232.

Eysenck, H. J., & Eysenck, M. W. (1985). *Personality and individual differences: A natural science approach.* New York: Plenum.

Eysenck, H. J., & Eysenck, M. W. (1995). *Mindwatching: Why we behave the way we do.* London: Prion Books.

Eysenck, H. J., & Rachman, S. (1965). *The causes and cures of neurosis: An introduction to modern behavior therapy based on learning theory and the principles of conditioning.* San Diego, CA: Knapp.

Fairweather, G. W. (1964). *Social psychology in treating mental illness: An experimental approach.* New York: Wiley.

Fairweather, G. W. (1967). *Methods in experimental social innovation.* New York: Wiley.

Fairweather, G. W., Sanders, D. H., Cressler, D. L., & Maynard, H. (1969). *Community life for the mentally ill: An alternative to institutional care.* Chicago: Aldine.

Farquhar, J. W., Wood, P. D., Breitrose, H., Haskell, W. L., Meyer, A. J., Maccoby, N., Alexander, J. K., Brown, B. W., Jr., McAlister, A. L., Nash, J. D., & Stern, M. P. (1977). Community education for cardiovascular health. *The Lancet,* June 4.

Fazio, R. H., Sanbonmatsu, D. M., Powell, M. C., & Kardes, F. (1986). On the automatic activation of attitudes. *Journal of Personality and Social Psychology, 50,* 229–238.

Feather, N. T. (1990). Bridging the gap between values and actions: Recent applications of the expectancy-value model. In E. T. Higgins & R. M. Sorrentino (Eds.), *Handbook on motivation and cognition: Foundations of social behavior* (Vol. 3, pp. 151–191). New York: Guilford Press.

Feld, B. G. (1997). An object relations perspective on couples group therapy. *International Journal of Group Psychotherapy, 47,* 315–332.

Feldman, S., & Downey, G. (1994). Rejection sensitivity as a mediator of the impact of childhood exposure to family violence on adult attachment behavior. *Development and Psychopathology, 6,* 231–247.

Fenz, W. D. (1964). Conflict and stress as related to physiological activation and sensory, perceptual and cognitive functioning. *Psychological Monographs, 78,* No. 8 (Whole No. 585).

Ferster, C. B., & Demyer, M. K. (1961). The development of performances in autistic children in an automatically controlled environment. *Journal of Chronic Diseases, 13,* 312–345.

Ferster, C. B., & Skinner, B. F. (1957). *Schedules of reinforcement.* New York: Appleton.

Festinger, L. (1957). *A theory of cognitive dissonance.* Stanford, CA: Stanford University Press.

Festinger, L. (1964). Behavioral support for opinion change. *Public Opinion Quarterly, 28,* 404–417.

Fischer, W. F. (1970). *Theories of anxiety.* New York: Harper.

Fisher, J. D., Fisher, W. A., Misovich, S. J., Kimble, D. L., & Malloy, T. E. (1996). Changing AIDS risk behavior: Effects of an intervention emphasizing AIDS risk reduction information, motivation, and behavioral skills in a college student population. *Health Psychology, 15,* 114–123.

Fiske, S. T., & Taylor, S. E. (1991). *Social cognition* (2nd ed.). New York: McGraw-Hill.

Fitch, G. (1970). Effects of self-esteem, perceived performance, and choice on causal attribution. *Journal of Personality and Social Psychology, 16,* 311–315.

Flavell, J. H., & Ross, L. (Eds.). (1981). *Social cognitive development: Frontiers and possible futures.* New York: Cambridge University Press.

Fleming, J., & Darley, J. M. (1986). *Perceiving intention in constrained behavior: The role of purposeful and constrained action cues in correspondence bias effects.* Unpublished manuscript, Princeton University, Princeton, NJ.

Flint, J., Corley, R., DeFries, J. C., Fulker, D. W., Gary, J. A., Miller, S., & Collins, A. C. (1995). A simple genetic basis for a complex psychological trait in laboratory mice. *Science, 269,* 1432–1435.

Foa, E. B., & Kozak, M. J. (1986). Emotional processing of fear: Exposure to corrective information. *Psychological Bulletin, 99,* 20–35.

Fodor, I. (1987). Moving beyond cognitive-behavior therapy: Integrating Gestalt therapy to facilitate personal and interpersonal awareness. In N. S. Jacobson (Ed.), *Psychotherapists in clinical practice: Cognitive and behavioral perspectives* (pp. 190–231). New York: Guilford Press.

Folkman, S., Lazarus, R., Dunkel-Schetter, C., DeLongis, A., & Gruen, R. (1986). The dynamics of a stressful encounter: Cognitive appraisal, coping, and encounter outcomes. *Journal of Personality and Social Psychology, 50,* 992–1003.

Forgas, J. P. (1983). Episode cognition and personality: A multidimensional analysis. *Journal of Personality, 51,* 34–48.

Forgas, J. P. (1992). Affect in social judgments and decisions: A multi-process model. In M. Zanna (Ed.), *Advances in experimental social psychology.* New York: Academic Press.

Forgas, J. P., Bower, G. H., & Moylan, S. J. (1990). Praise or blame? Affective influences on attributions for achievement. *Journal of Personality and Social Psychology, 59,* 809–819.

Foucault, M., (1980) *Power/knowledge: Selected interviews and other writings, 1972–1977.* C. Gordon (Ed. and Trans.). Brighton, England: Harvester.

Fraley, R. C., & Shaver, P. R. (1997). Adult attachment and the suppression of unwanted thoughts. *Journal of Personality and Social Psychology, 73,* 1080–1091.

Frank, K. G., & Hudson, S. M. (1990). Behavior management of infant sleep disturbance. *Journal of Applied Behavior Analysis, 23,* 91–98.

Frank, L. K. (1939). Projective methods for the study of personality. *Journal of Psychology, 8,* 389–413.

Fransella, F. (1995). *George Kelly.* London: Sage Publications.

Frawley, P. J., & Smith, J. W. (1990). Chemical aversion therapy in the treatment of cocaine dependence as part of a multimodal treatment program: Treatment outcome. *Journal of Substance Abuse Treatment, 7,* pp. 21–29.

Fremoux, W., & Heyneman, N. (1984). Obesity. In M. Hersen (Ed.), *Outpatient behavior theory: A clinical guide* (pp. 137–151). New York: Grune & Stratton.

Freud, S. (1899). The interpretation of dreams. *Standard edition, Vol. 4.* London: Hogarth, 1955.

Freud, S. (1901). Psychopathology of everyday life. *Standard edition, Vol. 6.* London: Hogarth, 1960.

Freud, S. (1905). Fragments of an analysis of a case of hysteria. *Standard edition, Vol. 7.* London: Hogarth, 1953.

Freud, S. (1909). Leonardo da Vinci: A study in psychosexuality. *Standard edition, Vol. 2.* London: Hogarth, 1957.

Freud, S. (1911). Formulations regarding the two principles of mental functioning. *Collected papers, Vol. IV.* New York: Basic Books, 1959.

Freud, S. (1915). Instincts and their vicissitudes. *Standard edition, Vol. 14.* London: Hogarth, 1957.

Freud, S. (1917). On transformations of instinct as exemplified in anal eroticism. *Standard edition, Vol. 18.* London: Hogarth, 1955.

Freud, S. (1920). *A general introduction to psychoanalysis.* New York: Boni and Liveright, 1924.

Freud, S. (1933). *New introductory lectures on psychoanalysis* (W. J. H. Sproutt, Trans.). New York: Norton.

Freud, S. (1940). An outline of psychoanalysis. *International Journal of Psychoanalysis, 21,* 27–84.

Freud, S. (1958). A note on the unconscious in psychoanalysis. In J. Strachey (Ed. and Trans.), *The standard edition of the complete psychological works of Sigmund Freud* (Vol. 12, pp. 255–266). London: Hogarth Press. (Original work published 1912)

Freud, S. (1959). *Collected papers, Vols. I–V.* New York: Basic Books.

Freud, S. (1963). *The sexual enlightenment of children.* New York: Macmillan.

Freud, A. (1990). Transference. In A. H. Esman et al. (Eds.), *Essential papers on transference. Essential papers in psychoanalysis* (pp. 110–114). New York: New York University Press.

Friedman, M., & Roseman, R. H. (1974). *Type A behavior and your heart.* New York: Knopf.

Fromm, E. (1941). *Escape from freedom.* New York: Holt, Rinehart and Winston.

Fromm, E. (1947). *Man for himself.* New York: Holt, Rinehart and Winston.

Frueh, B. C., Gold, P. B., de Arellano, M. A., & Brady, K. L. (1997). A racial comparison of combat veterans evaluated for PTSD. *Journal of Personality Assessment, 68,* 692–702.

Funder, D. C. (1987). Errors and mistakes: Evaluating the accuracy of social judgment. *Psychological Bulletin, 101,* 75–90.

Funder, D. C. (1991). Global traits: a neo-Allportian approach to personality. *Psychological Science, 2,* 31–39.

Funder, D. C. (1994). Explaining traits. *Psychological Inquiry, 5,* 125–127.

Funder, D. C., & Colvin, C. R. (1997). Congruence of others' and self-judgments of personality. In R. Hogan, J. Johnson, & S. Briggs (Eds.), *Handbook of personality psychology* (pp. 617–647). San Diego, CA: Academic Press.

Garcia, J., Mcgowan, B. K., & Green, K. F. (1972). Biological constraints on conditioning. In A. H. Black & W. F. Prokasy (Eds.), *Classical conditioning II: Current research and theory.* New York: Appleton-Century-Crofts.

Geen, R. G. (1997). Psychophysiological approaches to personality. In R. Hogan, J. A. Johnson, & S. R. Briggs (Eds.), *Handbook of personality psychology* (pp. 387–416). San Diego, CA: Academic Press.

Geer, J. H. (1965). The development of a scale to measure fear. *Behavior Research and Therapy, 3,* 45–53.

Geertz, C. (1986). Making experiences, authoring selves. In V. Turner & E. Bruner (Eds.), *The anthropology of experience.* Chicago: University of Illinois Press.

Gendlin, E. T. (1962). Client-centered developments and work with schizophrenics. *Journal of Counseling Psychology, 9,* 205–211.

Giese, H., & Schmidt, S. (1968). *Studenten sexualitat.* Hamburg: Rowohlt.

Gitlin, M. J. (1990). *The psychotherapist's guide to psychopharmacology.* New York: Free Press.

Glass, D. C. (1977). *Behavior patterns, stress, and coronary disease.* Hillsdale, NJ: Erlbaum.

Glass, D. C., Singer, J. E., & Friedman, L. N. (1969). Psychic costs of adaptation to an environmental stressor. *Journal of Personality and Social Psychology, 12,* 200–210.

Gleaves, D. H., & Eberenz, K. P. (1995). Correlates of dissociative symptoms among women with eating disorders. *Journal of Psychiatric Research, 29,* 417–426.

Goldberg, L. R. (1973). The exploitation of the English language for the development of a descriptive personality taxonomy. Paper delivered at the 81st Annual Convention of the American Psychological Association, Montreal, Canada.

Goldberg, L. R. (1990). An alternative "description of personality": The big-five factor structure. *Journal of Personality and Social Psychology, 59,* 1216–1229.

Goldberg, L. R. (1992). The development of markers for the big-five factor structure. *Psychological Assessment, 4,* 26–42.

Goldberg, L. R., & Werts, C. E. (1966). The reliability of clinician's judgments: A multitrait-multimethod approach. *Journal of Consulting Psychology, 30,* 199–206.

Golden, M. (1964). Some effects of combining psychological tests on clinical inferences. *Journal of Consulting Psychology, 28,* 440–446.

Goldfried, M. R., & Goldfried, A. P. (1980). Cognitive change methods. In F. H. Kanfer & A. P. Goldstein (Eds.), *Helping people change: A textbook of methods* (2nd ed.). Elmsford, NY: Pergamon.

Goldfried, M. R., & Sobocinski, D. (1975). Effect of irrational beliefs on emotional arousal. *Journal of Consulting and Clinical Psychology, 43,* 504–510.

Goldner, V., Penn, P., Sheinberg, M., & Walker, G. (1990). Love and violence: Gender paradoxes in volatile attachments. *Family Process, 29,* 343–364.

Goldsmith, H. H. (1983). Genetic influences on personality from infancy to childhood. *Child Development, 54,* 331–335.

Goldsmith, H. H. (1991). A zygosity questionnaire for young twins: A research note. *Behavior Genetics, 21,* 257–269.

Goldsmith, H. H., & Campos, J. J. (1982). Genetic influences on individual differences in emotionality. *Infant Behavior and Development, 5,* 99 (Abstract).

Goldsmith, H. H., & Campos, J. J. (1986). Fundamental issues in the study of early temperament: The Denver twin temperament study. In M. E. Lamb, A. L. Brown, & B. Rogoff (Eds.), *Advances in developmental psychology* (pp. 231–283). Hillsdale, NJ: Erlbaum.

Goleman, D. (1995). *Emotional intelligence.* New York: Bantam Books.

Gollwitzer, P. M. (1993). Goal achievement: The role of intentions. In W. Stroebe & M. Hewstone (Eds.), *European review of social psychology* (Vol. 4, pp. 141–185). London, England: Wiley.

Gollwitzer, P. M. (1996). The volitional benefits of planning. In P. M. Gollwitzer & J. A. Bargh (Eds.), *The psychology of action: Linking cognition and motivation to behavior* (pp. 297–312). New York: Guilford Press.

Gollwitzer, P. M., & Bargh, J. A. (Eds.). (1996). *The psychology of action: Linking cognition and motivation to behavior.* New York: Guilford Press.

Gollwitzer, P. M., & Moskowitz, G. B. (1996). Goal effects on action and cognition. In E. T. Higgins & A. W. Kruglamski (Eds.), *Social psychology: Handbook of basic principles* (pp. 361–399). New York: Guilford Press.

Gormly, J., & Edelberg, W. (1974). Validation in personality trait attribution. *American Psychologist, 29,* 189–193.

Gottesman, I. I. (1991). *Schizophrenia genesis: The origins of madness.* New York: W. H. Freeman.

Gough, H. G. (1957). *Manual, California Psychological Inventory.* Palo Alto, CA: Consulting Psychologists Press.

Gough, H. G., & Hall, W. B. (1975). An attempt to predict graduation from medical school. *Journal of Medical Education, 50,* 940–950.

Gough, H. G., Hall, R. E., & Harris, W. B. (1963). Admissions procedures as forecasters of performance in medical education. *Journal of Medical Education, 38,* 983–998.

Gove, F. L., Arend, R. A., & Sroufe, L. A. (1979). *Competence in preschool and kindergarten predicted from infancy.* Paper presented at the Meeting of the Society for Research in Child Development, San Francisco.

Grant, H., & Dweck, C. S. (1999). A goal analysis of personality and personality coherence. In D. Cervone and Y. Shoda (Eds.), *Social-cognitive approaches to personality coherence.* New York: Guilford Press.

Gray, J. A. (1991). The neuropsychology of temperament. In J. Strelau & A. Angleitner (Eds.), *Explorations in temperament: International perspective on theory and measurement.* New York: Plenum Press.

Greenberg, J. R., & Mitchell, S. (1983). *Object relations in psychoanalytic theory.* Cambridge, MA: Harvard University Press.

Greenwald, A. G. (1980). The totalitarian ego: Fabrication and revision of personal history. *American Psychologist, 7,* 603–618.

Greenwald, A. G. (1992). New look 3: Unconscious cognition reclaimed. *American Psychologist, 47,* 766–779.

Griffin, D. W., & Ross, L. (1991). Subjective construal, social inference, and human misunderstanding. *Advances in Experimental Social Psychology, 24,* 319–359.

Griffit, W., & Guay, P. (1969). "Object" evaluation and conditioned affect. *Journal of Experimental Research in Personality, 4,* 1–8.

Grilly, D. M. (1989). *Drugs and human behavior.* Boston: Allyn and Bacon.

Grinker, R. R., & Spiegel, J. P. (1945). *Men under stress.* Philadelphia: Blakiston.

Grossberg, J. M. (1964). Behavior therapy: A review. *Psychological Bulletin, 62,* 73–88.

Grunbaum, A. (1984). *The foundations of psychoanalysis.* Berkeley, CA: University of California Press.

Guilford, J. P. (1959). *Personality.* New York: McGraw-Hill.

Guilford, J. P. (1967). *The nature of human intelligence.* New York: McGraw-Hill.

Gur, R. C., & Sackeim, H. A. (1979). Self-deception: A concept in search of a phenomenon. *Journal of Personality and Social Psychology, 37,* 147–169.

Guthrie, E. R. (1935). *The psychology of learning.* New York: Harper & Brothers.

Haddock, G., Zanna, M. P., & Esses, V. M. (1993). Assessing the structure of prejudicial attitudes: The case of attitudes toward homosexuals. *Journal of Personality and Social Psychology, 65,* 1105–1118.

Hall, S. S. (1998, February 15). Our memories, our selves. *New York Times Magazine,* p. 28.

Halverson, C. (1971a). Longitudinal relations between newborn tactile threshold, preschool barrier behaviors, and early school-age imagination and verbal development. *Newborn and preschooler: Organization of behavior and relations between period.* SRCD Monograph, Vol. 36.

Halverson, C. (1971b). *Relation of preschool verbal communication to later verbal intelligence, social maturity, and distribution of play bouts.* Paper presented at the meeting of the American Psychological Association.

Halverson, C. F., Jr., & Waldrop, M. R. (1974). Relations between preschool barrier behaviors and early school-age measures of coping, imagination, and verbal development. *Development Psychology, 10,* 716–720.

Hamer, D., & Copeland, P. (in press). *Living with our genes.* New York: Doubleday.

Harackiewicz, J. M., Abrahams, S., & Wageman, R. (1987). Performance evaluation and intrinsic motivation: The effects of evaluative focus, rewards, and achievement orientation. *Journal of Personality and Social Psychology, 53,* 1015–1023.

Harackiewicz, J. M., Manderlink, G., & Sansone, C. (1984). Rewarding pinball wizardry: Effects of evaluation and cue on intrinsic motivation. *Journal of Personality and Social Psychology, 47,* 287–300.

Haring, T. G., & Breen, C. J. (1992). A peer-mediated social network intervention to enhance the social integration of persons with moderate and severe disabilities. *Journal of Applied Behavior Analysis, 25,* 319–333.

Harris, A. H., Gilliam, W. J., Findley, J. D., & Brady, J. B. (1973). Instrumental conditioning of large-magnitude, daily, 12-hour blood pressure elevations in the baboon. *Science, 182,* 175–177.

Harris, F. R., Johnston, M. K., Kelley, S. C., & Wolf, M. M. (1964). Effects of positive social reinforcement on regressed crawling of a nursery school child. *Journal of Educational Psychology, 55,* 35–41.

Harter, S. (1983). Developmental perspectives on the self-system. In P. H. Mussen (Ed.), *Handbook of child psychology* (Vol. 4, E. M. Hetherington, Ed.). New York: Wiley.

Hartig, M., & Kanfer, F. H. (1973). The role of verbal self-instructions in children's resistance to temptation. *Journal of Personality and Social Psychology, 25,* 259–267.

Hartmann, H., Kris, E., & Loewenstein, R. M. (1947). Comments on the formation of psychic structure. In A. Freud et al. (Eds.), *The psychoanalytic study of the child* (Vol. 2, pp. 11–38). New York: International Universities Press.

Hartshorne, H., & May, A. (1928). *Studies in the nature of character, Vol. 1. Studies in deceit.* New York: Macmillan.

Hawkins, R. P., Peterson, R. F., Schweid, E., & Bijou, S. W. (1966). Behavior therapy in the home: Amelioration of problem parent-child relations with the parent in a therapeutic role. *Journal of Experimental Child Psychology, 4,* 99–107.

Heatherton, T. F., & Weinberger, J. L. (Eds.). (1994). *Can personality change?* Washington, DC: American Psychological Association.

Heckhausen, H. (1969). Achievement motive research: Current problems and some contributions towards a general theory of motivation. In W. J. Arnold (Ed.), *Nebraska symposium on motivation* (pp. 103–174). Lincoln: Nebraska University Press.

Heider, F. (1958). *The psychology of interpersonal relations.* New York: Wiley.

Heider, F., & Simmel, M. (1944). An experimental study of apparent behavior. *American Journal of Psychology, 57,* 243–259.

Heitzman, A. J., & Alimena, M. J. (1991). Differential reinforcement to reduce disruptive behaviors in a blind boy with a learning disability. *Journal of Visual Impairment and Blindness, 85,* 176–177.

Henderson, V., & Dweck, C. S. (1990). Adolescence and achievement. In S. Feldman & G. Elliot (Eds.), *At the threshold: Adolescent development.* Cambridge, MA: Harvard University Press.

Herman, C. P. (1992). Review of W. H. Sheldon "Varieties of Temperament." *Contemporary Psychology, 37,* 525–528.

Hershberger, S. L., Lichtenstein, P., & Knox, S. S. (1994). Genetic and environmental influences on perceptions of organizational climate. *Journal of Applied Psychology, 79,* 24–33.

Heston, L. (1970). The genetics of schizophrenia and schizoid disease. *Science, 167,* 249–256.

Hetherington, E. M., & Clingempeel, W. G. (1992). Coping with marital transitions: A family systems perspective. *Monographs of the Society for Research in Child Development,* Nos. 2–3, Serial No. 277.

Higgins, E. T. (1987). Self-discrepancy: A theory relating self and affect. *Psychological Review, 94,* 319–340.

Higgins, E. T. (1990). Personality, social psychology, and person-situation relations: Standards and knowledge activation as a common language. In L. A. Pervin (Ed.), *Handbook of personality: Theory and research* (pp. 301–338). New York: Guilford Press.

Higgins, E. T. (1996a) Knowledge activation: Accessibility, applicability, and salience. In E. T. Higgins & A. W. Kruglanski, (Eds.), *Social psychology: Handbook of basic principles* (pp. 133–168). New York: Guilford Press.

Higgins, E. T. (1996b). Ideals, oughts, and regulatory focus: Affect and motivation from distinct pains and pleasures. In P. M. Gollwitzer & J. A. Bargh (Eds.), *The psychology of action: Linking cognition and motivation to behavior* (pp. 91–114). New York: Guilford Press.

Higgins, E. T. (1996c). Emotional experiences: The pains and pleasures of distinct regulatory systems. In R. D. Kavanaugh, B. Zimmerberg, & S. Fein (Eds.), *Emotion: Interdisciplinary perspectives* (pp. 203–241). Mahwah, NJ: Erlbaum.

Higgins, E. T., & Kruglanski, A. W. (Eds.). (1996). *Social psychology: Handbook of basic principles.* New York: Guilford Press.

Higgins, E. T., & Sorrentino, R. M. (Eds.). (1990). *Handbook of motivation and cognition: Foundations of social behavior, Vol. 2.* New York: Guilford Press.

Higgins, E. T., King, G. A., & Mavin, G. H. (1982). Individual construct accessibility and subjective impressions and recall. *Journal of Personality and Social Psychology, 43,* 35–47.

Hoffman, C., Mischel, W., & Baer, J. S. (1984). Language and person cognition: Effects of communicative set on trait attribution. *Journal of Personality and Social Psychology, 46,* 1029–1043.

Hogan, R., Johnson, J. A., & Briggs, S. R. (Eds.). (1997). *Handbook of personality psychology.* San Diego, CA: Academic Press.

Holahan, C. J., & Moos, R. N. (1990). Life stressors, resistance factors, and improved psychological functioning: An extension of the stress resistance paradigm. *Journal of Personality and Social Psychology, 58,* 909–917.

Holland, J. L., & Richards, J. M., Jr. (1965). Academic and nonacademic accomplishment: Correlated or uncorrelated? *Journal of Educational Psychology, 56,* 165–174.

Hollander, E., Liebowitz, M. R., Gorman, J. M., Cohen, B., Fyer, A., & Klein, D. F. (1989). Cortisol and sodium lactate-induced panic. *Archives of General Psychiatry, 46,* 135–140.

Hollon, S. D., DeRubeis, R. J., & Seligman, M. E. P. (1992). Cognitive therapy and the prevention of depression. *Applied and Preventive Psychology, 1,* 89–95.

Holmes, D. S. (1974). Investigations of repression: Differential recall of material experimentally or naturally associated with ego threat. *Psychological Bulletin, 81,* 632–653.

Holmes, D. S. (1992). The evidence for repression: An examination of sixty years of research. In J. L. Singer (Ed.), *Repression and dissociation* (pp. 85–102). Chicago: University of Chicago Press.

Holmes, D. S., & Houston, K. B. (1974). Effectiveness of situation redefinition and affective isolation in coping with stress. *Journal of Personality and Social Psychology, 29,* 212–218.

Holmes, D. S., & Schallow, J. R. (1969). Reduced recall after ego threat: Repression or response competition? *Journal of Personality and Social Psychology, 13,* 145–152.

Holmes, J. (1993). *John Bowlby and attachment theory.* New York: Routledge.

Holmes, T. H., & Rahe, R. H. (1967). The social readjustment rating scale. *Journal of Psychosomatic Research, 11,* 213–218.

Horowitz, L. M., Rosenberg, S. E., Ureno, G., Kalehzan, B. M., & O'Halloran, P. (1989). Psychodynamic formulation, consensual response method, and interpersonal problems. *Journal of Consulting and Clinical Psychology, 57,* 599–606.

Horowitz, M. J., & Stinson, C. H. (1995). Defense aspects of person schemas and control processes. In R. Plutchik & H. Conte (Eds.), *Ego defenses: Theory and measurement* (pp. 79–97). New York: Wiley.

Howard, V. F., Sweeney, W. J., & McLaughlin, T. F. (1993). Use of contingency contracting to increase on-task behavior with primary students. *Psychological Reports, 72,* 905–906.

Howes, D. H., & Solomon, R. L. (1951). Visual duration threshold as a function of word-probability. *Journal of Experimental Psychology, 41,* 401–410.

Howland, R. H. (1991). Pharmacotherapy of dysthymia: A review. *Journal of Clinical Psychopharmacology, 11,* 83–92.

Hunsberger, B. (1995). Religion and prejudice: The role of religious fundamentalism, quest, and right-wing authoritarianism. *Journal of Social Issues, 51,* 113–129.

Ickovics, J. (1997, August). Smithsonian seminar on health and well-being sponsored by Society for the Psychological Study of Social Issues and American Psychological Society, conducted at the Ninth Annual Conference of the American Psychological Society, Washington, DC.

Isen, A. M., Niedenthal, P. M., & Cantor, N. (1992). An influence of positive affect on social categorization. *Motivation and Emotion, 16,* 65–78.

Isen, A. M., Shalker, T. E., Clark, M., & Karp, L. (1978). Affect, accessibility of material in memory, and behavior: A cognitive loop? *Journal of Personality and Social Psychology, 36,* 1–12.

Jaccard, J. J. (1974). Predicting social behavior from personality traits. *Journal of Research in Personality, 7,* 358–367.

Jackson, D. N., & Paunonen, S. V. (1980). Personality structure and assessment. In M. R. Rosenzweig & L. W. Porter (Eds.), *Annual review of psychology* (Vol. 31). Palo Alto, CA: Annual Reviews, Inc.

Jackson, D. N., Chan, D. W., & Stricker, L. J. (1979). Implicit personality theory: Is it illusory? *Journal of Personality, 47,* 1–10.

Jacobs, L. (1989). Dialogues in Gestalt theory and therapy. *The Gestalt Journal, 12,* 25–67.

Jacobs, W. J., & Nadel, L. (1985). Stress-induced recovery of fears and phobias. *Psychological Review, 92,* 512–531.

Jahoda, M. (1958). *Current concepts of positive mental health.* New York: Basic Books.

James, W. (1890). *The principles of psychology* (Vols. 1 and 2). New York: Holt.

Jang, K. L. (1993). *A behavioral genetic analysis of personality, personality disorder, the environment, and the search for sources of nonshared environmental influences.* Unpublished doctoral dissertation, University of Western Ontario, London, Ontario.

Janis, I. L. (1971). *Stress and frustration.* New York: Harcourt.

Jasper, H. H. (1941). Electroencephalography. In W. Penfield & T. Erickson (Eds.), *Epilepsy and cerebral localization.* Springfield, IL: Charles C. Thomas.

Jemmott, J. B., Jemmott, L. S., Spears, H., Hewitt, N., & Cruz-Collins, M. (1992). Self-efficacy, hedonistic expectancies, and condom-use intentions among inner-city black adolescent women: A social cognitive approach to AIDS risk behavior. *Journal of Adolescent Health, 13,* 512–519.

Jersild, A. (1931). Memory for the pleasant as compared with the unpleasant. *Journal of Experimental Psychology, 14,* 284–288.

John, O. P. (1990). The big-five factor taxonomy: Dimensions of personality in the natural language and questionnaires. In L. A. Pervin (Ed.), *Handbook of personality: Theory and research* (pp. 66–100). New York: Guilford Press.

John, O. P., Hampson, S. E., & Goldberg, L. R. (1991). The basic level in personality-trait hierarchies: Studies of traits use and accessibility in different contexts. *Journal of Personality and Social Psychology, 60,* 348–361.

Jones, A. (1966). Information deprivation in humans. In B. A. Maher (Ed.), *Progress in experimental personality research* (Vol. 3, pp. 241–307). New York: Academic Press.

Jones, E. E., & Davis, K. E. (1965). From acts to dispositions: The attribution process in person perception. In L. Berkowitz (Ed.), *Advances in experimental social psychology* (Vol. 2). New York: Academic Press.

Jones, E. E., & Nisbett, R. E. (1971). The actor and the observer: Divergent perceptions of the causes of behavior. In E. E. Jones et al. (Eds.), *Attribution: Perceiving the causes of behavior.* Morristown, NJ: General Learning Press.

Jourard, S. M. (1967). Experimenter-subject dialogue: A paradigm for a humanistic science of psychology. In J. Bugental (Ed.), *Challenges of humanistic psychology* (pp. 109–116). New York: McGraw-Hill.

Jourard, S. M. (1974). *Healthy personality: An approach from the viewpoint of humanistic psychology.* New York: Macmillan.

Joy, V. L. (1963). Repression-sensitization and interpersonal behavior. Paper presented at the meeting of the American Psychological Association, Philadelphia, August 1963.

Jung, C. G. (1963). *Memories, dreams, reflections.* New York: Pantheon.

Jung, C. G. (1964). *Man and his symbols.* Garden City, NY: Doubleday.

Kagan, J., Reznick, J. S., & Snidman, N. (1988). Biological bases of childhood shyness. *Science, 240,* 167–171.

Kahle, A. L., & Kelley, M. L. (1994). Children's homework problems: A comparison of goal setting and parent training. *Behavior Therapy, 25*, 275–290.

Kahneman, D., & Snell, J. (1990). Predicting utility. In R. M. Hogarth (Ed.), *Handbook of personality: Theory and research* (pp. 66–100). New York: Guilford Press.

Kahneman, D., & Triesman, A. (1984). Changing views of attention and automaticity. In R. Parasuraman & D. R. Davies (Eds.), *Varieties of attention* (pp. 29–61). New York: Academic Press.

Kahneman, D., & Tversky, A. (1973). On the psychology of prediction. *Psychological Review, 80*, 237–251.

Kahneman, D., & Tversky, A. (1984). Choices, values, and frames. *American Psychologist, 39*, 341–350.

Kallman, F. J. (1953). *Heredity in health and mental disorder.* New York: Norton.

Kamps, D. M., Leonard, B. R., Vernon, S., Dugan, E. P., Delquadri, C., Gershon, B., Wade, L., & Folk, L. (1992). Teaching social skills to students with autism to increase peer interactions in an integrated first-grade classroom. *Journal of Applied Behavior Analysis, 25*, 281–288.

Kandel, E. R., & Hawkins, R. D. (1992). The biological basis of learning and individuality. *Scientific American, 267* (3), 78–86.

Kanfer, F. H. (1980). Self-management methods. In F. H. Kanfer & A. P. Goldstein (Eds.), *Helping people change: A textbook of methods* (2nd ed.). Elmsford, NY: Pergamon.

Kanfer, F. H., & Goldstein, A. P. (Eds.). (1991). *Helping people change: A textbook of methods* (4th ed.). Elmsford, NY: Pergamon.

Kanfer, F. H., & Karoly, P. (1972). Self control: A behavioristic excursion into the lion's den. *Behavior Therapy, 3*, 398–416.

Kanfer, F. H., & Phillips, J. S. (1970). *Learning foundations of behavior therapy.* New York: Wiley.

Kanfer, F. H., & Seidner, M. L. (1973). Self-control: Factors enhancing tolerance of noxious stimulation. *Journal of Personality and Social Psychology, 25*, 381–389.

Kanfer, F. H., & Zich, J. (1974). Self-control training: The effects of external control on children's resistance to temptation. *Developmental Psychology, 10*, 108–115.

Karoly, P. (1980). Operant methods. In F. H. Kanfer & A. P. Goldstein (Eds.), *Helping people change: A textbook of methods* (2nd ed.). Elmsford, NY: Pergamon.

Kayser A., Robinson, D. S., Yingling, K., Howard, D. B., Corcella, J., & Laux, D. (1988). The influence of panic attacks on response to phenelzine and amitriptyline in depressed outpatients. *Journal of Clinical Psychopharmacology, 8*, 246–253.

Kazdin, A. E. (1974). Effects of covert modeling and model reinforcement on assertive behavior. *Journal of Abnormal Psychology, 83*, 240–252.

Kazdin, A. E. (1975). Covert modeling, imagery assessment, and assertive behavior. *Journal of Consulting and Clinical Psychology, 43*, 716–724.

Kazdin, A. E., & Wilson, G. T. (1978). *Evaluation of behavior therapy: Issues, evidence and research strategies.* Cambridge, MA: Ballinger.

Kelley, H. H. (1973). The processes of causal attribution. *American Psychologist, 28*, 107–128.

Kelley, H. H., & Stahelski, A. J. (1970). The social interaction basis of cooperators' and competitors' beliefs about others. *Journal of Personality and Social Psychology, 16*, 66–91.

Kelly, E. L. (1955). Consistency of the adult personality. *American Psychologist, 10*, 659–681.

Kelly, G. A. (1955). *The psychology of personal constructs* (Vols. 1 and 2). New York: Norton.

Kelly, G. A. (1958). Man's construction of his alternatives. In G. Lindzey (Ed.), *Assessment of human motives* (pp. 33–64). New York: Holt, Rinehart and Winston.

Kelly, G. A. (1962). Quoted in B. A. Maher (Ed.), (1979), *Clinical psychology and personality: The selected papers of George Kelly.* Huntington, NY: Kreiger.

Kelly, G. A. (1966). Quoted in B. A. Maher (Ed.), (1979), *Clinical psychology and personality: The selected papers of George Kelly.* Huntington, NY: Kreiger.

Kendall, P. C., & Panichelli-Mindel, S. M. (1995). Cognitive-behavioral treatments. *Journal of Abnormal Child Psychology, 26*, 107–124.

Kendler, K. S., & Eaves, L. J. (1986). Models for the joint effects of genotype and environment on liability to psychiatric illness. *American Journal of Psychiatry, 143*, 279–289.

Kendler, K. S., Neale, M. C., Kessler, R. C., Heath, A. C., & Eaves, L. J. (1993). A twin study of recent life events and difficulties. *Archives of General Psychiatry, 50*, 789–796.

Kennard, D. (1983). *An introduction to the therapeutic community.* London, England: Routledge & Kegan Paul.

Kenrick, D. T., & Funder, D. C. (1988). Profiting from controversy: Lessons from the person-situation debate. *American Psychologist, 43*, 23–34.

Kenrick, D. T., Sadalla, E. K., Groth, G., & Trost, M. R. (1990). Evolution, traits, and the stages of human courtship: Qualifying the parental investment model. *Journal of Personality, 58*, 97–116.

Kernberg, O. (1976). *Object relations theory and clinical psychoanalysis.* New York: Jason Aronson.

Kernberg, O. (1984). *Severe personality disorders.* New Haven, CT: Yale University Press.

Kessler, R. C., Kendler, K. S., Heath, A., Neale, M. C., & Eaves, L. J. (1992). Social support, depressed mood, and adjustment to stress: A genetic epidemiologic investigation. *Journal of Personality and Social Psychology, 62*, 257–272.

Kety, S. S., Rosenthal, D., Wender, P. H., Schulsinger, F., & Jacobson, B. (1975). Mental illness in the biological and adoptive families of adopted individuals who have become schizophrenics. In R. R. Fieve, D. Rosenthal, & H. Brill (Eds.), *Genetic research in psychiatry.* Baltimore: Johns Hopkins University Press.

Kihlstrom, J. F. (1987). The cognitive unconscious. *Science, 237*, 1445–1452.

Kihlstrom, J. F. (1990). The psychological unconscious. In L.A. Pervin (Ed.), *Handbook of personality: Theory and research* (pp. 445–464). New York: Guilford Press.

Kim, M. P., & Rosenberg, S. (1980). Comparison of two-structured models of implicit personality theory. *Journal of Personality and Social Psychology, 38,* 375–389.

Klein, D. F., & Klein, H. M. (1989). The definition and psychopharmacology of spontaneous panic and phobia: A critical review I. In P. J. Tyrer (Ed.), *Psychopharmacology of anxiety.* New York: Oxford University Press.

Klein, D. F., Gittelman, R., Quitkin, F., & Rifkin, A. (1980). *Diagnosis and drug treatment of psychiatric disorders: Adults and children* (2nd ed.). Baltimore: Williams & Wilkins.

Klinger, E. (1975). Consequences of commitment to and disengagement from incentives. *Psychological Review, 82,* 1–25.

Klinger, E. (1977). The nature of fantasy and its clinical uses. *Psychotherapy: Theory, Research and Practice, 14,* 223–231.

Kobak, R. R., & Sceery, A. (1988). Attachment in late adolescence: Working models, affect regulation, and representations of self and others. *Child Development, 59,* 135–146.

Kobasa, S. C. (1979). Stressful life events, personality, and health: An inquiry into hardiness. *Journal of Personality and Social Psychology, 37,* 1–11.

Kobasa, S. C., Maddi, S. R., & Kahn, S. (1982). Hardiness and health: A prospective study. *Journal of Personality and Social Psychology, 42,* 168–177.

Koestner, R., & McClelland, D. C. (1990). Perspectives on competence motivation. In L. A. Pervin (Ed.), *Handbook of personality: Theory and research* (pp. 549–575). New York: Guilford Press.

Kohut, H. (1971). *The analysis of the self.* New York: International Universities Press.

Kohut, H. (1977). *The restoration of the self.* New York: International Universities Press.

Kohut, H. (1980). *Advances in self psychology.* New York: International Universities Press.

Kohut, H. (1984). *How does analysis cure?* Chicago, IL: University of Chicago Press.

Kopp, C. G. (1982). Antecedents of self-regulation: A developmental perspective. *Developmental Psychology, 18,* 199–214.

Koriat, A., Melkman, R., Averill, J. R., & Lazarus, R. S. (1972). The self-control of emotional reactions to a stressful film. *Journal of Personality, 40,* 601–619.

Kostlan, A. (1954). A method for the empirical study of psychodiagnosis. *Journal of Consulting Psychology, 18,* 83–88.

Krahe, B. (1990). *Situation cognition and coherence in personality: An individual-centered approach.* Cambridge, England: Cambridge University Press.

Kramer, P. D. (1993). *Listening to Prozac.* New York: Viking.

Krantz, D. S., Grunberg, N. B., & Baum, A. (1985). Health psychology. In M. R. Rosenzweig & L. W. Porter (Eds.), *Annual review of psychology* (pp. 349–384). Palo Alto, CA: Annual Reviews, Inc.

Krasner, L., & Ullmann, L. F. (1973). *Behavior influence and personality: The social matrix of human action.* New York: Holt, Rinehart and Winston.

Krumboltz, J. D., Mitchell, A. M., & Jones, G. B. (1976). A social learning theory of career selection. *The Counseling Psychologist, 6,* 71–81.

Kuhl, J. (1984). Volitional aspects of achievement motivation and learned helplessness: Toward a comprehensive theory of action control. In B. A. Maher (Ed.), *Progress in experimental personality research* (Vol. 13, pp. 91–171). New York: Academic Press.

Kuhl, J. (1985). From cognition to behavior: Perspectives for future research on action control. In J. Kuhl (Ed.), *Action control from cognition to behavior.* New York: Springer-Verlag.

Kunda, Z. (1990). The case for motivated reasoning. *Psychological Bulletin, 108,* 480–498.

Lader, M. (1980). *Introduction to psychopharmacology.* Kalamazoo, MI: Upjohn.

LaHoste, G. J., Swanson, J. M., Wigal, S. S., Glabe, C., Wigal, T., King, N., & Kennedy, J. L. (1996). Dopamine D4 receptor gene polymorphism is associated with attention deficit hyperactivity disorder. *Molecular Psychiatry, 1,* 128–131.

Lakin, M. (1972). *Experiential groups: The uses of interpersonal encounter, psychotherapy groups, and sensitivity training.* Morristown, NJ: General Learning Press.

Lamiell, J. T. (1997). Individuals and the differences between them. In R. Hogan, J. Johnson, & S. Briggs (Eds.), *Handbook of personality psychology* (pp. 117–141). San Diego, CA.: Academic Press.

Landfield, A. W., Stern, M., & Fjeld, S. (1961). Social conceptual processes and change in students undergoing psychotherapy. *Psychological Reports, 8,* 63–68.

Lang, P. J., & Lazovik, A. D. (1963). Experimental desensitization of a phobia. *Journal of Abnormal and Social Psychology, 66,* 519–525.

Langer, E. J. (1975). The illusion of control. *Journal of Personality and Social Psychology, 32,* 311–328.

Langer, E. J. (1977). The psychology of chance. *Journal for the Theory of Social Behavior, 7,* 185–207.

Langer, E. J. (1978). Rethinking the role of thought in social interaction. In J. H. Harvey, W. J. Ickes, & R. F. Kidd (Eds.), *New directions in attribution research* (Vol. 2). Hillsdale, NJ: Erlbaum.

Langer, E. J., Janis, I. L., & Wolfer, J.A. (1975). Reduction of psychological stress in surgical patients. Unpublished manuscript, Yale University.

Larsen, R. J. (1987). The stability of mood variability: A spectral analytic approach to daily mood assessments. *Journal of Personality and Social Psychology, 52,* 1195–1204.

Larsen, R. J. (1992). Neuroticism and selective encoding and recall of symptoms: Evidence from a combined concurrent-retrospective study. *Journal of Personality and Social Psychology, 62,* 480–488.

Larsen, R. J., & Cutler, S. E. (1996). The complexity of individual emotional lives: A within-subject analysis of affect structure. *Journal of Social and Clinical Psychology, 15,* 206–230.

Larsen, R. J., & Kasimatis, M. (1990). Individual differences in entrainment of mood to the weekly calendar. *Journal of Personality and Social Psychology, 58,* 164–171.

Larsen, R. J., & Kasimatis, M. (1991). Day-to-day physical symptoms: Individual differences in the occurrence, duration, and emotional concomitants of minor daily illnesses. *Journal of Personality, 59,* 387–424.

Larsen, R. J., Diener, E., & Emmons, R. A. (1986). Affect intensity and reactions to daily life. *Journal of Personality and Social Psychology, 51,* 803–814.

Lawson, G. W., & Cooperrider, C. A. (1988). *Clinical psychopharmacology: A practical reference for nonmedical psychotherapists.* Rockville, MD: Aspen Publishers.

Lazarus. A. A. (1963). The treatment of chronic frigidity by systematic desensitization. *Journal of Nervous and Mental Diseases, 136,* 272–278.

Lazarus, R. S. (1976). *Patterns of adjustment.* New York: McGraw-Hill.

Lazarus, R. S. (1981). The stress and coping paradigm. In C. Eisdorfer, D. Cohen, A. Kleinman, & P. Maxim (Eds.), *Models for clinical psychology* (pp. 177–214). New York: Spectrum Medical and Scientific Books.

Lazarus, R. S. (1990). Theory-based stress measurement. *Psychological Inquiry, 1,* 3–13.

Lazarus, R. S., & Folkman, S. (1984). *Stress, appraisal, and coping.* New York: Springer.

Lazarus, R. S., & Longo, N. (1953). The consistency of psychological defense against threat. *Journal of Abnormal and Social Psychology, 48,* 495–499.

Lazarus, R. S., Eriksen, C. W., & Fonda, C. P. (1951). Personality dynamics and auditory perceptual recognition. *Journal of Personality, 58,* 113–122.

Leary, T. (1957). *Interpersonal diagnosis of personality.* New York: Ronald Press.

Leary, T., Litwin, G. H., & Metzner, R. (1963). Reactions to psilocybin administered in a supportive environment. *Journal of Nervous and Mental Diseases, 137,* 561–573.

Ledoux, J. (1996). *The emotional brain.* New York: Simon & Schuster.

Lepper, M. R., & Greene, D. (1975) Turning play into work: Effects of adult surveillance and extrinsic rewards on children's intrinsic motivation. *Journal of Personality and Social Psychology, 31,* 479–486.

Lepper, M. R., Greene, D., & Nisbett, R. E. (1973). Undermining children's intrinsic interest with extrinsic reward: A test of the "overjustification" hypothesis. *Journal of Personality and Social Psychology, 28,* 129–137.

Lesch, K., Bengel, D., Heils, A., & Sabol, S. Z. (1996). Association of anxiety-related traits with a polymorphism in the serotonin transporter gene regulatory region. *Science, 274,* 1527–1531.

Leventhal, H. (1984). A perceptual-motor theory of emotion. In L. Berkowitz (Ed.), *Advances in experimental social psychology, Vol. 17. Theorizing in social psychology: Special topics* (pp. 118–173). New York: Academic Press.

Leventhal, H., Jacobs, R. L., & Kudirka, N. Z. (1964). Authoritarianism, ideology, and political candidate choice. *Journal of Abnormal and Social Psychology, 69,* 539–549.

Levine, R. (1991). *New developments in pharmacology* (Vol. 8, pp. 1–3). New York: Gracie Square Hospitals Publication.

Levy, S. R., Stroessner, S. J., & Dweck, C. S. (in press). Stereotype formation and endorsement: The role of implicit theories. *Journal of Personality and Social Psychology.*

Lewicki, P. (1986). *Nonconscious social information processing.* New York: Academic Press.

Lewicki, P., Hill, T., & Czyzewska, M. (1992). Nonconscious acquisition of information. *American Psychologist, 47,* 796–801.

Lewin, K. (1935). *A dynamic theory of personality.* New York: McGraw-Hill.

Lewin, K. (1936). *Principles of topological psychology.* New York: McGraw-Hill.

Lewin, K. (1951). *Field theory in social science; selected theoretical papers.* D. Cartwright (Ed.). New York: Harper & Row.

Lewinsohn, P. M. (1975). The behavioral study and treatment of depression. In M. Hersen (Ed.), *Progress in behavior modification* (pp. 19–63). New York: Academic Press.

Lewinsohn, P. M., Clarke, G. N., Hops, H., & Andrews, A. (1990). Cognitive-behavioral treatment for depressed adolescents. *Behavior Therapy, 21,* 385–401.

Lewinsohn, P. M., Mischel, W., Chaplin, W., & Barton, R. (1980). Social competence and depression: The role of illusory self-perceptions. *Journal of Abnormal Psychology, 89,* 203–212.

Lieberman, M. A., Yalom, I. D., & Miles, M. B. (1973). *Encounter groups: First facts.* New York: Basic Books.

Liebert, R. M. (1986). Effects of television on children and adolescents. *Journal of Developmental and Behavioral Pediatrics, 7,* 43–48.

Liebert, R. M., & Allen, K. M. (1967). The effects of rule structure and reward magnitude on the acquisition and adoption of self-reward criteria. Unpublished manuscript, Vanderbilt University, Nashville, TN.

Liebert, R. M., & Baron, R. A. (1972). Some immediate effects of televised violence on children's behavior. *Developmental Psychology, 6,* 469–475.

Lief, H. I., & Fox, R. S. (1963). Training for "detached concern" in medical students. In H. I. Lief, V. F. Lief, & N. R. Lief (Eds.), *The psychological basis of medical practice* (pp. 12–35). New York: Harper.

Lietaer, G. (1993). Authenticity, congruence, and transparency. In D. Brazier (Ed.), *Beyond Carl Rogers* (pp. 17–46). London, England: Constable.

Linehan, E., & O'Toole, J. (1982). The effect of subliminal stimulation of symbiotic fantasies on college student self-disclosure in group counseling. *Journal of Counseling Psychology, 29,* 151–157.

Linscheid, T. R., & Meinhold, P. (1990). The controversy over aversives: Basic operant research and the side effects of punishment. In A. C. Repp & N. N. Singh (Eds.), *Perspectives on the use of nonaversive and aversive interventions for persons with developmental disabilities* (pp. 435–450). Sycamore, IL: Sycamore Publishing Company.

Linville, P. W., & Carlston, D. E. (1994). Social cognition of the self. In P. G. Devine, D. C. Hamilton, & T. M. Ostrom (Eds.), *Social cognition: Impact on social psychology* (pp. 143–193). New York: Academic Press.

Little, K. B., & Shneidman, E. S. (1959). Congruencies among interpretations of psychological test and anamnestic data. *Psychological Monographs, 73,* No. 6 (Whole No. 476).

Loehlin, J. C. (1992). *Genes and environment in personality development.* Newbury Park, CA: Sage Publications.

Loehlin, J. C., & Nichols, R. C. (1976). *Heredity, environment, and personality: A study of 850 sets of twins.* Austin, TX: University of Texas Press.

Loevinger, J. (1957). Objective tests as instruments of psychological theory. *Psychological Reports Monographs,* No. 9. Southern University Press.

Loftus, E. F. (1993). The reality of repressed memories. *American Psychologist, 48,* 518–537.

Loftus, E. F. (1994). The repressed memory controversy. *American Psychologist, 49,* 443–445.

Loftus, E. F., & Klinger, M. R. (1992). Is the unconscious smart or dumb? *American Psychologist, 47,* 761–765.

LoPicolo, J., & Lobitz, W. C. (1972). The role of masturbation in the treatment of orgasmic dysfunction. *Archives of Sexual Behavior, 2,* 163–171.

Lott, A. J., & Lott, B. E. (1968). A learning theory approach to interpersonal attitudes. In A. G. Greenwald, T. C. Brock, & T. M. Ostrom (Eds.), *Psychological foundations of attitudes.* New York: Academic Press.

Lovaas, O. I., Berberich, J. P., Perloff, B. F., & Schaeffer, B. (1966). Acquisition of imitative speech by schizophrenic children. *Science, 151,* 705–707.

Lovaas, O. I., Berberich, J. P., Perloff, B. F., & Schaeffer, B. (1991). Acquisition of imitative speech by schizophrenic children. *Focus on Autistic Behavior, 6,* 1–5.

Lovaas, O. I., Freitag, G., Gold, V. J., & Kassorla, I. C. (1965a). Experimental studies in childhood schizophrenia: I. Analysis of self-destructive behavior. *Journal of Experimental Child Psychology, 2,* 67–84.

Lovaas, O. I., Freitag, G., Gold, V. J., & Kassorla, I. C. (1965b). Recording apparatus for observation of behaviors of children in free play settings. *Journal of Experimental Child Psychology, 2,* 108–120.

Lyons, D. (1997). The feminine in the foundations of organizational psychology. *Journal of Applied Behavioral Science, 33,* 7–26.

Lyons, M. J., Goldberg, J., Eisen, S. A., True, W., Tsuang, M. T., Meyer, J. M., & Henderson, W. G. (1993). Do genes influence exposure to trauma: A twin study of combat. *American Journal of Medical Genetics (Neuropsychiatric Genetics), 48,* 22–27.

Lytton, H. (1977). Do parents create or respond to differences in twins? *Developmental Psychology, 13,* 456–459.

MacFarlane, J. W., & Tuddenham, R. D. (1951). Problems in the validation of projective techniques. In H. H. Anderson & G. L. Anderson (Eds.), *Projective techniques* (pp. 26–54). New York: Prentice-Hall.

MacLeod, C., & Rutherford, E. M. (1992). Anxiety and the selective processing of emotional information: Mediating roles of awareness, trait and state variables, and personal relevance of stimulus materials. *Behavior Research and Therapy, 30,* 479–491.

Madison, P. (1960). *Freud's concept of repression and defense: Its theoretical and observational language.* Minneapolis: University of Minnesota Press.

Magnusson, D. (Ed.). (1980). *The situation: An interactional perspective.* Hillsdale, NJ: Erlbaum.

Magnusson, D. (1990). Personality development from an interactional perspective. In L. A. Pervin (Ed.), *Handbook of personality: Theory and research* (pp. 193–224). New York: Guilford Press.

Magnusson, D., & Allen, V. L. (Eds.). (1983). *Human development: An interactional perspective.* New York: Academic Press.

Magnusson, D., & Ekehammar, B. (1973). An analysis of situational dimensions: A replication. *Multivariate Behavioral Research, 8,* 331–339.

Magnusson, D., & Endler, N. S. (1977). Interactional psychology: Present status and future prospects. In D. Magnusson & N. S. Endler (Eds.), *Personality at the crossroads: Current issues in interactional psychology.* Hillsdale, NJ: Erlbaum.

Magnusson, D., & Endler, N. S. (Eds.). (1977). *Personality at the crossroads: Current issues in interactional psychology.* Hillsdale, NJ: Erlbaum.

Maher, B. A. (1966). *Principles of psychotherapy: An experimental approach.* New York: McGraw-Hill.

Maher, B. A. (1979). *Clinical psychology and personality: The selected papers of George Kelly.* Huntington, NY: Wiley.

Mahoney, M. J. (1974). Self-reward and self-monitoring techniques for weight control. *Behavior Therapy, 5,* 48–57.

Mahoney, M. J., & Mahoney, K. (1976). *Weight control as a personal science.* New York: Norton.

Mahoney, M. J., Moura, N. G., & Wade, T. C. (1973). Relative efficacy of self-reward, self-punishment, and self-monitoring techniques for weight loss. *Journal of Consulting and Clinical Psychology, 40,* 404–407.

Main, M., & Goldwyn, R. (1984). Predicting rejection of her infant from mother's representation of her own experience: Implications for the abused-abusing intergenerational cycle. *Child Abuse and Neglect, 8,* 203–217.

Main, M., Kaplan, N., & Cassidy, J. (1985). Security in infancy, childhood, and adulthood: A move to the level of representation. In I. Bretherton & E. Waters (Eds.), *Growing Points in Attachment Theory and Research. Monographs of the Society for Research in Child Development,* No. 209, Vol. 50, 66–104.

Malcom, J. (1982). *Psychoanalysis: The impossible profession.* New York: Vintage.

Malmo, R. B. (1959). Activation: A neuropsychological dimension. *Psychological Review, 66,* 367–386.

Malmquist, C. P. (1986). Children who witness parental murder: Post traumatic aspects. *Journal of the American Academy of Child Psychiatry, 25,* 320–325.

Mandler, G. (1962). From association to structure. *Psychological Review, 69,* 415–427.

Manke, B., McGuire, S., Reiss, D., Hetherington, E. M., & Plomin, R. (1995). Genetic contributions to children's extrafamilial social interactions: Teachers, friends, and peers. *Social Development, 4,* 238–256.

Maricle, R. A., Kinzie, J. D., & Lewinsohn, P. (1988). Medication-associated depression: A two and one-half year follow-up of a community sample. *International Journal of Psychiatry in Medicine, 18,* 283–292.

Marks, I. M. (1987). *Fears, phobias, and rituals.* New York: Oxford University Press.

Marks, I. M., & Nesse, R. M. (1994). Fear and fitness: An evolutionary analysis of anxiety disorders. *Ethology and Sociobiology, 15,* 247–261.

Marks, J., Stauffacher, J. C., & Lyle, C. (1963). Predicting outcome in schizophrenia. *Journal of Abnormal and Social Psychology, 66,* 117–127.

Marks, P. A., & Seeman, W. (1963). *Actuarial description of abnormal personality.* Baltimore: Williams & Wilkins.

Markus, H. (1977). Self-schemata and processing information about the self. *Journal of Personality and Social Psychology, 35,* 63–78.

Markus, H., & Cross, S. (1990). The interpersonal self. In L. A. Pervin (Ed.), *Handbook of personality: Theory and research* (pp. 576–608). New York: Guilford Press.

Markus, H., & Nurius, P. (1986). Possible selves. *American Psychologist, 41,* 954–969.

Markus, H. R., & Kitayama, S. (1991). Culture and the self: Implications for cognition, emotion, and motivation. *Psychological Review, 98,* 224–253.

Markus, H. R., Kitayama, S., & Heiman, R. J. (1996). Culture and basic psychological principles. In. E. T. Higgins & A. W. Kruglanski (Eds.), *Social psychology: Handbook of basic principles.* New York: Guilford Press.

Marsden, G. (1971). Content analysis studies of psychotherapy: 1954 through 1968. In A. E. Bergin & S. L. Garfield (Eds.), *Handbook of psychotherapy and behavior change.* New York: Wiley.

Martin, L. L., & Tesser, A. (1989). Toward a motivational and structural theory of ruminative thought. In J. S. Uleman & J. A. Bargh (Eds.), *Unintended thought* (pp. 306–323). New York: Guilford Press.

Masling, J. M. (1959). The effects of warm and cold interaction on the administration and scoring of an intelligence test. *Journal of Consulting Psychology, 23,* 336–341.

Masling, J. M. (1960). The influence of situational and interpersonal variables in projective testing. *Psychological Bulletin, 57,* 65–85.

Maslow, A. H. (1965). Some basic propositions of a growth and self-actualization psychology. In G. Lyndzey & C. Hall (Eds.), *Theories of personality: Primary sources and research* (pp. 307–316). New York: Wiley.

Maslow, A. H. (1968). *Toward a psychology of being* (2nd ed.). New York: Van Nostrand.

Maslow, A. H. (1971). *The farther reaches of human nature.* New York: Viking.

Masters, W. H., & Johnson, V. (1970). *Human sexual inadequacy.* Boston: Little, Brown.

Matas, W. H., Arend, R. A., & Sroufe, L. A. (1978). Continuity of adaptation in the second year: The relationship between quality of attachment and later competence. *Child Development, 49,* 547–556.

Matthews, K. A. (1984). Assessment of type A, anger, and hostility in epidemiological studies of cardiovascular disease. In A. Ostfeld & E. Eaker (Eds.), *Measuring psychosocial variables in epidemiological studies of cardiovascular disease.* Bethesda, MD: National Institute of Health.

Matute, H. (1994). Learned helplessness and superstitious behavior as opposite effects of uncontrollable reinforcement in humans. *Learning and Motivation, 25,* 216–232.

May, R. (1961). Existential psychology. In R. May (Ed.), *Existential psychology* (pp. 11–51). New York: Random House.

McAdams, D. P., & Constantian, C. A. (1983). Intimacy and affiliation motives in daily living: An experience sampling analysis. *Journal of Personality and Social Psychology, 45,* 851–861.

McCall, R. B. (1977). Childhood IQs as predictors of adult educational and occupational status. *Science, 197,* 482–483.

McCardel, J. B., & Murray, E. J. (1974). Nonspecific factors in weekend encounter groups. *Journal of Consulting and Clinical Psychology, 42,* 337–345.

McClanahan, T. M. (1995). Operant learning (R-S) principles applied to nail-biting. *Psychological Report, 77,* 507–514.

McClelland, D. C. (1951). *Personality.* New York: Holt, Rinehart and Winston.

McClelland, D. C. (1961). *The achieving society.* New York: Van Nostrand.

McClelland, D. C. (1966). Longitudinal trends in the relation of thought to action. *Journal of Consulting Psychology, 30,* 479–483.

McClelland, D. C. (1985). How motives, skills and values determine what people do. *American Psychologist, 40,* 812–825.

McClelland, D. C. (1992). Motivational configurations. In C. P. Smith, J. W. Atkinson, D. C. McClelland, & J. Veroff (Eds.), *Motivation and personality: Handbook of thematic content analysis* (pp. 87–99). New York: Cambridge University Press.

McClelland, D. C., Atkinson, J. W., Clark, R. A., & Lowell, E. L. (1953). *The achievement motive.* New York: Appleton.

McCrae, R. R, & Costa, P. T. (1997). Conceptions and correlates of openness and to experience. In R. Hogan, J. Johnson, & S. Briggs (Eds.), *Handbook of personality psychology* (pp. 825–847). San Diego, CA: Academic Press.

McCrae, R. R., & Costa, P. T. (1989). The structure of personality traits: Wiggins' circumplex and the five-factor model. *Journal of Personality and Social Psychology, 56,* 586–595.

McCrae, R. R., & Costa, P. T., Jr. (1985). Updating Norman's "adequacy taxonomy": Intelligence and personality in dimensions in natural language and in questionnaires. *Journal of Personality and Social Psychology, 49,* 710–721.

McCrae, R. R., & Costa, P. T., Jr. (1987). Validation of the five-factor model of personality across instruments and observers. *Journal of Personality and Social Psychology, 52,* 81–90.

McCrae, R. R., & Costa, P. T., Jr. (1990). *Personality in adulthood.* New York: Guilford Press.

McCrae, R. R., & Costa, P. T., Jr. (1996). Toward a new generation of personality theories: Theoretical contexts for the five-factor model. In J. S. Wiggins (Ed.), *The five-factor model of personality: Theoretical perspectives* (pp. 51–87). New York: Guilford Press.

McFall, R. M., & Marston, A. (1970). An experimental investigation of behavior rehearsal in assertive training. *Journal of Abnormal Psychology, 76,* 295–303.

McFarland, C., & Buehler, R. (1997). Negative affective states and the motivated retrieval of positive life events: The role of affect acknowledgment. *Journal of Personality and Social Psychology, 73,* 200–214.

McGinnies, E. (1949). Emotionality and perceptual defense. *Psychological Review, 56,* 244–251.

McGregor, I., & Little, B. R. (1998). Personal projects, happiness, and meaning: On doing well and being yourself. *Journal of Personality and Social Psychology, 74,* 494–512.

McGue, M., & Lykken, D. T. (1992). Genetic influence on risk of divorce. *Psychological Science, 3,* 368–373.

McGuffin, P., Katz, R., & Rutherford, J. (1991). Nature, nurture, and depression: A twin study. *Psychological Medicine, 21,* 329–335.

McGuire, S., Neiderheiser, J. M., Reiss, D., Hetherington, E. M., & Plomin, R. (1994). Genetic and environmental influences on perceptions of self-worth and competence in adolescence: A study of twins, full siblings, and step siblings. *Child Development, 65,* 785–799.

Medin, D. L. (1989). Concepts and conceptual structure. *American Psychologist, 44,* 1469–1481.

Meehl, P. (1995) Bootstraps taxometrics: Solving the classification problem in psychopathology. *American Psychologist, 50,* 266–275.

Meehl, P. E. (1945). The dynamics of "structured" personality tests. *Journal of Clinical Psychology, 1,* 296–303.

Meehl, P. E. (1990). Why summaries of research on psychological theories are often uninterpretable. *Psychological Reports, 66,* 195–244.

Meichenbaum, D. (1992a). Evolution of cognitive behavior therapy: Origins, tenets, and clinical examples. In J. K. Zeig (Ed.), *The evolution of psychotherapy: The second conference* (pp. 114–128). New York: Brunner/Mazel.

Meichenbaum, D. (1992b). Stress inoculation training: A twenty year update. In R. L. Woolfolk & P. M. Lehrer (Eds.), *Principles and practice of stress management.* New York: Guilford Press.

Meichenbaum, D. (1993). Changing conceptions of cognitive behavior modification: Retrospect and prospect. *Journal of Consulting and Clinical Psychology, 61,* 202–204.

Meichenbaum, D. H. (1974). *Cognitive-behavior modification.* Morristown, NJ: General Learning Press.

Meichenbaum, D. H. (1977). *Cognitive-behavior modification.* New York: Plenum Press.

Meichenbaum, D. H. (1995). Cognitive-behavioral therapy in historical perspective. In B. Bongar & L. E. Beutler (Eds.), *Comprehensive textbook of psychotherapy* (pp. 140–158). New York: Oxford University Press.

Meichenbaum, D. H., & Goodman, J. (1971). Training impulsive children to talk to themselves: A means of developing self-control. *Journal of Abnormal Psychology, 77,* 115–126.

Meichenbaum, D. H., & Smart, I. (1971). Use of direct expectancy to modify academic performance and attitudes of college students. *Journal of Counseling Psychology, 18,* 531–535.

Meltzer, H. (1930). The present status of experimental studies of the relation of feeling to memory. *Psychological Review, 37,* 124–139.

Merluzzi, T. V., Glass, C. R., & Genest, M. (Eds.). (1981). *Cognitive assessment.* New York: Guilford Press.

Metcalfe, J., & Jacobs W. J. (1998). Emotional memory: The effects of stress on "cool" and "hot" memory systems. In D. L. Medin (Ed.), *The psychology of learning and motivation: Vol. 38. Advances in research and theory.* San Diego, CA: Academic Press.

Metcalfe, J., & Mischel, W. (1999). A hot/cool system analysis of delay of gratification: Dynamics of willpower. *Psychological Review.*

Michotte, A. (1954). *La perception de la causalité* (2nd ed.). Louvain: Publications Universitaires de Louvain.

Milgram, N. (1993). War-related trauma and victimization: Principles of traumatic stress prevention in Israel. In J. P. Wilson & B. Raphael (Eds.), *International handbook of traumatic stress syndromes. The Plenum series on stress and coping* (pp. 811–820). New York: Plenum Press.

Milgram, S. (1974). *Obedience to authority.* New York: Harper & Row.

Miller, D. T., & Prentice, D. A. (1994). Collective errors and errors about the collective. Special issue: The self and the collective. *Personality and Social Psychology Bulletin, 20,* 541–550.

Miller, G. A., Galanter, E., & Pribram, K. H. (1960). *Plans and the structure of behavior.* New York: Holt, Rinehart and Winston.

Miller, N. E. (1948). Theory and experiment relating psychoanalytic displacement to stimulus response generalization. *Journal of Abnormal and Social Psychology, 43,* 155–178.

Miller, N. E. (1959). Liberalization of basic S-R concepts: Extensions to conflict behavior, motivation, and social learning. In S. Koch (Ed.), *Psychology: A study of a science* (Vol. 2, pp. 196–292). New York: McGraw-Hill.

Miller, N. E. (1963). Some reflections on the law of effect produce a new alternative to drive reduction. In M. R. Jones (Ed.), *Nebraska symposium on motivation* (Vol. 11, pp. 65–112). Lincoln: University of Nebraska Press.

Miller, N. E. (1974). Applications of learning and biofeedback to psychiatry and medicine. In A. M. Freedman, H. I. Kaplan, &

B. J. Sadock (Eds.), *Comprehensive textbook of psychiatry* (2nd ed.). Baltimore: Williams & Wilkins.

Miller, N. E., & Dollard, J. (1941). *Social learning and imitation.* New Haven, CT: Yale University Press.

Miller, S. M. (1979). Coping with impending stress: Physiological and cognitive correlates of choice. *Psychophysiology, 16,* 572–581.

Miller, S. M. (1981). Predictability and human stress: Towards a clarification of evidence and theory. In L. Berkowitz (Ed.), *Advances in experimental social psychology* (Vol. 14, pp. 203–256). New York: Academic Press.

Miller, S. M. (1987). Monitoring and blunting: Validation of a questionnaire to assess styles of information seeking under threat. *Journal of Personality and Social Psychology, 52,* 345–353.

Miller, S. M. (1996). Monitoring and blunting of threatening information: Cognitive interference and facilitation in the coping process. In I. G. Sarason, G. R. Pierce, & B. R. Sarason (Eds.), *Cognitive interference: Theories, methods, and findings. The LEA series in personality and clinical psychology* (pp. 175–190). Mahwah, NJ: Erlbaum.

Miller, S. M., & Mangan, C. E. (1983a). Cognition, stress, and health. In K. Dobson & P. C. Kendall (Eds.), *Cognition and psychopathology.* New York: Academic Press.

Miller, S. M., & Mangan, C. E. (1983b). The interacting effects of information and coping style in adapting to gynecologic stress: Should the doctor tell all? *Journal of Personality and Social Psychology, 45,* 223–236.

Miller, S. M., & O'Leary, A. (1993). Cognition, stress, and health. In K. Dobson & P. C. Kendall (Eds.), *Cognition and psychopathology.* New York: Academic Press.

Miller, S. M., Shoda, Y., & Hurley, K. (1996). Applying cognitive-social theory to health-protective behavior: Breast self-examination in cancer screening. *Psychological Bulletin, 119,* 70–94.

Miller, T. Q., Smith, T. W., Turner, C. W., Guijarro, M. L., & Hallett, A. J. (1996). A meta-analytic review of research on hostility and physical health. *Psychological Bulletin, 119,* 322–348.

Mineka, S., & Zinbarg, R. (1996). Conditioning and ethological models of anxiety disorders: Stress-in-dynamic-context-anxiety models. In D. A. Hope (Ed.), *Nebraska symposium on motivation, 1995: Perspectives on anxiety, panic, and fear. Current theory and research in motivation, Vol. 43* (pp. 135–210). Lincoln, NE: University of Nebraska Press.

Minuchin, S., & Nichols, M. P. (1994). *Family healing: Strategies for hope and understanding.* New York: Simon & Schuster.

Minuchin, S., Lee, W., & Simon, G. M. (1996). *Mastering family therapy: Journeys of growth and transformation.* New York: Wiley.

Minuchin, S., Roseman, B. L., & Baker, L. (1978). *Psychosomatic families: Anorexia nervosa in context.* Cambridge, MA: Harvard University Press.

Mirels, H. L. (1976). Implicit personality theory and inferential illusions. *Journal of Personality, 44,* 467–487.

Mischel, T. (1964). Personal constructs, rules, and the logic of clinical activity. *Psychological Review, 71,* 180–192.

Mischel, W. (1965). Predicting the success of Peace Corps volunteers in Nigeria. *Journal of Personality and Social Psychology, 1,* 510.

Mischel, W. (1968). *Personality and assessment.* New York: Wiley.

Mischel, W. (1969). Continuity and change in personality. *American Psychologist, 24,* 1012–1018.

Mischel, W. (1973). Toward a cognitive social learning reconceptualization of personality. *Psychological Review, 80,* 252–283.

Mischel, W. (1974). Processes in delay of gratification. In L. Berkowitz (Ed.), *Advances in experimental social psychology* (Vol. 7). New York: Academic Press.

Mischel, W. (1980). Personality and cognition: Something borrowed, something new? In N. Cantor & J. Kihlstrom (Eds.), *Personality, cognition, and social interaction.* Hillsdale, NJ: Erlbaum.

Mischel, W. (1981). Metacognition and the rules of delay. In J. H. Flavell & L. Ross (Eds.), *Social cognitive development: Frontiers and possible futures.* New York: Cambridge University Press.

Mischel, W. (1984). Convergences and challenges in the search for consistency. *American Psychologist, 39,* 351–364.

Mischel, W. (1990). Personality dispositions revisited and revised: A view after three decades. In L. A. Pervin (Ed.), *Handbook of personality: Theory and research* (pp. 111–134). New York: Guilford Press.

Mischel, W. (1991). *Finding personality coherence in the pattern of variability.* Eastern Psychological Association Distinguished Lecture. New York.

Mischel, W. (1993). *Introduction to personality* (5th ed.). Fort Worth, TX: Harcourt Brace Jovanovich.

Mischel, W., & Baker, N. (1975). Cognitive transformations of reward objects through instructions. *Journal of Personality and Social Psychology, 31,* 254–261.

Mischel, W., & Ebbesen, E. B. (1970). Attention in delay of gratification. *Journal of Personality and Social Psychology, 16,* 239–337.

Mischel, W., & Liebert, R. M. (1966). Effects of discrepancies between observed and imposed reward criteria on their acquisition and transmission. *Journal of Personality and Social Psychology, 3,* 45–53.

Mischel, W., & Mischel, H. N. (1983). Development of children's knowledge of self-control strategies. *Child Development, 54,* 603–619.

Mischel, W., & Moore, B. (1973). Effects of attention to symbolically-presented rewards on self-control. *Journal of Personality and Social Psychology, 28,* 172–179.

Mischel, W., & Patterson, C. J. (1976). Substantive and structural elements of effective plans for self-control. *Journal of Personality and Social Psychology, 34,* 942–950.

Mischel, W., & Peake, P. K. (1982). In search of consistency: Measure for measure. In M. P. Zanna, E. T. Higgins, & C. P.

Herman (Eds.), *Consistency in social behavior: The Ontario symposium* (Vol. 2). Hillsdale, NJ: Erlbaum.

Mischel, W., & Shoda, Y. (1995). A cognitive-affective system theory of personality: Reconceptualizing situations, dispositions, dynamics, and invariance in personality structure. *Psychological Review, 102* (2), 246–268.

Mischel, W., & Shoda, Y. (1998). Reconciling processing dynamics and personality dispositions. *Annual Review of Psychology, 49,* 229–258.

Mischel, W., & Staub, E. (1965). Effects of expectancy on working and waiting for larger rewards. *Journal of Personality and Social Psychology, 2,* 625–633.

Mischel, W., Cantor, N., & Feldman, S. (1996). Principles of self-regulation: The nature of willpower and self-control. In E. T. Higgins & A. W. Kruglanski (Eds.), *Social psychology: Handbook of basic principles* (pp. 329–360). New York: Guilford Press.

Mischel, W., Ebbesen, E. B., & Zeiss, A. R. (1972). Cognitive and attentional mechanisms in delay of gratification. *Journal of Personality and Social Psychology, 21,* 204–218.

Mischel, W., Ebbesen, E. B., & Zeiss, A. R. (1973). Selective attention to the self: Situational and dispositional determinants. *Journal of Personality and Social Psychology, 27,* 129–142.

Mischel, W., Ebbesen, E. B., & Zeiss, A. R. (1976). Determinants of selective memory about the self. *Journal of Consulting and Clinical Psychology, 44,* 92–103.

Mischel, W., Shoda, Y., & Peake, P. K. (1988). The nature of adolescent competencies predicted by preschool delay of gratification. *Journal of Personality and Social Psychology, 54,* 687–696.

Mischel, W., Shoda, Y., & Rodriguez, M. L. (1989). Delay of gratification in children. *Science, 244,* 933–938.

Moghaddam, F. M., & Vuksanovic, V. (1990). Attitudes and behavior toward human rights across different contexts: The role of right-wing authoritarianism, political ideology, and religiosity. *International Journal of Psychology, 25,* 455–474.

Molina, M. A. N. (1996). Archetypes and spirits: A Jungian analysis of Puerto Rican espiritismo. *Journal of Analytical Psychology, 41,* 227–244.

Monro, R. (1955). *Schools of psychoanalytic thought.* New York: Holt, Rinehart and Winston.

Moore, B., Mischel, W., & Zeiss, A. R. (1976). Comparative effects of the reward stimulus and its cognitive representation in voluntary delay. *Journal of Personality and Social Psychology, 34,* 419–424.

Moos, R. H. (1968). Situational analysis of a therapeutic community milieu. *Journal of Abnormal Psychology, 73,* 49–61.

Moos, R. H. (1973). Conceptualizations of human environments. *American Psychologist, 28,* 652–665.

Moos, R. H. (1974). Systems for the assessment and classification of human environments. In R. H. Moos & P. M. Insel (Eds.), *Issues in social ecology.* Palo Alto, CA: National Press Books.

Moos, R. H., & Insel, P. M. (Eds.). (1974). *Issues in social ecology.* Palo Alto, CA: National Press Books.

Morokoff, P. J. (1985). Effects of sex guilt, repression, sexual "arousibility", and sexual experience on female sexual arousal during erotica and fantasy. *Journal of Personality and Social Psychology, 49,* 177–187.

Morris, J. (1975). Fear reduction methods. In F. H. Kanfer & A. P. Goldstein (Eds.), *Helping people change* (pp. 229–271). Elmsford, NY: Pergamon.

Morse, W. H., & Kelleher, R. T. (1966). Schedules using noxious stimuli I. Multiple fixed-ratio and fixed-interval termination of schedule complexes. *Journal of the Experimental Analysis of Behavior, 9,* 267–290.

Moskowitz, D. S. (1982). Coherence and cross-situational generality in personality: A new analysis of old problems. *Journal of Personality and Social Psychology, 43,* 754–768.

Moskowitz, D. S. (1994). Cross-situational generality and the interpersonal circumplex. *Journal of Personality and Social Psychology, 66,* 921–933.

Moskowitz, D. S., Suh, E. J., & Desaulniers, J. (1994). Situational influences on gender differences in agency and communion. *Journal of Personality and Social Psychology, 66,* 753–761.

Mulaik, S. A. (1964). Are personality factors raters' conceptual factors? *Journal of Consulting Psychology, 28,* 506–511.

Murphy, J. M. (1976). Psychiatric labeling in a cross-cultural perspective. *Science, 191,* 1019–1028.

Murphy, S. T., & Zajonc, R. B. (1993). Affect, cognition, and awareness: Affective priming with optimal and suboptimal stimulus exposures. *Journal of Personality and Social Psychology, 64,* 723–739.

Murray, E. J., Auld, F., Jr., & White, A. M. (1954). A psychotherapy case showing progress but no decrease in the discomfort-relief quotient. *Journal of Consulting Psychology, 18,* 349–353.

Murray, H. A., Barrett, W. G., & Homburger, E. (1938). *Explorations in personality.* New York: Oxford University Press.

Murray, J. (1973). Television and violence: Implications of the surgeon general's research program. *American Psychologist, 28,* 472–478.

Murstein, B. I. (1963). *Theory and research in projective techniques.* New York: Wiley.

Mussen, P. H., & Naylor, H. K. (1954). The relationship between overt and fantasy aggression. *Journal of Abnormal and Social Psychology, 49,* 235–240.

Neale, M. C., & Cardon, L. R. (1992). *Methodology for genetic studies of twins and families.* Dordrecht, Netherlands: Kluwer Academic Publishers.

Neisser, U. (1967). *Cognitive psychology.* New York: Appleton.

Nelson, R. J., Demas, G. E., Huang, P. L., Fishman, M. C., Dawson, V. L., Dawson, T. M., & Snyder, S. H. (1995). Behavioural abnormalities in male mice lacking neuronal nitric synthase. *Nature, 378* (6555), 383–386.

Nemeroff, C. J., & Karoly, P. (1991). Operant methods. In F. H. Kanfer & A. P. Goldstein (Eds.), *Helping people change: A textbook of methods* (4th ed.). Pergamon general psychology series, Vol. 52. New York: Pergamon.

Newcomb, T. M. (1929). *Consistency of certain extrovert-intro-vert behavior patterns in 51 problem boys.* New York: Columbia University, Teachers College, Bureau of Publications.

Niedenthal, P. M. (1990). Implicit perception of affective information. *Journal of Experimental Social Psychology, 25,* 505–527.

Nilson, D. C., Nilson, L. B., Olson, R. S., & McAllister, B. H. (1981). *The planning environment report for the Southern California Earthquake Safety Advisory Board.* Redlands, CA: The Social Research Advisory and Policy Research Center.

National Institute of Mental Health. (1975). *Research in the service of mental health.* (Rep. of the Research Task Force of the NIMH; DHEW Publication No. 75–236.) Washington, DC: Author.

Nisbett, R. (1997, May). Cultures of honor: Economics, history, and the tradition of violence. Address given at the Ninth Annual Convention of the American Psychological Society, Washington, DC.

Nisbett, R. E., & Ross, L. D. (1980). *Human inference: Strategies and shortcomings of social judgment.* Century Psychology Series. Englewood Cliffs, NJ: Prentice-Hall.

Nisbett, R., & Wilson, T. (1977). Telling more than we can know: Verbal reports on mental processes. *Psychological Review, 84,* 231–259.

Nolen-Hoeksema, S. (1991). Responses to depression and their effects on the duration of depressive episodes. *Journal of Abnormal Psychology, 100,* 569–582.

Nolen-Hoeksema, S. (1996). Chewing the cud and other ruminations. In R. S. Wyer, Jr. (Ed.), *Ruminative thoughts: Advances in social cognition* (pp. 135–144). Mahwah, NJ: Erlbaum.

Nolen-Hoeksema, S. (1997, May). Emotion regulation and depression. Closing plenary session at the Ninth Annual American Psychological Society Convention, Washington, DC.

Nolen-Hoeksema, S., Parker, L. E, & Larson, J. (1994). Ruminative coping with depressed mood following loss. *Journal of Personality and Social Psychology, 67,* 92–104.

Norem, J. K., & Cantor, N. (1986). Anticipatory and post hoc cushioning strategies: Optimism and defensive pessimism in "risky" situations. *Cognitive Therapy and Research, 10,* 347–362.

Norman, W. T. (1961). Development of self-report tests to measure personality factors identified from peer nominations. *USAF ASK Technical Note,* No. 61–44.

Norman, W. T. (1963). Toward an adequate taxonomy of personality attributes: Replicated factor structure in peer nomination personality ratings. *Journal of Abnormal and Social Psychology, 66,* 574–583.

O' Leary, V. (1997, August). Smithsonian seminar on health and well-being sponsored by Society for the Psychological Study of Social Issues and American Psychological Society, conducted at the Ninth Annual Conference of the American Psychological Society, Washington, DC.

O'Connell, D. F., & Alexander, C. N. (1994). Recovery from addictions using transcendental meditation and Maharishi Ayur-Veda. In D. F. O'Connell & C. N. Alexander (Eds.), *Self-recovery: Treating addictions using transcendental meditation and Maharishi Ayur-Veda* (pp. 1–12). New York: Haworth Press.

O'Connor, T. G., Hetherington, E. M., Reiss, D., & Plomin, R. (1995). A twin-sibling study of observed parent-adolescent interactions. *Child Development, 66,* 812–829.

O'Leary, K. D., & Kent, R. N. (1973). Behavior modification for social action: Research tactics and problems. In L. Hamerlynck et al. (Eds.), *Critical issues in research and practice.* New York: Research Press.

Office of Strategic Services Administration. (1948). *Assessment of men.* New York: Holt, Rinehart and Winston.

Ofshe, R. J. (1992). Inadvertent hypnosis during interrogation: False confession due to dissociative state, misidentified multiple personality and the satanic cult hypothesis. *International Journal of Clinical and Experimental Hypnosis, 40,* 125–156.

Ofshe, R. J., & Watters, E. (1993). Making monsters. *Society, 1,* 4–16.

Opler, M. K. (1967). Cultural induction of stress. In M. H. Appley & R. Trumbull (Eds.), *Psychological stress* (pp. 209–241). New York: Appleton.

Ornstein, R. E. (1972). *The psychology of consciousness.* San Francisco: W. H. Freeman.

Ornstein, R. E., & Naranjo, C. (1971). *On the psychology of meditation.* New York: Viking.

Osgood, C. E., Suci, G. J., & Tannenbaum, P. H. (1957). *The measurement of meaning.* Urbana, IL: The University of Illinois Press.

Oskamp, S. (1965). Overconfidence in case-study judgments. *Journal of Consulting Psychology, 29,* 261–265.

Overall, J. (1964). Note on the scientific status of factors. *Psychological Bulletin, 61,* 270–276.

Pagano, R. R., Rose, R. M., Stivers, R. M., & Warrenburg, S. (1976). Sleep during transcendental meditation. *Science, 191,* 308–309.

Patterson, C. J., & Mischel, W. (1975). Plans to resist distraction. *Developmental Psychology, 11,* 369–378.

Patterson, C. J., & Mischel, W. (1976). Effects of temptation-inhibiting and task-facilitating plans on self-control. *Journal of Personality and Social Psychology, 33,* 209–217.

Patterson, G. R. (1976). The aggressive child: Victim and architect of a coercive system. In L. A. Hamerlynck, L. C. Handy, & E. J. Mash (Eds.), *Behavior modification and families, Vol. 1. Theory and research.* New York: Brunner/Mazel.

Patterson, G. R. (Ed.). (1990). *Depression and aggression in family interaction.* Hillsdale, NJ: Erlbaum.

Patterson, G. R., & Cobb, J. A. (1971). Stimulus control for classes of noxious behaviors. In J. F. Knutson (Ed.), *The control of aggression: Implications from basic research.* Chicago: Aldine.

Paul, G. L. (1966). *Insight vs. desensitization in psychotherapy.* Stanford, CA: Stanford University Press.

Paul, G. L. (1967). Insight vs. desensitization in psychotherapy two years after termination. *Journal of Consulting Psychology, 31,* 333–348.

Paul, G. L., & Shannon, D. T. (1966). Treatment of anxiety through systematic desensitization in therapy groups. *Journal of Abnormal Psychology, 71*, 124–135.

Paulhus, D. L., Fridhandler, B., & Hayes, S. (1997). Psychological defense: Contemporary theory and research. In R. Hogan, J. A. Johnson, & S. R. Briggs (Eds.), *Handbook of personality psychology* (pp. 543–579) San Diego, CA: Academic Press.

Pedersen, N. L., Plomin, R., McClearn, G. E., & Friberg, L. (1988). Neuroticism, extraversion, and related traits in adult twins reared apart and reared together. *Journal of Personality and Social Psychology, 55*, 950–957.

Pederson, F. A. (1958). Consistency data on the role construct repertory test. Unpublished manuscript, Ohio State University, Columbus.

Pennebaker, J. W. (1993). Social mechanisms of constraint. In D. M. Wegener & J. W. Pennebaker (Eds.), *Handbook of mental control* (pp. 200–219). Englewoood Cliff, NJ: Prentice-Hall.

Pennebaker, J. W. (1997). Writing about emotional experiences as a therapeutic process. *Psychological Science, 8*, 162–166.

Pennebaker, J. W., Barger, S. D., & Tiebout, J. (1989). Disclosure of traumas and health among Holocaust survivors. *Psychosomatic Medicine, 51*, 577–589.

Pennebaker, J. W., Czajka, J. A., Cropanzano, R., Richards, B. C., Brumbelow, S., Ferrarra, K., Thompson, R., & Thyssen, T. (1990). Levels of thinking. *Personality and Social Psychology Bulletin, 16*, 743–757.

Pennebaker, J. W., Kiecolt-Glaser, J. K., & Glaser, R. (1988). Disclosure of traumas and immune function: Health implications for psychotherapy. *Journal of Consulting and Clinical Psychology, 56*, 239–245.

Perls, F. S. (1969). *Gestalt therapy verbatim.* Lafayette, CA: Real People Press.

Perry, J. C., & Cooper, S. H. (1989). An empirical study of defense mechanisms, I. Clinical interviews and life vignette ratings. *Archives of General Psychiatry, 46*, 444–452.

Pervin, L. A. (1977). The representative design of person-situation research. In D. Magnusson & N. S. Endler (Eds.), *Personality at the crossroads: Current issues in interactional psychology.* Hillsdale, NJ: Erlbaum.

Pervin, L. A. (1989). Goal concepts: Themes, issues, and questions. In L. A. Pervin (Ed.), *Goal concepts in personality and social psychology* (pp. 473–479). Hillsdale, NJ: Erlbaum.

Pervin, L. A. (1994). A critical analysis of trait theory. *Psychological Inquiry, 5*, 103–113.

Pervin, L. A. (1996). *The science of personality.* New York: Wiley.

Pervin, L. A. (Ed.). (1990). *Handbook of personality: Theory and research.* New York: Guilford Press.

Peterson, B. E., Doty, R. M., & Winter, D. G. (1993). Authoritarianism and attitudes toward contemporary social issues. *Personality and Social Psychology Bulletin, 19*, 174–184.

Peterson, C., & Seligman, M. E. P. (1987). Explanatory style and illness. *Journal of Personality, 55*, 237–265.

Peterson, C., Maier, S. F., & Seligman, M. E. P. (1993). *Learned helplessness: A theory for the age of personal control.* New York: Oxford University Press.

Peterson, C., Seligman, M. E. P., & Vaillant, G. E. (1988). Pessimistic explanatory style is a risk factor of physical illness: A thirty-five-year longitudinal study. *Journal of Personality and Social Psychology, 55*, 23–27.

Peterson, D. R. (1965). Scope and generality of verbally defined personality factors. *Psychological Review, 72*, 48–59.

Peterson, D. R. (1968). *The clinical study of social behavior.* New York: Appleton.

Phares, E. J. (1978). Locus of control. In H. London & J. E. Exner, Jr. (Eds.), *Dimensions of personality.* New York: Wiley.

Phillips, K., & Mathews, A. P., Jr. (1995). Quantitative genetic analysis of injury liability in infants and toddlers. *American Journal of Medical Genetics (Neuropsychiatric Genetics), 60*, 64–71.

Piaget, J. (1932). *The moral judgment of the child.* London: Kegan Paul.

Pike, A., Reiss, D., Hetherington, E. M., & Plomin, R. (1996). Using MZ differences in the search for nonshared environmental effects. *Journal of Child Psychology and Psychiatry, 37*, 695–704.

Pinker, S. (1997). *How the mind works.* New York: Norton.

Plaud, J. J., & Gaither, G. A. (1996). Human behavioral momentum: Implications for applied behavior analysis and therapy. *Journal of Behavior Therapy and Experimental Psychiatry, 27*, 139–148.

Plomin, R. (1990). The role of inheritance in behavior. *Science, 248*, 183–188.

Plomin, R. (1994a). *Genetics and experience: The developmental interplay between nature and nurture.* Newbury Park, CA: Sage Publications.

Plomin, R. (1994b). The Emanuel Miller Memorial Lecture 1993: Genetic research and identification of environmental influences. *Journal of Child Psychology and Psychiatry, 35*, 817–834.

Plomin, R., & Daniels, D. (1987). Why are children in the same family so different from each other? *The Behavioral and Brain Sciences, 10*, 1–16.

Plomin, R., & Foch, T. T. (1980). A twin study of objectively assessed personality in childhood. *Journal of Personality and Social Psychology, 39*, 680–688.

Plomin, R., & Saudino, K. J. (1994). Quantitative genetics and molecular genetics. In J. E. Bates & T. D. Watts (Eds.), *Temperament: Individual differences at the interface of biology and behavior* (pp. 143–171). Washington, DC: American Psychological Association.

Plomin, R., Chipuer, H. M., & Loehlin, J. C. (1990). Behavioral genetics and personality. In L. A. Pervin (Ed.), *Handbook of personality: Theory and research* (pp. 225–243). New York: Guilford Press.

Plomin, R., Chipuer, H. M., & Neiderhiser, J. M. (1994). Behavioral genetic evidence for the importance of nonshared environment. In E. M. Hetherington, D. Reiss, & R. Plomin

(Eds.), *Separate social worlds of siblings: Impact of non-shared environment on development* (pp. 1–31). Hillsdale, NJ: Erlbaum.

Plomin, R., DeFries, J. C., & Loehlin, J. C. (1977). Genotype-environment interaction and correlation in the analysis of human behavior. *Psychological Bulletin, 84,* 309–322.

Plomin, R., Manke, B., & Pike, A. (1996). Siblings, behavioral genetics, and competence. In G. H. Brody (Ed.), *Sibling relationships: Their causes and consequences* (pp. 75–104). Norwood, NJ: Ablex Publishing.

Plomin, R., DeFries, J. C., McClearn, G. E., & Rutter, M. (1997). *Behavioral genetics* (3rd ed.). New York: W. H. Freeman.

Plomin, R., Owen, M. J., & McGuffin, P. (1994). The genetic basis of complex human behaviors. *Science, 264,* 1733–1739.

Plomin, R., Lichtenstein, P., Pedersen, N. L., McClearn, G. E., & Nesselroade, J. R. (1990). Genetic influence on life events during the last half of the life span. *Psychology and Aging, 5,* 25–30.

Plomin, R., McClearn, G. E., Pedersen, N. L., Nesselroade, J. R., & Bergeman, C. S. (1988). Genetic influence on childhood family environment perceived retrospectively from the last half of the life span. *Developmental Psychology, 24,* 738–745.

Polster, E., & Polster, M. (1993). Frederick Perls: Legacy and invitation. *Gestalt Journal, 16,* 23–25.

Posner, M. I. (1997, April). *Cognitive neuroscience and the development of attention.* Paper presented at the Biennial Meeting for the Society for Research in Child Development, Washington, DC.

Potter, W. Z., Rudorfer, M. V., & Manji, H. K. (1991). The pharmacologic treatment of depression. *New England Journal of Medicine, 325,* 633–642.

Powell, G. E. (1973). Negative and positive mental practice in motor skill acquisition. *Perceptual and Motor Skills, 37,* 312–313.

Prentice, D. A. (1990). Familiarity and differences in self- and other-representations. *Journal of Personality and Social Psychology, 59,* 369–383.

Prentice, D. A., & Miller, C. T. (1993). Pluralistic ignorance and alcohol use on campus: Some consequences of misperceiving the social norm. *Journal of Personality and Social Psychology, 64,* 243–256.

Proshansky, H. M. (1976). Environmental psychology and the real world. *American Psychologist, 31,* 303–310.

Proshansky, H. M., Fabian, A. K., & Kaminoff, R. (1983). Place-identity: Physical world socialization of the self. *Journal of Environmental Psychology, 3,* 57–83.

Proshansky, H. M., Ittelson, W. H., & Rivlin, L. G. (Eds.). (1970). *Environmental psychology.* New York: Holt, Rinehart and Winston.

Pyszczynski, T., Holt, J., & Greenberg, J. (1987). Depression, self-focused attention, and expectancies for positive and negative future life events for self and others. *Journal of Personality and Social Psychology, 52,* 994–1001.

Rabkin, J. G., & Struening, E. L. (1976). Life events, stress, and illness. *Science, 194,* 1013–1020.

Rachman, S. (1967). Systematic desensitization. *Psychological Bulletin, 67,* 93–103.

Rachman, S., & Cuk, M. (1992). Fearful distortions. *Behaviour Research and Therapy, 30,* 583–589.

Rachman, S., & Hodgeson, R. J. (1980). *Obsessions and compulsions.* Englewood Cliffs, NJ: Prentice-Hall.

Rachman, S., & Wilson, G. T. (1980). *The effects of psychological therapy.* Oxford, England: Pergamon.

Rachman, S. J. (1996). Trends in cognitive and behavioural therapies. In P. M. Salkovskis (Ed.), *Trends in cognitive and behavioural therapies* (pp. 1–23). New York: Wiley.

Raffety, B. D., Smith, R. E., & Ptacek, J. T. (1997). Facilitating and debilitating trait anxiety, situational anxiety, and coping with an anticipated stressor: A process analysis. *Journal of Personality and Social Psychology, 72,* 892–906.

Ramsey, E., Patterson, G. R., & Walker, H. M. (1990). Generalization of the antisocial trait from home to school settings. *Journal of Applied Developmental Psychology, 11,* 209–223.

Rapaport, D. (1951). The autonomy of the ego. *Bulletin of the Menninger Clinic, 15,* 113–123.

Rapaport, D. (1967). On the psychoanalytic theory of thinking. In M. M. Gill (Ed.), *The collected papers of David Rapaport.* New York: Basic Books.

Raush, H. L., Barry, W. A., Hertel, R. K., & Swain, M. A. (1974). *Communication conflict and marriage.* San Francisco: Jossey-Bass.

Raymond, M. S. (1956). Case of fetishism treated by aversion therapy. *British Medical Journal, 2,* 854–857.

Read, S. J., & Miller, L. C. (1989a). Inter-personalism: Toward a goal-based theory of persons in relationships. In L. A. Pervin (Ed.), *Goal concepts in personality and social psychology* (pp. 413–472). Hillsdale, NJ: Erlbaum.

Read, S. J., & Miller, L. C. (1989b). The importance of goals in personality: Toward a coherent model of persons. In R. S. Wyer, Jr., & T. K. Srull (Eds.), *Advances in social cognition: Vol 2. Social intelligence and cognitive assessments of personality* (pp. 163–174). Hillsdale, NJ: Erlbaum.

Record, R. G., McKeown, T., & Edwards, J. H. (1970). An investigation of the difference in measured intelligence between twins and single births. *Annals of the Human Genetic Society, 84,* 11–20.

Redd, W. H. (1995). Behavioral research in cancer as a model for health psychology. *Health Psychology, 14,* 99–100.

Redd, W. H., Porterfield, A. L., & Anderson, B. L. (1978). *Behavior modification: Behavioral approaches to human problems.* New York: Random House.

Reece, M. M. (1954). The effect of shock on recognition thresholds. *Journal of Abnormal and Social Psychology, 49,* 165–172.

Reisenzein, R. (1983). The Schachter theory of emotions: Two decades later. *Psychological Bulletin, 84,* 239–264.

Reiss, D., Neiderhiser, J. M., Hetherington, E. M., & Plomin, R. (in press). *The relationship code.* Cambridge, MA: Harvard University Press.

Revelle, W. (1995). Personality processes. *Annual Review of Psychology, 46,* 295–328.

Riemann, R., Angleitner, A., & Strelau, J. (1997). Genetic and environmental influences on personality: A study of twins reared together using the self- and peer report NEO-FFI scales. *Journal of Personality, 65,* 449–476.

Rimm, D. C., & Masters, J. C. (1974). *Behavior therapy: Techniques and empirical findings.* New York: Academic Press.

Ritson, B. (1992). Treatment of alcohol-related disorders and alcohol abuse. *International Journal of Mental Health, 21,* 43–67.

Roazen, P. (1974). *Freud and his followers.* New York: Meridian.

Robbins, A. S., Spence, J. T., & Clark, H. (1991). Psychological determinants of health and performance: The tangled web of desirable and undesirable characteristics. *Journal of Personality and Social Psychology, 61,* 755–765.

Robbins, L. N. (1972). Dissecting the "broken home" as a predictor of deviance. Paper presented at the National Institute of Mental Health conference on developmental aspects of self-regulation, La Jolla, CA, February.

Robinson, J. L., Kagan, J., Reznick, J. S., & Corley, R. (1992). The heritability of inhibited and uninhibited behavior: A twin study. *Developmental Psychology, 28,* 1030–1037.

Rogers, C. R. (1942). *Counseling and psychotherapy: Newer concepts in practice.* Boston: Houghton Mifflin.

Rogers, C. R. (1947). Some observations on the organization of personality. *American Psychologist, 2,* 358–368.

Rogers, C. R. (1951). *Client-centered therapy: Its current practice, implications and theory.* Boston: Houghton Mifflin.

Rogers, C. R. (1955). Persons or science? A philosophical question. *American Psychologist, 10,* 267–278.

Rogers, C. R. (1959). A theory of therapy, personality and interpersonal relationships, as developed in the client-centered framework. In S. Koch (Ed.), *Psychology: A study of a science* (Vol. 3, pp. 184–526). New York: McGraw-Hill.

Rogers, C. R. (1963). The actualizing tendency in relation to "motives" and to consciousness. In M. R. Jones (Ed.), *Nebraska symposium on motivation* (pp. 1–24). Lincoln: University of Nebraska Press.

Rogers, C. R. (1970). *Carl Rogers on encounter groups.* New York: Harper & Row.

Rogers, C. R. (1974). In retrospect: Forty-six years. *American Psychologist, 29,* 115–123.

Rogers, C. R. (1980). *A way of being.* Boston: Houghton Mifflin.

Rogers, C. R., & Dymond, R. F. (Eds.). (1954). *Psychotherapy and personality change, co-ordinated studies in the client-centered approach.* Chicago: University of Chicago Press.

Rogers, T. B. (1977). Self-reference in memory: Recognition of personality items. *Journal of Research in Personality, 11,* 295–305.

Rogers, T. B., Kuiper, N. A., & Kirker, W. S. (1977). Self-reference and the encoding of personal information. *Journal of Personality and Social Psychology, 35,* 677–688.

Romer, D., & Revelle, W. (1984). Personality traits: Fact or fiction? A critique of the Shweder and D'Andrade systematic distortion hypothesis. *Journal of Personality and Social Psychology, 47,* 1028–1042.

Rorer, L. G. (1990). Personality assessment: A conceptual survey. In L.A. Pervin (Ed.), *Handbook of personality: Theory and research* (pp. 693–720). New York: Guilford Press.

Rosch, E. (1975). Cognitive reference points. *Cognitive Psychology, 1,* 532–547.

Rosch, E., Mervis, C., Gray, W., Johnson, D., & Boyce-Braem, P. (1976). Basic objects in natural categories. *Cognitive Psychology, 8,* 382–439.

Rosen, A. C. (1954). Change in perceptual threshold as a protective function of the organism. *Journal of Personality, 23,* 182–195.

Rosenbaum, M. (1980). Individual differences in self-control behaviors and tolerance of painful simulation. *Journal of Abnormal Psychology, 89,* 581–590.

Rosenhan, D. L. (1973). On being sane in insane places. *Science, 179,* 250–258.

Rosenthal, D. (1971). *Genetics of psychopathology.* New York: McGraw-Hill.

Rosenzweig, S., & Mason, G. (1934). An experimental study of memory in relation to the theory of repression. *British Journal of Psychology, 24,* 247–265.

Ross, L., & Nisbett, R. E. (1991). *The person and the situation: Perspectives of social psychology.* New York: McGraw-Hill.

Ross, L. D. (1977). The intuitive psychologist and his shortcomings: Distortions in the attribution process. In L. Berkowitz (Ed.), *Advances in experimental social psychology* (Vol. 10). New York: Academic Press.

Rossini, E. D., & Moretti, R. J. (1997). Thematic Apperception Test (TAT) interpretation: Practice recommendations from a survey of clinical psychology doctoral programs accredited by the American Psychological Association. *Professional Psychology Research and Practice, 28,* 393–398.

Roth, S., & Newman, E. (1990). The process of coping with sexual trauma. *Journal of Traumatic Stress, 4,* 279–297.

Rothbart, M. K., Derryberry, D., & Posner, M. I. (1994). A psychobiological approach to the development of temperament. In J. E. Bates & T. D. Wachs (Eds.), *Temperament: Individual differences at the interface of biology and behavior* (pp. 83–116). Washington, DC: American Psychological Association.

Rothbart, M. K., Posner, M. I., & Gerardi, G. M. (1997, April 4). *Effortful control and the development of temperament.* Symposium presented at the 1997 Biennial Meeting of the Society for Research in Child Development, Washington, DC.

Rotter, J. B. (1954). *Social learning and clinical psychology.* Englewood Cliffs, NJ: Prentice-Hall.

Rotter, J. B. (1966). Generalized expectancies for internal versus external control of reinforcement. *Psychological Monographs, 80* (Whole No. 609).

Rotter, J. B. (1972). Beliefs, social attitudes, and behavior: A social learning analysis. In J. B. Rotter, J. E. Chance, & E. J.

Phares (Eds.), *Applications of a social learning theory of personality.* New York: Holt, Rinehart and Winston.

Rowan, J. (1992). What is humanistic psychotherapy? *British Journal of Psychotherapy, 9,* 74–83.

Rowe, D. C. (1981). Environmental and genetic influences on dimensions of perceived parenting: A twin study. *Developmental Psychology, 17,* 203–208.

Rowe, D. C. (1983). A biometrical analysis of perceptions of family environment: A study of twin and singleton sibling kinships. *Child Development, 54,* 416–423.

Rowe, D. C. (1991). Heredity. In V. J. Derlega, B. A. Winstead, & W. H. Jones (Eds.), *Personality: Contemporary theory and research* (pp. 55–88). Chicago: Nelson-Hall.

Rowe, D. C. (1997). Genetics, temperament, and personality. In R. Hogan, J. Johnson, & S. Briggs (Eds.), *Handbook of personality psychology* (pp. 367–386). San Diego, CA: Academic Press.

Royce, J. E. (1973). Does person or self imply dualism? *American Psychologist, 28,* 833–866.

Rubin, I. J. (1967). The reduction of prejudice through laboratory training. *Journal of Applied Behavioral Science, 3,* 29–50.

Ruebush, B. E. (1963). In H. A. Stevenson, et al. (Eds.), *Child psychology. The sixty-second yearbook of the National Society for the Study of Education* (pp. 460–516). Chicago: University of Chicago Press.

Runyan, W. M. (1997). Studying lives: Psychobiography and the conceptual structure of personality psychology. In R. Hogan, J. Johnson, & S. Briggs (Eds.), *Handbook of personality psychology* (pp. 41–69). San Diego, CA: Academic Press.

Rushton, J. P., Fulker, D. W., Neale, M. C., Nias, D. K. B., & Eysenck, H. J. (1986). Altruism and aggression: The heritability of individual differences. *Journal of Personality and Social Psychology, 50,* 1192–1198.

Rutter, M. (1987). Psychosocial resilience and protective mechanisms. *American Journal of Orthopsychiatry, 57,* 316–331.

Rutter, M., Dunn, J., Plomin, R., Simonoff, E., Pickles, A., Maughan, B., Ormel, J., Meyer, J., & Eaves, L. (1997). Integrating nature and nurture: Implications of person-environment correlations and interactions for developmental psychopathology. *Development and Psychopathology, 9,* 335–364.

Saley, E., & Holdstock, L. (1993). Encounter group experiences of black and white South Africans in exile. In D. Brazier (Ed.), *Beyond Carl Rogers* (pp. 201–216). London, England: Constable.

Salovey, (1997, August). *Emotion regulation in everyday life.* Discussant for symposium at Ninth Annual Conference of the American Psychological Society, Washington, DC.

Salovey, P., & Mayer, J. D. (1990). Emotional intelligence. *Imagination, Cognition, and Personality, 9,* 185–211.

Sapolsky, R. M. (1996). Why stress is bad for your brain. *Science, 273,* 749–750.

Sarason, I. G. (1966). *Personality: An objective approach.* New York: Wiley.

Sarason, I. G. (1978). The Test Anxiety Scale: Concept and research. In C. D. Spielberger & I. G. Sarason (Eds.), *Stress and anxiety* (Vol. 5). Washington, DC: Hemisphere.

Sarason, I. G. (1979). Life stress, self-preoccupation, and social supports. Presidential address, Western Psychological Association.

Sarason, I. G., & Sarason, B. R. (1990). Test anxiety. In H. Leitenberg (Ed.), *Handbook of social and evaluation anxiety* (pp. 475–496). New York: Plenum.

Sarason, S. B., Davidson, K. S., Lighthall, F. F., Waite, R. R., & Ruebush, B. K. (1960). *Anxiety in elementary school children.* New York: Wiley.

Saudino, K. J., & Eaton, W. O. (1991). Infant temperament and genetics: An objective twin study of motor activity level. *Child Development, 62,* 1167–1174.

Saudino, K. J., & Plomin, R. (1996). Personality and behavioral genetics: Where have we been and where are we going? *Journal of Research in Personality, 30,* 335–347.

Saudino, K. J., Plomin, R., & DeFries, J. C. (1996). Tester-rated temperament at 14, 20, and 24 months: Environmental change and genetic continuity . *British Journal of Developmental Psychology, 14,* 129–144.

Saudino, K. J., Pedersen, N. L., Lichtenstein, P., McClearn, G. E., & Plomin, R. (1997). Can personality explain genetic influences on life events? *Journal of Personality and Social Psychology: Personality Processes and Individual Differences, 72,* 196–206.

Saudou, F., Amara, D. A., Dierich, A., LeMur, M., Ramboz, S., Segu, L., Buhot, M. C., & Hen, R. (1994). Enhanced aggressive behavior in mice lacking 5-HT$_{1B}$ receptor. *Science, 265,* 1875–1878.

Schacter, D. L. (1996). *Searching for memory: The brain, the mind, and the past.* New York: Basic Books.

Schachter, S. (1964). The interaction of cognitive and physiological determinants of emotional state. In L. Berkowitz (Ed.), *Advances in experimental social psychology* (Vol. 1, pp. 49–80). New York: Academic Press.

Schachter, S., & Rodin, J. (1974). *Obese humans and rats.* Potomac, MD: Erlbaum.

Schachter, S., & Singer, J. E. (1962). Cognitive, social and physiological determinants of emotional state. *Psychological Review, 69,* 379–399.

Schachter, S., & Singer, J. E. (1979). Comments on the Maslach and Marshall-Zimbardo experiments. *Journal of Personality and Social Psychology, 37,* 989–995.

Schachter, S., Goldman, R., & Gordon, A. (1968). Effects of fear, food deprivation and obesity on eating. *Journal of Personality and Social Psychology, 10,* 91–97.

Schaffer, H. R., & Emerson, P. E. (1964). Patterns of response to physical contact in early human development. *Journal of Child Psychology and Psychiatry, 5,* 1–13.

Schank, R., & Abelson, R. P. (1977). *Scripts, plans, goals, and understanding.* Hillsdale, NJ: Erlbaum.

Scheier, M. F., & Carver, C. S. (1987). Dispositional optimism and physical well-being: The influence of generalized outcome expectancies on health. *Journal of Personality, 55,* 169–210.

Scheier, M. F., & Carver, C. S. (1988a). Individual differences in self-concept and self-processes. In D. M. Wegner & R. R. Vallacher (Eds.), *The self in social psychology.* New York: Oxford University Press.

Scheier, M. F., & Carver, C. S. (1988b). A model of behavioral self-regulation: Translating intention into action. In L. Berkowitz (Ed.), *Advances in experimental social psychology* (Vol. 21, pp. 322–343). San Diego, CA: Academic Press.

Scheier, M. F., & Carver, C. S. (1992). Effects of optimism on psychological and physical well-being: Theoretical overview and empirical update. *Cognitive Therapy and Research, 16,* 201–228.

Scheier, M. F., Weintraub, J. K., & Carver, C. S. (1986). Coping with stress: Divergent strategies of optimists and pessimists. *Journal of Personality and Social Psychology, 51,* 1257–1264.

Schneider, D. J. (1973). Implicit personality theory: A review. *Psychological Bulletin, 73,* 294–309.

Schneider, D. J., Hastorf, A. H., & Ellsworth, P. C. (1979). *Person perception* (2nd ed.). Reading, MA: Addison-Wesley.

Schooler, J. W. (1994). Seeking the core: The issues and evidence surrounding recovered accounts of sexual trauma. *Consciousness and Cognition, 3,* 452–469.

Schooler, J. W. (1997) Reflections on a memory discovery. *Child Maltreatment, 2,* 126–133.

Schooler, J. W., Bendiksen, M., & Ambadar, Z. (1997). Taking the middle line: Can we accommodate both fabricated and recovered memories of sexual abuse? In M. Conway (Ed.), *False and recovered memories* (pp. 251–292). Oxford, England: Oxford University Press.

Schutte, N. S., Kenrick, D. T., & Sadalla, E. K. (1985). The search for predictable settings: Situational prototypes, constraints, and behavioral variation. *Journal of Personality and Social Psychology, 49,* 121–128.

Schutz, W. C. (1967). *Joy: Expanding human awareness.* New York: Grove.

Schwartz, G. E. (1973). Biofeedback as therapy. *American Psychologist, 28,* 666–673.

Schwartz, M. S. (1987). *Biofeedback: A practitioner's guide.* New York: Guilford Press.

Schwarz, N. (1990). Feelings and information: Informational and motivational functions of affective states. In R. M. Sorrentino & E. T. Higgins (Eds.), *Handbook of motivation and cognition: Foundations of social behavior* (Vol. 2, pp. 527–561). New York: Guilford Press.

Scott, W. A., & Johnson, R. C. (1972). Comparative validities of direct and indirect personality tests. *Journal of Consulting and Clinical Psychology, 38,* 301–318.

Sears, R. R. (1936). Functional abnormalities of memory with special reference to amnesia. *Psychological Bulletin, 33,* 229–274.

Seligman, M. E., & Hager, J. L. (1972). *Biological boundaries of learning.* New York: Appleton-Century-Crofts.

Seligman, M. E., Abramson, L. Y., Semmel, A., & von Baeyer, C. (1979). Depressive attributional style. *Journal of Abnormal Psychology, 88,* 242–247.

Seligman, M. E. P. (1971). Phobias and preparedness. *Behavior Therapy, 2,* 307–320.

Seligman, M. E. P. (1975). *Helplessness—On depression, development, and death.* San Francisco: W. H. Freeman.

Seligman, M. E. P. (1978). Comment and integration. *Journal of Abnormal Psychology, 87,* 165–179.

Seligman, M. E. P. (1990). *Learned optimism.* New York: Knopf.

Seligman, M. E. P., Reivich, K., Jaycox, L., & Gillham, J. (1995). *The optimistic child.* Boston, MA: Houghton Mifflin.

Sewall, K. W. (1995). Personal construct therapy and the relation between cognition and affect. In M. J. Mahoney (Ed.), *Cognitive and constructive psychotherapies: Theory, research, and practice* (pp. 121–138). New York: Springer.

Sheline, Y., Wang, P. W., Gado, M. H., Csernansky, J. G., & Vannier, M. W. (1996). Hippocampal atrophy in recurrent major depression. Proceedings of the National Academy of Sciences of the United States of America. 93(9): 3908–3913.

Shevrin, H., & Dickman, S. (1980). The psychological unconscious: A necessary assumption for all psychological theory? *American Psychologist, 12,* 421–434.

Shoda, Y. (1990). Conditional analyses of personality coherence and dispositions. Unpublished doctoral dissertation, Columbia University, New York.

Shoda, Y., & Mischel, W. (1993). Cognitive social approach to dispositional inferences: What if the perceiver is a cognitive-social theorist? *Personality and Social Psychology Bulletin, 19,* 574–585.

Shoda, Y., & Mischel, W. (1996). Toward a unified, intra-individual dynamic conception of personality. *Journal of Research in Personality, 30,* 414–428.

Shoda, Y., & Mischel, W. (1998). Reconciling processing dynamics and personality dispositions. *Annual Review of Psychology, 49,* 229–258.

Shoda, Y., Mischel, W., & Peake, P. K. (1990). Predicting adolescent cognitive and self-regulatory competencies from preschool delay of gratification: Identifying diagnostic conditions. *Developmental Psychology, 26,* 978–986.

Shoda, Y., Mischel, W., & Wright, J. C. (1989). Intuitive interactionism in person perception: Effects of situation-behavior relations on dispositional judgments. *Journal of Personality and Social Psychology, 56,* 41–53.

Shoda, Y., Mischel, W., & Wright, J. C. (1993a). The role of situational demands and cognitive competencies in behavior organization and personality coherence. *Journal of Personality and Social Psychology, 56,* 41–53.

Shoda, Y., Mischel, W., & Wright, J. C. (1993b). Links between personality judgments and contextualized behavior patterns: Situation-behavior profiles of personality prototypes. *Social Cognition, 4,* 399–429.

Shoda, Y. Mischel, W., & Wright, J. C. (1994). Intra-individual stability in the organization and patterning of behavior: Incorporating psychological situations into the idiographic analysis of personality. *Journal of Personality and Social Psychology, 65,* 1023–1035.

Shure, G. H., & Rogers, M. S. (1965). Note of caution on the factor analysis of the MMPI. *Psychological Bulletin, 63,* 14–18.

Shweder, R. A. (1975). How relevant is an individual difference theory of personality? *Journal of Personality, 43,* 455–485.

Silverman, L. H. (1976). Psychoanalytic theory: The reports of my death are greatly exaggerated. *American Psychologist, 31,* 621–637.

Silverman, L. H., & Weinberger, J. (1985). Mommy and I are one: Implications for psychotherapy. *American Psychologist, 12,* 1296–1308.

Simons, A. D., & Thase, M. E. (1992). Biological markers, treatment outcome, and 1-year follow-up in endogenous depression: Electroencephalographic sleep studies and response to cognitive therapy. *Journal of Consulting and Clinical Psychology, 60,* 392–401.

Singer, J. A., & Bonanno, G. A. (1990). Personality and private experience: Individual variations in consciousness and in attention to subjective phenomena. In L. A. Pervin (Ed.), *Handbook of personality: Theory and research* (pp. 419–444). New York: Guilford Press.

Singer, J. A., & Salovey, P. (1993). *The remembered self: Emotion and memory in personality.* New York: Free Press.

Singer, J. L. (1955). Delayed gratification and ego development: Implications for clinical and experimental research. *Journal of Consulting Psychology, 19,* 259–266.

Skinner, B. F. (1953). *Science and human behavior.* New York: Macmillan.

Skinner, B. F. (1955). Freedom and the control of men. *American Scholar, 25,* 47–65.

Skinner, B. F. (1964). Behaviorism at fifty. In T. W. Wann (Ed.), *Behaviorism and phenomenology* (pp. 79–108). Chicago: University of Chicago Press.

Skinner, B. F. (1971). *Beyond freedom and dignity.* New York: Knopf.

Skinner, B. F. (1974). *About behaviorism.* New York: Knopf.

Skinner, B. F. (1990). Can psychology be a science of the mind? *American Psychologist, 45,* 1206–1210.

Skolnick, A. (1966). Motivational imagery and behavior over twenty years. *Journal of Consulting Psychology, 30,* 463–478.

Smith, C. A., & Lazarus, R. S. (1990). Emotion and adaptation. In L. A. Pervin (Ed.), *Handbook of personality: Theory and research.* (pp. 609–637). New York: Guilford Press.

Smith, R. G., Iwata, B. A., Vollmer, R., & Pace, G. M. (1992). On the relationship between self-injurious behavior and self-restraint. *Journal of Applied Behavior Analysis, 25,* 433–445.

Snyder, M. (1983). The influence of individuals on situations: Implications for understanding the links between personality and social behavior. *Journal of Personality, 51,* 497–516.

Snyder, M., & Uranowitz, S. (1978). Reconstructing the past: Some cognitive consequences of person perception. *Journal of Personality and Social Psychology, 36,* 941–950.

Snyder, S. H., Banerjee, S. P., Yamomura, H. I., & Greenberg, D. (1974). Drugs, neurotransmitters, and schizophrenia. *Science, 184,* 1243–1253.

Snygg, D., & Combs, A. W. (1949). *Individual behavior.* New York: Harper & Row.

Soskin, W. F. (1959). Influence of four types of data on diagnostic conceptualization in psychological testing. *Journal of Abnormal and Social Psychology, 58,* 69–78.

Sperry, L. (1994). Helping people control their weight: Research and practice. In J. Lewis (Ed.), *Addictions: Concepts and strategies for treatment* (pp. 83–97). Gaithersberg, MD: Aspen Publishers.

Spiegel, D. (1981). Vietnam grief work using hypnosis. *The American Journal of Clinical Hypnosis, 24,* 33–40.

Spiegel, D. (1991). Neurophysiological correlates of hypnosis and dissociation. *Journal of Neuropsychiatry, 3,* 440–445.

Spiegel, D. (1994). Cancer and depression. *Verhaltenstherapie, 4,* 81–88.

Spiegel, D. (1996). Cancer and depression. *British Journal of Psychiatry, 168,* 109–116.

Spiegel, D., & Cardena, E. (1990). New uses of hypnosis in the treatment of posttraumatic stress disorder. *Journal of Clinical Psychiatry, 51,* (10 Suppl.), 39–43.

Spiegel, D., & Cardena, E. (1991). Disintegrated experience: The dissociative disorders revisited. *Journal of Abnormal Psychology, 100,* 366–378.

Spiegel, D., Koopman, C., & Classen, C. (1994). Acute distress disorder and dissociation. *Australian Journal of Clinical and Experimental Hypnosis, 22* (1), 11–23.

Spiegel, D., Kraemer, H. C., Bloom, J. R., & Gottheil, E. (October 14, 1989). Effect of psychosocial treatment on survival of patients with metastatic breast cancer. *The Lancet,* 888–891.

Spielberger, C. D., & DeNike, L. D. (1966). Descriptive behaviorism versus cognitive theory in verbal operant conditioning. *Psychological Review, 73,* 306–326.

Spinelli, E. (1989). *The interpreted world: An introduction to phenomenological psychology.* London: Sage Publications.

Sroufe, L. A. (1977). *Knowing and enjoying your baby.* Englewood Cliffs, NJ: Prentice-Hall.

Sroufe, L. A., & Fleeson, J. (1986). Attachment and the construction of relationships. In W. Harte & Z. Rubin (Eds.), *The nature of relationships.* Hillsdale, NJ: Erlbaum.

Staats, C. K., & Staats, A. W. (1957). Meaning established by classical conditioning. *Journal of Experimental Psychology, 54,* 74–80.

Staub, E. (1978). *Positive social behavior and morality* (Vol. 1). New York: Academic Press.

Staub, E., Tursky, B., & Schwartz, G. E. (1971). Self-control and predictability: Their effects on reactions to aversive stimulation. *Journal of Personality and Social Psychology, 18,* 157–162.

Stayton, D. J., & Ainsworth, M. D. S. (1973). Individual differences in infant responses to brief, everyday separations as related to infant and maternal behaviors. *Developmental Psychology, 9,* 226–235.

Stelmack, R. M., & Michaud-Achorn, A. (1985). Extraversion, attention, and habituation of the auditory evoked response. *Journal of Research in Personality, 19,* 416–428.

Stelmack, R. M. (1990). Biological bases of extraversion: Psychophysiological evidence. *Journal of Personality, 58,* 293–311.

Stemmler, G. (1997). Selective activation of traits: Boundary conditions for the activation of anger. *Personality and Individual Differences, 22,* 213–233.

Stephenson, W. (1953). *The study of behavior.* Chicago: University of Chicago Press.

Sternberg, R. (1998). On memory. In E. Tulving & F. I. M. Craik (Eds.), *The Oxford handbook of memory.* Oxford University Press.

Sternberg, R. (1984). Toward a triarchic theory of human intelligence. *The Behavioral and Brain Sciences, 7,* 269–315.

Sternberg, R. J. (Ed.). (1982). *Handbook of human intelligence.* New York: Cambridge University Press.

Sternberg, R. J. (Ed.). (1989). *Advances in the psychology of human intelligence* (Vol. 5). Hillsdale, NJ: Erlbaum.

Sternberg, R. J., & Detterman, D. K. (1986). *What is intelligence? Contemporary viewpoints.* Norwood, NJ: Ablex Publishing.

Sternberg, R. J., & Kolligian, J., Jr. (Eds.). (1990). *Competence considered.* New Haven, CT: Yale University Press.

Steuer, F. B., Applefield, J. M., & Smith, R. (1971). Televised aggression and the interpersonal aggression of preschool children. *Journal of Experimental Child Psychology, 11,* 442–447.

Stigler, J. W., Shweder, R. A., & Herdt, G. (1990). *Cultural psychology: Essays on comparative human development.* New York: Cambridge University Press.

Stokols, D. (1978). Environmental psychology. *Annual Review of Psychology, 29,* 253–295.

Stokols, D. (1990). Instrumental and spiritual views of people-environment relations. *American Psychologist, 45,* 641–646.

Strauman, T. J., Vookles, J., Berenstein, V., Chaiken, S., & Higgins, E. T. (1991). Self-discrepancies and vulnerability to body dissatisfaction and disordered eating. *Journal of Personality and Social Psychology, 61,* 946–956.

Stuart, B. (1967). Behavioral control over eating. *Behavior Research and Therapy, 5,* 357–365.

Stuart, R. B. (1971). A three-dimensional program for the treatment of obesity. *Behavior Research and Therapy, 9,* 177–186.

Sulloway, F. J. (1996). *Born to rebel: Birth order, family dynamics, and creative lives.* London, England: Little, Brown.

Swann, W. B., Jr. (1983). Self-verification: Bringing social reality into harmony with the self. In J. Suls & A. G. Greenwald (Eds.), *Social psychology perspectives* (Vol. 2, pp. 33–66). Hillsdale, NJ: Erlbaum.

Szasz, T. (1989). *Law, liberty, and psychiatry: An inquiry into the social uses of mental health practices.* Syracuse, NY: Syracuse University Press.

Szasz, T. S. (1960). The myth of mental illness. *American Psychologist, 15,* 113–118.

Szasz, T. S. (1970). *The manufacture of madness.* New York: Dell.

Tart, C. (1970). Increases in hypnotizability resulting from a prolonged program for enhancing personal growth. *Journal of Abnormal Psychology, 75,* 260–266.

Taylor, J. A. (1953). A personality scale of manifest anxiety. *Journal of Abnormal and Social Psychology, 48,* 285–290.

Taylor, S., & Armor, D. (1996). Positive illusions and coping with adversity. *Journal of Personality, 64,* 873–898.

Taylor, S., Repetti, R. L., & Seeman, T. (1997). Health psychology: What is an unhealthy environment and how does it get under the skin? *Annual Review of Psychology, 48,* 411–447.

Taylor, S. E. (1983). Adjustment to threatening events. *American Psychologist, 38,* 1161–1173.

Taylor, S. E. (1995). *Health psychology* (3rd ed.). New York: McGraw-Hill.

Taylor, S. E., & Armor, D. A. (1996). Positive illusions and coping with adversity. *Journal of Personality, 64,* 873–898.

Taylor, S. E., & Brown, J. D. (1988). Illusion and well-being: A social psychological perspective on mental health. *Psychological Bulletin, 103,* 193–210.

Taylor, S. E., & Schneider, S. (1989). Coping and the simulation of events. *Social Cognition, 7,* 174–194.

Tellegen, A., Lykken, D., Bouchard, T., Wilcox, K., Segal, N., & Rich, S. (1988). Personality similarity in twins reared apart. *Journal of Personality and Social Psychology, 54,* 1031–1039.

Tennen, H., Suls, J., & Affleck, G. (1991). Personality and daily experience: The promise and the challenge. *Journal of Personality, 59* (3), 313–338.

Tesser, A. (1993). The importance of heritability in psychological research: The case of attitudes. *Psychological Review, 100,* 129–142.

Testa, T. J. (1974). Causal relationships and the acquisition of avoidance responses. *Psychological Review, 81,* 491–505.

Thomas, A., & Chess, S. (1977). *Temperament and development.* New York: Brunner/Mazel.

Thoresen, C., & Mahoney, M. J. (1974). *Self-control.* New York: Holt, Rinehart and Winston.

Thurstone, L. L. (1938). Primary mental abilities. *Psychometric Monographs, No. 1.* Chicago: University of Chicago Press.

Titus, H. E., & Hollander, E. P. (1957). The California F scale in psychological research: 1950–1955. *Psychological Bulletin, 54,* 47–64.

Toner, I. J. (1981). Role involvement and delay maintenance behavior in preschool children. *The Journal of Genetic Psychology, 138,* 245–251.

Toner, I. J., & Smith, R. A. (1977). Age and overt verbalization in delay-maintenance behavior in children. *Journal of experimental child psychology, 24,* 123–128.

Truax, C. B., & Mitchell, K. M. (1971). Research on certain therapist interpersonal skills in relation to process and outcome. In A. E. Bergin & S. I. Garfield (Eds.), *Handbook of psychotherapy and behavior change* (pp. 299–344). New York: Wiley.

Tsuang, M. T., Lyons, M. J., Eisen, S. A., True, W. T., Goldberg, J., & Henderson, W. (1992). A twin study of drug exposure and initiation of use. *Behavior Genetics, 22,* 756 (abstract).

Tudor, T. G., & Holmes, D. S. (1973). Differential recall of successes and failures: Its relationship to defensiveness, achievement motivation, and anxiety. *Journal of Research in Personality, 7,* 208–224.

Tupes, E. C., & Christal, R. E. (1958). Stability of personality trait rating factors obtained under diverse conditions. *USAF WADC Technical Note,* No. 58–61.

Tupes, E. C., & Christal, R. E. (1961). Recurrent personality factors based on trait ratings. *USAF ASD Technical Report,* No. 61-67.

Tversky, A. (1977). Features of similarity. *Psychological Review, 84,* 327–352.

Tversky, A., & Kahneman, D. (1974). Judgment under uncertainty: Heuristics and biases. *Science, 185,* 1124–1131.

Tyler, L. E. (1956). *The psychology of human differences.* New York: Appleton.

Uleman, J. S., & Bargh, J. A. (Eds.). (1989). *Unintended thought.* New York: Guilford Press.

Ullmann, L. F., & Krasner, L. (1969). *A psychological approach to abnormal behavior.* Englewood Cliffs, NJ: Prentice-Hall.

Ulrich, R. E., Stachnik, T. J., & Stainton, N. R. (1963). Student acceptance of generalized personality interpretations. *Psychological Reports, 13,* 831–834.

Urban, M. S., & Witt, L. A. (1990). Self-serving bias in group member attributions of success and failure. *Journal of Social Psychology, 130,* 417–418.

Vaillant, G. E. (1977). *Adaptation to life.* Boston: Little, Brown.

Van De Reit, V., Korb, M., & Gorrell, J. (1989). *Gestalt therapy: An introduction* (3rd ed.). New York: Pergamon.

Vanaerschot, G. (1993). Empathy as releasing several microprocesses in the client. In D. Brazier (Ed.), *Beyond Carl Rogers* (pp. 47–71). London, England: Constable.

Vandenberg, S. G. (1971). What do we know today about the inheritance of intelligence and how do we know it? In R. Cancro (Ed.), *Intelligence: Genetic and environmental influences* (pp. 182–218). New York: Grune & Stratton.

Venn, J. R., & Short, J. G. (1973). Vicarious classical conditioning of emotional responses in nursery school children. *Journal of Personality and Social Psychology, 28,* 249–255.

Vernon, P. E. (1964). *Personality assessment: A critical survey.* New York: Wiley.

Viglione, D. J. (1997). Problems in Rorschach research and what to do about them. *Journal of Personality Assessment, 68,* 590–599.

Wachs, T. D., & King, B. (1994). Behavioral research in the brave new world of neuroscience: A guide to the biologically perplexed. In J. E. Bates & T. D. Wachs (Eds.), *Temperament: Individual differences at the interface of biology and behavior* (pp. 307–336). Washington, DC: American Psychological Association.

Wade, T. C., & Baker, T. B. (1977). Opinions and use of psychological tests: A survey of clinical psychologists. *American Psychologist, 32,* 874–882.

Walker, G. (1991). *In the midst of winter: Systematic therapy with families, couples, and individuals with AIDS.* New York: Norton.

Walker, L. E. (1979). *The battered women.* New York: Harper & Row.

Wallach, M. A., & Wing, C. W., Jr. (1969). *The talented student.* New York: Holt.

Waller, N. G., & Shaver, P. R. (1994). The importance of nongenetic influences on romantic love styles: A twin-family study. *Psychological Science, 5,* 268–274.

Walters, G. C., & Grusec, J. E. (1977). *Punishment.* San Francisco: W. H. Freeman.

Walters, R. H., & Parke, R. D. (1967). The influence of punishment and related disciplinary techniques on the social behavior of children: Theory and empirical findings. In B. A. Maher (Ed.), *Progress in experimental personality research* (Vol. 4, pp. 179–228). New York: Academic Press.

Watkins, C. E., Campbell, V. L., Nieberding, R., & Hallmark, R. (1995). Contemporary practice of psycholgical assessment by clinical psychologists. *Professional Psychology, Research and Practice, 26,* 54–60.

Watson, J. B., & Rayner, R. (1920). Conditioned emotional reaction. *Journal of Experimental Psychology, 3,* 1–14.

Watson, R. I. (1959). Historical review of objective personality testing: The search for objectivity. In B. M. Bass & I. A. Berg (Eds.), *Objective approaches to personality assessment* (pp. 1–23). Princeton, NJ: Van Nostrand.

Weidner, G., & Matthews, K. A. (1978). Reported physical symptoms elicited by unpredictable events and the type A coronary-prone behavior pattern. *Journal of Personality and Social Psychology, 36,* 1213–1220.

Weigel, R. H., & Newman, S. L. (1976). Increasing attitude-behavior correspondence by broadening the scope of the behavioral measure. *Journal of Personality and Social Psychology, 33,* 793–802.

Weiner, B. (1968). Motivated forgetting and the study of repression. *Journal of Personality, 36,* 213–234.

Weiner, B. (1972). *Theories of motivation: From mechanism to cognition.* Chicago: Markham.

Weiner, B. (1974). An attributional interpretation of expectancy value theory. Paper presented at the AAAS Meetings, San Francisco.

Weiner, B. (1990). Attribution in personality psychology. In L. A. Pervin (Ed.), *Handbook of personality: Theory and research* (pp. 465–484). New York: Guilford Press.

Weiner, B. (1995). *Judgments of responsibility: A foundation for a theory of social conduct.* New York: Guilford Press.

Weir, M. W. (1965). Children's behavior in a two-choice task as a function of patterned reinforcement following forced-choice trials. *Journal of Experimental Child Psychology, 2,* 85–91.

Weiss, T., & Engel, B. T. (1971). Operant conditioning of heart rate in patients with premature ventricular contractions. *Psychosomatic Medicine, 33,* 301–321.

West, S. G., & Finch, J. F. (1997). Personality measurement: Reliability and validity issues. In R. Hogan, J. Johnson, & S. Briggs (Eds.), *Handbook of personality psychology* (pp. 143–165). San Diego, CA: Academic Press.

Westen, D. (1985). *Self and society: Narcissism, collectivism, and the development of morals.* New York: Cambridge University Press.

Westen, D. (1990). Psychoanalytic approaches to personality. In L. A. Pervin (Ed.), *Handbook of personality: Theory and research* (pp. 21–65). New York: Guilford Press.

Westen, D. (1991). Social cognition and object relations. *Psychological Bulletin, 109,* 429–455.

Westen, D. (1998). The scientific legacy of Sigmund Freud: Toward a psychodynamically informed psychological science. *Psychological Bulletin.*

Wheeler, G. (1991). *Gestalt reconsidered: A new approach to contact and resistance.* New York: Gardner Press.

White, B. L. (1967). An experimental approach to the effects of experience on early human behavior. In J. P. Hill (Ed.), *Minnesota symposia on child psychology* (Vol. 1, pp. 201–226). Minneapolis: University of Minnesota Press.

White, B. L., & Held, R. (1966). Plasticity of sensorimotor development in the human infant. In J. F Rosenblith & W. Allinsmith (Eds.), *The causes of behavior, II.* Boston: Allyn & Bacon.

White, M., & Epston, D. (1990). *Narrative means to therapeutic ends.* New York: Norton.

White, R. W. (1952). *Lives in progress.* New York: Dryden.

White, R. W. (1959). Motivation reconsidered: The concept of competence. *Psychological Review, 66,* 297–333.

White, R. W. (1964). *The abnormal personality.* New York: Ronald.

White, R. W. (1972). *The enterprise of living.* New York: Holt.

Wiedenfield, S. A., Bandura, A., Levine, S., O'Leary, A., Brown, S., & Raska, K. (1990). Impact of perceived self-efficacy in coping with stressors on components of the immune system. *Journal of Personality and Social Psychology, 59,* 1082–1094.

Wiggins, J. S. (1973). *Personality and prediction: Principles of personality assessment.* Reading, MA: Addison-Wesley.

Wiggins, J. S. (1979). A psychological taxonomy of trait-descriptive terms: The interpersonal domain. *Journal of Personality and Social Psychology, 37,* 395–412.

Wiggins, J. S. (1980). Circumplex models of interpersonal behavior in personality and social psychology. *The Review of Personality and Social Psychology.*

Wiggins, J. S. (1997). In defense of traits. In R. Hogan, J. Johnson, & S. Briggs (Eds.), *Handbook of personality psychology* (pp. 95–115). San Diego, CA: Academic Press.

Wiggins, J. S., Phillips, N., & Trapnell, P. (1989). Circular reasoning about interpersonal behavior: Evidence concerning some untested assumptions underlying diagnostic classification. *Journal of Personality and Social Psychology, 56,* 296–305.

Wiley, R. C. (1979). *The self concept, Vol. 2. Theory and research on selected topics.* Lincoln: University of Nebraska Press.

Wilson, G. T., & O'Leary, K. D. (1980). *Principles of behavior therapy.* Englewood Cliffs, NJ: Prentice-Hall.

Wilson, W. R. (1979). Feeling more than we can know: Exposure effects without learning. *Journal of Personality and Social Psychology, 37,* 811–821.

Winder, C. L., & Wiggins, J. S. (1964). Social reputation and social behavior: A further validation of the peer nomination inventory. *Journal of Abnormal and Social Psychology, 68,* 681–685.

Winter, D. G., John, O. P., Stewart, A. J., Klohnen, E. C., & Duncan, L. E. (1998). Traits and motives: Toward an integration of two traditions in personality research. *Psychological Review, 105,* 230–250.

Wissler, C. (1901). The correlation of mental and physical tests. *Psychological Review Monograph Supplement, 3,* No. 16.

Wittgenstein, L. (1953). *Philosophical investigations.* New York: Macmillan.

Wolf, R. (1966). The measurement of environments. In A. Anastasi (Ed.), *Testing problems in perspective* (pp. 491–503). Washington, DC: American Council on Education.

Wolpe, J. (1958). *Psychotherapy by reciprocal inhibition.* Stanford, CA: Stanford University Press.

Wolpe, J. (1963). Behavior therapy in complex neurotic states. *British Journal of Psychiatry, 110,* 28–34.

Wolpe, J. (1997). From psychoanalytic to behavioral methods in anxiety disorders: A continuing evolution. In J. K. Zeig (Ed.), *The evolution of psychotherapy: The third conference* (pp. 107–116). New York: Brunner/Mazel.

Wolpe, J., & Lazarus, A. A. (1966). *Behavior therapy techniques: A guide to the treatment of neuroses.* Elmsford, NY: Pergamon.

Wolpe, J., & Rachman, S. (1960). Psychoanalytic evidence: A critique based on Freud's case of Little Hans. *Journal of Nervous and Mental Diseases, 31,* 134–147.

Wood, J. M., Nezworski, M. T., & Stejskal, W. J. (1996). The comprehensive system for the Rorschach: A critical examination. *Psychological Science, 7,* 3–10.

Woodall, K. L., & Matthews, K. A. (1989). Familial environments associated with Type A behaviors and psychophysiological responses to stress in children. *Health Psychology, 8,* 403–426.

Woody, S. R., Chambless, D. L., & Glass, C. R. (1997). Self-focused attention in the treatment of social phobia. *Behaviour and Research Therapy, 35,* 117–129.

Wortman, C. B., & Brehm, J. W. (1975). Responses to uncontrollable outcomes. In L. Berkowitz (Ed.), *Advances in experimental social psychology* (Vol. 8, pp. 278–336). New York: Academic Press.

Wortman, C. B., Costanzo, P. R., & Witt, T. R. (1973). Effect of anticipated performance on the attributions of causality to self and others. *Journal of Personality and Social Psychology, 27,* 372–381.

Wright, J. C., & Mischel, W. (1982). The influence of affect on cognitive social learning person variables. *Journal of Personality and Social Psychology, 43,* 901–914.

Wright, J. C., & Mischel, W. (1987). A conditional approach to dispositional constructs: The local predictability of social behavior. *Journal of Personality and Social Psychology, 53,* 1159–1177.

Wright, J. C., & Mischel, W. (1988). Conditional hedges and the intuitive psychology of traits. *Journal of Personality and Social Psychology, 55,* 454–469.

Wright, L. (1998). *Twins and what they tell us about who we are.* New York: Wiley.

Yates, B. T. (1985). *Self-management: Science and the art of helping yourself.* Belmont, CA: Wadsworth.

Yates, B. T., & Mischel, W. (1979). Young children's preferred attentional strategies for delaying gratification. *Journal of Personality and Social Psychology, 37,* 286–300.

Youngblade, L. M., & Belsky, J. (1992). Parent-child antecedents of 5-year-olds' close friendships: A longitudinal analysis. *Developmental Psychology, 28,* 700–713.

Zahn-Waxler, C., Robinson, J. L., & Emde, R. N. (1992). The development of empathy in twins. *Developmental Psychology, 28,* 1038–1047.

Zajonc, R. B. (1980). Feeling and thinking: Preferences need no inferences. *American Psychologist, 35,* 151–175.

Zajonc, R. B. (1986). The decline and rise of scholastic aptitude scores: A prediction derived from the confluence model. *American Psychologist, 41,* 862–867.

Zajonc, R. B., & Mullally, P. R. (1997). Birth order: Reconciling conflicting effects. *American Psychologist, 53,* 685–699.

Zajonc, R. B., Markus, H., & Markus, G. B. (1979). The birth order puzzle. *Journal of Personality and Social Psychology, 37,* 1325–1341.

Zeller, A. (1950). An experimental analogue of repression, I. Historical summary. *Psychological Bulletin, 47,* 39–51.

Zimmerman, B. J. (1983). Social learning theory: A contextualist accounting of social functioning. In C. J. Braimerd (Ed.), *Recent advances in cognitive-developmental theory* (pp. 1–50). New York: Springer-Verlag.

Zirkel, S. (1992). Developing independence in a life transition: Investing the self in the concerns of the day. *Journal of Personality and Social Psychology, 62,* 506–521.

Ziv, A., Kruglanski, A. W., & Shulman, S. (1974). Children's psychological reactions to war-time stress. *Journal of Personality and Social Psychology, 30,* 24–30.

Zubin, J., Eron, L. D., & Schumer, F. (1965). *An experimental approach to projective techniques.* New York: Wiley.

Zuckerman, M., Kolin, E. A., Price, L., & Zoob, I., (1964). Development of a sensation seeking scale. *Journal of Consulting Psychology, 28,* 477–482.

Zuckerman, M. (1979). Attribution of success and failure revisited: Or the motivational bias is alive and well in attribution theory. *Journal of Personality, 47,* 245–287.

Zuckerman, M. (1983). A rejoinder to Notarius. *Journal of Personality and Social Psychology, 45,* 1165–1166.

Zuckerman, M. (1984). Sensation seeking: A comparative approach to a human trait. *Behavioral and Brain Sciences, 7,* 413–471.

Zuckerman, M. (1990). The psychophysiology of sensation seeking. *Journal of Personality, 58,* 313–345.

Zuckerman, M. (1991). *The psychobiology of personality.* Cambridge, England: Cambridge University Press.

Zuckerman, M. (1994). *Behavioral expressions and biosocial bases of sensation seeking.* New York: Cambridge University Press.

Zuckerman, M., Persky, H., Link, K. E., & Basu, G. K. (1968). Responses to confinement: An investigation of sensory deprivation, social isolation, restriction of movement and set factors. *Perceptual and Motor Skills, 27,* 319–334.

Zuckerman, M., Porac, J., Lathin, D., Smith, R., & Deci, E. L. (1978). On the importance of self-determination for intrinsically motivated behavior. *Personality and Social Psychology Bulletin, 4,* 443–446.

Zuckerman, M., Koestner, R., DeBoy, T., Garcia, T., Maresca, B. C., & Sartoris, J. M. (1988). To predict some of the people some of the time: A reexamination of the moderator variable approach in personality theory. *Journal of Personality and Social Psychology, 54,* 1006–1019.

Chapter 1   p. 13, © Roger Tully/Tony Stone Images; p. 26, © Marcia Weinstein.

Chapter 2   p. 36, National Library of Medicine, Bethesda, Maryland; p. 43, © Elizabeth Crews/Stock, Boston; p. 47, © Gregory G. Dimijian/Photo Researchers, Inc.; p. 60, © Bud Gray/Stock, Boston.

Chapter 3   p. 68, Corbis–The Bettmann Archive; p. 71, AP/Wide World Photos; p. 72, Corbis–Bettmann Newsphotos; p. 74, Corbis–Bettmann Newsphotos; p. 75, © J. Nourok/Photo Edit; p. 80, *The Restoration of Self,* by Heinz Kohut, International Universities Press, Inc.; p. 83, © Jerome Tisne/Tony Stone Images.

Chapter 5   p. 129, AP/Wide World Photos.

Chapter 6   p. 144, © Photo by Jean-Claude Lejeune/Stock, Boston; p. 146, Louis Fenandez/Black Star; p. 150, Harvard University News Office, Cambridge, Massachusetts; p. 152, Times Newspapers Ltd., London; p. 153, courtesy of Hans J. Eysenck; p. 159, left, courtesy of Robert McCrae; p. 159, right, courtesy of Paul Costa.

Chapter 7   p. 167, © Comstock; p. 173, © Robert E. Daemmrich/Tony Stone Images; p. 198, courtesy of Jack Block.

Chapter 8   p. 202, left, © Mary Kate Denny/PhotoEdit; p. 202, right, © Renee Lynn/Tony Stone Images; p. 209, Robert Plomin, Deputy Director, Social Genetic & Developmental Psychiatry Research Centre, Institute of Psychiatry.

Chapter 9   p. 226, Wellcome Centre Medical Photographic Library; p. 227, courtesy of David Buss; p. 235, courtesy of Norman S. Endler.

Chapter 10   p. 254, AP/Wide World Photos; p. 256, Douglas A. Land, La Jolla, California; p. 258, © Spencer Grant/PhotoEdit;

p. 261, Brandeis University, Waltham, Massachusetts; p. 265, © David Young-Wolff/PhotoEdit; p. 268, courtesy of Hazel Markus.

Chapter 11   p. 292, © Bruce Ayres/Tony Stone Images; p. 298, courtesy of Shelly Taylor.

Chapter 12   p. 314, Corbis–The Bettmann Archive; p. 316, © Milton Feinberg/Stock, Boston; p. 321, Helena Frost, New York; p. 323, Corbis–The Bettmann Archive; p. 327, Bob Daemmrich Photo, Inc.; p. 333, courtesy of Albert Bandura, Stanford University Psychology Department, California; p. 334, © F. Martinez/PhotoEdit; p. 338, courtesy of Albert Bandura, Stanford University Psychology Department, California; p. 341, © Superstock.

Chapter 13   p. 360, © Mark E. Gibson.

Chapter 14   p. 369, © Bob Daemmrich/Stock, Boston; p. 375, from Bandura, Blanchard & Ritter (1969); p. 382, photos by Allan Grant, Los Angeles, California, courtesy of Dr. Ivor Lovaas, UCLA; p. 397, © Burke Uzzle/Woodfin Camp; p. 403, University of Waterloo, Graphics Photo/Imaging.

Chapter 15   p. 418, courtesy of Walter Mischel; p. 419, © Sean Arbabi/Tony Stone Images; p. 422, © Superstock; p. 424, courtesy of Julian B. Rotter.

Chapter 16   p. 440, courtesy of Columbia University, New York; p. 445, © Superstock; p. 452, © Robin Sachs; p. 454, courtesy of Carol Dweck; p. 457, © Hazel Hankin/Stock, Boston; p. 458, courtesy of Columbia University, New York.

Chapter 17   p. 476, © Mark Richards/PhotoEdit; p. 479, based on Mischel, Ebbesen, & Zeiss (1972); p. 487, © David Frazier/Tony Stone Images; p. 488, photo by Bob Kalmbach.

Chapter 18   p. 508, © John Maher/Stock, Boston; p. 511, © Deborah Kahn/Stock, Boston.